PDF Reference
second edition

Adobe Portable Document Format
Version 1.3

Adobe Systems Incorporated

D1733119

ADDISON–WESLEY

Boston • San Francisco • New York • Toronto • Montreal
London • Munich • Paris • Madrid
Capetown • Sydney • Tokyo • Singapore • Mexico City

Library of Congress Cataloging-in-Publication Data

Adobe portable document format, version 1.3 / Adobe Systems Incorporated. — 2nd ed.
     p. cm.
  Includes bibliographical references and index.
  ISBN 0-201-61588-6
    1. Text processing (Computer science). 2. Adobe Acrobat. 3. Portable document
software. I. Adobe Systems.

  QA76.76.T49 A36 2000
  005.7′2—dc21

00-040581

1 2 3 4 5 6 7 8 9-MA-0403020100
First printing, July 2000

Contents

Figures

Tables

Preface

THE ORIGINS OF THE Portable Document Format and the Adobe® Acrobat® product family date to early 1990. At that time, the PostScript® page description language was rapidly becoming the worldwide standard for the production of the printed page. PDF builds on the PostScript page description language by layering a document structure and interactive navigation features on PostScript's underlying imaging model, providing a convenient, efficient mechanism enabling documents to be reliably viewed and printed anywhere.

The PDF specification was first published at the same time the first Acrobat products were introduced in 1993. Since then, updated versions of the specification have been and continue to be available from Adobe via the World Wide Web. This book is the first version of the specification that is completely self-contained, including the precise documentation of the underlying imaging model from PostScript along with the PDF-specific features that are combined in version 1.3 of the PDF standard.

Over the past seven years, aided by the explosive growth of the Internet, PDF has become the *de facto* standard for the electronic exchange of documents. Well over 100 million copies of the Acrobat Reader application have been distributed around the world, facilitating efficient electronic access to and sharing of information. In addition, PDF is now the industry standard for the intermediate representation of printed material in electronic prepress systems for conventional printing applications. As major corporations, government agencies, and educational institutions streamline their operations by replacing paper-based workflow with electronic exchange of information, the impact and opportunity for the application of PDF will continue to grow at a rapid pace.

Adobe offers a collection of PDF-based applications, the Adobe Acrobat products, that provide a broad range of capabilities for its customers. Adobe Acrobat provides the basic tools to create and enhance documents prepared by essentially any software product on the popular operating system platforms. The Acrobat Reader, available free of charge for downloading from myriad Web sites (including Adobe.com), is frequently bundled with consumer products to provide paperless documentation that customers can view on-line or print to paper.

Acrobat Capture converts paper documents into PDF format, using state-of-the-art character recognition combined with a highly compressed representation of graphics, enabling the conversion of legacy information into electronic form. A significant number of third-party developers and systems integrators offer customized enhancements and extensions to the core family of products.

The emergence of PDF as a *de facto* standard for electronic information exchange is the result of concerted effort by many individuals in both the private and public sectors. Without the dedication of Adobe employees, our industry partners, and our customers, the widespread acceptance of PDF could not have been achieved. We thank all of you for your continuing support and creative contributions to the success of PDF.

Chuck Geschke and John Warnock
March 2000

CHAPTER 1

Introduction

THIS BOOK DESCRIBES the Adobe Portable Document Format (PDF), the native file format of the Adobe® Acrobat® family of products. The goal of these products is to enable users to exchange and view electronic documents easily and reliably, independently of the environment in which they were created. PDF relies on the imaging model of the PostScript® page description language to describe text and graphics in a device-independent and resolution-independent manner. To improve performance for interactive viewing, PDF defines a more structured format than that used by most PostScript language programs. PDF also includes objects, such as annotations and hypertext links, that are not part of the page itself but are useful for interactive viewing and document interchange.

1.1 About This Book

This book provides a description of the PDF file format and is intended primarily for application developers wishing to develop *PDF generator* applications that create PDF files directly. It also contains enough information to allow developers to write *PDF consumer* applications that read existing PDF files and interpret or modify their contents.

Although the PDF specification is independent of any particular software implementation, some PDF features are best explained by describing the way they are processed by a typical application program. In such cases, this book uses the Adobe Acrobat family of PDF viewer applications as its model. (The prototypical viewer is the fully capable Acrobat product, not the limited Acrobat Reader product.) Similarly, Appendix C discusses some implementation limits in the Acrobat viewer applications, even though these limits are not part of the file format itself. To provide guidance to implementors of PDF generator and consumer applications, implementation notes in Appendix H describe the behavior of Acrobat viewer applications when they encounter newer features they do not understand.

- Chapter 2, "Overview," briefly introduces the overall architecture of PDF and the design considerations behind it, compares it with the PostScript language, and describes the underlying imaging model that they share.

- Chapter 3, "Syntax," presents the syntax of PDF at the object, file, and document level. It sets the stage for subsequent chapters, which describe how that information is interpreted as page descriptions, interactive navigational aids, and application-level logical structure.

- Chapter 4, "Graphics," describes the graphics operators used to describe the appearance of pages in a PDF document.

- Chapter 5, "Fonts," discusses PDF's special facilities for presenting text in the form of character shapes, or glyphs, defined by fonts.

- Chapter 6, "Rendering," considers how device-independent content descriptions are matched to the characteristics of a particular output device.

- Chapter 7, "Interactive Features," describes those features of PDF that allow a user to interact with a document on the screen, using the mouse and keyboard.

- Chapter 8, "Document Interchange," shows how PDF documents can incorporate higher-level information that is useful for the interchange of documents among applications.

- Appendix A, "Operator Summary," lists all the operators used in describing the visual content of a PDF document.

- Appendix B, "Operators in Type 4 Functions," summarizes the PostScript operators that can be used in PostScript calculator functions, which contain code written in a small subset of the PostScript language.

- Appendix C, "Implementation Limits," describes typical size and quantity limits imposed by the Acrobat viewer applications.

- Appendix D, "Character Sets and Encodings," lists the character sets and encodings that are assumed to be predefined in any PDF viewer application.

- Appendix E, "PDF Name Registry," discusses a registry, maintained for developers by Adobe Systems, that contains private names and formats used by PDF producers or Acrobat plug-in extensions.

- Appendix F, "Linearized PDF," describes a special form of PDF file organization designed to work efficiently in network environments.

- Appendix G, "Example PDF Files," presents several examples showing the structure of actual PDF files, ranging from one containing a minimal one-page document to one showing how the structure of a PDF file evolves over the course of several revisions.

- Appendix H, "Compatibility and Implementation Notes," provides details on the behavior of Acrobat viewer applications and describes how viewer applications should handle PDF files containing features that they do not recognize.

The book concludes with a Bibliography and an Index.

The enclosed CD-ROM contains the entire text of this book in PDF form.

1.2 Introduction to PDF 1.3 Features

This second edition of the *PDF Reference* describes version 1.3 of the Portable Document Format. (See implementation note 1 in Appendix H.) Throughout the book, information specific to particular versions of PDF is marked with indicators of the form *(PDF 1.0)*, *(PDF 1.1)*, *(PDF 1.2)*, or *(PDF 1.3)*. Features so marked may be new in the indicated version or may have been substantially redefined in that version. Features designated *(PDF 1.0)* have generally been superseded in later versions; unless otherwise stated, features identified as specific to other versions are understood to be available in later versions as well. PDF viewer applications designed for a specific PDF version generally ignore newer features that they do not recognize.

PDF 1.3 adds support for the new features of the Adobe imaging model embodied in PostScript LanguageLevel 3, as well as other new features, including the following:

- Data structures for efficiently mapping strings and numbers to PDF objects (Sections 3.8.4, "Name Trees," and 3.8.5, "Number Trees")

- New types of functions (Section 3.9, "Functions")

- Embedding of files of any type within a PDF document (Section 3.10.3, "Embedded File Streams")

- New color spaces: **ICCBased** and **DeviceN** ("ICCBased Color Spaces" on page 173 and "DeviceN Color Spaces" on page 186)

- Smooth shading (Section 4.6.3, "Shading Patterns")

- Alternate representations for a single image ("Alternate Images" on page 255)

- Masked images (Section 4.8.5, "Masked Images")

- Additional support for CIDFonts (Section 5.6, "Composite Fonts")

- Enhanced page numbering (Section 7.3.1, "Page Labels")

- Many new annotation types (Section 7.4.5, "Annotation Types")

- Digital signatures ("Signature Fields" on page 451)

- Support for JavaScript ("JavaScript Actions" on page 458)

- A facility for representing the logical structure of a document independently of its graphic structure (Section 8.4.3, "Logical Structure")

- A facility for capturing information from the World Wide Web and converting it to PDF form (Section 8.5, "Web Capture")

- Information useful in prepress production workflows (Section 8.6, "Prepress Support")

1.3 Related Publications

PDF and the PostScript page description language share the same underlying Adobe imaging model. A document can be converted straightforwardly between PDF and the PostScript language; the two representations produce the same output when printed. However, PostScript includes a general-purpose programming language framework not present in PDF. The *PostScript Language Reference* is the comprehensive reference for the PostScript language and its imaging model.

PDF and PostScript support several standard formats for font programs, including Adobe Type 1, CFF (Compact Font Format), TrueType®, and CID-keyed fonts. The PDF manifestations of these fonts are documented in this book. However, the specifications for the font files themselves are published separately, because they are highly specialized and are of interest to a different user community. A variety of Adobe publications are available on the subject of font formats, most notably the following:

- *Adobe Type 1 Font Format* and Adobe Technical Note #5015, *Type 1 Font Format Supplement*

- Adobe Technical Note #5176, *The Compact Font Format Specification*

- Adobe Technical Note #5177, *The Type 2 Charstring Format*

- Adobe Technical Note #5014, *Adobe CMap and CID Font Files Specification*

See the Bibliography for additional publications related to PDF and the contents of this book.

1.4 Copyright Permission

The general idea of using an interchange format for electronic documents is in the public domain. Anyone is free to devise a set of unique data structures and operators that define an interchange format for electronic documents. However, Adobe Systems Incorporated owns the copyright for the particular data structures and operators and the written specification constituting the interchange format called the Portable Document Format. Thus, these elements of the Portable Document Format may not be copied without Adobe's permission.

Adobe will enforce its copyright. Adobe's intention is to maintain the integrity of the Portable Document Format standard. This enables the public to distinguish between the Portable Document Format and other interchange formats for electronic documents. However, Adobe desires to promote the use of the Portable Document Format for information interchange among diverse products and applications. Accordingly, Adobe gives copyright permission to anyone to:

- Prepare files whose content conforms to the Portable Document Format

- Write drivers and applications that produce output represented in the Portable Document Format

- Write software that accepts input in the form of the Portable Document Format and displays, prints, or otherwise interprets the contents

- Copy Adobe's copyrighted list of data structures and operators, as well as the example code and PostScript language function definitions in the written specification, to the extent necessary to use the Portable Document Format for the purposes above

The only condition of such copyright permission is that anyone who uses the copyrighted list of data structures and operators in this way must include an appropriate copyright notice. This limited right to use the copyrighted list of data structures and operators does not include the right to copy this book, other copyrighted material from Adobe, or the software in any of Adobe's products that use the Portable Document Format, in whole or in part, nor does it include the right to use any Adobe patents (except as may be permitted by an official Adobe Patent Clarification Notice).

CHAPTER 2

Overview

THE ADOBE *PORTABLE DOCUMENT FORMAT (PDF)* is a file format for representing documents in a manner independent of the application software, hardware, and operating system used to create them and of the output device on which they are to be displayed or printed. A *PDF document* consists of a collection of *objects* that together describe the appearance of one or more *pages*, possibly accompanied by additional interactive elements and higher-level application data. A *PDF file* contains the objects making up a PDF document along with associated structural information, all represented as a single self-contained sequence of bytes.

A document's pages (and other visual elements) may contain any combination of text, graphics, and images. A page's appearance is described by a PDF *content stream*, which contains a sequence of *graphics objects* to be painted on the page. This appearance is fully specified; all layout and formatting decisions have already been made by the application that generated the content stream.

In addition to describing the static appearance of pages, a PDF document may contain interactive elements that are possible only in an electronic representation. PDF supports *annotations* of many kinds for such things as text notes, hypertext links, markup, file attachments, sounds, and movies. A document can define its own user interface; keyboard and mouse input can trigger *actions* that are specified by PDF objects. The document can contain *interactive form* fields to be filled in by the user, and can import the values of these fields from or export them to other applications.

Finally, a PDF document can contain higher-level information that is useful for interchange among applications. In addition to specifying appearance, a document's content can include identification and structural information that allows it to be searched, edited, or extracted for reuse elsewhere. PDF is particularly well suited for representing a document as it moves through successive stages of a pre-press production workflow.

2.1 Imaging Model

At the heart of PDF is its ability to describe the appearance of sophisticated graphics and typography. This is achieved through the use of the *Adobe imaging model*, the same high-level, device-independent representation used in the Post-Script page description language.

Although application programs could theoretically describe any page as a full-resolution pixel array, the resulting file would be bulky, device-dependent, and impractical for high-resolution devices. A high-level *imaging model* enables applications to describe the appearance of pages containing text, graphical shapes, and sampled images in terms of abstract graphical elements rather than directly in terms of device pixels. Such a description is economical and device-independent, and can be used to produce high-quality output on a broad range of printers and displays.

2.1.1 Page Description Languages

Among its other roles, PDF serves as a *page description language*: a language for describing the graphical appearance of pages with respect to an imaging model. An application program produces output through a two-stage process:

1. The application generates a device-independent description of the desired output in the page description language.

2. A program controlling a specific output device interprets the description and *renders* it on that device.

The two stages may be executed in different places and at different times; the page description language serves as an interchange standard for the compact, device-independent transmission and storage of printable or displayable documents.

2.1.2 Adobe Imaging Model

The Adobe imaging model is a simple and unified view of two-dimensional graphics borrowed from the graphic arts. In this model, "paint" is placed on a page in selected areas.

- The painted figures may be in the form of character shapes (*glyphs*), geometric shapes, lines, or sampled images such as digital representations of photographs.

- The paint may be in color or in black, white, or any shade of gray; it may also take the form of a repeating *pattern (PDF 1.2)* or a smooth transition between colors *(PDF 1.3)*.

- Any of these elements may be *clipped* to appear within other shapes as they are placed onto the page.

A page's content stream contains *operands* and *operators* describing a sequence of graphics objects. A PDF viewer application maintains an implicit *current page* that accumulates the marks made by the painting operators. Initially, the current page is completely blank. For each graphics object encountered in the content stream, the viewer places marks on the current page, which completely obscure any previous marks they may overlay (subject to the effects of the *overprint parameter* in the graphics state; see Section 4.5.6, "Overprint Control"). This method is known as a *painting model*: no matter what color a mark has—white, black, gray, or color—it is placed on the current page as if it were applied with opaque paint. Once the page has been completely composed, the accumulated marks are rendered on the output medium and the current page is cleared to blank again.

The principal graphics objects (among others) are as follows:

- A *path object* consists of a sequence of connected and disconnected points, lines, and curves that together describe shapes and their positions. It is built up through the sequential application of *path construction operators*, each of which appends one or more new elements. The path object is ended by a *path-painting operator*, which paints the path on the page in some way. The principal path-painting operators are **S** (stroke), which paints a line along the path, and **f** (fill), which paints the interior of the path.

- A *text object* consists of one or more glyph shapes representing characters of text. The glyph shapes for the characters are described in a separate data structure called a *font*. Like path objects, text objects can be stroked or filled.

- An *image object* is a rectangular array of *sample values*, each representing a color at a particular position within the rectangle. Image objects are typically used to represent photographs.

The painting operators require various parameters, some explicit and others implicit. Implicit parameters include the current color, current line width, current font (typeface and size), and many others. Together, these implicit parameters make up the *graphics state*. There are operators for setting the value of each implicit parameter in the graphics state; painting operators use the values currently in effect at the time they are invoked.

One additional implicit parameter in the graphics state modifies the results of painting graphics objects. The *current clipping path* outlines the area of the current page within which paint can be placed. Although painting operators may attempt to place marks anywhere on the current page, only those marks falling within the current clipping path will affect the page; those falling outside it will not. Initially, the current clipping path encompasses the entire imageable area of the page. It can temporarily be reduced to the shape defined by a path or text object, or to the intersection of multiple such shapes. Marks placed by subsequent painting operators will then be confined within that boundary.

2.1.3 Raster Output Devices

Much of the power of the Adobe imaging model derives from its ability to deal with the general class of *raster output devices*. These encompass such technologies as laser, dot-matrix, and ink-jet printers, digital imagesetters, and raster-scan displays. The defining property of a raster output device is that a printed or displayed image consists of a rectangular array, or *raster*, of dots called *pixels* (picture elements) that can be addressed individually. On a typical *bilevel* output device, each pixel can be made either black or white. On some devices, pixels can be set to intermediate shades of gray or to some color. The ability to set the colors of individual pixels makes it possible to generate printed or displayed output that can include text, arbitrary graphical shapes, and reproductions of sampled images.

The *resolution* of a raster output device measures the number of pixels per unit of distance along the two linear dimensions. Resolution is typically—but not necessarily—the same horizontally and vertically. Manufacturers' decisions on device technology and price/performance tradeoffs create characteristic ranges of resolution:

- Computer displays have relatively low resolution, typically 75 to 110 pixels per inch.

- Dot-matrix printers generally range from 100 to 250 pixels per inch.

- Ink-jet and laser-scanned xerographic printing technologies achieve medium-level resolutions of 300 to 1400 pixels per inch.

- Photographic technology permits high resolutions of 2400 pixels per inch or more.

Higher resolution yields better quality and fidelity of the resulting output, but is achieved at greater cost. As the technology improves and computing costs decrease, products evolve to higher resolutions.

2.1.4 Scan Conversion

An abstract graphical element (such as a line, a circle, a character glyph, or a sampled image) is rendered on a raster output device by a process known as *scan conversion*. Given a mathematical description of the graphical element, this process determines which pixels to adjust and what values to assign to those pixels to achieve the most faithful rendition possible at the available device resolution.

The pixels on a page can be represented by a two-dimensional array of pixel values in computer memory. For an output device whose pixels can only be black or white, a single bit suffices to represent each pixel. For a device that can reproduce gray levels or colors, multiple bits per pixel are required.

Note: *Although the ultimate representation of a printed or displayed page is logically a complete array of pixels, its actual representation in computer memory need not consist of one memory cell per pixel. Some implementations use other representations, such as display lists. The Adobe imaging model has been carefully designed not to depend on any particular representation of raster memory.*

For each graphical element that is to appear on the page, the scan converter sets the values of the corresponding pixels. When the interpretation of the page description is complete, the pixel values in memory represent the appearance of the page. At this point, a raster output process can *render* this representation (make it visible) on a printed page or display screen.

Scan-converting a graphical shape, such as a rectangle or circle, entails determining which device pixels lie inside the shape and setting their values appropriately (for example, to black). Because the edges of a shape do not always fall precisely on the boundaries between pixels, some policy is required for deciding how to set the pixels along the edges. Scan-converting a glyph representing a text character is conceptually the same as scan-converting an arbitrary graphical shape; however, character glyphs are much more sensitive to legibility requirements and must meet more rigid objective and subjective measures of quality.

Rendering grayscale elements on a bilevel device is accomplished by a technique known as *halftoning*. The array of pixels is divided into small clusters according to some pattern (called the *halftone screen*). Within each cluster, some pixels are set to black and some to white in proportion to the level of gray desired at that location on the page. When viewed from a sufficient distance, the individual dots become imperceptible and the perceived result is a shade of gray. This enables a bilevel raster output device to reproduce shades of gray and to approximate natural images such as photographs. Some color devices use a similar technique.

2.2 Other General Properties

This section describes other notable general properties of PDF, aside from its imaging model.

2.2.1 Portability

PDF files are represented as sequences of 8-bit binary bytes. A PDF file is designed to be portable across all platforms and operating systems. The binary representation is intended to be generated, transported, and consumed directly, without translation between native character sets, end-of-line representations, or other conventions used on various platforms.

Any PDF file can also be represented in a form that uses only 7-bit ASCII (American Standard Code for Information Interchange) character codes. This is useful for the purpose of exposition, as in this book. However, this representation is not recommended for actual use, since it is less efficient than the normal binary representation. Regardless of which representation is used, PDF files must be transported and stored as *binary* files, not as *text* files; inadvertent changes, such as conversion between text end-of-line conventions, will damage the file and may render it unusable.

2.2.2 Compression

To reduce file size, PDF supports a number of industry-standard compression filters:

- JPEG compression of color and grayscale images

- CCITT Group 3, CCITT Group 4, and run-length compression of monochrome images

- LZW (Lempel-Ziv-Welch) and Flate compression *(PDF 1.2)* of text, graphics, and images

Using JPEG compression, color and grayscale images can be compressed by a factor of 10 or more. Effective compression of monochrome images depends on the compression filter used and the properties of the image, but reductions of 2:1 to 8:1 are common. LZW or Flate compression of the content streams describing all other text and graphics in the document results in compression ratios of approximately 2:1. All of these compression filters produce binary data, which can then be further converted to ASCII base-85 encoding if a 7-bit ASCII representation is desired.

2.2.3 Font Management

Managing fonts is a fundamental challenge in document interchange. Generally, the receiver of a document must have the same fonts that were originally used to create it. If a different font is substituted, its character set, glyph shapes, and metrics may differ from those in the original font. This can produce unexpected and undesirable results, such as lines of text extending into margins or overlapping with graphics.

PDF provides various means for dealing with font management:

- The original font programs can be embedded in the PDF file. PDF supports various font formats, including Type 1, TrueType®, and CID-keyed fonts. This ensures the most predictable and dependable results.

- To conserve space, a font subset can be embedded, containing just the glyph descriptions for those characters that are actually used in the document. Also, Type 1 fonts can be represented in a special compact format.

- PDF prescribes a set of 14 standard fonts that can be used without prior definition. These include four faces of each of three Latin text typefaces (Courier, Helvetica*, and Times*) and two symbolic fonts (Symbol and ITC Zapf Dingbats®). These fonts, or suitable substitute fonts with the same metrics, are guaranteed to be available in all PDF viewer applications.

- A PDF file can refer by name to fonts that are not embedded in the PDF file. In this case, a viewer application will use those fonts if they are available in the viewer's environment. This approach suffers from the uncertainties noted above.

- A PDF file contains a *font descriptor* for each font that it uses (other than the standard 14). The font descriptor includes font metrics and style information, enabling a viewer application to select or synthesize a suitable substitute font if necessary. Although the glyphs' shapes will differ from those intended, their placement will be accurate.

Font management is primarily concerned with producing the correct appearance of text—that is, the shape and placement of glyphs. However, it is sometimes necessary for a PDF application to extract the meaning of the text, represented in some standard information encoding such as Unicode®. In some cases, this information can be deduced from the encoding used to represent the text in the PDF file. Otherwise, the PDF creator application should specify the mapping explicitly by including a special object, the ***ToUnicode** CMap*.

2.2.4 Single-Pass File Generation

Because of system limitations and efficiency considerations, it may be necessary or desirable for an application program to generate a PDF file in a single pass. For example, the program may have limited memory available or be unable to open temporary files. For this reason, PDF supports single-pass generation of files. Although some PDF objects must specify their length in bytes, a mechanism is provided allowing the length to follow the object itself in the PDF file. In addition, information such as the number of pages in the document can be written into the file after all pages have been generated.

A PDF file that is generated in a single pass is generally not ordered for most efficient viewing, particularly when accessing the contents of the file over a network. When generating a PDF file that is intended to be viewed many times, it is worthwhile to perform a second pass to optimize the order in which objects occur in the file. PDF specifies a particular file organization, *Linearized PDF*, which is documented in Appendix F. Other optimizations are also possible, such as detecting duplicated sequences of graphics objects and collapsing them to a single shared sequence that is specified only once.

2.2.5   Random Access

A PDF file should be thought of as a flattened representation of a data structure consisting of a collection of objects that can refer to each other in any arbitrary way. The order of the objects' occurrence in the PDF file has no semantic significance. In general, a viewing application should process a PDF file by following references from object to object, rather than by processing objects sequentially. This is particularly important for interactive document viewing, or for any application in which pages or other objects in the PDF file are accessed out of sequence.

To support such random access to individual objects, every PDF file contains a *cross-reference table* that can be used to locate and directly access pages and other important objects within the file. The cross-reference table is stored at the end of the file, allowing applications that generate PDF files in a single pass to store it easily and applications that read PDF files to locate it easily. Using the cross-reference table makes the time needed to locate a page or other object nearly independent of the length of the document. This allows PDF documents containing hundreds or thousands of pages to be accessed efficiently.

2.2.6 Security

PDF has two security features that can be used, separately or together, in any document:

- The document can be *encrypted* so that only authorized users can access it. There is separate authorization for the owner of the document and for all other users; the users' access can be selectively restricted to allow only certain operations, such as viewing, printing, or editing.

- The document can be digitally *signed* to certify its authenticity. The signature may take many forms, including a document digest that has been encrypted with a public/private key, a biometric signature such as a fingerprint, and others. Any subsequent changes to a signed PDF file will invalidate the signature.

2.2.7 Incremental Update

Applications may allow users to modify PDF documents. Users should not have to wait for the entire file—which can contain hundreds of pages or more—to be rewritten each time modifications to the document are saved. PDF allows modifications to be appended to a file, leaving the original data intact. The addendum appended when a file is incrementally updated contains only those objects that were actually added or modified, and includes an update to the cross-reference table. Incremental update allows an application to save modifications to a PDF document in an amount of time proportional to the size of the modification instead of the size of the file.

In addition, because the original contents of the document are still present in the file, it is possible to undo saved changes by deleting one or more addenda. The ability to recover the exact contents of an original document is critical when digital signatures have been applied and subsequently need to be verified.

2.2.8 Extensibility

PDF is designed to be extensible. Not only can new features be added, but applications based on earlier versions of PDF can behave reasonably when they encounter newer features that they do not understand. Appendix H describes how a PDF viewer application should behave in such cases.

Additionally, PDF provides means for applications to store their own private information in a PDF file. This information can be recovered when the file is imported by the same application, but is ignored by other applications. This allows PDF to serve as an application's native file format while allowing its documents be viewed and printed by other applications. Application-specific data can be stored either as *marked content* annotating the graphics objects in a PDF content stream or as entirely separate objects unconnected with the PDF content.

2.3 Using PDF

PDF files may be produced either directly by application programs or indirectly by conversion from other file formats or imaging models. As PDF documents and applications that process them become more prevalent, new ways of creating and using PDF will be invented. One of the goals of this book is to make the file format accessible so that application developers can expand on the ideas behind PDF and the applications that initially support it.

Many applications can produce PDF files directly, and some can import them as well. This is the most desirable approach, since it gives the application access to the full capabilities of PDF, including the imaging model and the interactive and document interchange features. Alternatively, existing applications that do not generate PDF directly can still be used to produce PDF output by indirect methods. There are two principal ways of doing this:

* The application describes its printable output by making calls to an application programming interface (API), such as GDI in Microsoft® Windows® or Quick-Draw® in the Apple® Mac® OS. A software component called a *printer driver* intercepts these calls and interprets them to generate output in the form of a PDF file.

* The application produces printable output directly in some other file format, such as PostScript, PCL, HPGL, or DVI, which is then converted into PDF by a separate translation program.

Note, however, that while these indirect strategies are often the easiest way to obtain PDF output from an existing application, the resulting PDF files may not make the best use of the high-level Adobe imaging model. This is because the information embodied in the application's API calls or in the intermediate output file often describes the desired results at too low a level; any higher-level information maintained by the original application has been lost and is not available to the printer driver or translator.

Figures 2.1 and 2.2 show how Adobe Acrobat products support these indirect approaches. PDF Writer (Figure 2.1), available on the Windows and Mac OS platforms, acts as a printer driver, intercepting graphics and text operations generated by a running application program through the operating system's API. Instead of converting these operations into printer commands and transmitting them directly to a printer, however, PDF Writer converts them to equivalent PDF operators and embeds them in a PDF file. The result is a platform-independent file that can be viewed and printed by a PDF viewer application, such as Adobe Acrobat, running on any supported platform—even a different platform from the one on which the file was originally generated.

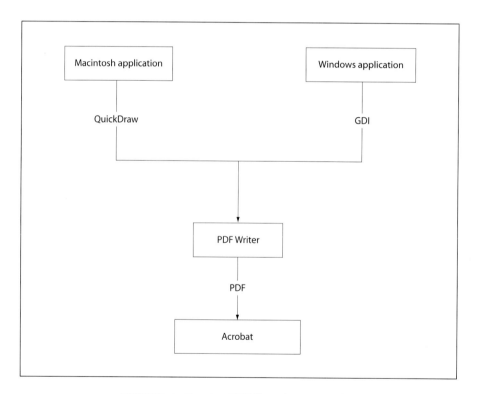

FIGURE 2.1 *Creating PDF files using PDF Writer*

| 2.4 | 19 | *PDF and the PostScript Language* |

Instead of describing their printable output via API calls, some applications produce PostScript page descriptions directly—either because of limitations in the QuickDraw or GDI imaging models or because the applications run on platforms such as DOS or UNIX®, where there is no system-level printer driver. PostScript files generated by such applications can be converted into PDF files using the Acrobat Distiller® application (see Figure 2.2). Because PostScript and PDF share the same Adobe imaging model, Acrobat Distiller can preserve the exact graphical content of the PostScript file in the translation to PDF. Additionally, Distiller supports a PostScript language extension, called **pdfmark**, that allows the producing application to embed instructions in the PostScript file for creating hypertext links, logical structure, and other interactive and document interchange features of PDF. Again, the resulting PDF file can be viewed with a viewer application, such as Adobe Acrobat, on any supported platform.

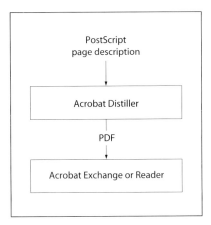

FIGURE 2.2 *Creating PDF files using Acrobat Distiller*

2.4 PDF and the PostScript Language

The PDF operators for setting the graphics state and painting graphics objects are similar to the corresponding operators in the PostScript language. Unlike PostScript, however, PDF is not a full-scale programming language; it trades reduced flexibility for improved efficiency and predictability. PDF therefore differs from PostScript in the following significant ways:

- PDF enforces a strictly defined file structure that allows an application to access parts of a document in arbitrary order.

- To simplify the processing of content streams, PDF does not include common programming language features such as procedures, variables, and control constructs.

- PDF files contain information such as font metrics to ensure viewing fidelity.

- A PDF file may contain additional information that is not directly connected with the imaging model, such as hypertext links for interactive viewing and logical structure information for document interchange.

Because of these differences, a PDF file generally cannot be transmitted directly to a PostScript output device for printing (although a few such devices do also support PDF directly). An application printing a PDF document to a PostScript device must carry out the following steps:

1. Insert *procedure sets* containing PostScript procedure definitions to implement the PDF operators.

2. Extract the content for each page. Each content stream is essentially the script portion of a traditional PostScript program using very specific procedures, such as **m** for **moveto** and **l** for **lineto**.

3. Decode compressed text, graphics, and image data as necessary. The compression filters used in PDF are compatible with those used in PostScript; they may or may not be supported, depending on the LanguageLevel of the target output device.

4. Insert any needed resources, such as fonts, into the PostScript file. These can be either the original fonts themselves or suitable substitute fonts based on the font metrics in the PDF file. Fonts may need to be converted to a format that the PostScript interpreter recognizes, such as Type 1 or Type 42.

5. Put the information in the correct order. The result is a traditional PostScript program that fully represents the visual aspects of the document but no longer contains PDF elements such as hypertext links, annotations, and bookmarks.

6. Send the PostScript program to the output device.

CHAPTER 3

Syntax

THIS CHAPTER COVERS everything about the syntax of PDF at the object, file, and document level. It sets the stage for subsequent chapters, which describe how the contents of a PDF file are interpreted as page descriptions, interactive navigational aids, and application-level logical structure.

PDF syntax is best understood by thinking of it in four parts, as shown in Figure 3.1:

- *Objects.* A PDF document is a data structure composed from a small set of basic types of data object. Section 3.1, "Lexical Conventions," describes the character set used to write objects and other syntactic elements. Section 3.2, "Objects," describes the syntax and essential properties of the objects themselves. Section 3.3, "Details of Filtered Streams," provides complete details of the most complex data type, the stream object.

- *File structure.* The PDF file structure determines how objects are stored in a PDF file, how they are accessed, and how they are updated. This structure is independent of the semantics of the objects. Section 3.4, "File Structure," describes the file structure. Section 3.5, "Encryption," describes a file-level mechanism for protecting a document's contents from unauthorized access.

- *Document structure.* The PDF document structure specifies how the basic object types are used to represent components of a PDF document: pages, fonts, annotations, and so forth. Section 3.6, "Document Structure," describes the overall document structure; later chapters address the detailed semantics of the components.

- *Content streams.* A PDF *content stream* contains a sequence of instructions describing the appearance of a page or other graphical entity. These instructions, while also represented as objects, are conceptually distinct from the objects that represent the document structure and are described separately. Section 3.7, "Content Streams and Resources," discusses PDF content streams and their associated resources.

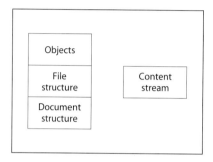

FIGURE 3.1 *PDF components*

In addition, this chapter describes some data structures, built from basic objects, that are so widely used that they can almost be considered basic object types in their own right. These objects are covered in Sections 3.8, "Common Data Structures"; 3.9, "Functions"; and 3.10, "File Specifications."

PDF's object and file syntax is also used as the basis for other file formats. These include the Forms Data Format (FDF), described in Section 7.6.6, "Forms Data Format," and the Portable Job Ticket Format (PJTF), described in Adobe Technical Note #5620, *Portable Job Ticket Format.*

3.1 Lexical Conventions

At the most fundamental level, a PDF file is a sequence of 8-bit bytes. These bytes can be grouped into *tokens* according to the syntax rules described below. One or more tokens are then assembled to form higher-level syntactic entities, principally *objects*, which are the basic data values from which a PDF document is constructed.

PDF can be entirely represented using byte values corresponding to the visible printable subset of the ASCII character set, plus characters that appear as "white space," such as space, tab, carriage return, and line feed characters. ASCII is the American Standard Code for Information Interchange, a widely used convention for encoding a specific set of 128 characters as binary numbers. However, a PDF file is not restricted to the ASCII character set; it can contain arbitrary 8-bit bytes, subject to the following considerations:

- The tokens that delimit objects and that describe the structure of a PDF file are all written in the ASCII character set, as are all the reserved words and the names used as keys in standard dictionaries.

- The data values of certain types of object—strings and streams—can be but need not be written entirely in ASCII. For the purpose of exposition (as in this book), ASCII representation is preferred. However, in actual practice, data that is naturally binary, such as sampled images, is represented directly in binary for the sake of compactness and efficiency.

- A PDF file containing binary data must be transported and stored by means that preserve all bytes of the file faithfully; that is, as a binary file rather than a text file. Such a file is not portable to environments that impose reserved character codes, maximum line lengths, end-of-line conventions, or other restrictions.

Note: *In this chapter, the term* character *is synonymous with* byte *and merely refers to a particular 8-bit value. This is entirely independent of any logical meaning that the value may have when it is treated as data in specific contexts, such as representing human-readable text or selecting a glyph from a font.*

3.1.1 Character Set

The PDF character set is divided into three classes, called *regular, delimiter,* and *white-space* characters. This classification determines the grouping of characters into tokens, except within strings, streams, and comments; different rules apply in those contexts.

White-space characters (see Table 3.1) separate syntactic constructs such as names and numbers from each other. All white-space characters are equivalent, except in comments, strings, and streams. In all other contexts, PDF treats any sequence of consecutive white-space characters as if there were just one.

TABLE 3.1 White-space characters			
DECIMAL	HEXADECIMAL	OCTAL	NAME
0	00	000	Null (NUL)
9	09	011	Tab (HT)
10	0A	012	Line feed (LF)
12	0C	014	Form feed (FF)
13	0D	015	Carriage return (CR)
32	20	040	Space (SP)

The carriage return (CR) and line feed (LF) characters, also called *newline characters*, are treated as *end-of-line* (EOL) markers. The combination of a carriage return followed immediately by a line feed is treated as one EOL marker. For the most part, EOL markers are treated the same as any other white-space characters. However, there are certain instances in which an EOL marker is required or recommended—that is, the following token must appear at the beginning of a line.

Note: The examples in this book illustrate a recommended convention for arranging tokens into lines. However, the examples' use of white space for indentation is purely for clarity of exposition and is not recommended for practical use.

The *delimiter characters* (,), <, >, [,], {, }, /, and % are special. They delimit syntactic entities such as strings, arrays, names, and comments. Any of these characters terminates the entity preceding it and is not included in the entity.

All characters besides the white-space characters and delimiters are referred to as *regular characters*. These include 8-bit binary characters that are outside the ASCII character set. A sequence of consecutive regular characters comprises a single token.

Note: PDF is case-sensitive; corresponding uppercase and lowercase letters are considered distinct.

3.1.2 Comments

Any occurrence of the percent sign character (%) outside a string or stream introduces a *comment*. The comment consists of all characters between the percent sign and the end of the line, including regular, delimiter, space, and tab characters. PDF ignores comments, treating them as if they were single white-space characters. That is, a comment separates the token preceding it from the one following; thus the PDF fragment

```
abc% comment {/%) blah blah blah
123
```

is syntactically equivalent to just the tokens abc and 123.

Comments (other than the %PDF–1.3 and %%EOF comments described in Section 3.4, "File Structure") have no semantics. They are not necessarily preserved by applications that edit PDF files (see implementation note 2 in Appendix H). In particular, there is no PDF equivalent of the PostScript document structuring conventions (DSC).

3.2 Objects

PDF supports eight basic types of object:

- Boolean values
- Integer and real numbers
- Strings
- Names
- Arrays
- Dictionaries
- Streams
- The null object

Objects may be labeled so that they can be referred to by other objects. A labeled object is called an *indirect object*.

The following sections describe each object type, as well as how to create and refer to indirect objects.

3.2.1 Boolean Objects

PDF provides *boolean objects* with values *true* and *false*. The keywords **true** and **false** represent these values. Boolean objects can be used as the values of array elements and dictionary entries, and can also occur in PostScript calculator functions as the results of boolean and relational operators and as operands to the conditional operators **if** and **ifelse** (see Section 3.9.4, "Type 4 (PostScript Calculator) Functions").

3.2.2 Numeric Objects

PDF provides two types of numeric object: integer and real. *Integer objects* represent mathematical integers within a certain interval centered at 0. *Real objects* approximate mathematical real numbers, but with limited range and precision; they are typically represented in fixed-point, rather than floating-point, form. The range and precision of numbers are limited by the internal representations used in the machine on which the PDF viewer application is running; Appendix C gives these limits for typical implementations.

An integer is written one or more decimal digits optionally preceded by a sign:

    123 43445 +17 −98 0

The value is interpreted as a signed decimal integer and is converted to an integer object. If it exceeds the implementation limit for integers, it is converted to a real object.

A real value is written as one or more decimal digits with an optional sign and a leading, trailing, or embedded period (decimal point):

    34.5 −3.62 +123.6 4. −.002 0.0

The value is interpreted as a real number and is converted to a real object. If it exceeds the implementation limit for real numbers, an error occurs.

Note: PDF does not support the PostScript syntax for numbers with nondecimal radices (such as 16#FFFE) or in exponential format (such as 6.02E23).

Throughout this book, the term *number* refers to an object whose type may be either integer or real. Wherever a real number is expected, an integer may be used instead and will be automatically converted to an equivalent real value. For example, it is not necessary to write the number 1.0 in real format; the integer 1 will suffice.

3.2.3 String Objects

A *string object* consists of a series of bytes—unsigned integer values in the range 0 to 255. The string elements are not integer objects, but are stored in a more compact format. The length of a string is subject to an implementation limit; see Appendix C.

There are two conventions, described in the following sections, for writing a string object in PDF:

• As a sequence of literal characters enclosed in parentheses ( )

• As hexadecimal data enclosed in angle brackets < >

This section describes only the basic syntax for writing a string as a sequence of bytes. Strings can be used for many purposes and can be formatted in a variety of ways. When a string is used for a specific purpose (to represent a date, for example), it is useful to have a standard format for that purpose (see Section 3.8.2, "Dates"). Such formats are merely conventions for interpreting the contents of a string and are not in themselves separate object types. The use of a particular format is described with the definition of the string object that uses that format.

Literal Strings

A *literal string* is written as an arbitrary number of characters enclosed in parentheses. Any characters may appear in a string except unbalanced parentheses and the backslash, which must be treated specially. Balanced pairs of parentheses within a string require no special treatment.

The following are valid literal strings:

```
(This is a string)
(Strings may contain newlines
and such.)
(Strings may contain balanced parentheses ( ) and
special characters (*!&}^% and so on).)
(The following is an empty string.)
()
(It has zero (0) length.)
```

Within a literal string, the backslash (\) is used as an escape character for various purposes, such as to include newline characters, nonprinting ASCII characters, unbalanced parentheses, or the backslash character itself in the string. The character immediately following the backslash determines its precise interpretation (see Table 3.2). If the character following the backslash is not one of those shown in the table, the backslash is ignored.

TABLE 3.2 Escape sequences in literal strings	
SEQUENCE	**MEANING**
\n	Line feed
\r	Carriage return
\t	Horizontal tab
\b	Backspace
\f	Form feed
\(	Left parenthesis
\)	Right parenthesis
\\	Backslash
\ddd	Character code *ddd* (octal)

If a string is too long to be conveniently placed on a single line, it may be split across multiple lines by using the backslash character at the end of a line to indicate that the string continues on the following line. The backslash and the end-of-line marker following it are not considered part of the string. For example:

    (These \
    two strings \
    are the same.)
    (These two strings are the same.)

If an end-of-line marker appears within a literal string without a preceding backslash, the result is equivalent to \n (regardless of whether the end-of-line marker itself was a carriage return, a line feed, or both). For example:

    (This string has an end–of–line at the end of it.
)
    (So does this one.\n)

The \ddd escape sequence provides a way to represent characters outside the printable ASCII character set. For example:

    (This string contains \245two octal characters\307.)

The number *ddd* may consist of one, two, or three octal digits, with high-order overflow ignored. It is required that three octal digits be used, with leading zeros as needed, if the next character of the string is also a digit. For example, the literal

    (\0053)

denotes a string containing two characters, \005 (Control-E) followed by the digit 3, whereas both

    (\053)

and

    (\53)

denote strings containing the single character \053, a plus sign (+).

This notation provides a way to specify characters outside the 7-bit ASCII character set using ASCII characters only. However, any 8-bit value may appear in a string. In particular, when a document is encrypted (see Section 3.5, "Encryption"), all of its strings are encrypted and often contain arbitrary 8-bit values. Note that the backslash character is still required as an escape to specify unbalanced parentheses or the backslash character itself.

Hexadecimal Strings

Strings may also be written in hexadecimal form; this is useful for including arbitrary binary data in a PDF file. A hexadecimal string is written as a sequence of hexadecimal digits (0–9 and either A–F or a–f) enclosed within angle brackets (< and >):

    <4E6F762073686D6F7A206B6120706F702E>

Each pair of hexadecimal digits defines one byte of the string. White-space characters (such as space, tab, carriage return, line feed, and form feed) are ignored.

If the final digit of a hexadecimal string is missing—that is, if there is an odd number of digits—the final digit is assumed to be 0. For example,

    <901FA3>

is a 3-byte string consisting of the characters whose hexadecimal codes are 90, 1F, and A3, but

    <901FA>

is a 3-byte string containing the characters whose hexadecimal codes are 90, 1F, and A0.

3.2.4 Name Objects

A *name object* is an atomic symbol uniquely defined by a sequence of characters. *Uniquely defined* means that any two name objects defined by the same sequence of characters are identically the same object. *Atomic* means that a name has no internal structure; although it is defined by a sequence of characters, those characters are not "elements" of the name.

A slash character (/) introduces a name. The slash is not part of the name itself, but a prefix indicating that the following sequence of characters constitutes a name. There can be no white-space characters between the slash and the first character in the name. The name may include any regular characters, but not delimiter or white-space characters (see Section 3.1, "Lexical Conventions"). Uppercase and lowercase letters are considered distinct; /A and /a are different names. The following are examples of valid literal names:

```
/Name1
/ASomewhatLongerName
/A;Name_With–Various***Characters?
/1.2
/$$
/@pattern
/.notdef
```

Note: *The token / (a slash followed by no regular characters) is a valid name.*

In PDF 1.2 and higher, any character except null (character code 0) may be included in a name by writing its 2-digit hexadecimal code, preceded by the number sign character (#); see implementation notes 3 and 4 in Appendix H. This syntax is required in order to represent any of the delimiter or white-space characters or the number sign character itself; it is recommended but not required for characters whose codes are outside the range 33 (!) to 126 (~). The examples shown in Table 3.3 are valid literal names in PDF 1.2 and higher.

TABLE 3.3   Examples of literal names using the # character

LITERAL NAME	RESULT
/Adobe#20Green	Adobe Green
/PANTONE#205757#20CV	PANTONE 5757 CV
/paired#28#29parentheses	paired()parentheses
/The_Key_of_F#23_Minor	The_Key_of_F#_Minor
/A#42	AB

The length of a name is subject to an implementation limit; see Appendix C. The limit applies to the number of characters in the name's internal representation. For example, the name /A#20B has 4 characters (/, A, space, B), not 6.

In PDF, name objects always begin with the slash character /, unlike keywords such as **true, false,** and **obj.** This book follows a typographic convention of writing names in boldface without the leading slash when they appear in running text and tables. For example, **Type** and **DecodeParms** denote names that would actually be written in a PDF file (and in code examples in this book) as /Type and /DecodeParms.

3.2.5 Array Objects

An *array object* is a one-dimensional collection of objects arranged sequentially. Unlike arrays in many other computer languages, PDF arrays may be heterogeneous; that is, an array's elements may be any combination of numbers, strings, dictionaries, or any other objects, including other arrays. The number of elements in an array is subject to an implementation limit; see Appendix C.

An array is written as a sequence of objects enclosed in square brackets ([and]):

```
[549 3.14 false (Ralph) /SomeName]
```

PDF directly supports only one-dimensional arrays. Arrays of higher dimension can be constructed by using arrays as elements of arrays, nested to any depth.

3.2.6 Dictionary Objects

A *dictionary object* is an associative table containing pairs of objects, known as the dictionary's *entries.* The first element of each entry is the *key* and the second element is the *value.* The key must be a name (unlike dictionary keys in Post-Script, which may be objects of any type). The value can be any kind of object, including another dictionary. A dictionary entry whose value is **null** (see Section 3.2.8, "The Null Object") is equivalent to an absent entry. (Note that this differs from PostScript, where **null** behaves like any other object as the value of a dictionary entry.) The number of entries in a dictionary is subject to an implementation limit; see Appendix C.

Note: *No two entries in the same dictionary should have the same key. If a key does appear more than once, its value is undefined.*

A dictionary is written as a sequence of key-value pairs enclosed in double angle brackets (<< and >>). For example:

```
<< /Type  /Example
   /Subtype  /DictionaryExample
   /Version  0.01
   /IntegerItem  12
   /StringItem  (a string)
   /Subdictionary  << /Item1  0.4
                      /Item2  true
                      /LastItem  (not!)
                      /VeryLastItem  (OK)
                   >>
>>
```

Note: *Do not confuse the double angle brackets with single angle brackets (< and >), which delimit a hexadecimal string (see "Hexadecimal Strings" on page 30).*

Dictionary objects are the main building blocks of a PDF document. They are commonly used to collect and tie together the attributes of a complex object, such as a font or a page of the document, with each entry in the dictionary specifying the name and value of an attribute. By convention, the **Type** entry of such a dictionary identifies the type of object the dictionary describes. In some cases, a **Subtype** entry (sometimes abbreviated **S**) is used to further identify a specialized subcategory of the general type. The value of the **Type** or **Subtype** entry is always a name. For example, in a font dictionary, the value of the **Type** entry is always **Font**, whereas that of the **Subtype** entry may be **Type1**, **TrueType**, or one of several other values.

The value of the **Type** entry can almost always be inferred from context. The operand of the **Tf** operator, for example, must be a font object, so the **Type** entry in a font dictionary serves primarily as documentation and as information for error checking. The **Type** entry is not required unless so stated in its description; however, if the entry is present, it must have the correct value. In addition, the value of the **Type** entry in any dictionary, even in private data, must be either a name defined in this book or a registered name; see Appendix E for details.

3.2.7   Stream Objects

A *stream object*, like a string object, is a sequence of bytes. However, a PDF application can read a stream incrementally, while a string must be read in its entirety.

Furthermore, a stream can be of unlimited length, whereas a string is subject to an implementation limit. For this reason, objects with potentially large amounts of data, such as images and page descriptions, are represented as streams.

Note: As with strings, this section describes only the syntax for writing a stream as a sequence of bytes. What those bytes represent is determined by the context in which the stream is referenced.

A stream consists of a dictionary that describes a sequence of bytes, followed by zero or more lines of bytes bracketed between the keywords **stream** and **endstream**:

> *dictionary*
> **stream**
> *… Zero or more lines of bytes …*
> **endstream**

All streams must be indirect objects (see Section 3.2.9, "Indirect Objects") and the stream dictionary must be a direct object. The keyword **stream** that follows the stream dictionary should be followed by either a carriage return and a line feed or by just a line feed, and not by a carriage return alone. The sequence of bytes that make up a stream lie between the **stream** and **endstream** keywords, or, in PDF 1.2, may be contained in an external file. If the data is in an external file, the stream dictionary specifies the file, and any bytes between **stream** and **endstream** are ignored. (See implementation note 5 in Appendix H.)

*Note: Without the restriction against following the keyword **stream** by a carriage return alone, it would be impossible to differentiate a stream that uses carriage return as its end-of-line marker and has a line feed as its first byte of data from one that uses a carriage return–line feed sequence to denote end-of-line.*

Table 3.4 lists the entries common to all stream dictionaries; certain types of stream may have additional dictionary entries, as indicated where those streams are described. The optional entries regarding *filters* for the stream indicate whether and how the data in the stream must be transformed ("decoded") before it is used.

TABLE 3.4   Entries common to all stream dictionaries

KEY	TYPE	VALUE
Length	integer	*(Required)* The number of bytes from the beginning of the line following the keyword **stream** to the last byte just before the keyword **endstream**. (There may be an additional EOL marker, preceding **endstream**, that is not included in the count and is not logically part of the stream data.)
Filter	name or array	*(Optional)* The name of a filter to be applied in processing the stream data found between the keywords **stream** and **endstream**, or an array of such names. Multiple filters should be specified in the order in which they are to be applied.
DecodeParms	dictionary or array	*(Optional)* A parameter dictionary, or an array of such dictionaries, used by the filters specified by **Filter**. If there is only one filter and that filter has parameters, **DecodeParms** must be set to the filter's parameter dictionary unless all the filter's parameters have their default values, in which case the **DecodeParms** entry may be omitted. If there are multiple filters and any of the filters has parameters set to non-default values, **DecodeParms** must be an array with one entry for each filter: either the parameter dictionary for that filter, or the null object if that filter has no parameters (or if all of its parameters have their default values). If none of the filters have parameters, or if all their parameters have default values, the **DecodeParms** entry may be omitted. (See implementation note 6 in Appendix H.)
F	file specification	*(Optional; PDF 1.2)* The file containing the stream data. If this entry is present, the bytes between **stream** and **endstream** are ignored, the filters are specified by **FFilter** rather than **Filter**, and the filter parameters are specified by **FDecodeParms** rather than **DecodeParms**. However, the **Length** entry should still specify the number of those bytes. (Usually there are no bytes and **Length** is 0.)
FFilter	name or array	*(Optional; PDF 1.2)* The name of a filter to be applied in processing the data found in the stream's external file, or an array of such names. The same rules apply as for **Filter**.
FDecodeParms	dictionary or array	*(Optional; PDF 1.2)* A parameter dictionary, or an array of such dictionaries, used by the filters specified by **FFilter**. The same rules apply as for **DecodeParms**.

Stream Extent

Every stream dictionary has a **Length** entry that indicates how many bytes of the PDF file are used for the stream's data. (If the stream has a filter, **Length** is the number of bytes of *encoded* data.) In addition, most filters are defined so that the data is self-limiting; that is, they use an encoding scheme in which an explicit *end-of-data* (EOD) marker delimits the extent of the data. Finally, streams are used to represent many objects from whose attributes a length can be inferred. *All of these constraints must be consistent.*

For example, an image with 10 rows and 20 columns, using a single color component and 8 bits per component, requires exactly 200 bytes of image data. If the stream uses a filter, there must be enough bytes of encoded data in the PDF file to produce those 200 bytes. An error occurs if **Length** is too small, if an explicit EOD marker occurs too soon, or if the decoded data does not contain 200 bytes.

It is also an error if the stream contains too *much* data, with the exception that there may be an extra end-of-line marker in the PDF file before the keyword **endstream**.

Filters

A *filter* is an optional part of the specification of a stream, indicating how the data in the stream must be decoded before it is used. For example, if a stream has an **ASCIIHexDecode** filter, an application reading the data in that stream will transform the ASCII hexadecimal-encoded data in the stream into binary data.

An application program that produces a PDF file can encode certain information (for example, data for sampled images) to compress it or to convert it to a portable ASCII representation. Then an application that reads ("consumes") the PDF file can invoke the corresponding decoding filter to convert the information back to its original form.

The filter or filters for a stream are specified by the **Filter** key in the stream's dictionary (or the **FFilter** key if the stream is external). Filters can be cascaded to form a *pipeline* that passes the stream through two or more decoding transformations in sequence. For example, data encoded using LZW and ASCII base-85 encoding (in that order) can be decoded using the following entry in the stream dictionary:

   /Filter [/ASCII85Decode /LZWDecode]

Some filters may take parameters to control how they operate. These optional parameters are specified by the **DecodeParms** entry in the stream's dictionary (or the **FDecodeParms** entry if the stream is external).

Standard Filters

PDF supports a standard set of filters that fall into two main categories:

- *ASCII filters* enable arbitrary 8-bit binary data to be represented in the printable subset of the ASCII character set. (See Section 3.1, "Lexical Conventions," for an explanation of why this might be useful. Note that ASCII filters serve no useful purpose in a PDF file that is encrypted; see Section 3.5, "Encryption.")

- *Decompression filters* enable data to be represented in a compressed form. Compression is particularly valuable for large sampled images, since it reduces storage requirements and transmission time. Note that the compressed data is always in 8-bit binary format, even if the original data happens to be ASCII text.

These filters are summarized in Table 3.5, which also indicates whether they accept any optional parameters. The filters and their parameters (if any) are described further in Section 3.3, "Details of Filtered Streams." (See also implementation notes 7 and 8 in Appendix H.)

Example Encoded Stream

Example 3.1 shows a stream, containing the marking instructions for a page, that was compressed using the LZW compression method and then encoded in ASCII base-85 representation. Example 3.2 shows the same stream without any encoding. (The stream's contents are explained in Section 3.7.1, "Content Streams," and the operators used there are further described in Chapter 5.)

TABLE 3.5 Standard filters

FILTER NAME	PARAMETERS?	DESCRIPTION
ASCIIHexDecode	no	Decodes data encoded in an ASCII hexadecimal representation, reproducing the original binary data.
ASCII85Decode	no	Decodes data encoded in an ASCII base-85 representation, reproducing the original binary data.
LZWDecode	yes	Decompresses data encoded using the LZW (Lempel-Ziv-Welch) adaptive compression method, reproducing the original text or binary data.
FlateDecode	yes	*(PDF 1.2)* Decompresses data encoded using the public-domain zlib/deflate compression method, reproducing the original text or binary data. (See implementation note 9 in Appendix H.)
RunLengthDecode	no	Decompresses data encoded using a byte-oriented run-length encoding algorithm, reproducing the original text or binary data (typically monochrome image data, or any data that contains frequent long runs of a single byte value).
CCITTFaxDecode	yes	Decompresses data encoded using the CCITT facsimile standard, reproducing the original data (typically monochrome image data at 1 bit per pixel).
DCTDecode	yes	Decompresses data encoded using a DCT (discrete cosine transform) technique based on the JPEG standard, reproducing image sample data that approximates the original data.

Example 3.1

```
<< /Length 534
    /Filter [/ASCII85Decode /LZWDecode]
>>
stream
J..)6T`?p&<!J9%_[umg"B7/Z7KNXbN'S+,*Q/&"OLT'F
LIDK#!n`$"<Atdi`\Vn%b%)&'cA*VnK\CJY(sF>c!Jnl@
RM]WM;jjH6Gnc75idkL5]+cPZKEBPWdR>FF(kj1_R%W_d
&/jS!;iuad7h?[L−F$+]]0A3Ck*$I0KZ?;<)CJtqi65Xb
Vc3\n5ua:Q/=0$W<#N3U;H,MQKqfg1?:IUpR;6oN[C2E4
ZNr8Udn.'p+?#X+1>0Kuk$bCDF/(3fL5]Oq)^kJZ!C2H1
'TO]Rl?Q:&'<5&iP!$Rq;BXRecDN[IJB`,)o8XJOSJ9sD
S]hQ;Rj@!ND)bD_q&C\g:inYC%)&u#:u,M6Bm%IY!Kb1+
```

```
":aAa'S`ViJglLb8<W9k6Yl\\0McJQkDeLWdPN?9A'jX*
al>iG1p&i;eVoK&juJHs9%;Xomop"5KatWRT"JQ#qYuL,
JD?M$0QP)lKn06l1apKDC@\qJ4B!!(5m+j.7F790m(Vj8
8l8Q:_CZ(Gm1%X\N1&u!FKHMB~>
endstream
```

Example 3.2

```
<< /Length 568 >>
stream
2 J
BT
/F1 12 Tf
0 Tc
0 Tw
72.5 712 TD
[(Unencoded streams can be read easily) 65 (,)] TJ
0 –14 TD
[(b) 20 (ut generally tak) 10 (e more space than \311)] TJ
T* (encoded streams.) Tj
0 –28 TD
[(Se) 25 (v) 15 (eral encoding methods are a) 20 (v) 25 (ailable in PDF) 80 (.)] TJ
0 –14 TD
(Some are used for compression and others simply) Tj
T* [(to represent binary data in an ) 55 (ASCII format.)] TJ
T* (Some of the compression encoding methods are \
suitable ) Tj
T* (for both data and images, while others are \
suitable only ) Tj
T* (for continuous–tone images.) Tj
ET
endstream
```

3.2.8 The Null Object

The *null object* is used to fill empty or uninitialized positions in an array or dictionary. There is only one object of type null, denoted by the keyword **null**. As noted in Section 3.2.6, "Dictionary Objects," specifying the null object as the value of a dictionary entry is equivalent to omitting the entry entirely.

3.2.9 Indirect Objects

Any object in a PDF file may be labeled as an *indirect object.* This gives the object a unique *object identifier* by which other objects can refer to it (for example, as an element of an array or as the value of a dictionary entry). The object identifier consists of two parts:

- A positive integer *object number.* Indirect objects are often numbered sequentially within a PDF file, but this is not required; object numbers may be assigned in any arbitrary order.

- A nonnegative integer *generation number.* In a newly created file, all indirect objects have generation numbers of 0. Nonzero generation numbers may be introduced when the file is later updated; see Sections 3.4.3, "Cross-Reference Table," and 3.4.5, "Incremental Updates."

Together, the combination of an object number and a generation number uniquely identifies an indirect object. The object retains the same object number and generation number throughout its existence, even if its value is modified.

The definition of an indirect object in a PDF file consists of its object number and generation number, followed by the value of the object itself bracketed between the keywords **obj** and **endobj**. For example, the definition

```
12 0 obj
   (Brillig)
endobj
```

defines an indirect string object with an object number of 12, a generation number of 0, and the value Brillig. The object can then be referred to from elsewhere in the file by an *indirect reference* consisting of the object number, the generation number, and the keyword **R**:

```
12 0 R
```

An indirect reference to an undefined object is not an error; it is simply treated as a reference to the null object. For example, if a file contains the indirect reference

```
17 0 R
```

but does not contain the corresponding definition

```
17  0  obj
    …
endobj
```

then the indirect reference is considered to refer to the null object.

Note: In the data structures that make up a PDF document, certain values are required to be specified as indirect object references. Except where this is explicitly called out, any object (other than a stream) may be specified either directly or as an indirect object reference; the semantics are entirely equivalent. Note in particular that content streams, which define the visible contents of the document, may not contain indirect references (see Section 3.7.1, "Content Streams").

Example 3.3 shows the use of an indirect object to specify the length of a stream. The value of the stream's **Length** entry is an integer object that follows the stream itself in the file. This allows applications that generate PDF in a single pass to defer specifying the stream's length until after its contents have been generated.

Example 3.3

```
7  0  obj
    << /Length  8 0 R  >>              % An indirect reference to object 8
stream
    BT
        /F1  12  Tf
        72  712  Td
        (A stream with an indirect length)  Tj
    ET
endstream
endobj

8  0  obj
    77                                 % The length of the preceding stream
endobj
```

3.3 Details of Filtered Streams

Stream filters are introduced under "Filters" on page 36. This section describes the semantics of filters in more detail, including specifications of encoding algorithms for some filters.

3.3.1 ASCIIHexDecode Filter

The **ASCIIHexDecode** filter decodes data that has been encoded in ASCII hexadecimal form. ASCII hexadecimal encoding and ASCII base-85 encoding (described in the next section) convert binary data, such as image data, to 7-bit ASCII characters. In general, ASCII base-85 encoding is preferred to ASCII hexadecimal encoding because it is more compact: it expands the data by a factor of $4:5$, compared with $1:2$ for ASCII hexadecimal encoding.

For each pair of ASCII hexadecimal digits (0–9 and A–F or a–f), the **ASCIIHexDecode** filter produces one byte of binary data. All white-space characters (see Section 3.1, "Lexical Conventions") are ignored. A right angle bracket character (>) indicates EOD. Any other characters will cause an error. If the filter encounters the EOD marker after reading an odd number of hexadecimal digits, it will behave as if a 0 followed the last digit.

3.3.2 ASCII85Decode Filter

The **ASCII85Decode** filter decodes data that has been encoded in ASCII base-85 encoding and produces binary data. The following paragraphs describe the process for encoding binary data in ASCII base-85; the **ASCII85Decode** filter reverses this process.

The ASCII base-85 encoding uses the characters ! through u and the character z, with the 2-character sequence ~> as its EOD marker. The **ASCII85Decode** filter ignores all white-space characters (see Section 3.1, "Lexical Conventions"). Any other characters, and any character sequences that represent impossible combinations in the ASCII base-85 encoding, will cause an error.

Specifically, ASCII base-85 encoding produces 5 ASCII characters for every 4 bytes of binary data. Each group of 4 binary input bytes, $(b_1\ b_2\ b_3\ b_4)$, is converted to a group of 5 output bytes, $(c_1\ c_2\ c_3\ c_4\ c_5)$, using the relation

$$(b_1 \times 256^3) + (b_2 \times 256^2) + (b_3 \times 256^1) + b_4 =$$
$$(c_1 \times 85^4) + (c_2 \times 85^3) + (c_3 \times 85^2) + (c_4 \times 85^1) + c_5$$

In other words, 4 bytes of binary data are interpreted as a base-256 number and then converted into a base-85 number. The five "digits" of the base-85 number are then converted to ASCII characters by adding 33 (the ASCII code for the character !) to each. The resulting encoded data contains only printable ASCII characters with codes in the range 33 (!) to 117 (u). As a special case, if all five digits are 0, they are represented by the character with code 122 (z) instead of by five exclamation points (!!!!!).

If the length of the binary data to be encoded is not a multiple of 4 bytes, the last, partial group of 4 is used to produce a last, partial group of 5 output characters. Given n (1, 2, or 3) bytes of binary data, the encoder first appends $4 - n$ zero bytes to make a complete group of 4. It then encodes this group in the usual way, but without applying the special z case. Finally, it writes only the first $n + 1$ characters of the resulting group of 5. These characters are immediately followed by the ~> EOD marker.

The following conditions (which never occur in a correctly encoded byte sequence) will cause errors during decoding:

- The value represented by a group of 5 characters is greater than $2^{32} - 1$.

- A z character occurs in the middle of a group.

- A final partial group contains only one character.

3.3.3 LZWDecode and FlateDecode Filters

The **LZWDecode** and (in PDF 1.2) **FlateDecode** filters have much in common and so are discussed together in this section. They decode data that has been encoded using the LZW or Flate data compression method, respectively.

- LZW (Lempel-Ziv-Welch) is a variable-length, adaptive compression method that has been adopted as one of the standard compression methods in the *Tag Image File Format* (TIFF) standard. Details on LZW encoding follow in the next section.

- The Flate method is based on the public-domain zlib/deflate compression method, which is a variable-length Lempel-Ziv adaptive compression method cascaded with adaptive Huffman coding. It is fully defined in Internet RFCs 1950, *ZLIB Compressed Data Format Specification*, and 1951, *DEFLATE Compressed Data Format Specification* (see the Bibliography).

Both of these methods compress either binary data or ASCII text but (like all compression methods) always produce binary data, even if the original data was text.

The LZW and Flate compression methods can discover and exploit many patterns in the input data, whether the data is text or images. As described later, both filters support optional transformation by a *predictor function*, which improves the compression of sampled image data. Thanks to its cascaded adaptive Huffman coding, Flate-encoded output is usually much more compact than LZW-encoded output for the same input. Flate and LZW decoding speeds are comparable, but Flate encoding is considerably slower than LZW encoding.

Usually, both Flate and LZW encodings compress their input substantially. However, in the worst case (in which no pair of adjacent characters appears twice), Flate encoding *expands* its input by no more than 11 bytes or a factor of 1.003 (whichever is larger), plus the effects of algorithm tags added by PNG predictors. For LZW encoding, the best case (all zeros) provides a compression approaching 1365:1 for long files, but the worst-case expansion is at least a factor of 1.125, which can increase to nearly 1.5 in some implementations (plus the effects of PNG tags as with Flate encoding).

Details of LZW Encoding

Data encoded using the LZW compression method consists of a sequence of codes that are 9 to 12 bits long. Each code represents a single character of input data (0–255), a clear-table marker (256), an EOD marker (257), or a table entry representing a multiple-character sequence that has been encountered previously in the input (258 or greater).

Initially, the code length is 9 bits and the LZW table contains only entries for the 258 fixed codes. As encoding proceeds, entries are appended to the table, associating new codes with longer and longer sequences of input characters. The encoder and the decoder maintain identical copies of this table.

Whenever both the encoder and the decoder independently (but synchronously) realize that the current code length is no longer sufficient to represent the number of entries in the table, they increase the number of bits per code by 1. The first output code that is 10 bits long is the one following the creation of table entry 511, and similarly for 11 (1023) and 12 (2047) bits. Codes are never longer than 12 bits, so entry 4095 is the last entry of the LZW table.

The encoder executes the following sequence of steps to generate each output code:

1. Accumulate a sequence of one or more input characters matching a sequence already present in the table. For maximum compression, the encoder looks for the longest such sequence.

2. Emit the code corresponding to that sequence.

3. Create a new table entry for the first unused code. Its value is the sequence found in step 1 followed by the next input character.

For example, suppose the input consists of the following sequence of ASCII character codes:

    45 45 45 45 45 65 45 45 45 66

Starting with an empty table, the encoder proceeds as shown in Table 3.6.

TABLE 3.6   Typical LZW encoding sequence

INPUT SEQUENCE	OUTPUT CODE	CODE ADDED TO TABLE	SEQUENCE REPRESENTED BY NEW CODE
–	256 (clear-table)	–	–
45	45	258	45 45
45 45	258	259	45 45 45
45 45	258	260	45 45 65
65	65	261	65 45
45 45 45	259	262	45 45 45 66
–	257 (EOD)	–	–

Codes are packed into a continuous bit stream, high-order bit first. This stream is then divided into 8-bit bytes, high-order bit first. Thus, codes can straddle byte boundaries arbitrarily. After the EOD marker (code value 257), any leftover bits in the final byte are set to 0.

In the example above, all the output codes are 9 bits long; they would pack into bytes as follows (represented in hexadecimal):

```
80 0B 60 50 22 0C 0E 02
```

To adapt to changing input sequences, the encoder may at any point issue a clear-table code, which causes both the encoder and the decoder to restart with initial tables and a 9-bit code length. By convention, the encoder begins by issuing a clear-table code. It must issue a clear-table code when the table becomes full; it may do so sooner.

Note: The LZW compression method is the subject of United States patent number 4,558,302 and corresponding foreign patents owned by the Unisys Corporation. Adobe Systems has licensed this patent for use in its Acrobat products; however, independent software vendors (ISVs) may be required to license this patent directly from Unisys to develop software that uses the LZW method to compress data in PDF files. For information on Unisys licensing policies, send e-mail to <lzw_info@unisys.com>; or visit the Unisys Web site at <http://www.unisys.com>.

LZWDecode and FlateDecode Parameters

The **LZWDecode** and **FlateDecode** filters accept optional parameters to control the decoding process. Most of these parameters are related to techniques that reduce the size of compressed sampled images (rectangular arrays of color values, described in Section 4.8, "Images"). For example, image data frequently changes very little from sample to sample; subtracting the values of adjacent samples (a process called *differencing*), and encoding the differences rather than the raw sample values, can reduce the size of the output data. Furthermore, when the image data contains several color components (red-green-blue or cyan-magenta-yellow-black) per sample, taking the difference between the values of corresponding components in adjacent samples, rather than between different color components in the same sample, often reduces the output data size.

Table 3.7 shows the parameters that can optionally be specified for **LZWDecode** and **FlateDecode** filters. Except where otherwise noted, all values supplied to the decoding filter for any optional parameters must match those used when the data was encoded.

TABLE 3.7 Optional parameters for LZWDecode and FlateDecode filters

KEY	TYPE	VALUE
Predictor	integer	A code that selects the predictor algorithm, if any. If the value of this entry is 1, the filter assumes that the normal algorithm was used to encode the data, without prediction. If the value is greater than 1, the filter assumes that the data was differenced before being encoded, and **Predictor** selects the predictor algorithm. For more information regarding **Predictor** values greater than 1, see "LZW and Flate Predictor Functions," below. Default value: 1.
Colors	integer	*(Used only if **Predictor** is greater than 1)* The number of interleaved color components per sample. Valid values are 1 to 4 in PDF 1.2 or earlier, and 1 or greater in PDF 1.3. Default value: 1.
BitsPerComponent	integer	*(Used only if **Predictor** is greater than 1)* The number of bits used to represent each color component in a sample. Valid values are 1, 2, 4, and 8. Default value: 8.
Columns	integer	*(Used only if **Predictor** is greater than 1)* The number of samples in each row. Default value: 1.
EarlyChange	integer	*(**LZWDecode** only)* An indication of when to increase the code length. If the value of this entry is 0, code length increases are postponed as long as possible. If it is 1, they occur one code early. This parameter is included because LZW sample code distributed by some vendors increases the code length one code earlier than necessary. Default value: 1.

LZW and Flate Predictor Functions

LZW and Flate encoding compress more compactly if their input data is highly predictable. One way of increasing the predictability of many continuous-tone sampled images is to replace each sample with the difference between that sample and a *predictor function* applied to earlier neighboring samples. If the predictor function works well, the postprediction data will cluster toward 0.

Two groups of predictor functions are supported. The first, the *TIFF* group, consists of the single function that is Predictor 2 in the TIFF standard. (In the TIFF standard, Predictor 2 applies only to LZW compression, but here it applies to Flate compression as well.) TIFF Predictor 2 predicts that each color component of a sample will be the same as the corresponding color component of the sample immediately to its left.

The second supported group of predictor functions, the *PNG* group, consists of the "filters" of the World Wide Web Consortium's Portable Network Graphics recommendation, documented in Internet RFC 2083, *PNG (Portable Network Graphics) Specification* (see the Bibliography). The term *predictors* is used here instead of *filters* to avoid confusion. There are five basic PNG predictor algorithms (and a sixth that chooses the optimum predictor function separately for each row):

None	No prediction
Sub	Predicts the same as the sample to the left
Up	Predicts the same as the sample above
Average	Predicts the average of the sample to the left and the sample above
Paeth	A nonlinear function of the sample above, the sample to the left, and the sample to the upper left

The predictor algorithm to be used, if any, is indicated by the **Predictor** filter parameter (see Table 3.7), which can have any of the values listed in Table 3.8.

TABLE 3.8 Predictor values

VALUE	MEANING
1	No prediction (the default value)
2	TIFF Predictor 2
10	PNG prediction (on encoding, PNG None on all rows)
11	PNG prediction (on encoding, PNG Sub on all rows)
12	PNG prediction (on encoding, PNG Up on all rows)
13	PNG prediction (on encoding, PNG Average on all rows)
14	PNG prediction (on encoding, PNG Paeth on all rows)
15	PNG prediction (on encoding, PNG optimum)

For **LZWDecode** and **FlateDecode**, a **Predictor** value greater than or equal to 10 merely indicates that a PNG predictor is in use; the specific predictor function used is explicitly encoded in the incoming data. The value of **Predictor** supplied by the decoding filter need not match the value used when the data was encoded if they are both greater than or equal to 10.

The two groups of predictor functions have some commonalities. Both assume the following:

- Data is presented in order, from the top row to the bottom row and, within a row, from left to right.

- A row occupies a whole number of bytes, rounded up if necessary.

- Samples and their components are packed into bytes from high-order to low-order bits.

- All color components of samples outside the image (which are necessary for predictions near the boundaries) are 0.

The predictor function groups also differ in significant ways:

- The postprediction data for each PNG-predicted row begins with an explicit algorithm tag, so different rows can be predicted with different algorithms to improve compression. TIFF Predictor 2 has no such identifier; the same algorithm applies to all rows.

- The TIFF function group predicts each color component from the prior instance of that component, taking into account the number of bits per component and components per sample. In contrast, the PNG function group predicts each byte of data as a function of the corresponding byte of one or more previous image samples, regardless of whether there are multiple color components in a byte or whether a single color component spans multiple bytes. This can yield significantly better speed at the cost of somewhat worse compression.

3.3.4 RunLengthDecode Filter

The **RunLengthDecode** filter decodes data that has been encoded in a simple byte-oriented format based on run length. The encoded data is a sequence of *runs*, where each run consists of a *length* byte followed by 1 to 128 bytes of data. If the *length* byte is in the range 0 to 127, the following *length* + 1 (1 to 128) bytes are copied literally during decompression. If *length* is in the range 129 to 255, the following single byte is to be copied 257 − *length* (2 to 128) times during decompression. A *length* value of 128 denotes EOD.

The compression achieved by run-length encoding depends on the input data. In the best case (all zeros), a compression of approximately 64:1 is achieved for long files. The worst case (the hexadecimal sequence 00 alternating with FF) results in an expansion of 127:128.

3.3.5 CCITTFaxDecode Filter

The **CCITTFaxDecode** filter decodes image data that has been encoded using either Group 3 or Group 4 CCITT facsimile (fax) encoding. CCITT encoding is designed to achieve efficient compression of monochrome (1 bit per pixel) image data at relatively low resolutions, and so is useful only for bitmap image data, not for color images, grayscale images, or text.

The CCITT encoding standard is defined by the International Telecommunications Union (ITU), formerly known as the Comité Consultatif International Téléphonique et Télégraphique (International Coordinating Committee for Telephony and Telegraphy). The encoding algorithm is not described in detail here, but can be found in ITU Recommendations T.4 and T.6 (see the Bibliography). For historical reasons, we refer to these documents as the CCITT standard.

CCITT encoding is bit-oriented, not byte-oriented. This means that, in principle, encoded or decoded data might not end at a byte boundary. This problem is dealt with in the following ways:

• Unencoded data is treated as complete scan lines, with unused bits inserted at the end of each scan line to fill out the last byte. This is compatible with the PDF convention for sampled image data.

• Encoded data is ordinarily treated as a continuous, unbroken bit stream. The **EncodedByteAlign** parameter (described in Table 3.9) can be used to cause each encoded scan line to be filled to a byte boundary; although this is not prescribed by the CCITT standard and fax machines never do this, some software packages find it convenient to encode data this way.

• When a filter reaches EOD, it always skips to the next byte boundary following the encoded data.

If the **CCITTFaxDecode** filter encounters improperly encoded source data, an error will occur. The filter will not perform any error correction or resynchronization, except as noted for the **DamagedRowsBeforeError** parameter in Table 3.9.

Table 3.9 lists the optional parameters that can be used to control the decoding. Except where noted otherwise, all values supplied to the decoding filter by any of these parameters must match those used when the data was encoded.

TABLE 3.9 Optional parameters for the CCITTFaxDecode filter

KEY	TYPE	VALUE
K	integer	A code identifying the encoding scheme used:
		<0 Pure two-dimensional encoding (Group 4)
		0 Pure one-dimensional encoding (Group 3, 1-D)
		>0 Mixed one- and two-dimensional encoding (Group 3, 2-D), in which a line encoded one-dimensionally can be followed by at most **K** $-$ 1 lines encoded two-dimensionally
		The filter distinguishes among negative, zero, and positive values of **K** to determine how to interpret the encoded data; however, it does not distinguish between different positive **K** values. Default value: 0.
EndOfLine	boolean	A flag indicating whether end-of-line bit patterns are required to be present in the encoding. The **CCITTFaxDecode** filter always accepts end-of-line bit patterns, but requires them only if **EndOfLine** is *true*. Default value: *false*.
EncodedByteAlign	boolean	A flag indicating whether the filter expects extra 0-bits before each encoded line so that the line begins on a byte boundary. If *true*, the filter skips over encoded bits to begin decoding each line at a byte boundary. If *false*, the filter does not expect extra bits in the encoded representation. Default value: *false*.
Columns	integer	The width of the image in pixels. If the value is not a multiple of 8, the filter adjusts the width of the unencoded image to the next multiple of 8, so that each line starts on a byte boundary. Default value: 1728.
Rows	integer	The height of the image in scan lines. If the value is 0 or absent, the image's height is not predetermined, and the encoded data must be terminated by an end-of-block bit pattern or by the end of the filter's data. Default value: 0.

EndOfBlock   boolean   A flag indicating whether the filter expects the encoded data to be terminated by an end-of-block pattern, overriding the **Rows** parameter. If *false*, the filter stops when it has decoded the number of lines indicated by **Rows** or when its data has been exhausted, whichever occurs first. The end-of-block pattern is the CCITT end-of-facsimile-block (EOFB) or return-to-control (RTC) appropriate for the **K** parameter. Default value: *true*.

BlackIs1   boolean   A flag indicating whether 1-bits are to be interpreted as black pixels and 0-bits as white pixels, the reverse of the normal PDF convention for monochrome image data. Default value: *false*.

DamagedRowsBeforeError   integer   The number of damaged rows of data to be tolerated before an error occurs. This entry applies only if **EndOfLine** is *true* and **K** is nonnegative. Tolerating a damaged row means locating its end in the encoded data by searching for an **EndOfLine** pattern and then substituting decoded data from the previous row if the previous row was not damaged, or a white scan line if the previous row was also damaged. Default value: 0.

The compression achieved using CCITT encoding depends on the data, as well as on the value of various optional parameters. For Group 3 one-dimensional encoding, in the best case (all zeros), each scan line compresses to 4 bytes, and the compression factor depends on the length of a scan line. If the scan line is 300 bytes long, a compression ratio of approximately 75:1 is achieved. The worst case, an image of alternating ones and zeros, produces an expansion of 2:9.

3.3.6 DCTDecode Filter

The **DCTDecode** filter decodes grayscale or color image data that has been encoded in the JPEG baseline format. (JPEG stands for the Joint Photographic Experts Group, a group within the International Organization for Standardization that developed the format; DCT stands for discrete cosine transform, the primary technique used in the encoding.)

JPEG encoding is a "lossy" compression method, meaning that the data produced by the decoder is not exactly the same as the data originally presented to the encoder. This method is designed specifically for compression of sampled continuous-tone images, not for general data compression.

Data to be encoded consists of a stream of image samples, each consisting of one, two, three, or four color components. The color component values for a particular sample must appear consecutively. Each component value occupies an 8-bit byte.

During encoding, several parameters control the algorithm and the information loss. The values of these parameters, which include the dimensions of the image and the number of components per sample, are entirely under the control of the encoder and are stored in the encoded data. **DCTDecode** generally obtains the parameter values it requires directly from the encoded data. However, in one instance, the parameter might not be present in the encoded data but must be specified in the filter parameter dictionary; see Table 3.10.

TABLE 3.10   Optional parameter for the DCTDecode filter

KEY	TYPE	VALUE
ColorTransform	integer	A code specifying the transformation to be performed on the sample values:

0   No transformation.

1   If the image has three color components, transform *RGB* values to *YUV* before encoding and from *YUV* to *RGB* after decoding. If the image has four components, transform *CMYK* values to *YUVK* before encoding and from *YUVK* to *CMYK* after decoding. This option is ignored if the image has one or two color components.

Note: *The* RGB *and* YUV *used here have nothing to do with the color spaces defined as part of the Adobe imaging model. The purpose of converting from* RGB *to* YUV *is to separate luminance and chrominance information (see below).*

The default value of **ColorTransform** is 1 if the image has three components and 0 otherwise. In other words, conversion between *RGB* and *YUV* is performed for all three-component images unless explicitly disabled by setting **ColorTransform** to 0. Additionally, the encoding algorithm inserts an Adobe-defined marker code in the encoded data indicating the **ColorTransform** value used. If present, this marker code overrides the **ColorTransform** value given to **DCTDecode**. Thus it is necessary to specify **ColorTransform** only when decoding data that does not contain the Adobe-defined marker code.

The details of the encoding algorithm are not presented here but can be found in the ISO specification and in *JPEG: Still Image Data Compression Standard*, by Pennebaker and Mitchell (see the Bibliography). Briefly, the JPEG algorithm breaks an image up into blocks 8 samples wide by 8 high. Each color component in an image is treated separately. A two-dimensional DCT is performed on each block. This operation produces 64 coefficients, which are then quantized. Each coefficient may be quantized with a different step size. It is this quantization that results in the loss of information in the JPEG algorithm. The quantized coefficients are then compressed.

The encoding algorithm can reduce the information loss by making the step size in the quantization smaller at the expense of reducing the amount of compression achieved by the algorithm. The compression achieved by the JPEG algorithm depends on the image being compressed and the amount of loss that is acceptable. In general, a compression of 15:1 can be achieved without perceptible loss of information, and 30:1 compression causes little impairment of the image.

Better compression is often possible for color spaces that treat luminance and chrominance separately than for those that do not. The *RGB-to-YUV* conversion provided by the filters is one attempt to separate luminance and chrominance; it conforms to CCIR recommendation 601-1. Other color spaces, such as the CIE 1976 *L*a*b** space, may also achieve this objective. The chrominance components can then be compressed more than the luminance by using coarser sampling or quantization, with no degradation in quality.

The JPEG filter implementation in Adobe Acrobat products does not support features of the JPEG standard that are irrelevant to images. In addition, certain choices have been made regarding reserved marker codes and other optional features of the standard. For details, see Adobe Technical Note #5116, *Supporting the DCT Filters in PostScript Level 2.*

In addition to the baseline JPEG format, in PDF 1.3 the **DCTDecode** filter supports the progressive JPEG extension. This extension does not add any entries to the **DCTDecode** parameter dictionary; the distinction between baseline and progressive JPEG is represented in the encoded data.

Note: *There is no benefit to using progressive JPEG for stream data that is embedded in a PDF file. Decoding progressive JPEG is slower and consumes more memory than baseline JPEG. The purpose of this feature is to enable a stream to refer to an external file whose data happens to be already encoded in progressive JPEG. (See also implementation note 10 in Appendix H.)*

3.4 File Structure

The preceding sections describe the syntax of individual objects. This section describes how objects are organized in a PDF file for efficient random access and incremental update. A canonical PDF file initially consists of four elements (see Figure 3.2):

- A one-line *header* identifying the version number of the PDF specification to which the file conforms

- A *body* containing the objects that make up the document contained in the file

- A *cross-reference table* containing information about the indirect objects in the file

- A *trailer* giving the location of the cross-reference table and of certain special objects within the body of the file

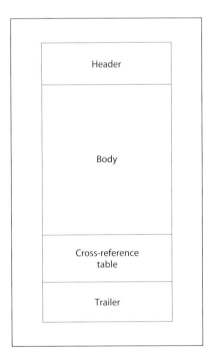

FIGURE 3.2 *Initial structure of a PDF file*

This initial structure may be modified by later updates, which append additional elements to the end of the file; see Section 3.4.5, "Incremental Updates," for details.

As a matter of convention, the tokens in a PDF file are arranged into lines; see Section 3.1, "Lexical Conventions." Each line is terminated by an end-of-line (EOL) marker, which may be a carriage return (character code 13), a line feed (character code 10), or both. PDF files with binary data may have arbitrarily long lines. However, to increase compatibility with other applications that process PDF files, lines that are not part of stream object data are limited to no more than 255 characters (see implementation notes 11 and 12 in Appendix H).

The rules described here are sufficient to produce a well-formed PDF file. However, there are some additional rules for organizing a PDF file to enable efficient incremental access to a document's components in a network environment. This form of organization, called *Linearized PDF*, is described in Appendix F.

3.4.1 File Header

The first line of a PDF file is a *header* identifying the version number of the PDF specification to which the file conforms. For a file conforming to PDF version 1.3, the header should be

```
%PDF–1.3
```

However, since any file conforming to an earlier version of PDF also conforms to version 1.3, an application that processes PDF 1.3 can also accept files with any of the following headers:

```
%PDF–1.0
%PDF–1.1
%PDF–1.2
```

(See also implementation notes 13 and 14 in Appendix H.)

Furthermore, under some conditions, a viewer application may be able to process PDF files conforming to a later version than it was designed to accept. New PDF features are often introduced in such a way that they can safely be ignored by a viewer that does not understand them (see Section H.1, "PDF Version Numbers").

Note: *If a PDF file contains binary data, as most do (see Section 3.1, "Lexical Conventions"), it is recommended that the header line be immediately followed by a comment line containing at least four binary characters—that is, characters whose codes are 128 or greater. This will ensure proper behavior of file transfer applications that inspect data near the beginning of a file to determine whether to treat the file's contents as text or as binary.*

3.4.2 File Body

The *body* of a PDF file consists of a sequence of indirect objects representing the contents of a document. The objects, which are of the basic types described in Section 3.2, "Objects," represent components of the document such as fonts, pages, and sampled images.

3.4.3 Cross-Reference Table

The *cross-reference table* contains information that permits random access to indirect objects within the file, so that the entire file need not be read to locate any particular object. The table contains a one-line entry for each indirect object, specifying the location of that object within the body of the file.

The cross-reference table is the only part of a PDF file with a fixed format; this permits entries in the table to be accessed randomly. The table comprises one or more *cross-reference sections*. Initially, the entire table consists of a single section; one additional section is added each time the file is updated (see Section 3.4.5, "Incremental Updates").

Each cross-reference section begins with a line containing the keyword **xref**. Following this line are one or more *cross-reference subsections*, which may appear in any order. The subsection structure is useful for incremental updates, since it allows a new cross-reference section to be added to the PDF file, containing entries only for objects that have been added or deleted. For a file that has never been updated, the cross-reference section contains only one subsection, whose object numbering begins at 0.

Each cross-reference subsection contains entries for a contiguous range of object numbers. The subsection begins with a line containing two numbers, separated by a space: the object number of the first object in this subsection and the number of entries in the subsection. For example, the line

28 5

introduces a subsection containing five objects, numbered consecutively from 28 to 32.

Following this line are the cross-reference entries themselves, one per line. Each entry is exactly 20 bytes long, including the end-of-line marker. There are two kinds of cross-reference entry: one for objects that are in use and another for objects that have been deleted and so are free. Both types of entry have similar basic formats, distinguished by the keyword **n** (for an in-use entry) or **f** (for a free entry). The format of an in-use entry is as follows:

nnnnnnnnnn ggggg **n** *eol*

where

nnnnnnnnnn is a 10-digit byte offset

ggggg is a 5-digit generation number

n is a literal keyword identifying this as an in-use entry

eol is a 2-character end-of-line sequence

The byte offset is a 10-digit number, padded with leading zeros if necessary, giving the number of bytes from the beginning of the file to the beginning of the object. It is separated from the generation number by a single space. The generation number is a 5-digit number, also padded with leading zeros if necessary. Following the generation number is a single space, the keyword **n**, and then a 2-character end-of-line sequence. If the file's end-of-line marker is a single character (either a carriage return or a line feed), it is preceded by a single space; if the marker is 2 characters (both a carriage return and a line feed), it is not preceded by a space. Thus the overall length of the entry is always exactly 20 bytes.

The cross-reference entry for a free object has essentially the same format, except that the keyword is **f** instead of **n** and the interpretation of the first item is different:

   nnnnnnnnnn ggggg **f** *eol*

where

   nnnnnnnnnn is the 10-digit object number of the next free object

   ggggg is a 5-digit generation number

   f is a literal keyword identifying this as a free entry

   eol is a 2-character end-of-line sequence

The free entries in the cross-reference table form a linked list, with each free entry containing the object number of the next. The first entry in the table (object number 0) is always free and has a generation number of 65,535; it is the head of the linked list of free objects. The last free entry (the tail of the linked list) links back to object number 0.

Except for object number 0, all objects in the cross-reference table initially have generation numbers of 0. When an indirect object is deleted, its cross-reference entry is marked free and it is added to the linked list of free entries. The entry's generation number is incremented by 1 to indicate the generation number to be used the next time an object with that object number is created. Thus each time the entry is reused, it is given a new generation number. The maximum generation number is 65,535; when a cross-reference entry reaches this value, it will never be reused.

The cross-reference table (comprising the original cross-reference section and all update sections) must contain one entry for each object number from 0 to the maximum object number used in the file, even if one or more of the object numbers in this range do not actually occur in the file.

Example 3.4 shows a cross-reference section consisting of a single subsection with six entries: four that are in use (objects number 1, 2, 4, and 5) and two that are free (objects number 0 and 3). Object number 3 has been deleted, and the next object created with that object number will be given a generation number of 7.

Example 3.4

```
xref
0  6
0000000003  65535  f
0000000017  00000  n
0000000081  00000  n
0000000000  00007  f
0000000331  00000  n
0000000409  00000  n
```

Example 3.5 shows a cross-reference section with four subsections, containing a total of five entries. The first subsection contains one entry, for object number 0, which is free. The second subsection contains one entry, for object number 3, which is in use. The third subsection contains two entries, for objects number 23 and 24, both of which are in use. Object number 23 has been reused, as can be seen from the fact that it has a generation number of 2. The fourth subsection contains one entry, for object number 30, which is in use.

Example 3.5

```
xref
0  1
0000000000  65535  f
3  1
0000025325  00000  n
23  2
0000025518  00002  n
0000025635  00000  n
30  1
0000025777  00000  n
```

See Section G.6, "Updating Example," for a more extensive example of the structure of a PDF file that has been updated several times.

3.4.4 File Trailer

The *trailer* of a PDF file enables an application reading the file to quickly find the cross-reference table and certain special objects. Applications should read a PDF file from its end. The last line of the file contains only the end-of-file marker, %%EOF. (See implementation note 15 in Appendix H.) The two preceding lines contain the keyword **startxref** and the byte offset from the beginning of the file to the beginning of the **xref** keyword in the last cross-reference section. The **start-xref** line is preceded by the *trailer dictionary,* consisting of the keyword **trailer** followed by a series of key-value pairs enclosed in double angle brackets. Thus the trailer has the following overall structure:

```
trailer
    <<  key₁  value₁
        key₂  value₂
        …
        keyₙ  valueₙ
    >>
startxref
Byte_offset_of_last_cross-reference_section
%%EOF
```

Table 3.11 shows the contents of the trailer dictionary.

TABLE 3.11   Entries in the trailer dictionary

KEY	TYPE	VALUE
Size	integer	*(Required)* The total number of entries in the file's cross-reference table, as defined by the combination of the original section and all update sections. Equivalently, this value is 1 greater than the highest object number used in the file.
Prev	integer	*(Present only if the file has more than one cross-reference section)* The byte offset from the beginning of the file to the beginning of the previous cross-reference section.
Root	dictionary	*(Required; must be an indirect reference)* The catalog object for the PDF document contained in the file (see Section 3.6.1, "Document Catalog").
Encrypt	dictionary	*(Required if document is encrypted; PDF 1.1)* The document's encryption dictionary (see Section 3.5, "Encryption").
Info	dictionary	*(Optional; must be an indirect reference)* The document's information dictionary (see Section 8.2, "Document Information Dictionary").
ID	array	*(Optional; PDF 1.1)* An array of two strings, each of which is a file identifier (see Section 8.3, "File Identifiers"). The first identifier is established permanently when the file is created; the second is changed each time the file is updated.

Example 3.6 shows an example trailer for a file that has never been updated (as indicated by the absence of a **Prev** entry in the trailer dictionary).

Example 3.6

```
trailer
    << /Size  22
        /Root  2 0 R
        /Info  1 0 R
        /ID [ <81b14aafa313db63dbd6f981e49f94f4>
              <81b14aafa313db63dbd6f981e49f94f4>
            ]
    >>
startxref
18799
%%EOF
```

3.4.5 Incremental Updates

The contents of a PDF file can be updated incrementally without rewriting the entire file. Changes are appended to the end of the file, leaving its original contents intact. Any new or changed objects are appended, a cross-reference section is added, and a new trailer is inserted. The resulting file has the structure shown in Figure 3.3. A complete example of an updated file is shown in Section G.6, "Updating Example."

The cross-reference section added when a file is updated contains entries only for objects that have been changed, replaced, or deleted, plus the entry for object 0. Deleted objects are left unchanged in the file, but are marked as deleted via their cross-reference entries. The added trailer contains all the entries (perhaps modified) from the previous trailer, as well as a **Prev** entry giving the location of the previous cross-reference section (see Table 3.11 on page 61). As shown in Figure 3.3, a file that has been updated several times contains several trailers; note that each trailer is terminated by its own end-of-file (%%EOF) marker.

Because updates are appended to PDF files, it is possible to end up with several copies of an object with the same object identifier (object number and generation number). This can occur, for example, if a text annotation (see Section 7.4, "Annotations") is changed several times, with the file being saved between changes. Because the text annotation object is not deleted, it retains the same object number and generation number as before. An updated copy of the object is included in the new update section added to the file; the update's cross-reference section includes a byte offset to this new copy of the object, overriding the old byte offset contained in the original cross-reference section. When a viewer application reads the file, it must build its cross-reference information in such a way that the most recent copy of each object is the one accessed in the file.

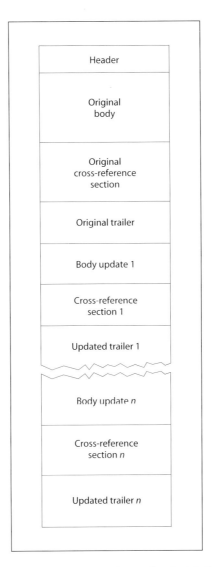

FIGURE 3.3 *Structure of an updated PDF file*

3.5 Encryption

A PDF document can be *encrypted (PDF 1.1)* to protect its contents from un-authorized access. Encryption applies to all strings and streams in the document's PDF file, but not to other object types such as integers and boolean values, which are used primarily to convey information about the document's structure rather than its content. Leaving these values unencrypted allows random access to the objects within a document, while encrypting the strings and streams protects the document's substantive contents.

Note: *When a PDF stream object (see Section 3.2.7, "Stream Objects") refers to an external file, the stream's contents are not encrypted, since they are not part of the PDF file itself. However, if the contents of the stream are embedded within the PDF file (see Section 3.10.3, "Embedded File Streams"), they are encrypted like any other stream in the file.*

Encryption is controlled by an *encryption dictionary,* which is the value of the **Encrypt** entry in the document's trailer dictionary (see Table 3.11 on page 61). If this entry is absent from the trailer dictionary, the document is not encrypted. The entries shown in Table 3.12 are common to all encryption dictionaries.

TABLE 3.12 Entries common to all encryption dictionaries

KEY	TYPE	VALUE
Filter	name	*(Required)* The name of the security handler for this document; see below. Default value: **Standard**, for the built-in security handler. (Names for nonstandard security handlers can be registered using the procedure described in Appendix E.)
V	number	*(Optional)* A code specifying the algorithm to be used in encrypting and decrypting the document:

1   Algorithm 3.1 on page 66

0   An alternate algorithm that is undocumented and no longer supported, and whose use is strongly discouraged

The default value if this entry is omitted is 0, but a value of 1 is strongly recommended. Values greater than 1 are not defined for PDF 1.3, and documents specifying such values cannot be opened by PDF 1.3 viewer applications.

The encryption dictionary's **Filter** entry identifies the file's *security handler,* a software module that implements various aspects of the encryption process and controls access to the contents of the encrypted document. PDF specifies a standard security handler that all viewer applications are expected to support, but applications may optionally substitute alternate security handlers of their own. The remaining contents of the encryption dictionary are determined by the security handler, and may vary from one handler to another. Those for the standard security handler are described below in Section 3.5.2, "Standard Security Handler."

Unlike strings within the body of the document, those in the encryption dictionary must be direct objects and are *not* encrypted by the usual methods. The security handler itself is responsible for encrypting and decrypting strings in the encryption dictionary, using whatever encryption algorithm it chooses.

Note: *If the standard encryption methods provided by PDF are not sufficient to their needs, document creators have two choices: they can provide an alternate, more secure security handler or they can encrypt whole PDF documents themselves, bypassing PDF security entirely.*

3.5.1 General Encryption Algorithm

PDF's standard encryption methods use the MD5 message-digest algorithm (described in Internet RFC 1321, *The MD5 Message-Digest Algorithm;* see the Bibliography) and a proprietary encryption algorithm known as RC4. RC4 is a symmetric stream cipher—the same algorithm is used for both encryption and decryption, and the algorithm does not change the length of the data.

Note: *RC4 is a copyrighted, proprietary algorithm of RSA Security, Inc. Adobe Systems has licensed this algorithm for use in its Acrobat products. Independent software vendors may be required to license RC4 in order to develop software that encrypts or decrypts PDF documents. For further information, visit the RSA Web site at <http://www.rsasecurity.com> or send e-mail to <products@rsasecurity.com>.*

The encryption of data in a PDF file is based on the use of an *encryption key* computed by the security handler. Different security handlers can compute the key in a variety of ways, more or less cryptographically secure. In particular, PDF's standard encryption handler limits the key to 5 bytes (40 bits) in length, in accordance with U.S. cryptographic export requirements in effect at the time of initial publication of the PDF 1.3 specification. Regardless of how the key is computed, its use in the encryption of data is always the same (see Algorithm 3.1). Because the RC4 algorithm is symmetric, this same sequence of steps can be used (given a key) both to encrypt and to decrypt data.

Algorithm 3.1 *Encryption of data using an encryption key*

1. Obtain the object number and generation number from the object identifier of the string or stream to be encrypted (see Section 3.2.9, "Indirect Objects"). If the string is a direct object, use the identifier of the indirect object containing it.

2. Treating the object number and generation number as binary integers, extend the original 5-byte key to 10 bytes by appending the low-order 3 bytes of the object number and the low-order 2 bytes of the generation number in that order, low-order byte first.

3. Pass the resulting 10-byte string as input to the MD5 hash function.

4. Use the first 10 bytes of the output from the MD5 function as the key for the RC4 encryption function, along with the string or stream data to be encrypted. The output is the encrypted data to be stored in the PDF file.

Stream data is encrypted after applying all stream encoding filters, and is decrypted before applying any stream decoding filters; the number of bytes to be encrypted or decrypted is given by the **Length** entry in the stream dictionary. Decryption of strings (other than those in the encryption dictionary) is done after escape-sequence processing and hexadecimal decoding as appropriate to the string representation described in Section 3.2.3, "String Objects."

3.5.2 Standard Security Handler

PDF's standard security handler allows two passwords to be specified for a document: an *owner password* and a *user password*. Correctly supplying either password allows a user to open the document, decrypt it, and display it on the screen. The owner password allows the following additional operations:

• Modifying the document's contents

• Copying text and graphics from the document

• Adding or modifying text annotations (see Section 7.4, "Annotations") and interactive form fields (Section 7.6, "Interactive Forms")

• Printing the document

Access to any of these operations may be restricted if the user password is supplied instead of the owner password. Access information in the document's encryption dictionary specifies which, if any, of these additional operations are permitted by the user password. The owner password must be supplied in order to change these restrictions or the passwords themselves.

Note: PDF cannot enforce the document access privileges specified in the encryption dictionary. It is up to the implementors of PDF viewer applications to respect the intent of the document creator by restricting access to an encrypted PDF file according to the passwords and permissions contained in the file.

Note: If the owner and user passwords are the same, the document is always opened with user access privileges. It is therefore impossible in these circumstances to obtain owner privileges for the document.

Encryption Dictionary

Table 3.13 shows the encryption dictionary entries for the standard security handler (in addition to those in Table 3.12). The values of the **O** and **U** entries are used to determine whether a password string supplied by the user is the correct owner password, user password, or neither. If the user password is supplied, the **P** entry determines which operations are to be permitted. A document is encrypted if an owner password, user password, or any access restriction was specified when the document was created. However, the user is prompted for a password on opening the document only if the document has a user password; this can be determined by testing the empty string as the user password (see Algorithm 3.5 on page 70).

The value of the encryption dictionary's **P** entry is an unsigned 32-bit integer containing a set of flags specifying which access privileges should be granted when the document is opened with the user password. Table 3.14 shows the meanings of these flags. Bit positions within the flag word are numbered from 1 (low-order) to 32 (high-order); a 1-bit in any position enables the corresponding access privilege.

*Note: PDF integer objects in fact are represented internally in signed twos-complement form. Since all the reserved high-order flag bits in the encryption dictionary's **P** value are required to be 1, the value must be specified as a negative integer. For example, the value -44 allows printing and copying but disallows modifying the content and annotations.*

TABLE 3.13 Additional encryption dictionary entries for the standard security handler

KEY	TYPE	VALUE
R	number	*(Required)* The revision number of the standard security handler that created this dictionary. At the time of publication, the current revision number is 2.
O	string	*(Required)* A 32-byte string used in determining whether a valid owner password was entered. Contains an encrypted version of the padded user password (see step 1 of Algorithm 3.2 below).
U	string	*(Required)* A 32-byte string used in determining whether a valid user password was entered. Contains an encrypted version of the fixed padding string shown in step 1 of Algorithm 3.2 below.
P	integer	*(Required)* A set of flags specifying which operations are permitted when the document is opened with the user password (see Table 3.14).

TABLE 3.14 User password access privileges

BIT POSITION	MEANING
1–2	Reserved; must be 0
3	Print document
4	Modify contents of document (other than text annotations and interactive form fields)
5	Copy text and graphics from document
6	Add or modify text annotations and interactive form fields
7–32	Reserved; must be 1

Key Generation Algorithms

As noted earlier, one function of a security handler is to generate a 5-byte encryption key for use in encrypting and decrypting the contents of a document. Given a password string, the standard security handler computes an encryption key as shown in Algorithm 3.2.

Algorithm 3.2 *Computing an encryption key*

1. Pad or truncate the password string to exactly 32 bytes. If the password string is more than 32 bytes long, use only its first 32 bytes; if it is less than 32 bytes long, pad it by appending the required number of additional bytes from the beginning of the following padding string:

   < 28 BF 4E 5E 4E 75 8A 41 64 00 4E 56 FF FA 01 08
     2E 2E 00 B6 D0 68 3E 80 2F 0C A9 FE 64 53 69 7A >

   That is, if the password string is *n* bytes long, append the first 32 − *n* bytes of the padding string to the end of the password string. If the password is omitted, treat it as an empty (zero-length) string and substitute the entire padding string in its place.

2. Pass the result of step 1 as input to the MD5 hash function, followed by the value of the encryption dictionary's **O** entry. (Algorithm 3.3 shows how the **O** value is computed.)

3. Treat the value of the **P** entry as an unsigned 4-byte integer and pass these bytes to the MD5 hash function, low-order byte first.

4. Pass the first element of the file's file identifier to the MD5 hash function (see Section 8.3, "File Identifiers").

5. The first 5 bytes of the output from the MD5 algorithm constitute the encryption key.

This algorithm, when applied to the user password, produces the encryption key used to encrypt or decrypt string and stream data according to Algorithm 3.1 on page 66. Parts of this algorithm are also used in the algorithms described below.

In addition to the encryption key, the standard security handler must provide the contents of the encryption dictionary (Tables 3.12 on page 64 and 3.13 on page 68). The values of the **Filter**, **R**, **P**, and **V** entries are straightforward, but the computation of the **O** (owner password) and **U** (user password) entries requires further explanation. Algorithms 3.3 and 3.4 show how to compute the values of these entries.

Algorithm 3.3 *Computing the O (owner) value in the encryption dictionary*

1. Pad or truncate the owner password string as described in step 1 of Algorithm 3.2. If there is no owner password, use the user password instead. (See implementation note 16 in Appendix H.)

2. Pass the result of step 1 as input to the MD5 hash function.

3. Create an RC4 key using the first 5 bytes of the MD5 output.

4. Pad or truncate the user password string as described in step 1 of Algorithm 3.2.

5. Encrypt the padded user password string with the RC4 algorithm, using the key obtained in step 3.

6. Store the result of step 5 as the value of the **O** entry in the encryption dictionary.

Algorithm 3.4 *Computing the U (user) value in the encryption dictionary*

1. Create an encryption key based on the user password string, as described in Algorithm 3.2.

2. Encrypt the 32-byte padding string shown in step 1 of Algorithm 3.2, using the RC4 algorithm with the encryption key from the preceding step.

3. Store the result of step 2 as the value of the **U** entry in the encryption dictionary.

Given a password string supplied by the user, the standard security handler uses the contents of the encryption dictionary to determine whether the document should be opened and what access privileges should be granted. If the password supplied is the correct user password, the document is opened with only the access privileges specified by the **P** entry in the encryption dictionary. If the password supplied is the correct owner password (but not the same as the user password), full access privileges are granted.

The standard security handler uses Algorithms 3.5 and 3.6 to determine whether a supplied password string is the correct user or owner password.

Algorithm 3.5 *Checking the user password*

1. Compute an encryption key from the supplied password string, as described in Algorithm 3.2.

2. Decrypt the value of the encryption dictionary's **U** entry, using the RC4 algorithm with the encryption key computed in step 1.

3. If the result of step 2 is identical to the fixed padding string shown in step 1 of Algorithm 3.2, the password supplied is the correct user password. The key obtained in step 1 can be used to decrypt the document using Algorithm 3.1 on page 66.

Algorithm 3.6 *Checking the owner password*

1. Compute an encryption key from the supplied password string, as described in steps 1 to 3 of Algorithm 3.3.

2. Decrypt the value of the encryption dictionary's **O** entry, using the RC4 algorithm with the encryption key computed in step 1.

3. Use Algorithm 3.2 to compute an encryption key from the decrypted value obtained in step 2.

4. Decrypt the value of the encryption dictionary's **U** entry, using the RC4 algorithm with the encryption key computed in step 3.

5. If the result of step 4 is identical to the fixed padding string shown in step 1 of Algorithm 3.2, the password supplied is the correct owner password. The key obtained in step 3 can be used to decrypt the document using Algorithm 3.1 on page 66.

3.6 Document Structure

A PDF document can be regarded as a hierarchy of objects contained in the body section of a PDF file. At the root of the hierarchy is the document's *catalog* dictionary (see Section 3.6.1, "Document Catalog"). Most of the objects in the hierarchy are dictionaries. For example, each page of the document is represented by a *page object*—a dictionary that includes references to the page's contents and other attributes, such as its thumbnail image (Section 7.2.3, "Thumbnail Images") and any annotations (Section 7.4, "Annotations") associated with it. The individual page objects are tied together in a structure called the *page tree* (described in *Section 3.6.2, "Page Tree"*), which in turn is located via an indirect reference in the document catalog. Parent, child, and sibling relationships within the hierarchy are defined by dictionary entries whose values are indirect references to other dictionaries. Figure 3.4 illustrates the structure of the object hierarchy.

Note: *The data structures described in this section, particularly the catalog and page dictionaries, combine entries describing document structure with ones dealing with the detailed semantics of documents and pages. All entries are listed here, but many of their descriptions are deferred to subsequent chapters.*

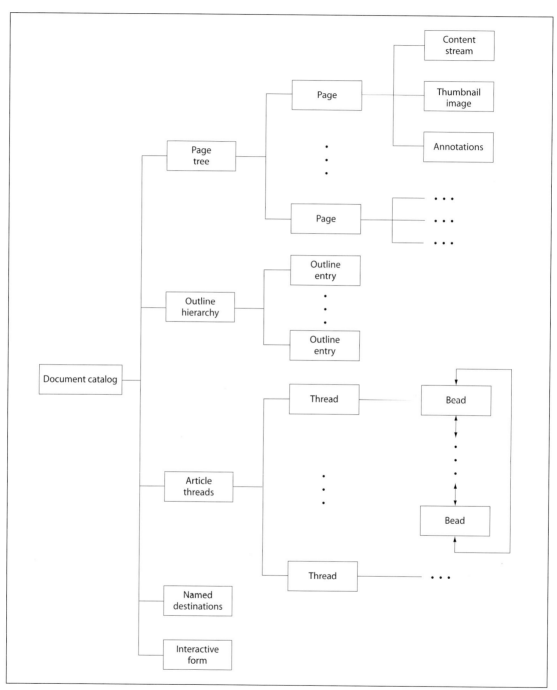

FIGURE 3.4 *Structure of a PDF document*

3.6.1 Document Catalog

The root of a document's object hierarchy is the *catalog* dictionary, located via the **Root** entry in the trailer of the PDF file (see Section 3.4.4, "File Trailer"). The catalog contains references to other objects defining the document's contents, outline, article threads *(PDF 1.1)*, named destinations, and other attributes. In addition, it contains information about how the document should be displayed on the screen, such as whether its outline and thumbnail page images should be displayed automatically and whether some location other than the first page should be shown when the document is opened.

Table 3.15 shows the entries in the catalog dictionary. (See also implementation note 17 in Appendix H.)

TABLE 3.15 Entries in the catalog dictionary

KEY	TYPE	VALUE
Type	name	*(Required)* The type of PDF object that this dictionary describes; must be **Catalog** for the catalog dictionary.
Pages	dictionary	*(Required, must be an indirect reference)* The page tree node that is the root of the document's page tree (see *Section 3.6.2, "Page Tree"*).
PageLabels	number tree	*(Optional; PDF 1.3)* A number tree (see Section 3.8.5, "Number Trees") defining the page labeling for the document. The keys in this tree are page indices; the corresponding values are page label dictionaries (see Section 7.3.1, "Page Labels"). Each page index denotes the first page to which the specified page label dictionary applies. The tree must include a value for page index 0.
Names	dictionary	*(Optional; PDF 1.2)* The document's name dictionary (see Section 3.6.3, "Name Dictionary").
Dests	dictionary	*(Optional; PDF 1.1; must be an indirect reference)* A dictionary of names and corresponding destinations (see "Named Destinations" on page 387).
ViewerPreferences	dictionary	*(Optional; PDF 1.2)* A viewer preferences dictionary (see Section 7.1, "Viewer Preferences") specifying the way the document is to be displayed on the screen. If this entry is absent, viewer applications should use their own current user preference settings.

PageLayout	name	*(Optional)* A name object specifying the page layout to be used when the document is opened:

SinglePage	Display one page at a time.
OneColumn	Display the pages in one column.
TwoColumnLeft	Display the pages in two columns, with odd-numbered pages on the left.
TwoColumnRight	Display the pages in two columns, with odd-numbered pages on the right.

(See implementation note 18 in Appendix H.) Default value: SinglePage.

PageMode	name	*(Optional)* A name object specifying how the document should be displayed when opened:

UseNone	Neither document outline nor thumbnail images visible
UseOutlines	Document outline visible
UseThumbs	Thumbnail images visible
FullScreen	Full-screen mode, with no menu bar, window controls, or any other window visible

Default value: UseNone.

Outlines	dictionary	*(Optional; must be an indirect reference)* The outline dictionary that is the root of the document's outline hierarchy (see Section 7.2.2, "Document Outline").
Threads	array	*(Optional; PDF 1.1; must be an indirect reference)* An array of thread dictionaries representing the document's article threads (see Section 7.3.2, "Articles").
OpenAction	array or dictionary	*(Optional; PDF 1.1)* A value specifying a destination to be displayed or an action to be performed when the document is opened. The value is either an array defining a destination (see Section 7.2.1, "Destinations") or an action dictionary representing an action (Section 7.5, "Actions"). If this entry is absent, the document should be opened to the top of the first page at the default magnification factor.
URI	dictionary	*(Optional)* A dictionary containing document-level information for uniform resource identifier (URI) actions (see "URI Actions" on page 428).
AcroForm	dictionary	*(Optional; PDF 1.2)* The document's interactive form (AcroForm) dictionary (see Section 7.6.1, "Interactive Form Dictionary").

StructTreeRoot	dictionary	*(Optional; PDF 1.3)* The document's structure tree root dictionary (see "Structure Hierarchy" on page 486).
SpiderInfo	dictionary	*(Optional; PDF 1.3)* A dictionary containing state information used by the Acrobat Web Capture (AcroSpider) plug-in extension (see Section 8.5.1, "Web Capture Information Dictionary").

Example 3.7 shows a sample catalog object.

Example 3.7

```
1 0 obj
    << /Type /Catalog
       /Pages  2 0 R
       /Outlines  3 0 R
       /PageMode  /UseOutlines
    >>
endobj
```

3.6.2 Page Tree

The pages of a document are accessed through a structure known as the *page tree*, which defines their ordering within the document. The tree structure allows PDF viewer applications to quickly open a document containing thousands of pages using only limited memory. The tree contains nodes of two types—intermediate nodes, called *page tree nodes*, and leaf nodes, called *page objects*—whose form is described in the sections below. Viewer applications should be prepared to handle any form of tree structure built of such nodes. The simplest structure would consist of a single page tree node that references all of the document's page objects directly; however, to optimize the performance of viewer applications, the Acrobat Distiller and PDF Writer programs construct trees of a particular form, known as *balanced trees*. Further information on this form of tree can be found in *Data Structures and Algorithms*, by Aho, Hopcroft, and Ullman (see the Bibliography).

Page Tree Nodes

Table 3.16 shows the required entries in a page tree node.

TABLE 3.16 Required entries in a page tree node

KEY	TYPE	VALUE
Type	name	*(Required)* The type of PDF object that this dictionary describes; must be **Pages** for a page tree node.
Parent	dictionary	*(Required except in root node; must be an indirect reference)* The page tree node that is the immediate parent of this one.
Kids	array	*(Required)* An array of indirect references to the immediate children of this node. The children may be page objects or other page tree nodes.
Count	integer	*(Required)* The number of leaf nodes (page objects) that are descendants of this node within the page tree.

Note: The structure of the page tree is not necessarily related to the logical structure of the document itself; that is, page tree nodes do not represent chapters, sections, and so forth. (Other data structures are defined for that purpose; see Section 8.4.3, "Logical Structure.") Applications that consume or produce PDF files are not required to preserve the existing structure of the page tree.

Example 3.8 illustrates the page tree for a document with three pages. See "Page Objects," below, for the contents of the individual page objects, and Section G.4, "Page Tree Example," for a more extended example showing the page tree for a longer document.

Example 3.8

```
2 0 obj
    << /Type /Pages
        /Kids [ 4 0 R
                10 0 R
                24 0 R
              ]
        /Count 3
    >>
endobj

4 0 obj
    << /Type /Page
        … Additional entries describing the attributes of this page …
    >>
endobj
```

```
10  0  obj
  << /Type /Page
      … Additional entries describing the attributes of this page …
  >>
endobj
24  0  obj
  << /Type /Page
      … Additional entries describing the attributes of this page …
  >>
endobj
```

In addition to the entries shown in Table 3.16, a page tree node may contain further entries defining *inherited attributes* for the page objects that are its descendants (see "Inheritance of Page Attributes" on page 80).

Page Objects

The leaves of the page tree are *page objects*, each of which is a dictionary specifying the attributes of a single page of the document. Table 3.17 shows the contents
of this dictionary (see also implementation note 19 in Appendix H). The table
also identifies which attributes a page may inherit from its ancestor nodes in the
page tree, as described under "Inheritance of Page Attributes" on page 80.
Attributes that are not explicitly identified in the table as inheritable cannot be
inherited.

TABLE 3.17 Entries in a page object

KEY	TYPE	VALUE
Type	name	*(Required)* The type of PDF object that this dictionary describes; must be **Page** for a page object.
Parent	dictionary	*(Required; must be an indirect reference)* The page tree node that is the im-mediate parent of this page object.
Resources	dictionary	*(Required; inheritable)* A dictionary containing any resources required by the page (see Section 3.7.2, "Resource Dictionaries"). If the page requires no resources, the value of this entry should be an empty dictionary; omit-ting the entry entirely, or specifying a null value, indicates that the re-sources are to be inherited from an ancestor node in the page tree.

MediaBox	rectangle	*(Required; inheritable)* A rectangle (see Section 3.8.3, "Rectangles"), expressed in default user space units, defining the maximum imageable area of the physical medium on which the page is to be printed (see Section 8.6.1, "Page Boundaries").
CropBox	rectangle	*(Optional; inheritable)* A rectangle, expressed in default user space units, defining the region to which the contents of the page are to be clipped (cropped) when displayed or printed (see Section 8.6.1, "Page Boundaries"). Default value: the value of **MediaBox**.
BleedBox	rectangle	*(Optional; PDF 1.3)* A rectangle, expressed in default user space units, defining the region to which the contents of the page should be clipped when output in a production environment (see Section 8.6.1, "Page Boundaries"). Default value: the value of **CropBox**.
TrimBox	rectangle	*(Optional; PDF 1.3)* A rectangle, expressed in default user space units, defining the intended dimensions of the finished page after trimming (see Section 8.6.1, "Page Boundaries"). Default value: the value of **CropBox**.
ArtBox	rectangle	*(Optional; PDF 1.3)* A rectangle, expressed in default user space units, defining the extent of the page's meaningful content (including potential white space) as intended by the page's creator (see Section 8.6.1, "Page Boundaries"). Default value: the value of **CropBox**.
Contents	stream or array	*(Optional)* A content stream (see Section 3.7.1, "Content Streams") describing the contents of this page. If this entry is absent, the page is empty.
		The value may be either a single stream or an array of streams. If it is an array, the effect is as if all of the streams in the array were concatenated, in order, to form a single stream. This allows a program generating a PDF file to create image objects and other resources as they occur, even though they interrupt the content stream. The division between streams may occur only at the boundaries between lexical tokens (see Section 3.1, "Lexical Conventions"), but is unrelated to the page's logical content or organization. Applications that consume or produce PDF files are not required to preserve the existing structure of the **Contents** array.
Rotate	integer	*(Optional; inheritable)* The number of degrees by which the page should be rotated clockwise when displayed or printed. The value must be a multiple of 90. Default value: 0.
Thumb	stream	*(Optional)* A stream object defining the page's thumbnail image (see Section 7.2.3, "Thumbnail Images").
B	array	*(Optional; PDF 1.1; recommended if the page contains article beads)* An array of indirect references to article beads appearing on the page (see Section 7.3.2, "Articles"; see also implementation note 20 in Appendix H). The beads are listed in the array in natural reading order.

Dur	number	*(Optional; PDF 1.1)* The page's *display duration* (also called its *advance timing*): the maximum length of time, in seconds, that the page will be displayed during presentations before the viewer application automatically advances to the next page (see Section 7.3.3, "Presentations"). By default, the viewer does not advance automatically.
Trans	dictionary	*(Optional; PDF 1.1)* A transition dictionary describing the transition effect to be used when displaying the page during presentations (see Section 7.3.3, "Presentations").
Annots	array	*(Optional)* An array of annotation dictionaries representing annotations associated with the page (see Section 7.4, "Annotations").
AA	dictionary	*(Optional; PDF 1.2)* An additional-actions dictionary defining actions to be performed when the page is opened or closed (see Section 7.5.2, "Trigger Events"; see also implementation note 21 in Appendix H).
PieceInfo	dictionary	*(Optional; PDF 1.3)* A page-piece dictionary associated with the page (see Section 8.4.1, "Page-Piece Dictionaries").
LastModified	date	*(Optional unless **PieceInfo** is present; PDF 1.3)* The date and time (see Section 3.8.2, "Dates") when the page's contents were most recently modified.
StructParents	integer	*(Required if the page contains structural content items; PDF 1.3)* The integer key of the page's entry in the structural parent tree (see "Finding Structure Elements from Content Items" on page 496).
ID	string	*(Optional; PDF 1.3; indirect reference preferred)* The digital identifier of the page's parent Web Capture content set (see Section 8.5.5, "Object Attributes Related to Web Capture").
PZ	number	*(Optional; PDF 1.3)* The page's preferred zoom (magnification) factor: the factor by which it should be scaled to achieve the "natural" display magnification (see Section 8.5.5, "Object Attributes Related to Web Capture").
SeparationInfo	dictionary	*(Optional; PDF 1.3)* A separation dictionary containing information needed to generate color separations for the page (see Section 8.6.2, "Separation Dictionaries").

Example 3.9 shows the definition of a page object with a thumbnail image and two annotations. The media box specifies that the page is to be printed on letter-size paper. In addition, the resource dictionary is specified as a direct object and shows that the page makes use of three fonts, named F3, F5, and F7.

Example 3.9

```
3 0 obj
   << /Type /Page
      /Parent  4 0 R
      /MediaBox [0  0  612  792]
      /Resources << /Font << /F3  7 0 R
                             /F5  9 0 R
                             /F7  11 0 R
                          >>
                    /ProcSet [/PDF]
               >>
      /Contents  12 0 R
      /Thumb  14 0 R
      /Annots [ 23 0 R
               24 0 R
            ]
   >>
endobj
```

Inheritance of Page Attributes

Some of the page attributes shown in Table 3.17 are designated as *inheritable*. If such an attribute is omitted from a page object, its value is inherited from an ancestor node in the page tree. If the attribute is a required one, a value must be supplied in an ancestor node; if it is optional and no inherited value is specified, the default value is used.

An attribute can thus be defined once for a whole set of pages, by specifying it in an intermediate page tree node and arranging the pages that share the attribute as descendants of that node. For example, a document might specify the same media box for all of its pages by including a **MediaBox** entry in the root node of the page tree. If necessary, an individual page object could then override this inherited value with a **MediaBox** entry of its own.

Note: *In a document conforming to the Linearized PDF organization (see Appendix F), all page attributes must be specified explicitly as entries in the page dictionaries to which they apply; they may not be inherited from an ancestor node.*

Figure 3.5 illustrates the inheritance of attributes. In the page tree shown, pages 1, 2, and 4 are rotated clockwise by 90 degrees, page 3 by 270 degrees, page 6 by 180 degrees, and pages 5 and 7 not at all (0 degrees).

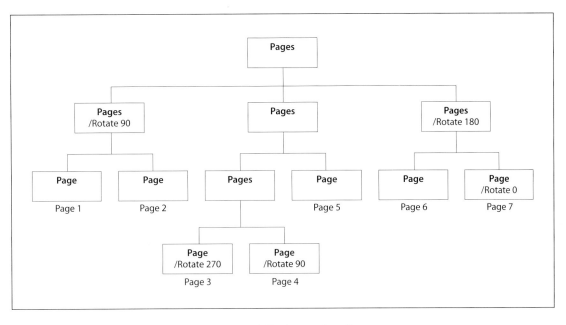

FIGURE 3.5 *Inheritance of attributes*

3.6.3 Name Dictionary

Some categories of objects in a PDF file can be referred to by name rather than by object reference. The correspondence between names and objects is established by the document's *name dictionary (PDF 1.2)*, located via the **Names** entry in the document's catalog (see Section 3.6.1, "Document Catalog"). Each entry in this dictionary designates the root of a name tree (Section 3.8.4, "Name Trees") defining names for a particular category of objects. Table 3.18 shows the contents of the name dictionary.

TABLE 3.18 Entries in the name dictionary

KEY	TYPE	VALUE
Dests	name tree	*(Optional; PDF 1.2)* A name tree mapping name strings to destinations (see "Named Destinations" on page 387).
AP	name tree	*(Optional; PDF 1.3)* A name tree mapping name strings to annotation appearance streams (see Section 7.4.4, "Appearance Streams").
JavaScript	name tree	*(Optional; PDF 1.3)* A name tree mapping name strings to document-level JavaScript actions (see "JavaScript Actions" on page 458).

Pages	name tree	*(Optional; PDF 1.3)* A name tree mapping name strings to visible pages for use in interactive forms (see Section 7.6.5, "Named Pages").
Templates	name tree	*(Optional; PDF 1.3)* A name tree mapping name strings to invisible pages for use in interactive forms (see Section 7.6.5, "Named Pages").
IDS	name tree	*(Optional; PDF 1.3)* A name tree mapping content set IDs to Web Capture content sets (see Section 8.5.3, "Content Sets").
URLS	name tree	*(Optional; PDF 1.3)* A name tree mapping uniform resource locators (URLs) to Web Capture content sets (see Section 8.5.3, "Content Sets").

3.7 Content Streams and Resources

Content streams are the primary means for describing the appearance of pages and other graphical elements. A content stream depends on information contained in an associated resource dictionary; in combination, these two objects form a self-contained entity. This section describes these objects.

3.7.1 Content Streams

A *content stream* is a PDF stream object whose data consists of a sequence of instructions describing the graphical elements to be painted on a page. The instructions are represented in the form of PDF objects, using the same object syntax as in the rest of the PDF document. However, whereas the document as a whole is a static, random-access data structure, the objects in the content stream are intended to be interpreted and acted upon sequentially.

Each page of a document is represented by one or more content streams. Content streams are also used to package up sequences of instructions as self-contained graphical elements, such as forms (see Section 4.9, "Form XObjects"), patterns (Section 4.6, "Patterns"), certain fonts (Section 5.5.4, "Type 3 Fonts"), and annotation appearances (Section 7.4.4, "Appearance Streams").

A content stream, after decoding with any specified filters, is interpreted according to the PDF syntax rules described in Section 3.1, "Lexical Conventions." It consists of PDF objects denoting operands and operators. The operands needed by an operator precede it in the stream. See Example 3.2 on page 39 for an example of a content stream.

An *operand* is a direct object belonging to any of the basic PDF data types except a stream. Dictionaries are permitted as operands only by certain specific operators. Indirect objects and object references are not permitted at all.

An *operator* is a PDF keyword that specifies some action to be performed, such as painting a graphical shape on the page. An operator keyword is distinguished from a name object by the absence of an initial slash character (/). Operators are meaningful only inside a content stream.

Note: *This "postfix" notation, in which an operator is preceded by its operands, is superficially the same as in the PostScript language. However, PDF has no concept of an operand stack as PostScript has. In PDF, all of the operands needed by an operator must immediately precede that operator. Operators do not return results, and there may not be operands left over when an operator finishes execution.*

Most operators have to do with painting graphical elements on the page or with specifying parameters that affect subsequent painting operations. The individual operators are described in the chapters devoted to their functions:

• Chapter 4 describes operators that paint general graphics, such as filled areas, strokes, and sampled images, and that specify device-independent graphical parameters, such as color.

• Chapter 5 describes operators that paint text using character glyphs defined in fonts.

• Chapter 6 describes operators that specify device-dependent rendering parameters.

• Chapter 8 describes the marked-content operators that associate higher-level logical information with objects in the content stream. These operators do not affect the rendered appearance of the content; rather, they specify information useful to applications that use PDF for document interchange.

Ordinarily, when a viewer application encounters an operator in a content stream that it does not recognize, an error will occur. (See implementation note 22 in Appendix H.) A pair of compatibility operators, **BX** and **EX** *(PDF 1.1)*, modify this behavior (see Table 3.19). These operators must occur in pairs and may be nested. They bracket a *compatibility section*, a portion of a content stream within which unrecognized operators are to be ignored without error. This mechanism enables a PDF document to use operators defined in newer versions of PDF without sacrificing compatibility with older viewers; it should be used only in cases where ignoring such newer operators is the appropriate thing to do. The **BX** and **EX** operators are not themselves part of any graphics object (see Section 4.1, "Graphics Objects") or of the graphics state (Section 4.3, "Graphics State").

TABLE 3.19 Compatibility operators

OPERANDS	OPERATOR	DESCRIPTION
—	**BX**	*(PDF 1.1)* Begin a compatibility section. Unrecognized operators (along with their operands) will be ignored without error until the balancing **EX** operator is encountered.
—	**EX**	*(PDF 1.1)* End a compatibility section begun by a balancing **BX** operator.

3.7.2 Resource Dictionaries

As stated above, the operands supplied to operators in a content stream may only be direct objects; indirect objects and object references are not permitted. In some cases, an operator needs to refer to a PDF object that is defined outside the content stream, such as a font dictionary or a stream containing image data. This can be accomplished by defining such objects as *named resources* and referring to them by name from within the content stream.

Note: *Named resources are meaningful only in the context of a content stream. The scope of a resource name is local to a particular content stream, and is unrelated to externally known identifiers for objects such as fonts. References from one object to another outside of content streams should be made by means of indirect object references rather than named resources.*

A content stream's named resources are defined by a *resource dictionary*, which enumerates the named resources needed by the operators in the content stream and the names by which they can be referred to. For example, if a text operator appearing within the content stream needed a certain font, the content stream's resource dictionary might associate the name F42 with the corresponding font dictionary. The text operator could then use this name to refer to the font.

A resource dictionary is associated with a content stream in one of the following ways:

- For a content stream that is the value of a page's **Contents** entry (or is an element of an array that is the value of that entry), the resource dictionary is designated by the page dictionary's **Resources** entry. (Since a page's **Resources** attribute is inheritable, as described under "Inheritance of Page Attributes" on page 80, it may actually reside in some ancestor node of the page object.)

- For other content streams, the resource dictionary is specified by the **Resources** entry in the stream dictionary of the content stream itself. This applies to content streams that define form XObjects, patterns, Type 3 fonts, and annotation appearances.

- A form XObject or a Type 3 font's glyph description may omit the **Resources** entry, in which case resources will be looked up in the **Resources** entry of the page on which the form or font is used. This practice is *not recommended*.

In the context of a given content stream, the term *current resource dictionary* refers to the resource dictionary associated with the stream in one of the ways described above.

Each key in a resource dictionary is the name of a resource type, as shown in Table 3.20. For most resource types, the corresponding value is a subdictionary whose keys, in turn, are the names of resources of the given type and whose values are the PDF objects representing those resources. (For resource type **Proc-Set**, the value is an array of procedure set names instead of a subdictionary.)

TABLE 3.20 Entries in a resource dictionary

KEY	TYPE	VALUE
ExtGState	dictionary	(*Optional*) A dictionary mapping resource names to graphics state parameter dictionaries (see Section 4.3.4, "Graphics State Parameter Dictionaries").
ColorSpace	dictionary	(*Optional*) A dictionary mapping each resource name to either the name of a device-dependent color space or an array describing a color space (see Section 4.5, "Color Spaces").
Pattern	dictionary	(*Optional*) A dictionary mapping resource names to pattern objects (see Section 4.6, "Patterns").
Shading	dictionary	(*Optional; PDF 1.3*) A dictionary mapping resource names to shading dictionaries (see "Shading Dictionaries" on page 214).

XObject	stream	*(Optional)* A dictionary mapping resource names to external objects (see Section 4.7, "External Objects").
Font	dictionary	*(Optional)* A dictionary mapping resource names to font dictionaries (see Chapter 5).
ProcSet	array	*(Optional)* An array of predefined procedure set names (see Section 8.1, "Procedure Sets").
Properties	dictionary	*(Optional; PDF 1.2)* A dictionary mapping resource names to property list dictionaries for marked content (see "Property Lists" on page 481).

Example 3.10 shows a resource dictionary containing procedure sets, fonts, and external objects. The procedure sets are specified by an array, as described in Section 8.1, "Procedure Sets." The fonts are specified with a subdictionary associating the names F5, F6, F7, and F8 with objects 6, 8, 10, and 12, respectively. Likewise, the **XObject** subdictionary associates the names Im1 and Im2 with objects 13 and 15, respectively.

Example 3.10

```
<< /ProcSet [/PDF /ImageB]
   /Font << /F5 6 0 R
            /F6 8 0 R
            /F7 10 0 R
            /F8 12 0 R
        >>
   /XObject << /Im1 13 0 R
               /Im2 15 0 R
           >>
>>
```

3.8 Common Data Structures

As mentioned at the beginning of this chapter, there are some general-purpose data structures that are built from the basic object types described in Section 3.2, "Objects," and are used in many places throughout PDF. This section describes data structures for text strings, dates, rectangles, name trees, and number trees. The subsequent two sections describe more complex data structures for functions and file specifications.

All of these data structures are meaningful only as part of the document hierarchy; they cannot appear within content streams. In particular, the special conventions for interpreting the values of string objects apply only to strings outside content streams. An entirely different convention is used within content streams for using strings to select sequences of glyphs to be painted on the page (see Chapter 5). Table 3.21 summarizes the basic and higher-level data types that are used throughout this book to describe the values of dictionary entries and other PDF data values.

	TABLE 3.21 PDF data types		
TYPE	**DESCRIPTION**	**SECTION**	**PAGE**
array	Array object	3.2.5	32
boolean	Boolean value	3.2.1	26
date	Date (string)	3.8.2	89
dictionary	Dictionary object	3.2.6	32
file specification	File specification (string or dictionary)	3.10	107
function	Function (dictionary or stream)	3.9	95
integer	Integer number	3.2.2	26
name	Name object	3.2.4	30
name tree	Name tree (dictionary)	3.8.4	90
null	Null object	3.2.8	39
number	Number (integer or real)	3.2.2	26
number tree	Number tree (dictionary)	3.8.5	94
rectangle	Rectangle (array)	3.8.3	90
stream	Stream object	3.2.7	33
string	String object	3.2.3	27
text string	Text string	3.8.1	88

3.8.1 Text Strings

Certain strings contain information that is intended to be human-readable, such as text annotations, bookmark names, article names, document information, and so forth. Such strings are referred to as *text strings*. Text strings are encoded in either **PDFDocEncoding** or Unicode character encoding. **PDFDocEncoding** is a superset of the ISO Latin 1 encoding and is documented in Appendix D. Unicode is described in the document *The Unicode Standard* (see the Bibliography).

For text strings encoded in Unicode, the first two bytes must be 254 followed by 255, representing the Unicode byte order marker, U+FEFF. (This sequence conflicts with the **PDFDocEncoding** character sequence thorn ydieresis, which is unlikely to be a meaningful beginning of a word or phrase.) The remainder of the string consists of Unicode character codes, according to the UTF-16 encoding specified in the Unicode standard, version 2.0. Commonly used Unicode values are represented as 2 bytes per character, with the high-order byte appearing first in the string.

Anywhere in a Unicode text string, an escape sequence may appear to indicate the language in which subsequent text is written; this is useful when the language cannot be determined from the character codes used in the text itself. The escape sequence consists of the following elements, in order:

1. The Unicode value U+001B (that is, the byte sequence 0 followed by 27)

2. A 2-character ISO 639 language code—for example, EN for English or JA for Japanese

3. *(Optional)* A 2-character ISO 3166 country code—for example, US for the United States or JP for Japan

4. The Unicode value U+001B

The complete list of codes defined by ISO 639 and ISO 3166 can be obtained from the International Organization for Standardization (see the Bibliography).

3.8.2 Dates

PDF defines a standard date format, which closely follows that of the international standard ASN.1 (Abstract Syntax Notation One), defined in ISO/IEC 8824 (see the Bibliography). A date is a string of the form

(D:*YYYYMMDDHHmmSSOHH'mm'*)

where

YYYY is the year

MM is the month

DD is the day (01–31)

HH is the hour (00–23)

mm is the minute (00–59)

SS is the second (00–59)

O is the relationship of local time to Universal Time (UT), denoted by one of the characters +, –, or Z (see below)

HH followed by ' is the absolute value of the offset from UT in hours (00–23)

mm followed by ' is the absolute value of the offset from UT in minutes (00–59)

The quotation mark character (') after *HH* and *mm* is part of the syntax. All fields after the year are optional. (The prefix D:, although also optional, is strongly recommended.) The default values for *MM* and *DD* are both 01; all other numerical fields default to zero values. A plus sign (+) as the value of the *O* field signifies that local time is later than UT, a minus sign (–) that local time is earlier than UT, and the letter Z that local time is equal to UT. If no UT information is specified, the relationship of the specified time to UT is considered to be unknown. Whether or not the time zone is known, the rest of the date should be specified in local time.

For example, December 23, 1998, at 7:52 PM, U.S. Pacific Standard Time, is represented by the string

D:199812231952–08'00'

3.8.3 Rectangles

Rectangles are used to describe locations on a page and bounding boxes for a variety of objects, such as fonts. A rectangle is written as an array of four numbers giving the coordinates of a pair of diagonally opposite corners. Typically, the array takes the form

$$[ll_x \ ll_y \ ur_x \ ur_y]$$

specifying the lower-left x, lower-left y, upper-right x, and upper-right y coordinates of the rectangle, in that order.

Note: Although rectangles are conventionally specified by their lower-left and upper-right corners, it is acceptable to specify any two diagonally opposite corners. Applications that process PDF should be prepared to normalize such rectangles in situations where specific corners are required.

3.8.4 Name Trees

A *name tree* serves a similar purpose to a dictionary—associating keys and values—but by different means. A name tree differs from a dictionary in the following important ways:

- Unlike the keys in a dictionary, which are name objects, those in a name tree are strings.

- The keys are ordered.

- The values associated with the keys may be objects of any type, but they must always be specified via indirect object references.

- The data structure can represent an arbitrarily large collection of key-value pairs, which can be looked up efficiently without requiring the entire data structure to be read from the PDF file. (In contrast, a dictionary is subject to an implementation limit on the number of entries it can contain.)

A name tree is constructed of *nodes*, each of which is a dictionary object. Table 3.22 shows the entries in a node dictionary. The nodes are of three kinds, depending on the specific entries they contain. The tree always has exactly one *root node*, which contains a single entry: either **Kids** or **Names** but not both. If the root node has a **Names** entry, it is the only node in the tree. If it has a **Kids** entry, then each of the remaining nodes is either an *intermediate node*, containing a **Limits** entry and a **Kids** entry, or a *leaf node*, containing a **Limits** entry and a **Names** entry.

TABLE 3.22   Entries in a name tree node dictionary

KEY	TYPE	VALUE
Kids	array	*(Root and intermediate nodes only; required in intermediate nodes; present in the root node if and only if **Names** is not present)* An array of indirect references to the immediate children of this node. The children may be intermediate or leaf nodes.
Names	array	*(Root and leaf nodes only; required in leaf nodes; present in the root node if and only if **Kids** is not present)* An array of the form $[key_1\ value_1\ \ key_2\ value_2\ \ \ldots\ \ key_n\ value_n]$ where each key_i is a string and the corresponding $value_i$ is an indirect reference to the object associated with that key. The keys are sorted in lexical order, as described below.
Limits	array	*(Intermediate and leaf nodes only; required)* An array of two strings, specifying the (lexically) least and greatest keys included in the **Names** array of a leaf node or in the **Names** arrays of any leaf nodes that are descendants of an intermediate node.

The **Kids** entries in the root and intermediate nodes define the tree's structure by identifying the immediate children of each node. The **Names** entries in the leaf (or root) nodes contain the tree's keys and their associated values, arranged in key-value pairs and sorted lexically in ascending order by key. Shorter keys appear before longer ones beginning with the same byte sequence. The encoding of the keys is immaterial as long as it is self-consistent; keys are compared for equality on a simple byte-by-byte basis.

The keys contained within the various nodes' **Names** entries do not overlap; that is, each **Names** entry contains a single contiguous range of all the keys in the tree. In a leaf node, the **Limits** entry specifies the least and greatest keys contained within the node's **Names** entry; in an intermediate node, it specifies the least and greatest keys contained within the **Names** entries of any of that node's descendants. The value associated with a given key can thus be found by walking the tree in order, searching for the leaf node whose **Names** entry contains that key.

Table 3.23 is an abbreviated outline, showing object numbers and nodes, of a name tree that maps the names of all the chemical elements, from actinium to zirconium, to their atomic numbers. Example 3.11 shows the representation of this tree in a PDF file.

TABLE 3.23   Example of a name tree

1: Root node
  2: Intermediate node: Actinium to Gold
    5: Leaf node: Actinium = 25, …, Astatine = 31
      25: Integer: 89

      …

      31: Integer: 85

    …

    11: Leaf node: Gadolinium = 56, …, Gold = 59
      56: Integer: 64

      …

      59: Integer: 79
  3: Intermediate node: Hafnium to Protactinium
    12: Leaf node: Hafnium = 60, …, Hydrogen = 65
      60: Integer: 72

      …

      65: Integer: 1

    …

    19: Leaf node: Palladium = 92, …, Protactinium = 100
      92: Integer: 46

      …

      100: Integer: 91
  4: Intermediate node: Radium to Zirconium
    20: Leaf node: Radium = 101, …, Ruthenium = 107
      88: Integer: 89

      …

      44: Integer: 85

    …

    24: Leaf node: Xenon = 129, …, Zirconium = 133
      129: Integer: 54

      …

      133: Integer: 40

Example 3.11

```
1  0  obj
        /Kids  [  2 0 R                          % Root node
                  3 0 R
                  4 0 R
               ]
     >>
endobj

2  0  obj
     <<  /Limits  [(Actinium)  (Gold)]           % Intermediate node
        /Kids  [  5 0 R
                  6 0 R
                  7 0 R
                  8 0 R
                  9 0 R
                 10 0 R
                 11 0 R
               ]
     >>
endobj

3  0  obj
     <<  /Limits  [(Hafnium)  (Protactinium)]     % Intermediate node
        /Kids  [ 12 0 R
                 13 0 R
                 14 0 R
                 15 0 R
                 16 0 R
                 17 0 R
                 18 0 R
                 19 0 R
               ]
     >>
endobj

4  0  obj
     <<  /Limits  [(Radium)  (Zirconium)]         % Intermediate node
        /Kids  [ 20 0 R
                 21 0 R
                 22 0 R
                 23 0 R
                 24 0 R
               ]
     >>
endobj
```

```
5  0  obj
    <<  /Limits  [(Actinium)  (Astatine)]              % Leaf node
        /Names  [  (Actinium)   25 0 R
                   (Aluminum)   26 0 R
                   (Americium)  27 0 R
                   (Antimony)   28 0 R
                   (Argon)      29 0 R
                   (Arsenic)    30 0 R
                   (Astatine)   31 0 R
                ]
    >>
endobj

...

24 0  obj
    <<  /Limits  [(Xenon)  (Zirconium)]                % Leaf node
        /Names  [  (Xenon)      129 0 R
                   (Ytterbium)  130 0 R
                   (Yttrium)    131 0 R
                   (Zinc)       132 0 R
                   (Zirconium)  133 0 R
                ]
    >>
endobj

25 0  obj
    89                                                 % Atomic number (Actinium)
endobj

...

133  0  obj
    40                                                 % Atomic number (Zirconium)
endobj
```

3.8.5 Number Trees

A *number tree* is similar to a name tree (see Section 3.8.4, "Name Trees"), except that its keys are integers instead of strings, sorted in ascending numerical order. The entries in the leaf (or root) nodes containing the key-value pairs are named **Nums** instead of **Names** as in a name tree. Table 3.24 shows the entries in a number tree's node dictionaries.

		TABLE 3.24 Entries in a number tree node dictionary
KEY	**TYPE**	**VALUE**
Kids	array	*(Root and intermediate nodes only; required in intermediate nodes; present in the root node if and only if **Nums** is not present)* An array of indirect references to the immediate children of this node. The children may be intermediate or leaf nodes.
Nums	array	*(Root and leaf nodes only; required in leaf nodes; present in the root node if and only if **Kids** is not present)* An array of the form $$[key_1\ value_1\ \ key_2\ value_2\ \ ...\ \ key_n\ value_n]$$ where each key_i is an integer and the corresponding $value_i$ is an indirect reference to the object associated with that key. The keys are sorted in numerical order, analogously to the arrangement of keys in a name tree as described in Section 3.8.4, "Name Trees."
Limits	array	*(Intermediate and leaf nodes only; required)* An array of two integers, specifying the (numerically) least and greatest keys included in the **Nums** array of a leaf node or in the **Nums** arrays of any leaf nodes that are descendants of an intermediate node.

3.9 Functions

PDF is not a programming language, and a PDF file is not a program; however, PDF does provide several types of *function object (PDF 1.2)* that represent parameterized classes of functions, including mathematical formulas and sampled representations with arbitrary resolution. Functions are used in various ways in PDF: device-dependent rasterization information for high-quality printing (halftone spot functions and transfer functions), color transform functions for certain color spaces, and specification of colors as a function of position for smooth shadings.

Functions in PDF represent static, self-contained numerical transformations. A function to add two numbers has two input values and one output value:

$$f(x_0, x_1) = x_0 + x_1$$

Similarly, a function that computes the arithmetic and geometric mean of two numbers could be viewed as a function of two input values and two output values:

$$f(x_0, x_1) = \frac{x_0 + x_1}{2}, \sqrt{x_0 \times x_1}$$

In general, a function can take any number (m) of input values and produce any number (n) of output values:

$$f(x_0, \ldots, x_{m-1}) = y_0, \ldots, y_{n-1}$$

In PDF functions, all the input values and all the output values are numbers, and functions have no side effects.

Each function definition includes a *domain*, the set of legal values for the input. Some types of function also define a *range*, the set of legal values for the output. Input values passed to the function are clipped to the domain, and output values produced by the function are clipped to the range. For example, suppose the function

$$f(x) = x + 2$$

is defined with a domain of [−1 1]. If the function is called with the input value 6, that value is replaced with the nearest value in the defined domain, 1, before the function is evaluated; the resulting output value is therefore 3. Similarly, if the function

$$f(x_0, x_1) = 3 \times x_0 + x_1$$

is defined with a range of [0 100], and if the input values −6 and 4 are passed to the function (and are within its domain), then the output value produced by the function, −14, is replaced with 0, the nearest value in the defined range.

A function object may be a dictionary or a stream, depending on the type of function; the term *function dictionary* will be used generically in this section to refer to either a dictionary object or the dictionary portion of a stream object. A function dictionary specifies the function's representation, the set of attributes that parameterize that representation, and the additional data needed by that representation. Four types of function are available, as indicated by the dictionary's **FunctionType** entry:

- *(PDF 1.2)* A *sampled function* (type 0) uses a table of *sample values* to define the function. Various techniques are used to interpolate values between the sample values.

- *(PDF 1.3)* An *exponential interpolation function* (type 2) defines a set of coefficients for an exponential function.

- *(PDF 1.3)* A *stitching function* (type 3) is a combination of other functions, partitioned across a domain.

- *(PDF 1.3)* A *PostScript calculator function* (type 4) uses operators from the PostScript language to describe an arithmetic expression.

All function dictionaries share the entries listed in Table 3.25.

TABLE 3.25 Entries common to all function dictionaries

KEY	TYPE	VALUE
FunctionType	integer	*(Required)* The function type:
		0 Sampled function
		2 Exponential interpolation function
		3 Stitching function
		4 PostScript calculator function
Domain	array	*(Required)* An array of $2 \times m$ numbers, where m is the number of input values. For each i from 0 to $m-1$, **Domain**$_{2i}$ must be less than or equal to **Domain**$_{2i+1}$, and the ith input value, x_i, must lie in the interval **Domain**$_{2i} \leq x_i \leq$ **Domain**$_{2i+1}$. Input values outside the declared domain are clipped to the nearest boundary value.
Range	array	*(Required for type 0 and type 4 functions, optional otherwise; see below)* An array of $2 \times n$ numbers, where n is the number of output values. For each j from 0 to $n-1$, **Range**$_{2j}$ must be less than or equal to **Range**$_{2j+1}$, and the jth output value, y_j, must lie in the interval **Range**$_{2j} \leq y_j \leq$ **Range**$_{2j+1}$. Output values outside the declared range are clipped to the nearest boundary value. If this entry is absent, no clipping is done.

In addition, each type of function dictionary must include entries appropriate to the particular function type. The number of output values can usually be inferred from other attributes of the function; if not (as is always the case for type 0 and type 4 functions), the **Range** entry is required. The dimensionality of the function implied by the **Domain** and **Range** entries must be consistent with that implied by other attributes of the function.

3.9.1 Type 0 (Sampled) Functions

Type 0 functions use a sequence of *sample values* (contained in a stream) to provide an approximation for functions whose domains and ranges are bounded. The samples are organized as an *m*-dimensional table in which each entry has *n* components.

Sampled functions are highly general and offer reasonably accurate representations of arbitrary analytic functions at low expense. For example, a 1-input sinusoidal function can be represented over the range [0 180] with an average error of only 1 percent, using just ten samples and linear interpolation. Two-input functions require significantly more samples, but usually not a prohibitive number, so long as the function does not have high frequency variations.

The dimensionality of a sampled function is restricted only by implementation limits. However, the number of samples required to represent high-dimensionality functions multiplies rapidly unless the sampling resolution is very low. Also, the process of multilinear interpolation becomes computationally intensive if the number of inputs *m* is greater than 2. The multidimensional spline interpolation is even more computationally intensive.

In addition to the entries in Table 3.25, a type 0 function dictionary includes those shown in Table 3.26.

TABLE 3.26 Additional entries specific to a type 0 function dictionary

KEY	TYPE	VALUE
Size	array	*(Required)* An array of *m* positive integers specifying the number of samples in each input dimension of the sample table.
BitsPerSample	integer	*(Required)* The number of bits used to represent each sample. (If the function has multiple output values, each one occupies **BitsPerSample** bits.) Valid values are 1, 2, 4, 8, 12, 16, 24, and 32.
Order	integer	*(Optional)* The order of interpolation between samples. Valid values are 1 and 3, specifying linear and cubic spline interpolation, respectively. (See implementation note 23 in Appendix H.) Default value: 1.
Encode	array	*(Optional)* An array of $2 \times m$ numbers specifying the linear mapping of input values into the domain of the function's sample table. Default value: [0 ($Size_0 - 1$) 0 ($Size_1 - 1$) ...].

| **Decode** | array | *(Optional)* An array of $2 \times n$ numbers specifying the linear mapping of sample values into the range appropriate for the function's output values. Default value: Same as the value of **Range**. |
| *other stream attributes* | (various) | *(Optional)* Other attributes of the stream that provides the sample values, as appropriate (see Table 3.4 on page 35). |

The **Domain, Encode,** and **Size** entries determine how the function's input variable values are mapped into the sample table. For example, if **Size** is [21 31], the default **Encode** array is [0 20 0 30], which maps the entire domain into the full set of sample table entries. Other values of **Encode** may be used.

To explain the relationship between **Domain, Encode, Size, Decode,** and **Range,** we use the following notation:

$$y = \text{Interpolate}\,(x, x_{\min}, x_{\max}, y_{\min}, y_{\max}) = (x - x_{\min}) \times \frac{(y_{\max} - y_{\min})}{(x_{\max} - x_{\min})} + y_{\min}$$

For a given value of x, Interpolate calculates the y value on the line defined by the two points $(x_{\min}, y_{\min})$ and $(x_{\max}, y_{\max})$.

When a sampled function is called, each input value x_i, for $0 \le i < m$, is clipped to the domain:

$$x_i' = \min\,(\max\,(x_i, \text{\textbf{Domain}}_{2i}),\, \text{\textbf{Domain}}_{2i+1})$$

That value is encoded:

$$e_i = \text{Interpolate}\,(x_i', \text{\textbf{Domain}}_{2i}, \text{\textbf{Domain}}_{2i+1}, \text{\textbf{Encode}}_{2i}, \text{\textbf{Encode}}_{2i+1})$$

That value is clipped to the size of the sample table in that dimension:

$$e_i' = \min\,(\max\,(e_i, 0),\, \text{\textbf{Size}}_i - 1)$$

The encoded input values are real numbers, not restricted to integers. Interpolation is then used to determine output values from the nearest surrounding values in the sample table. Each output value r_j, for $0 \le j < n$, is then decoded:

$$r_j' = \text{Interpolate}\,(r_j, 0, 2^{\text{BitsPerSample}} - 1, \text{\textbf{Decode}}_{2j}, \text{\textbf{Decode}}_{2j+1})$$

Finally, each decoded value is clipped to the range:

$$y_j = \min(\max(r'_j, \mathbf{Range}_{2j}), \mathbf{Range}_{2j+1})$$

Sample data is represented as a stream of unsigned 8-bit bytes (integers in the range 0 to 255). The bytes constitute a continuous bit stream, with the high-order bit of each byte first. Each sample value is represented as a sequence of **BitsPer-Sample** bits. Successive values are adjacent in the bit stream; there is no padding at byte boundaries.

For a function with multidimensional input (more than one input variable), the sample values in the first dimension vary fastest, and the values in the last dimension vary slowest. For example, for a function $f(a, b, c)$, where a, b, and c vary from 0 to 9 in steps of 1, the sample values would appear in this order: $f(0, 0, 0)$, $f(1, 0, 0)$, ..., $f(9, 0, 0)$, $f(0, 1, 0)$, $f(1, 1, 0)$, ..., $f(9, 1, 0)$, $f(0, 2, 0)$, $f(1, 2, 0)$, ..., $f(9, 9, 0), f(0, 0, 1), f(1, 0, 1)$, and so on.

For a function with multidimensional output (more than one output value), the values are stored in the same order as **Range**.

The stream data must be long enough to contain the entire sample array, as indicated by **Size**, **Range**, and **BitsPerSample**; see "Stream Extent" on page 36.

Example 3.12 illustrates a sampled function with 4-bit samples in an array containing 21 columns and 31 rows (651 values). The function takes two arguments, x and y, in the domain [−1.0 1.0], and returns one value, z, in that same range. The x argument is linearly transformed by the encoding to the domain [0 20] and the y argument to the domain [0 30]. Using bilinear interpolation between sample points, the function computes a value for z, which (because **BitsPer-Sample** is 4) will be in the range [0 15], and the decoding transforms z to a number in the range [−1.0 1.0] for the result. The sample array is stored in a string of 326 bytes, calculated as follows (rounded up):

326 bytes = 31 rows × 21 samples/row × 4 bits/sample ÷ 8 bits/byte

The first byte contains the sample for the point $(−1.0, −1.0)$ in the high-order 4 bits and the sample for the point $(−0.9, −1.0)$ in the low-order 4 bits.

Example 3.12

```
14  0  obj
    <<  /FunctionType  0
        /Domain  [−1.0  1.0  −1.0  1.0]
        /Size  [21  31]
        /Encode  [0  20   0  30]
        /BitsPerSample  4
        /Range  [−1.0  1.0]
        /Decode  [−1.0  1.0]
        /Length  …
        /Filter  …
    >>
stream
… 651 sample values …
endstream
endobj
```

The **Decode** entry can be used creatively to increase the accuracy of encoded samples corresponding to certain values in the range. For example, if the desired range of the function is [−1.0 1.0] and **BitsPerSample** is 4, the usual value of **Decode** would be [−1.0 1.0] and the sample values would be integers in the interval [0 15] (as shown in Figure 3.6). But if these values were used, the midpoint of the range, 0.0, would not be represented exactly by any sample value, since it would fall halfway between 7 and 8. On the other hand, if the **Decode** array were [−1.0 +1.1429] (1.1429 being approximately equal to 16 ÷ 14) and the sample values supplied were in the interval [0 14], then the desired effective range of [−1.0 1.0] would be achieved, and the range value 0.0 would be represented by the sample value 7.

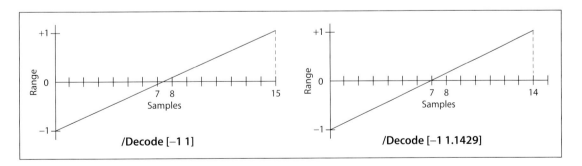

FIGURE 3.6 *Mapping with the **Decode** array*

The **Size** value for an input dimension can be 1, in which case all input values in that dimension will be mapped to the single allowed value. If **Size** is less than 4, cubic spline interpolation is not possible and **Order** 3 will be ignored if specified.

3.9.2 Type 2 (Exponential Interpolation) Functions

Type 2 functions *(PDF 1.3)* include a set of parameters that define an *exponential interpolation* of one input value and *n* output values:

$$f(x) = y_0, ..., y_{n-1}$$

In addition to the entries in Table 3.25 on page 97, a type 2 function dictionary includes those; listed in Table 3.27. (See implementation note 24 in Appendix H.)

		TABLE 3.27 Additional entries specific to a type 2 function dictionary
KEY	**TYPE**	**VALUE**
C0	array	*(Optional)* An array of *n* numbers defining the function result when $x = 0.0$ (hence the "0" in the name). Default value: [0.0].
C1	array	*(Optional)* An array of *n* numbers defining the function result when $x = 1.0$ (hence the "1" in the name). Default value: [1.0].
N	number	*(Required)* The interpolation exponent. Each input value *x* will return *n* values, given by $y_j = C0_j + x^N \times (C1_j - C0_j)$, for $0 \le j < n$.

Values of **Domain** must constrain *x* in such a way that if **N** is not an integer, all values of *x* must be nonnegative, and if **N** is negative, no value of *x* may be zero. Typically, **Domain** will be declared as [0.0 1.0], and **N** will be a positive number. The **Range** parameter is optional and can be used to clip the output to a desired range. Note that when **N** is 1, the function performs a linear interpolation between **C0** and **C1**. This can also be expressed as a sampled function (type 0).

3.9.3 Type 3 (Stitching) Functions

Type 3 functions *(PDF 1.3)* define a "stitching" of the subdomains of several
1-input functions to produce a single new 1-input function. Since the resulting
stitching function is a 1-input function, the domain is given by a two-element
array, [**Domain$_0$ Domain$_1$**].

In addition to the entries in Table 3.25 on page 97, a type 3 function dictionary
includes those listed in Table 3.28. (See implementation note 25 in Appendix H.)

TABLE 3.28   Additional entries specific to a type 3 function dictionary

KEY	TYPE	VALUE
Functions	array	*(Required)* An array of k 1-input functions making up the stitching function. The output dimensionality of all functions must be the same, and compatible with the value of **Range** if **Range** is present.
Bounds	array	*(Required)* An array of $k-1$ numbers that, in combination with **Domain**, define the intervals to which each function from the **Functions** array applies. **Bounds** elements must be in order of increasing value, and each value must be within the domain defined by **Domain**.
Encode	array	*(Required)* An array of $2 \times k$ numbers that, taken in pairs, map each subset of the domain defined by **Domain** and the **Bounds** array to the domain of the corresponding function.

Domain must be of size 2 (that is, $m = 1$), and **Domain$_0$** must be strictly less than
Domain$_1$ unless $k = 1$. The domain is partitioned into k subdomains, as indicated
by the dictionary's **Bounds** entry, which is an array of $k-1$ numbers that obey the
following relationships (with exceptions as noted below):

$$\textbf{Domain}_0 < \textbf{Bounds}_0 < \textbf{Bounds}_1 < \ldots < \textbf{Bounds}_{k-2} < \textbf{Domain}_1$$

The **Bounds** array describes a series of half-open intervals, closed on the left and
open on the right (except the last, which is closed on the right as well). The value
of the **Functions** entry is an array of k functions. The first function applies to x
values in the first subdomain, **Domain$_0$** $\leq x <$ **Bounds$_0$**; the second function applies to x values in the second subdomain, **Bounds$_0$** $\leq x <$ **Bounds$_1$**; and so on.
The last function applies to x values in the last subdomain, which includes the
upper bound: **Bounds$_{k-2}$** $\leq x \leq$ **Domain$_1$**. The value of k may be 1, in which case

the **Bounds** array is empty and the single item in the **Functions** array applies to all x values, $\textbf{Domain}_0 \leq x \leq \textbf{Domain}_1$.

The **Encode** array contains $2 \times k$ numbers. A value x from the ith subdomain is encoded as follows:

$$x' = \text{Interpolate}\,(x,\, \textbf{Bounds}_{i-1},\, \textbf{Bounds}_i,\, \textbf{Encode}_{2i},\, \textbf{Encode}_{2i+1})$$

for $0 \leq i < k$. In this equation, $\textbf{Bounds}_{-1}$ means $\textbf{Domain}_0$, and $\textbf{Bounds}_{k-1}$ means $\textbf{Domain}_1$. If the last bound, $\textbf{Bounds}_{k-2}$, is equal to $\textbf{Domain}_1$, then x' is defined to be $\textbf{Encode}_{2i}$.

The stitching function is designed to make it easy to combine several functions to be used within one shading pattern, over different parts of the shading's domain. (Shading patterns are discussed in Section 4.6.3, "Shading Patterns.") The same effect could be achieved by creating a separate shading dictionary for each of the functions, with adjacent domains. However, since each shading would have similar parameters, and because the overall effect is one shading, it is more convenient to have a single shading with multiple function definitions.

Also, function type 3 provides a general mechanism for inverting the domains of 1-input functions. For example, consider a function f with a **Domain** of [0.0 1.0], and a stitching function g with a **Domain** of [0.0 1.0], a **Functions** array containing f, and an **Encode** array of [1.0 0.0]. In effect, $g(x) = f(1 - x)$.

3.9.4 Type 4 (PostScript Calculator) Functions

A type 4 function *(PDF 1.3)*, also called a *PostScript calculator function*, is represented as a stream containing code written in a small subset of the PostScript language. While any function can be sampled (in a type 0 PDF function) and others can be described with exponential functions (type 2 in PDF), type 4 functions offer greater flexibility and potentially greater accuracy. For example, a tint transformation function for a hexachrome (six-component) **DeviceN** color space with an alternate color space of **DeviceCMYK** (see "DeviceN Color Spaces" on page 186) requires a 6-in, 4-out function. If such a function were sampled with m values for each input variable, the number of samples, $4 \times m^6$, could be prohibitively large. In practice, such functions are often written as short, simple PostScript functions. (See implementation note 26 in Appendix H.)

Type 4 functions also make it possible to include a wide variety of halftone spot functions without the loss of accuracy that comes from sampling, and without adding to the list of predefined spot functions (see Section 6.4.2, "Spot Functions"). All of the predefined spot functions can be written as type 4 functions.

The language that can be used in a type 4 function contains expressions involving integers, real numbers, and boolean values only. There are no composite data structures such as strings or arrays, no procedures, and no variables or names. Table 3.29 lists the operators that can be used in this type of function. (For more information on these operators, see Appendix B or the *PostScript Language Reference*, Third Edition.) Although the semantics are those of the corresponding PostScript operators, a PostScript interpreter is not required.

TABLE 3.29   Operators in type 4 functions

OPERATOR TYPE	OPERATORS				
Arithmetic operators	abs	cvi	floor	mod	sin
	add	cvr	idiv	mul	sqrt
	atan	div	ln	neg	sub
	ceiling	exp	log	round	truncate
	cos				
Relational, boolean, and bitwise operators	and	false	le	not	true
	bitshift	ge	lt	or	xor
	eq	gt	ne		
Conditional operators	if	ifelse			
Stack operators	copy	exch	pop		
	dup	index	roll		

The operand syntax for type 4 functions follows PDF conventions rather than PostScript conventions. The entire code stream defining the function is enclosed in braces { }. Braces also delimit expressions that are executed conditionally by the **if** and **ifelse** operators:

boolean {*expression*} if
boolean {*expression*$_1$} {*expression*$_2$} ifelse

Note that this is a purely syntactic construct; unlike in PostScript, no "procedure objects" are involved.

A type 4 function dictionary includes the entries in Table 3.25 on page 97, as well as other stream attributes as appropriate (see Table 3.4 on page 35). Example 3.13 shows a type 4 function equivalent to the predefined spot function **DoubleDot** (see Section 6.4.2, "Spot Functions").

Example 3.13

```
10  0  obj
    << /FunctionType  4
        /Domain  [−1.0 1.0  −1.0 1.0]
        /Range  [−1.0  1.0]
        /Length  71
    >>
stream
    { 360  mul  sin
      2 div
      exch  360  mul  sin
      2 div
      add
    }
endstream
endobj
```

The **Domain** and **Range** keys are both required. The input variables constitute the initial operand stack; the items remaining on the operand stack after execution of the function are the output variables. It is an error for the number of remaining operands to differ from the number of output variables specified by **Range**, or for any of them to be objects other than numbers.

Implementations of type 4 functions must provide a stack with room for at least 100 entries. No implementation is required to provide a larger stack, and it is an error to overflow the stack.

Although any integers or real numbers that may appear in the stream fall under the same implementation limits (defined in Appendix C) as in other contexts, the *intermediate* results in type 4 function computations do not. An implementation may use a representation that exceeds those limits. Operations on real numbers, for example, might use single-precision or double-precision floating-point numbers. (See implementation note 27 in Appendix H.)

Errors in Type 4 Functions

The code that reads a type 4 function (analogous to the PostScript *scanner*) must detect and report syntax errors. It may also be able to detect some errors that will occur when the function is used, although this is not always possible. Any errors detected by the scanner are considered to be errors in the PDF file itself and are handled like other errors in the file.

The code that executes a type 4 function (analogous to the PostScript *interpreter*) must detect and report errors. PDF does not define a representation for the errors; those details are provided by the application that processes the PDF file. The following types of error can occur (among others):

- Stack overflow

- Stack underflow

- A type error (for example, applying **not** to a real number)

- A range error (for example, applying **sqrt** to a negative number)

- An undefined result (for example, dividing by 0)

3.10 File Specifications

A PDF file can refer to the contents of another file by using a *file specification (PDF 1.1)*, which can take either of two forms. A *simple* file specification gives just the name of the target file in a standard format, independent of the naming conventions of any particular file system; a *full* file specification includes information related to one or more specific file systems. A simple file specification may take the form of either a string or a dictionary; a full file specification can only be represented as a dictionary.

Although the file designated by a file specification is normally external to the PDF file referring to it, PDF 1.3 permits a copy of the external file to be embedded within the PDF file itself, allowing its contents to be stored or transmitted along with the PDF file. However, embedding a file does not change the presumption that it is external to the PDF file. Consequently, in order for the PDF file to be processed correctly, it may be necessary to copy the embedded files it contains back into a local file system.

3.10.1 File Specification Strings

The standard format for representing a simple file specification in string form divides the string into component substrings separated by the slash character (/). The slash is a generic component separator that is mapped to the appropriate platform-specific separator when generating a platform-dependent file name. Any of the components may be empty. If a component contains one or more literal slashes, each must be preceded by a backslash (\), which in turn must be preceded by another backslash to indicate that it is part of the string and not an escape character. For example, the string

    (in\\/out)

represents the file name

    in/out

The backslashes are removed in processing the string; they are needed only to distinguish the component values from the component separators. The component substrings are stored as bytes and are passed to the operating system without interpretation or conversion of any sort.

Absolute and Relative File Specifications

A simple file specification that begins with a slash is an *absolute* file specification. The last component is the file name; the preceding components specify its context. In some file specifications, the file name may be empty; for example, URL (uniform resource locator) specifications can specify directories instead of files. A file specification that does not begin with a slash is a *relative* file specification giving the location of the file relative to that of the PDF file containing it.

In the case of a URL file system, the rules of Internet RFC 1808, *Relative Uniform Resource Locators* (see the Bibliography), are used to compute an absolute URL from a relative file specification and the specification of the PDF file. Prior to this process, the relative file specification is converted to a relative URL by using the escape mechanism of RFC 1738, *Uniform Resource Locators*, to represent any bytes that would be either "unsafe" according to RFC 1738 or not representable in 7-bit U.S. ASCII. In addition, such URL-based relative file specifications are limited to paths as defined in RFC 1808; the scheme, network location/login, fragment identifier, query information, and parameter sections are not allowed.

In the case of other file systems, a relative file specification is converted to an absolute file specification by removing the file name component from the specification of the containing PDF file and appending the relative file specification in its place. For example, the relative file specification

   ArtFiles/Figure1.pdf

appearing in a PDF file whose specification is

   /HardDisk/PDFDocuments/AnnualReport/Summary.pdf

yields the absolute specification

   /HardDisk/PDFDocuments/AnnualReport/ArtFiles/Figure1.pdf

The special component .. (two periods) can be used in a relative file specification to move up a level in the file system hierarchy. When the component immediately preceding .. is not another .., the two cancel each other; both are eliminated from the file specification and the process is repeated. Thus in the example above, the relative file specification

   ../../ArtFiles/Figure1.pdf

would yield the absolute specification

   /HardDisk/ArtFiles/Figure1.pdf

Conversion to Platform-Dependent File Names

The conversion of a file specification into a platform-dependent file name depends on the specific file naming conventions of each platform. For example:

- For the Apple Macintosh®, all components are separated by colons (:).

- For UNIX, all components are separated by slashes (/). An initial slash, if present, is preserved.

- For DOS, the initial component is either a physical or logical drive identifier or a network resource name as returned by the Microsoft Windows function WNetGetConnection, and is followed by a colon. A network resource name is constructed from the first two components; the first component is the server name and the second is the share name (volume name). All components are then separated by backslashes. It is possible to specify an absolute DOS path without a drive by making the first component empty. (Empty components are ignored by other platforms.)

Strings used to specify a file name are interpreted in the standard encoding for the platform on which the document is being viewed. Table 3.30 shows examples of file specifications on the most common platforms.

TABLE 3.30 Examples of file specifications		
SYSTEM	**SYSTEM-DEPENDENT PATHS**	**WRITTEN FORM**
Macintosh	Mac HD:PDFDocs:spec.pdf	(/Mac HD/PDFDocs/spec.pdf)
DOS	\pdfdocs\spec.pdf (no drive)	(//pdfdocs/spec.pdf)
	r:\pdfdocs\spec.pdf	(/r/pdfdocs/spec.pdf)
	pclib/eng:\pdfdocs\spec.pdf	(/pclib/eng/pdfdocs/spec.pdf)
UNIX	/user/fred/pdfdocs/spec.pdf	(/user/fred/pdfdocs/spec.pdf)
	pdfdocs/spec.pdf (relative)	(pdfdocs/spec.pdf)

When creating documents that are to be viewed on multiple platforms, care must be taken to ensure file name compatibility. Only a subset of the U.S. ASCII character set should be used in file specifications: the uppercase alphabetic characters (A–Z), the numeric characters (0–9), and the underscore (_). The period (.) has special meaning in DOS and Windows file names, and as the first character in a Macintosh pathname. In file specifications, the period should be used only to separate a base file name from a file extension.

Some file systems are case-insensitive, so names within a directory should remain distinguishable if lowercase letters are changed to uppercase or vice versa. On DOS and Windows 3.1 systems and on some CD-ROM file systems, file names are limited to 8 characters plus a 3-character extension. File system software typically converts long names to short names by retaining the first 6 or 7 characters of the file name and the first 3 characters after the last period, if any. Since characters beyond the sixth or seventh are often converted to other values unrelated to the original value, file names must be distinguishable from the first 6 characters.

Multiple-Byte Strings in File Specifications

In PDF 1.2 or higher, a file specification may contain multiple-byte character codes, represented in hexadecimal form between angle brackets (< and >). Since the slash character <2F> is used as a component delimiter and the backslash <5C> is used as an escape character, any occurrence of either of these bytes in a multiple-byte character must be preceded by the ASCII code for the backslash character. For example, a file name containing the 2-byte character code <89 5C> must write it as <89 5C 5C>. When the viewer application encounters this sequence of bytes in a file name, it replaces the sequence with the original 2-byte code.

3.10.2 File Specification Dictionaries

The dictionary form of file specification provides more flexibility than the string form, allowing different files to be specified for different file systems or platforms, or for file systems other than the standard ones (Macintosh, DOS/Windows, and UNIX). Table 3.31 shows the entries in a file specification dictionary. Viewer applications running on a particular platform should use the appropriate platform-specific entry (**Mac**, **DOS**, or **Unix**) if available. If the required platform-specific entry is not present and there is no file system entry (**FS**), the generic **F** entry should be used as a simple file specification.

TABLE 3.31 Entries in a file specification dictionary

KEY	TYPE	VALUE
Type	name	*(Required if an **EF** or **RF** entry is present; recommended always)* The type of PDF object that this dictionary describes; must be **Filespec** for a file specification dictionary.
FS	name	*(Optional)* The name of the file system to be used to interpret this file specification. If this entry is present, all other entries in the dictionary are interpreted by the designated file system. PDF defines only one standard file system, URL (see Section 3.10.4, "URL Specifications"); a viewer application or plug-in extension can register a different one (see Appendix E). Note that this entry is independent of the **F**, **Mac**, **DOS**, and **Unix** entries.
F	string	*(Required if the **Mac**, **DOS**, and **Unix** entries are all absent)* A file specification string of the form described in Section 3.10.1, "File Specification Strings," or (if the file system is **URL**) a uniform resource locator, as described in Section 3.10.4, "URL Specifications."

Mac	string	*(Optional)* A file specification string (see Section 3.10.1, "File Specification Strings") representing a Macintosh file name.
DOS	string	*(Optional)* A file specification string (see Section 3.10.1, "File Specification Strings") representing a DOS file name.
Unix	string	*(Optional)* A file specification string (see Section 3.10.1, "File Specification Strings") representing a UNIX file name.
ID	array	*(Optional)* An array of two strings, each of which is a file identifier (see Section 8.3, "File Identifiers") that is also included in the referenced file. The first identifier is established permanently when the file is created; the second is changed each time the file is updated. This improves a viewer application's chances of finding the intended file and allows it to warn the user if the file has changed since the link was made.
V	boolean	*(Optional; PDF 1.2)* A flag indicating whether the file referenced by the file specification is *volatile* (changes frequently with time). If the value is *true*, viewer applications should never cache a copy of the file. For example, a movie annotation referencing a URL to a live video camera could set this flag to *true*, notifying the application that it should reacquire the movie each time it is played. Default value: *false*.
EF	dictionary	*(Optional; PDF 1.3)* A dictionary containing a subset of the file name entries **F**, **Mac**, **DOS**, and **Unix**. The value of each such key is an embedded file stream (see Section 3.10.3, "Embedded File Streams") containing the corresponding file. This entry is required if **RF** is present. If this entry is present, the **Type** entry is required and the file specification dictionary must be indirectly referenced.
RF	dictionary	*(Optional; PDF 1.3)* A dictionary with the same structure as the **EF** dictionary, which must also be present. Each entry in the **RF** dictionary must also be present in the **EF** dictionary. Each value is a related files array (see "Related Files Arrays" on page 114) identifying files that are related to the corresponding file in the **EF** dictionary. If this entry is present, the **Type** entry is required and the file specification dictionary must be indirectly referenced.

3.10.3 Embedded File Streams

File specifications ordinarily refer to files external to the PDF file in which they occur. To preserve the integrity of the PDF file, this requires that all external files it refers to must accompany it when it is archived or transmitted. *Embedded file streams (PDF 1.3)* address this problem by allowing the contents of the referenced files to be embedded directly within the body of the PDF file itself. For example, if the file contains OPI (Open Prepress Interface) dictionaries that refer to externally stored high-resolution images (see Section 8.6.4, "Open Prepress Interface (OPI)"), the image data can be incorporated into the PDF file with embedded file streams. This makes the PDF file a self-contained unit that can be stored or transmitted as a single entity. (The embedded files are included purely for convenience, and need not be directly processed by any PDF consumer application.)

The stream dictionary describing an embedded file contains the standard entries for any stream, such as **Length** and **Filter** (see Table 3.4 on page 35), as well as the additional entries shown in Table 3.32.

TABLE 3.32 Additional entries in an embedded file stream dictionary

KEY	TYPE	VALUE
Type	name	*(Optional)* The type of PDF object that this dictionary describes; if present, must be **EmbeddedFile** for an embedded file stream.
Subtype	name	*(Optional)* The subtype of the embedded file. The value of this entry must be a first-class name, as defined in Appendix E. Names without a registered prefix must conform to the MIME media type names defined in Internet RFC 2046, *Multipurpose Internet Mail Extensions (MIME), Part Two: Media Types* (see the Bibliography), with the provision that characters not allowed in names must use the 2-character hexadecimal code format described in Section 3.2.4, "Name Objects."
Params	dictionary	*(Optional)* An *embedded file parameter dictionary* containing additional, file-specific information (see Table 3.33).

TABLE 3.33 Entries in an embedded file parameter dictionary

KEY	TYPE	VALUE
Size	integer	*(Optional)* The size of the embedded file, in bytes.
CreationDate	date	*(Optional)* The date and time when the embedded file was created.
ModDate	date	*(Optional)* The date and time when the embedded file was last modified.
Mac	dictionary	*(Optional)* A subdictionary containing additional information specific to Macintosh files (see Table 3.34).
CheckSum	string	*(Optional)* A 16-byte string that is the checksum of the bytes of the uncompressed embedded file. The checksum is calculated by applying the standard MD5 message-digest algorithm (described in Internet RFC 1321, *The MD5 Message-Digest Algorithm*; see the Bibliography) to the bytes of the embedded file stream.

For Macintosh files, the **Mac** entry in the embedded file parameter dictionary holds a further subdictionary containing Macintosh-specific file information. Table 3.34 shows the contents of this subdictionary.

TABLE 3.34 Entries in a Macintosh-specific file information dictionary

KEY	TYPE	VALUE
Subtype	string	*(Optional)* The embedded file's file type.
Creator	string	*(Optional)* The embedded file's creator signature.
ResFork	stream	*(Optional)* The binary contents of the embedded file's resource fork.

Related Files Arrays

In some circumstances, a PDF file can refer to a group of related files, such as the set of five files that make up a DCS 1.0 color-separated image. The file specification explicitly names only one of the files; the rest are identified by some systematic variation of that file name (such as by altering the extension). When such a file is to be embedded in a PDF file, the related files must be embedded as well. This is accomplished by including a *related files array (PDF 1.3)* as the value of the **RF** entry in the file specification dictionary. The array has $2 \times n$ elements, which are paired in the form

> [$string_1$ $stream_1$
> $string_2$ $stream_2$
>   …
> $string_n$ $stream_n$
>]

The first element of each pair is a string giving the name of one of the related files; the second element is an embedded file stream holding the file's contents.

In Example 3.14, objects 21, 31, and 41 are embedded file streams containing the Macintosh file Sunset.eps, the DOS file SUNSET.EPS, and the UNIX file Sunset.eps, respectively. The file specification dictionary's **RF** entry specifies an array, object 20, identifying a set of embedded files related to the Macintosh file, forming a DCS 1.0 set. The example shows only the first two embedded file streams in the set; an actual PDF file would of course include all of them.

Example 3.14

```
10 0 obj                        % File specification dictionary
   << /Type /Filespec
      /Mac (Sunset.eps)         % Name of the Macintosh file
      /DOS (SUNSET.EPS)
      /Unix (Sunset.eps)
      /EF << /Mac  21 0 R       % Embedded Macintosh file
             /DOS  31 0 R
             /Unix 41 0 R
          >>
      /RF << /Mac 20 0 R >>     % Related files array for the Macintosh file
   >>
endobj

20 0 obj                        % Related files array for the Macintosh file
   [ (Sunset.eps) 21 0 R        % Includes file Sunset.eps itself
     (Sunset.C) 22 0 R
     (Sunset.M) 23 0 R
     (Sunset.Y) 24 0 R
     (Sunset.K) 25 0 R
   ]
endobj

21 0 obj                        % Embedded file stream for file Sunset.eps
   << /Type /EmbeddedFile
      /Length ...
      /Filter ...
   >>
stream
... Data for Sunset.eps ...
endstream
endobj

22 0 obj                        % Embedded file stream for file Sunset.C
   << /Type /EmbeddedFile
      /Length ...
      /Filter ...
   >>
stream
... Data for Sunset.C ...
endstream
endobj
```

3.10.4 URL Specifications

When the **FS** entry in a file specification dictionary has the value **URL**, the value of the **F** entry in that dictionary is not a file specification string, but a uniform resource locator (URL) of the form defined in Internet RFC 1738, *Uniform Resource Locators* (see the Bibliography). Example 3.15 shows a URL specification.

Example 3.15

```
<< /FS /URL
    /F (ftp://www.beatles.com/Movies/AbbeyRoad.mov)
>>
```

The URL must adhere to the character-encoding requirements specified in RFC 1738. Because 7-bit U.S. ASCII is a strict subset of **PDFDocEncoding**, this value may also be considered to be in that encoding.

3.10.5 Maintenance of File Specifications

The techniques described in this section can be used to maintain the integrity of the file specifications within a PDF file during operations such as the following:

- Updating the relevant file specification when a referenced file is renamed

- Determining the complete collection of files that must be copied to a mirror site

- When creating new links to external files, discovering existing file specifications that refer to the same files and sharing them

- Finding the file specifications associated with embedded files to be packed or unpacked

It is not possible, in general, to find all file specification strings in a PDF file, because there is no way to determine whether a given string is a file specification string. It is possible, however, to find all file specification *dictionaries*, provided that they meet the following conditions:

- They are indirect objects.

- They contain a **Type** entry whose value is the name **Filespec**.

An application can then locate all of the file specification dictionaries by traversing the PDF file's cross-reference table (see Section 3.4.3, "Cross-Reference Table") and finding all dictionaries with **Type** keys whose value is **Filespec**. For this reason, it is highly recommended that all file specifications be expressed in dictionary form and meet the conditions stated above. Note that any file specification dictionary specifying embedded files (that is, one that contains an **EF** entry) *must* satisfy these conditions (see Table 3.31 on page 111).

Note: *It may not be possible to locate file specification dictionaries that are direct objects, since they are neither self-typed nor necessarily reachable via any standard path of object references.*

Files may be embedded in a PDF file either directly, using the **EF** entry in a file specification dictionary, or indirectly, using related files arrays specified in the **RF** entry. If a file is embedded indirectly, its name is given by the string that precedes the embedded file stream in the related files array; if it is embedded directly, its name is obtained from the value of the corresponding entry in the file specification dictionary. In Example 3.14 on page 115, for instance, the **EF** dictionary has a **DOS** entry identifying object number 31 as an embedded file stream; the name of the embedded DOS file, SUNSET.EPS, is given by the **DOS** entry in the file specification dictionary.

A given external file may be referenced from more than one file specification. Therefore, when embedding a file with a given name, it is necessary to check for other occurrences of the same name as the value associated with the corresponding key in other file specification dictionaries. This requires finding all embeddable file specifications and, for each matching key, checking for both of the following conditions:

• The string value associated with the key matches the name of the file being embedded.

• A value has not already been embedded for the file specification. (If there is already a corresponding key in the **EF** dictionary, then a file has already been embedded for that use of the file name.)

Note that there is no requirement that the files associated with a given file name be unique. The same file name, such as readme.txt, may be associated with different embedded files in distinct file specifications.

CHAPTER 4

Graphics

THE GRAPHICS OPERATORS used in PDF content streams describe the appearance of pages that are to be reproduced on a raster output device. The facilities described in this chapter are intended for both printer and display applications.

The graphics operators form six main groups:

- *Graphics state operators* manipulate the data structure called the *graphics state*, the global framework within which the other graphics operators execute. The graphics state includes the *current transformation matrix* (CTM), which maps user space coordinates used within a PDF content stream into output device coordinates. It also includes the *current color*, the *clipping path*, and many other parameters that are implicit operands of the painting operators.

- *Path construction operators* specify *paths*, which define shapes, line trajectories, and regions of various sorts. They include operators for beginning a new path, adding line segments and curves to it, and closing it.

- *Path-painting operators* fill a path with a color, paint a stroke along it, or use it as a clipping boundary.

- *Other painting operators* paint certain self-describing graphics objects. These include sampled images, geometrically defined shadings, and entire content streams that in turn contain sequences of graphics operators.

- *Text operators* select and paint *character glyphs* from *fonts* (descriptions of typefaces for representing text characters). Because PDF treats glyphs as general graphical shapes, many of the text operators could be grouped with the graphics state or painting operators. However, the data structures and mechanisms for dealing with glyph and font descriptions are sufficiently specialized that Chapter 5 focuses on them.

- *Marked-content operators* associate higher-level logical information with objects in the content stream. This information does not affect the rendered appearance of the content; it is useful to applications that use PDF for document interchange. Marked content is described in Section 8.4.2, "Marked Content."

This chapter presents general information about device-independent graphics in PDF: how a PDF content stream describes the abstract appearance of a page. *Rendering*—the device-dependent part of graphics—is covered in Chapter 6. The Bibliography lists a number of books that give details of these computer graphics concepts and their implementation.

4.1 Graphics Objects

As discussed in Section 3.7.1, "Content Streams," the data in a content stream is interpreted as a sequence of *operators* and their *operands*, expressed as basic data objects according to standard PDF syntax. A content stream can describe the appearance of a page, or it can be treated as a graphical element in certain other contexts.

The operands and operators are written sequentially using postfix notation. This notation resembles the sequential execution model of the PostScript language. However, a PDF content stream is not a program to be interpreted; rather, it is a static description of a sequence of *graphics objects*. There are specific rules, described below, for writing the operands and operators that describe a graphics object.

PDF provides five types of graphics object:

- A *path object* is an arbitrary shape made up of straight lines, rectangles, and cubic Bézier curves. A path may intersect itself and may have disconnected sections and holes. A path object ends with one or more painting operators that specify whether the path is filled, stroked, used as a clipping path, or some combination of these operations.

- A *text object* consists of one or more character strings that identify sequences of glyphs to be painted. Like a path, text can be filled, stroked, or used as a clipping path.

- An *external object* (*XObject*) is an object defined outside the content stream and referenced as a named resource (see Section 3.7.2, "Resource Dictionaries"). The interpretation of an XObject depends on its type. An *image XObject* defines a rectangular array of color samples to be painted; a *form XObject* is an entire content stream to be treated as a single graphics object. (There is also a *PostScript XObject*, whose use is not recommended.)

- An *in-line image object* is a means of expressing the data for a small image directly in the content stream, using a special syntax.

- A *shading object* describes a geometric shape whose color is an arbitrary function of position within the shape. (A shading can also be treated as a color when painting other graphics objects; it is not considered to be a graphics object in that case.)

Each graphics object is painted on the page in sequence, obscuring any previously painted objects that it overlaps, in accordance with the opaque painting model introduced in Section 2.1.2, "Adobe Imaging Model." Although this painting behavior is often attributed to individual operators making up the object, it is always the object as a whole that is painted. Figure 4.1 shows the ordering rules for the operations that define graphics objects. Some operations are permitted only in certain types of graphics object or in the intervals between graphics objects (called the *page description level* in the figure). Every content stream begins at the page description level, where changes can be made to the graphics state, such as colors and text attributes, as discussed in the following sections.

In the figure, arrows indicate the operators that mark the beginning or end of each type of graphics object. Some operators are identified individually, others by general category. Table 4.1 summarizes these categories for all PDF operators. For example, the path construction operators **m** and **re** signal the beginning of a path object. Inside the path object, additional path construction operators are permitted, as are the clipping path operators **W** and **W***, but not general graphics state operators such as **w** or **J**. A path-painting operator, such as **S** or **f**, ends the path object and returns to the page description level.

Note: *A content stream whose operations violate these rules for describing graphics objects can produce unpredictable behavior, even though it may display and print correctly. Applications that attempt to extract graphics objects for editing or other purposes depend on the objects' being well formed. The rules for graphics objects are also important for the proper interpretation of marked content (see Section 8.4.2, "Marked Content").*

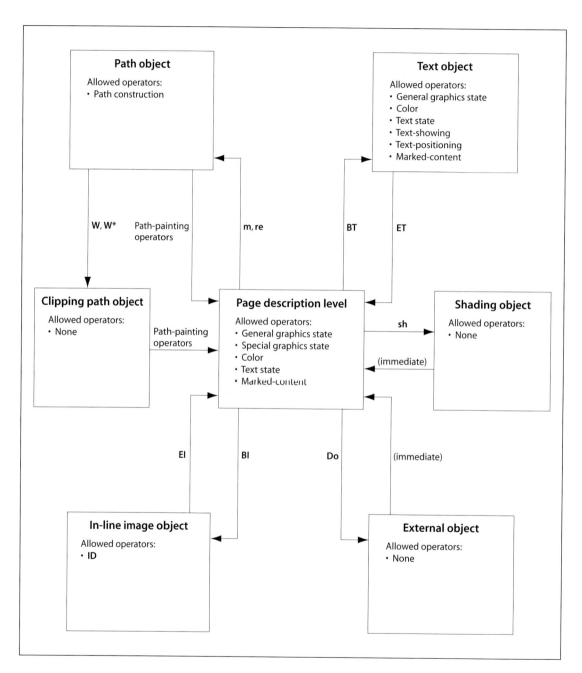

FIGURE 4.1 *Graphics objects*

TABLE 4.1 Operator categories

CATEGORY	OPERATORS	TABLE	PAGE
General graphics state	w, J, j, M, d, ri, i, gs	4.7	142
Special graphics state	q, Q, cm	4.7	142
Path construction	m, l, c, v, y, h, re	4.9	149
Path painting	S, s, f, F, f*, B, B*, b, b*, n	4.10	152
Clipping paths	W, W*	4.11	156
Text objects	BT, ET	5.4	286
Text state	Tc, Tw, Tz, TL, Tf, Tr, Ts	5.2	280
Text positioning	Td, TD, Tm, T*	5.5	287
Text showing	Tj, TJ, ', "	5.6	289
Type 3 fonts	d0, d1	5.10	303
Color	cs, CS, sc, scn, SC, SCN, g, G, rg, RG, k, K	4.21	198
Shading patterns	sh	4.24	214
In-line images	BI, ID, EI	4.38	260
XObjects	Do	4.34	243
Marked content	BMC, BDC, EMC, MP, DP	8.5	480
Compatibility	BX, EX	3.19	84

A graphics object also implicitly includes all graphics state parameters that affect its behavior. For instance, a path object depends on the value of the current color parameter at the moment the path object is defined. The effect is as if this parameter were specified as part of the definition of the path object. However, the operators that are invoked at the page description level to set graphics state parameters are *not* considered to belong to any particular graphics object. Graphics state parameters need to be specified only when they change. A graphics object may depend on parameters that were defined much earlier.

Similarly, the individual character strings within a text object implicitly include the graphics state parameters on which they depend. Most of these parameters may be set either inside or outside the text object. The effect is as if they were separately specified for each text string.

The important point is that there is no semantic significance to the exact arrangement of graphics state operators. An application that reads and writes a PDF content stream is not required to preserve this arrangement, but is free to change it to any other arrangement that achieves the same values of the relevant graphics state parameters for each graphics object. An application should not infer any higher-level logical semantics from the arrangement of tokens constituting a graphics object. A separate mechanism, *marked content*, allows such higher-level information to be explicitly associated with the graphics objects; see Section 8.4.2, "Marked Content."

4.2 Coordinate Systems

Coordinate systems define the canvas on which all painting occurs. They determine the position, orientation, and size of the text, graphics, and images that appear on a page. This section describes each of the coordinate systems used in PDF, how they are related, and how transformations among them are specified.

4.2.1 Coordinate Spaces

Paths and positions are defined in terms of pairs of *coordinates* on the Cartesian plane. A coordinate pair is a pair of real numbers x and y that locate a point horizontally and vertically within a two-dimensional *coordinate space*. A coordinate space is determined by the following properties with respect to the current page:

• The location of the origin

• The orientation of the x and y axes

• The lengths of the units along each axis

PDF defines several coordinate spaces in which the coordinates specifying graphics objects are interpreted. The following sections describe these spaces and the relationships among them.

Transformations among coordinate spaces are defined by *transformation matrices*, which can specify any linear mapping of two-dimensional coordinates, including translation, scaling, rotation, reflection, and skewing. Transformation matrices are discussed in Sections 4.2.2, "Common Transformations," and 4.2.3, "Transformation Matrices."

Device Space

The contents of a page ultimately appear on a raster output device such as a display or a printer. Such devices vary greatly in the built-in coordinate systems they use to address pixels within their imageable areas. A particular device's coordinate system is called its *device space*. The origin of the device space on different devices can fall in different places on the output page; on displays, the origin can vary depending on the window system. Because the paper or other output medium moves through different printers and imagesetters in different directions, the axes of their device spaces may be oriented differently; for instance, vertical (*y*) coordinates may increase from the top of the page to the bottom on some devices and from bottom to top on others. Finally, different devices have different resolutions; some even have resolutions that differ in the horizontal and vertical directions.

If coordinates in a PDF file were specified in device space, the file would be device-dependent and would appear differently on different devices. For example, images specified in the typical device spaces of a 72-pixel-per-inch display and a 600-dot-per-inch printer would differ in size by more than a factor of 8; an 8-inch line segment on the display would appear less than 1 inch long on the printer. Figure 4.2 shows how the same graphics object, specified in device space, can appear drastically different when rendered on different output devices.

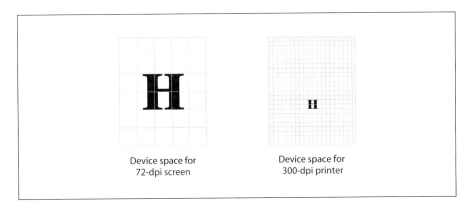

Device space for
72-dpi screen

Device space for
300-dpi printer

FIGURE 4.2 *Device space*

User Space

To avoid the device-dependent effects of specifying objects in device space, PDF defines a device-independent coordinate system that always bears the same relationship to the current page, regardless of the output device on which printing or displaying will occur. This device-independent coordinate system is called *user space*.

The user space coordinate system is initialized to a default state for each page of a document. Initially, the origin is located at the lower-left corner of the output page or display window, with the positive x axis extending horizontally to the right and the positive y axis extending vertically upward, as in standard mathematical practice. The length of a unit along both the x and y axes is 1/72 inch. This coordinate system is the *default user space*, in which all points on a page have positive x and y coordinate values.

Note: The unit size in default user space (1/72 inch) is approximately the same as a point, a unit widely used in the printing industry. It is not exactly the same, however; there is no universal definition of a point.

Conceptually, user space is an infinite plane. Only a small portion of this plane corresponds to the imageable area of the output device: a rectangular area above and to the right of the origin in default user space. The region of default user space that is viewed or printed can be different for each page, and is described in Section 8.6.1, "Page Boundaries."

The default user space origin coincides with the lower-left corner of the physical output medium. Portions of the physical medium may not be imageable on some output devices; for example, many laser printers cannot place marks at the extreme edges of the physical sheet of paper. Thus, in particular, it may not be possible to place marks at or near the default user space origin. However, the correspondence of physical corner to default origin ensures that marks within the imageable portion of the output page will be consistently positioned with respect to the edges of the medium.

Note: Because coordinates in user space (as in any other coordinate space) may be specified as either integers or real numbers, the unit size in default user space does not constrain positions to any arbitrary grid. The resolution of coordinates in user space is not related in any way to the resolution of pixels in device space.

The transformation from user space to device space is defined by the *current transformation matrix* (CTM), an element of the PDF graphics state (see Section 4.3, "Graphics State"). A PDF viewer application can adjust the CTM for the native resolution of a particular output device, maintaining the device-independence of the PDF page description itself. Figure 4.3 shows how this allows an object specified in user space to appear the same regardless of the device on which it is rendered.

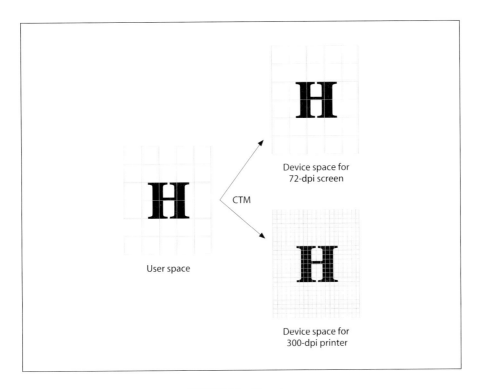

FIGURE 4.3 *User space*

The default user space provides a consistent, dependable starting place for PDF page descriptions regardless of the output device used. If necessary, a PDF content stream may then modify user space to be more suitable to its needs by applying the *coordinate transformation operator*, **cm** (see Section 4.3.3, "Graphics State Operators"). Thus what may appear to be absolute coordinates in a content stream are not absolute with respect to the current page, because they are expressed in a coordinate system that may slide around and shrink or expand. Coordinate system transformation not only enhances device-independence but is a useful tool in its own right. For example, a content stream originally composed to occupy an entire page can be incorporated without change as an element of another page by shrinking the coordinate system in which it is drawn.

Other Coordinate Spaces

In addition to device space and user space, PDF uses a variety of other coordinate spaces for specialized purposes:

- The coordinates of text are specified in *text space*. The transformation from text space to user space is defined by a *text matrix* in combination with several text-related parameters in the graphics state (see Section 5.3.1, "Text-Positioning Operators").

- Character glyphs in a font are defined in *glyph space* (see Section 5.1.3, "Glyph Positioning and Metrics"). The transformation from glyph space to text space is defined by the *font matrix*. For most types of font, this matrix is predefined to map 1000 units of glyph space to 1 unit of text space; for Type 3 fonts, the font matrix is given explicitly in the font dictionary (see Section 5.5.4, "Type 3 Fonts").

- All sampled images are defined in *image space*. The transformation from image space to user space is predefined and cannot be changed. All images are 1 unit wide by 1 unit high in user space, regardless of the number of samples in the image. To be painted, an image must be mapped to the desired region of the page by temporarily altering the current transformation matrix (CTM).

   Note: *In PostScript, unlike PDF, the relationship between image space and user space can be specified explicitly. The fixed transformation prescribed in PDF corresponds to the convention that is recommended for use in PostScript.*

- A form XObject (discussed in Section 4.9, "Form XObjects") is a self-contained content stream that can be treated as a graphical element within another content stream. The space in which it is defined is called *form space*. The transformation from form space to user space is specified by a matrix contained in the form XObject.

- PDF 1.2 defines a type of color known as a *pattern*, discussed in Section 4.6, "Patterns." A pattern is defined either by a content stream that is invoked repeatedly to tile an area or by a shading whose color is a function of position. The space in which a pattern is defined is called *pattern space*. The transformation from pattern space to user space is specified by a matrix contained in the pattern.

Relationships among Coordinate Spaces

Figure 4.4 shows the relationships among the coordinate spaces described above. Each arrow in the figure represents a transformation from one coordinate space to another. PDF allows modifications to many of these transformations.

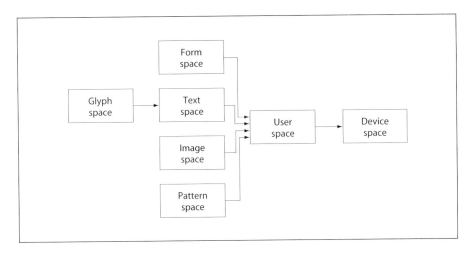

FIGURE 4.4 *Relationships among coordinate systems*

Because PDF coordinate spaces are defined relative to one another, changes made to one transformation can affect the appearance of objects defined in several coordinate spaces. For example, a change in the CTM, which defines the transformation from user space to device space, will affect forms, text, images, and patterns, since they are all "upstream" from user space.

4.2.2   Common Transformations

A *transformation matrix* specifies the relationship between two coordinate spaces. By modifying a transformation matrix, objects can be scaled, rotated, translated, or transformed in other ways.

A transformation matrix in PDF is specified by six numbers, usually in the form of an array containing six elements. In its most general form, this array is denoted [*a b c d e f*]; it can represent any linear transformation from one coordinate system to another. This section lists the arrays that specify the most common transformations; Section 4.2.3, "Transformation Matrices," discusses more mathematical details of transformations, including information on specifying transformations that are combinations of those listed here.

- Translations are specified as $[1\ 0\ 0\ 1\ t_x\ t_y]$, where t_x and t_y are the distances to translate the origin of the coordinate system in the horizontal and vertical dimensions, respectively.

- Scaling is obtained by $[s_x\ 0\ 0\ s_y\ 0\ 0]$. This scales the coordinates so that 1 unit in the horizontal and vertical dimensions of the new coordinate system is the same size as s_x and s_y units, respectively, in the previous coordinate system.

- Rotations are produced by $[\cos\theta\ \sin\theta\ -\sin\theta\ \cos\theta\ 0\ 0]$, which has the effect of rotating the coordinate system axes by an angle θ counterclockwise.

- Skew is specified by $[1\ \tan\alpha\ \tan\beta\ 1\ 0\ 0]$, which skews the x axis by an angle α and the y axis by an angle β.

Figure 4.5 shows examples of each transformation. The directions of translation, rotation, and skew shown in the figure correspond to positive values of the array elements.

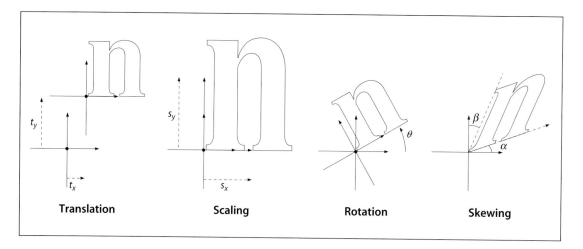

FIGURE 4.5 *Effects of coordinate transformations*

If several transformations are combined, the order in which they are applied is significant. For example, first scaling and then translating the x axis is not the same as first translating and then scaling it. In general, to obtain the expected results, transformations should be done in the following order:

1. Translate

2. Rotate

3. Scale or skew

Figure 4.6 shows the effect of the order in which transformations are applied. The figure shows two sequences of transformations applied to a coordinate system. After each successive transformation, an outline of the letter n is drawn.

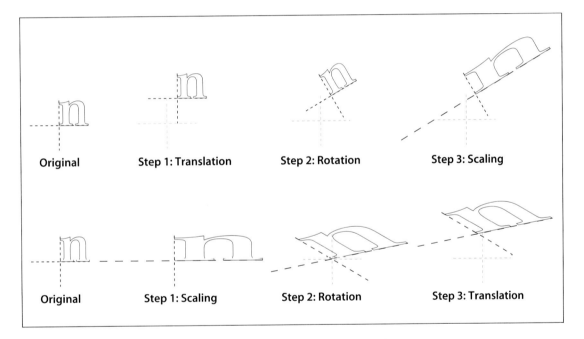

FIGURE 4.6 *Effect of transformation order*

The transformations shown in the figure are as follows:

• A translation of 10 units in the *x* direction and 20 units in the *y* direction

• A rotation of 30 degrees

• A scaling by a factor of 3 in the *x* direction

In the figure, the axes are shown with a dash pattern having a 2-unit dash and a 2-unit gap. In addition, the original (untransformed) axes are shown in a lighter color for reference. Notice that the scale-rotate-translate ordering results in a distortion of the coordinate system, leaving the *x* and *y* axes no longer perpendicular, while the recommended translate-rotate-scale ordering does not.

4.2.3 Transformation Matrices

This section discusses the mathematics of transformation matrices. It is not necessary to read this section in order to use the transformations described previously; the information is presented for the benefit of readers who want to gain a deeper understanding of the theoretical basis of coordinate transformations.

To understand the mathematics of coordinate transformations in PDF, it is vital to remember two points:

- *Transformations alter coordinate systems, not graphics objects.* All objects painted before a transformation is applied are unaffected by the transformation. Objects painted after the transformation is applied will be interpreted in the transformed coordinate system.

- *Transformation matrices specify the transformation from the new (transformed) coordinate system to the original (untransformed) coordinate system.* All coordinates used after the transformation are expressed in the transformed coordinate system. PDF applies the transformation matrix to find the equivalent coordinates in the untransformed coordinate system.

Note: Many computer graphics textbooks consider transformations of graphics objects rather than of coordinate systems. Although either approach is correct and self-consistent, some details of the calculations differ depending on which point of view is taken.

PDF represents coordinates in a two-dimensional space. The point (x, y) in such a space can be expressed in vector form as [x y 1]. The constant third element of this vector (1) is needed so that the vector can be used with 3-by-3 matrices in the calculations described below.

The transformation between two coordinate systems is represented by a 3-by-3 transformation matrix written as

$$\begin{bmatrix} a & b & 0 \\ c & d & 0 \\ e & f & 1 \end{bmatrix}$$

Because a transformation matrix has only six elements that can be changed, it is usually specified in PDF as the six-element array [*a b c d e f*].

Coordinate transformations are expressed as matrix multiplications:

$$[x'\ y'\ 1] = [x\ y\ 1] \times \begin{bmatrix} a & b & 0 \\ c & d & 0 \\ e & f & 1 \end{bmatrix}$$

Because PDF transformation matrices specify the conversion from the transformed coordinate system to the original (untransformed) coordinate system, x' and y' in this equation are the coordinates in the untransformed coordinate system, while x and y are the coordinates in the transformed system. Carrying out the multiplication, we have

$$x' = a \times x + c \times y + e$$
$$y' = b \times x + d \times y + f$$

If a series of transformations is carried out, the matrices representing each of the individual transformations can be multiplied together to produce a single equivalent matrix representing the composite transformation.

Matrix multiplication is not commutative—the order in which matrices are multiplied is significant. Consider a sequence of two transformations: a scaling transformation applied to the user space coordinate system, followed by a conversion from the resulting scaled user space to device space. Let M_S be the matrix specifying the scaling and M_C the current transformation matrix, which transforms user space to device space. Recalling that coordinates are always specified in the transformed space, the correct order of transformations must first convert the scaled coordinates to default user space and then the default user space coordinates to device space. This can be expressed as

$$X_D = X_U \times M_C = (X_S \times M_S) \times M_C = X_S \times (M_S \times M_C)$$

where

X_D denotes the coordinates in device space

X_U denotes the coordinates in default user space

X_S denotes the coordinates in scaled user space

This shows that when a new transformation is concatenated with an existing one, the matrix representing it must be multiplied *before* (*premultiplied* with) the existing transformation matrix.

This result is true in general for PDF: when a sequence of transformations is carried out, the matrix representing the combined transformation (M') is calculated by premultiplying the matrix representing the additional transformation (M_T) with the one representing all previously existing transformations (M):

$$M' = M_T \times M$$

4.3 Graphics State

A PDF viewer application maintains an internal data structure called the *graphics state* that holds current graphics control parameters. These parameters define the global framework within which the graphics operators execute. For example, the **f** (fill) operator implicitly uses the *current color* parameter, and the **S** (stroke) operator additionally uses the *current line width* parameter from the graphics state.

The graphics state is initialized at the beginning of each page, using the default values specified in Tables 4.2 and 4.3. Table 4.2 lists those graphics state parameters that are device-independent and are appropriate to specify in page descriptions. The parameters listed in Table 4.3 control details of the rendering (scan conversion) process and are device-dependent; a page description that is intended to be device-independent should not modify these parameters.

TABLE 4.2 Device-independent parameters of the graphics state

PARAMETER	TYPE	VALUE
CTM	array	The *current transformation matrix*, which maps positions from user coordinates to device coordinates (see Section 4.2, "Coordinate Systems"). This matrix is modified by each application of the coordinate transformation operator, **cm**. Initial value: a matrix that transforms default user coordinates to device coordinates.
clipping path	(internal)	A path defining the current *clipping boundary* against which all output is to be cropped (see Section 4.4.3, "Clipping Path Operators"). Initial value: the boundary of the entire imageable portion of the output page.
color space	name or array	The *current color space* in which color values are to be interpreted (see Section 4.5, "Color Spaces"). There are two separate color space parameters: one for stroking and one for all other painting operations. Initial value: **DeviceGray**.
color	(various)	The *current color* to use during painting operations (see Section 4.5, "Color Spaces"). The type and interpretation of this parameter depend on the current color space; for most color spaces, a color value consists of one to four numbers. There are two separate color parameters: one for stroking and one for all other painting operations. Initial value: black.
text state	(various)	A set of eight graphics state parameters that pertain only to the painting of text. These include parameters that select the font, scale the glyphs to an appropriate size, and accomplish other effects. The text state parameters are described in Section 5.2, "Text State Parameters and Operators."
line width	number	The thickness, in user space units, of paths to be stroked (see "Line Width" on page 139). Initial value: 1.0.
line cap	integer	A code specifying the shape of the endpoints for any open path that is stroked (see "Line Cap Style" on page 139). Initial value: 0, for square butt caps.
line join	integer	A code specifying the shape of joints between connected segments of a stroked path (see "Line Join Style" on page 140). Initial value: 0, for mitered joins.
miter limit	number	The maximum length of mitered line joins for stroked paths (see "Miter Limit" on page 140). This parameter limits the length of

"spikes" produced when line segments join at sharp angles. Initial value: 10.0, for a miter cutoff below approximately 11.5 degrees.

dash pattern	array and number	A description of the dash pattern to be used when paths are stroked (see "Line Dash Pattern" on page 141). Initial value: a solid line.
rendering intent	name	The *rendering intent* to use when converting CIE-based colors to device colors (see "Rendering Intents" on page 179). Default value: **RelativeColorimetric**.
stroke adjustment	boolean	*(PDF 1.2)* A flag specifying whether to compensate for possible rasterization effects when stroking a path with a line width that is small relative to the pixel resolution of the output device (see Section 6.5.4, "Automatic Stroke Adjustment"). Note that this is considered a device-independent parameter, even though the details of its effects are device-dependent. Initial value: *false*.

TABLE 4.3 Device-dependent parameters of the graphics state

PARAMETER	TYPE	VALUE
overprint	boolean	*(PDF 1.2)* A flag specifying (on output devices that support the overprint control feature) whether painting in one set of colorants should cause the corresponding areas of other colorants to be erased (*false*) or left unchanged (*true*); see Section 4.5.6, "Overprint Control." In PDF 1.3, there are two separate overprint parameters: one for stroking and one for all other painting operations. Initial value: *false*.
overprint mode	number	*(PDF 1.3)* A code specifying whether a color component value of 0 in a **DeviceCMYK** color space should erase that component (0) or leave it unchanged (1) when overprinting (see Section 4.5.6, "Overprint Control"). Initial value: 0.
black generation	function or name	*(PDF 1.2)* A function that calculates the level of black colorant to use when converting *RGB* colors to *CMYK* (see Section 6.2.3, "Conversion from DeviceRGB to DeviceCMYK"). Initial value: installation-dependent.
undercolor removal	function or name	*(PDF 1.2)* A function that calculates the reduction in the levels of cyan, magenta, and yellow colorants to compensate for the amount of black added by black generation (see Section 6.2.3, "Conversion from DeviceRGB to DeviceCMYK"). Initial value: installation-dependent.

transfer	function, array, or name	*(PDF 1.2)* A function that adjusts device gray or color component levels to compensate for nonlinear response in a particular output device (see Section 6.3, "Transfer Functions"). Initial value: installation-dependent.
halftone	dictionary, stream, or name	*(PDF 1.2)* A halftone screen for gray and color rendering, specified as a halftone dictionary or stream (see Section 6.4, "Halftones"). Initial value: installation-dependent.
flatness	number	The precision with which curves are to be rendered on the output device (see Section 6.5.1, "Flatness Tolerance"). The value of this parameter gives the maximum error tolerance, measured in output device pixels; smaller numbers give smoother curves at the expense of more computation and memory use. Initial value: 1.0.
smoothness	number	*(PDF 1.3)* The precision with which color gradients are to be rendered on the output device (see Section 6.5.2, "Smoothness Tolerance"). The value of this parameter gives the maximum error tolerance, expressed as a fraction of the range of each color component; smaller numbers give smoother color transitions at the expense of more computation and memory use. Initial value: installation-dependent.

Some graphics state parameters are set with specific PDF operators, some are set by including a particular entry in a *graphics state parameter dictionary*, and some can be specified either way. The current line width, for example, can be set either with the **w** operator or (in PDF 1.3) with the **LW** entry in a graphics state parameter dictionary, whereas the current color is set only with specific operators and the current halftone is set only with a graphics state parameter dictionary. It is expected that all future graphics state parameters will be specified with new entries in the graphics state parameter dictionary rather than with new operators.

In general, the operators that set graphics state parameters simply store them unchanged for later use by the painting operators. However, some parameters have special properties or behavior:

• Most parameters must be of the correct type or have values that fall within a certain range.

• Parameters that are numeric values, such as color, line width, and miter limit, are forced into valid range, if necessary. However, they are *not* adjusted to reflect capabilities of the raster output device, such as resolution or number of distinguishable colors. Painting operators perform such adjustments, but the adjusted values are not stored back into the graphics state.

• Paths are internal objects that are not directly represented in PDF.

Note: As indicated in Tables 4.2 and 4.3, some of the parameters—color space, color, and overprint—have two values, one used for stroking (of path and text objects) and one for all other painting operations. The two parameter values can be set independently, allowing for operations such as combined filling and stroking of the same path with different colors. Except where noted, a term such as current color *should be interpreted to refer to whichever color parameter applies to the operation being performed. When necessary, the individual color parameters are distinguished explicitly as the* stroking color *and the* nonstroking color.

4.3.1 Graphics State Stack

A well-structured PDF document typically contains many graphical elements that are essentially independent of each other and sometimes nested to multiple levels. The *graphics state stack* allows these elements to make local changes to the graphics state without disturbing the graphics state of the surrounding environment. The stack is a LIFO (last in, first out) data structure in which the contents of the graphics state can be saved and later restored using the following operators:

• The **q** operator pushes a copy of the entire graphics state onto the stack.

• The **Q** operator restores the entire graphics state to its former value by popping it from the stack.

These operators can be used to encapsulate a graphical element so that it can modify parameters of the graphics state and later restore them to their previous values. Occurrences of the **q** and **Q** operators must be balanced within a given content stream (or within the sequence of streams specified in a page dictionary's **Contents** array).

4.3.2 Details of Graphics State Parameters

This section gives details of several of the device-independent graphics state parameters listed in Table 4.2 on page 135.

Line Width

The *line width* parameter specifies the thickness of the line used to stroke a path. It is a nonnegative number expressed in user space units; stroking a path entails painting all points whose perpendicular distance from the path in user space is less than or equal to half the line width. The effect produced in device space depends on the current transformation matrix (CTM) in effect at the time the path is stroked. If the CTM specifies scaling by different factors in the *x* and *y* dimensions, the thickness of stroked lines in device space will vary according to their orientation. The actual line width achieved can differ from the requested width by as much as 2 device pixels, depending on the positions of lines with respect to the pixel grid. Automatic stroke adjustment can be used to ensure uniform line width; see Section 6.5.4, "Automatic Stroke Adjustment."

A line width of 0 denotes the thinnest line that can be rendered at device resolution: 1 device pixel wide. However, some devices cannot reproduce 1-pixel lines, and on high-resolution devices, they are nearly invisible. Since the results of rendering such "zero-width" lines are device-dependent, their use is not recommended.

Line Cap Style

The *line cap style* specifies the shape to be used at the ends of open subpaths (and dashes, if any) when they are stroked. Table 4.4 shows the possible values.

TABLE 4.4   Line cap styles

STYLE	APPEARANCE	DESCRIPTION
0		*Butt cap.* The stroke is squared off at the endpoint of the path. There is no projection beyond the end of the path.
1		*Round cap.* A semicircular arc with a diameter equal to the line width is drawn around the endpoint and filled in.
2		*Projecting square cap.* The stroke continues beyond the endpoint of the path for a distance equal to half the line width and is then squared off.

Line Join Style

The *line join style* specifies the shape to be used at the corners of paths that are stroked. Table 4.5 shows the possible values. Join styles are significant only at points where consecutive segments of a path connect at an angle; segments that meet or intersect fortuitously receive no special treatment.

TABLE 4.5 Line join styles		
STYLE	APPEARANCE	DESCRIPTION
0		*Miter join.* The outer edges of the strokes for the two segments are extended until they meet at an angle, as in a picture frame. If the segments meet at too sharp an angle (as defined by the miter limit parameter— see "Miter Limit," below), a bevel join is used instead.
1		*Round join.* A circle with a diameter equal to the line width is drawn around the point where the two segments meet and is filled in, producing a rounded corner. **Note:** *If path segments shorter than half the line width meet at a sharp angle, an unintended "wrong side" of the circle may appear.*
2		*Bevel join.* The two segments are finished with butt caps (see "Line Cap Style" on page 139) and the resulting notch beyond the ends of the segments is filled with a triangle.

Miter Limit

When two line segments meet at a sharp angle and mitered joins have been specified as the line join style, it is possible for the miter to extend far beyond the thickness of the line stroking the path. The *miter limit* imposes a maximum on the ratio of the miter length to the line width (see Figure 4.7). When the limit is exceeded, the join is converted from a miter to a bevel.

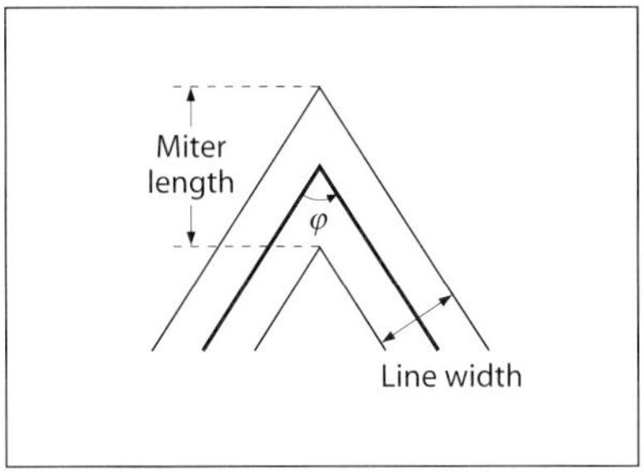

FIGURE 4.7 *Miter length*

The ratio of miter length to line width is directly related to the angle φ between the segments in user space by the formula

$$\frac{miterLength}{lineWidth} = \frac{1}{\sin\left(\dfrac{\varphi}{2}\right)}$$

For example, a miter limit of 1.414 converts miters to bevels for φ less than 90 degrees, a limit of 2.0 converts them for φ less than 60 degrees, and a limit of 10.0 converts them for φ less than approximately 11.5 degrees.

Line Dash Pattern

The *line dash pattern* controls the pattern of dashes and gaps used to stroke paths. It is specified by a *dash array* and a *dash phase*. The dash array's elements are numbers that specify the lengths of alternating dashes and gaps; the dash phase specifies the distance into the dash pattern at which to start the dash. The elements of both the dash array and the dash phase are expressed in user space units.

Before beginning to stroke a path, the dash array is cycled through, adding up the lengths of dashes and gaps. When the accumulated length equals the value specified by the dash phase, stroking of the path begins, using the dash array cyclically from that point onward. Table 4.6 shows examples of line dash patterns. As can be seen from the table, an empty dash array and zero phase can be used to restore the dash pattern to a solid line.

TABLE 4.6 Examples of line dash patterns

DASH ARRAY AND PHASE	APPEARANCE	DESCRIPTION
[] 0		No dash; solid, unbroken lines
[3] 0		3 units on, 3 units off, …
[2] 1		1 on, 2 off, 2 on, 2 off, …
[2 1] 0		2 on, 1 off, 2 on, 1 off, …
[3 5] 6		2 off, 3 on, 5 off, 3 on, 5 off, …
[2 3] 11		1 on, 3 off, 2 on, 3 off, 2 on, …

Dashed lines wrap around curves and corners just as solid stroked lines do. The ends of each dash are treated with the current line cap style, and corners within dashes are treated with the current line join style. A stroking operation takes no measures to coordinate the dash pattern with features of the path; it simply dispenses dashes and gaps along the path in the pattern defined by the dash array.

When a path consisting of several subpaths is stroked, each subpath is treated independently—that is, the dash pattern is restarted and the dash phase is reapplied to it at the beginning of each subpath.

4.3.3 Graphics State Operators

Table 4.7 shows the operators that set the values of parameters in the graphics state. (See also the color operators listed in Table 4.21 on page 198 and the text state operators in Table 5.2 on page 280.)

TABLE 4.7 Graphics state operators

OPERANDS	OPERATOR	DESCRIPTION
—	q	Save the current graphics state on the graphics state stack (see "Graphics State Stack" on page 138).
—	Q	Restore the graphics state by removing the most recently saved state from the stack and making it the current state (see "Graphics State Stack" on page 138).

a b c d e f	**cm**	Modify the CTM by concatenating the specified matrix (see Section 4.2.1, "Coordinate Spaces"). Although the operands specify a matrix, they are written as six separate numbers, not as an array.
lineWidth	**w**	Set the line width in the graphics state (see "Line Width" on page 139).
lineCap	**J**	Set the line cap style in the graphics state (see "Line Cap Style" on page 139).
lineJoin	**j**	Set the line join style in the graphics state (see "Line Join Style" on page 140).
miterLimit	**M**	Set the miter limit in the graphics state (see "Miter Limit" on page 140).
dashArray dashPhase	**d**	Set the line dash pattern in the graphics state (see "Line Dash Pattern" on page 141).
intent	**ri**	*(PDF 1.1)* Set the color rendering intent in the graphics state (see "Rendering Intents" on page 179).
flatness	**i**	Set the flatness tolerance in the graphics state (see Section 6.5.1, "Flatness Tolerance"). *flatness* is a number in the range 0 to 100; a value of 0 specifies the output device's default flatness tolerance.
dictName	**gs**	*(PDF 1.2)* Set the specified parameters in the graphics state. *dictName* is the name of a graphics state parameter dictionary in the **ExtGState** subdictionary of the current resource dictionary (see the next section).

4.3.4 Graphics State Parameter Dictionaries

While some parameters in the graphics state can be set with individual operators, as shown in Table 4.7, others cannot. The latter can only be set with the generic graphics state operator **gs** *(PDF 1.2)*. The operand supplied to this operator is the name of a *graphics state parameter dictionary* whose contents specify the values of one or more graphics state parameters. This name is looked up in the **ExtGState** subdictionary of the current resource dictionary. (The name **ExtGState**, for "extended graphics state," is a vestige of earlier versions of PDF.)

Note: The graphics state parameter dictionary is also used by type 2 patterns, which do not have a content stream in which the graphics state operators could be invoked (see Section 4.6.3, "Shading Patterns").

Each entry in the parameter dictionary specifies the value of an individual graphics state parameter, as shown in Table 4.8. It is not necessary for all entries to be present for every invocation of the **gs** operator; the parameter dictionary supplied may include any desired combination of parameter entries. The results of **gs** are cumulative; parameter values established in previous invocations will persist until explicitly overridden. Note that some parameters appear in both Tables 4.7 and 4.8; these parameters can be set either with individual graphics state operators or with **gs**. It is expected that any future extensions to the graphics state will be implemented by adding new keys to the graphics state parameter dictionary, rather than by introducing new graphics state operators.

TABLE 4.8   Entries in a graphics state parameter dictionary

KEY	TYPE	DESCRIPTION
Type	name	*(Optional)* The type of PDF object that this dictionary describes; must be **ExtGState** for a graphics state parameter dictionary.
Font	array	*(Optional; PDF 1.3)* An array of the form [*font size*], where *font* is an indirect reference to a font dictionary and *size* is a number expressed in text space units. These two objects correspond to the operands of the **Tf** operator (see Section 5.2, "Text State Parameters and Operators"); however, the first operand is an indirect object reference instead of a resource name.
LW	number	*(Optional; PDF 1.3)* The line width (see "Line Width" on page 139).
LC	integer	*(Optional; PDF 1.3)* The line cap style (see "Line Cap Style" on page 139).
LJ	integer	*(Optional; PDF 1.3)* The line join style (see "Line Join Style" on page 140).
ML	number	*(Optional; PDF 1.3)* The miter limit (see "Miter Limit" on page 140).
D	array	*(Optional; PDF 1.3)* The line dash pattern, expressed as an array of the form [*dashArray dashPhase*], where *dashArray* is itself an array and *dashPhase* is an integer (see "Line Dash Pattern" on page 141).
RI	name	*(Optional; PDF 1.3)* The name of the rendering intent (see "Rendering Intents" on page 179).
SA	boolean	*(Optional)* A flag specifying whether to apply automatic stroke adjustment (see Section 6.5.4, "Automatic Stroke Adjustment").
OP	boolean	*(Optional)* A flag specifying whether to apply overprint (see Section 4.5.6, "Overprint Control"). In PDF 1.2 and earlier, there is a single overprint parameter that applies to all painting operations. In PDF 1.3, there are two separate overprint parameters: one for stroking and one for all other painting operations. Specifying an **OP** entry sets both parameters unless there is also an **op** entry in the same graphics state parameter dictionary, in which case the **OP** entry sets only the overprint parameter for stroking.

op	boolean	*(Optional; PDF 1.3)* A flag specifying whether to apply overprint (see Section 4.5.6, "Overprint Control") for painting operations other than stroking. If this entry is absent, the **OP** entry, if any, sets this parameter.
OPM	integer	*(Optional; PDF 1.3)* The overprint mode (see Section 4.5.6, "Overprint Control").
BG	function	*(Optional)* The black-generation function, which maps the interval $[0.0 \ 1.0]$ to the interval $[0.0 \ 1.0]$ (see Section 6.2.3, "Conversion from DeviceRGB to DeviceCMYK").
BG2	function or name	*(Optional; PDF 1.3)* Same as **BG** except that the value may also be the name **Default**, denoting the black-generation function that was in effect at the start of the page. If both **BG** and **BG2** are present, **BG2** takes precedence.
UCR	function	*(Optional)* The undercolor-removal function, which maps the interval $[0.0 \ 1.0]$ to the interval $[-1.0 \ 1.0]$ (see Section 6.2.3, "Conversion from DeviceRGB to DeviceCMYK").
UCR2	function or name	*(Optional; PDF 1.3)* Same as **UCR** except that the value may also be the name **Default**, denoting the undercolor-removal function that was in effect at the start of the page. If both **UCR** and **UCR2** are present, **UCR2** takes precedence.
TR	function, array, or name	*(Optional)* The transfer function, which maps the interval $[0.0 \ 1.0]$ to the interval $[0.0 \ 1.0]$ (see Section 6.3, "Transfer Functions"). The value is either a single function (which applies to all process colorants) or an array of four functions (which apply to the process colorants individually). The name **Identity** may be used to represent the identity function.
TR2	function, array, or name	*(Optional; PDF 1.3)* Same as **TR** except that the value may also be the name **Default**, denoting the transfer function that was in effect at the start of the page. If both **TR** and **TR2** are present, **TR2** takes precedence.
HT	dictionary, stream, or name	*(Optional)* The halftone dictionary or stream (see Section 6.4, "Halftones") or the name **Default**, denoting the halftone that was in effect at the start of the page.
FL	number	*(Optional; PDF 1.3)* The flatness tolerance (see Section 6.5.1, "Flatness Tolerance").
SM	number	*(Optional; PDF 1.3)* The smoothness tolerance (see Section 6.5.2, "Smoothness Tolerance").

Example 4.1 shows two graphics state parameter dictionaries. In the first, automatic stroke adjustment is turned on, and the dictionary includes a transfer function that inverts its value, $f(x) = 1 - x$. In the second, overprint is turned off, and

the dictionary includes a parabolic transfer function, $f(x) = (2x - 1)^2$, with a sample of 21 values. The domain of the transfer function, $[0.0 \ 1.0]$, is mapped to $[0 \ 20]$, and the range of the sample values, $[0 \ 255]$, is mapped to the range of the transfer function, $[0.0 \ 1.0]$.

Example 4.1

```
10 0 obj                         % Page object
    << /Type /Page
       /Parent  5 0 R
       /Resources  20 0 R
       /Contents  40 0 R
    >>
endobj

20 0 obj                         % Resource dictionary for page
    << /ProcSet [/PDF /Text]
       /Font << /F1 25 0 R >>
       /ExtGState << /GS1  30 0 R
                     /GS2  35 0 R
                  >>
    >>
endobj

30 0 obj                         % First graphics state parameter dictionary
    << /Type /ExtGState
       /SA  true
       /TR  31 0 R
    >>
endobj

31 0 obj                         % First transfer function
    << /FunctionType  0
       /Domain  [0.0 1.0]
       /Range  [0.0 1.0]
       /Size  2
       /BitsPerSample  8
       /Length  7
       /Filter /ASCIIHexDecode
    >>
stream
01 00 >
endstream
endobj
```

```
35  0  obj                              % Second graphics state parameter dictionary
    <<  /Type  /ExtGState
        /OP  false
        /TR  36 0 R
    >>
endobj

36  0  obj                              % Second transfer function
    <<  /FunctionType  0
        /Domain  [0.0  1.0]
        /Range  [0.0  1.0]
        /Size  21
        /BitsPerSample  8
        /Length  63
        /Filter  /ASCIIHexDecode
    >>
stream
FF CE A3 7C 5B 3F 28 16 0A 02 00 02 0A 16 28 3F 5B 7C A3 CE FF >
endstream
endobj
```

4.4 Path Construction and Painting

Paths define shapes, trajectories, and regions of all sorts. They are used to draw lines, define the shapes of filled areas, and specify boundaries for clipping other graphics. The graphics state includes a *clipping path* that defines the clipping boundary for the current page. At the beginning of each page, the clipping path is initialized to include the entire page.

A path is composed of straight and curved line segments, which may connect to one another or may be disconnected. A pair of segments are said to *connect* only if they are defined consecutively, with the second segment starting where the first one ends. Thus the order in which the segments of a path are defined is significant. Nonconsecutive segments that meet or intersect fortuitously are not considered to connect.

A path is made up of one or more disconnected *subpaths*, each comprising a sequence of connected segments. The topology of the path is unrestricted: it may be concave or convex, may contain multiple subpaths representing disjoint areas, and may intersect itself in arbitrary ways. There is an operator, **h**, that explicitly connects the end of a subpath back to its starting point; such a subpath is said to be *closed*. A subpath that has not been explicitly closed is *open*.

As discussed in Section 4.1, "Graphics Objects," a path object is defined by a sequence of operators to construct the path, followed by one or more operators to paint the path or to use it as a clipping path. PDF path operators fall into three categories:

- *Path construction operators* (Section 4.4.1) define the geometry of a path. A path is constructed by sequentially applying one or more of these operators.

- *Path-painting operators* (Section 4.4.2) end a path object, usually causing the object to be painted on the current page in any of a variety of ways.

- *Clipping path operators* (Section 4.4.3), invoked immediately prior to a path-painting operator, cause the path object also to be used for clipping of subsequent graphics objects.

4.4.1 Path Construction Operators

A page description begins with an empty path and builds up its definition by invoking one or more path construction operators to add segments to it. The path construction operators may be invoked in any sequence, but the first one invoked must be **m** or **re** to begin a new subpath. The path definition concludes with the application of a path-painting operator such as **S**, **f**, or **b** (see Section 4.4.2, "Path-Painting Operators"); this may optionally be preceded by one of the clipping path operators **W** or **W*** (Section 4.4.3, "Clipping Path Operators"). Note that the path construction operators in themselves do not place any marks on the page; only the painting operators do that. A path definition is not complete until a path-painting operator has been applied to it.

The path currently under construction is called the *current path*. In PDF (unlike PostScript), the current path is *not* part of the graphics state and is *not* saved and restored along with the other graphics state parameters. PDF paths are strictly internal objects with no explicit representation. Once a path has been painted, it is no longer defined; there is then no current path until a new one is begun with the **m** or **re** operator.

The trailing endpoint of the segment most recently added to the current path is referred to as the *current point*. If the current path is empty, the current point is undefined. Most operators that add a segment to the current path start at the current point; if the current point is undefined, they generate an error.

Table 4.9 shows the path construction operators. All operands are numbers denoting coordinates in user space.

TABLE 4.9 **Path construction operators**

OPERANDS	OPERATOR	DESCRIPTION
x y	m	Begin a new subpath by moving the current point to coordinates (x, y), omitting any connecting line segment. If the previous path construction operator in the current path was also **m**, the new **m** overrides it; no vestige of the previous **m** operation remains in the path.
x y	l (lowercase **L**)	Append a straight line segment from the current point to the point (x, y). The new current point is (x, y).
$x_1\ y_1\ x_2\ y_2\ x_3\ y_3$	c	Append a cubic Bézier curve to the current path. The curve extends from the current point to the point (x_3, y_3), using (x_1, y_1) and (x_2, y_2) as the Bézier control points (see "Cubic Bézier Curves," below). The new current point is (x_3, y_3).
$x_2\ y_2\ x_3\ y_3$	v	Append a cubic Bézier curve to the current path. The curve extends from the current point to the point (x_3, y_3), using the current point and (x_2, y_2) as the Bézier control points (see "Cubic Bézier Curves," below). The new current point is (x_3, y_3).
$x_1\ y_1\ x_3\ y_3$	y	Append a cubic Bézier curve to the current path. The curve extends from the current point to the point (x_3, y_3), using (x_1, y_1) and (x_3, y_3) as the Bézier control points (see "Cubic Bézier Curves," below). The new current point is (x_3, y_3).
—	h	Close the current subpath by appending a straight line segment from the current point to the starting point of the subpath. This operator terminates the current subpath; appending another segment to the current path will begin a new subpath, even if the new segment begins at the endpoint reached by the **h** operation. If the current subpath is already closed or the current path is empty, **h** does nothing.
x y width height	re	Append a rectangle to the current path as a complete subpath, with lower-left corner (x, y) and dimensions *width* and *height* in user space. The operation

    x y width height re

is equivalent to

    x y m
    $(x + width)$ *y* l
    $(x + width)$ $(y + height)$ l
    x $(y + height)$ l
    h |

Cubic Bézier Curves

Curved path segments are specified as *cubic Bézier curves*. Such curves are defined by four points: the two endpoints (the current point P_0 and the final point P_3) and two *control points* P_1 and P_2. Given the coordinates of the four points, the curve is generated by varying the parameter t from 0.0 to 1.0 in the following equation:

$$R(t) = (1-t)^3 P_0 + 3t(1-t)^2 P_1 + 3t^2(1-t)P_2 + t^3 P_3$$

When $t = 0.0$, the value of the function $R(t)$ coincides with the current point P_0; when $t = 1.0$, $R(t)$ coincides with the final point P_3. Intermediate values of t generate intermediate points along the curve. The curve does not, in general, pass through the two control points P_1 and P_2.

Cubic Bézier curves have two desirable properties:

• The curve can be very quickly split into smaller pieces for rapid rendering.

• The curve is contained within the convex hull of the four points defining the curve, most easily visualized as the polygon obtained by stretching a rubber band around the outside of the four points. This property allows rapid testing of whether the curve lies completely outside the visible region, and hence does not have to be rendered.

The Bibliography lists several books that describe cubic Bézier curves in more depth.

The most general PDF operator for constructing curved path segments is **c**, which specifies the coordinates of points P_1, P_2, and P_3 explicitly, as shown in Figure 4.8. (The starting point, P_0, is defined implicitly by the current point.) Two more operators, **v** and **y**, each specify one of the two control points implicitly (see Figure 4.9). In each case, one control point and the final point of the curve are supplied as operands; the other control point is implied, as follows:

• For the **v** operator, the first control point coincides with initial point of the curve.

• For the **y** operator, the second control point coincides with final point of the curve.

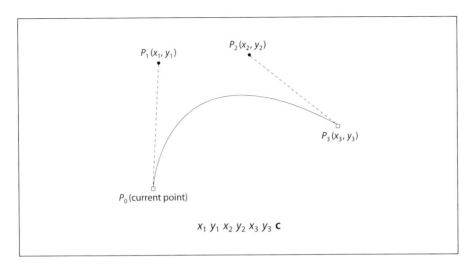

FIGURE 4.8 *Cubic Bézier curve generated by the **c** operator*

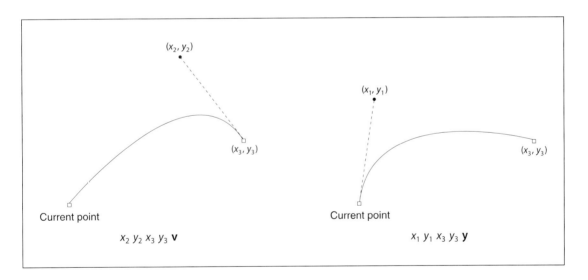

FIGURE 4.9 *Cubic Bézier curves generated by the **v** and **y** operators*

4.4.2 Path-Painting Operators

The path-painting operators end a path object, causing it to be painted on the current page in the manner that the operator specifies. The principal path-painting operators are **S** (for *stroking*) and **f** (for *filling*). Variants of these operators combine stroking and filling in a single operation or apply different rules for determining the area to be filled. Table 4.10 lists all the path-painting operators.

TABLE 4.10 Path-painting operators

OPERANDS	OPERATOR	DESCRIPTION
—	S	Stroke the path.
—	s	Close and stroke the path. This operator has the same effect as the sequence h S.
—	f	Fill the path, using the nonzero winding number rule to determine the region to fill (see "Nonzero Winding Number Rule" on page 154).
—	F	Equivalent to f; included only for compatibility. Although applications that read PDF files must be able to accept this operator, those that generate PDF files should use f instead.
—	f*	Fill the path, using the even-odd rule to determine the region to fill (see "Even-Odd Rule" on page 155).
—	B	Fill and then stroke the path, using the nonzero winding number rule to determine the region to fill. This produces the same result as constructing two identical path objects, painting the first with f and the second with S. Note, however, that the filling and stroking portions of the operation consult different values of several graphics state parameters, such as the color.
—	B*	Fill and then stroke the path, using the even-odd rule to determine the region to fill. This operator produces the same result as B, except that the path is filled as if with f* instead of f.
—	b	Close, fill, and then stroke the path, using the nonzero winding number rule to determine the region to fill. This operator has the same effect as the sequence h B.
—	b*	Close, fill, and then stroke the path, using the even-odd rule to determine the region to fill. This operator has the same effect as the sequence h B*.
—	n	End the path object without filling or stroking it. This operator is a "path-painting no-op," used primarily for the side effect of changing the clipping path (see Section 4.4.3, "Clipping Path Operators").

Stroking

The S operator paints a line along the current path. The stroked line follows each straight or curved segment in the path, centered on the segment with sides parallel to it. Each of the path's subpaths is treated separately.

The results of the **S** operator depend on the current settings of various parameters in the graphics state. See Section 4.3, "Graphics State," for further information on these parameters.

- The width of the stroked line is determined by the *line width* parameter ("Line Width" on page 139).

- The color or pattern of the line is determined by the *color* and *color space* parameters for stroking.

- The line can be painted either solid or with a dash pattern, as specified by the *dash pattern* parameter ("Line Dash Pattern" on page 141).

- If a subpath is open, the unconnected ends are treated according to the *line cap* parameter, which may be butt, rounded, or square ("Line Cap Style" on page 139).

- Wherever two consecutive segments are connected, the joint between them is treated according to the *line join* parameter, which may be mitered, rounded, or beveled ("Line Join Style" on page 140). Mitered joins are also subject to the *miter limit* parameter ("Miter Limit" on page 140).

  Note: *Points at which unconnected segments happen to meet or intersect receive no special treatment. In particular, "closing" a subpath with an explicit l operator rather than with h may result in a messy corner, because line caps will be applied instead of a line join.*

- The *stroke adjustment* parameter *(PDF 1.2)* specifies that coordinates and line widths be adjusted automatically to produce strokes of uniform thickness despite rasterization effects (Section 6.5.4, "Automatic Stroke Adjustment").

If a subpath is degenerate (consists of a single-point closed path or of two or more points at the same coordinates), the **S** operator paints it only if round line caps have been specified, producing a filled circle centered at the single point. If butt or projecting square line caps have been specified, **S** produces no output, because the orientation of the caps would be indeterminate. A single-point open subpath (specified by a trailing **m** operator) produces no output.

Filling

The **f** operator uses the current nonstroking color to paint the entire region enclosed by the current path. If the path consists of several disconnected subpaths, **f** paints the insides of all subpaths, considered together. Any subpaths that are open are implicitly closed before being filled.

If a subpath is degenerate (consists of a single-point closed path or of two or more points at the same coordinates), **f** paints the single device pixel lying under that point; the result is device-dependent and not generally useful. A single-point open subpath (specified by a trailing **m** operator) produces no output.

For a simple path, it is intuitively clear what region lies inside. However, for a more complex path—for example, a path that intersects itself or has one subpath that encloses another—the interpretation of "inside" is not always obvious. The path machinery uses one of two rules for determining which points lie inside a path: the *nonzero winding number rule* and the *even-odd rule*, both discussed in detail below.

The nonzero winding number rule is more versatile than the even-odd rule and is the standard rule the **f** operator uses. Similarly, the **W** operator uses this rule to determine the inside of the current clipping path. The even-odd rule is occasionally useful for special effects or for compatibility with other graphics systems; the **f*** and **W*** operators invoke this rule.

Nonzero Winding Number Rule

The *nonzero winding number rule* determines whether a given point is inside a path by conceptually drawing a ray from that point to infinity in any direction and then examining the places where a segment of the path crosses the ray. Starting with a count of 0, the rule adds 1 each time a path segment crosses the ray from left to right and subtracts 1 each time a segment crosses from right to left. After counting all the crossings, if the result is 0 then the point is outside the path; otherwise it is inside.

Note: *The method just described does not specify what to do if a path segment coincides with or is tangent to the chosen ray. Since the direction of the ray is arbitrary, the rule simply chooses a ray that does not encounter such problem intersections.*

For simple convex paths, the nonzero winding number rule defines the inside and outside as one would intuitively expect. The more interesting cases are those involving complex or self-intersecting paths like the ones shown in Figure 4.10. For a path consisting of a five-pointed star, drawn with five connected straight line segments intersecting each other, the rule considers the inside to be the entire area enclosed by the star, including the pentagon in the center. For a path composed of two concentric circles, the areas enclosed by both circles are considered to be inside, *provided that both are drawn in the same direction.* If the circles are drawn in opposite directions, only the "doughnut" shape between them is inside, according to the rule; the "doughnut hole" is outside.

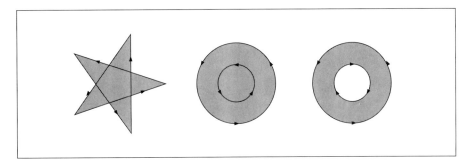

FIGURE 4.10 *Nonzero winding number rule*

Even-Odd Rule

An alternative to the nonzero winding number rule is the *even-odd rule.* This rule determines the "insideness" of a point by drawing a ray from that point in any direction and simply counting the number of path segments that cross the ray, regardless of direction. If this number is odd, the point is inside; if even, the point is outside. This yields the same results as the nonzero winding number rule for paths with simple shapes, but produces different results for more complex shapes.

Figure 4.11 shows the effects of applying the even-odd rule to complex paths. For the five-pointed star, the rule considers the triangular points to be inside the path, but not the pentagon in the center. For the two concentric circles, only the "doughnut" shape between the two circles is considered inside, regardless of the directions in which the circles are drawn.

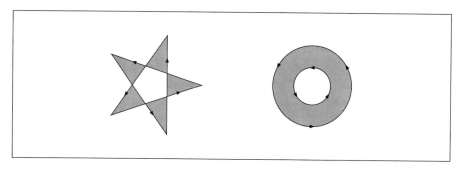

FIGURE 4.11 *Even-odd rule*

4.4.3 Clipping Path Operators

The graphics state contains a *clipping path* that limits the regions of the page affected by painting operators. The closed subpaths of this path define the area that can be painted. Marks falling inside this area will be applied to the page; those falling outside it will not. (Precisely what is considered to be "inside" a path is discussed under "Filling," above.)

The initial clipping path includes the entire page. A clipping path operator (**W** or **W***, shown in Table 4.11) may appear after the last path construction operator and before the path-painting operator that terminates a path object. Although the clipping path operator appears before the painting operator, it does not alter the clipping path at the point where it appears. Rather, it modifies the effect of the succeeding painting operator. *After* the path has been painted, the clipping path in the graphics state is set to the intersection of the current clipping path and the newly constructed path.

TABLE 4.11 Clipping path operators

OPERANDS	OPERATOR	DESCRIPTION
—	W	Modify the current clipping path by intersecting it with the current path, using the nonzero winding number rule to determine which regions lie inside the clipping path.
—	W*	Modify the current clipping path by intersecting it with the current path, using the even-odd rule to determine which regions lie inside the clipping path.

Note: *In addition to path objects, text objects can also be used for clipping; see Section 5.2.5, "Text Rendering Mode."*

The **n** operator (see Table 4.10 on page 152) is a "no-op" path-painting operator; it causes no marks to be placed on the page, but it can be used with a clipping path operator to establish a new clipping path. That is, after a path has been constructed, the sequence W n will intersect that path with the current clipping path to establish a new clipping path.

There is no way to enlarge the current clipping path or to set a new clipping path without reference to the current one. However, since the clipping path is part of the graphics state, its effect can be localized to specific graphics objects by enclosing the modification of the clipping path and the painting of those objects between a pair of **q** and **Q** operators (see Section 4.3.1, "Graphics State Stack"). Execution of the **Q** operator causes the clipping path to revert to the value that was saved by the **q** operator, before the clipping path was modified.

4.5 Color Spaces

PDF includes powerful facilities for specifying the colors of graphics objects to be painted on the current page. The color facilities are divided into two parts:

- *Color specification.* A PDF file can specify abstract colors in a device-independent way. Colors can be described in any of a variety of color systems, or *color spaces.* Some color spaces are related to device color representation (grayscale, *RGB*, *CMYK*), others to human visual perception (CIE-based). Certain special features are also modeled as color spaces: patterns, color mapping, separations, and high-fidelity and multitone color.

- *Color rendering.* The viewer application reproduces colors on the raster output device by a multiple-step process that includes some combination of color conversion, gamma correction, halftoning, and scan conversion. Some aspects of this process use information that is specified in PDF. However, unlike the facilities for color specification, the color rendering facilities are device-dependent and ordinarily should not be included in a page description.

Figures 4.12 and 4.13 on pages 158 and 159 illustrate the division between PDF's (device-independent) color specification and (device-dependent) color rendering facilities. This section describes the color specification features, covering everything that most PDF documents need in order to specify colors. The facilities for controlling color rendering are described in Chapter 6; a PDF document should use these facilities only to configure or calibrate an output device or to achieve special device-dependent effects.

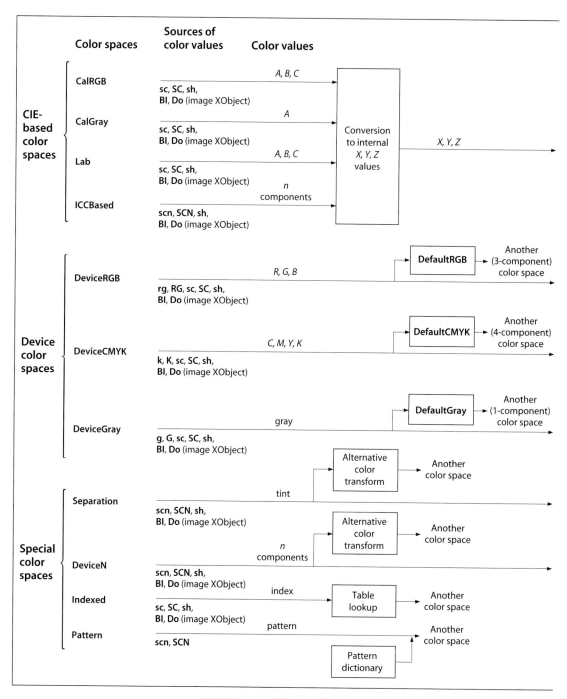

FIGURE 4.12 *Color specification*

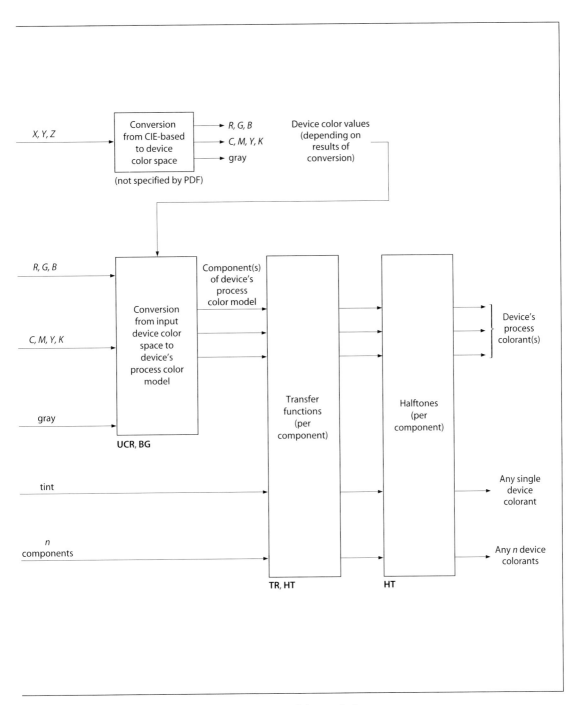

FIGURE 4.13 *Color rendering*

4.5.1 Color Values

As described in Section 4.4.2, "Path-Painting Operators," marks placed on the page by operators such as **f** and **S** have a color that is determined by the *current color* parameter of the graphics state. A color value consists of one or more *color components*, which are usually numbers. For example, a gray level can be specified by a single number ranging from 0.0 (black) to 1.0 (white). Full color values can be specified in any of several ways; a common method uses three numeric values to specify red, green, and blue components.

Color values are interpreted according to the *current color space*, another parameter of the graphics state. A PDF content stream first selects a color space by invoking the **cs** operator (for the nonstroking color) or the **CS** operator (for the stroking color). It then selects color values within that color space with the **sc** operator (nonstroking) or the **SC** operator (stroking). There are also convenience operators—**g**, **G**, **rg**, **RG**, **k**, and **K**—that select both a color space and a color value within it in a single step. Table 4.21 on page 198 lists all the color-setting operators.

Sampled images (see Section 4.8, "Images") specify the color values of individual samples with respect to a color space designated by the image object itself. While these values are independent of the current color space and color parameters in the graphics state, all later stages of color processing treat them in exactly the same way as color values specified with the **sc** or **SC** operator.

4.5.2 Types of Color Space

Color spaces can be classified into *color space families*. Spaces within a family share the same general characteristics; they are distinguished by parameter values supplied at the time the space is specified. The families, in turn, fall into three broad categories:

- *Device color spaces* directly specify colors or shades of gray that the output device is to produce. They provide a variety of color specification methods, including gray level, *RGB* (red-green-blue), and *CMYK* (cyan-magenta-yellow-black), corresponding to the color space families **DeviceGray**, **DeviceRGB**, and **DeviceCMYK**. Since each of these families consists of just a single color space with no parameters, they are sometimes loosely referred to as the **DeviceGray**, **DeviceRGB**, and **DeviceCMYK** color spaces.

- *CIE-based color spaces* are based on an international standard for color specification created by the Commission Internationale de l'Éclairage (International Commission on Illumination). These spaces allow colors to be specified in a way that is independent of the characteristics of any particular output device. Color space families in this category include **CalGray**, **CalRGB**, **Lab**, and **ICC-Based**. Individual color spaces within these families are specified by means of dictionaries containing the parameter values needed to define the space.

- *Special color spaces* add features or properties to an underlying color space. They include facilities for patterns, color mapping, separations, and high-fidelity and multitone color. The corresponding color space families are **Pattern**, **Indexed**, **Separation**, and **DeviceN**. Individual color spaces within these families are specified by means of additional parameters.

Table 4.12 summarizes the color space families supported by PDF. (See implementation note 28 in Appendix H.)

TABLE 4.12 Color space families		
DEVICE	**CIE-BASED**	**SPECIAL**
DeviceGray *(PDF 1.1)*	**CalGray** *(PDF 1.1)*	**Indexed** *(PDF 1.1)*
DeviceRGB *(PDF 1.1)*	**CalRGB** *(PDF 1.1)*	**Pattern** *(PDF 1.2)*
DeviceCMYK *(PDF 1.1)*	**Lab** *(PDF 1.1)*	**Separation** *(PDF 1.2)*
	ICCBased *(PDF 1.3)*	**DeviceN** *(PDF 1.3)*

A color space is defined by an array object whose first element is a name object identifying the color space family. The remaining array elements, if any, are parameters that further characterize the color space; their number and types vary according to the particular family. For families that do not require parameters, the color space can be specified simply by the family name itself instead of an array.

There are two principal ways in which a color space can be specified:

- Within a content stream, the **cs** or **CS** operator establishes the color space parameter in the graphics state. The operand is always a name object, which either identifies one of the color spaces that need no additional parameters (**DeviceGray**, **DeviceRGB**, **DeviceCMYK**, or some cases of **Pattern**) or is used as a key in the **ColorSpace** subdictionary of the current resource dictionary (see Section 3.7.2, "Resource Dictionaries"). In the latter case, the value of the dictionary entry is in turn a color space array or name. A color space array is never permitted in-line within a content stream.

• Outside a content stream, certain objects, such as image XObjects, specify a color space as an explicit parameter, often associated with the key **ColorSpace**. In this case, the color space array or name is always defined directly as a PDF object, not by an entry in the **ColorSpace** resource subdictionary. This convention also applies when color spaces are defined in terms of other color spaces.

The following operators set the color space and color value parameters in the graphics state:

• **cs** sets the nonstroking color space; **CS** sets the stroking color space.

• **sc** and **scn** set the nonstroking color; **SC** and **SCN** set the stroking color. Depending on the color space, these operators require one or more operands, each specifying one component of the color value.

• **g**, **rg**, and **k** set the nonstroking color space implicitly and the nonstroking color as specified by the operands; **G**, **RG**, and **K** do the same for the stroking color space and color.

4.5.3 Device Color Spaces

The device color spaces enable a page description to specify color values that are *directly* related to their representation on an output device. Color values in these spaces map directly (or via simple conversions) to the application of device colorants, such as quantities of ink or intensities of display phosphors. This enables a PDF document to control colors precisely for a *particular* device, but the results may not be consistent between *different* devices.

Output devices form colors either by adding light sources together or by subtracting light from an illuminating source. Computer displays and film recorders typically add colors, while printing inks typically subtract them. These two ways of forming colors give rise to two complementary forms of color specification, the additive *RGB* specification and the subtractive *CMYK* specification. The corresponding device color spaces are as follows:

- **DeviceGray** controls the intensity of achromatic light, on a scale from black to white.

- **DeviceRGB** controls the intensities of red, green, and blue light, the three additive primary colors used in displays.

- **DeviceCMYK** controls the concentrations of cyan, magenta, yellow, and black inks, the four subtractive process colors used in printing.

Although the notion of explicit color spaces is a PDF 1.1 feature, the operators for specifying colors in the device color spaces—**g**, **G**, **rg**, **RG**, **k**, and **K**—are available in all versions of PDF. In PDF 1.2, colors specified in device color spaces can optionally be remapped systematically into other color spaces; see "Default Color Spaces" on page 177.

DeviceGray Color Space

Black, white, and intermediate shades of gray are special cases of full color. A grayscale value is represented by a single number in the range 0.0 to 1.0, where 0.0 corresponds to black, 1.0 to white, and intermediate values to different gray levels. Example 4.2 shows alternative ways to select the **DeviceGray** color space and a specific gray level within that space for nonstroking operations.

Example 4.2

```
/DeviceGray  cs          % Set DeviceGray color space
gray  sc                 % Set gray level

gray  g                  % Set both in one operation
```

The **cs** and **sc** operators select the color space and color value separately; **g** sets them in combination. (The **CS**, **SC**, and **G** operators perform the same functions for stroking operations.) When the specified color space is **DeviceGray**, the **cs** or **CS** operator sets the corresponding color value to 0.0.

DeviceRGB Color Space

Colors in the **DeviceRGB** color space are specified according to the additive *RGB* (red-green-blue) color model, in which color values are defined by three components representing the intensities of the additive primary colors red, green, and blue. Each component is specified by a number in the range 0.0 to 1.0, where 0.0 denotes the complete absence of a primary component and 1.0 denotes maximum intensity. If all three components have equal intensity, the perceived result theoretically is a pure gray on the scale from black to white. If the intensities are not all equal, the result is some color other than a pure gray.

Example 4.3 shows alternative ways to select the **DeviceRGB** color space and a specific color within that space for nonstroking operations.

Example 4.3

```
/DeviceRGB cs              % Set DeviceRGB color space
red green blue sc          % Set color

red green blue rg          % Set both in one operation
```

The **cs** and **sc** operators select the color space and color value separately; **rg** sets them in combination. (The **CS**, **SC**, and **RG** operators perform the same functions for stroking operations.) When the specified color space is **DeviceRGB**, the **cs** or **CS** operator sets the red, green, and blue components of the corresponding color value to 0.0.

DeviceCMYK Color Space

The **DeviceCMYK** color space allows colors to be specified according to the subtractive *CMYK* (cyan-magenta-yellow-black) model typical of printers and other paper-based output devices. In theory, each of the three standard *process colorants* used in printing (cyan, magenta, and yellow) absorbs one of the additive primary colors (red, green, and blue, respectively). Black, a fourth standard process colorant, absorbs all of the additive primaries in equal amounts. The four components in a **DeviceCMYK** color value represent the concentrations of these process colorants. Each component is specified by a number in the range 0.0 to 1.0, where 0.0 denotes the complete absence of a process colorant (that is, absorbs none of the corresponding additive primary) and 1.0 denotes maximum concentration (absorbs as much as possible of the additive primary). Note that the sense of these numbers is opposite to that of *RGB* color components.

Example 4.4 shows alternative ways to select the **DeviceCMYK** color space and a specific color within that space for nonstroking operations.

Example 4.4

/DeviceCMYK cs	% Set DeviceCMYK color space
cyan magenta yellow black sc	% Set color
cyan magenta yellow black k	% Set both in one operation

The **cs** and **sc** operators select the color space and color value separately; **k** sets them in combination. (The **CS**, **SC**, and **K** operators perform the same functions for stroking operations.) When the specified color space is **DeviceCMYK**, the **cs** or **CS** operator sets the cyan, magenta, and yellow components of the corresponding color value to 0.0 and the black component to 1.0.

4.5.4 CIE-Based Color Spaces

Calibrated color in PDF is defined in terms of an international standard used in the graphic arts, television, and printing industries. *CIE-based* color spaces enable a page description to specify color values in a way that is related to human visual perception. The goal is for the same color specification to produce consistent results on different output devices, within the limitations of each device. PDF 1.1 supports three CIE-based color space families, named **CalGray**, **CalRGB**, and **Lab**; PDF 1.3 adds a fourth, named **ICCBased**.

*Note: In PDF 1.1, a color space family named **CalCMYK** was partially defined, with the expectation that its definition would be completed in a future version. However, this is no longer being considered. PDF 1.3 supports calibrated four-component color spaces by means of ICC profiles (see "ICCBased Color Spaces" on page 173). PDF consumer applications should ignore **CalCMYK** color space attributes and render colors specified in this family as if they had been specified using **DeviceCMYK**.*

The details of the CIE colorimetric system and the theory on which it is based are beyond the scope of this book; see the Bibliography for sources of further information. The semantics of CIE-based color spaces are defined in terms of the relationship between the space's components and the tristimulus values *X*, *Y*, and *Z* of the CIE 1931 *XYZ* space. The **CalRGB** and **Lab** color spaces *(PDF 1.1)* are special cases of three-component CIE-based color spaces, known as *CIE-based ABC* color spaces. These spaces are defined in terms of a two-stage, nonlinear transformation of the CIE 1931 *XYZ* space. The formulation of such color spaces models a simple *zone theory* of color vision, consisting of a nonlinear trichromatic first stage combined with a nonlinear opponent-color second stage. This formulation allows colors to be digitized with minimum loss of fidelity, an important consideration in sampled images.

Color values in a CIE-based *ABC* color space have three components, arbitrarily named *A*, *B*, and *C*. The first stage transforms these components by first forcing their values to a specified range, then applying *decoding functions*, and finally multiplying the results by a 3-by-3 matrix, producing three intermediate components arbitrarily named *L*, *M*, and *N*. The second stage transforms these intermediate components in a similar fashion, producing the final *X*, *Y*, and *Z* components of the CIE 1931 *XYZ* space (see Figure 4.14).

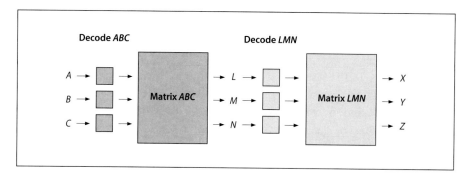

FIGURE 4.14 *Component transformations in a CIE-based* ABC *color space*

Color spaces in the CIE-based families are defined by an array

[*name dictionary*]

where *name* is the name of the family and *dictionary* is a dictionary containing parameters that further characterize the space. The entries in this dictionary have specific interpretations that vary depending on the color space; some entries are required and some are optional.

When any CIE-based color space is established, its initial color value has all components set to 0.0 (unless the range of valid values for a given component does not include 0.0, in which case the nearest valid value is substituted.)

*Note: The model and terminology used here—CIE-based ABC (above) and CIE-based A (below)—are derived from the PostScript language, which supports these classes of spaces in their full generality. PDF supports specific useful cases of CIE-based ABC and CIE-based A spaces; most others can be represented as **ICCBased** spaces.*

CalGray Color Spaces

A **CalGray** color space *(PDF 1.1)* is a special case of a single-component CIE-based color space, known as a *CIE-based A* color space. This type of space is the one-dimensional (and usually achromatic) analog of CIE-based *ABC* spaces. Color values in a CIE-based *A* space have a single component, arbitrarily named *A*. Figure 4.15 illustrates the transformations of the *A* component to *X*, *Y*, and *Z* components of the CIE 1931 *XYZ* space.

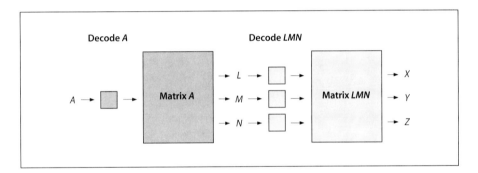

FIGURE 4.15 *Component transformations in a CIE-based A color space*

A **CalGray** color space is a CIE-based *A* color space with only one transformation stage instead of two. In this type of space, *A* represents the gray component of a calibrated gray space. This component must be in the range 0.0 to 1.0. The decoding function (denoted by "Decode *A*" in Figure 4.15) is a gamma function whose coefficient is specified by the **Gamma** entry in the color space dictionary (see Table 4.13). The transformation matrix denoted by "Matrix *A*" in the figure is derived from the dictionary's **WhitePoint** entry, as described below. Since there is no second transformation stage, "Decode *LMN*" and "Matrix *LMN*" are implicitly taken to be identity transformations.

TABLE 4.13 Entries in a CalGray color space dictionary

KEY	TYPE	VALUE
WhitePoint	array	(Required) An array of three numbers $[X_W\, Y_W\, Z_W]$ specifying the tristimulus value, in the CIE 1931 *XYZ* space, of the diffuse white point; see "CalRGB Color Spaces," below, for further discussion. The numbers X_W and Z_W must be positive, and Y_W must be equal to 1.0.
BlackPoint	array	(Optional) An array of three numbers $[X_B\, Y_B\, Z_B]$ specifying the tristimulus value, in the CIE 1931 *XYZ* space, of the diffuse black point; see "CalRGB Color Spaces," below, for further discussion. All three of these numbers must be nonnegative. Default value: [0.0 0.0 0.0].
Gamma	array	(Optional) A number *G* defining the gamma for the gray (*A*) component. *G* must be positive and will generally be greater than or equal to 1. Default value: 1.

The transformation defined by the **Gamma** and **WhitePoint** entries is

$$X = L = X_W \times A^G$$
$$Y = M = Y_W \times A^G$$
$$Z = N = Z_W \times A^G$$

In other words, the *A* component is first decoded by the gamma function, and the result is multiplied by the components of the white point to obtain the *L*, *M*, and *N* components of the intermediate representation. Since there is no second stage, these are also the *X*, *Y*, and *Z* components of the final representation.

The following examples illustrate various interesting and useful special cases of **CalGray** spaces. Example 4.5 establishes a space consisting of the *Y* dimension of the CIE 1931 *XYZ* space with the CCIR XA/11–recommended D65 white point.

Example 4.5

```
[ /CalGray
     << /WhitePoint [0.9505 1.0000 1.0890] >>
]
```

Example 4.6 establishes a calibrated gray space with the CCIR XA/11–recommended D65 white point and opto-electronic transfer function.

Example 4.6

```
[ /CalGray
     << /WhitePoint [0.9505 1.0000 1.0890]
        /Gamma 2.222
     >>
]
```

CalRGB Color Spaces

A **CalRGB** color space is a CIE-based *ABC* color space with only one transformation stage instead of two. In this type of space, *A*, *B*, and *C* represent calibrated red, green, and blue color values. These three color components must be in the range 0.0 to 1.0; component values falling outside that range will be adjusted to the nearest valid value without error indication. The decoding functions (denoted by "Decode *ABC*" in Figure 4.14 on page 166) are gamma functions whose coefficients are specified by the **Gamma** entry in the color space dictionary (see Table 4.14). The transformation matrix denoted by "Matrix *ABC*" in Figure 4.14 is defined by the dictionary's **Matrix** entry. Since there is no second transformation stage, "Decode *LMN*" and "Matrix *LMN*" are implicitly taken to be identity transformations.

TABLE 4.14   Entries in a CalRGB color space dictionary

KEY	TYPE	VALUE
WhitePoint	array	*(Required)* An array of three numbers $[X_W \ Y_W \ Z_W]$ specifying the tristimulus value, in the CIE 1931 *XYZ* space, of the diffuse white point; see below for further discussion. The numbers X_W and Z_W must be positive, and Y_W must be equal to 1.0.
BlackPoint	array	*(Optional)* An array of three numbers $[X_B \ Y_B \ Z_B]$ specifying the tristimulus value, in the CIE 1931 *XYZ* space, of the diffuse black point; see below for further discussion. All three of these numbers must be nonnegative. Default value: [0.0 0.0 0.0].
Gamma	array	*(Optional)* An array of three numbers $[G_R \ G_G \ G_B]$ specifying the gamma for the red, green, and blue (*A*, *B*, and *C*) components of the color space. Default value: [1.0 1.0 1.0].
Matrix	array	*(Optional)* An array of nine numbers $[X_A \ Y_A \ Z_A \ X_B \ Y_B \ Z_B \ X_C \ Y_C \ Z_C]$ specifying the linear interpretation of the decoded *A*, *B*, and *C* components of the color space with respect to the final *XYZ* representation. Default value: the identity matrix [1 0 0 0 1 0 0 0 1].

The **WhitePoint** and **BlackPoint** entries in the color space dictionary control the overall effect of the CIE-based gamut mapping function described in Section 6.1, "CIE-Based Color to Device Color." Typically, the colors specified by **WhitePoint** and **BlackPoint** are mapped to the nearly lightest and nearly darkest achromatic colors that the output device is capable of rendering in a way that preserves color appearance and visual contrast.

WhitePoint is assumed to represent the diffuse achromatic highlight, not a specular highlight. Specular highlights, achromatic or otherwise, are often reproduced lighter than the diffuse highlight. **BlackPoint** is assumed to represent the diffuse achromatic shadow; its value is typically limited by the dynamic range of the input device. In images produced by a photographic system, the values of **White-Point** and **BlackPoint** vary with exposure, system response, and artistic intent; hence, their values are image-dependent.

The transformation defined by the **Gamma** and **Matrix** entries in the **CalRGB** color space dictionary is

$$X = L = X_A \times A^{G_R} + X_B \times B^{G_G} + X_C \times C^{G_B}$$
$$Y = M = Y_A \times A^{G_R} + Y_B \times B^{G_G} + Y_C \times C^{G_B}$$
$$Z = N = Z_A \times A^{G_R} + Z_B \times B^{G_G} + Z_C \times C^{G_B}$$

In other words, the A, B, and C components are first decoded individually by the gamma functions. The results are treated as a three-element vector and multiplied by **Matrix** (a 3-by-3 matrix) to obtain the L, M, and N components of the intermediate representation. Since there is no second stage, these are also the X, Y, and Z components of the final representation.

Example 4.7 shows an example of a **CalRGB** color space for the CCIR XA/11– recommended D65 white point with 1.8 gammas and Sony Trinitron® phosphor chromaticities.

Example 4.7

```
[ /CalRGB
        << /WhitePoint [0.9505  1.0000  1.0890]
           /Gamma [1.8000  1.8000  1.8000]
           /Matrix [ 0.4497  0.2446  0.0252
                     0.3163  0.6720  0.1412
                     0.1845  0.0833  0.9227
                   ]
        >>
]
```

In some cases, the parameters of a **CalRGB** color space may be specified in terms of the CIE 1931 chromaticity coordinates (x_R, y_R), (x_G, y_G), (x_B, y_B) of the red, green, and blue phosphors, respectively, and the chromaticity (x_W, y_W) of the diffuse white point corresponding to some linear *RGB* value (R, G, B), where usually $R = G = B = 1.0$. Note that standard CIE notation uses lowercase letters to specify chromaticity coordinates and uppercase letters to specify tristimulus values. Given this information, **Matrix** and **WhitePoint** can be found as follows:

$$z = y_W \times ((x_G - x_B) \times y_R - (x_R - x_B) \times y_G + (x_R - x_G) \times y_B)$$

$$Y_A = \frac{y_R}{R} \times \frac{(x_G - x_B) \times y_W - (x_W - x_B) \times y_G + (x_W - x_G) \times y_B}{z}$$

$$X_A = Y_A \times \frac{x_R}{y_R} \qquad Z_A = Y_A \times \left(\frac{1 - x_R}{y_R} - 1\right)$$

$$Y_B = -\frac{y_G}{G} \times \frac{(x_R - x_B) \times y_W - (x_W - x_B) \times y_R + (x_W - x_R) \times y_B}{z}$$

$$X_B = Y_B \times \frac{x_G}{y_G} \qquad Z_B = Y_B \times \left(\frac{1 - x_G}{y_G} - 1\right)$$

$$Y_C = \frac{y_B}{B} \times \frac{(x_R - x_G) \times y_W - (x_W - x_G) \times y_W + (x_W - x_R) \times y_G}{z}$$

$$X_C = Y_C \times \frac{x_B}{y_B} \qquad Z_C = Y_C \times \left(\frac{1 - x_B}{y_B} - 1\right)$$

$$X_W = X_A \times R + X_B \times G + X_C \times B$$
$$Y_W = Y_A \times R + Y_B \times G + Y_C \times B$$
$$Z_W = Z_A \times R + Z_B \times G + Z_C \times B$$

Lab Color Spaces

A **Lab** color space is a CIE-based *ABC* color space with two transformation stages (see Figure 4.14 on page 166). In a this type of space, *A*, *B*, and *C* represent the $L^\star$, $a^\star$, and $b^\star$ components of a CIE 1976 $L^\star a^\star b^\star$ space. The range of the first ($L^\star$) component is always 0 to 100. The ranges of the second and third ($a^\star$ and $b^\star$)

components are defined by the **Range** entry in the color space dictionary (see Table 4.15).

TABLE 4.15 Entries in a Lab color space dictionary

KEY	TYPE	VALUE
WhitePoint	array	*(Required)* An array of three numbers $[X_W \, Y_W \, Z_W]$ specifying the tristimulus value, in the CIE 1931 *XYZ* space, of the diffuse white point; see "CalRGB Color Spaces" on page 169 for further discussion. The numbers X_W and Z_W must be positive, and Y_W must be equal to 1.0.
BlackPoint	array	*(Optional)* An array of three numbers $[X_B \, Y_B \, Z_B]$ specifying the tristimulus value, in the CIE 1931 *XYZ* space, of the diffuse black point; see "CalRGB Color Spaces" on page 169 for further discussion. All three of these numbers must be nonnegative. Default value: [0.0 0.0 0.0].
Range	array	*(Optional)* An array of four numbers $[a_{min} \, a_{max} \, b_{min} \, b_{max}]$ specifying the range of valid values for the $a^\star$ and $b^\star$ (*B* and *C*) components of the color space—that is, $$a_{min} \leq a^\star \leq a_{max}$$ and $$b_{min} \leq b^\star \leq b_{max}$$ Component values falling outside the specified range will be adjusted to the nearest valid value without error indication. Default value: [−100 100 −100 100].

A **Lab** color space does not specify explicit decoding functions or matrix coefficients for either stage of the transformation from $L^\star a^\star b^\star$ space to *XYZ* space (denoted by "Decode *ABC*," "Matrix *ABC*," "Decode *LMN*," and "Matrix *LMN*" in Figure 4.14 on page 166). Instead, these parameters have constant implicit values. The first transformation stage is defined by the equations

$$L = \frac{L^\star + 16}{116} + \frac{a^\star}{500}$$

$$M = \frac{L^\star + 16}{116}$$

$$N = \frac{L^\star + 16}{116} - \frac{b^\star}{200}$$

The second transformation stage is given by

$$X = X_W \times g(L)$$

$$Y = Y_W \times g(M)$$

$$Z = Z_W \times g(N)$$

where the function $g(x)$ is defined as

$$g(x) = x^3 \qquad\qquad \text{if } x \geq \frac{6}{29}$$

$$g(x) = \frac{108}{841} \times \left(x - \frac{4}{29} \right) \qquad \text{otherwise}$$

Example 4.8 defines the CIE 1976 $L^\star a^\star b^\star$ space with the CCIR XA/11–recommended D65 white point. The $a^\star$ and $b^\star$ components, although theoretically unbounded, are defined to lie in the useful range −128 to +127.

Example 4.8

```
[ /Lab
      << /WhitePoint [0.9505  1.0000  1.0890]
         /Range [−128  127  −128  127]
      >>
]
```

ICCBased Color Spaces

ICCBased color spaces *(PDF 1.3)* are based on a cross-platform *color profile* as defined by the International Color Consortium (ICC). Unlike the **CalGray**, **CalRGB**, and **Lab** color spaces, which are characterized by entries in the color space dictionary, an **ICCBased** color space is characterized by a sequence of bytes in a standard format. Details of the profile format can be found in the ICC specification (see the Bibliography).

An **ICCBased** color space is specified as an array:

```
[/ICCBased  stream]
```

The stream contains the ICC profile. Besides the usual entries common to all streams (see Table 3.4 on page 35), the profile stream has the additional entries listed in Table 4.16.

TABLE 4.16 Entries in an ICC profile stream dictionary

KEY	TYPE	VALUE
N	integer	*(Required)* The number of color components in the color space described by the ICC profile data. This number must match the number of components actually in the ICC profile. In PDF 1.3, **N** must be 1, 3, or 4.
Alternate	array or name	*(Optional)* An alternate color space to be used in case the one specified in the stream data is not supported (for example, by viewer applications designed for earlier versions of PDF). The alternate space may be any valid color space, except a **Pattern** color space, that has the number of components specified by **N**. If this entry is omitted and the viewer application does not understand the ICC profile data, the color space used will be **DeviceGray**, **DeviceRGB**, or **DeviceCMYK**, depending on whether the value of **N** is 1, 3, or 4, respectively.
		Note that there is no conversion of color values, such as a tint transformation, when using the alternate color space. Color values that are within the range of the **ICC-Based** color space might not be within the range of the alternate color space. In this case, the nearest values within the range of the alternate space will be substituted.
Range	array	*(Optional)* An array of $2 \times N$ numbers [min_0 max_0 min_1 max_1 ...] specifying the minimum and maximum valid values of the corresponding color components. These values must match the information in the ICC profile. Default value: [0.0 1.0 0.0 1.0 ...].

The ICC specification is an evolving standard. The **ICCBased** color spaces supported in PDF 1.3 are based on version 3.3 of the ICC specification. Early versions of the ICC specification are also supported. (The version number is available in the ICC profile's header.)

PDF 1.3 supports only the profile types shown in Table 4.17; other types may be supported in the future. (In particular, note that *XYZ* and 16-bit $L^*a^*b^*$ profiles are not supported.) Each of the indicated fields must have one of the values listed for that field in the second column of the table. (Profiles must satisfy *both* the criteria shown in the table.) The terminology is taken from the ICC specifications.

TABLE 4.17   ICC profile types

HEADER FIELD	REQUIRED VALUE
deviceClass	icSigInputClass ('scnr')
	icSigDisplayClass ('mntr')
	icSigOutputClass ('prtr')
	icSigColorSpaceClass ('spac')
colorSpace	icSigGrayData ('GRAY')
	icSigRgbData ('RGB ')
	icSigCmykData ('CMYK')
	icSigLabData ('Lab ')

The terminology used in PDF color spaces and ICC color profiles is similar, but sometimes the same terms are used with different meanings. For example, the default value for each component in an **ICCBased** color space is 0. The range of each color component is a function of the color space specified by the profile and is indicated in the ICC specification. The ranges for several ICC color spaces are shown in Table 4.18.

TABLE 4.18   Ranges for typical ICC color spaces

ICC COLOR SPACE	COMPONENT RANGES
Gray	$[0.0\ \ 1.0]$
RGB	$[0.0\ \ 1.0]$
CMYK	$[0.0\ \ 1.0]$
L*a*b*	$L^\star$: $[0\ \ 100]$; $a^\star$ and $b^\star$: $[-128\ \ 127]$

Since the **ICCBased** color space is being used as a source color space, only the "to CIE" profile information (*AToB* in ICC terminology) is used; the "from CIE" (*BToA*) information is ignored when present. Additionally, an ICC profile may specify a *rendering intent*; however, a PDF viewer application ignores this information. The rendering intent is specified in PDF by a separate parameter; see "Rendering Intents" on page 179.

The representations of **ICCBased** color spaces are less compact than **CalGray, Cal-RGB**, and **Lab**, but can represent a wider range of color spaces. In those cases where a given color space can be expressed by more than one of the CIE-based color space families, the resulting colors are expected to be rendered similarly, regardless of the method selected for representation.

One particular color space is the so-called "standard *RGB*" or *sRGB*, defined in the International Electrotechnical Commission (IEC) document *Colour Measurement and Management in Multimedia Systems and Equipment* (see the Bibliography). In PDF, the *sRGB* color space can be expressed precisely only as an **ICCBased** color space, although it can be approximated by a **CalRGB** color space.

Example 4.9 shows an **ICCBased** color space for a typical three-component *RGB* space. The profile's data has been encoded in hexadecimal representation for readability; in actual practice, a lossless decompression filter such as **FlateDecode** should be used.

Example 4.9

```
10  0  obj                           % Color space
    [/ICCBased  15 0 R]
endobj

15  0  obj                           % ICC profile stream
    <<  /N  3
        /Alternate  /DeviceRGB
        /Length  1605
        /Filter  /ASCIIHexDecode
    >>
stream
00 00 02 0C 61 70 70 6C 02 00 00 00 6D 6E 74 72
52 47 42 20 58 59 5A 20 07 CB 00 02 00 16 00 0E
00 22 00 2C 61 63 73 70 41 50 50 4C 00 00 00 00
61 70 70 6C 00 00 04 01 00 00 00 00 00 00 00 02
00 00 00 00 00 00 F6 D4 00 01 00 00 00 00 D3 2B
00 00 00 00 00 00 00 00 00 00 00 00 00 00 00 00
00 00 00 00 00 00 00 00 00 00 00 00 00 00 00 00
00 00 00 00 00 00 00 00 00 00 00 00 00 00 00 00
00 00 00 09 64 65 73 63 00 00 00 F0 00 00 00 71
72 58 59 5A 00 00 01 64 00 00 00 14 67 58 59 5A
00 00 01 78 00 00 00 14 62 58 59 5A 00 00 01 8C
00 00 00 14 72 54 52 43 00 00 01 A0 00 00 00 0E
67 54 52 43 00 00 01 B0 00 00 00 0E 62 54 52 43
```

```
00 00 01 C0 00 00 00 0E 77 74 70 74 00 00 01 D0
00 00 00 14 63 70 72 74 00 00 01 E4 00 00 00 27
64 65 73 63 00 00 00 00 00 00 00 17 41 70 70 6C
65 20 31 33 22 20 52 47 42 20 53 74 61 6E 64 61
72 64 00 00 00 00 00 00 00 00 00 00 00 17 41 70
70 6C 65 20 31 33 22 20 52 47 42 20 53 74 61 6E
64 61 72 64 00 00 00 00 00 00 00 00 00 00 00 00
00 00 00 00 00 00 00 00 00 00 00 00 00 00 00 00
00 00 00 00 00 00 00 00 00 00 00 00 00 00 00 00
00 58 59 5A 58 59 5A 20 00 00 00 00 00 00 63 0A
00 00 35 0F 00 00 03 30 58 59 5A 20 00 00 00 00
00 00 53 3D 00 00 AE 37 00 00 15 76 58 59 5A 20
00 00 00 00 00 00 40 89 00 00 1C AF 00 00 BA 82
63 75 72 76 00 00 00 00 00 00 00 01 01 CC 63 75
63 75 72 76 00 00 00 00 00 00 00 01 01 CC 63 75
63 75 72 76 00 00 00 00 00 00 00 01 01 CC 58 59
58 59 5A 20 00 00 00 00 00 00 F3 1B 00 01 00 00
00 01 67 E7 74 65 78 74 00 00 00 00 20 43 6F 70
79 72 69 67 68 74 20 41 70 70 6C 65 20 43 6F 6D
70 75 74 65 72 73 20 31 39 39 34 00
endstream
endobj
```

Default Color Spaces

Specifying colors in a device color space (**DeviceGray**, **DeviceRGB**, or **Device-CMYK**) makes them device-dependent. By setting *default color spaces (PDF 1.1),* a PDF document can request that such colors be systematically transformed into device-independent CIE-based color spaces. This capability can be useful in a variety of circumstances, such as the following:

• A document originally intended for one output device is redirected to a different device.

• A document is intended to be compatible with viewer applications designed for earlier versions of PDF, and thus cannot specify CIE-based colors directly.

• Color corrections or rendering intents need to be applied to device colors (see "Rendering Intents" on page 179).

A color space is selected for painting each graphics object. This is either the current color space parameter in the graphics state or a color space given as an entry in an image XObject, in-line image, or shading dictionary. Regardless of how the color space is specified, it may be subject to remapping as described below.

When a device color space is selected, the **ColorSpace** subdictionary of the current resource dictionary (see Section 3.7.2, "Resource Dictionaries") is checked for the presence of an entry designating a corresponding default color space (**DefaultGray**, **DefaultRGB**, or **DefaultCMYK**, corresponding to **DeviceGray**, **DeviceRGB**, or **DeviceCMYK**, respectively). If such an entry is present, its value is used as the color space for the operation currently being performed. (If the viewer application does not recognize this color space, no remapping will occur; the original device color space will be used.)

Color values in the original device color space are passed unchanged to the default color space, which must have the same number of components as the original space. The default color space should be chosen to be compatible with the original, taking into account the components' ranges and whether the components are additive or subtractive. If a color value lies outside the range of the default color space, it will be adjusted to the nearest valid value.

*Note: Any color space other than a **Lab**, **Indexed**, or **Pattern** color space may be used as a default color space, provided that it is compatible with the original device color space as described above.*

If the selected space is a special color space based on an underlying device color space, the default color space will be used in place of the underlying space. This applies to the following:

- The base color space of an **Indexed** color space

- The underlying color space of a **Pattern** color space

- The alternate color space of a **Separation** or **DeviceN** color space (but only if the alternate color space is actually selected)

See Section 4.5.5, "Special Color Spaces," for details on these color spaces.

Note: *Note that there is no conversion of color values, such as a tint transformation, when using the default color space. Color values that are within the range of the device color space might not be within the range of the default color space (particularly if the default is an **ICCBased** color space). In this case, the nearest values within the range of the default space will be used. For this reason, a **Lab** color space is not permitted as the **DefaultRGB** color space.*

Rendering Intents

Although CIE-based color specifications are theoretically device-independent, they are subject to practical limitations in the color reproduction capabilities of the output device. Such limitations may sometimes require compromises to be made among various properties of a color specification when rendering colors for a given device. Specifying a *rendering intent (PDF 1.1)* allows a PDF file to set priorities regarding which of these properties to preserve and which to sacrifice. For example, the PDF file might request that colors falling within the output device's gamut (the range of colors it can reproduce) be rendered exactly while sacrificing the accuracy of out-of-gamut colors, or that a scanned image such as a photograph be rendered in a perceptually "pleasing" manner at the cost of strict colorimetric accuracy.

Rendering intents are specified with the **ri** operator and with the **Intent** entry in image dictionaries. The value is a name identifying the desired rendering intent. Table 4.19 lists the standard rendering intents recognized in the initial release of PDF viewer applications from Adobe Systems. These have been deliberately chosen to correspond closely to the rendering intents defined by the International Color Consortium (ICC), an industry organization that has developed standards for device-independent color. Note, however, that the exact set of rendering intents supported may vary from one output device to another; a particular device may not support all possible intents, or may support additional ones beyond those listed in the table. If the viewer application does not recognize the specified name, it uses the **RelativeColorimetric** intent by default. (See implementation note 29 in Appendix H.)

TABLE 4.19 Rendering intents

NAME	DESCRIPTION
AbsoluteColorimetric	Colors are represented solely with respect to the light source; no correction is made for the output medium's white point (such as the color of unprinted paper). Thus, for example, a monitor's white point, which is bluish compared to that of a printer's paper, would be reproduced with a blue cast. In-gamut colors are reproduced exactly; out-of-gamut colors are mapped to the nearest value within the reproducible gamut. This style of reproduction has the advantage of providing exact color matches from one output medium to another. It has the disadvantage of causing colors with Y values between the medium's white point and 1.0 to be out of gamut. A typical use might be for logos and solid colors that require exact reproduction across different media.
RelativeColorimetric	Colors are represented with respect to the combination of the light source and the output medium's white point (such as the color of unprinted paper). Thus, for example, a monitor's white point would be reproduced on a printer by simply leaving the paper unmarked, ignoring color differences between the two media. In-gamut colors are reproduced exactly; out-of-gamut colors are mapped to the nearest value within the reproducible gamut. This style of reproduction has the advantage of adapting for the varying white points of different output media. It has the disadvantage of not providing exact color matches from one medium to another. A typical use might be for vector graphics.
Saturation	Colors are represented in a manner that preserves or emphasizes saturation. Reproduction of in-gamut colors may or may not be colorimetrically accurate. A typical use might be for business graphics, where saturation is the most important attribute of the color.
Perceptual	Colors are represented in a manner that provides a pleasing perceptual appearance. This generally means that both in-gamut and out-of-gamut colors are modified from their precise colorimetric values in order to preserve color relationships. A typical use might be for scanned images.

4.5.5 Special Color Spaces

Special color spaces add features or properties to an underlying color space. There are four special color space families: **Pattern**, **Indexed**, **Separation**, and **DeviceN**.

Pattern Color Spaces

A **Pattern** color space *(PDF 1.2)* enables a PDF content stream to paint an area with a "color" defined as a *pattern*, which may be either a *tiling pattern* (**PatternType** 1) or a *shading pattern* (**PatternType** 2). Section 4.6, "Patterns," discusses patterns in detail.

Indexed Color Spaces

An **Indexed** color space allows a PDF content stream to select from a *color map* or *color table* of arbitrary colors in some other space, using small integers as indices. A PDF viewer application treats each sample value as an index into the color table and uses the color value it finds there. This technique can considerably reduce the amount of data required to represent a sampled image—for example, by using 8-bit index values as samples instead of 24-bit *RGB* color values.

An **Indexed** color space is defined by a four-element array, as follows:

> [/Indexed *base hival lookup*]

The first element is the color space family name **Indexed**. The remaining elements are parameters that an **Indexed** color space requires; their meanings are discussed below. When the color space is set to an **Indexed** color space, the current color is set to 0.

The *base* parameter is an array or name that identifies the *base color space* in which the values in the color table are to be interpreted. It can be any device or CIE-based color space or (in PDF 1.3) a **Separation** or **DeviceN** space, but not a **Pattern** space or another **Indexed** space. For example, if the base color space is **DeviceRGB**, the values in the color table are to be interpreted as red, green, and blue components; if the base color space is a CIE-based *ABC* space such as a **Cal-RGB** or **Lab** space, the values are to be interpreted as *A*, *B*, and *C* components.

*Note: Attempting to use a **Separation** or **DeviceN** color space as the base for an **Indexed** color space will generate an error in PDF 1.2.*

The *hival* parameter is an integer that specifies the maximum valid index value. In other words, the color table is to be indexed by integers in the range 0 to *hival*. *hival* can be no greater than 255, which is what would be required to index a table with 8-bit index values.

The color table is defined by the *lookup* parameter, which can be either a stream or (in PDF 1.2) a string. It provides the mapping between index values and the corresponding colors in the base color space.

The color table data must be $m \times (hival + 1)$ bytes long, where m is the number of color components in the base color space. Each byte is an unsigned integer in the range 0 to 255 that is scaled to the range of the corresponding color component in the base color space; that is, 0 corresponds to the minimum value in the range for that component, and 255 corresponds to the maximum value in the range.

*Note: This is different from the interpretation of an **Indexed** color space's color table in PostScript. In PostScript, the component value is always scaled to the range 0.0 to 1.0, regardless of the range of color values in the base color space.*

The color components for each entry in the table appear consecutively in the string or stream. For example, if the base color space is **DeviceRGB** and the indexed color space contains two colors, the order of bytes in the string or stream is $R_0 \ G_0 \ B_0 \ R_1 \ G_1 \ B_1$, where letters denote the color component and numeric subscripts denote the table entry.

Example 4.10 illustrates the specification of an **Indexed** color space that maps 8-bit index values to three-component color values in the **DeviceRGB** color space.

Example 4.10

```
[ /Indexed
    /DeviceRGB
    255
    <000000 FF0000 00FF00 0000FF B57342 ...>
]
```

The example shows only the first five color values in the *lookup* string; in all, there should be 256 color values and the string should be 768 bytes long. Having established this color space, the program can now specify colors using single-component values in the range 0 to 255. For example, a color value of 4 selects an *RGB* color whose components are coded as the hexadecimal integers B5, 73, and 42. Dividing these by 255 and scaling the results to the range 0.0 to 1.0 yields a color with red, green, and blue components of 0.710, 0.451, and 0.259, respectively.

Although an **Indexed** color space is useful mainly for images, index values can also be used with the color selection operators **sc**, **scn**, **SC**, and **SCN**. For example,

    123 sc

selects the same color as does an image sample value of 123. The index value should be an integer in the range 0 to *hival*. If it is a real number, it is rounded to the nearest integer; if it is outside the range 0 to *hival*, it is adjusted to the nearest value within that range.

Separation Color Spaces

Color output devices produce full color by combining *primary* or *process colorants* in varying amounts. On a display, the primary colorants consist of red, green, and blue phosphors; on a printer, they typically consist of cyan, magenta, yellow, and sometimes black inks. In addition, some devices can apply special colorants, often called *spot colorants*, to produce effects that cannot be achieved with the standard process colorants alone. Examples include metallic and fluorescent colors and special textures.

When printing a page, most devices produce a single *composite* page on which all process colorants (and spot colorants, if any) are combined. However, some devices, such as imagesetters, produce a separate, monochromatic rendition of the page, called a *separation*, for each individual colorant. When the separations are later combined—on a printing press, for example—and the proper inks or other colorants are applied to them, a full-color page results.

A **Separation** color space *(PDF 1.2)* provides a means for specifying the use of additional colorants or for isolating the control of individual color components of a device color space. When such a space is the current color space, the current color is a single-component value, called a *tint*, that controls the application of the given colorant or color component only.

Note: *The term* separation *is often misused as a synonym for an individual device colorant. In the context of this discussion, a printing system that produces separations generates a separate piece of physical medium (generally film) for each colorant. It is these pieces of physical medium that are correctly referred to as separations. A particular colorant properly constitutes a separation only if the device is generating physical separations, one of which corresponds to the given colorant. The* **Separation** *color space is so named for historical reasons, but it has evolved to the broader purpose of controlling the application of individual colorants in general, whether or not they are actually realized as physical separations.*

Note also that the operation of a **Separation** color space itself is independent of the characteristics of any particular output device. Depending on the device, the space may or may not correspond to a true, physical separation or to an actual colorant. For example, a **Separation** color space could be used to control the application of a single process colorant (such as cyan) on a composite device that does not produce physical separations, or could represent a color (such as orange) for which no specific colorant exists on the device. A **Separation** color space provides consistent, predictable behavior, even on devices that cannot directly generate the requested color.

A **Separation** color space is defined as follows:

    [/Separation *name alternateSpace tintTransform*]

In other words, it is a four-element array whose first element is the color space family name **Separation**. The remaining elements are parameters that a **Separation** color space requires; their meanings are discussed below.

A color value in a **Separation** color space consists of a single tint component in the range 0.0 to 1.0. The value 0.0 represents the minimum amount of colorant that can be applied; 1.0 represents the maximum. Tints are always treated as *subtractive* colors, even if the device produces output for the designated component by an additive method. Thus a tint value of 0.0 denotes the lightest color that can be achieved with the given colorant, and 1.0 the darkest. (Note that this is the same as the convention for **DeviceCMYK** color components, but opposite to the one for **DeviceGray** and **DeviceRGB**.) The **scn** and **SCN** operators respectively set the current fill and stroke color in the graphics state to a tint value; the initial value in either case is 1.0. A sampled image with single-component samples can also be used as a source of tint values.

The *name* parameter in the color space array is a name object specifying the name of the colorant that this **Separation** color space is intended to represent (or one of the special names **All** or **None**; see below). Such colorant names are arbitrary, and there can be any number of them, subject to implementation limits.

The special colorant name **All** refers collectively to all colorants available on an output device, including those for the standard process colorants. When a **Separation** space with this colorant name is the current color space, painting operators apply tint values to all available colorants at once. This is useful for purposes such as painting registration marks in the same place on every separation. Such marks would typically be painted as the last step in composing a page, to ensure that they are not overwritten by subsequent painting operations.

The special colorant name **None** will never produce any visible output. Painting operations in a **Separation** space with this colorant name have no effect on the current page.

All devices support **Separation** color spaces with the colorant names **All** and **None**, even if they do not support any others. **Separation** spaces with either of these colorant names ignore the *alternateSpace* and *tintTransform* parameters (discussed below), although valid values must still be provided.

At the moment the color space is set to a **Separation** space, the viewer application determines whether the device has an available colorant corresponding to the name of the requested space. If so, the application ignores the *alternateSpace* and *tintTransform* parameters; subsequent painting operations within the space will apply the designated colorant directly, according to the tint values supplied.

If the colorant name associated with a **Separation** color space does not correspond to a colorant available on the device, the viewer application arranges instead for subsequent painting operations to be performed in an *alternate color space*. This enables the intended colors to be approximated by colors in some device or CIE-based color space, which are then rendered using the usual primary or process colorants. This works as follows:

• The *alternateSpace* parameter must be an array or name object that identifies the alternate color space. This can be any device or CIE-based color space, but not another special color space (**Pattern**, **Indexed**, **Separation**, or **DeviceN**).

- The *tintTransform* parameter must be a function (see Section 3.9, "Functions"). During subsequent painting operations, a viewer application will call this function to transform a tint value into color component values in the alternate color space. The function is called with the tint value and must return the corresponding color component values. That is, the number of components and the interpretation of their values depend on the alternate color space.

Example 4.11 illustrates the specification of a **Separation** color space (object 5) that is intended to produce a color named LogoGreen. If the output device has no colorant corresponding to this color, **DeviceCMYK** will be used as the alternate color space; the tint transformation function provided (object 12) maps tint values linearly into shades of a *CMYK* color value approximating the "logo green" color.

Example 4.11

```
5 0 obj                                    % Color space
    [ /Separation
        /LogoGreen
        /DeviceCMYK
        12 0 R
    ]
endobj

12 0 obj                                   % Tint transformation function
    << /FunctionType 4
        /Domain [0.0 1.0]
        /Range [0.0 1.0  0.0 1.0  0.0 1.0  0.0 1.0]
        /Length 62
    >>
stream
    { dup 0.84 mul
      exch 0.00 exch dup 0.44 mul
      exch 0.21 mul
    }
endstream
endobj
```

DeviceN Color Spaces

DeviceN color spaces *(PDF 1.3)* support the use of high-fidelity and multitone color. *High-fidelity* color is the use of more than the standard *CMYK* process colorants to produce an extended *gamut,* or range of colors. A popular example of such a system is the PANTONE® Hexachrome™ system, which uses six color-ants: the usual cyan, magenta, yellow, and black, plus orange and green.

Multitone color systems use a single-component image to specify multiple color components. In a *duotone,* for example, a single-component image can be used to specify both the black component and a spot color component. The tone reproduction is generally different for the different components; for example, the black component might be painted with the exact sample data from the single-component image, while the spot color component might be generated as a non-linear function of the image data in a manner that emphasizes the shadows.

DeviceN color spaces allow any subset of the available device colorants to be treated as a device color space with multiple components. This provides greater flexibility than is possible with standard device color spaces such as **DeviceCMYK** or with individual **Separation** color spaces. For example, it is possible to create a **DeviceN** color space consisting of only the cyan, magenta, and yellow color com-ponents, while excluding the black component. If overprinting is enabled (see Section 4.5.6, "Overprint Control"), painting in this color space will leave the black component unchanged.

A **DeviceN** color space is specified as follows:

    [/DeviceN *names alternateSpace tintTransform*]

or

    [/DeviceN *names alternateSpace tintTransform attributes*]

It is a four- or five-element array whose first element is the color space family name **DeviceN**. The remaining elements are parameters that a **DeviceN** color space requires; their meanings are discussed below.

Color values in the **DeviceN** color space are tint components in the range 0.0 to 1.0. The value 0.0 represents the minimum amount of colorant; 1.0 represents the maximum. The **scn** and **SCN** operators set the current color in the graphics state to a set of tint values; the initial value is 1.0 for each tint. A sampled image can also be treated as a source of tint values.

A **DeviceN** color space works almost the same as a **Separation** color space—in fact, a **DeviceN** color space with only one component is exactly equivalent to a **Separation** color space. The following are the only differences between **DeviceN** and **Separation**:

- Color values in a **DeviceN** color space consist of multiple tint components, rather than only one. The number of components is subject to an implementation limit; see Appendix C.

- The *names* parameter in the color space array is an array of name objects specifying the individual colorants. (The special colorant name **All** is not allowed.) The length of the array determines the number of components, and hence the number of operands required by the **scn** and **SCN** operators when this space is the current color space. Operand values supplied to **scn** or **SCN** are interpreted as color component values in the order in which the colors are given in the *names* array.

- At the moment the color space is set to a **DeviceN** space, the viewer application will select the requested set of colorants only if all of them are available on the device; otherwise, it will select the alternate color space designated by the *alternateSpace* parameter.

- The tint transformation function is called with *n* tint values and must return the corresponding *m* color component values, where *n* is the number of components needed to specify a color in the **DeviceN** color space and *m* is the number required by the alternate color space.

In a **DeviceN** color space, one or more of the colorant names in the *names* array may be the name **None**. This indicates that the corresponding color component is never painted on the page, as in a **Separation** color space for the **None** colorant. When a **DeviceN** color space is painting the named device colorants directly, color components corresponding to **None** colorants are discarded. However, when the **DeviceN** color space reverts to its alternate color space, those components are passed to the tint transformation function, which may use them in any desired manner.

The optional *attributes* parameter is a dictionary containing additional information about the color space. At the time of publication, only one entry is defined in this dictionary, as shown in Table 4.20.

TABLE 4.20 Entry in a DeviceN color space attributes dictionary

KEY	TYPE	VALUE
Colorants	dictionary	*(Optional)* A dictionary describing the individual colorants used in the **DeviceN** color space. For each entry in this dictionary, the key is a colorant name and the value is an array defining a **Separation** color space for that colorant (see "Separation Color Spaces" on page 183). The key must match the colorant name given in that color space. The dictionary need not list all colorants used in the **DeviceN** color space and may list additional colorants.

This dictionary has no effect on the operation of the **DeviceN** color space itself or the appearance that it produces. However, it provides information about the individual colorants that may be useful to some applications. In particular, the alternate color space and tint transformation function of a **Separation** color space describe the appearance of that colorant alone, whereas those of a **DeviceN** color space describe only the appearance of its colorants in combination. |

Example 4.12 shows a **DeviceN** color space consisting of three color components named **Orange**, **Green**, and **None**. In this example, the **DeviceN** color space, object 30, has an attributes dictionary whose **Colorants** entry is an indirect reference to object 45 (which might also be referenced by attributes dictionaries of other **DeviceN** color spaces). *tintTransform1*, whose definition is not shown, maps three color components (tints of the colorants **Orange**, **Green**, and **None**) to four color components in the alternate color space, **DeviceCMYK**. *tintTransform2* maps a single color component (an orange tint) to four components in **DeviceCMYK**. Likewise, *tintTransform3* maps a green tint to **DeviceCMYK**, and *tintTransform4* maps a tint of PANTONE 131 to **DeviceCMYK**.

Example 4.12

```
30  0  obj                          % Color space
   [  /DeviceN
         [/Orange /Green /None]
         /DeviceCMYK
         tintTransform1
         << /Colorants  45 0 R  >>
   ]
   endobj
```

```
45  0  obj                                              % Colorants dictionary
    <<  /Orange  [ /Separation
                    /Orange
                    /DeviceCMYK
                    tintTransform2
                ]
        /Green [ /Separation
                  /Green
                  /DeviceCMYK
                  tintTransform3
              ]
        /PANTONE#20131  [ /Separation
                            /PANTONE#20131
                            /DeviceCMYK
                            tintTransform4
                        ]
    >>
    endobj
```

Multitone Examples

The following examples illustrate various interesting and useful special cases of the use of **Indexed** and **DeviceN** color spaces in combination to produce multi-tone colors.

Examples 4.13 and 4.14 illustrate the use of **DeviceN** to create duotone color spaces. In Example 4.13, an **Indexed** color space maps index values in the range 0 to 255 to a duotone **DeviceN** space in cyan and black. In effect, the index values are treated as if they were tints of the duotone space, which are then mapped into tints of the two underlying colorants. Only the beginning of the lookup table string for the **Indexed** color space is shown; the full table would contain 256 two-byte entries, each specifying a tint value for cyan and black, for a total of 512 bytes. If the alternate color space of the **DeviceN** space is selected, the tint trans-formation function (object 15 in the example) maps the two tint components for cyan and black to the four components for a **DeviceCMYK** color space by supply-ing zero values for the other two components. Example 4.14 shows the definition of another duotone color space, this time using black and gold colorants (where gold is a spot colorant) and using a **CalRGB** space as the alternate color space. This could be defined in the same way as in the preceding example, with a tint trans-formation function that converts from the two tint components to colors in the alternate **CalRGB** color space.

Example 4.13

```
10  0  obj                                      % Color space
   [  /Indexed
        [  /DeviceN
                [/Cyan  /Black]
                /DeviceCMYK
                15 0 R
        ]
        255
        <6605  6806  6907  6B09  6C0A  …>
   ]
endobj

15  0  obj                                      % Tint transformation function
   <<  /FunctionType  4
       /Domain  [0.0  1.0   0.0  1.0]
       /Range  [0.0 1.0  0.0 1.0  0.0 1.0  0.0 1.0]
       /Length  16
   >>
stream
   {0  0  3  −1  roll}
endstream
endobj
```

Example 4.14

```
30  0  obj                                      % Color space
   [  /Indexed
        [  /DeviceN
                [/Black  /Gold]
                [   /CalRGB
                    <<  /WhitePoint  [1.0  1.0  1.0]
                        /Gamma  [2.2  2.2  2.2]
                    >>
                ]
                35 0 R                           % Tint transformation function
        ]
        255
        … Lookup table …
   ]
endobj
```

Given a formula for converting any combination of black and gold tints to calibrated *RGB*, a 2-in, 3-out type 4 function could be used for the tint transformation. Alternatively, a type 0 function could be used, but this would require a large number of sample points to represent the function accurately; for example, sampling each input variable for 256 tint values between 0.0 and 1.0 would require $256^2 = 65,536$ samples. But since the **DeviceN** color space is being used as the base of an **Indexed** color space, there are actually only 256 possible combinations of black and gold tint values. A more compact way to represent this information is to put the alternate color values directly into the lookup table alongside the **DeviceN** color values, as in Example 4.15.

Example 4.15

```
10  0  obj                                    % Color space
   [ /Indexed
       [ /DeviceN
            [/Black /Gold /None /None /None]
            [   /CalRGB
                 <<  /WhitePoint [1.0  1.0  1.0]
                     /Gamma  [2.2  2.2  2.2]
                 >>
            ]
            20 0 R                            % Tint transformation function
       ]
       255
       ... Lookup table ...
   ]
 endobj
```

In this example, each entry in the lookup table has *five* components: two for the black and gold colorants and three more (specified as **None**) for the equivalent **CalRGB** color components. If the black and gold colorants are available on the output device, the **None** components will be ignored; if black and gold are not available, the tint transformation function will be used to convert a five-component color into a three-component equivalent in the alternate **CalRGB** color space. But since, by construction, the third, fourth, and fifth components *are* the **CalRGB** components, the tint transformation function can merely discard the first two components and return the last three. This can be easily expressed with a type 4 function, as shown in Example 4.16.

Example 4.16

```
20 0 obj                                    % Tint transformation function
   << /FunctionType 4
      /Domain [0.0 1.0  0.0 1.0  0.0 1.0  0.0 1.0  0.0 1.0]
      /Range [0.0 1.0  0.0 1.0  0.0 1.0]
      /Length 27
   >>
stream
   {5 3 roll pop pop}
endstream
endobj
```

For a final example, consider Figure 4.16, which shows a quadtone (four-component) image produced using **Indexed** and **DeviceN** color spaces by an extension of the techniques described above. (See implementation note 30 in Appendix H.)

Single-component (grayscale) image

Quadtone image

FIGURE 4.16 *Quadtone image using **Indexed DeviceN***

This example starts with the grayscale image shown on the left and paints it with four colorants: black and three PANTONE spot colors. The alternate color space is a simple calibrated *RGB*. Thus the **DeviceN** color space has seven components: the four desired colorants plus the three components of the alternate space. Example 4.17 shows the image XObject (see Section 4.8.4, "Image Dictionaries") representing the quadtone image, followed by the color space used to interpret the image data.

Example 4.17

```
5 0 obj                              % Image XObject
   << /Type /XObject
      /Subtype /Image
      /Width 288
      /Height 288
      /ColorSpace 10 0 R
      /BitsPerComponent 8
      /Length 105278
      /Filter /ASCII85Decode
   >>
stream
… Data for grayscale image …
endstream
endobj

10 0 obj                             % Indexed color space for image
   [ /Indexed
         15 0 R                      % Base color space
         255                         % Table has 256 entries
         30 0 R                      % Lookup table
   ]
endobj

15 0 obj                             % Base color space (DeviceN) for Indexed space
   [ /DeviceN
         [ /Black                    % Four colorants (black plus three spot colors)
           /PANTONE#20216#20CVC
           /PANTONE#20409#20CVC
           /PANTONE#202985#20CVC
           /None                     % Three components for alternate space
           /None
           /None
         ]
         16 0 R                      % Alternate color space
         20 0 R                      % Tint transformation function
   ]
endobj
```

```
16  0  obj                              % Alternate color space for DeviceN space
   [ /CalRGB
          << /WhitePoint  [1.0  1.0  1.0]  >>
   ]
endobj

20  0  obj                              % Tint transformation function for DeviceN space
   <<  /FunctionType  4
        /Domain  [0.0 1.0  0.0 1.0  0.0 1.0  0.0 1.0  0.0 1.0  0.0 1.0  0.0 1.0]
        /Range  [0.0 1.0  0.0 1.0  0.0 1.0]
        /Length  44
   >>
stream
   { 7  3  roll                          % Just discard first four values
     pop  pop  pop  pop
   }
endstream
endobj

30  0  obj                              % Lookup table for Indexed color space
   <<  /Length  1975
        /Filter  [/ASCII85Decode  /FlateDecode]
   >>
stream
8;T1BB2"M7*!"psYBt1k\gY1T<D&tO]r*F7Hga*
... Additional data (seven components for each table entry) ...
endstream
endobj
```

4.5.6 Overprint Control

The graphics state contains an *overprint parameter*, controlled by the **op** and **OP**
entries in a graphics state parameter dictionary. Overprint control is useful mainly on devices that produce true physical separations, but it is available on some
composite devices as well. Although the operation of this parameter is device-
dependent, it is described here, rather than in the chapter on color rendering,
because it pertains to an aspect of painting in device color spaces that is important to many applications.

Any painting operation marks some specific set of device colorants, depending
on the color space in which the painting takes place. In a **Separation** or **DeviceN**
color space, the colorants to be marked are specified explicitly; in a device or CIE-
based color space, they are implied by the process color model of the output

device (see Chapter 6). The overprint parameter is a boolean flag that determines how painting operations affect colorants other than those explicitly or implicitly specified by the current color space.

If the overprint parameter is *false* (the default value), painting a color in any color space causes the corresponding areas of unspecified colorants to be erased (painted with a tint value of 0.0). The effect is that the color at any position on the page is whatever was painted there last; this is consistent with the normal opaque painting behavior of the Adobe imaging model.

If the overprint parameter is *true* and the output device supports overprinting, no such erasing actions are performed; anything previously painted in other colorants is left undisturbed. Consequently, the color at a given position on the page may be a combined result of several painting operations in different colorants. The effect produced by such overprinting is device-dependent and is not defined by the PDF language.

Note: *Not all devices support overprinting. Furthermore, many PostScript printers support it only when separations are being produced, and not for composite output. If overprinting is not supported, the value of the overprint parameter is ignored.*

An additional graphics state parameter, the *overprint mode (PDF 1.3)* affects the interpretation of a tint value of 0.0 for a color component in a **DeviceCMYK** color space when overprinting is enabled. This parameter is controlled by the **OPM** entry in a graphics state parameter dictionary; it has an effect only when the overprint parameter is *true*, as described above.

When colors are specified in a **DeviceCMYK** color space and the output device has a native color space that is also **DeviceCMYK**, each of the source color components controls the corresponding device colorant directly. Ordinarily, each source color component value replaces the value previously painted for the corresponding device colorant, no matter what the new value is; this is the default behavior, specified by overprint mode 0.

When the overprint mode is 1 (also called *nonzero overprint mode*), a tint value of 0.0 for a source color component leaves the corresponding component of the previously painted color unchanged. The effect is equivalent to painting in a **DeviceN** color space that includes only those components whose values are nonzero. For example, if the overprint parameter is *true* and the overprint mode is 1, the operation

    0.2 0.3 0.0 1.0 k

is equivalent to

    0.2 0.3 1.0 scn

in the color space shown in Example 4.18.

Example 4.18

```
10  0  obj                          % Color space
   [ /DeviceN
        [/Cyan /Magenta /Black]
        /DeviceCMYK
        15 0 R
   ]
endobj

15  0  obj                          % Tint transformation function
   << /FunctionType  4
      /Domain  [0.0 1.0  0.0 1.0  0.0 1.0]
      /Range  [0.0 1.0  0.0 1.0  0.0 1.0  0.0 1.0]
      /Length  13
   >>
stream
   {0  exch}
endstream
endobj
```

Nonzero overprint mode applies only to painting operations that use the current color in the graphics state when the current color space is **DeviceCMYK**. It does not apply to the painting of images or to any colors that are the result of a computation, such as those in a shading pattern or conversions from some other color space. It also does not apply if the device's native color space is not **DeviceCMYK**; in that case, source colors must be converted to the device's native color space, and all components participate in the conversion, whatever their values. (This is shown explicitly in the alternate color space and tint transformation function of the **DeviceN** color space in Example 4.18.)

4.5.7 Color Operators

Table 4.21 lists the PDF operators that control color spaces and color values. (Also color-related is the graphics state operator **ri**, listed in Table 4.7 on page 142 and discussed under "Rendering Intents" on page 179.) Color operators may appear at the page description level or inside text objects (see Figure 4.1 on page 122).

TABLE 4.21 Color operators

OPERANDS	OPERATOR	DESCRIPTION
name	cs	*(PDF 1.1)* Set the color space to use for nonstroking operations. The operand *name* must be a name object. If the color space is one that can be specified by a name and no additional parameters (**DeviceGray, DeviceRGB, DeviceCMYK,** and certain cases of **Pattern**), the name may be specified directly. Otherwise, it must be a name defined in the **ColorSpace** subdictionary of the current resource dictionary (see Section 3.7.2, "Resource Dictionaries"); the associated value is an array describing the color space (see Section 4.5.2, "Types of Color Space").
		The **cs** operator also sets the current nonstroking color to its initial value, which depends on the color space:
		• In a device, **CalGray,** or **CalRGB** color space, the initial color is black.
		• In a **Lab** or **ICCBased** color space, the initial color is black unless that falls outside the intervals specified by the space's **Range** entry, in which case the nearest valid value is substituted.
		• In an **Indexed** color space, the initial color value is 0.
		• In a **Separation** or **DeviceN** color space, the initial tint value is 1.0 for all colorants.
		• In a **Pattern** color space, the initial color is a pattern object that causes nothing to be painted.
name	CS	*(PDF 1.1)* Same as **cs**, but for stroking operations.
$c_1 \ldots c_n$	sc	*(PDF 1.1)* Set the color to use for nonstroking operations in a device, CIE-based (other than **ICCBased**), or **Indexed** color space. The number of operands required and their interpretation depends on the current nonstroking color space:
		• For **DeviceGray, CalGray,** and **Indexed** color spaces, one operand is required ($n = 1$).
		• For **DeviceRGB, CalRGB,** and **Lab** color spaces, three operands are required ($n = 3$).
		• For **DeviceCMYK**, four operands are required ($n = 4$).

$c_1 \dots c_n$ $c_1 \dots c_n$ *name*	**scn** **scn**	*(PDF 1.2)* Same as **sc**, but also supports **Pattern**, **Separation**, **DeviceN**, and **ICCBased** color spaces.
		If the current nonstroking color space is a **Separation**, **DeviceN** *(PDF 1.3)*, or **ICCBased** *(PDF 1.3)* color space, the operands $c_1 \dots c_n$ are numbers. The number of operands and their interpretation depends on the color space.
		If the current nonstroking color space is a **Pattern** color space, *name* is the name of an entry in the **Pattern** subdictionary of the current resource dictionary (see Section 3.7.2, "Resource Dictionaries"). For an uncolored tiling pattern (**PatternType** = 1 and **PaintType** = 2), $c_1 \dots c_n$ are component values specifying a color in the pattern's underlying color space. For other types of pattern, these operands must not be specified.
$c_1 \dots c_n$	**SC**	*(PDF 1.1)* Same as **sc**, but for stroking operations.
$c_1 \dots c_n$ $c_1 \dots c_n$ *name*	**SCN** **SCN**	*(PDF 1.2)* Same as **scn**, but for stroking operations.
gray	**g**	Set the color space to **DeviceGray** (or the **DefaultGray** color space; see "Default Color Spaces" on page 177) and set the gray level to use for nonstroking operations. *gray* is a number between 0.0 (black) and 1.0 (white).
gray	**G**	Same as **g**, but for stroking operations.
r g b	**rg**	Set the color space to **DeviceRGB** (or the **DefaultRGB** color space; see "Default Color Spaces" on page 177) and set the color to use for nonstroking operations. Each operand must be a number between 0.0 (minimum intensity) and 1.0 (maximum intensity).
r g b	**RG**	Same as **rg**, but for stroking operations.
c m y k	**k**	Set the color space to **DeviceCMYK** (or the **DefaultCMYK** color space; see "Default Color Spaces" on page 177) and set the color to use for nonstroking operations. Each operand must be a number between 0.0 (zero concentration) and 1.0 (maximum concentration). The behavior of this operator is affected by the overprint mode (see Section 4.5.6, "Overprint Control").
c m y k	**K**	Same as **k**, but for stroking operations.

In certain circumstances, invoking operators that specify colors or other color-related parameters in the graphics state is not allowed. This restriction occurs when defining graphical figures whose colors are to be specified separately each time they are used. Specifically, the restriction applies:

• In any glyph definition that uses the **d1** operator (see Section 5.5.4, "Type 3 Fonts")

• In the content stream of an uncolored tiling pattern (see "Uncolored Tiling Patterns" on page 209)

In these circumstances, the following will cause an error:

• Invoking any of the following operators:

cs	SCN	k
CS	g	K
sc	G	ri
SC	rg	sh
scn	RG	

• Invoking the **gs** operator with any of the following entries in the graphics state parameter dictionary:

HT	BG	UCR
TR	BG2	UCR2
TR2		

• Painting an image. However, painting an *image mask* (see "Stencil Masking" on page 257) is permitted, because it does not specify colors, but rather designates places where the current color is to be painted.

4.6 Patterns

When operators such as **S** (stroke), **f** (fill), and **Tj** (show text) paint an area of the page with the current color, they ordinarily apply a single color that covers the area uniformly. However, it is also possible to apply "paint" that consists of a repeating graphical figure or a smoothly varying color gradient instead of a simple color. Such a repeating figure or smooth gradient is called a *pattern*. Patterns are quite general, and have many uses; for example, they can be used to create various graphical textures, such as weaves, brick walls, sunbursts, and similar geometrical and chromatic effects. (See implementation note 31 in Appendix H.)

Patterns come in two varieties:

- *Tiling patterns* consist of a small graphical figure (called a *pattern cell*) that is replicated at fixed horizontal and vertical intervals to fill the area to be painted. The graphics objects to use for tiling are described by a content stream.

- *Shading patterns* define a *gradient fill* that produces a smooth transition between colors across the area. The color to use is specified as a function of position using any of a variety of methods.

Note: *The ability to paint with patterns is a feature of PDF 1.2 (tiling patterns) and PDF 1.3 (shading patterns). With some effort, it is possible to achieve a limited form of tiling patterns in PDF 1.1 by defining them as character glyphs in a special font and painting them repeatedly with the* **Tj** *operator. Another technique, defining patterns as halftone screens, is not recommended, because the effects produced are device-dependent.*

Patterns are specified in a special family of color spaces named **Pattern**, whose "color values" are *pattern objects* instead of the numeric component values used with other color spaces. A pattern object may be a dictionary or a stream, depending on the type of pattern; the term *pattern dictionary* will be used generically in this section to refer to either a dictionary object or the dictionary portion of a stream object. This section describes **Pattern** color spaces and the specification of color values within them; see Section 4.5, "Color Spaces," for information about color spaces and color values in general.

4.6.1 General Properties of Patterns

A pattern dictionary contains descriptive information defining the appearance and properties of a pattern. All pattern dictionaries contain an entry named **PatternType**, whose value identifies the kind of pattern the dictionary describes: type 1 for a tiling pattern or type 2 for a shading pattern. The remaining contents of the dictionary depend on the pattern type, and are detailed below in the sections on individual pattern types.

All patterns are treated as colors; a **Pattern** color space is established with the **cs** or **CS** operator just like other color spaces, and a particular pattern is installed as the current color with the **scn** or **SCN** operator (see Table 4.21 on page 198).

A pattern's appearance is described with respect to its own internal coordinate system. Every pattern has a *pattern matrix,* a transformation matrix that maps the pattern's internal coordinate system to the default coordinate system of the pattern's *parent content stream* (the content stream in which the pattern is defined as a resource). The concatenation of the pattern matrix with that of the parent content stream establishes the *pattern coordinate space*, within which all graphics objects in the pattern are interpreted.

For example, if a pattern is used on a page, the pattern will appear in the **Pattern** subdictionary of that page's resource dictionary, and the pattern matrix maps pattern space to the default (initial) coordinate space of the page. Changes to the page's transformation matrix that occur within the page's content stream, such as rotation and scaling, have no effect on the pattern; it maintains its original relationship to the page no matter where on the page it is used. Similarly, if a pattern is used within a form XObject (see Section 4.9, "Form XObjects"), the pattern matrix maps pattern space to the form's default user space (that is, the form coordinate space at the time the form is painted with the **Do** operator). Finally, a pattern may used within another pattern; the inner pattern's matrix defines its relationship to the pattern space of the outer pattern.

Note: PostScript allows a pattern to be defined in one context but used in another. For example, a pattern might be defined on a page (that is, its pattern matrix maps the pattern coordinate space to the user space of the page) but be used in a form on that page, so that its relationship to the page is independent of each individual placement of the form. PDF does not support this feature; in PDF, all patterns are local to the context in which they are defined.

4.6.2 Tiling Patterns

A *tiling pattern* consists of a small graphical figure called a *pattern cell.* Painting with the pattern replicates the cell at fixed horizontal and vertical intervals to fill an area. The effect is as if the figure were painted on the surface of a clear glass tile, identical copies of which were then laid down in an array covering the area and trimmed to its boundaries. This is called *tiling* the area.

The pattern cell can include graphical elements such as filled areas, text, and sampled images. Its shape need not be rectangular, and the spacing of tiles can differ from the dimensions of the cell itself. When performing painting operations such as **S** (stroke) or **f** (fill), the viewer application paints the cell on the current page as many times as necessary to fill an area. The order in which individual tiles (instances of the cell) are painted is unspecified and unpredictable; it is inadvisable for the figures on adjacent tiles to overlap.

The appearance of the pattern cell is defined by a content stream containing the painting operators needed to paint one instance of the cell. Table 4.22 lists the entries in this stream's dictionary.

TABLE 4.22 Entries in a type 1 pattern dictionary

KEY	TYPE	VALUE
Type	name	*(Optional)* The type of PDF object that this dictionary describes; if present, must be **Pattern** for a pattern dictionary.
PatternType	integer	*(Required)* A code identifying the type of pattern that this dictionary describes; must be 1 for a tiling pattern.
PaintType	integer	*(Required)* A code that determines how the color of the pattern cell is to be specified:

1   *Colored tiling pattern.* The pattern's content stream itself specifies the colors used to paint the pattern cell. When the content stream begins execution, the current color is the one that was initially in effect in the pattern's parent content stream. (This is similar to the definition of the pattern matrix; see above.)

2   *Uncolored tiling pattern.* The pattern's content stream does not specify any color information. Instead, the entire pattern cell is painted with a separately specified color each time the pattern is used. Essentially, the content stream describes a *stencil* through which the current color is to be poured. The content stream must not invoke operators that specify colors or other color-related parameters in the graphics state; otherwise, an error will occur (see Section 4.5.7, "Color Operators"). The content stream may paint an image mask, however, since it does not specify any color information (see "Stencil Masking" on page 257).

TilingType	integer	*(Required)* A code that controls adjustments to the spacing of tiles relative to the device pixel grid:

> 1   *Constant spacing.* Pattern cells are spaced consistently—that is, by a multiple of a device pixel. To achieve this, the viewer application may need to distort the pattern cell slightly by making small adjustments to **XStep**, **YStep**, and the transformation matrix. The amount of distortion does not exceed 1 device pixel.
>
> 2   *No distortion.* The pattern cell is not distorted, but the spacing between pattern cells may vary by as much as 1 device pixel, both horizontally and vertically, when the pattern is painted. This achieves the spacing requested by **XStep** and **YStep** *on average*, but not necessarily for each individual pattern cell.
>
> 3   *Constant spacing and faster tiling.* Pattern cells are spaced consistently as in tiling type 1, but with additional distortion permitted to enable a more efficient implementation.

BBox	rectangle	*(Required)* An array of four numbers in the pattern coordinate system giving the coordinates of the left, bottom, right, and top edges, respectively, of the pattern cell's bounding box. These boundaries are used to clip the pattern cell.
XStep	number	*(Required)* The desired horizontal spacing between pattern cells, measured in the pattern coordinate system.
YStep	number	*(Required)* The desired vertical spacing between pattern cells, measured in the pattern coordinate system. Note that **XStep** and **YStep** may differ from the dimensions of the pattern cell implied by the **BBox** entry. This allows tiling with irregularly shaped figures. **XStep** and **YStep** may be either positive or negative, but not zero.
Resources	dictionary	*(Required)* A resource dictionary containing all of the named resources required by the pattern's content stream (see Section 3.7.2, "Resource Dictionaries").
Matrix	array	*(Optional)* An array of six numbers defining the pattern matrix (see Section 4.6.1, "General Properties of Patterns"). Default value: the identity matrix [1 0 0 1 0 0].

The pattern dictionary's **BBox**, **XStep**, and **YStep** values are interpreted in the pattern coordinate system, and the graphics objects in the pattern's content stream are defined with respect to that coordinate system. The placement of pattern cells in the tiling is based on the location of one *key pattern cell*, which is then displaced by multiples of **XStep** and **YStep** to replicate the pattern. The origin of the key pattern cell coincides with the origin of the pattern coordinate system; the phase of the tiling can be controlled by the translation components of the **Matrix** entry in the pattern dictionary.

The first step in painting with a tiling pattern is to establish the pattern as the current color in the graphics state. Subsequent painting operations will tile the painted areas with the pattern cell described by the pattern's content stream. Whenever it needs to obtain the pattern cell, the viewer application does the following:

1. Saves the current graphics state (as if by invoking the **q** operator)

2. Installs the graphics state that was in effect at the beginning of the pattern's parent content stream, with the current transformation matrix altered by the pattern matrix as described in Section 4.6.1, "General Properties of Patterns"

3. Paints the graphics objects specified in the pattern's content stream

4. Restores the saved graphics state (as if by invoking the **Q** operator)

Note: *The pattern's content stream should not set any of the device-dependent parameters in the graphics state (see Table 4.3 on page 136). Doing so may result in incorrect output.*

Colored Tiling Patterns

A *colored tiling pattern* is one whose color is self-contained. In the course of painting the pattern cell, the pattern's content stream explicitly sets the color of each graphical element it paints. A single pattern cell can contain elements that are painted different colors; it can also contain sampled grayscale or color images. This type of pattern is identified by a pattern type of 1 and a paint type of 1 in the pattern dictionary.

When the current color space is a **Pattern** space, a colored tiling pattern can be selected as the current color by supplying its name as the single operand to the **scn** or **SCN** operator. This name must be the key of an entry in the **Pattern** subdictionary of the current resource dictionary (see Section 3.7.2, "Resource Dictionaries"), whose value is the stream object representing the pattern. Since the pattern defines its own color information, no additional operands representing color components are specified to **scn** or **SCN**. For example, if P1 is the name of a pattern resource in the current resource dictionary, the following code establishes it as the current nonstroking color:

```
/Pattern cs
/P1 scn
```

Subsequent executions of nonstroking painting operators, such as **f** (fill), **Tj** (paint text), or **Do** (paint external object) with an image mask, will use the designated pattern to tile the areas to be painted.

Example 4.19 defines a page (object 5) that paints a rectangle and a character glyph using a colored tiling pattern (object 15). Figure 4.17 shows the results.

Example 4.19

```
5  0  obj                          % Page object
   << /Type /Page
      /Parent  2 0 R
      /Resources  10 0 R
      /Contents  20 0 R
   >>
endobj

10  0  obj                         % Resource dictionary for page
   << /ProcSet  [/PDF /Text]
      /Font  << /F1  12 0 R >>
      /Pattern  << /P1  15 0 R >>
   >>
endobj

12  0  obj
   << /Type /Font
      /Subtype /Type1
      /BaseFont /Times–Roman
   >>
endobj
```

```
15  0  obj                                  % Pattern definition
    << /Type  /Pattern
        /PatternType  1                     % Tiling pattern
        /PaintType  1                       % Colored
        /TilingType  1
        /BBox  [0  0  60  60]
        /XStep  60
        /YStep  60
        /Resources  16 0 R
        /Length  404
    >>
stream
    0.3  g                                  % Set color for dark gray stars
    15.000  27.000  m                       % Construct star-shaped path
    7.947  5.292  l
    26.413  18.708  l
    3.587  18.708  l
    22.053  5.292  l
    f                                       % Fill with dark gray
    45.000  57.000  m                       % Construct star-shaped path
    37.947  35.292  l
    56.413  48.708  l
    33.587  48.708  l
    52.053  35.292  l
    f                                       % Fill with dark gray
    0.7  g                                  % Set color for light gray stars
    15.000  57.000  m                       % Construct star-shaped path
    7.947  35.292  l
    26.413  48.708  l
    3.587  48.708  l
    22.053  35.292  l
    f                                       % Fill with light gray
    45.000  27.000  m                       % Construct star-shaped path
    37.947  5.292  l
    56.413  18.708  l
    33.587  18.708  l
    52.053  5.292  l
    f                                       % Fill with light gray
endstream
endobj

16  0  obj                                  % Resource dictionary for pattern
    << /ProcSet  [/PDF] >>
endobj
```

```
20 0 obj                                  % Contents of page
   << /Length 246 >>
stream
   /Pattern cs                            % Set pattern color space
   /P1 scn                                % Set star pattern as nonstroking color
   0.0 G                                  % Set stroking color to black
   120 120 184 120 re                     % Construct rectangular path
   B                                      % Fill and stroke path
   BT                                     % Begin text object
      /F1 1 Tf                            % Set font and size
      270 0 0 270 160 100 Tm             % Set text matrix
      0.9 g                               % Set nonstroking color to light gray
      (A) Tj                              % Fill glyph with gray
      /Pattern cs                         % Set pattern color space
      /P1 scn                             % Set star pattern as nonstroking color
      0 0 TD                              % Return to start of line
      (A) Tj                              % Fill glyph with stars
   ET                                     % End text object
endstream
endobj
```

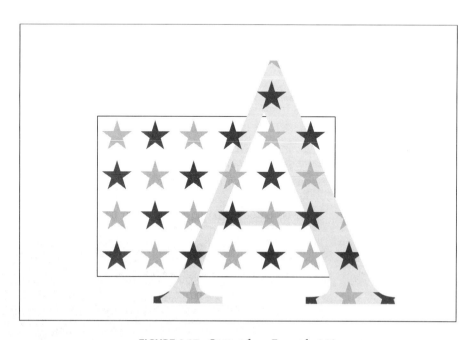

FIGURE 4.17 *Output from Example 4.19*

The pattern consists of four stars in two different colors. The pattern's content stream specifies the colors of the stars. Several features of Example 4.19 are noteworthy:

• The rectangle and the glyph representing the letter A are painted with the same pattern. The pattern cells align, even though the current transformation matrix is altered between the two uses of the pattern.

• The pattern cell does not completely cover the tile: it leaves the spaces between the stars unpainted. When the tiling pattern is used as a color, the existing background shows through these unpainted areas, as the appearance of the A glyph in Figure 4.17 demonstrates. The letter is first painted solid gray; when it is painted again with the star pattern, the gray continues to show between the stars.

Uncolored Tiling Patterns

An *uncolored tiling pattern* is one that has no inherent color: the color must be specified separately whenever the pattern is used. This type of pattern is identified by a pattern type of 1 and a paint type of 2 in the pattern dictionary. The pattern's content stream does not explicitly specify any colors; it can paint an image mask (see "Stencil Masking" on page 257), but no other kind of image. This provides a way to tile different regions of the page with pattern cells having the same shape but different colors.

A **Pattern** color space representing an uncolored tiling pattern requires a parameter: an object identifying the *underlying color space* in which the actual color of the pattern is to be specified. The underlying color space is given as the second element of the array that defines the **Pattern** color space. For example, the array

    [/Pattern /DeviceRGB]

defines a **Pattern** color space with **DeviceRGB** as its underlying color space.

*Note: The underlying color space cannot be another **Pattern** color space.*

Operands supplied to the **scn** or **SCN** operator in such a color space must include a color value in the underlying color space, specified by one or more numeric color components, as well as the name of a pattern object representing an uncolored tiling pattern. For example, if the current resource dictionary (see

Section 3.7.2, "Resource Dictionaries") defines Cs3 as the name of a **ColorSpace** resource whose value is the **Pattern** color space shown above, and P2 as a **Pattern** resource denoting an uncolored tiling pattern, then the code

```
/Cs3  cs
0.30  0.75  0.21  /P2  scn
```

establishes Cs3 as the current nonstroking color space and P2 as the current non-stroking color, to be painted in the color represented by the specified components in the **DeviceRGB** color space. Subsequent executions of nonstroking painting operators, such as **f** (fill), **Tj** (show text), and **Do** (paint external object) with an image mask, will use the designated pattern and color to tile the areas to be painted. The same pattern can be used repeatedly with a different color each time.

Example 4.20 defines an uncolored tiling pattern and then uses it to paint a rectangle and a circle in different colors; Figure 4.18 shows the results.

Example 4.20

```
5  0  obj                        % Page object
   <<  /Type  /Page
       /Parent  2 0 R
       /Resources  10 0 R
       /Contents  20 0 R
   >>
endobj

10  0  obj                       % Resource dictionary for page
   <<  /ProcSet  [/PDF]
       /ColorSpace  <<  /Cs9  12 0 R  >>
       /Pattern  <<  /P1  15 0 R  >>
   >>
endobj

12  0  obj                       % Color space
   [/Pattern  /DeviceGray]
endobj

15  0  obj                       % Pattern definition
   <<  /Type  /Pattern
       /PatternType  1           % Tiling pattern
       /PaintType  2             % Uncolored
       /TilingType  1
       /BBox  [−12  −12  12  12]
```

```
        /XStep  30
        /YStep  30
        /Resources  16 0 R
        /Length  95
   >>
stream
   0.000  12.000  m                    % Construct star-shaped path
   −7.053  −9.708  l
   11.413  3.708  l
   −11.413  3.708  l
   7.053  −9.708  l
   f                                   % Fill with current color
endstream
endobj

16  0  obj                            % Resource dictionary for pattern
   << /ProcSet  [/PDF] >>
endobj

20  0  obj                            % Contents of page
   << /Length  243 >>
stream
   0.9 g                              % Set nonstroking color to light gray
   140 210 170 −100 re                % Construct rectangular path
   f                                  % Fill with light gray
   /Cs9 cs                            % Set pattern color space
   1.0 /P1 scn                        % Set fill pattern and underlying color (white)
   140 110 170 100 re                 % Construct rectangular path
   f                                  % Fill with white stars
   0.0 /P1 scn                        % Set fill pattern and underlying color (black)
   0.0 G                              % Set stroking color to black
   285.00 185.04  m                   % Construct circular path
   285.00 218.16 258.12 245.04 225.00 245.04 c
   191.88 245.04 165.00 218.16 165.00 185.04 c
   165.00 151.92 191.88 125.04 225.00 125.04 c
   258.12 125.04 285.00 151.92 285.00 185.04 c
   B                                  % Fill and stroke path
endstream
endobj
```

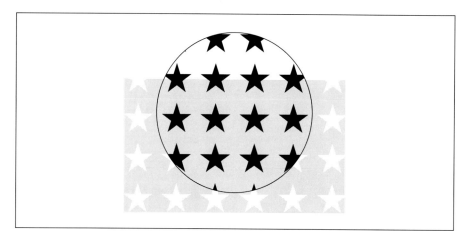

FIGURE 4.18 *Output from Example 4.20*

The pattern consists of a single star, which the pattern paints without specifying a color. Most of the remarks following Example 4.19 on page 206 also apply to Example 4.20. Additionally:

- The program paints the rectangle twice, first with light gray and then with the tiling pattern. To paint with the pattern, it supplies two operands to the **scn** operator: the number 1.0, denoting white in the underlying **DeviceGray** color space, and the name of the pattern.

- The program paints the interior of the circle with the same pattern, but with the underlying color set to 0.0 (black).

4.6.3 Shading Patterns

Shading patterns (PDF 1.3) provide a smooth transition between colors across an area to be painted, independent of the resolution of any particular output device and without specifying the number of steps in the color transition. Patterns of this type are described by pattern dictionaries with a pattern type of 2. Table 4.23 shows the contents of this type of dictionary.

TABLE 4.23   Entries in a type 2 pattern dictionary

KEY	TYPE	VALUE
Type	integer	*(Optional)* The type of PDF object that this dictionary describes; if present, must be **Pattern** for a pattern dictionary.
PatternType	integer	*(Required)* A code identifying the type of pattern that this dictionary describes; must be 2 for a shading pattern.
Shading	dictionary or stream	*(Required)* A shading object (see below) defining the shading pattern's gradient fill. The contents of the dictionary consist of the entries in Table 4.25 on page 216, plus those in one of Tables 4.26 to 4.31 on pages 219 to 235.
Matrix	array	*(Optional)* An array of six numbers defining the pattern matrix (see Section 4.6.1, "General Properties of Patterns"). Default value: the identity matrix [1 0 0 1 0 0].
ExtGState	dictionary	*(Optional)* A graphics state parameter dictionary (see Section 4.3.4, "Graphics State Parameter Dictionaries") containing graphics state parameters to be put into effect temporarily while the shading pattern is painted. Any parameters that are not so specified are inherited from the graphics state that was in effect at the beginning of the content stream in which the pattern is defined as a resource.

The most significant additional entry is **Shading**, whose value is a *shading object* defining the properties of the shading pattern's *gradient fill*. This is a complex "paint" that determines the type of color transition the shading pattern produces when painted across an area. A shading object may be a dictionary or a stream, depending on the type of shading; the term *shading dictionary* will be used generically in this section to refer to either a dictionary object or the dictionary portion of a stream object.

By setting a shading pattern as the current color in the graphics state, a PDF content stream can use it with painting operators such as **f** (fill), **S** (stroke), **Tj** (show text), or **Do** (paint external object) with an image mask to paint a path, character glyph, or mask with a smooth color transition. When a shading is used in this way, the geometry of the gradient fill is independent of that of the object being painted.

Shading Operator

When the area to be painted is a relatively simple shape whose geometry is the same as that of the gradient fill itself, the **sh** operator can be used instead of the usual painting operators. **sh** accepts a shading dictionary as an operand and applies the corresponding gradient fill directly to current user space. This operator does not require the creation of a pattern dictionary or a path and works without reference to the current color in the graphics state. Table 4.24 describes the **sh** operator.

*Note: Patterns defined by type 2 pattern dictionaries do not tile. To create a tiling pattern containing a gradient fill, invoke the **sh** operator from within the content stream of a type 1 (tiling) pattern.*

TABLE 4.24 Shading operator

OPERANDS	OPERATOR	DESCRIPTION
name	**sh**	*(PDF 1.3)* Paint the shape and color shading described by a shading dictionary, subject to the current clipping path. The current color in the graphics state is neither used nor altered. The effect is different from that of painting a path using a shading pattern as the current color.
		name is the name of a shading dictionary resource in the **Shading** subdictionary of the current resource dictionary (see Section 3.7.2, "Resource Dictionaries"). All coordinates in the shading dictionary are interpreted relative to the current user space. (By contrast, when a shading dictionary is used in a type 2 pattern, the coordinates are expressed in pattern space.) All colors are interpreted in the color space identified by the shading dictionary's **ColorSpace** entry (see Table 4.25 on page 216). The **Background** entry, if present, is ignored.
		This operator should be applied only to bounded or geometrically defined shadings. If applied to an unbounded shading, it will paint the shading's gradient fill across the entire clipping region, which may be time-consuming.

Shading Dictionaries

A shading dictionary specifies details of a particular gradient fill, including the type of shading to be used, the geometry of the area to be shaded, and the geometry of the gradient fill itself. Various shading types are available, depending on the value of the dictionary's **ShadingType** entry:

- *Function-based shadings* (type 1) define the color of every point in the domain using a mathematical function (not necessarily smooth or continuous).

- *Axial shadings* (type 2) define a color blend along a line between two points, optionally extended beyond the boundary points by continuing the boundary colors.

- *Radial shadings* (type 3) define a blend between two circles, optionally extended beyond the boundary circles by continuing the boundary colors. This type of shading is commonly used to represent three-dimensional spheres and cones.

- *Free-form Gouraud-shaded triangle meshes* (type 4) define a common construct used by many three-dimensional applications to represent complex colored and shaded shapes. Vertices are specified in free-form geometry.

- *Lattice-form Gouraud-shaded triangle meshes* (type 5) are based on the same geometrical construct as type 4, but with vertices specified as a pseudo-rectangular lattice.

- *Coons patch meshes* (type 6) construct a shading from one or more color patches, each bounded by four cubic Bézier curves.

- *Tensor-product patch meshes* (type 7) are similar to type 6, but with additional control points in each patch, affording greater control over color mapping.

Table 4.25 shows the entries that all shading dictionaries share in common; entries specific to particular shading types are described in the relevant sections below.

Note: *The term* target coordinate space, *used in many of the following descriptions, refers to the coordinate space into which a shading is painted. For shadings used with a type 2 pattern dictionary, this is the pattern coordinate space, discussed in Section 4.6.1, "General Properties of Patterns." For shadings used directly with the **sh** operator, it is the current user space.*

TABLE 4.25   Entries common to all shading dictionaries

KEY	TYPE	VALUE
ShadingType	integer	*(Required)* The shading type:

		1 Function-based shading 2 Axial shading 3 Radial shading 4 Free-form Gouraud-shaded triangle mesh 5 Lattice-form Gouraud-shaded triangle mesh 6 Coons patch mesh 7 Tensor-product patch mesh
ColorSpace	name or array	*(Required)* The color space in which color values are expressed. This may be any device, CIE-based, or special color space except a **Pattern** space. See "Color Space: Special Considerations," below, for further information.
Background	array	*(Optional)* An array of color components appropriate to the color space, specifying a single background color value. If present, this color is used before any painting operation involving the shading, to fill the entire area to be painted. The effect is as if the painting operation were performed twice: first with the background color and then again with the shading.
BBox	rectangle	*(Optional)* An array of four numbers giving the left, bottom, right, and top coordinates, respectively, of the shading's bounding box. The coordinates are interpreted in the shading's target coordinate space. If present, this bounding box is applied as a temporary clipping boundary when the shading is painted, in addition to the current clipping path and any other clipping boundaries in effect at that time.
AntiAlias	boolean	*(Optional)* A flag indicating whether to filter the shading function to prevent *aliasing* artifacts. The shading operators sample shading functions at a rate determined by the resolution of the output device. Aliasing can occur if the function is not smooth—that is, if it has a high spatial frequency relative to the sampling rate. Anti-aliasing can be computationally expensive and is usually unnecessary, since most shading functions are smooth enough, or are sampled at a high enough frequency, to avoid aliasing effects. Anti-aliasing may not be implemented on some output devices, in which case this flag is ignored. Default value: *false*.

Shading types 4 to 7 are defined by a stream containing descriptive data characterizing the shading's gradient fill. In these cases, the shading dictionary is also a stream dictionary and can contain any of the standard entries common to all streams (see Table 3.4 on page 35). In particular, it will always include a **Length** entry, which is required for all streams.

In addition, some shading dictionaries also include a **Function** entry whose value is a function (dictionary or stream) defining how colors vary across the area to be shaded. In such cases, the shading dictionary usually defines the geometry of the shading, while the function defines the color transitions across that geometry. The function is required for some types of shading and optional for others. Functions are described in detail in Section 3.9, "Functions."

Note: *Discontinuous color transitions, or those with high spatial frequency, may exhibit aliasing effects when painted at low effective resolutions.*

Color Space: Special Considerations

Conceptually, a shading determines a color value for each individual point within the area to be painted. In practice, however, the shading may actually be used to compute color values only for some subset of the points in the target area, with the colors of the intervening points determined by interpolation between the ones computed. Viewer applications are free to use this strategy as long as the interpolated color values approximate those defined by the shading to within the smoothness tolerance specified in the graphics state (see Section 6.5.2, "Smoothness Tolerance"). The **ColorSpace** entry common to all shading dictionaries not only defines the color space in which the shading specifies its color values, but also determines the color space in which color interpolation is performed.

Note: *Some shading types (4 to 7) perform interpolation on a parametric value supplied as* input *to the shading's color mapping function, as described in the relevant sections below. This form of interpolation is conceptually distinct from the interpolation described here, which operates on the* output *color values produced by the color mapping function and takes place within the shading's target color space.*

Gradient fills between colors defined by most shadings are implemented using a variety of interpolation algorithms, and these algorithms are sensitive to the characteristics of the color space. Linear interpolation, for example, may have observably different results when applied in a **DeviceCMYK** color space than in a **Lab** color space, even if the starting and ending colors are perceptually identical. The difference arises because the two color spaces are not linear relative to each other. Shadings are rendered according to the following rules:

- If **ColorSpace** is a device color space different from the native color space of the output device, color values in the shading will be converted to the native color space using the standard conversion formulas described in Section 6.2, "Conversions among Device Color Spaces." To optimize performance, these conversions may take place at any time (either before or after any interpolation on the color values in the shading). Thus, shadings defined with device color spaces may have color gradient fills that are less accurate and somewhat device-dependent. (This does not apply to axial and radial shadings—shading types 2 and 3—because those shading types perform gradient fill calculations on a single variable and then convert to parametric colors.)

- If **ColorSpace** is a CIE-based color space, all gradient fill calculations will be performed in that space. Conversion to device colors will occur only after all interpolation calculations have been performed. Thus, the color gradients will be device-independent for the colors generated at each point.

- If **ColorSpace** is a **Separation** or **DeviceN** color space and the specified colorants are supported, no color conversion calculations are needed. If the specified colorants are not supported (so that the space's alternate color space must be used), gradient fill calculations will be performed in the designated **Separation** or **DeviceN** color space before conversion to the alternate space. Thus, nonlinear tint transformation functions will be accommodated for the best possible representation of the shading.

- If **ColorSpace** is an **Indexed** color space, all color values specified in the shading will be immediately converted to the base color space. Depending on whether the base color space is a device or CIE-based space, gradient fill calculations will be performed as stated above. Interpolation never occurs in an **Indexed** color space, which is quantized and therefore inappropriate for calculations that assume a continuous range of colors. For similar reasons, an **Indexed** color space is not allowed in any shading whose color values are generated by a function; this applies to any shading dictionary that contains a **Function** entry.

Shading Types

In addition to the entries listed in Table 4.25 on page 216, all shading dictionaries have entries specific to the type of shading they represent, as indicated by the value of their **ShadingType** key. The following sections describe the available shading types and the dictionary entries specific to each.

Type 1 (Function-Based) Shadings

In type 1 (function-based) shadings, the color at every point in the domain is defined by a specified mathematical function. The function need not be smooth or continuous. This is the most general of the available shading types, and is useful for shadings that cannot be adequately described with any of the other types. Table 4.26 shows the shading dictionary entries specific to this type of shading, in addition to those common to all shading dictionaries (Table 4.25 on page 216).

Note: *This type of shading may not be used with an* **Indexed** *color space.*

TABLE 4.26 Additional entries specific to a type 1 shading dictionary

KEY	TYPE	VALUE
Domain	array	*(Optional)* An array of four numbers $[x_{min} \ x_{max} \ y_{min} \ y_{max}]$ specifying the rectangular domain of coordinates over which the color function(s) are defined. Default value: [0.0 1.0 0.0 1.0].
Matrix	array	*(Optional)* A transformation matrix mapping the coordinate space specified by the **Domain** entry into the shading's target coordinate space. For example, to map the domain rectangle [0.0 1.0 0.0 1.0] to a 1-inch square with lower-left corner at coordinates (100, 100) in default user space, the **Matrix** value would be [72 0 0 72 100 100]. Default value: the identity matrix [1 0 0 1 0 0].
Function	function	*(Required)* A 2-in, *n*-out function or an array of *n* 2-in, 1-out functions (where *n* is the number of color components in the shading dictionary's color space). Each function's domain must be a superset of that of the shading dictionary. If the value returned by the function for a given color component is out of range, it will be adjusted to the nearest valid value.

The domain rectangle (**Domain**) establishes an internal coordinate space for the shading that is independent of the target coordinate space in which it is to be painted. The color function(s) (**Function**) specify the color of the shading at each point within this domain rectangle. The transformation matrix (**Matrix**) then maps the domain rectangle into a corresponding rectangle or parallelogram in the target coordinate space. Points within the shading's bounding box (**BBox**) that fall outside this transformed domain rectangle will be painted with the shading's background color (**Background**); if the shading dictionary has no **Background** entry, such points will be left unpainted. If the function is undefined at any point within the declared domain rectangle, an error may occur, even if the corresponding transformed point falls outside the shading's bounding box.

Type 2 (Axial) Shadings

Type 2 (axial) shadings define a color blend that varies along a linear axis between two endpoints and extends indefinitely perpendicular to that axis. The shading may optionally be extended beyond either or both endpoints by continuing the boundary colors indefinitely. Table 4.27 shows the shading dictionary entries specific to this type of shading, in addition to those common to all shading dictionaries (Table 4.25 on page 216).

*Note: This type of shading may not be used with an **Indexed** color space.*

TABLE 4.27   Additional entries specific to a type 2 shading dictionary

KEY	TYPE	VALUE
Coords	array	*(Required)* An array of four numbers $[x_0 \ y_0 \ x_1 \ y_1]$ specifying the starting and ending coordinates of the axis, expressed in the shading's target coordinate space.
Domain	array	*(Optional)* An array of two numbers $[t_0 \ t_1]$ specifying the limiting values of a parametric variable t. The variable is considered to vary linearly between these two values as the color gradient varies between the starting and ending points of the axis. The variable t becomes the input argument to the color function(s). Default value: [0.0 1.0].
Function	function	*(Required)* A 1-in, n-out function or an array of n 1-in, 1-out functions (where n is the number of color components in the shading dictionary's color space). The function(s) are called with values of the parametric variable t in the domain defined by the **Domain** entry. Each function's domain must be a superset of that of the shading dictionary. If the value returned by the function for a given color component is out of range, it will be adjusted to the nearest valid value.
Extend	array	*(Optional)* An array of two boolean values specifying whether to extend the shading beyond the starting and ending points of the axis, respectively. Default value: [*false false*].

The color blend is accomplished by linearly mapping each point (x, y) along the axis between the endpoints (x_0, y_0) and (x_1, y_1) to a corresponding point in the domain specified by the shading dictionary's **Domain** entry. The points $(0, 0)$ and $(1, 0)$ in the domain correspond respectively to (x_0, y_0) and (x_1, y_1) on the axis. Since all points along a line in domain space perpendicular to the line from $(0, 0)$ to $(1, 0)$ will have the same color, only the new value of x needs to be computed:

$$x' = \frac{(x_1 - x_0) \times (x - x_0) + (y_1 - y_0) \times (y - y_0)}{(x_1 - x_0)^2 + (y_1 - y_0)^2}$$

The value of the parametric variable t is then determined from x' as follows:

• For $0 \leq x' \leq 1$, $t = t_0 + (t_1 - t_0) \times x'$.

• For $x' < 0$, if the first element of the **Extend** array is *true*, then $t = t_0$; otherwise, t is undefined and the point is left unpainted.

• For $x' > 1$, if the second element of the **Extend** array is *true*, then $t = t_1$; otherwise, t is undefined and the point is left unpainted.

The resulting value of t is then passed as input to the function(s) defined by the shading dictionary's **Function** entry, yielding the component values of the color with which to paint the point (x, y).

Type 3 (Radial) Shadings

Type 3 (radial) shadings define a color blend that varies between two circles. Shadings of this type are commonly used to depict three-dimensional spheres and cones. Table 4.28 shows the shading dictionary entries specific to this type of shading, in addition to those common to all shading dictionaries (Table 4.25 on page 216).

*Note: This type of shading may not be used with an **Indexed** color space.*

TABLE 4.28 **Additional entries specific to a type 3 shading dictionary**

KEY	TYPE	VALUE
Coords	array	*(Required)* An array of six numbers $[x_0\ y_0\ r_0\ x_1\ y_1\ r_1]$ specifying the centers and radii of the starting and ending circles, expressed in the shading's target coordinate space. The radii r_0 and r_1 must both be greater than or equal to 0. If one radius is 0, the corresponding circle is treated as a point; if both are 0, nothing is painted.
Domain	array	*(Optional)* An array of two numbers $[t_0\ t_1]$ specifying the limiting values of a parametric variable *t*. The variable is considered to vary linearly between these two values as the color gradient varies between the starting and ending circles. The variable *t* becomes the input argument to the color function(s). Default value: [0 1].
Function	function	*(Required)* A 1-in, *n*-out function or an array of *n* 1-in, 1-out functions (where *n* is the number of color components in the shading dictionary's color space). The function(s) are called with values of the parametric variable *t* in the domain defined by the shading dictionary's **Domain** entry. Each function's domain must be a superset of that of the shading dictionary. If the value returned by the function for a given color component is out of range, it will be adjusted to the nearest valid value.
Extend	array	*(Optional)* An array of two boolean values specifying whether to extend the shading beyond the starting and ending circles, respectively. Default value: [*false false*].

The color blend is based on a family of *blend circles* interpolated between the starting and ending circles that are defined by the shading dictionary's **Coords** entry. The blend circles are defined in terms of a subsidiary parametric variable

$$s = \frac{t - t_0}{t_1 - t_0}$$

which varies linearly between 0.0 and 1.0 as *t* varies across the domain from t_0 to t_1, as specified by the dictionary's **Domain** entry. The center and radius of each blend circle are given by the parametric equations

$$x_c(s) = x_0 + s \times (x_1 - x_0)$$
$$y_c(s) = y_0 + s \times (y_1 - y_0)$$
$$r(s) = r_0 + s \times (r_1 - r_0)$$

Each value of s between 0.0 and 1.0 determines a corresponding value of *t*, which is then passed as the input argument to the function(s) defined by the shading dictionary's **Function** entry. This yields the component values of the color with which to fill the corresponding blend circle. For values of *s* not lying between 0.0 and 1.0, the boolean elements of the shading dictionary's **Extend** array determine whether and how the shading will be extended. If the first of the two elements is *true*, the shading is extended beyond the defined starting circle to values of *s* less than 0.0; if the second element is *true*, the shading is extended beyond the defined ending circle to *s* values greater than 1.0.

Note that either of the starting and ending circles may be larger than the other. If the shading is extended at the smaller end, the family of blend circles continues as far as that value of *s* for which the radius of the blend circle $r(s) = 0$; if the shading is extended at the larger end, the blend circles continue as far as that *s* value for which $r(s)$ is large enough to encompass the shading's entire bounding box (**BBox**). Extending the shading can thus cause painting to extend beyond the areas defined by the two circles themselves.

Conceptually, all of the blend circles are painted in order of increasing values of *s*, from smallest to largest. Blend circles extending beyond the starting circle are painted in the same color defined by the shading dictionary's **Function** entry for the starting circle ($t = t_0$, $s = 0.0$); those extending beyond the ending circle are painted in the color defined for the ending circle ($t = t_1$, $s = 1.0$). The painting is opaque, with the color of each circle completely overlaying those preceding it; thus if a point lies within more than one blend circle, its final color will be that of the last of the enclosing circles to be painted, corresponding to the greatest value of *s*. Note the following points:

- If one of the starting and ending circles entirely contains the other, the shading will depict a sphere.

- If neither circle contains the other, the shading will depict a cone. If the starting circle is larger, the cone will appear to point out of the page; if the ending circle is larger, the cone will appear to point into the page.

Example 4.21 paints the leaf-covered branch shown in Figure 4.19. Each leaf is filled with the same radial shading (object number 5). The color function (object 10) is a stitching function (described in Section 3.9.3, "Type 3 (Stitching) Functions") whose two subfunctions (objects 11 and 12) are both exponential interpolation functions (see Section 3.9.2, "Type 2 (Exponential Interpolation)

Functions"). Each leaf is drawn as a path and then filled with the shading, using code such as that shown in Example 4.22 (where the name Sh1 is associated with object 5 by the **Shading** subdictionary of the current resource dictionary; see Section 3.7.2, "Resource Dictionaries").

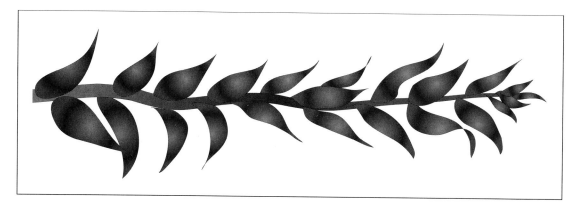

FIGURE 4.19 *Radial shading*

Example 4.21

```
5 0 obj                                           % Shading dictionary
   << /ShadingType 3
      /ColorSpace /DeviceCMYK
      /Coords [0.0 0.0 0.096 0.0 0.0 1.000]       % Concentric circles
      /Function 10 0 R
      /Extend [true true]
   >>
endobj

10 0 obj                                          % Color function
   << /FunctionType 3
      /Domain [0.0 1.0]
      /Functions [11 0 R 12 0 R]
      /Bounds [0.708]
      /Encode [1.0 0.0 0.0 1.0]
   >>
endobj
```

```
11  0  obj                                              % First subfunction
    <<  /FunctionType  2
        /Domain  [0.0  1.0]
        /C0  [0.929  0.357  1.000  0.298]
        /C1  [0.631  0.278  1.000  0.027]
        /N  1.048
    >>
endobj

12  0  obj                                              % Second subfunction
    <<  /FunctionType  2
        /Domain  [0.0  1.0]
        /C0  [0.929  0.357  1.000  0.298]
        /C1  [0.941  0.400  1.000  0.102]
        /N  1.374
    >>
endobj
```

Example 4.22

```
316.789  140.311  m                                         % Move to start of leaf
303.222  146.388  282.966  136.518  279.122  121.983  c     % Curved segment
277.322  120.182  l                                         % Straight line
285.125  122.688  291.441  121.716  298.156  119.386  c     % Curved segment
336.448  119.386  l                                         % Straight line
331.072  128.643  323.346  137.376  316.789  140.311  c     % Curved segment
W  n                                                        % Set clipping path
q                                                           % Save graphics state
    27.7843  0 .0000  0.0000  −27.7843  310.2461  121.1521  cm    % Set matrix
    /Sh1  sh                                                       % Paint shading
Q                                                                  % Restore graphics state
```

Type 4 Shadings (Free-Form Gouraud-Shaded Triangle Meshes)

Type 4 shadings (free-form Gouraud-shaded triangle meshes) are commonly used to represent complex colored and shaded three-dimensional shapes. The area to be shaded is defined by a path composed entirely of triangles. The color at each vertex of the triangles is specified, and a technique known as *Gouraud interpolation* is used to color the interiors. The interpolation functions defining the shading may be linear or nonlinear. Table 4.29 shows the entries specific to this type of shading dictionary, in addition to those common to all shading dictionaries (Table 4.25 on page 216) and stream dictionaries (Table 3.4 on page 35).

KEY	TYPE	VALUE
TABLE 4.29 Additional entries specific to a type 4 shading dictionary		
BitsPerCoordinate	integer	*(Required)* The number of bits used to represent each vertex coordinate. Valid values are 1, 2, 4, 8, 12, 16, 24, and 32.
BitsPerComponent	integer	*(Required)* The number of bits used to represent each color component. Valid values are 1, 2, 4, 8, 12, and 16.
BitsPerFlag	integer	*(Required)* The number of bits used to represent the edge flag for each vertex (see below). Valid values of **BitsPerFlag** are 2, 4, and 8, but only the least significant 2 bits in each flag value are used. Valid values for the edge flag itself are 0, 1, and 2.
Decode	rectangle	*(Required)* An array of numbers specifying how to map vertex coordinates and color components into the appropriate ranges of values. The decoding method is similar to that used in image dictionaries (see "Decode Arrays" on page 252). The ranges are specified as follows: $$[x_{min} \ x_{max} \ y_{min} \ y_{max} \ c_{1,min} \ c_{1,max} \ \cdots \ c_{n,min} \ c_{n,max}]$$ Note that only one pair of c values should be specified if a **Function** entry is present.
Function	function	*(Optional)* A 1-in, n-out function or an array of n 1-in, 1-out functions (where n is the number of color components in the shading dictionary's color space). If this entry is present, the color data for each vertex must be specified by a single parametric variable rather than by n separate color components; the designated function(s) will be called with each interpolated value of the parametric variable to determine the actual color at each point. Each input value will be forced into the range interval specified for the corresponding color component in the shading dictionary's **Decode** array. Each function's domain must be a superset of that interval. If the value returned by the function for a given color component is out of range, it will be adjusted to the nearest valid value. This entry may not be used with an **Indexed** color space.

Unlike shading types 1 to 3, types 4 to 7 are represented as streams. Each stream contains a sequence of vertex coordinates and color data that defines the triangle mesh. In a type 4 shading, each vertex is specified by the following values, in the order shown:

$$f \; x \; y \; c_1 \ldots c_n$$

where

f is the vertex's edge flag (discussed below)

x and y are its horizontal and vertical coordinates

$c_1 \ldots c_n$ are its color components

All vertex coordinates are expressed in the shading's target coordinate space. If the shading dictionary includes a **Function** entry, then only a single parametric value, t, is permitted for each vertex in place of the color components $c_1 \ldots c_n$.

The *edge flag* associated with each vertex determines the way it connects to the other vertices of the triangle mesh. A vertex v_a with an edge flag value $f_a = 0$ begins a new triangle, unconnected to any other. At least two more vertices (v_b and v_c) must be provided, but their edge flags will be ignored. These three vertices define a triangle (v_a, v_b, v_c), as shown in Figure 4.20.

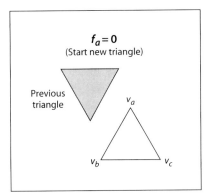

FIGURE 4.20 *Starting a new triangle in a free-form Gouraud-shaded triangle mesh*

Subsequent triangles are defined by a single new vertex combined with two vertices of the preceding triangle. Given triangle (v_a, v_b, v_c), where vertex v_a precedes vertex v_b in the data stream and v_b precedes v_c, a new vertex v_d can form a new triangle on side v_{bc} or side v_{ac}, as shown in Figure 4.21. (Side v_{ab} is assumed to be shared with a preceding triangle and so is not available for continuing the mesh.) If the edge flag is $f_d = 1$ (side v_{bc}), the next vertex forms the triangle (v_b, v_c, v_d); if the edge flag is $f_d = 2$ (side v_{ac}), the next vertex forms the triangle (v_a, v_c, v_d). An edge flag of $f_d = 0$ would start a new triangle, as described above.

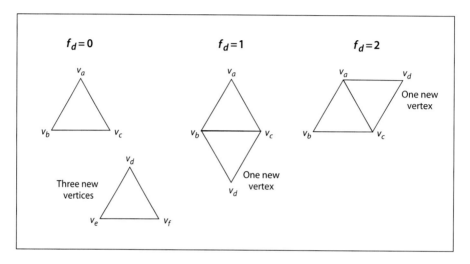

FIGURE 4.21 *Connecting triangles in a free-form Gouraud-shaded triangle mesh*

Complex shapes can be created by using the edge flags to control the edge on which subsequent triangles are formed. Figure 4.22 shows two simple examples. Mesh 1 begins with triangle 1 and uses the following edge flags to draw each succeeding triangle:

1 $(f_a = f_b = f_c = 0)$ 7 $(f_i = 2)$

2 $(f_d = 1)$ 8 $(f_j = 2)$

3 $(f_e = 1)$ 9 $(f_k = 2)$

4 $(f_f = 1)$ 10 $(f_l = 1)$

5 $(f_g = 1)$ 11 $(f_m = 1)$

6 $(f_h = 1)$

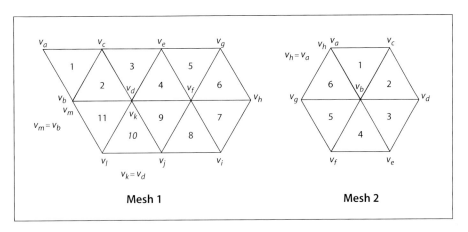

FIGURE 4.22 *Varying the value of the edge flag to create different shapes*

Mesh 2 again begins with triangle 1 and uses the edge flags

1 $(f_a = f_b = f_c = 0)$ 4 $(f_f = 2)$

2 $(f_d = 1)$ 5 $(f_g = 2)$

3 $(f_e = 2)$ 6 $(f_h = 2)$

The stream must provide vertex data for a whole number of triangles with appropriate edge flags; otherwise, an error will occur.

The data for each vertex consists of the following items, reading in sequence from higher-order to lower-order bit positions:

- An edge flag, expressed in **BitsPerFlag** bits

- A pair of horizontal and vertical coordinates, each expressed in **BitsPerCoordinate** bits

- A set of *n* color components (where *n* is the number of components in the shading's color space), each expressed in **BitsPerComponent** bits, in the order expected by the **sc** operator

Each set of vertex data must occupy a whole number of bytes; if the total number of bits required is not divisible by 8, the last data byte for each vertex is padded at the end with extra bits, which are ignored. The coordinates and color values are decoded according to the **Decode** array in the same way as in an image dictionary (see "Decode Arrays" on page 252).

If the shading dictionary contains a **Function** entry, the color data for each vertex must be specified by a single parametric value t, rather than by n separate color components. All linear interpolation within the triangle mesh is done using the t values; after interpolation, the results are passed to the function(s) specified in the **Function** entry to determine the color at each point.

Type 5 Shadings (Lattice-Form Gouraud-Shaded Triangle Meshes)

Type 5 shadings (lattice-form Gouraud-shaded triangle meshes) are similar to type 4, but instead of using free-form geometry, their vertices are arranged in a *pseudorectangular lattice*, which is topologically equivalent to a rectangular grid. The vertices are organized into rows, which need not be geometrically linear (see Figure 4.23). Table 4.30 shows the shading dictionary entries specific to this type of shading, in addition to those common to all shading dictionaries (Table 4.25 on page 216) and stream dictionaries (Table 3.4 on page 35).

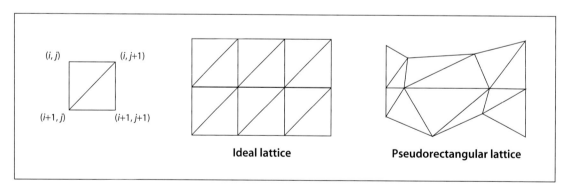

FIGURE 4.23 *Lattice-form triangular meshes*

231

TABLE 4.30 Additional entries specific to a type 5 shading dictionary

KEY	TYPE	VALUE
BitsPerCoordinate	integer	*(Required)* The number of bits used to represent each vertex coordinate. Valid values are 1, 2, 4, 8, 12, 16, 24, and 32.
BitsPerComponent	integer	*(Required)* The number of bits used to represent each color component. Valid values are 1, 2, 4, 8, 12, and 16.
VerticesPerRow	integer	*(Required)* The number of vertices in each row of the lattice; the value must be greater than or equal to 2. The number of rows need not be specified.
Decode	array	*(Required)* An array of numbers specifying how to map vertex coordinates and color components into the appropriate ranges of values. The decoding method is similar to that used in image dictionaries (see "Decode Arrays" on page 252). The ranges are specified as follows: $$[x_{min}\ x_{max}\ y_{min}\ y_{max}\ c_{1,min}\ c_{1,max}\ \cdots\ c_{n,min}\ c_{n,max}]$$ Note that only one pair of c values should be specified if a **Function** entry is present.
Function	function	*(Optional)* A 1-in, n-out function or an array of n 1-in, 1-out functions (where n is the number of color components in the shading dictionary's color space). If this entry is present, the color data for each vertex must be specified by a single parametric variable rather than by n separate color components; the designated function(s) will be called with each interpolated value of the parametric variable to determine the actual color at each point. Each input value will be forced into the range interval specified for the corresponding color component in the shading dictionary's **Decode** array. Each function's domain must be a superset of that interval. If the value returned by the function for a given color component is out of range, it will be adjusted to the nearest valid value. This entry may not be used with an **Indexed** color space.

The data stream for a type 5 shading has the same format as for type 4, except that it does not use edge flags to define the geometry of the triangle mesh. The data for each vertex thus consists of the following values, in the order shown:

$$x\ y\ c_1 \ldots c_n$$

where

x and y are the vertex's horizontal and vertical coordinates

$c_1 \ldots c_n$ are its color components

All vertex coordinates are expressed in the shading's target coordinate space. If the shading dictionary includes a **Function** entry, then only a single parametric value, t, is permitted for each vertex in place of the color components $c_1 \ldots c_n$.

The **VerticesPerRow** entry in the shading dictionary gives the number of vertices in each row of the lattice. All of the vertices in a row are specified sequentially, followed by those for the next row. Given m rows of k vertices each, the triangles of the mesh are constructed using the following triplets of vertices, as shown in Figure 4.23:

$$(V_{i,j}, V_{i,j+1}, V_{i+1,j}) \qquad \text{for } 0 \le i \le m-2,\ 0 \le j \le k-2$$
$$(V_{i,j+1}, V_{i+1,j}, V_{i+1,j+1})$$

See "Type 4 Shadings (Free-Form Gouraud-Shaded Triangle Meshes)" on page 225 for further details on the format of the vertex data.

Type 6 Shadings (Coons Patch Meshes)

Type 6 shadings (Coons patch meshes) are constructed from one or more *color patches*, each bounded by four cubic Bézier curves. Degenerate Bézier curves are allowed and are useful for certain graphical effects. At least one complete patch must be specified.

A Coons patch generally has two independent aspects:

• Colors are specified for each corner of the unit square, and bilinear interpolation is used to fill in colors over the entire unit square.

• Coordinates are mapped from the unit square into a four-sided patch whose sides are not necessarily linear. The mapping is continuous: the corners of the unit square map to corners of the patch, and the sides of the unit square map to sides of the patch, as shown in Figure 4.24.

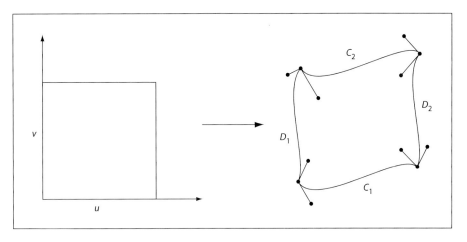

FIGURE 4.24 *Coordinate mapping from a unit square to a four-sided Coons patch*

The sides of the patch are given by four cubic Bézier curves, C_1, C_2, D_1, and D_2, defined over a pair of parametric variables u and v that vary horizontally and vertically across the unit square. The four corners of the Coons patch satisfy the equations

$$C_1(0) = D_1(0)$$
$$C_1(1) = D_2(0)$$
$$C_2(0) = D_1(1)$$
$$C_2(1) = D_2(1)$$

Two surfaces can be described that are linear interpolations between the boundary curves. Along the u axis, the surface S_C is defined by

$$S_C(u, v) = (1 - v) \times C_1(u) + v \times C_2(u)$$

Along the v axis, the surface S_D is given by

$$S_D(u, v) = (1 - u) \times D_1(v) + u \times D_2(v)$$

A third surface is the bilinear interpolation of the four corners:

$$S_B(u, v) = (1 - v) \times [(1 - u) \times C_1(0) + u \times C_1(1)]$$
$$+ v \times [(1 - u) \times C_2(0) + u \times C_2(1)]$$

The coordinate mapping for the shading is given by the surface S, defined as

$$S = S_C + S_D - S_B$$

This defines the geometry of each patch. A patch mesh is constructed from a sequence of one or more such colored patches.

Patches can sometimes appear to fold over on themselves—for example, if a boundary curve intersects itself. As the value of parameter u or v increases in parameter space, the location of the corresponding pixels in device space may change direction, so that new pixels are mapped onto previous pixels already mapped. If more than one point (u, v) in parameter space is mapped to the same point in device space, the point selected will be the one with the largest value of v; if multiple points have the same v, the one with the largest value of u will be selected. If one patch overlaps another, the patch that appears later in the data stream paints over the earlier one.

Note also that the patch is a control surface, rather than a painting geometry. The outline of a projected square (that is, the painted area) might not be the same as the patch boundary if, for example, the patch folds over on itself, as shown in Figure 4.25.

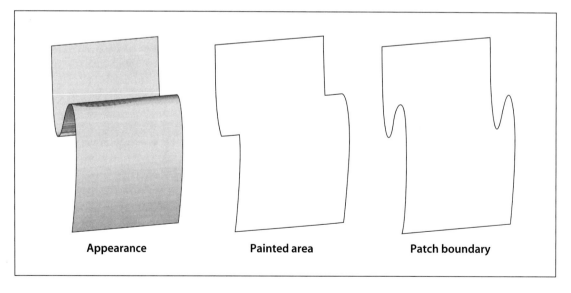

Appearance   **Painted area**   **Patch boundary**

FIGURE 4.25 *Painted area and boundary of a Coons patch*

Table 4.31 shows the shading dictionary entries specific to this type of shading, in addition to those common to all shading dictionaries (Table 4.25 on page 216) and stream dictionaries (Table 3.4 on page 35).

TABLE 4.31 **Additional entries specific to a type 6 shading dictionary**

KEY	TYPE	VALUE
BitsPerCoordinate	integer	*(Required)* The number of bits used to represent each geometric coordinate. Valid values are 1, 2, 4, 8, 12, 16, 24, and 32.
BitsPerComponent	integer	*(Required)* The number of bits used to represent each color component. Valid values are 1, 2, 4, 8, 12, and 16.
BitsPerFlag	integer	*(Required)* The number of bits used to represent the edge flag for each patch (see below). Valid values of **BitsPerFlag** are 2, 4, and 8, but only the least significant 2 bits in each flag value are used. Valid values for the edge flag itself are 0, 1, 2, and 3.
Decode	array	*(Required)* An array of numbers specifying how to map coordinates and color components into the appropriate ranges of values. The decoding method is similar to that used in image dictionaries (see "Decode Arrays" on page 252). The ranges are specified as follows: $$[x_{min}\ x_{max}\ y_{min}\ y_{max}\ c_{1,min}\ c_{1,max}\ \cdots\ c_{n,min}\ c_{n,max}]$$ Note that only one pair of *c* values should be specified if a **Function** entry is present.
Function	function	*(Optional)* A 1-in, *n*-out function or an array of *n* 1-in, 1-out functions (where *n* is the number of color components in the shading dictionary's color space). If this entry is present, the color data for each vertex must be specified by a single parametric variable rather than by *n* separate color components; the designated function(s) will be called with each interpolated value of the parametric variable to determine the actual color at each point. Each input value will be forced into the range interval specified for the corresponding color component in the shading dictionary's **Decode** array. Each function's domain must be a superset of that interval. If the value returned by the function for a given color component is out of range, it will be adjusted to the nearest valid value. This entry may not be used with an **Indexed** color space.

The data stream provides a sequence of Bézier control points and color values that define the shape and colors of each patch. All of a patch's control points are given first, followed by the color values for its corners. Note that this differs from a triangle mesh (shading types 4 and 5), in which the coordinates and color of each vertex are given together. All control point coordinates are expressed in the shading's target coordinate space.

As in free-form triangle meshes (type 4), each patch has an *edge flag* that tells which edge, if any, it shares with the previous patch. An edge flag of 0 begins a new patch, unconnected to any other. This must be followed by 12 pairs of coordinates, $x_1 y_1$ $x_2 y_2$ ... $x_{12} y_{12}$, which specify the Bézier control points that define the four boundary curves. Figure 4.26 shows how these control points correspond to the cubic Bézier curves C_1, C_2, D_1, and D_2 identified in Figure 4.24 on page 233. Color values are then given for the four corners of the patch, in the same order as the control points corresponding to the corners. Thus, c_1 is the color at coordinates (x_1, y_1), c_2 at (x_4, y_4), c_3 at (x_7, y_7), and c_4 at (x_{10}, y_{10}), as shown in the figure.

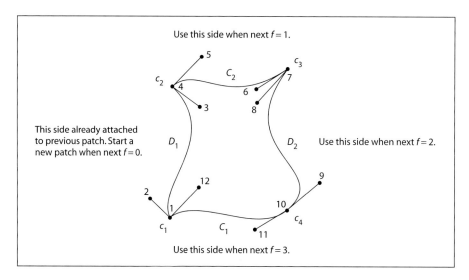

FIGURE 4.26 *Color values and edge flags in Coons patch meshes*

Figure 4.26 also shows how nonzero values of the edge flag ($f = 1, 2,$ or 3) connect a new patch to one of the edges of the previous patch. In this case, some of the previous patch's control points serve implicitly as control points for the new patch as well (see Figure 4.27), and so are not explicitly repeated in the data stream. Table 4.32 summarizes the required data values for various values of the edge flag.

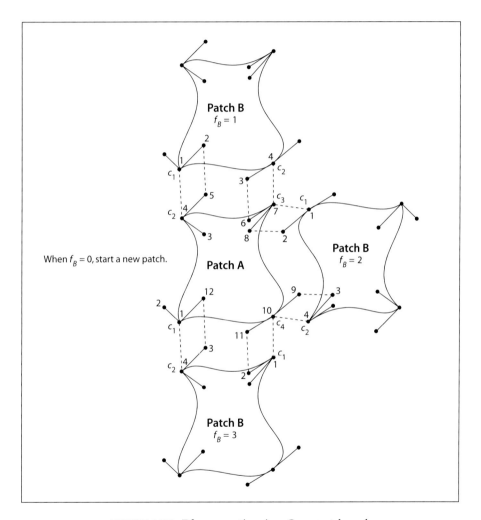

FIGURE 4.27 *Edge connections in a Coons patch mesh*

TABLE 4.32 Data values in a Coons patch mesh

EDGE FLAG	NEXT SET OF DATA VALUES
$f = 0$	$x_1\ y_1\ x_2\ y_2\ x_3\ y_3\ x_4\ y_4\ x_5\ y_5\ x_6\ y_6$ $x_7\ y_7\ x_8\ y_8\ x_9\ y_9\ x_{10}\ y_{10}\ x_{11}\ y_{11}\ x_{12}\ y_{12}$ $c_1\ c_2\ c_3\ c_4$ New patch; no implicit values
$f = 1$	$x_5\ y_5\ x_6\ y_6\ x_7\ y_7\ x_8\ y_8\ x_9\ y_9\ x_{10}\ y_{10}\ x_{11}\ y_{11}\ x_{12}\ y_{12}$ $c_3\ c_4$ Implicit values: $(x_1, y_1) = (x_4, y_4)$ previous $\quad\quad c_1 = c_2$ previous $(x_2, y_2) = (x_5, y_5)$ previous $\quad\quad c_2 = c_3$ previous $(x_3, y_3) = (x_6, y_6)$ previous $(x_4, y_4) = (x_7, y_7)$ previous
$f = 2$	$x_5\ y_5\ x_6\ y_6\ x_7\ y_7\ x_8\ y_8\ x_9\ y_9\ x_{10}\ y_{10}\ x_{11}\ y_{11}\ x_{12}\ y_{12}$ $c_3\ c_4$ Implicit values: $(x_1, y_1) = (x_7, y_7)$ previous $\quad\quad c_1 = c_3$ previous $(x_2, y_2) = (x_8, y_8)$ previous $\quad\quad c_2 = c_4$ previous $(x_3, y_3) = (x_9, y_9)$ previous $(x_4, y_4) = (x_{10}, y_{10})$ previous
$f = 3$	$x_5\ y_5\ x_6\ y_6\ x_7\ y_7\ x_8\ y_8\ x_9\ y_9\ x_{10}\ y_{10}\ x_{11}\ y_{11}\ x_{12}\ y_{12}$ $c_3\ c_4$ Implicit values: $(x_1, y_1) = (x_{10}, y_{10})$ previous $\quad\quad c_1 = c_4$ previous $(x_2, y_2) = (x_{11}, y_{11})$ previous $\quad\quad c_2 = c_1$ previous $(x_3, y_3) = (x_{12}, y_{12})$ previous $(x_4, y_4) = (x_1, y_1)$ previous

If the shading dictionary contains a **Function** entry, the color data for each corner of a patch must be specified by a single parametric value t, rather than by n separate color components $c_1 \ldots c_n$. All linear interpolation within the mesh is done using the t values; after interpolation, the results are passed to the function(s) specified in the **Function** entry to determine the color at each point.

Type 7 Shadings (Tensor-Product Patch Meshes)

Type 7 shadings (tensor-product patch meshes) are identical to type 6, except that they are based on a bicubic tensor-product patch defined by 16 control points, instead of the 12 control points that define a Coons patch. The shading dictionaries representing the two patch types differ only in the value of the **ShadingType** entry and in the number of control points specified for each patch in the data stream. Although the Coons patch is more concise and easier to use, the tensor-product patch affords greater control over color mapping.

Note: *The data format for type 7 shadings (as for types 4 through 6) is the same in PDF as it is in PostScript. However, the numbering and order of control points was described incorrectly in the first printing of the* PostScript Language Reference, Third Edition. *That description has been corrected here.*

Like the Coons patch mapping, the tensor-product patch mapping is controlled by the location and shape of four cubic Bézier curves marking the boundaries of the patch. However, the tensor-product patch has four additional, "internal" control points to adjust the mapping. The 16 control points can be arranged in a 4-by-4 array indexed by row and column, as follows (see Figure 4.28):

$$
\begin{array}{cccc}
p_{03} & p_{13} & p_{23} & p_{33} \\
p_{02} & p_{12} & p_{22} & p_{32} \\
p_{01} & p_{11} & p_{21} & p_{31} \\
p_{00} & p_{10} & p_{20} & p_{30}
\end{array}
$$

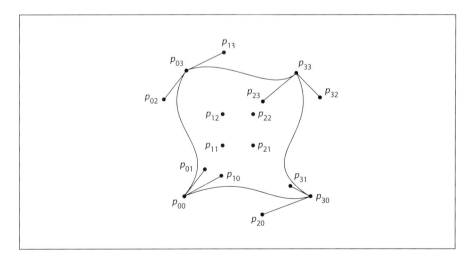

FIGURE 4.28 *Control points in a tensor-product mesh*

As in a Coons patch mesh, the geometry of the tensor-product patch is described by a surface defined over a pair of parametric variables, u and v, which vary horizontally and vertically across the unit square. The surface is defined by the equation

$$S(u, v) = \sum_{i=0}^{3} \sum_{j=0}^{3} p_{ij} \times B_i(u) \times B_j(v)$$

where p_{ij} is the control point in column i and row j of the tensor, and B_i and B_j are the *Bernstein polynomials*

$$B_0(t) = (1-t)^3$$

$$B_1(t) = 3t \times (1-t)^2$$

$$B_2(t) = 3t^2 \times (1-t)$$

$$B_3(t) = t^3$$

Since each point p_{ij} is actually a pair of coordinates (x_{ij}, y_{ij}), the surface can also be expressed as

$$x(u, v) = \sum_{i=0}^{3} \sum_{j=0}^{3} x_{ij} \times B_i(u) \times B_j(v)$$

$$y(u, v) = \sum_{i=0}^{3} \sum_{j=0}^{3} y_{ij} \times B_i(u) \times B_j(v)$$

The geometry of the tensor-product patch can be visualized in terms of a cubic Bézier curve moving from the bottom boundary of the patch to the top. At the bottom and top, the control points of this curve coincide with those of the patch's bottom ($p_{00} \dots p_{30}$) and top ($p_{03} \dots p_{33}$) boundary curves, respectively. As the curve moves from the bottom edge of the patch to the top, each of its four control points follows a trajectory that is in turn a cubic Bézier curve defined by the four control points in the corresponding column of the array. That is, the starting point of the moving curve follows the trajectory defined by control points $p_{00} \dots p_{03}$, the trajectory of the ending point is defined by points $p_{30} \dots p_{33}$, and those of the two intermediate control points by $p_{10} \dots p_{13}$ and $p_{20} \dots p_{23}$. Equivalently, the patch can be considered to be traced by a cubic Bézier curve moving from the left edge to the right, with its control points following the trajectories defined by the rows of the coordinate array instead of the columns.

The Coons patch (type 6) is actually a special case of the tensor-product patch (type 7) in which the four internal control points $(p_{11}, p_{12}, p_{21}, p_{22})$ are implicitly defined by the boundary curves. The values of the internal control points are given by the equations

$$p_{11} = S(\tfrac{1}{3}, \tfrac{1}{3})$$
$$p_{12} = S(\tfrac{1}{3}, \tfrac{2}{3})$$
$$p_{21} = S(\tfrac{2}{3}, \tfrac{1}{3})$$
$$p_{22} = S(\tfrac{2}{3}, \tfrac{2}{3})$$

where S is the Coons surface equation

$$S = S_C + S_D - S_B$$

discussed above under "Type 6 Shadings (Coons Patch Meshes)" on page 232. In the more general tensor-product patch, the values of these four points are unrestricted.

The coordinates of the control points in a tensor-product patch are actually specified in the shading's data stream in the following order:

4	5	6	7
3	14	15	8
2	13	16	9
1	12	11	10

All control point coordinates are expressed in the shading's target coordinate space. These are followed by the color values for the four corners of the patch, in the same order as the corners themselves. If the patch's edge flag f is 0, all 16 control points and four corner colors must be explicitly specified in the data stream; if f is 1, 2, or 3, the control points and colors for the patch's shared edge are implicitly understood to be the same as those along the specified edge of the previous patch, and are not repeated in the data stream. Table 4.33 summarizes the data values for various values of the edge flag f, expressed in terms of the row and column indices used in Figure 4.28 above.

TABLE 4.33   Data values in a tensor-product patch mesh

EDGE FLAG	NEXT SET OF DATA VALUES
$f = 0$	x_{00} y_{00} x_{01} y_{01} x_{02} y_{02} x_{03} y_{03} x_{13} y_{13} x_{23} y_{23} x_{33} y_{33} x_{32} y_{32} x_{31} y_{31} x_{30} y_{30} x_{20} y_{20} x_{10} y_{10} x_{11} y_{11} x_{12} y_{12} x_{22} y_{22} x_{21} y_{21} c_{00} c_{03} c_{33} c_{30} New patch; no implicit values

$f = 1$

x_{13} y_{13} x_{23} y_{23} x_{33} y_{33} x_{32} y_{32} x_{31} y_{31} x_{30} y_{30}
x_{20} y_{20} x_{10} y_{10} x_{11} y_{11} x_{12} y_{12} x_{22} y_{22} x_{21} y_{21}
c_{33} c_{30}

Implicit values:

$(x_{00}, y_{00}) = (x_{03}, y_{03})$ previous $c_{00} = c_{03}$ previous
$(x_{01}, y_{01}) = (x_{13}, y_{13})$ previous $c_{03} = c_{33}$ previous
$(x_{02}, y_{02}) = (x_{23}, y_{23})$ previous
$(x_{03}, y_{03}) = (x_{33}, y_{33})$ previous

$f = 2$

x_{13} y_{13} x_{23} y_{23} x_{33} y_{33} x_{32} y_{32} x_{31} y_{31} x_{30} y_{30}
x_{20} y_{20} x_{10} y_{10} x_{11} y_{11} x_{12} y_{12} x_{22} y_{22} x_{21} y_{21}
c_{33} c_{30}

Implicit values:

$(x_{00}, y_{00}) = (x_{33}, y_{33})$ previous $c_{00} = c_{33}$ previous
$(x_{01}, y_{01}) = (x_{32}, y_{32})$ previous $c_{03} = c_{30}$ previous
$(x_{02}, y_{02}) = (x_{31}, y_{31})$ previous
$(x_{03}, y_{03}) = (x_{30}, y_{30})$ previous

$f = 3$

x_{13} y_{13} x_{23} y_{23} x_{33} y_{33} x_{32} y_{32} x_{31} y_{31} x_{30} y_{30}
x_{20} y_{20} x_{10} y_{10} x_{11} y_{11} x_{12} y_{12} x_{22} y_{22} x_{21} y_{21}
c_{33} c_{30}

Implicit values:

$(x_{00}, y_{00}) = (x_{30}, y_{30})$ previous $c_{00} = c_{30}$ previous
$(x_{01}, y_{01}) = (x_{20}, y_{20})$ previous $c_{03} = c_{00}$ previous
$(x_{02}, y_{02}) = (x_{10}, y_{10})$ previous
$(x_{03}, y_{03}) = (x_{00}, y_{00})$ previous

4.7 External Objects

An *external object* (commonly called an *XObject*) is a graphics object whose contents are defined by a self-contained content stream, separate from the content stream in which it is used. There are three types of external object:

- An *image XObject* (Section 4.8.4, "Image Dictionaries") represents a sampled visual image such as a photograph.

- A *form XObject* (Section 4.9, "Form XObjects") is a self-contained description of an arbitrary sequence of graphics objects.

- A *PostScript XObject* (Section 4.10, "PostScript XObjects") contains a fragment of code expressed in the PostScript page description language.

Any XObject can be painted as part of another content stream by means of the **Do** operator (see Table 4.34). This operator applies to any type of XObject—image, form, or PostScript. The syntax is the same in all cases, though details of the operator's behavior differ depending on the type. (See implementation note 32 in Appendix H.)

TABLE 4.34 XObject operator

OPERANDS	OPERATOR	DESCRIPTION
name	**Do**	Paint the specified XObject. The operand *name* must appear as a key in the **XObject** subdictionary of the current resource dictionary (see Section 3.7.2, "Resource Dictionaries"); the associated value must be a stream whose **Type** entry, if present, is **XObject**. The effect of **Do** depends on the value of the XObject's **Subtype** entry, which may be **Image** (see Section 4.8.4, "Image Dictionaries"), **Form** (Section 4.9, "Form XObjects"), or **PS** (Section 4.10, "PostScript XObjects").

4.8 Images

PDF's painting operators include general facilities for dealing with sampled images. A *sampled image* (or just *image* for short) is a rectangular array of *sample values*, each representing a color. The image may approximate the appearance of some natural scene obtained through an input scanner or a video camera, or it may be generated synthetically.

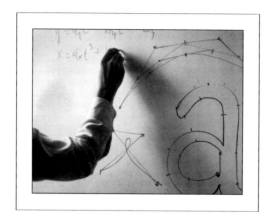

FIGURE 4.29 *Typical sampled image*

An image is defined by a sequence of samples obtained by scanning the image array in row or column order. Each sample in the array consists of as many color components as are needed for the color space in which they are specified—for example, one component for **DeviceGray**, three for **DeviceRGB**, four for **Device-CMYK**, or whatever number is required by a particular **DeviceN** space. Each component is a 1-, 2-, 4-, or 8-bit integer, permitting the representation of 2, 4, 16, or 256 distinct values for each component.

PDF provides two means for specifying images:

• An *image XObject* (described in Section 4.8.4, "Image Dictionaries") is a stream object whose dictionary specifies attributes of the image and whose data contains the image samples. Like all external objects, it is painted on the page by invoking the **Do** operator in a content stream (see Section 4.7, "External Objects"). Image XObjects have other uses as well, such as for alternate images (see "Alternate Images" on page 255), image masks (Section 4.8.5, "Masked Images"), and thumbnail images (Section 7.2.3, "Thumbnail Images").

- An *in-line image* is a small image that is completely defined—both attributes and data—directly in-line within a content stream. The kinds of image that can be represented in this way are limited; see Section 4.8.6, "In-Line Images," for details.

4.8.1 Image Parameters

The properties of an image—resolution, orientation, scanning order, and so forth—are entirely independent of the characteristics of the raster output device on which the image is to be rendered. A PDF viewer application usually renders images by a sampling technique that attempts to approximate the color values of the source as accurately as possible. The actual accuracy achieved depends on the resolution and other properties of the output device.

To paint an image, four interrelated items must be specified:

- The format of the image: number of columns (width), number of rows (height), number of color components per sample, and number of bits per color component

- The sample data constituting the image's visual content

- The correspondence between coordinates in user space and those in the image's own internal coordinate space, defining the region of user space that will receive the image

- The mapping from color component values in the image data to component values in the image's color space

All of these items are specified explicitly or implicitly by an image XObject or an in-line image.

Note: For convenience, the following sections refer consistently to the object defining an image as an image dictionary. *Although this term properly refers only to the dictionary portion of the stream object representing an image XObject, it should be understood to apply equally to the stream's data portion or to the parameters and data of an in-line image.*

4.8.2 Sample Representation

The source format for an image can be described by four parameters:

- The width of the image in samples
- The height of the image in samples
- The number of color components per sample
- The number of bits per color component

The image dictionary specifies the width, the height, and the number of bits per component explicitly; the number of color components can be inferred from the color space specified in the dictionary.

Sample data is represented as a stream of bytes, interpreted as 8-bit unsigned integers in the range 0 to 255. The bytes constitute a continuous bit stream, with the high-order bit of each byte first. This bit stream, in turn, is divided into units of n bits each, where n is the number of bits per component. Byte boundaries are ignored, except that each row of sample data must begin on a byte boundary. If the number of data bits per row is not a multiple of 8, the end of the row is padded with extra bits to fill out the last byte. A PDF viewer application ignores these padding bits.

Each n-bit unit within the bit stream is interpreted as an unsigned integer in the range 0 to $2^n - 1$, with the high-order bit first; the image dictionary's **Decode** entry maps this to a color component value, equivalent to what could be used with color operators such as **sc** or **g**. Color components are interleaved sample by sample; for example, in a three-component *RGB* image, the red, green, and blue components for one sample are followed by the red, green, and blue components for the next.

Normally, the color samples in an image are interpreted according to the color space specified in the image dictionary (see Section 4.5, "Color Spaces"), without reference to the color parameters in the graphics state. However, if the image dictionary's **ImageMask** entry is *true*, the sample data is interpreted as a *stencil mask* for applying the graphics state's nonstroking color parameters (see "Stencil Masking" on page 257).

4.8.3 Image Coordinate System

Each image has its own internal coordinate system, or *image space*. The image occupies a rectangle in image space w units wide and h units high, where w and h are the width and height of image in samples. Each sample occupies one square unit. The coordinate origin $(0, 0)$ is at the upper-left corner of the image, with coordinates ranging from 0 to w horizontally and 0 to h vertically.

The image's sample data is ordered by row, with the horizontal coordinate varying most rapidly. This is shown in Figure 4.30, where the numbers inside the squares indicate the order of the samples, counting from 0. The upper-left corner of the first sample is at coordinates $(0, 0)$, the second at $(1, 0)$, and so on through the last sample of the first row, whose upper-left corner is at $(w - 1, 0)$ and whose upper-right corner is at $(w, 0)$. The next samples after that are at coordinates $(0, 1)$, $(1, 1)$, and so on, until the final sample of the image, whose upper-left corner is at $(w - 1, h - 1)$ and whose lower-right corner is at (w, h).

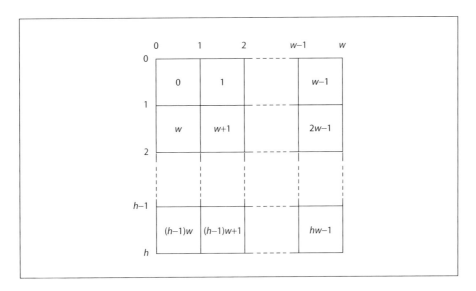

FIGURE 4.30 *Source image coordinate system*

Note: The image coordinate system and scanning order imposed by PDF do not preclude using different conventions in the actual image. Coordinate transformations can be used to map from other conventions to the PDF convention.

The correspondence between image space and user space is constant: the unit square of user space, bounded by user coordinates $(0, 0)$ and $(1, 1)$, corresponds to the boundary of the image in image space (see Figure 4.31). Following the normal convention for user space, the coordinate $(0, 0)$ is at the *lower-left* corner of this square, corresponding to coordinates $(0, h)$ in image space. The transformation from image space to user space could be described by the matrix $[1/w \ 0 \ 0 \ -1/h \ 0 \ 1]$.

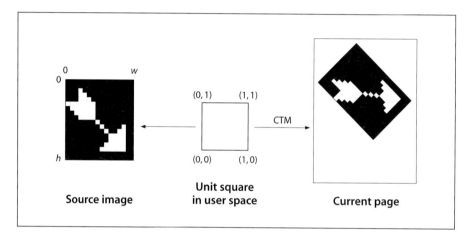

FIGURE 4.31 *Mapping the source image*

An image can be placed on the output page in any desired position, orientation, and size by using the **cm** operator to modify the current transformation matrix (CTM) so as to map the unit square of user space to the rectangle or parallelogram in which the image is to be painted. Typically, this is done within a pair of **q** and **Q** operators to isolate the effect of the transformation, which can include translation, rotation, reflection, and skew (see Section 4.2, "Coordinate Systems"). For example, if the **XObject** subdictionary of the current resource dictionary defines the name Image1 to denote an image XObject, the code shown in Example 4.23 paints the image in a rectangle whose lower-left corner is at coordinates $(100, 200)$, that is rotated 45 degrees counterclockwise, and that is 150 units wide and 80 units high.

Example 4.23

```
q                              % Save graphics state
    1 0 0 1 100 200 cm         % Translate
    0.7071 0.7071 −0.7071 0.7071 0 0 cm   % Rotate
    150 0 0 80 0 0 cm          % Scale
    /Image1 Do                 % Paint image
Q                              % Restore graphics state
```

(As discussed in Section 4.2.3, "Transformation Matrices," these three transformations could be combined into one.) Of course, if the aspect ratio (width to height) of the original image in this example is different from 150:80, the result will be distorted.

4.8.4 Image Dictionaries

Table 4.35 lists the entries in an image dictionary (that is, in the dictionary portion of a stream representing an image XObject). There are many relationships among these entries, and the current color space may limit the choices for some of them. Attempting to use an image dictionary whose entries are inconsistent with each other or with the current color space will cause an error.

Note: *The entries described here are those that are appropriate for a base image—one that is invoked directly with the **Do** operator. Some of these entries are not relevant for images used in other ways, such as for alternate images (see "Alternate Images" on page 255), image masks (Section 4.8.5, "Masked Images"), or thumbnail images (Section 7.2.3, "Thumbnail Images"). Except as noted, such irrelevant entries are simply ignored.*

TABLE 4.35 Entries in an image dictionary

KEY	TYPE	VALUE
Type	name	(*Optional*) The type of PDF object that this dictionary describes; if present, must be **XObject** for an image XObject.
Subtype	name	(*Required*) The type of XObject that this dictionary describes; must be **Image** for an image XObject.
Width	integer	(*Required*) The width of the image, in samples.
Height	integer	(*Required*) The height of the image, in samples.

ColorSpace	name or array	(*Required except for image masks; not allowed for image masks*) The color space in which image samples are specified. This may be any type of color space except **Pattern**.
BitsPerComponent	integer	(*Required except for image masks; optional for image masks*) The number of bits used to represent each color component. Only a single value may be specified; the number of bits is the same for all color components. Valid values are 1, 2, 4, and 8. If **ImageMask** is *true*, this entry is optional, and if specified, its value must be 1.
		If the image stream uses a filter, the value of **BitsPerComponent** must be consistent with the size of the data samples that the filter delivers. In particular, a **CCITTFaxDecode** filter always delivers 1-bit samples, a **RunLengthDecode** or **DCTDecode** filter delivers 8-bit samples, and an **LZWDecode** or **FlateDecode** filter delivers samples of a specified size if a predictor function is used.
Intent	name	(*Optional; PDF 1.1*) The name of a color rendering intent to be used in rendering the image (see "Rendering Intents" on page 179). Default value: the rendering intent parameter in the graphics state.
ImageMask	boolean	(*Optional*) A flag indicating whether the image is to be treated as an image mask (see Section 4.8.5, "Masked Images"). If this flag is *true*, the value of **BitsPerComponent** must be 1 and **Mask** and **ColorSpace** should not be specified; unmasked areas will be painted using the current nonstroking color. Default value: *false*.
Mask	stream or array	(*Optional except for image masks; not allowed for image masks; PDF 1.3*) An image XObject defining an image mask to be applied to this image (see "Explicit Masking" on page 258), or an array specifying a range of colors to be applied to it as a color key mask (see "Color Key Masking" on page 259). If **ImageMask** is *true*, this entry must not be present. (See implementation note 33 in Appendix H.)
Decode	array	(*Optional*) An array of numbers describing how to map image samples into the range of values appropriate for the image's color space (see "Decode Arrays," below). If **ImageMask** is *true*, the array must be either [0 1] or [1 0]; otherwise, its length must be twice the number of color components required by **ColorSpace**. Default value: see "Decode Arrays" on page 252.
Interpolate	boolean	(*Optional*) A flag indicating whether image interpolation is to be performed (see "Image Interpolation" on page 255). Default value: *false*.

Alternates	array	*(Optional; PDF 1.3)* An array of alternate image dictionaries for this image (see "Alternate Images" on page 255). The order of elements within the array has no significance. This entry may not be present in an image XObject that is itself an alternate image.
Name	name	*(Required in PDF 1.0; optional otherwise)* The name by which this image XObject is referenced in the **XObject** subdictionary of the current resource dictionary (see Section 3.7.2, "Resource Dictionaries"). **Note:** *This entry is obsolescent and its use is no longer recommended. (See implementation note 34 in Appendix H.)*
StructParents	integer	*(Required if the image is a structural content item; PDF 1.3)* The integer key of the image's entry in the structural parent tree (see "Finding Structure Elements from Content Items" on page 496).
ID	string	*(Optional; PDF 1.3; indirect reference preferred)* The digital identifier of the image's parent Web Capture content set (see Section 8.5.5, "Object Attributes Related to Web Capture").
OPI	dictionary	*(Optional; PDF 1.2)* An OPI version dictionary for this image (see Section 8.6.4, "Open Prepress Interface (OPI)"). If **ImageMask** is *true*, this entry is ignored.

Example 4.24 defines an image 256 samples wide by 256 high, with 8 bits per sample in the **DeviceGray** color space. It paints the image on a page with its lower-left corner positioned at coordinates (45, 140) in current user space and scaled to a width and height of 132 user space units.

Example 4.24

```
20 0 obj                        % Page object
   << /Type /Page
      /Parent  1 0 R
      /Resources  21 0 R
      /MediaBox  [0 0 612 792]
      /Contents  23 0 R
   >>
endobj
21 0 obj                        % Resource dictionary for page
   << /ProcSet [/PDF /ImageB]
      /XObject << /Im1 22 0 R >>
   >>
endobj
```

```
22 0 obj                                    % Image XObject
    << /Type /XObject
        /Subtype /Image
        /Width 256
        /Height 256
        /ColorSpace /DeviceGray
        /BitsPerComponent 8
        /Length 83183
        /Filter /ASCII85Decode
    >>
stream
9LhZl9h\GY9i+bb;,p:e;G9SP92/)X9MJ>^:f14d;,U(X8P;cO;G9e];c$=k9Mn\]
... Image data representing 65,536 samples ...
8P;cO;G9e];c$=k9Mn\]~>
endstream
endobj

23 0 obj                                    % Contents of page
    << /Length 56 >>
stream
    q                                       % Save graphics state
        132 0 0 132 45 140 cm               % Translate to (45,140) and scale by 132
        /Im1 Do                             % Paint image
    Q                                       % Restore graphics state
endstream
endobj
```

Decode Arrays

An image's data stream is initially decomposed into integers in the range 0 to $2^n - 1$, where n is the value of the image dictionary's **BitsPerComponent** entry. The image's **Decode** array specifies a linear mapping of each integer component value to a number that would be appropriate as a component value in the image's color space.

Each pair of numbers in a **Decode** array specifies the lower and upper values to which the range of sample values in the image is mapped. A **Decode** array contains one pair of numbers for each component in the color space specified by the image's **ColorSpace** entry. The mapping for each color component is a linear transformation. That is, it uses the following formula for linear interpolation:

$$y = \text{Interpolate}(x, x_{min}, x_{max}, y_{min}, y_{max}) = (x - x_{min}) \times \frac{(y_{max} - y_{min})}{(x_{max} - x_{min})} + y_{min}$$

Generally, this is used to convert a value x between x_{min} and x_{max} to a corresponding value y between y_{min} and y_{max}, projecting along the line defined by the points (x_{min}, y_{min}) and (x_{max}, y_{max}). While this formula applies to values outside the range x_{min} to x_{max} and does not require that $x_{min} < x_{max}$, note that interpolation used for color conversion, such as the **Decode** array, does require that $x_{min} < x_{max}$ and "clips" x values to this range, so that $y = y_{min}$ for all $x \leq x_{min}$, and $y = y_{max}$ for all $x \geq x_{max}$.

For a **Decode** array of the form $[D_{min} \; D_{max}]$, this can be written as

$$y = \text{Interpolate}(x, 0, 2^n - 1, D_{min}, D_{max})$$

$$= D_{min} + x \times \left(\frac{D_{max} - D_{min}}{2^n - 1} \right)$$

where

n is the value of **BitsPerComponent**

x is the input value, in the range 0 to $2^n - 1$

D_{min} and D_{max} are the values specified in the **Decode** array

y is the output value, to be interpreted in the image's color space

Samples with a value of 0 are mapped to D_{min}, those with a value of $2^n - 1$ are mapped to D_{max}, and those with intermediate values are mapped linearly between D_{min} and D_{max}. Table 4.36 lists the default **Decode** arrays for use with the various color spaces. For most color spaces, the **Decode** arrays listed in the table map into the full range of allowed component values. For an **Indexed** color space, the default **Decode** array ensures that component values that index a color table are passed through unchanged.

TABLE 4.36 Default Decode arrays

COLOR SPACE	Decode ARRAY
DeviceGray	[0.0 1.0]
DeviceRGB	[0.0 1.0 0.0 1.0 0.0 1.0]
DeviceCMYK	[0.0 1.0 0.0 1.0 0.0 1.0 0.0 1.0]
CalGray	[0.0 1.0]
CalRGB	[0.0 1.0 0.0 1.0 0.0 1.0]
Lab	[0 100 a_{min} a_{max} b_{min} b_{max}] where a_{min}, a_{max}, b_{min}, and b_{max} correspond to the values in the **Range** array of the image's color space
ICCBased	Same as the value of **Range** in the image's color space
DeviceN	[0.0 1.0 0.0 1.0 ... 0.0 1.0] (one pair of elements for each color component)
Separation	[0.0 1.0]
Indexed	[0 N], where $N = 2^n - 1$
Pattern	(Not permitted with images)

It is possible to specify a mapping that *inverts* sample color intensities, by specifying a D_{min} value greater than D_{max}. For example, if the image's color space is **DeviceGray** and the **Decode** array is [1.0 0.0], an input value of 0 will be mapped to 1.0 (white), while an input value of $2^n - 1$ will be mapped to 0.0 (black).

The D_{min} and D_{max} parameters for a color component are not required to fall within the range of values allowed for that component. For instance, if an application uses 6-bit numbers as its native image sample format, it can represent those samples in PDF in 8-bit form, setting the two unused high-order bits of each sample to 0. The image dictionary should then specify a **Decode** array of [0.00000 4.04762], which maps input values from 0 to 63 into the range 0.0 to 1.0 (4.04762 being approximately equal to 255 ÷ 63). If an output value falls outside the range allowed for a component, it will automatically be adjusted to the nearest allowed value.

Image Interpolation

When the resolution of a source image is significantly lower than that of the output device, each source sample covers many device pixels. This can cause images to appear "jaggy" or "blocky." These visual artifacts can be reduced by applying an *image interpolation* algorithm during rendering. Instead of painting all pixels covered by a source sample with the same color, image interpolation attempts to produce a smooth transition between adjacent sample values. Because it may increase the time required to render the image, image interpolation is disabled by default; setting the **Interpolate** entry in the image dictionary to *true* enables it.

Note: The interpolation algorithm is implementation-dependent and is not specified by PDF. Image interpolation may not always be performed for some classes of images or on some output devices.

Alternate Images

Alternate images (PDF 1.3) provide a straightforward and backward-compatible way to include multiple versions of an image in a PDF file for different purposes. These variant representations of the image may differ, for example, in resolution or in color space. The primary goal is to reduce the need to maintain separate versions of a PDF document for low-resolution on-screen viewing and high-resolution printing.

In PDF 1.3, a *base image* (that is, the image XObject referred to in a resource dictionary) can contain an **Alternates** entry. The value of this entry is an array of *alternate image dictionaries* specifying variant representations of the base image. Each alternate image dictionary contains an image XObject for one variant and specifies its properties. Table 4.37 shows the contents of an alternate image dictionary.

TABLE 4.37 Entries in an alternate image dictionary

KEY	TYPE	VALUE
Image	stream	*(Required)* The image XObject for the alternate image.
DefaultForPrinting	boolean	*(Optional)* A flag indicating whether this alternate image is the default version to be used for printing. At most one alternate for a given base image may be so designated. If no alternate has this entry set to *true*, the base image itself is used for printing.

Example 4.25 shows an image with a single alternate. The base image is a gray-scale image, and the alternate is a high-resolution *RGB* image stored on a Web server.

Example 4.25

```
10 0 obj                          % Image XObject
    << /Type /XObject
       /Subtype /Image
       /Width 100
       /Height 200
       /ColorSpace /DeviceGray
       /BitsPerComponent 8
       /Alternates 15 0 R
       /Length 2167
       /Filter /DCTDecode
    >>
stream
… Image data …
endstream
endobj

15 0 obj                          % Alternate images array
    [ << /Image 16 0 R
         /DefaultForPrinting true
      >>
    ]
endobj

16 0 obj                          % Alternate image
    << /Type /XObject
       /Subtype /Image
       /Width 1000
       /Height 2000
       /ColorSpace /DeviceRGB
       /BitsPerComponent 8
       /Length 0                   % This is an external stream
       /F << /FS /URL
             /F (http://www.myserver.mycorp.com/images/exttest.jpg)
          >>
       /FFilter /DCTDecode
    >>
stream
endstream
endobj
```

4.8.5 Masked Images

Ordinarily, images mark all areas they occupy on the page as if with opaque paint. All portions of the image, whether black, white, gray, or color, completely obscure any marks that may previously have existed in the same place on the page. In the graphic arts industry and page layout applications, however, it is common to crop or "mask out" the background of an image and then place the masked image on a different background, allowing the existing background to show through the masked areas. A number of PDF features are available for achieving such masking effects (see implementation note 35 in Appendix H):

- The **ImageMask** entry in the image dictionary, available in all versions of PDF, specifies that the image data is to be used as a *stencil mask* for painting in the current color.

- The **Mask** entry in the image dictionary *(PDF 1.3)* may specify a separate image XObject to be used as an *explicit mask* specifying which areas of the image to paint and which to mask out.

- Alternatively, the **Mask** entry *(PDF 1.3)* may specify a range of colors to be masked out wherever they occur within the image; this technique is known as *color key masking.*

Note: *Although the **Mask** entry is a PDF 1.3 feature, its effects are commonly simulated in earlier versions of PDF by defining a clipping path enclosing only those of an image's samples that are to be painted. However, implementation limits can cause errors if the clipping path is very complex (or if there is more than one clipping path). An alternative way to achieve the effect of an explicit mask in PDF 1.2 is to define the image being clipped as a pattern, make it the current color, and then paint the explicit mask as an image whose **ImageMask** entry is* true. *In any case, the PDF 1.3 features allow masked images to be placed on the page without regard to the complexity of the clipping path.*

Stencil Masking

An *image mask* (an image XObject whose **ImageMask** entry is *true*) is a monochrome image, in which each sample is specified by a single bit. However, instead of being painted in opaque black and white, the image mask is treated as a *stencil mask* that is partly opaque and partly transparent. Sample values in the image do not represent black and white pixels; rather, they designate places on the page that should either be marked with the current color or masked out (not marked at all). Areas that are masked out retain their former contents. The effect is like applying paint in the current color through a cut-out stencil, which allows the paint to reach the page in some places and masks it out in others.

An image mask differs from an ordinary image in the following significant ways:

- The image dictionary does not contain a **ColorSpace** entry, because sample values represent masking properties (1 bit per sample) rather than colors.

- The value of the **BitsPerComponent** entry must be 1.

- The **Decode** entry determines how the source samples are to be interpreted. If the **Decode** array is [0 1] (the default for an image mask), a sample value of 0 marks the page with the current color and a 1 leaves the previous contents unchanged; if the **Decode** array is [1 0], these meanings are reversed.

One of the most important uses of stencil masking is for painting character glyphs represented as bitmaps. Using such a glyph as a stencil mask transfers only its "black" bits to the page, while leaving the "white" bits (which are really just background) unchanged. For reasons discussed in Section 5.5.4, "Type 3 Fonts," an image mask rather than an image should almost always be used to paint glyph bitmaps.

Note: If image interpolation (see "Image Interpolation" on page 255) is requested during stencil masking, the effect is to smooth the edges of the mask, not to interpolate the painted color values. This can minimize the "jaggy" appearance of a low-resolution stencil mask.

Explicit Masking

In PDF 1.3, the **Mask** entry in an image dictionary may be an image mask, as described above under "Stencil Masking," which serves as an *explicit mask* for the primary (base) image. The base image and the image mask need not have the same resolution (**Width** and **Height** values), but since all images are defined on the unit square in user space, their boundaries on the page will coincide; that is, they will overlay each other. The image mask indicates which places on the page are to be painted and which are to be masked out (left unchanged). Unmasked areas are painted with the corresponding portions of the base image; masked areas are not.

Color Key Masking

In PDF 1.3, the **Mask** entry in an image dictionary may alternatively be an array specifying a range of colors to be masked out. Samples in the image that fall within this range are not painted, allowing the existing background to show through. The effect is similar to that of the video technique known as *chroma-key*.

For color key masking, the value of the **Mask** entry is an array of $2 \times n$ integers, $[min_1 \ max_1 \ \dots \ min_n \ max_n]$, where n is the number of color components in the image's color space. Each integer must be in the range 0 to $2^{\text{BitsPerComponent}} - 1$, representing color values *before* decoding with the **Decode** array. An image sample is masked (not painted) if all of its color components before decoding, $c_1 \dots c_n$, fall within the specified ranges (that is, if $min_i \le c_i \le max_i$ for all $1 \le i \le n$).

Note: *When color key masking is specified, the use of a **DCTDecode** filter for the stream is not recommended. **DCTDecode** is a "lossy" filter, meaning that the output is only an approximation of the original input data. This can lead to slight changes in the color values of image samples, possibly causing samples that were intended to be masked to be unexpectedly painted instead, in colors slightly different from the mask color.*

4.8.6 In-Line Images

As an alternative to the image XObjects described in Section 4.8.4, "Image Dictionaries," a sampled image may be specified in the form of an *in-line image*. This type of image is defined directly within the content stream in which it will be painted, rather than as a separate object. Because the in-line format gives the viewer application less flexibility in managing the image data, it should be used only for small images (4 KB or less).

An in-line image object is delimited in the content stream by the operators **BI** (begin image), **ID** (image data), and **EI** (end image); these operators are summarized in Table 4.38. **BI** and **ID** bracket a series of key-value pairs specifying the characteristics of the image, such as its dimensions and color space; the image data follows between the **ID** and **EI** operators. The format is thus analogous to that of a stream object such as an image XObject:

BI
> *… Key-value pairs …*

ID
> *… Image data …*

EI

TABLE 4.38 In-line image operators

OPERANDS	OPERATOR	DESCRIPTION
—	BI	Begin an in-line image object.
—	ID	Begin the image data for an in-line image object.
—	EI	End an in-line image object.

In-line image objects may not be nested; that is, two **BI** operators may not appear without an intervening **EI** to close the first object. Similarly, an **ID** operator may appear only between a **BI** and its balancing **EI**. Unless the image uses **ASCII-HexDecode** or **ASCII85Decode** as one of its filters, the **ID** operator should be followed by a single white-space character; the next character after that is interpreted as the first byte of image data.

The key-value pairs appearing between the **BI** and **ID** operators are analogous to those in the dictionary portion of an image XObject (though the syntax is different). Table 4.39 shows the entries that are valid for an in-line image, all of which have the same meanings as in a stream dictionary (Table 3.4 on page 35) or an image dictionary (Table 4.35 on page 249). Entries other than those listed will be ignored; in particular, the **Type**, **Subtype**, and **Length** entries normally found in a stream or image dictionary are unnecessary. For convenience, the abbreviations shown in the table may be used in place of the fully spelled-out keys; Table 4.40 shows additional abbreviations that can be used for the names of filters and color spaces. (Note, however, that these abbreviations are valid only in in-line images; they may *not* be used in image XObjects.)

TABLE 4.39 Entries in an in-line image object

FULL NAME	ABBREVIATION
BitsPerComponent	BPC
ColorSpace	CS
Decode	D
DecodeParms	DP
Filter	F
Height	H
ImageMask	IM
Intent *(PDF 1.1)*	No abbreviation
Interpolate	I (uppercase I)
Width	W

TABLE 4.40 Additional abbreviations in an in-line image object

FULL NAME	ABBREVIATION
DeviceCMYK	CMYK
DeviceGray	G
DeviceRGB	RGB
Indexed	I (uppercase I)
ASCIIHexDecode	AHx
ASCII85Decode	A85
CCITTFaxDecode	CCF
DCTDecode	DCT
FlateDecode *(PDF 1.2)*	Fl (uppercase F, lowercase L)
LZWDecode	LZW
RunLengthDecode	RL

The color space specified by the **ColorSpace** (or **CS**) entry may be any of the standard device color spaces (**DeviceGray**, **DeviceRGB**, or **DeviceCMYK**). It may not be a CIE-based color space or a special color space, with the exception of a limited form of **Indexed** color space whose base color space is a device space and whose color table is a specified by a string (see "Indexed Color Spaces" on page 181). In PDF 1.2, the value of the **ColorSpace** entry may also be the name of a color space in the **ColorSpace** subdictionary of the current resource dictionary (see Section 3.7.2, "Resource Dictionaries"); in this case, the name may designate any color space that can be used with an image XObject.

The image data in an in-line image may be encoded using any of the standard PDF filters. The bytes between the **ID** and **EI** operators are treated much the same as a stream object's data (see Section 3.2.7, "Stream Objects"), even though they do not follow the standard stream syntax. (This is an exception to the usual rule that the data in a content stream is interpreted according to the standard PDF syntax for objects.)

Example 4.26 shows an in-line image 17 samples wide by 17 high with 8 bits per component in the **DeviceRGB** color space. The image has been encoded using LZW and ASCII base-85 encoding. The **cm** operator is used to scale it to a width and height of 17 units in user space and position it at coordinates (298, 388). The **q** and **Q** operators encapsulate the **cm** operation to limit its effect to resizing the image.

Example 4.26

```
q                                              % Save graphics state
17  0  0  17  298  388  cm                     % Scale and translate coordinate space
BI                                             % Begin in-line image object
    /W  17                                     % Width in samples
    /H  17                                     % Height in samples
    /CS  /RGB                                  % Color space
    /BPC  8                                    % Bits per component
    /F  [/A85  /LZW]                           % Filters
ID                                             % Begin image data
J1/gKA>.]AN&J?]-<HW]aRVcg*bb.\eKAdVV%/PcZ
... Omitted data ...
R.s(4KE3&d&7hb*7[%Ct2HCqC~>
EI                                             % End in-line image object
Q                                              % Restore graphics state
```

4.9 Form XObjects

A *form XObject* is a self-contained description of any sequence of graphics objects (including path objects, text objects, and sampled images), defined as a PDF content stream. It may be painted multiple times—either on several pages or at several locations on the same page—and will produce the same output each time, subject only to the graphics state at the time it is invoked. Not only is this shared definition economical to represent in the PDF file, but under suitable circumstances, the PDF viewer can optimize execution by caching the results of rendering the form XObject for repeated reuse.

Note: *The term* form *also refers to a completely different kind of object, an* interactive form *(sometimes called an* AcroForm*), discussed in Section 7.6, "Interactive Forms." Unlike the form XObjects described in this section, which correspond to the notion of forms in the PostScript language, interactive forms are the PDF equivalent of the familiar paper instrument. Any unqualified use of the word* form *is understood to refer to an interactive form; the type of form described here is always referred to explicitly as a* form XObject.

Form XObjects have various uses:

• As its name suggests, a form XObject can serve as the template for an entire page. For example, a program that prints filled-in tax forms can first paint the fixed template as a form XObject and then paint the variable information on top of it.

• Any graphical element that is to be used repeatedly, such as a company logo or a standard component in the output from a computer-aided design system, can be defined as a form XObject.

• Certain document elements that are not part of a page's contents, such as annotation appearances (see Section 7.4.4, "Appearance Streams"), are represented as form XObjects.

The use of form XObjects requires two steps:

1. *Define the appearance of the form XObject.* A form XObject is a PDF content stream. The dictionary portion of the stream (called the *form dictionary*) contains descriptive information about the form XObject, while the body of the stream describes the graphics objects that produce its appearance.

2. *Paint the form XObject.* The **Do** operator (see Section 4.7, "External Objects") paints a form XObject whose name is supplied as an operand. (The name is defined in the **XObject** subdictionary of the current resource dictionary.) Before invoking this operator, the content stream in which it appears should set appropriate parameters in the graphics state; in particular, it should alter the current transformation matrix to control the position, size, and orientation of the form XObject in user space.

Every form XObject has a *form type*, which determines the format and meaning of the entries in its form dictionary. At the time of publication, only one form type, type 1, has been defined. Table 4.41 shows the contents of the form dictionary for this type of form XObject.

TABLE 4.41 Entries in a type 1 form dictionary

KEY	TYPE	VALUE
Type	name	(Optional) The type of PDF object that this dictionary describes; if present, must be **XObject** for a form XObject.
Subtype	name	(Required) The type of XObject that this dictionary describes; must be **Form** for a form XObject.
FormType	integer	(Optional) A code identifying the type of form XObject that this dictionary describes. The only valid value defined at the time of publication is 1. Default value: 1.
BBox	rectangle	(Required) An array of four numbers in the form coordinate system (see below), giving the coordinates of the left, bottom, right, and top edges, respectively, of the form XObject's bounding box. These boundaries are used to clip the form XObject and to determine its size for caching.
Matrix	array	(Optional) An array of six numbers specifying a transformation matrix (see Section 4.2.3, "Transformation Matrices") that maps form space into user space. Default value: the identity matrix [1 0 0 1 0 0].
Resources	dictionary	(Optional but strongly recommended; PDF 1.2) A dictionary specifying any resources (such as fonts and images) required by the form XObject (see Section 3.7, "Content Streams and Resources"). In PDF 1.1 and earlier, all named resources used in the form XObject must be included in the resource dictionary of each page object on which the form XObject appears, whether or not they also appear in the resource dictionary of the form XObject itself. It can be useful to specify these resources in the form XObject's own resource dictionary as well, in order to determine which

resources are used inside the form XObject. If a resource is included in both dictionaries, it should have the same name in both locations.

In PDF 1.2 and later versions, form XObjects can be independent of the content streams in which they appear, and this is strongly recommended although not required. In an independent form XObject, the resource dictionary of the form XObject is required and contains all named resources used by the form XObject. These resources are not "promoted" to the outer content stream's resource dictionary, although that stream's resource dictionary will refer to the form XObject itself.

Name	name	*(Required in PDF 1.0; optional otherwise)* The name by which this form XObject is referenced in the **XObject** subdictionary of the current resource dictionary (see Section 3.7.2, "Resource Dictionaries").
		Note: This entry is obsolescent and its use is no longer recommended. (See implementation note 36 in Appendix H.)
PieceInfo	dictionary	*(Optional; PDF 1.3)* A page-piece dictionary associated with the form XObject (see Section 8.4.1, "Page-Piece Dictionaries").
LastModified	date	*(Optional unless **PieceInfo** is present; PDF 1.3)* The date and time (see Section 3.8.2, "Dates") when the form XObject's contents were most recently modified.
StructParents	integer	*(Required if the form XObject is a structural content item or contains such items; PDF 1.3)* The integer key of the form XObject's entry in the structural parent tree (see "Finding Structure Elements from Content Items" on page 496).
OPI	dictionary	*(Optional; PDF 1.2)* An OPI version dictionary for this form XObject (see Section 8.6.4, "Open Prepress Interface (OPI)").

Each form XObject is defined in its own coordinate system, called *form space*. The **BBox** entry in the form dictionary is expressed in form space, as are any coordinates used in the form XObject's content stream, such as path coordinates. The **Matrix** entry in the form dictionary specifies the mapping from form space to the current user space; each time the form XObject is painted by the **Do** operator, this matrix is concatenated with the current transformation matrix to define the mapping from form space to device space. (This is different from the **Matrix** entry in a pattern dictionary, which maps pattern space to the *initial* user space of the content stream in which the pattern is used.)

When the **Do** operator is applied to a form XObject, it does the following:

1. Saves the current graphics state (as if by invoking the **q** operator)

2. Concatenates the matrix from the form dictionary's **Matrix** entry with the current transformation matrix (CTM)

3. Clips according to the form dictionary's **BBox** entry

4. Paints the graphics objects specified in the form's content stream

5. Restores the saved graphics state (as if by invoking the **Q** operator)

Except as described above, the initial graphics state for the form is inherited from the graphics state that is in effect at the time **Do** is invoked.

Example 4.27 shows a simple form XObject that paints a filled square 1000 units on each side.

Example 4.27

```
6 0 obj                             % Form XObject
   << /Type /XObject
      /Subtype /Form
      /FormType 1
      /BBox [0 0 1000 1000]
      /Matrix [1 0 0 1 0 0]
      /Resources << /ProcSet [/PDF] >>
      /Length 58
   >>
stream
   0 0 m
   0 1000 l
   1000 1000 l
   1000 0 l
   f
endstream
endobj
```

4.10 PostScript XObjects

In PDF 1.1, a content stream can include PostScript language fragments. These fragments are used only when printing to a PostScript output device; they have no effect either when viewing the document on-screen or when printing to a non-PostScript device. In addition, applications that understand PDF are unlikely to be able to interpret the PostScript fragments. Hence, this capability should be used with extreme caution and only if there is no other way to achieve the same result. Inappropriate use of PostScript XObjects can cause PDF files to print incorrectly.

Note: Since PDF 1.3 encompasses all of the Adobe imaging model features of the PostScript language, there is no longer any reason to use PostScript XObjects. This feature is likely to be removed from PDF in a future version.

A *PostScript XObject* is an XObject stream whose **Subtype** entry has the value **PS**. Table 4.42 shows the contents of a PostScript XObject stream dictionary.

TABLE 4.42   Entries in a PostScript XObject dictionary

KEY	TYPE	VALUE
Type	name	*(Optional)* The type of PDF object that this dictionary describes; if present, must be **XObject** for a PostScript XObject.
Subtype	name	*(Required)* The type of XObject that this dictionary describes; must be **PS** for a PostScript XObject.
Level1	stream	*(Optional)* A stream whose contents are to be used in place of the PostScript XObject's stream when the PDF viewer knows that the target PostScript interpreter supports only LanguageLevel 1.

When a PDF content stream is translated into the PostScript language, any **Do** operation that references a PostScript XObject is replaced by the contents of the XObject stream itself. The stream is copied without interpretation. The PostScript fragment may use Type 1 and TrueType fonts listed in the **Font** subdictionary of the current resource dictionary (see Section 3.7.2, "Resource Dictionaries"), accessing them by their **BaseFont** names using the PostScript **findfont** operator. The fragment may not use other types of font listed there. It should not reference the PostScript definitions corresponding to PDF procedure sets (see Section 8.1, "Procedure Sets"), which are subject to change.

CHAPTER 5

Fonts

THIS CHAPTER DESCRIBES the special facilities in PDF for dealing with text—specifically, for representing characters with *glyphs* from *fonts*. A glyph is a graphical shape and is subject to all graphical manipulations, such as coordinate transformation. Because of the importance of text in most page descriptions, PDF provides higher-level facilities that permit an application to describe, select, and render glyphs conveniently and efficiently.

The first section is a general description of how glyphs from fonts are painted on the page. Subsequent sections cover the following topics in detail:

- *Text state.* A subset of the graphics state parameters pertain to text, including parameters that select the font, scale the glyphs to an appropriate size, and accomplish other graphical effects.

- *Text objects and operators.* The text operators specify the glyphs to be painted, represented by string objects whose values are interpreted as sequences of character codes. A text object encloses a sequence of text operators and associated parameters.

- *Font data structures.* Font dictionaries and associated data structures provide information that a viewer application needs to interpret the text and position the glyphs properly. The definitions of the glyphs themselves are contained in *font programs*, which may be embedded in the PDF file, built into the viewer application, or obtained from an external font file.

5.1 Organization and Use of Fonts

A *character* is an abstract symbol, whereas a *glyph* is a specific graphical rendering of a character. For example, the glyphs A, **A**, and *A* are renderings of the abstract

"A" character. Historically these two terms have often been used interchangeably in computer typography (as evidenced by the names chosen for some PDF dictionary keys and PostScript operators), but advances in this area have made the distinction more meaningful in recent times. Consequently, this book distinguishes between characters and glyphs, though with some residual names that are inconsistent.

Glyphs are organized into *fonts*. A font defines glyphs for a particular character set; for example, the Helvetica and Times-Roman fonts define glyphs for a set of standard Latin characters. A font for use with a PDF viewer application is prepared in the form of a program. Such a *font program* is written in a special-purpose language, such as the *Type 1* or *TrueType* font format, that is understood by a specialized font interpreter.

In PDF, the term *font* refers to a *font dictionary*, a PDF object that identifies the font program and contains additional information about it. There are several different types of font, identified by the **Subtype** entry of the font dictionary.

For most types of font, the font program itself is defined in a separate *font file*, which may be either embedded in a PDF stream object or obtained from an external source. The font program contains *glyph descriptions* that generate glyphs.

A content stream paints glyphs on the page by specifying a font dictionary and a string object that is interpreted as a sequence of one or more character codes identifying glyphs in the font. This operation is called *showing* the text string. The glyph description consists of a sequence of graphics operators that produce the specific shape for that character in this font. To render a glyph, the viewer application executes the glyph description.

Programmers who have experience with scan conversion of general shapes may be concerned about the amount of computation that this description seems to imply. However, this is only the abstract behavior of glyph descriptions and font programs, not how they are implemented. In fact, the font machinery works very efficiently.

5.1.1 The Basics of Showing Text

Example 5.1 illustrates the most straightforward use of a font. It places the text ABC 10 inches from the bottom of the page and 4 inches from the left edge, using 12-point Helvetica.

Example 5.1

```
BT
    /F13  12  Tf
    288  720  Td
    (ABC)  Tj
ET
```

The five lines of this example perform the following steps:

1. Begin a text object.

2. Set the font and font size to use, installing them as parameters in the text state. (The font resource identified by the name F13 specifies the font externally known as Helvetica.)

3. Specify a starting position on the page, setting parameters in the text object.

4. Paint the glyphs for a string of characters there.

5. End the text object.

The following paragraphs explain these operations in more detail.

To paint glyphs, a content stream must first identify the font to be used. The **Tf** operator specifies the name of a font resource—that is, an entry in the **Font** subdictionary of the current resource dictionary. The value of that entry is a font dictionary. The font dictionary in turn identifies the font's externally known name, such as Helvetica, and supplies some additional information that the viewer application needs to paint glyphs from that font; it optionally provides the definition of the font program itself.

Note: *The font resource name presented to the* **Tf** *operator is arbitrary, as are the names for all kinds of resources. It bears no relationship to an actual font name, such as Helvetica.*

Example 5.2 illustrates an excerpt from the current page's resource dictionary, defining the font dictionary that is referenced as F13 in Example 5.1.

Example 5.2

```
/Resources
    << /Font << /F13 23 0 R >>
    >>
23 0 obj
    << /Type /Font
        /Subtype /Type1
        /BaseFont /Helvetica
    >>
endobj
```

A font defines the glyphs for one standard size. This standard is so arranged that the nominal height of tightly spaced lines of text is 1 unit. In the default user coordinate system, this means the standard glyph size is 1 unit in user space, or 1/72 inch. The standard-size font must then be scaled to be usable. The scale factor is specified as the second operand of the **Tf** operator, thereby setting the *text font size* parameter in the graphics state. Example 5.1 establishes the Helvetica font with a 12-unit size in the graphics state.

Once the font has been selected and scaled, it can be used to paint glyphs. The **Td** operator adjusts the current text position (actually, the translation components of the text matrix, as described in Section 5.3.1, "Text-Positioning Operators"). When executed for the first time after **BT**, it establishes the text position in the current user coordinate system. This determines the position on the page at which to begin painting glyphs.

The **Tj** operator takes a string operand and paints the corresponding glyphs using the current font and other text-related parameters in the graphics state. In Example 5.1, the **Tj** operator treats each element of the string (an integer in the range 0 to 255) as a character code. Each code selects a glyph description in the font, and the glyph description is executed to paint that glyph on the page. This is the behavior of **Tj** for simple fonts, such as ordinary Latin text fonts; interpretation of the string as a sequence of character codes is more complex for composite fonts, described in Section 5.6, "Composite Fonts."

Note: What these steps produce on the page is not a 12-point glyph, but rather a 12-unit glyph, where the unit size is that of the text space at the time the glyphs are rendered on the page. The actual size of the glyph is determined by the text matrix (T_m) *in the text object, several text state parameters, and the current transformation matrix (CTM) in the graphics state; see Section 5.3.3, "Text Space Details." If the text space is later scaled to make the unit size 1 centimeter, painting glyphs from the same 12-unit font will generate results that are 12 centimeters high.*

5.1.2 Achieving Special Graphical Effects

Normal uses of **Tj** and other glyph-painting operators cause black-filled glyphs to be painted. Other effects can be obtained by combining font operators with general graphics operators.

The color used for painting glyphs is the current color in the graphics state: either the nonstroking or the stroking color (or both), depending on the text rendering mode (see Section 5.2.5, "Text Rendering Mode"). The default color is black, but other colors can be obtained by executing an appropriate color-setting operator or operators (see Section 4.5.7, "Color Operators") before painting the glyphs. Example 5.3 uses text rendering mode 0 and the **g** operator to fill glyphs in 50 percent gray, as shown in Figure 5.1.

Example 5.3

```
BT
    /F13 48 Tf
    20 40 Td
    0 Tr
    0.5 g
    (ABC) Tj
ET
```

FIGURE 5.1 *Glyphs painted in 50% gray*

Other graphical effects can be achieved by treating the glyph outline as a path instead of filling it. The *text rendering mode* parameter in the graphics state specifies whether glyph outlines are to be filled, stroked, used as a clipping path, or some combination of these effects. (This parameter does not apply to Type 3 fonts.)

Example 5.4 treats glyph outlines as a path to be stroked. The **Tr** operator sets the text rendering mode to 1 (stroke). The **w** operator sets the line width to 2 units in user space. Given those graphics state parameters, the **Tj** operator strokes the glyph outlines with a line 2 points thick (see Figure 5.2).

Example 5.4

```
BT
    /F13 48 Tf
    20 38 Td
    1 Tr
    2 w
    (ABC) Tj
ET
```

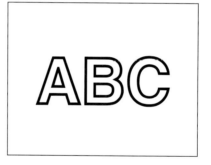

FIGURE 5.2 *Glyph outlines treated as a stroked path*

Example 5.5 treats the glyphs' outlines as a clipping path. The **Tr** operator sets the text rendering mode to 7 (clip), causing the subsequent **Tj** operator to impose the glyph outlines as a clipping path. All subsequent painting operations will mark the page only within this path, as illustrated in Figure 5.3. This state persists until some earlier clipping path is reinstated by the **Q** operator.

Example 5.5

```
BT
    /F13  48  Tf
    20  38  Td
    7  Tr
    (ABC)  Tj
ET
```
… Graphics operators to draw a starburst …

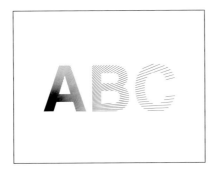

FIGURE 5.3   *Graphics clipped by a glyph path*

5.1.3   Glyph Positioning and Metrics

A glyph's *width*—formally, its *horizontal displacement*—is the amount of space it occupies along the baseline of a line of text that is written horizontally. In other words, it is the distance the current text position moves (by translating text space) when the glyph is painted. Note that the width is distinct from the dimensions of the glyph outline.

In some fonts, the width is constant; it does not vary from glyph to glyph. Such fonts are called *fixed-pitch* or *monospaced*. They are used mainly for typewriter-style printing. However, most fonts used for high-quality typography associate a different width with each glyph. Such fonts are called *proportional* or *variable-pitch* fonts. In either case, the **Tj** operator positions the glyphs for consecutive characters of a string according to their widths.

The width information for each glyph is stored in the font dictionary. The operators for showing text are designed on the assumption that glyphs are ordinarily positioned according to their standard widths. However, means are provided to vary the positioning in certain limited ways. For example, the **TJ** operator enables the text position to be adjusted between any consecutive pair of glyphs corresponding to characters in a text string. There are graphics state parameters to adjust character and word spacing systematically.

In addition to width, a glyph has several other metrics that influence glyph positioning and painting. For most font types, this information is largely internal to the font program and is not specified explicitly in the PDF font dictionary; however, in a Type 3 font, all metrics are specified explicitly (see Section 5.5.4, "Type 3 Fonts").

The *glyph coordinate system* is the space in which an individual character's glyph is defined. All path coordinates and metrics are interpreted in glyph space. For all font types except Type 3, the units of glyph space are one-thousandth of a unit of text space; for a Type 3 font, the transformation from glyph space to text space is defined by an explicit **FontMatrix** entry in the font. Figure 5.4 shows a typical glyph outline and its metrics.

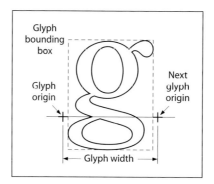

FIGURE 5.4 *Glyph metrics*

The *glyph origin* is the point $(0, 0)$ in the glyph coordinate system. **Tj** and other glyph-painting operators position the origin of the first glyph to be painted at the origin of text space. For example, the code

```
BT
    40  50  Td
    (ABC)  Tj
ET
```

adjusts the origin of text space to (40, 50) in the user coordinate system, and then places the origin of the A glyph at that point.

The *glyph displacement* is the distance from the glyph's origin to the point at which the origin of the *next* glyph should normally be placed when painting the consecutive glyphs of a line of text. This distance is a vector (called the *displacement vector*) in the glyph coordinate system; it has *x* and *y* components. (A displacement that is horizontal is usually called a *width*.) Most Indo-European alphabets, including the Latin alphabet, have a positive *x* displacement and a zero *y* displacement; some Asian writing systems have a nonzero *y* displacement. In all cases, the glyph-painting operators transform the displacement vector into text space and then translate text space by that amount.

The *glyph bounding box* is the smallest rectangle (oriented with the axes of the glyph coordinate system) that will just enclose the entire glyph shape. The bounding box is expressed in terms of its left, bottom, right, and top coordinates relative to the glyph origin in the glyph coordinate system.

In some writing systems, text is frequently aligned in two different directions. For example, it is common to write Japanese and Chinese glyphs either horizontally or vertically. To handle this, a font can optionally contain a second set of metrics for each glyph. Which set of metrics to use is selected according to a *writing mode*, where 0 specifies horizontal writing and 1 specifies vertical writing. This feature is available only for composite fonts, discussed in Section 5.6, "Composite Fonts."

When a glyph has two sets of metrics, each set specifies a glyph origin and a displacement vector for that writing mode. In vertical writing, the glyph position is described by a *position vector* from the origin used for horizontal writing (origin 0) to the origin used for vertical writing (origin 1). Figure 5.5 illustrates the metrics for the two writing modes, as follows:

- The left diagram illustrates the glyph metrics associated with writing mode 0, horizontal writing. The coordinates *ll* and *ur* specify the bounding box of the glyph relative to origin 0. *w0* is the displacement vector that specifies how the text position is changed after the glyph is painted in writing mode 0; its *y* component is always 0.

- The center diagram illustrates writing mode 1, vertical writing. *w1* is the displacement vector for writing mode 1; its *x* component is always 0.

- In the right diagram, *v* is a *position vector* defining the position of origin 1 relative to origin 0.

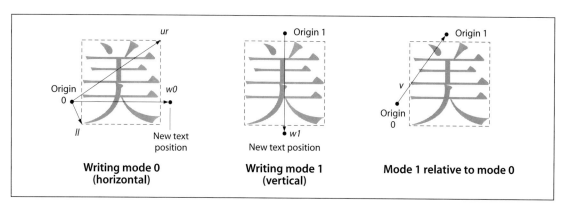

FIGURE 5.5 *Metrics for horizontal and vertical writing modes*

Glyph metric information is also available separately in the form of Adobe font metrics (AFM) and Adobe composite font metrics (ACFM) files. These files are for use by application programs that generate PDF page descriptions and must make formatting decisions based on the widths and other metrics of glyphs. Also available in the AFM and ACFM files is kerning information, which allows an application generating a PDF file to determine spacing adjustments between characters depending on context. Specifications for the AFM and ACFM file formats are available in Adobe Technical Note #5004, *Adobe Font Metrics File Format Specification*; the files themselves can be obtained from the ASN Developer Program Web site (see the Bibliography).

5.2   Text State Parameters and Operators

The text state comprises those graphics state parameters that only affect text. There are eight parameters in the text state (see Table 5.1).

TABLE 5.1 Text state parameters	
PARAMETER	**DESCRIPTION**
T_c	Character spacing
T_w	Word spacing
T_h	Horizontal scaling
T_l	Leading
T_f	Text font
T_{fs}	Text font size
T_{mode}	Text rendering mode
T_{rise}	Text rise

Except for the self-explanatory T_f and T_{fs}, these parameters are discussed further in the following sections. (As described in Section 5.3, "Text Objects," three additional text-related parameters are defined only within a text object: T_m, the text matrix; T_{LM}, the text line matrix; and T_{RM}, the text rendering matrix.) The values of the text state parameters are consulted when text is positioned and shown (using the operators described in Sections 5.3.1, "Text-Positioning Operators," and 5.3.2, "Text-Showing Operators"). In particular, the spacing and scaling parameters participate in a computation described in Section 5.3.3, "Text Space Details." The text state parameters can be set using the operators listed in Table 5.2.

The text state operators can appear outside text objects, and the values they set are retained across text objects in a single content stream. Like other graphics state parameters, these parameters are initialized to their default values at the beginning of each page.

Note that some of these parameters are expressed in *unscaled* text space units. This means that they are specified in a coordinate system that is defined by the text matrix, T_m, but is not scaled by the font size parameter, T_{fs}.

TABLE 5.2 Text state operators

OPERANDS	OPERATOR	DESCRIPTION
charSpace	Tc	Set the character spacing, T_c, to *charSpace*, which is a number expressed in unscaled text space units. Character spacing is used by the **Tj**, **TJ**, and **'** operators. Default value: 0.
wordSpace	Tw	Set the word spacing, T_w, to *wordSpace*, which is a number expressed in unscaled text space units. Word spacing is used by the **Tj**, **TJ**, and **'** operators. Default value: 0.
scale	Tz	Set the horizontal scaling, T_h, to (*scale* ÷ 100). *scale* is a number specifying the percentage of the normal width. Default value: 100 (normal width).
leading	TL	Set the text leading, T_l, to *leading*, which is a number expressed in unscaled text space units. Text leading is used only by the **T***, **'**, and **"** operators. Default value: 0.
font size	Tf	Set the font, T_f, to *font* and the font size, T_{fs}, to *size*. *font* is the name of a font resource in the **Font** subdictionary of the current resource dictionary. *size* is a number representing a scale factor. There is no default value for either *font* or *size*; they must be specified using **Tf** before any text is shown.
render	Tr	Set the text rendering mode, T_{mode}, to *render*, which is an integer. Default value: 0.
rise	Ts	Set the text rise, T_{rise}, to *rise*, which is a number expressed in unscaled text space units. Default value: 0.

5.2.1 Character Spacing

The character spacing parameter, T_c, is a number specified in unscaled text space units (although it is subject to scaling by the T_h parameter if the writing mode is horizontal). When the glyph for each character in the string is rendered, T_c is *added* to the *x* component of the glyph's displacement in horizontal writing mode or to the *y* component of the displacement in vertical writing mode. (See Section 5.1.3, "Glyph Positioning and Metrics," for a discussion of glyph displacements.) In the default coordinate system, horizontal coordinates increase from left to right and vertical coordinates from bottom to top. So for horizontal writing, a positive value of T_c has the effect of expanding the distance between glyphs (see Figure 5.6), whereas for vertical writing, a *negative* value of T_c has the effect of expanding the distance between glyphs.

$T_c = 0$ (default)	Character
$T_c = 0.25$	Character

FIGURE 5.6 *Character spacing in horizontal writing*

5.2.2 Word Spacing

Word spacing works the same way as character spacing, but applies only to the space character, code 32. The word spacing parameter, T_w, is added to the glyph's x or y displacement (depending on writing mode). For horizontal writing, a positive value for T_w has the effect of increasing the spacing between words. For vertical writing, a positive value for T_w *decreases* the spacing between words (and a negative value increases it), since y coordinates increase from bottom to top. Figure 5.7 illustrates the effect of word spacing in horizontal writing.

$T_w = 0$ (default)	Word Space
$T_w = 2.5$	Word Space

FIGURE 5.7 *Word spacing in horizontal writing*

Note: *Word spacing is applied to every occurrence of the single-byte character code 32 in a string. This can occur when using a simple font or a composite font that defines code 32 as a single-byte code. It does not apply to occurrences of the byte value 32 in multiple-byte codes.*

5.2.3 Horizontal Scaling

The horizontal scaling parameter, T_h, adjusts the width of glyphs by stretching or shrinking them in the horizontal direction. Its value is specified as a percentage of the normal width of the glyphs, with 100 being the normal width. The scaling always applies to the x coordinate in text space, independently of the writing mode. It affects both the glyph's shape and its horizontal displacement (that is, its displacement vector). If the writing mode is horizontal, it also affects the spacing parameters T_c and T_w, as well as any positioning adjustments performed by the **TJ** operator. Figure 5.8 shows the effect of horizontal scaling.

$T_h = 100$ (default)	Word
$T_h = 50$	WordWord

FIGURE 5.8 *Horizontal scaling*

5.2.4 Leading

The leading parameter, T_l, is measured in unscaled text space units. It specifies the vertical distance between the baselines of adjacent lines of text, as shown in Figure 5.9. The leading parameter is used by the **TD**, **T***, **'**, and **"** operators; see Table 5.5 on page 287 for a precise description of its effects. This parameter always applies to the y coordinate in text space, independently of the writing mode.

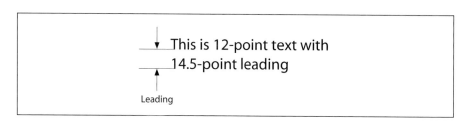

This is 12-point text with
14.5-point leading

Leading

FIGURE 5.9 *Leading*

5.2.5 Text Rendering Mode

The text rendering mode, T_{mode}, determines whether showing text causes glyph outlines to be stroked, filled, used as a clipping path, or some combination of these operations. Stroking, filling, and clipping have the same effects for a text object as they do for a path object, although they are specified in an entirely different way; see Sections 4.4.2, "Path-Painting Operators," and 4.4.3, "Clipping Path Operators." The graphics state parameters affecting those operations, such as line width, are interpreted in user space, not in text space.

Note: The text rendering mode has no effect on text displayed in a Type 3 font (see Section 5.5.4, "Type 3 Fonts").

If the text rendering mode calls for filling, the current nonstroking color in the graphics state is used; if it calls for stroking, the current stroking color is used. If it calls for both filling and stroking, the effect is as if each glyph outline were filled and then stroked with separate operations.

The text rendering modes are shown in Table 5.3. In the examples, a stroke color of black and a fill color of light gray are used. For the clipping modes (4 to 7), a series of lines has been drawn through the glyphs to show where the clipping occurs.

The behavior of the clipping modes requires further explanation. Glyph outlines begin accumulating if a **BT** operator is executed while the text rendering mode is set to a clipping mode or if it is set to a clipping mode within a text object. Glyphs accumulate until the text object is ended by an **ET** operator; the text rendering mode must not be changed back to a nonclipping mode before that point.

At the end of the text object, the accumulated glyph outlines, if any, are combined into a single path, treating the individual outlines as subpaths of that path and applying the nonzero winding number rule (see "Nonzero Winding Number Rule" on page 154). The clipping path in the graphics state is set to the intersection of this path and the current clipping path. As is the case for path objects, this clipping occurs *after* all filling and stroking operations for the text object have occurred. It remains in effect until some previous clipping path is restored by an invocation of the **Q** operator.

Note: If no glyphs are shown, or if the only glyphs shown have no outlines (in other words, they are space characters), no clipping occurs.

TABLE 5.3 Text rendering modes

MODE	EXAMPLE	DESCRIPTION
0		Fill text.
1		Stroke text.
2		Fill, then stroke, text.
3		Neither fill nor stroke text (invisible).
4		Fill text and add to path for clipping (see above).
5		Stroke text and add to path for clipping.
6		Fill, then stroke, text and add to path for clipping.
7		Add text to path for clipping.

5.2.6 Text Rise

Text rise, T_{rise}, specifies the distance, in unscaled text space units, to move the baseline up or down from its default location. Positive values of text rise move the baseline up. Adjustments to the baseline are useful for drawing superscripts or subscripts. The default location of the baseline can be restored by setting the text rise to 0. Figure 5.10 illustrates the effect of the text rise. Text rise always applies to the *y* coordinate in text space, regardless of the writing mode.

(This text is) Tj 5 Ts (superscripted) Tj	This text is ^{superscripted}
(This text is) Tj –5 Ts (subscripted) Tj	This text is _{subscripted}
(This) Tj –5 Ts (text) Tj 5 Ts (moves) Tj 0 Ts (around) Tj	This _{text} ^{moves} around

FIGURE 5.10 *Text rise*

5.3 Text Objects

A PDF *text object* consists of operators that can show text strings, move the text position, and set text state and certain other parameters. In addition, there are three parameters that are defined only within a text object (and do not persist from one text object to the next):

- T_m, the *text matrix*

- T_{LM}, the *text line matrix*

- T_{RM}, the *text rendering matrix*, actually just an intermediate result that combines the effects of text state parameters, the text matrix (T_m), and the current transformation matrix

A text object begins with the **BT** operator and ends with the **ET** operator, as shown below and described in Table 5.4.

>**BT**
> *… Zero or more text operators or other allowed operators …*
>**ET**

OPERANDS	OPERATOR	DESCRIPTION
—	BT	Begin a text object, initializing the text matrix, T_m, and the text line matrix, T_{LM}, to the identity matrix. Text objects cannot be nested; a second BT cannot appear before an ET.
—	ET	End a text object, discarding the text matrix.

TABLE 5.4 Text object operators

The specific categories of text-related operators that can appear in a text object are:

• *Text state operators,* described in Section 5.2, "Text State Parameters and Operators."

• *Text-positioning operators* and *text-showing operators,* described in Sections 5.3.1, "Text-Positioning Operators," and 5.3.2, "Text-Showing Operators." These sections also provide further details about the text object parameters mentioned above.

The other operators that can appear in a text object are those related to the general graphics state, color, and marked content, as shown in Figure 4.1 on page 122.

*Note: If a content stream does not contain any text, the **Text** procedure set may be omitted (see Section 8.1, "Procedure Sets"). In those circumstances, no text operators (including operators that merely set the text state) may be present in the content stream, since those operators are defined in the same procedure set.*

Note: Although text objects cannot be statically nested, text might be shown using a Type 3 font whose glyph descriptions include any graphics objects, including another text object. Likewise, the current color might be a pattern whose definition includes a text object.

5.3.1 Text-Positioning Operators

Text space is the coordinate system in which text is shown. It is defined by the text matrix, T_m, and the text state parameters T_{fs}, T_h, and T_{rise}, which together determine the transformation from text space to user space. Specifically, the origin of the first glyph shown by a text-showing operator will be placed at the origin of text space. If text space has been translated, scaled, or rotated, then the position, size, or orientation of the glyph in user space will be correspondingly altered.

At the beginning of a text object, T_m is the identity matrix, so the origin of text space is initially the same as that of user space. The *text-positioning operators*, described in Table 5.5, alter T_m and thereby control the placement of glyphs that are subsequently painted. Also, the *text-showing operators*, described in Table 5.6 on page 289, update T_m (by altering its e and f translation components) to take into account the horizontal or vertical displacement of each glyph painted as well as any character or word spacing parameters in the text state.

Additionally, a text object keeps track of a text line matrix, T_{LM}, which captures the value of T_m at the beginning of a line of text. This is convenient for aligning evenly spaced lines of text. The text-positioning and text-showing operators read and set T_{LM} on specific occasions mentioned in Tables 5.5 and 5.6.

Note: *The text-positioning operators can appear only within text objects.*

TABLE 5.5 Text-positioning operators

OPERANDS	OPERATOR	DESCRIPTION
t_x t_y	**Td**	Move to the start of the next line, offset from the start of the current line by (t_x, t_y). t_x and t_y are numbers expressed in unscaled text space units. More precisely, this operator performs the following assignments: $$T_m = T_{LM} = \begin{bmatrix} 1 & 0 & 0 \\ 0 & 1 & 0 \\ t_x & t_y & 1 \end{bmatrix} \times T_{LM}$$
t_x t_y	**TD**	Move to the start of the next line, offset from the start of the current line by (t_x, t_y). As a side effect, this operator sets the leading parameter in the text state. This operator has the same effect as the code $-t_y$ TL t_x t_y Td

a b c d e f	**Tm**	Set the text matrix, T_m, and the text line matrix, T_{LM}, as follows:

$$T_m = T_{LM} = \begin{bmatrix} a & b & 0 \\ c & d & 0 \\ e & f & 1 \end{bmatrix}$$

The operands are all numbers, and the initial value for T_m and T_{LM} is the identity matrix, [1 0 0 1 0 0]. Although the operands specify a matrix, they are passed to **Tm** as six separate numbers, not as an array.

The matrix specified by the operands is not concatenated onto the current text matrix, but replaces it.

—	**T***	Move to the start of the next line. This operator has the same effect as the code

$$0 \; T_l \; \text{Td}$$

where T_l is the leading parameter in the text state.

5.3.2 Text-Showing Operators

The *text-showing operators* (Table 5.6) show text on the page, repositioning text space as they do so. All of the operators interpret the text string and apply the text state parameters as described below.

Note: The text-showing operators can appear only within text objects.

A string operand of a text-showing operator is interpreted as a sequence of character codes identifying the glyphs to be painted. With most font types, each byte of the string is treated as a separate character code. The character code is then looked up in the font's encoding to select the glyph, as described in Section 5.5.5, "Character Encoding."

In PDF 1.2, a string may be shown in a composite font that uses multiple-byte codes to select some of its glyphs. In that case, one or more consecutive bytes of the string are treated as a single character code. The code lengths and the mappings from codes to glyphs are defined in a data structure called a *CMap*, described in Section 5.6, "Composite Fonts."

TABLE 5.6 Text-showing operators

OPERANDS	OPERATOR	DESCRIPTION
string	**Tj**	Show a text string.

string	**'**	Move to the next line and show a text string. This operator has the same effect as
		
		    T*
		    string Tj

a_w a_c *string*	**"**	Move to the next line and show a text string, using a_w as the word spacing and a_c as the character spacing (setting the corresponding parameters in the text state). a_w and a_c are numbers expressed in unscaled text space units. This operator has the same effect as
		
		    a_w Tw
		    a_c Tc
		    string '

array	**TJ**	Show one or more text strings, allowing individual glyph positioning (see implementation note 37 in Appendix H). Each element of *array* can be a string or a number. If the element is a string, this operator shows the string. If it is a number, the operator adjusts the text position by that amount; that is, it translates the text matrix, T_m. The number is expressed in thousandths of a unit of text space (see Section 5.3.3, "Text Space Details," and implementation note 38 in Appendix H). This amount is *subtracted* from the current x coordinate in horizontal writing mode or from the current y coordinate in vertical writing mode. In the default coordinate system, a positive adjustment has the effect of moving the next glyph painted either to the left or down by the given amount. Figure 5.11 shows an example of the effect of passing offsets to **TJ**.

[(AWAY again)] TJ	AWAY again
[(A) 120 (W) 120 (A) 95 (Y again)] TJ	AWAY again

FIGURE 5.11 *Operation of **TJ** operator in horizontal writing*

The strings must conform to the syntax for string objects. When a string is written by enclosing the data in parentheses, bytes whose values are the same as those of the ASCII characters left parenthesis (40), right parenthesis (41), and backslash (92) must be preceded by a backslash character. All other byte values between 0 and 255 may be used in a string object. These rules apply to each individual byte in a string object, regardless of whether the string is interpreted by the text-showing operators as single-byte or multiple-byte character codes.

Strings presented to the text-showing operators may be of any length—even a single character per string—and may be placed on the page in any order. However, the performance of text searching (and other text extraction operations) is significantly better if the text strings are as long as possible and are shown in natural reading order.

5.3.3 Text Space Details

As stated in Section 5.3.1, "Text-Positioning Operators," text is shown in text space, which is defined by the combination of the text matrix, T_m, and the text state parameters T_{fs}, T_h, and T_{rise}. This determines how text coordinates are transformed into user space. Both the glyph's shape and its displacement (horizontal or vertical) are interpreted in text space.

The entire transformation of the glyph onto the current page can be represented by a *text rendering matrix*, T_{RM}:

$$T_{RM} = \begin{bmatrix} T_{fs} \times T_h & 0 & 0 \\ 0 & T_{fs} & 0 \\ 0 & T_{rise} & 1 \end{bmatrix} \times T_m \times CTM$$

T_{RM} is a temporary matrix; conceptually, it is recomputed before each glyph is painted during a text-showing operation.

After the glyph is painted, the text matrix is updated according to the glyph displacement and any spacing parameters that apply. First, a combined displacement is computed, denoted by either t_x (in horizontal writing mode) or t_y (in vertical writing mode); the variable corresponding to the other writing mode is set to 0.

$$t_x = \left(\left(w0 - \frac{T_j}{1000} \right) \times T_{fs} + T_c + T_w \right) \times T_h$$

$$t_y = \left(w1 - \frac{T_j}{1000} \right) \times T_{fs} + T_c + T_w$$

where

w0 and *w1* are the glyph's horizontal and vertical displacements

T_j is a position adjustment specified by a number in a **TJ** array, if any

T_c and T_w are the character and word spacing parameters in the graphics state, if applicable

The text matrix is then updated as follows:

$$T_m = \begin{bmatrix} 1 & 0 & 0 \\ 0 & 1 & 0 \\ t_x & t_y & 1 \end{bmatrix} \times T_m$$

5.4 Introduction to Font Data Structures

A font is represented in PDF as a dictionary specifying the type of font, its Post-Script name, its encoding, and information that can be used to provide a substitute when the font program is not available. Optionally, the font program itself can be embedded as a stream object in the PDF file.

The font types are distinguished by the **Subtype** entry in the font dictionary. Table 5.7 lists the font types defined in PDF. Type 0 fonts are called *composite fonts*; other types of font are called *simple fonts*. In addition to fonts, PDF supports two classes of font-related objects, called *CIDFonts* and *CMaps*, described in Section 5.6.1, "CID-Keyed Fonts Overview." CIDFonts are listed in Table 5.7 because, like fonts, they are collections of glyphs; however, a CIDFont is never used directly, but only as a component of a Type 0 font.

TABLE 5.7 Font types

TYPE	SUBTYPE VALUE	DESCRIPTION
Type 0	**Type0**	*(PDF 1.2)* A *composite* font—a font composed of other fonts, organized hierarchically (see Section 5.6, "Composite Fonts")
Type 1	**Type1**	A font that defines glyph shapes by using a special encoded format (see Section 5.5.1, "Type 1 Fonts")
	MMType1	A *multiple master* font—an extension of the Type 1 font that allows the generation of a wide variety of typeface styles from a single font (see "Multiple Master Fonts" on page 297)
Type 3	**Type3**	A font that defines glyphs with streams of PDF graphics operators (see Section 5.5.4, "Type 3 Fonts")
TrueType	**TrueType**	A font based on the TrueType font format (see Section 5.5.2, "TrueType Fonts")
CIDFont	**CIDFontType0**	*(PDF 1.2)* A CIDFont whose glyph descriptions are based on Type 1 font technology (see Section 5.6.3, "CIDFonts")
	CIDFontType2	*(PDF 1.2)* A CIDFont whose glyph descriptions are based on TrueType font technology (see Section 5.6.3, "CIDFonts")

For all font types, the term *font dictionary* refers to a PDF dictionary containing information about the font; likewise, a *CIDFont dictionary* contains information about a CIDFont. Except for Type 3, this dictionary is distinct from the *font program* that defines the font's glyphs. That font program may be embedded in the PDF file as a stream object or be obtained from some external source.

Note: This terminology differs from that used in the PostScript language. In PostScript, a font dictionary is a PostScript data structure that is created as a direct result of interpreting a font program. In PDF, a font program is always treated as if it were a separate file, even if its contents are embedded in the PDF file. The font program is interpreted by a specialized font interpreter when necessary; its contents never materialize as PDF objects.

Most font programs (and related programs, such as CIDFonts and CMaps) conform to external specifications, such as the *Adobe Type 1 Font Format.* This book does not include those specifications. See the Bibliography for more information about the specifications mentioned in this chapter.

The most predictable and dependable results are produced when all font programs used to show text are embedded in the PDF file. The following sections describe precisely how to do so. On the other hand, if a PDF file refers to font programs that are not embedded, the results depend on the availability of fonts in the viewer application's environment. The following sections specify some conventions for referring to external font programs; however, some details of font naming, font substitution, and glyph selection are implementation-dependent and may vary among different viewer applications and operating system environments.

5.5 Simple Fonts

There are several types of simple fonts, all of which have the following properties:

- Glyphs in the font are selected by single-byte character codes obtained from a string that is shown by the text-showing operators. Logically, these codes index into a table of 256 glyphs; the mapping from codes to glyphs is called the font's *encoding.* Each font program has a built-in encoding. Under some circumstances, the encoding can be altered by means described in Section 5.5.5, "Character Encoding."

- Each glyph has a single set of metrics, including a *horizontal displacement* or *width*, as described in Section 5.1.3, "Glyph Positioning and Metrics." That is, simple fonts support only horizontal writing mode.

- Except for Type 3 fonts and certain standard Type 1 fonts, every font dictionary contains a subsidiary dictionary, the *font descriptor*, containing fontwide metrics and other attributes of the font; see Section 5.7, "Font Descriptors." Among those attributes is an optional *font file* stream containing the font program itself.

5.5.1 Type 1 Fonts

A Type 1 font program is a stylized PostScript program that describes glyph shapes. It uses a compact encoding for the glyph descriptions, and it includes hint information that enables high-quality rendering even at small sizes and low resolutions. Details on this format are provided in a separate book, *Adobe Type 1 Font Format.* An alternative, more compact but functionally equivalent representation of a Type 1 font program is documented in Adobe Technical Note #5176, *The Compact Font Format Specification.*

Note: *Although a Type 1 font program uses PostScript language syntax, using it does not require a full PostScript interpreter; a specialized Type 1 font interpreter suffices.*

A Type 1 font dictionary contains the entries listed in Table 5.8. Some entries are optional for the 14 standard fonts listed under "The Standard Type 1 Fonts" on page 296, but are required otherwise.

		TABLE 5.8 Entries in a Type 1 font dictionary
KEY	**TYPE**	**VALUE**
Type	name	*(Required)* The type of PDF object that this dictionary describes; must be **Font** for a font dictionary.
Subtype	name	*(Required)* The type of font; must be **Type1**.
Name	name	*(Required in PDF 1.0; optional otherwise)* The name by which this font is referenced in the **Font** subdictionary of the current resource dictionary.
		Note: *This entry is obsolescent and its use is no longer recommended. (See implementation note 39 in Appendix H.)*
BaseFont	name	*(Required)* The PostScript name of the font. For Type 1 fonts, this is usually the value of the **FontName** entry in the font program; for more information, see Section 5.2 of the *PostScript Language Reference*, Third Edition. The PostScript name of the font can be used to find the font's definition in the viewer application or its environment. It is also the name that will be used when printing to a PostScript output device.
FirstChar	integer	*(Required except for the 14 standard fonts)* The first character code defined in the font's **Widths** array.
LastChar	integer	*(Required except for the 14 standard fonts)* The last character code defined in the font's **Widths** array.

Widths	array	*(Required except for the 14 standard fonts; indirect reference preferred)* An array of (**LastChar** − **FirstChar** + 1) widths, each element being the glyph width for the character whose code is **FirstChar** plus the array index. For character codes outside the range **FirstChar** to **LastChar**, the value of **MissingWidth** from the **FontDescriptor** entry for this font is used. The glyph widths are measured in units in which 1000 units corresponds to 1 unit in text space. These widths must be consistent with the actual widths given in the font program itself. For more information on glyph widths and other glyph metrics, see Section 5.1.3, "Glyph Positioning and Metrics."
FontDescriptor	dictionary	*(Required except for the 14 standard fonts; must be an indirect reference)* A font descriptor describing the font's metrics other than its glyph widths (see Section 5.7, "Font Descriptors").
Encoding	name or dictionary	*(Optional)* A specification of the font's character encoding, if different from its built-in encoding. The value of **Encoding** may be either the name of a predefined encoding (**MacRomanEncoding**, **MacExpertEncoding**, or **WinAnsiEncoding**, as described in Appendix D) or an encoding dictionary that specifies differences from the font's built-in encoding or from a specified predefined encoding (see Section 5.5.5, "Character Encoding").
ToUnicode	stream	*(Optional; PDF 1.2)* A stream containing a CMap file that maps character codes to Unicode values (see Section 5.9, "ToUnicode CMaps").

Example 5.6 shows the font dictionary for the Adobe Garamond™ Semibold font. The font has an encoding dictionary (object 25), although neither the encoding dictionary nor the font descriptor (object 7) is shown in the example.

Example 5.6

```
14 0 obj
    << /Type /Font
        /Subtype /Type1
        /BaseFont /AGaramond–Semibold
        /FirstChar 0
        /LastChar 255
        /Widths 21 0 R
        /FontDescriptor 7 0 R
        /Encoding 25 0 R
    >>
endobj
```

```
21 0 obj
   [ 255 255 255 255 255 255 255 255 255 255 255 255 255 255 255 255
     255 255 255 255 255 255 255 255 255 255 255 255 255 255 255 255
     255 280 438 510 510 868 834 248 320 320 420 510 255 320 255 347
     510 510 510 510 510 510 510 510 510 510 255 255 510 510 510 330
     781 627 627 694 784 580 533 743 812 354 354 684 560 921 780 792
     588 792 656 504 682 744 650 968 648 590 638 320 329 320 510 500
     380 420 510 400 513 409 301 464 522 268 259 484 258 798 533 492
     516 503 349 346 321 520 434 684 439 448 390 320 255 320 510 255
     627 627 694 580 780 792 744 420 420 420 420 420 420 402 409 409
     409 409 268 268 268 268 533 492 492 492 492 492 520 520 520 520
     486 400 510 510 506 398 520 555 800 800 1044 360 380 549 846 792
     713 510 549 549 510 522 494 713 823 549 274 354 387 768 615 496
     330 280 510 549 510 549 612 421 421 1000 255 627 627 792 1016 730
     500 1000 438 438 248 248 510 494 448 590 100 510 256 256 539 539
     486 255 248 438 1174 627 580 627 580 580 354 354 354 354 792 792
     790 792 744 744 744 268 380 380 380 380 380 380 380 380 380 380
   ]
endobj
```

The Standard Type 1 Fonts

The PostScript names of 14 Type 1 fonts, known as the *standard fonts*, are as follows:

Courier	Helvetica	Times–Roman	Symbol
Courier–Bold	Helvetica–Bold	Times–Bold	ZapfDingbats
Courier–Oblique	Helvetica–Oblique	Times–Italic	
Courier–BoldOblique	Helvetica–BoldOblique	Times–BoldItalic	

These fonts, or their font metrics and suitable substitution fonts, are guaranteed to be available to the viewer application. The character sets and encodings for these fonts are given in Appendix D. The Adobe font metrics (AFM) files for the standard 14 fonts are available from the ASN Developer Program Web site (see the Bibliography). For more information on font metrics, see Adobe Technical Note #5004, *Adobe Font Metrics File Format Specification*.

Ordinarily, a font dictionary that refers to one of the standard fonts should omit the **Widths** and **FontDescriptor** entries. However, it is permissible to override a standard font by including **Widths** and **FontDescriptor** entries and embedding the font program in the PDF file. (See implementation note 40 in Appendix H.)

Multiple Master Fonts

The *multiple master* font format is an extension of the Type 1 font format that allows the generation of a wide variety of typeface styles from a single font program. This is accomplished through the presence of various design dimensions in the font. Examples of design dimensions are weight (light to extra-bold) and width (condensed to expanded). Coordinates along these design dimensions (such as the degree of boldness) are specified by numbers. A particular choice of numbers selects an *instance* of the multiple master font. Adobe Technical Note #5015, *Type 1 Font Format Supplement*, describes multiple master fonts in detail.

The font dictionary for a multiple master font instance has the same entries as a Type 1 font dictionary (Table 5.8 on page 294), except note the following:

* The value of **Subtype** is **MMType1**.

* If the PostScript name of the instance contains spaces, the spaces are replaced by underscores in the value of **BaseFont**. For instance, as illustrated in Example 5.7, the name "MinionMM 366 465 11 " (which ends with a space character) becomes /MinionMM_366_465_11_.

Example 5.7

```
7 0 obj
   << /Type /Font
       /Subtype /MMType1
       /BaseFont /MinionMM_366_465_11_
       /FirstChar 32
       /LastChar 255
       /Widths 19 0 R
       /FontDescriptor 6 0 R
       /Encoding 5 0 R
   >>
endobj

19 0 obj
   [ 187 235 317 430 427 717 607 168 326 326 421 619 219 317 219 282 427
     … Omitted data …
     569 0 569 607 607 607 239 400 400 400 400 253 400 400 400 400 400
   ]
endobj
```

This example illustrates a convention for including the numeric values of the design coordinates as part of the instance's **BaseFont** name. This convention is commonly used for accessing multiple master font instances from an external source in the viewer application's environment; it is documented in Adobe Technical Note #5088, *Font Naming Issues*. However, this convention is not prescribed as part of the PDF specification. In particular, if the font program for this instance is embedded in the PDF file, it must be an ordinary Type 1 font program, not a multiple master font program. This font program is called a *snapshot* of the multiple master font instance, incorporating the chosen values of the design coordinates.

5.5.2 TrueType Fonts

The *TrueType* font format was developed by Apple Computer and has been adopted as a standard font format for Microsoft Windows. Specifications for the TrueType font file format are available in Apple's *TrueType Reference Manual* and Microsoft's *TrueType 1.0 Font Files Technical Specification*.

Note: *A TrueType font program can be embedded directly in a PDF file as a stream object. The Type 42 font format that is defined for PostScript does not apply to PDF.*

A TrueType font dictionary can contain the same entries as a Type 1 font dictionary (Table 5.8 on page 294), except note the following:

- The value of **Subtype** is **TrueType**.

- The value of **BaseFont** is derived differently, as described below.

- The value of **Encoding** is subject to limitations that are described in Section 5.5.5, "Character Encoding."

The PostScript name for the value of **BaseFont** is determined in one of two ways:

- Use the PostScript name that is an optional entry in the "name" table of the TrueType font itself.

- In the absence of such an entry in the "name" table, derive a PostScript name from the name by which the font is known in the host operating system: on a Windows system, it is based on the lfFaceName field in a LOGFONT structure; in the Mac OS, it is based on the name of the FOND resource. If the name contains any spaces, the spaces are removed.

If the font in a source document uses a bold or italic style, but there is no font data for that style, the host operating system will synthesize the style. In this case, a comma and the style name (one of Bold, Italic, or BoldItalic) are appended to the font name. For example, for a TrueType font that is a bold variant of the New York font, the **BaseFont** value is written as /NewYork,Bold (as illustrated in Example 5.8).

Example 5.8

```
17 0 obj
    << /Type /Font
       /Subtype /TrueType
       /BaseFont /NewYork,Bold
       /FirstChar 0
       /LastChar 255
       /Widths 23 0 R
       /FontDescriptor 7 0 R
       /Encoding /MacRomanEncoding
    >>
endobj

23 0 obj
    [ 0 333 333 333 333 333 333 333 0 333 333 333 333 333 333 333 333 333
      ... Omitted data ...
      803 790 803 780 780 780 340 636 636 636 636 636 636 636 636 636 636
    ]
endobj
```

Note that for CJK (Chinese, Japanese, and Korean) fonts, the host font system's "font name" is often encoded in the host operating system's script. For instance, a Japanese font may have a name that is written in Japanese using some (unidentified) Japanese encoding. Thus, TrueType font names may contain multiple-byte character codes, each of which requires multiple characters to represent in a PDF name object (using the # notation to quote special characters as needed).

5.5.3 Font Subsets

PDF 1.1 permits documents to include subsets of Type 1 and TrueType fonts. The font and font descriptor that describe a font subset are slightly different from those of ordinary fonts. These differences allow an application to recognize font subsets and to merge documents containing different subsets of the same font. (For more information on font descriptors, see Section 5.7, "Font Descriptors.")

For a font subset, the PostScript name of the font—the value of the font's **BaseFont** entry and the font descriptor's **FontName** entry—begins with a *tag* followed by a plus sign. The tag consists of exactly six uppercase letters; the choice of letters is arbitrary, but different subsets in the same PDF file must have different tags. For example, EOODIA+Poetica is the name of a subset of Poetica®, a Type 1 font. (See implementation note 41 in Appendix H.)

5.5.4 Type 3 Fonts

Type 3 fonts differ from the other fonts supported by PDF. A Type 3 font dictionary defines the font itself, while the other font dictionaries simply contain information *about* the font and refer to a separate font program for the actual glyph descriptions. In Type 3 fonts, glyphs are defined by streams of PDF graphics operators. These streams are associated with character names. A separate encoding entry maps character codes to the appropriate character names for the glyphs.

Type 3 fonts are more flexible than Type 1 fonts, because the glyph descriptions may contain arbitrary PDF graphics operators. However, Type 3 fonts have no hinting mechanism for improving output at small sizes or low resolutions. A Type 3 font dictionary contains the entries listed in Table 5.9.

TABLE 5.9 Entries in a Type 3 font dictionary

KEY	TYPE	VALUE
Type	name	(*Required*) The type of PDF object that this dictionary describes; must be **Font** for a font dictionary.
Subtype	name	(*Required*) The type of font; must be **Type3**.
Name	name	(*Required in PDF 1.0; optional otherwise*) See Table 5.8 on page 294.
CharProcs	dictionary	(*Required*) A dictionary in which each key is a character name and the value associated with that key is a content stream that constructs and paints the glyph for that character. The stream must include as its first operator either **d0** or **d1**. This is followed by operators describing one or more graphics objects, which may include path, text, or image objects. See below for more details about Type 3 glyph descriptions.
FontBBox	rectangle	(*Required*) A rectangle (see Section 3.8.3, "Rectangles"), expressed in the glyph coordinate system, specifying the *font bounding box*. This is the smallest rectangle enclosing the shape that would result if all of the glyphs of the font were placed with their origins coincident and then filled.

		If all four elements of the rectangle are zero, no assumptions are made based on the font bounding box. If any element is nonzero, it is essential that the font bounding box be accurate; if any glyph's marks fall outside this bounding box, incorrect behavior may result.
FontMatrix	array	*(Required)* An array of six numbers specifying the transformation from glyph space to text space (see Section 5.1.3, "Glyph Positioning and Metrics"). A common practice is to define glyphs in terms of a 1000-unit glyph coordinate system, so the font matrix is [0.001 0 0 0.001 0 0].
Encoding	name or dictionary	*(Required)* An encoding dictionary whose **Differences** array specifies the complete character encoding for this font (see Section 5.5.5, "Character Encoding"; also see implementation note 42 in Appendix H).
FirstChar	integer	*(Required)* See Table 5.8 on page 294.
LastChar	integer	*(Required)* See Table 5.8 on page 294.
Widths	array	*(Required; indirect reference preferred)* An array of (**LastChar** – **FirstChar** + 1) widths, each element being the glyph width for the character whose code is **FirstChar** plus the array index. For character codes outside the range **FirstChar** to **LastChar**, the width is 0. These widths are interpreted in glyph space as specified by **FontMatrix** (unlike the widths of a Type 1 font, which are in thousandths of a unit of text space).
		*Note: If **FontMatrix** specifies a rotation, only the x component of the transformed width is used. That is, the resulting displacement is always horizontal in text space, as is the case for all simple fonts.*
Resources	dictionary	*(Optional, but strongly recommended; PDF 1.2)* A list of the named resources, such as fonts and images, required by the glyph descriptions in this font (see Section 3.7.2, "Resource Dictionaries"). If any glyph descriptions refer to named resources but this dictionary is absent, the names are looked up in the resource dictionary of the page on which this font is used. (See implementation note 43 in Appendix H.)
ToUnicode	stream	*(Optional; PDF 1.2)* A stream containing a CMap file mapping character codes to Unicode values (see Section 5.9, "ToUnicode CMaps").

For each character shown by a text-showing operator using a Type 3 font, the viewer application does the following:

1. Looks up the character code in the font's **Encoding** entry, as described in Section 5.5.5, "Character Encoding," to obtain a character name.

2. Looks up the character name in the font's **CharProcs** dictionary to obtain a stream object containing a glyph description. (If the name is not present as a key in **CharProcs**, no glyph is painted.)

3. Invokes the glyph description, as described below. The graphics state is saved before this invocation and restored afterward, so any changes the glyph description makes to the graphics state do not persist after it finishes.

When the glyph description begins execution, the current transformation matrix (CTM) is the concatenation of the font matrix (**FontMatrix** in the current font dictionary) and the text space that was in effect at the time the text-showing operator was invoked (see Section 5.3.3, "Text Space Details"). This means that shapes described in the glyph coordinate system will be transformed into the user coordinate system and will appear in the appropriate size and orientation on the page. The glyph description should describe the glyph in terms of absolute coordinates in the glyph coordinate system, placing the glyph origin at $(0, 0)$ in this space. It should make no assumptions about the initial text position.

Aside from the CTM, the graphics state is inherited from the environment of the text-showing operator that caused the glyph description to be invoked. To ensure predictable results, the glyph description must initialize any graphics state parameters on which it depends. In particular, if it invokes the **S** (stroke) operator, it should explicitly set the line width, line join, line cap, and dash pattern to appropriate values. Normally, it is unnecessary and undesirable to initialize the current color parameter, because the text-showing operators are designed to paint glyphs with the current color.

The glyph description must execute one of the operators described in Table 5.10 to pass width and bounding box information to the font machinery. This must precede the execution of any path construction or painting operators describing the glyph.

Note: *Type 3 fonts in PDF are very similar to those in PostScript. Some of the information provided in Type 3 font dictionaries and glyph descriptions, while seemingly redundant or unnecessary, is nevertheless required for correct results when a PDF viewer application prints to a PostScript output device. This applies particularly to the operands of the* **d0** *and* **d1** *operators, which in PostScript are named* **setcharwidth** *and* **setcachedevice***. For further explanation, see Section 5.7 of the* PostScript Language Reference, *Third Edition.*

TABLE 5.10 Type 3 font operators

OPERANDS	OPERATOR	DESCRIPTION
w_x w_y	**d0**	Set width information for the glyph and declare that the glyph description specifies both its shape and its color. (Note that this operator name ends in the digit **0**.) w_x specifies the horizontal displacement in the glyph coordinate system; it must be consistent with the corresponding width in the font's **Widths** array. w_y must be 0 (see Section 5.1.3, "Glyph Positioning and Metrics"). This operator is typically used only if the glyph description executes operators to set the color explicitly.
w_x w_y ll_x ll_y ur_x ur_y	**d1**	Set width and bounding box information for the glyph and declare that the glyph description specifies only shape, not color. (Note that this operator name ends in the digit **1**.) w_x specifies the horizontal displacement in the glyph coordinate system; it must be consistent with the corresponding width in the font's **Widths** array. w_y must be 0 (see Section 5.1.3, "Glyph Positioning and Metrics").
		ll_x and ll_y are the coordinates of the lower-left corner, and ur_x an ur_y the upper-right corner, of the glyph bounding box. The glyph bounding box is the smallest rectangle, oriented with the axes of the glyph coordinate system, that completely encloses all marks placed on the page as a result of executing the glyph's description. The declared bounding box must be correct—in other words, sufficiently large to enclose the entire glyph. If any marks fall outside this bounding box, the result is unpredictable.
		A glyph description that begins with the **d1** operator should not execute any operators that set the color (or other color-related parameters) in the graphics state; any use of such operators will be ignored. The glyph description is executed solely to determine the glyph's shape; its color is determined by the graphics state in effect each time this glyph is painted by a text-showing operator. For the same reason, the glyph description may not include an image; however, an image mask is acceptable, since it merely defines a region of the page to be painted with the current color.

Example of a Type 3 Font

Example 5.9 shows the definition of a Type 3 font with only two glyphs—a filled square and a filled triangle, selected by the characters a and b. Figure 5.12 shows the result of showing the string (ababab) using this font.

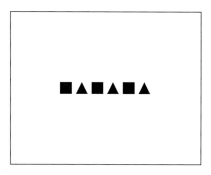

FIGURE 5.12 *Output from Example 5.9*

Example 5.9

```
4 0 obj
    << /Type /Font
        /Subtype /Type3
        /FontBBox [0 0 750 750]
        /FontMatrix [0.001 0 0 0.001 0 0]
        /FirstChar 97
        /LastChar 98
        /Encoding 9 0 R
        /CharProcs 10 0 R
        /Widths [1000 1000]
    >>
endobj

9 0 obj
    << /Type /Encoding
        /Differences [97 /square /triangle]
    >>
endobj

10 0 obj
    << /square 11 0 R
        /triangle 12 0 R
    >>
endobj
```

```
11 0 obj
  << /Length 39 >>
stream
  1000 0 0 0 750 750 d1
  0 0 750 750 re
  f
endstream
endobj

12 0 obj
  << /Length 48 >>
stream
  1000 0 0 0 750 750 d1
  0 0 m
  375 750 l
  750 0 l
  f
endstream
endobj
```

5.5.5 Character Encoding

A font's *encoding* is the association between character codes (obtained from text strings that are shown) and glyph descriptions. This section describes the character encoding scheme used with simple PDF fonts. Composite fonts (Type 0) use a different character mapping algorithm, as discussed in Section 5.6, "Composite Fonts."

Except for Type 3 fonts, every font program has a built-in encoding. Under certain circumstances, a PDF font dictionary can change a font's built-in encoding to match the requirements of the application generating the text being shown. This flexibility in character encoding is valuable for two reasons:

- It permits showing text that is encoded according to any of the various existing conventions. For example, the Microsoft Windows and Apple Mac OS operating systems use different standard encodings for Latin text, and many applications use their own special-purpose encodings.

- It allows applications to specify how characters selected from a large character set are to be encoded. Some character sets consist of more than 256 characters, including ligatures, accented characters, and other symbols required for high-quality typography or non-Latin writing systems. Different encodings can select different subsets of the same character set.

Latin-text font programs produced by Adobe Systems use the *Adobe standard encoding*, often referred to as **StandardEncoding**. The name **StandardEncoding** has no special meaning in PDF, but this encoding does play a role as a default encoding (as shown in Table 5.11 below). The regular encodings used for Latin-text fonts on Mac OS and Windows systems are named **MacRomanEncoding** and **WinAnsiEncoding**, respectively. Additionally, an encoding named **MacExpertEncoding** is used with "expert" fonts that contain additional characters useful for sophisticated typography. Complete details of these encodings and of the characters present in typical fonts are provided in Appendix D.

In PDF, a font is classified as either *nonsymbolic* or *symbolic* according to whether or not all of its characters are members of the Adobe standard Latin character set. This is indicated by flags in the font descriptor; see Section 5.7.1, "Font Descriptor Flags." Symbolic fonts contain other character sets, to which the encodings mentioned above ordinarily do not apply. Such font programs have built-in encodings that are usually unique to each font. The 14 standard fonts include two symbolic fonts, Symbol and ZapfDingbats, whose encodings and character sets are documented in Appendix D.

A font program's built-in encoding can be overridden or altered by including an **Encoding** entry in the PDF font dictionary. The possible encoding modifications depend on the font type, as discussed below. The value of the **Encoding** entry is either a named encoding (the name of one of the predefined encodings **MacRomanEncoding**, **MacExpertEncoding**, or **WinAnsiEncoding**) or an *encoding dictionary*. An encoding dictionary contains the entries listed in Table 5.11.

The value of the **Differences** entry is an array of character codes and character names organized as follows:

$$code_1 \; name_{1,1} \; name_{1,2} \; \ldots$$
$$code_2 \; name_{2,1} \; name_{2,2} \; \ldots$$
$$\ldots$$
$$code_n \; name_{n,1} \; name_{n,2} \; \ldots$$

Each code is the first index in a sequence of characters to be changed. The first character name after the code becomes the name corresponding to that code. Subsequent names replace consecutive code indices until the next code appears in the array or the array ends. These sequences may be specified in any order but should not overlap.

TABLE 5.11   Entries in an encoding dictionary

KEY	TYPE	VALUE
Type	name	*(Optional)* The type of PDF object that this dictionary describes; if present, must be **Encoding** for an encoding dictionary.
BaseEncoding	name	*(Optional)* The *base encoding*—that is, the encoding from which the **Differences** entry (if present) describes differences—specified as the name of a predefined encoding **MacRomanEncoding**, **MacExpertEncoding**, or **WinAnsiEncoding** (see Appendix D).
		If this entry is absent, the **Differences** entry describes differences from an implicit base encoding. For a font program that is embedded in the PDF file, the implicit base encoding is the font program's built-in encoding, as described above and further elaborated in the sections on specific font types below. Otherwise, for a nonsymbolic font, it is **StandardEncoding**, and for a symbolic font, it is the font's built-in encoding.
Differences	array	*(Optional; not recommended with TrueType fonts)* An array describing the differences from the encoding specified by **BaseEncoding** or, if **BaseEncoding** is absent, from an implicit base encoding. The **Differences** array is described above.

For example, in the encoding dictionary in Example 5.10, the name quotesingle (') is associated with character code 39, Adieresis (Ä) with code 128, Aring (Å) with 129, and trademark (™) with 170.

Example 5.10

```
25  0  obj
    <<  /Type /Encoding
        /Differences
            [    39 /quotesingle
                 96 /grave
                128 /Adieresis /Aring /Ccedilla /Eacute /Ntilde /Odieresis /Udieresis
                    /aacute /agrave /acircumflex /adieresis /atilde /aring /ccedilla
                    /eacute /egrave /ecircumflex /edieresis /iacute /igrave /icircumflex
                    /idieresis /ntilde /oacute /ograve /ocircumflex /odieresis /otilde
                    /uacute /ugrave /ucircumflex /udieresis /dagger /degree /cent
                    /sterling /section /bullet /paragraph /germandbls /registered
                    /copyright /trademark /acute /dieresis
                174 /AE /Oslash
                177 /plusminus
                180 /yen  /mu
```

```
       187 /ordfeminine /ordmasculine
       190 /ae /oslash /questiondown /exclamdown /logicalnot
       196 /florin
       199 /guillemotleft /guillemotright /ellipsis
       203 /Agrave /Atilde /Otilde /OE /oe /endash /emdash /quotedblleft
           /quotedblright /quoteleft /quoteright /divide
       216 /ydieresis /Ydieresis /fraction /currency /guilsinglleft /guilsinglright
           /fi /fl /daggerdbl /periodcentered /quotesinglbase /quotedblbase
           /perthousand /Acircumflex /Ecircumflex /Aacute /Edieresis /Egrave
           /Iacute /Icircumflex /Idieresis /Igrave /Oacute /Ocircumflex
       241 /Ograve /Uacute /Ucircumflex /Ugrave /dotlessi /circumflex /tilde
           /macron /breve /dotaccent /ring /cedilla /hungarumlaut /ogonek
           /caron
       ]
   >>
 endobj
```

By convention, the name .notdef can be used to indicate that there is no character name associated with a given character code.

Encodings for Type 1 Fonts

A Type 1 font program's glyph descriptions are keyed by character *names*, not by character *codes*. Character names are ordinary PDF name objects. Descriptions of Latin alphabetic characters are normally associated with names consisting of single letters, such as **A** or **a**. Other characters are associated with names composed of words, such as three, ampersand, or parenleft. A Type 1 font's built-in encoding is defined by an **Encoding** array that is part of the font program itself; this is not to be confused with the **Encoding** entry in the PDF font dictionary.

An **Encoding** entry can alter a Type 1 font's mapping from character codes to character names. The **Differences** array can map a code to the name of any glyph description that exists in the font program, whether or not that glyph is referenced by the font's built-in encoding or by the encoding specified in the **BaseEncoding** entry.

All Type 1 font programs contain an actual glyph for the character named .notdef. The effect produced by showing the .notdef character is at the discretion of the font designer; in Type 1 font programs produced by Adobe, it is the same as the space character. If an encoding maps to a character name that does not exist in the Type 1 font program, the .notdef character is substituted.

Encodings for Type 3 Fonts

A Type 3 font, like Type 1, contains glyph descriptions that are keyed by character names; in this case, they appear as explicit keys in the font's **CharProcs** dictionary. A Type 3 font's mapping from character codes to character names is entirely defined by its **Encoding** entry, which is required in this case.

Encodings for TrueType Fonts

A TrueType font program's built-in encoding maps directly from character codes to glyph descriptions, using an internal data structure called a "cmap" (not to be confused with the CMap described in Section 5.6.4, "CMaps"). A TrueType font program can contain multiple encodings that are intended for use on different platforms (such as Mac OS and Windows). The PDF font dictionary's **Encoding** entry can select among the available encodings; in the absence of this entry, an implementation-dependent encoding is chosen.

There is no standard support for named characters in TrueType, although some font programs have an optional "post" table listing character names for the glyphs. If the viewer application needs to select glyph descriptions by name in a font program lacking a "post" table, it translates from character names to codes in one of the encodings given in the font program's "cmap" table.

Because some aspects of TrueType glyph selection are dependent on the viewer implementation or the operating system, PDF files that use TrueType fonts should follow certain guidelines to ensure predictable behavior across all viewer applications. The font program should be embedded. A nonsymbolic font should specify **MacRomanEncoding** or **WinAnsiEncoding** as its **Encoding** entry, with no **Differences** array. A symbolic font should not specify an **Encoding** entry; its font program's "cmap" table should contain exactly one encoding. See below for specific guidelines on the contents of this "cmap" table.

Note: Some popular TrueType font programs contain incorrect encoding information. Implementations of TrueType font interpreters have evolved heuristics for dealing with such problems; those heuristics are not described here. For maximum portability, only well-formed TrueType font programs should be used in PDF files.

The following paragraphs describe the treatment of TrueType font encodings in PDF 1.3, as implemented in the Acrobat 4.0 viewers. This information does not necessarily apply to earlier versions or implementations.

A TrueType font program's "cmap" table consists of one or more subtables, each identified by the combination of a *platform ID* and a *platform-specific encoding ID*. If a named encoding (**WinAnsiEncoding**, **MacRomanEncoding**, or **MacExpertEncoding**) is specified in a font dictionary's **Encoding** entry or in an encoding dictionary's **BaseEncoding** entry, a "cmap" subtable is selected and used as described below.

- If a "cmap" subtable with platform ID 3 and encoding ID 1 (Microsoft Unicode) is present, it is used as follows: A character code is first mapped to a character name as specified by the font's **Encoding** entry. The character name is then mapped to a Unicode value by consulting the *Adobe Glyph List* (see the Bibliography). Finally, the Unicode value is mapped to a glyph description according to the (3, 1) subtable.

- If a "cmap" subtable with platform ID 1 and encoding 0 (Macintosh Roman) is present, it is used as follows: A character code is first mapped to a character name as specified by the font's **Encoding** entry. The character name is then mapped back to a character code according to **MacRomanEncoding** (see Appendix D). Finally, the code is mapped to a glyph description according to the (1, 0) subtable.

- In either of the cases above, if the character name cannot be mapped as specified, the character name is looked up in the font program's "post" table (if one is present) and the associated glyph description is used.

If no **Encoding** entry is specified in the font dictionary, the "cmap" subtable with platform ID 1 and encoding 0 will be used to map directly from character codes to glyph descriptions, without any consideration of character names. This is the normal convention for symbolic fonts.

If a character cannot be mapped in any of the ways described above, the results are implementation-dependent.

5.6 Composite Fonts

A *composite font* is one whose glyphs are obtained from other fonts or from font-like objects called *CIDFonts*, organized hierarchically. In PDF, a composite font is represented by a font dictionary whose **Subtype** value is **Type0**; this is also called a Type 0 font. The Type 0 font at the top level of the hierarchy is the *root font*. Fonts and CIDFonts immediately below a Type 0 font are called its *descendant* *fonts.* The Type 0 font immediately above a descendant font is called its *parent font.*

When the current font is composite, the text-showing operators behave different-ly than with simple fonts. Whereas for simple fonts each byte of a string to be shown selects one character, for composite fonts a sequence of one or more bytes can be decoded to select a character from any of the descendant fonts or CIDFonts. This facility supports the use of very large character sets, such as those for the Japanese and Chinese languages. It also simplifies the organization of fonts that have complex encoding requirements.

PDF 1.2 introduces a general architecture for composite fonts that theoretically allows a Type 0 font to have multiple descendants, which might themselves be Type 0 fonts. However, in versions up to and including PDF 1.3, only a single descendant is allowed, which must be a CIDFont (not a font). This restriction may be relaxed in a future PDF version.

Note: Composite fonts in PDF are analogous to composite fonts in PostScript, but with some limitations. In particular, PDF requires that the character encoding be de-fined by a CMap (described below), which is only one of several encoding methods available in PostScript.

This section first introduces the architecture of *CID-keyed fonts,* which are the only kind of composite font supported in PDF. Then it describes the *CIDFont* and *CMap* dictionaries, which are the PDF objects that represent the correspondingly named components of a CID-keyed font. Finally, it describes the Type 0 font dic-tionary, which combines a CIDFont and a CMap to produce a font whose glyphs can be accessed by means of variable-length character codes in a string to be shown.

5.6.1   CID-Keyed Fonts Overview

CID-keyed fonts provide a convenient and efficient method for defining multiple-byte character encodings, fonts with a large number of glyphs, and fonts that incorporate glyphs obtained from other fonts. These capabilities provide great flexibility for representing text in writing systems for languages with large character sets, such as Chinese, Japanese, and Korean (CJK).

The CID-keyed font architecture specifies the external representation of certain font programs, called *CMap* and *CIDFont* files, along with some conventions for combining and using those files. This architecture is independent of PDF; CID-keyed fonts can be used in other environments. For complete documentation on the architecture and the file formats, see Adobe Technical Notes #5092, *CID-Keyed Font Technology Overview*, and #5014, *Adobe CMap and CIDFont Files Specification*. This section describes only the PDF objects that represent these font programs.

The term *CID-keyed font* reflects the fact that *CID* (character identifier) numbers are used to index and access the glyph descriptions in the font. This method is more efficient for large fonts than the method of accessing by character name, as is used for some simple fonts. CIDs range from 0 to a maximum value that is subject to an implementation limit (see Appendix C).

A *character collection* is an ordered set of all characters needed to support one or more popular character sets for a particular language. The order of the characters in the character collection determines the CID number for each character. Each CID-keyed font must explicitly reference the character collection on which its CID numbers are based; see Section 5.6.2, "CIDSystemInfo Dictionaries."

A *CMap* (character map) file specifies the correspondence between character codes and the CID numbers used to identify characters. It is equivalent to the concept of an encoding in simple fonts. Whereas a simple font allows a maximum of 256 characters to be encoded and accessible at one time, a CMap can describe a mapping from multiple-byte codes to thousands of characters in a large CID-keyed font. For example, it can describe JIS, one of several widely used encodings for Japanese, or Unicode, an international standard encoding that covers many languages.

A CMap can reference an entire character collection, a subset, or multiple character collections. It can also reference characters in other fonts by character code or character name. The CMap mapping yields a *font number* and a *character selector* that can be a CID, a character code, or a character name. Furthermore, a CMap can incorporate another CMap by reference, without having to duplicate it. These features enable character collections to be combined or supplemented, and make all the constituent characters accessible to text-showing operations through a single encoding.

Note: *As mentioned earlier, PDF versions up to and including PDF 1.3 do not support the entire CID-keyed font architecture. In PDF, a CID-keyed font may have only a single descendant, whose characters must be referenced by CID.*

A *CIDFont* file contains the glyph descriptions for a character collection. The glyph descriptions themselves are typically in a format similar to those used in simple fonts, such as Type 1. However, they are identified by CIDs rather than by names, and they are organized differently.

In PDF, the CMap and CIDFont are represented by PDF objects, which are described below. The CMap and CIDFont programs themselves can be either referenced by name or embedded as stream objects in the PDF file. As stated earlier, the external file formats are not documented here, but in Adobe Technical Note #5014, *Adobe CMap and CIDFont Files Specification*.

A CID-keyed font, then, is the combination of a CMap with one or more CIDFonts, simple fonts, or composite fonts containing glyph descriptions. In PDF, a CID-keyed font is represented as a Type 0 font. It contains an **Encoding** entry whose value is a CMap dictionary, and its **DescendantFonts** array references the CIDFont or font dictionaries with which the CMap has been combined.

5.6.2 CIDSystemInfo Dictionaries

CIDFont and CMap dictionaries contain a **CIDSystemInfo** entry that specifies the character collection that the CIDFont assumes—that is, the interpretation of the CID numbers it uses. A character collection is uniquely identified by the **Registry**, **Ordering**, and **Supplement** entries in the **CIDSystemInfo** dictionary, as described in Table 5.12. Character collections whose **Registry** and **Ordering** values are the same are compatible.

In a CIDFont, the **CIDSystemInfo** entry is a dictionary that specifies the CIDFont's character collection. Note that the CIDFont need not contain glyph descriptions for all the CIDs in a collection; it can contain a subset. In a CMap, the **CIDSystemInfo** entry is either a single dictionary or an array of dictionaries, depending on whether it associates codes with a single character collection or with multiple character collections; see Section 5.6.4, "CMaps."

For proper behavior, the **CIDSystemInfo** entry of a CMap should be compatible with that of the CIDFont or CIDFonts with which it is used. If they are incompatible, the effects produced will be unpredictable.

TABLE 5.12 Entries in a CIDSystemInfo dictionary

KEY	TYPE	VALUE
Registry	string	*(Required)* A string identifying an issuer of character collections—for example, Adobe. For information about assigning a registry identifier, consult the ASN Developer Program Web site or contact the Adobe Solutions Network (see the Bibliography).
Ordering	string	*(Required)* A string that uniquely names a character collection issued by a specific registry—for example, Japan1.
Supplement	integer	*(Required)* The *supplement number* of the character collection. An original character collection has a supplement number of 0. Whenever additional CIDs are assigned in a character collection, the supplement number is increased. Supplements do not alter the ordering of existing CIDs in the character collection. This value is not used in determining compatibility between character collections.

5.6.3 CIDFonts

A CIDFont program contains glyph descriptions that are accessed using a CID as the character selector. There are two types of CIDFont. A Type 0 CIDFont contains glyph descriptions based on Adobe's Type 1 font format, whereas those in a Type 2 CIDFont are based on the TrueType font format.

A CIDFont dictionary is a PDF object that contains information about a CID-Font program. Although its **Type** value is **Font**, a CIDFont is not actually a font. It does not have an **Encoding** entry, it cannot be listed in the **Font** subdictionary of a resource dictionary, and it cannot be used as the operand of the **Tf** operator. It is used only as a descendant of a Type 0 font. The CMap in the Type 0 font is what defines the encoding that maps character codes to CIDs in the CIDFont. Table 5.13 lists the entries in a CIDFont dictionary.

TABLE 5.13 Entries in a CIDFont dictionary

KEY	TYPE	VALUE
Type	name	*(Required)* The type of PDF object that this dictionary describes; must be **Font** for a CIDFont dictionary.
Subtype	name	*(Required)* The type of CIDFont; **CIDFontType0** or **CIDFontType2**.

BaseFont	name	*(Required)* The PostScript name of the CIDFont. For Type 0 CIDFonts, this is usually the value of the **CIDFontName** entry in the CIDFont program. For Type 2 CIDFonts, it is derived the same way as for a simple TrueType font; see Section 5.5.2, "TrueType Fonts." In either case, the name can have a subset prefix if appropriate; see Section 5.5.3, "Font Subsets."
CIDSystemInfo	dictionary	*(Required)* A dictionary containing entries that define the character collection of the CIDFont. See Table 5.12 on page 314.
FontDescriptor	dictionary	*(Required; must be an indirect reference)* A font descriptor describing the CIDFont's default metrics other than its glyph widths (see Section 5.7, "Font Descriptors").
DW	integer	*(Optional)* The default width for glyphs in the CIDFont (see "Glyph Metrics in CIDFonts" on page 317). Default value: 0.
W	array	*(Optional)* A description of the widths for the glyphs in the CIDFont. The array's elements have a variable format that can specify individual widths for consecutive CIDs or one width for a range of CIDs (see "Glyph Metrics in CIDFonts" on page 317). Default value: none (the **DW** value is used for all glyphs).
DW2	array	*(Optional; applies only to CIDFonts used for vertical writing)* An array of two numbers specifying the default metrics for vertical writing (see "Glyph Metrics in CIDFonts" on page 317). Default value: [880 −1000].
W2	array	*(Optional; applies only to CIDFonts used for vertical writing)* A description of the metrics for vertical writing for the glyphs in the CIDFont (see "Glyph Metrics in CIDFonts" on page 317). Default value: none (the **DW2** value is used for all glyphs).
CIDToGIDMap	stream or name	*(Optional; Type 2 CIDFonts only)* A specification of the mapping from CIDs to glyph indices. If the value is a stream, the bytes in the stream contain the mapping from CIDs to glyph indices: the glyph index for a particular CID value c is a 2-byte value stored in bytes $2 \times c$ and $2 \times c + 1$, where the first byte is the high-order byte. If the value of **CIDToGIDMap** is a name, it must be **Identity**, indicating that the mapping between CIDs and glyph indices is the identity mapping. Default value: **Identity**. This entry may appear only in a Type 2 CIDFont whose associated TrueType font program is embedded in the PDF file (see the next section).

Glyph Selection in CIDFonts

Type 0 and Type 2 CIDFonts handle the mapping from CIDs to glyph descriptions in somewhat different ways.

For Type 0, the CIDFont program itself contains glyph descriptions that are identified by CIDs. The CIDFont program identifies the character collection by a **CIDSystemInfo** dictionary, which should simply be copied into the PDF CIDFont dictionary. CIDs are interpreted uniformly in all CIDFont programs supporting a given character collection, whether the program is embedded in the PDF file or obtained from an external source.

For Type 2, the CIDFont program is actually a TrueType font program, which has no native notion of CIDs. In a TrueType font program, glyph descriptions are identified by *glyph index* values. Glyph indices are internal to the font and are not defined consistently from one font to another. Instead, a TrueType font program contains a "cmap" table that provides mappings directly from character codes to glyph indices for one or more predefined encodings.

TrueType font programs are integrated with the CID-keyed font architecture in one of two ways, depending on whether the font program is embedded in the PDF file.

- If the TrueType font program is embedded, the Type 2 CIDFont dictionary must contain a **CIDToGIDMap** entry that maps CIDs to the glyph indices for the appropriate glyph descriptions in that font program.

- If the TrueType font program is not embedded but is referenced by name, the Type 2 CIDFont dictionary must *not* contain a **CIDToGIDMap** entry, since it is not meaningful to refer to glyph indices in an external font program. In this case, CIDs do not participate in glyph selection, and only predefined CMaps may be used with this CIDFont (see Section 5.6.4, "CMaps"). The viewer application selects glyphs by translating characters from the encoding specified by the predefined CMap to one of the encodings given in the TrueType font's "cmap" table. The means by which this is accomplished are implementation-dependent.

Even though the CIDs are sometimes not used to select glyphs in a Type 2 CID-Font, they are always used to determine the glyph metrics, as described in the next section.

Every CIDFont must contain a glyph description for CID 0, which is analogous to the .notdef character name in simple fonts (see "Handling Undefined Characters" on page 329).

Glyph Metrics in CIDFonts

As discussed in Section 5.1.3, "Glyph Positioning and Metrics," the *width* of a glyph refers to the horizontal displacement between the origin of the glyph and the origin of the next glyph when writing in horizontal mode. In this mode, the vertical displacement between origins is always 0. Widths for a CIDFont are defined using the **DW** and **W** entries in the CIDFont dictionary. These widths must be consistent with the actual widths given in the CIDFont program itself.

The **DW** entry defines the default width, which is used for all glyphs whose widths are not specified individually. This entry is particularly useful for Chinese, Japanese, and Korean fonts, in which many of the glyphs have the same width.

The **W** array allows the definition of widths for individual CIDs. The elements of the array are organized in groups of two or three, where each group is in one of the following two formats:

$$c \; [w_1 \; w_2 \; \dots \; w_n]$$
$$c_{first} \; c_{last} \; w$$

In the first format, c is an integer specifying a starting CID value; it is followed by an array of n numbers that specify the widths for n consecutive CIDs, starting with c. The second format defines the same width, w, for all CIDs in the range c_{first} to c_{last}.

The following is an example of a **W** entry:

```
/W [ 120 [400 325 500]
     7080 8032 1000
   ]
```

In this example, the glyphs for the characters having CIDs 120, 121, and 122 are 400, 325, and 500 units wide, respectively. CIDs in the range 7080 through 8032 all have a width of 1000 units.

Glyphs from a CIDFont can be shown in vertical writing mode. (This is selected by the **WMode** entry in the associated CMap dictionary; see Section 5.6.4, "CMaps.") To be used in this way, the CIDFont must define the vertical displacement for each glyph and the position vector that relates the horizontal and vertical writing origins.

The default position vector and vertical displacement vector are specified by the **DW2** entry in the CIDFont dictionary. **DW2** is an array of two values: the y component of the position vector v and the y component of the displacement vector $w1$ (see Figure 5.5 on page 278). The x component of the position vector is always half the glyph width, and that of the displacement vector is always 0. For example, if the **DW2** entry is

```
/DW2 [880 −1000]
```

then a glyph's position vector and vertical displacement vector are

$$v = (w0 \div 2, 880)$$
$$w1 = (0, -1000)$$

where $w0$ is the width (horizontal displacement) for the same glyph. Note that a negative value for the y component will place the origin of the next glyph *below* the current glyph, because y coordinates in a standard coordinate system increase from bottom to top.

The **W2** array allows the definition of vertical metrics for individual CIDs. The elements of the array are organized in groups of two or five, where each group is in one of the following two formats:

$$c\ [w1_{1y}\ v_{1x}\ v_{1y}\ w1_{2y}\ v_{2x}\ v_{2y}\ \ldots]$$
$$c_{first}\ c_{last}\ w1_{1y}\ v_{1x}\ v_{1y}$$

In the first format, c is a starting CID and is followed by an array containing numbers interpreted in groups of three. Each group consists of the y component of the vertical displacement vector $w1$ (whose x component is always 0) followed by the x and y components for the position vector v. Successive groups define the vertical metrics for consecutive CIDs starting with c. The second format defines a range of CIDs from c_{first} to c_{last}, followed by three numbers that define the vertical metrics for all CIDs in this range. For example:

```
/W2 [ 120 [−1000 250 772]
      7080 8032 −1000 500 900
    ]
```

This **W2** entry defines the vertical displacement vector for the character with CID 120 as $(0, -1000)$ and the position vector as $(250, 772)$. It also defines the displacement vector for CIDs in the range 7080 through 8032 as $(0, -1000)$ and the position vector as $(500, 900)$.

5.6.4 CMaps

As stated earlier, a CMap specifies the mapping from character codes to character selectors (CIDs, character names, or character codes) in one or more associated fonts or CIDFonts. It serves a function analogous to the **Encoding** dictionary for a simple font. The CMap does not refer directly to specific fonts or CIDFonts; instead, it is combined with them as part of a CID-keyed font, represented in PDF as a Type 0 font dictionary (see Section 5.6.5, "Type 0 Font Dictionaries").

Within the CMap, the character mappings refer to the associated fonts or CIDFonts by *font number*, indexing from 0. All of the mappings for a particular font number must specify the same kind of character selector. If the character selectors are CIDs, the associated dictionary is expected to be a CIDFont. If the character selectors are names or codes, the associated dictionary is expected to be a font.

Note: As mentioned earlier, PDF versions up to and including PDF 1.3 do not support the entire CID-keyed font architecture. In PDF, a CID-keyed font may have only a single descendant, selected by font number 0, whose characters must be referenced by CID.

A CMap also specifies the writing mode—horizontal or vertical—for any CIDFont with which the CMap is combined. This determines which metrics are to be used when glyphs are painted from that font. (Writing mode is specified as part of the CMap because some glyphs have different shapes when written horizontally and vertically. In that case, the horizontal and vertical variants of a CMap specify different CIDs for a given character code.)

A CMap may be specified in two ways:

• As a name object identifying a predefined CMap, whose definition is known to the viewer application.

• As a stream object whose contents are a CMap file. (See implementation note 44 in Appendix H.)

Predefined CMaps

Table 5.14 lists the predefined CMap names. These CMaps map character codes to CIDs in a single descendant CIDFont. CMaps whose names end in H specify horizontal writing mode; those ending in V specify vertical writing mode.

TABLE 5.14   Predefined CJK CMap names

NAME	DESCRIPTION
	Chinese (Simplified)
GB–EUC–H GB–EUC–V	Microsoft Code Page 936 (IfCharSet 0x86), GB 2312-80 character set, EUC-CN encoding Vertical version of GB–EUC–H
GBpc–EUC–H GBpc–EUC–V	Macintosh, GB 2312-80 character set, EUC-CN encoding, Script Manager code 2 Vertical version of GBpc–EUC–H
GBK–EUC–H GBK–EUC–V	Microsoft Code Page 936 (IfCharSet 0x86), GBK character set, GBK encoding Vertical version of GBK–EUC–H
UniGB–UCS2–H UniGB–UCS2–V	Unicode (UCS-2) encoding for the Adobe-GB1 character collection Vertical version of UniGB–UCS2–H
	Chinese (Traditional)
B5pc–H B5pc–V	Macintosh, Big Five character set, Big Five encoding, Script Manager code 2 Vertical version of B5pc–H
ETen–B5–H ETen–B5–V	Microsoft Code Page 950 (IfCharSet 0x88), Big Five character set with ETen extensions Vertical version of ETen–B5–H
ETenms–B5–H ETenms–B5–V	Same as ETen–B5–H, but replaces half-width Latin characters with proportional forms Vertical version of ETenms–B5–H
CNS–EUC–H CNS–EUC–V	CNS 11643-1992 character set, EUC-TW encoding Vertical version of CNS–EUC–H
UniCNS–UCS2–H UniCNS–UCS2–V	Unicode (UCS-2) encoding for the Adobe-CNS1 character collection Vertical version of UniCNS–UCS2–H
	Japanese
83pv–RKSJ–H	Macintosh, JIS X 0208 character set with KanjiTalk6 extensions, Shift-JIS encoding, Script Manager code 1
90ms–RKSJ–H	Microsoft Code Page 932 (IfCharSet 0x80), JIS X 0208 character set with NEC and IBM extensions
90ms–RKSJ–V	Vertical version of 90ms–RKSJ–H

90msp–RKSJ–H	Same as 90ms–RKSJ–H, but replaces half-width Latin characters with proportional forms
90msp–RKSJ–V	Vertical version of 90msp–RKSJ–H
90pv–RKSJ–H	Macintosh, JIS X 0208 character set with KanjiTalk7 extensions, Shift-JIS encoding, Script Manager code 1
Add–RKSJ–H	JIS X 0208 character set with Fujitsu FMR extensions, Shift-JIS encoding
Add–RKSJ–V	Vertical version of Add–RKSJ–H
EUC–H	JIS X 0208 character set, EUC-JP encoding
EUC–V	Vertical version of EUC–H
Ext–RKSJ–H	JIS C 6226 (JIS78) character set with NEC extensions, Shift-JIS encoding
Ext–RKSJ–V	Vertical version of Ext–RKSJ–H
H	JIS X 0208 character set, ISO-2022-JP encoding
V	Vertical version of H
UniJIS–UCS2–H	Unicode (UCS-2) encoding for the Adobe-Japan1 character collection
UniJIS–UCS2–V	Vertical version of UniJIS–UCS2–H
UniJIS–UCS2–HW–H	Same as UniJIS–UCS2–H, but replaces proportional Latin characters with half-width forms
UniJIS–UCS2–HW–V	Vertical version of UniJIS–UCS2–HW–H

Korean

KSC–EUC–H	KS X 1001:1992 character set, EUC-KR encoding
KSC–EUC–V	Vertical version of KSC–EUC–H
KSCms–UHC–H	Microsoft Code Page 949 (lfCharSet 0x81), KS X 1001:1992 character set plus 8822 additional hangul, Unified Hangul Code (UHC) encoding
KSCms–UHC–V	Vertical version of KSCms–UHC–H
KSCms–UHC–HW–H	Same as KSCms–UHC–H, but replaces proportional Latin characters with half-width forms
KSCms–UHC–HW–V	Vertical version of KSCms–UHC–HW–H
KSCpc–EUC–H	Macintosh, KS X 1001:1992 character set with Mac OS KH extensions, Script Manager Code 3
UniKS–UCS2–H	Unicode (UCS-2) encoding for the Adobe-Korea1 character collection
UniKS–UCS2–V	Vertical version of UniKS–UCS2–H

Generic

Identity–H	The horizontal identity mapping for 2-byte CIDs; may be used with CIDFonts using any **Registry**, **Ordering**, and **Supplement** values. It maps 2-byte character codes ranging from 0 to 65,535 to the same 2-byte CID value, interpreted high-order byte first (see below).
Identity–V	Vertical version of Identity–H. The mapping is the same as for Identity–H.

The CMap programs that define all of the predefined CMaps are available through the Adobe Developer Program and are also provided in conjunction with the book *CJKV Information Processing* (see the Bibliography).

The Identity–H and Identity–V CMaps can be used to refer to characters directly by their CIDs when showing a text string. When the current font is a Type 0 font whose **Encoding** entry is Identity–H or Identity–V, the string to be shown is interpreted as pairs of bytes representing CIDs, high-order byte first. This works with any CIDFont, independently of its character collection. Additionally, when used in conjunction with a Type 2 CIDFont whose **CIDToGIDMap** entry is **Identity**, the 2-byte CID values in fact represent glyph indices for the glyph descriptions in the TrueType font program. This works only if the TrueType font program is embedded in the PDF file.

Embedded CMap Files

For character encodings that are not predefined, the PDF file must contain a stream that defines the CMap. In addition to the standard entries for stream dictionaries (listed in Table 3.4 on page 35), the stream contains the entries listed in Table 5.15. The data in the stream defines the mapping from character codes to a font number and a character selector. The data must follow the syntax defined in Adobe Technical Note #5014, *Adobe CMap and CIDFont Files Specification*.

TABLE 5.15 Entries in a CMap dictionary		
KEY	**TYPE**	**VALUE**
Type	name	(*Required*) The type of PDF object that this dictionary describes; must be **CMap** for a CMap dictionary. (Note that although this object is the value of an entry named **Encoding** in a Type 0 font, its type is **CMap**.)
CMapName	name	(*Required*) The PostScript name of the CMap. This should be the same as the value of **CMapName** in the CMap file itself.
CIDSystemInfo	dictionary or array	(*Required*) A dictionary or array containing entries that define the character collection of the CIDFont. If the CMap refers to a single CIDFont, the entry may be a dictionary; see Table 5.12 on page 314. If the CMap refers to more than one descendant font, the entry must be an array that is indexed by font number; if the corresponding descendant font is a CIDFont, the array element must be a **CIDSystemInfo** dictionary, otherwise the element must be *null*.

*Note: In all PDF versions up to and including PDF 1.3, **CIDSystemInfo** must be either a dictionary or a one-element array containing a dictionary.*

WMode	integer	*(Optional)* A code that determines the writing mode of the Type 0 font that uses this CMap:

0	Horizontal
1	Vertical

Default value: 0.

UseCMap	name or stream	*(Optional)* The name of a predefined CMap, or a stream containing a CMap, that is to be used as the base for this CMap. This allows the CMap to be defined differentially, specifying only the character mappings that differ from the base CMap.

CMap Example and Operator Summary

The following example of a CMap stream object illustrates and partially explains the contents of a CMap file. This is fully documented in Adobe Technical Note #5014, *Adobe CMap and CIDFont Files Specification*. There are several reasons for including this material here:

- It documents some restrictions on the contents of a CMap file that can be embedded in a PDF file.

- It provides background to aid in understanding subsequent material, particularly "CMap Mapping" on page 328.

- It is the basis for a PDF feature, the **ToUnicode** CMap, which is a minor extension of the CMap file format. This extension is described in Section 5.9, "To-Unicode CMaps."

Example 5.11 is a sample CMap for a Japanese Shift-JIS encoding. Character codes in this encoding can be either 1 or 2 bytes in length. This CMap maps all character codes to CIDs in font number 0. It could be used with a CIDFont that uses the same CID ordering as specified in the **CIDSystemInfo** entry. Note that several of the entries in the stream dictionary are also replicated in the stream data itself.

Example 5.11

```
22 0 obj
    << /Type /CMap
        /CMapName /90ms–RKSJ–H
        /CIDSystemInfo << /Registry (Adobe)
                          /Ordering (Japan1)
                          /Supplement 2
                >>
        /WMode 0
        /Length 23 0 R
    >>

stream
%!PS–Adobe–3.0 Resource–CMap
%%DocumentNeededResources: ProcSet (CIDInit)
%%IncludeResource: ProcSet (CIDInit)
%%BeginResource: CMap (90ms–RKSJ–H)
%%Title: (90ms–RKSJ–H Adobe Japan1 2)
%%Version: 10.001
%%Copyright: Copyright 1990–1998 Adobe Systems Inc.
%%Copyright: All Rights Reserved.
%%EndComments
/CIDInit /ProcSet findresource begin
12 dict begin
begincmap
/CIDSystemInfo
3 dict dup begin
/Registry (Adobe) def
/Ordering (Japan1) def
/Supplement 2 def
end def

/CMapName /90ms–RKSJ–H def
/CMapVersion 10.001 def
/CMapType 1 def
/UIDOffset 950 def
/XUID [1 10 25343] def
/WMode 0 def
4 begincodespacerange
<00>    <80>
<8140>  <9FFC>
<A0>    <DF>
<E040>  <FCFC>
endcodespacerange
```

```
1  beginnotdefrange
<00>    <1F>    231
endnotdefrange

100  begincidrange
<20>    <7D>    231
<7E>    <7E>    631
<8140>  <817E>  633
<8180>  <81AC>  696
<81B8>  <81BF>  741
<81C8>  <81CE>  749
… Additional ranges …
<FB40>  <FB7E>  8518
<FB80>  <FBFC>  8581
<FC40>  <FC4B>  8706
endcidrange
endcmap
CMapName currentdict /CMap defineresource pop
end
end
%%EndResource
%%EOF
endstream
endobj
```

As can be seen from this example, a CMap file conforms to PostScript language syntax; however, a full PostScript interpreter is not needed to interpret it. Aside from some required boilerplate, the CMap file consists of one or more occurrences of several special CMap construction operators, invoked in a specific order. The following is a summary of these operators.

* **begincmap** and **endcmap** enclose the CMap definition.

* **usecmap** incorporates the code mappings from another CMap file. In PDF, the other CMap must also be identified in the **UseCMap** entry in the CMap dictionary (see Table 5.15 on page 322).

* **begincodespacerange** and **endcodespacerange** define *codespace ranges*—the valid input character code ranges—by specifying a pair of codes of some particular length giving the lower and upper bounds of each range; see "CMap Mapping" on page 328.

- **usefont** specifies a font number that is an implicit operand of all the character code mapping operations that follow. In PDF versions up to and including PDF 1.3, the font number must be 0; since this is the default, **usefont** typically does not appear at all.

- **beginbfchar** and **endbfchar** define mappings of individual input character codes to character codes or character names in the associated font. **beginbfrange** and **endbfrange** do the same, but for ranges of input codes. In PDF versions up to and including PDF 1.3, these operators may not appear in a CMap that is used as the **Encoding** entry of a Type 0 font; however, they may appear in the definition of a **ToUnicode** CMap (see Section 5.9, "ToUnicode CMaps").

- **begincidchar** and **endcidchar** define mappings of individual input character codes to CIDs in the associated CIDFont. **begincidrange** and **endcidrange** do the same, but for ranges of input codes.

- **beginnotdefchar**, **endnotdefchar**, **beginnotdefrange**, and **endnotdefrange** define notdef mappings from character codes to CIDs. As described in the section "Handling Undefined Characters" on page 329, a notdef mapping is used if the normal mapping produces a CID for which no glyph is present in the associated CIDFont.

The **beginrearrangedfont**, **endrearrangedfont**, **beginusematrix**, and **endusematrix** operators, described in Adobe Technical Note #5014, *Adobe CMap and CIDFont Files Specification*, may not be used in CMap files embedded in a PDF file.

5.6.5 Type 0 Font Dictionaries

A Type 0 font dictionary contains the entries listed in Table 5.16. Example 5.12 shows a Type 0 font that refers to a single CIDFont. The CMap used is one of the predefined CMaps listed in Table 5.14 on page 320, and is referenced by name.

TABLE 5.16   Entries in a Type 0 font dictionary

KEY	TYPE	VALUE
Type	name	*(Required)* The type of PDF object that this dictionary describes; must be **Font** for a font dictionary.
Subtype	name	*(Required)* The type of font; must be **Type0**.
BaseFont	name	*(Required)* The PostScript name of the font. In principle, this is an arbitrary name, since there is no font program associated directly with a Type 0 font dictionary. The conventions described here ensure maximum compatibility with existing Acrobat products. If the descendant is a Type 0 CIDFont, this name should be the concatenation of the CIDFont's **BaseFont** name, a hyphen, and the CMap name given in the **Encoding** entry (or the **CMapName** entry in the CMap program itself). If the descendant is a Type 2 CIDFont, this name should be the same as the CID-Font's **BaseFont** name.
Encoding	name or stream	*(Required)* The name of a predefined CMap, or a stream containing a CMap program, that maps character codes to font numbers and CIDs. If the descendant font is a Type 2 CIDFont whose associated TrueType font program is not embedded in the PDF file, the **Encoding** entry must be a predefined CMap name (see "Glyph Selection in CIDFonts" on page 315).
DescendantFonts	array	*(Required)* An array specifying one or more fonts or CIDFonts that are descendants of this composite font. This array is indexed by the font number that is obtained by mapping a character code through the CMap specified in the **Encoding** entry. *Note: In all PDF versions up to and including PDF 1.3, **DescendantFonts** must be a one-element array containing a CIDFont dictionary.*
ToUnicode	stream	*(Optional)* A stream containing a CMap file that maps character codes to Unicode values (see Section 5.9, "ToUnicode CMaps").

Example 5.12

```
14 0 obj
    << /Type /Font
       /Subtype /Type0
       /BaseFont /HeiseiMin–W5–90ms–RKSJ–H
       /Encoding /90ms–RKSJ–H
       /DescendantFonts [15 0 R]
    >>
endobj
```

CMap Mapping

When the current font is a Type 0 font, the text-showing operators (such as **Tj**) interpret the bytes in the string to be shown according to the CMap specified as the **Encoding** entry of the Type 0 font dictionary. The following paragraphs describe how the characters in the string are decoded and mapped into character selectors (which in PDF 1.3 must always be CIDs).

The number of bytes extracted from the string for each successive character is determined exclusively by the codespace ranges in the CMap (delimited by **begincodespacerange** and **endcodespacerange**). A codespace range is specified by a pair of codes of some particular length giving the lower and upper bounds of that range. A code is considered to match the range if it is the same length as the bounding codes and the value of each of its bytes lies between the corresponding bytes of the lower and upper bounds. The code length cannot exceed the number of bytes representable in an integer (see Appendix C).

A sequence of one or more bytes is extracted from the string and matched against the codespace ranges in the CMap. That is, the first byte is matched against 1-byte codespace ranges; if no match is found, a second byte is extracted, and the 2-byte code is matched against 2-byte codespace ranges. This continues for successively longer codes until a match is found or all codespace ranges have been tested. There will be at most one match, since codespace ranges do not overlap.

The code extracted from the string is then looked up in the character code mappings for codes of that length. (These are the mappings defined by **beginbfchar**, **endbfchar**, **begincidchar**, **endcidchar**, and corresponding operators for ranges.) Failing that, it is looked up in the notdef mappings, as described in the next section.

The results of the CMap mapping algorithm are a font number and a character selector. In PDF 1.3, the font number must always be 0 and the character selector must always be a CID; this is the only case described here. The font number is used as an index into the Type 0 font's **DescendantFonts** array, selecting a CIDFont. The CID is then used to select a glyph in the CIDFont. If the CIDFont contains no glyph for that CID, the notdef mappings are consulted, as described in the next section.

Handling Undefined Characters

A CMap mapping operation can fail to select a glyph for any of a variety of reasons. This section describes what happens when that occurs.

If a code maps to a CID for which there is no such glyph in the descendant CID-Font, the *notdef mappings* in the CMap are consulted to obtain a substitute character selector. These mappings (so called by analogy with the .notdef character mechanism in simple fonts) are delimited by the operators **beginnotdefchar**, **endnotdefchar**, **beginnotdefrange**, and **endnotdefrange**; they always map to a CID. If a matching notdef mapping is found, the CID selects a glyph in the associated descendant, which must be a CIDFont. If there is no glyph for that CID, the glyph for CID 0 (which is required to be present) is substituted.

If the CMap does not contain either a character mapping or a notdef mapping for the code, descendant 0 is selected and the glyph for CID 0 is substituted from the associated CIDFont.

If the code is invalid—that is, the bytes extracted from the string to be shown do not match any codespace range in the CMap—a substitute glyph is chosen as just described. The character mapping algorithm is reset to its original position in the string, and a modified mapping algorithm chooses the best partially matching codespace range, as follows:

1. If the first byte extracted from the string to be shown does not match the first byte of any codespace range, the range having the shortest codes is chosen.

2. Otherwise (that is, if there is a partial match), for each additional byte extracted, the code accumulated so far is matched against the beginnings of all longer codespace ranges until the longest such partial match has been found. If multiple codespace ranges have partial matches of the same length, the one having the shortest codes is chosen.

The length of the codes in the chosen codespace range determines the total number of bytes to consume from the string for the current mapping operation.

5.7 Font Descriptors

A *font descriptor* specifies metrics and other attributes of a simple font or a CID-Font as a whole, as distinct from the metrics of individual glyphs. These font metrics provide information that enable a viewing application to synthesize a substitute font or select a similar font when the font program is unavailable. The font descriptor may also be used to embed the font program in the PDF file. (Font descriptors are not used with Type 0 or Type 3 fonts.)

A font descriptor is a dictionary whose entries specify various font attributes. The entries common to all font descriptors—for both simple fonts and CIDFonts—are listed in Table 5.17; additional entries in the font descriptor for a CIDFont are described in Section 5.7.2, "Font Descriptors for CIDFonts." All integer values are units in glyph space. The conversion from glyph space to text space is described in Section 5.1.3, "Glyph Positioning and Metrics."

TABLE 5.17 Entries common to all font descriptors

KEY	TYPE	VALUE
Type	name	*(Required)* The type of PDF object that this dictionary describes; must be **FontDescriptor** for a font descriptor.
Ascent	number	*(Required)* The maximum height above the baseline reached by glyphs in this font, excluding the height of glyphs for accented characters.
CapHeight	number	*(Required)* The *y* coordinate of the top of flat capital letters, measured from the baseline.
Descent	number	*(Required)* The maximum depth below the baseline reached by glyphs in this font. The value is a negative number.
Flags	integer	*(Required)* A collection of flags defining various characteristics of the font (see Section 5.7.1, "Font Descriptor Flags").
FontBBox	rectangle	*(Required)* A rectangle (see Section 3.8.3, "Rectangles"), expressed in the glyph coordinate system, specifying the *font bounding box*. This is the smallest rectangle enclosing the shape that would result if all of the glyphs of the font were placed with their origins coincident and then filled.
FontName	name	*(Required)* The PostScript name of the font. This should be the same as the value of **BaseFont** in the font or CIDFont dictionary that refers to this font descriptor.

ItalicAngle	number	*(Required)* The angle, expressed in degrees counterclockwise from the vertical, of the dominant vertical strokes of the font. (For example, the 9-o'clock position is 90 degrees, and the 3-o'clock position is –90 degrees.) The value is negative for fonts that slope to the right, as almost all italic fonts do.
StemV	number	*(Required)* The width, measured in the *x* direction, of the dominant vertical stems of glyphs in the font.
AvgWidth	number	*(Optional)* The average width of glyphs in the font. Default value: 0.
FontFile	stream	*(Optional)* A stream containing a Type 1 font program (see Section 5.8, "Embedded Font Programs").
FontFile2	stream	*(Optional; PDF 1.1)* A stream containing a TrueType font program (see Section 5.8, "Embedded Font Programs").
FontFile3	stream	*(Optional; PDF 1.2)* A stream containing a font program other than Type 1 or TrueType. The format of the font program is specified by the **Subtype** entry in the stream dictionary (see Section 5.8, "Embedded Font Programs," and implementation note 45 in Appendix H).
		Note: *At most, only one of the* **FontFile**, **FontFile2**, *and* **FontFile3** *entries may be present.*
Leading	number	*(Optional)* The desired spacing between baselines of consecutive lines of text. Default value: 0.
MaxWidth	number	*(Optional)* The maximum width of glyphs in the font. Default value: 0.
MissingWidth	number	*(Optional)* The width to use for character codes whose widths are not specified in a font dictionary's **Widths** array. This has a predictable effect only if all such codes map to glyphs whose actual widths are the same as the **MissingWidth** value. Default value: 0.
StemH	number	*(Optional)* The vertical width of the dominant horizontal stems of glyphs in the font. Default value: 0.
XHeight	number	*(Optional)* The *y* coordinate of the top of flat nonascending lowercase letters, measured from the baseline. Default value: 0.
CharSet	string	*(Optional; meaningful only in Type 1 fonts; PDF 1.1)* A string listing the character names defined in a subset font. The names in this string must be in PDF syntax—that is, each name preceded by a slash (/). The names can appear in any order. The name .notdef should be omitted; it is assumed to exist in the font subset. If this entry is absent, the only indication of a subset font is the subset tag in the **FontName** entry (see Section 5.5.3, "Font Subsets").

5.7.1 Font Descriptor Flags

The value of the **Flags** entry in a font descriptor is an unsigned 32-bit integer containing flags specifying various characteristics of the font. Bit positions within the flag word are numbered from 1 (low-order) to 32 (high-order). Table 5.18 shows the meanings of the flags; all undefined flag bits are reserved and must be set to 0. Figure 5.13 shows examples of fonts with these characteristics.

TABLE 5.18 Font flags

BIT POSITION	NAME	MEANING
1	FixedPitch	All glyphs have the same width (as opposed to proportional or variable-pitch fonts, which have different widths).
2	Serif	Glyphs have serifs, which are short strokes drawn at an angle on the top and bottom of glyph stems (as opposed to *sans serif* fonts, which do not).
3	Symbolic	Font contains characters outside the Adobe standard Latin character set. Bits 3 and 6 cannot both be 0 or both be 1 (see below).
4	Script	Glyphs resemble cursive handwriting.
6	Nonsymbolic	Font uses the Adobe standard Latin character set or a subset of it (see below).
7	Italic	Glyphs have dominant vertical strokes that are slanted.
17	AllCap	Font contains no lowercase letters; typically used for display purposes such as titles or headlines.
18	SmallCap	Font contains both uppercase and lowercase letters. The uppercase letters are similar to ones in the regular version of the same typeface family. The glyphs for the lowercase letters have the same shapes as the corresponding uppercase letters, but they are sized and their proportions adjusted so that they have the same size and stroke weight as lowercase glyphs in the same typeface family.
19	ForceBold	See below.

Fixed-pitch font	The quick brown fox jumped.
Serif font	The quick brown fox jumped.
Sans serif font	The quick brown fox jumped.
Symbolic font	✳✲❊ ❑◆✳✳✳ ❂❑⬜◗■ ✳❑❘ ✳◆◯❑✳✳✎
Script font	*The quick brown fox jumped.*
Italic font	*The quick brown fox jumped.*
All-cap font	*THE QUICK BROWN FOX JUMPED*
Small-cap font	THE QUICK BROWN FOX JUMPED.

FIGURE 5.13 *Characteristics represented in the **Flags** entry of a font descriptor*

The Nonsymbolic flag (bit 6 in the **Flags** entry) indicates that the font's character set is the Adobe standard Latin character set (or a subset of it) and that it uses the standard names for those characters. The characters in this character set are shown in Section D.1, "Latin Character Set and Encodings." If the font uses any characters outside this set, the Symbolic flag should be set and the Nonsymbolic flag clear; in other words, any font whose character set is not a subset of the Adobe standard character set is considered to be symbolic. This influences the font's implicit base encoding and may affect a viewer application's font substitution strategies.

Note: This classification of nonsymbolic and symbolic fonts is peculiar to PDF. A font may contain additional characters that are used in Latin writing systems but are outside the Adobe standard Latin character set; PDF considers such a font to be symbolic. The use of two flags to represent a single binary choice is a historical accident.

The ForceBold flag (bit 19) determines whether bold glyphs are painted with extra pixels even at very small text sizes. Typically, when glyphs are painted at small sizes on very low-resolution devices such as display screens, features of bold glyphs may appear only one pixel wide. Because this is the minimum feature width on a pixel-based device, ordinary (nonbold) glyphs also appear with one-pixel-wide features, and so cannot be distinguished from bold glyphs. If the ForceBold flag is set, features of bold glyphs may be thickened at small text sizes.

Example 5.13 illustrates a font descriptor whose **Flags** entry has the Serif, Nonsymbolic, and ForceBold flags (bits 2, 6, and 19) set.

Example 5.13

```
7 0 obj
    << /Type /FontDescriptor
       /FontName /AGaramond–Semibold
       /Flags 262178                        % Bits 2, 6, and 19
       /FontBBox [−177 −269 1123 866]
       /MissingWidth 255
       /StemV 105
       /StemH 45
       /CapHeight 660
       /XHeight 394
       /Ascent 720
       /Descent −270
       /Leading 83
       /MaxWidth 1212
       /AvgWidth 478
       /ItalicAngle 0
    >>
endobj
```

5.7.2 Font Descriptors for CIDFonts

In addition to the entries in Table 5.17 on page 330, the **FontDescriptor** dictionaries of CIDFonts may contain the entries listed in Table 5.19.

TABLE 5.19 Additional font descriptor entries for CIDFonts

KEY	TYPE	VALUE
Style	dictionary	*(Optional)* A dictionary containing entries that describe the style of the glyphs in the font (see "Style," below).
Lang	name	*(Optional)* A name specifying the language of the font, used for encodings where the language is not implied by the encoding itself. The possible values are the 2-character codes defined by ISO 639—for example, EN for English and JA for Japanese. The complete list of these codes be obtained from the International Organization for Standardization (see the Bibliography).
FD	dictionary	*(Optional)* A dictionary whose keys identify a class of characters in a CIDFont. Each value is a dictionary containing entries that override the corresponding values in the main font descriptor dictionary for that class of characters (see "FD" on page 336).
CIDSet	stream	*(Optional)* A stream identifying which CIDs are present in the CIDFont file. If this entry is present, the CIDFont contains only a subset of the glyphs in the character collection defined by the **CIDSystemInfo** dictionary. If it is absent, the only indication of a subset CIDFont is the subset tag in the **FontName** entry (see Section 5.5.3, "Font Subsets").
		The stream's data is organized as a table of bits indexed by CID. The bits should be stored in bytes with the high-order bit first. Each bit corresponds to a CID. The first bit of the first byte corresponds to CID 0, the next bit to CID 1, and so on.

Style

The **Style** dictionary contains entries that define style attributes and values for the CIDFont. Currently, only the **Panose** entry is defined. The value of **Panose** is a 12-byte string consisting of the following:

- The font family class and subclass ID bytes, given in the sFamilyClass field of the "OS/2" table in a TrueType font. This field is documented in Microsoft's *TrueType 1.0 Font Files Technical Specification*.

- Ten bytes for the PANOSE classification number for the font. The PANOSE classification system is documented in the *PANOSE Classification Metrics Guide.*

See the Bibliography for more information about these documents. The following is an example of a **Style** entry in the font descriptor:

```
/Style << /Panose <01 05 02 02 03 00 00 00 00 00 00 00> >>
```

FD

A CIDFont may be made up of different classes of characters, each class requiring different sets of the fontwide attributes that appear in font descriptors. Latin characters, for example, may require different attributes than kanji characters. The font descriptor defines a set of default attributes that apply to all characters in the CIDFont; the **FD** entry in the font descriptor contains exceptions to these defaults.

The key for each entry in an **FD** dictionary is the name of a class of characters—that is, a particular subset of the CIDFont's character collection. The entry's value is a font descriptor whose contents are to override the fontwide attributes for that class only. This font descriptor should contain entries for metric information only; it should not include **FontFile**, **FontFile2**, **FontFile3**, or any of the entries listed in Table 5.19.

It is strongly recommended that the **FD** dictionary contain at least the metrics for the proportional Latin characters. With the information for these characters, a more accurate substitution font can be created.

The names of the character classes depend on the character collection, as identified by the **Registry**, **Ordering**, and **Supplement** values in the **CIDSystemInfo** entry of the CIDFont dictionary. Table 5.20 lists the valid keys for the Adobe-Japan1-2, Adobe-Japan2-0, Adobe-Korea1-1, Adobe-GB1-2, and Adobe-CNS1-0 character collections.

TABLE 5.20 Character classes in CJK fonts

CHARACTER COLLECTION	CLASS	CHARACTERS IN CLASS
Adobe-Japan1-2	**Alphabetic**	Full-width Latin, Greek, and Cyrillic characters
	AlphaNum	Numeric characters
	Dingbats	Special symbols
	Generic	Typeface-independent characters, such as line-drawing
	HKana	Half-width kana (katakana and hiragana) characters
	HRoman	Half-width Latin characters
	Kana	Full-width kana (katakana and hiragana) characters
	Kanji	Full-width kanji (Chinese) characters
	Proportional	Proportional Latin characters
Adobe-Japan2-0	**Alphabetic**	Full-width Latin, Greek, and Cyrillic characters
	Dingbats	Special symbols
	HojoKanji	Full-width kanji characters
Adobe-Korea1-1	**Alphabetic**	Full-width Latin, Greek, and Cyrillic characters
	Dingbats	Special symbols
	Hangul	Hangul and jamo characters
	Hanja	Full-width hanja (Chinese) characters
	HRoman	Half-width Latin characters
	Kana	Japanese kana (katakana and hiragana) characters
	Proportional	Proportional Latin characters
Adobe-GB1-2	**Alphabetic**	Full-width Latin, Greek, and Cyrillic characters
	Dingbats	Special symbols
	Hanzi	Full-width hanzi (Chinese) characters
	HRoman	Half-width Latin characters
	Kana	Japanese kana (katakana and hiragana) characters
	Proportional	Proportional Latin characters
Adobe-CNS1-0	**Alphabetic**	Full-width Latin, Greek, and Cyrillic characters
	Dingbats	Special symbols
	Hanzi	Full-width hanzi (Chinese) characters
	HRoman	Half-width Latin characters
	Kana	Japanese kana (katakana and hiragana) characters
	Proportional	Proportional Latin characters

Example 5.14 illustrates an **FD** dictionary containing two entries.

Example 5.14

```
/FD  <<  /Proportional  25 0 R
         /HKana  26 0 R
    >>

25  0  obj
   <<  /Type  /FontDescriptor
       /FontName  /HeiseiMin–W3–Proportional
       /Flags  2
       /AvgWidth  478
       /MaxWidth  1212
       /MissingWidth  250
       /StemV  105
       /StemH  45
       /CapHeight  660
       /XHeight  394
       /Ascent  720
       /Descent  –270
       /Leading  83
   >>
endobj

26  0  obj
   <<  /Type  /FontDescriptor
       /FontName  /HeiseiMin–W3–HKana
       /Flags  3
       /Style  << /Panose  <01 05 02 02 03 00 00 00 00 00 00 00> >>
       /AvgWidth  500
       /MaxWidth  500
       /MissingWidth  500
       /StemV  50
       /StemH  75
       /Ascent  720
       /Descent  0
       /Leading  83
   >>
endobj
```

5.8 Embedded Font Programs

A font program can be embedded in a PDF file as data contained in a PDF stream object. Such a stream object is also called a *font file*, by analogy with font programs that are available from sources external to the viewer application. (See also implementation note 46 in Appendix H.)

Table 5.21 summarizes the ways in which font programs are embedded in a PDF file, depending on the representation of the font program. The key is the name used in the font descriptor to refer to the font file stream; the subtype is the value of the **Subtype** key, if present, in the font file stream dictionary. Further details of specific font program representations are given below.

TABLE 5.21 Embedded font organization for various font types

KEY	SUBTYPE	DESCRIPTION
FontFile	—	Type 1 font program, in the original (noncompact) format described in *Adobe Type 1 Font Format*. This entry can appear in the font descriptor for a **Type1** or **MMType1** font dictionary.
FontFile2	—	*(PDF 1.1)* TrueType font program, as described in the *TrueType Reference Manual*. This entry can appear in the font descriptor for a **TrueType** font dictionary or (in PDF 1.3) for a **CIDFontType2** CIDFont dictionary.
FontFile3	Type1C	*(PDF 1.2)* Type 1–equivalent font program represented in the Compact File Format (CFF), as described in Adobe Technical Note #5176, *Compact File Format Specification*. This entry can appear in the font descriptor for a **Type1** or **MMType1** font dictionary.
	CIDFontType0C	*(PDF 1.3)* Type 0 CIDFont program represented in the Compact File Format (CFF), as described in Adobe Technical Note #5176, *Compact File Format Specification*. This entry can appear in the font descriptor for a **CIDFontType0** CIDFont dictionary.
	other name	Font or CIDFont program represented in some future format, identified by *other name* as the font file subtype.

The stream dictionary for a font file contains the normal entries for a stream, such as **Length** and **Filter** (listed in Table 3.4 on page 35), plus the additional entries listed in Table 5.22.

TABLE 5.22   Additional entries in a FontFile stream dictionary

KEY	TYPE	VALUE
Length1	integer	*(Required for Type 1 and TrueType fonts)* The length in bytes of the ASCII portion of the Type 1 font program (see below), or the entire TrueType font program, after it has been decoded using the filters specified by the stream's **Filter** entry, if any.
Length2	integer	*(Required for Type 1 fonts)* The length in bytes of the encrypted portion of the Type 1 font program (see below) after it has been decoded using the filters specified by the stream's **Filter** entry.
Length3	integer	*(Required for Type 1 fonts)* The length in bytes of the portion of the Type 1 font program that contains the 512 zeros, plus the **cleartomark** operator, plus any following data (see below), after it has been decoded using the filters specified by the stream's **Filter** entry. If **Length3** is 0, it indicates that the 512 zeros and **cleartomark** have not been included in the **FontFile** font program and must be added.
Subtype	name	*(Required if referenced from **FontFile3**; PDF 1.2)* A name specifying the format of the embedded font program. The name must be **Type1C** for Type 1 compact fonts or **CIDFontType0C** for Type 0 compact CIDFonts. When additional font formats are added to PDF, more values will be defined for **Subtype**.

A standard Type 1 font program, as described in *Adobe Type 1 Font Format*, consists of three parts: a clear text portion (written using PostScript syntax), an encrypted portion, and a fixed-content portion. The fixed-content portion contains 512 ASCII zeros followed by a **cleartomark** operator, and perhaps followed by additional data. While the encrypted portion of a standard Type 1 font may be in binary or ASCII hexadecimal format, PDF supports only the binary format; however, the entire font program may be encoded using any filters. Example 5.15 shows the structure of an embedded standard Type 1 font.

Example 5.15

```
12  0  obj
   <<  /Filter  /ASCII85Decode
        /Length  41116
        /Length1  2526
        /Length2  32393
        /Length3  570
   >>
stream
,p>`rDKJj'E+LaU0eP.@+AH9dBOu$hFD55nC
… Omitted data …
JJQ&Nt')<=^p&mGf(%:%h1%9c//K(/*o=.C>UXkbVGTrr~>
endstream
endobj
```

As indicated in Table 5.21 above, a Type 1–equivalent font program or a Type 0 CIDFont program can be represented in the Compact Font Format (CFF). The **Length1**, **Length2**, and **Length3** entries are not needed in that case. Although CFF enables multiple font or CIDFont programs to be bundled together in a single file, an embedded CFF font file in PDF must consist of exactly one font or CIDFont (as appropriate for the associated font dictionary).

A TrueType font program may be used as part of either a font or a CIDFont. Although the basic font file format is the same in both cases, there are different requirements for what information must be present in the font program. The following TrueType tables are always required: "head," "hhea," "loca," "maxp," "cvt_," "prep," "glyf," "hmtx," and "fpgm." If used with a simple font dictionary, the font program must additionally contain a "cmap" table defining one or more encodings, as discussed in Section 5.5.5, "Character Encoding." If used with a CIDFont dictionary, the "cmap" table is not needed, since the mapping from character codes to glyphs is provided separately.

*Note: The "vhea" and "vmtx" tables that specify vertical metrics are never used by a PDF viewer application. The only way to specify vertical metrics in PDF is by means of the **DW2** and **W2** entries in a CIDFont dictionary.*

As discussed in Section 5.5.3, "Font Subsets," an embedded font program may contain only the subset of glyphs that are used in the PDF document. This may be indicated by the presence of a **CharSet** or **CIDSet** entry in the font descriptor that refers to the font file, although subset fonts are not always so identified.

5.9 ToUnicode CMaps

The preceding sections describe all the facilities for showing text and causing the corresponding glyphs to be painted on the page. However, a viewer application sometimes needs to determine the information content of text—that is, its meaning according to some standard character identification, as opposed to its rendered appearance. This need arises during operations such as searching, indexing, and exporting of text to other applications.

The Unicode standard defines a system for numbering all of the common characters used in a large number of languages. It is a suitable scheme for representing the information content of text, but not its appearance, since Unicode values identify characters, not glyphs. For information about Unicode, see *The Unicode Standard* (see the Bibliography).

If a font's characters are identified according to a standard character set that is known to the viewer application, the viewer can easily convert text to Unicode values with no additional information. This character identification can occur if either the font uses a standard named encoding or the characters in the font are identified by standard character names or CIDs. A viewer application can identify characters if the font with which the text is shown is defined in any of the following ways:

* It uses one of the predefined encodings **MacRomanEncoding**, **WinAnsiEncoding**, **MacExpertEncoding**, or any of the predefined CMaps listed in Table 5.14 on page 320 except Identity–H and Identity–V.

* It is a Type 1 font whose character names are taken from the Adobe standard Latin character set and the set of named characters in the Symbol font, documented in Appendix D.

* It is a Type 0 font whose descendant CIDFont uses the Adobe-Japan1-2, Adobe-Korea1-1, Adobe-CNS1-0, or Adobe-GB1-2 character collection, as specified in the **CIDSystemInfo** dictionary. (Other supplements of these character collections can be used, but only the CIDs that are included in the supplements mentioned above are considered to be standard CIDs.)

If a font is not defined in one of these ways, the viewer application has no way to identify characters in the text. The glyphs can still be shown, but the characters cannot be converted to Unicode values without additional information. This information can be provided as an optional **ToUnicode** entry *(PDF 1.2)* in the font dictionary, whose value is a stream object containing a special kind of CMap file that maps character codes to Unicode values.

The CMap defined in the **ToUnicode** entry must follow the syntax for CMaps introduced in Section 5.6.4, "CMaps" and fully documented in Adobe Technical Note #5014, *Adobe CMap and CIDFont Files Specification*. This CMap differs from an ordinary one in the following ways:

• In the CMap stream dictionary, no CMap-specific entries are required. The only pertinent entry from the list in Table 5.15 on page 322 is **UseCMap**, which may be used if the CMap is based on another **ToUnicode** CMap.

• The CMap file must contain **begincodespacerange** and **endcodespacerange** operators that are consistent with the encoding that the font uses. In particular, for a simple font, the codespace must be one byte long.

• It must use the **beginbfrange**, **endbfrange**, **beginbfchar**, and **endbfchar** operators to define the mapping from character codes to 2-byte Unicode values, interpreted high-order byte first. These operators have been extended to handle cases where a single character code maps to one or more Unicode values, as described below.

Example 5.16 illustrates a Type 0 font that uses the Identity–H CMap to map from character codes to CIDs, and whose descendant CIDFont uses the **Identity** mapping from CIDs to TrueType glyph indices. Text strings shown using this font simply use a 2-byte glyph index for each character. In the absence of a **ToUnicode** entry, there would be no information available about what the characters mean.

Example 5.16

```
14 0 obj
    << /Type /Font
        /Subtype /Type0
        /BaseFont /Ryumin–Light
        /Encoding /Identity–H
        /DescendantFonts [15 0 R]
        /ToUnicode 16 0 R
    >>
endobj
```

```
15 0 obj
   << /Type /Font
      /Subtype /CIDFontType2
      /BaseFont /Ryumin–Light
      /CIDSystemInfo  17 0 R
      /FontDescriptor  18 0 R
      /CIDToGIDMap /Identity
   >>
endobj
```

The value of the **ToUnicode** entry is a stream object that contains the definition of the CMap, as shown in Example 5.17.

Example 5.17

```
16 0 obj
   << /Length 433 >>
stream
/CIDInit /ProcSet findresource begin
12 dict begin
begincmap
/CIDSystemInfo
<< /Registry (Adobe)
/Ordering (UCS)
/Supplement 0
>> def
/CMapName /Adobe–Identity–UCS def
/CMapType 2 def
1 begincodespacerange
<0000> <FFFF>
endcodespacerange
2 beginbfrange
<0000> <005E> <0020>
<005F> <0061> [<00660066> <00660069> <00660066006C>]
endbfrange
endcmap
CMapName currentdict /CMap defineresource pop
end
end
endstream
endobj
```

The **begincodespacerange** and **endcodespacerange** operators in Example 5.17 define the source character code range to be the 2-byte character codes from <00 00> to <FF FF>. The specific mappings for several of the character codes are shown. For example, <00 00> to <00 5E> are mapped to the Unicode values U+0020 to U+007E (where Unicode values are conventionally written as U+ followed by four hexadecimal digits). This is followed by the definition of a mapping used where each character code represents more than one Unicode value:

<005F> <0061> [<00660066> <00660069> <00660066006C>]

In this case, the original character codes are the glyph indices for the ligatures ff, fi, and ffl. The entry defines the mapping from the character codes <00 5F>, <00 60>, and <00 61> to the string of Unicode values with a code for each character in the ligature: U+0066 U+0066 are the Unicode values for the character sequence f f, U+0066 U+0069 for f i, and U+0066 U+0066 U+006c for f f l.

Example 5.17 illustrates several extensions to the way destination values can be defined. To support mappings from a source code to a string of destination codes, the following extension has been made to the ranges defined after a **beginbfchar** operator:

n **beginbfchar**
srcCode dstString
endbfchar

where *dstString* can be a string of up to 512 bytes. Likewise, mappings after the **beginbfrange** operator may be defined as:

n **beginbfrange**
$srcCode_1$ $srcCode_2$ *dstString*
endbfrange

In this case, the last byte of the string will be incremented for each consecutive code in the source code range. When defining ranges of this type, care must be taken to ensure that the value of the last byte in the string is less than or equal to $255 - (srcCode_2 - srcCode_1)$. This ensures that the last byte of the string will not be incremented past 255; otherwise the result of mapping is undefined and an error occurs.

To support more compact representations of mappings from a range of source character codes to a discontiguous range of destination codes, the CMaps used for the **ToUnicode** entry may use the following syntax for the mappings following a **beginbfrange** definition:

```
n  beginbfrange
srcCode₁ srcCodeₙ [dstString₁ dstString₂ … dstStringₙ]
endbfrange
```

Consecutive codes starting with $srcCode_1$ and ending with $srcCode_n$ are mapped to the destination strings in the array starting with $dstString_1$ and ending with $dstString_n$.

CHAPTER 6

Rendering

THE ADOBE IMAGING MODEL separates *graphics* (the specification of shapes and colors) from *rendering* (controlling a raster output device). Figures 4.12 and 4.13 on pages 158 and 159 illustrate this division. Chapter 4 describes the facilities for specifying the appearance of pages in a device-independent way. This chapter describes the facilities for controlling how shapes and colors are rendered on the raster output device. All of the facilities discussed here depend on the specific characteristics of the output device; PDF documents that are intended to be device-independent should limit themselves to the general graphics facilities described in Chapter 4.

Nearly all of the rendering facilities that are under the control of a PDF document have to do with the reproduction of color. Colors are rendered by a multiple-step process outlined below. (Depending on the current color space and on the characteristics of the device, it is not always necessary to perform every step.)

1. If a color has been specified in a CIE-based color space (see Section 4.5.4, "CIE-Based Color Spaces"), it must first be transformed to the *native color space* of the raster output device (also called its *process color model*).

2. If a color has been specified in a device color space that is inappropriate for the output device (for example, *RGB* color with a *CMYK* or grayscale device), a *color conversion function* is invoked.

3. The device color values are now mapped through *transfer functions*, one for each color component. The transfer functions compensate for peculiarities of the output device, such as nonlinear gray-level response. This step is sometimes called *gamma correction*.

4. If the device cannot reproduce continuous tones, but only certain discrete colors such as black and white pixels, a *halftone function* is invoked, which approximates the desired colors by means of patterns of pixels.

5. Finally, *scan conversion* is performed to mark the appropriate pixels of the raster output device with the requested colors.

Once these operations have been performed for all graphics objects on the page, the resulting raster data is used to mark the physical medium, such as pixels on a display or ink on a printed page. A PDF document specifies very little about the properties of the physical medium on which the output will be produced; that information is obtained from the following sources:

- The media box and a few other entries in the page dictionary (see Section 8.6.1, "Page Boundaries").

- An interactive dialog conducted when the user requests viewing or printing.

- A *job ticket*, either embedded in the PDF file or provided separately, specifying detailed instructions for imposing PDF pages onto media and for controlling special features of the output device. Job tickets are described in Adobe Technical Note #5620, *Portable Job Ticket Format*.

Some of the rendering facilities described in this chapter are controlled by device-dependent graphics state parameters, listed in Table 4.3 on page 136. These parameters can be changed by invoking the **gs** operator with a parameter dictionary containing entries shown in Table 4.8 on page 144.

6.1 CIE-Based Color to Device Color

To render CIE-based colors on an output device, the viewer application must convert from the specified CIE-based color space to the device's native color space (typically **DeviceGray**, **DeviceRGB**, or **DeviceCMYK**), taking into account the known properties of the device. As discussed in Section 4.5.4, "CIE-Based Color Spaces," CIE-based color is based on a model of human color perception. The goal of CIE-based color rendering is to produce output in the device's native color space that accurately reproduces the requested CIE-based color values as perceived by a human observer. CIE-based color specification and rendering are a feature of PDF 1.1 (**CalGray**, **CalRGB**, and **Lab**) and PDF 1.3 (**ICCBased**).

The conversion from CIE-based color to device color is complex, and the theory on which it is based is beyond the scope of this book; see the Bibliography for sources of further information. The algorithm has many parameters, including an optional, full three-dimensional color lookup table. The color fidelity of the output depends on having these parameters properly set, usually by a method that includes some form of calibration. The colors that a device can produce are characterized by a *device profile*, which is usually specified by an ICC profile associated with the device (and entirely separate from the profile that is specified in an **ICCBased** color space).

Note: *PDF has no equivalent of the PostScript color rendering dictionary. The means by which a device profile is associated with a viewer application's output device are implementation-dependent and cannot be specified in a PDF file. Typically, this is done through a color management system (CMS) that is provided by the operating system.*

Conversion from a CIE-based color value to a device color value requires two main operations:

1. Adjust the CIE-based color value according to a *CIE-based gamut mapping function.* A *gamut* is a subset of all possible colors in some color space. A page description has a *source gamut* consisting of all the colors it uses. An output device has a *device gamut* consisting of all the colors it can reproduce. This step transforms colors from the source gamut to the device gamut in a way that attempts to preserve color appearance, visual contrast, or some other explicitly specified *rendering intent* (see "Rendering Intents" on page 179).

2. Generate a corresponding device color value according to a *CIE-based color mapping function.* For a given CIE-based color value, this function computes a color value in the device's native color space.

The CIE-based gamut and color mapping functions are applied only to color values presented in a CIE-based color space. By definition, color values in device color spaces directly control the device color components (though this can be altered by the **DefaultGray**, **DefaultRGB**, and **DefaultCMYK** color space resources; see "Default Color Spaces" on page 177).

The source gamut is specified by a page description when it selects a CIE-based color space. This specification is device-independent. The corresponding properties of the output device are given in the device profile associated with the device. The gamut mapping and color mapping functions are part of the implementation of the viewer application.

6.2 Conversions among Device Color Spaces

Each raster output device has a *native color space*, which typically is one of the standard device color spaces (**DeviceGray, DeviceRGB**, or **DeviceCMYK**). In other words, most devices support reproduction of colors according to a grayscale (monochrome), red-green-blue, or cyan-magenta-yellow-black model. If the device supports continuous-tone output, reproduction occurs directly. Otherwise, it is accomplished by means of halftoning.

A device's native color space is also called its *process color model.* Process colors are ones that are produced by combinations of one or more standard *process colorants.* Colors specified in any device or CIE-based color space are rendered as process colors. (A device can also support additional *spot colorants*, which can be painted only by means of **Separation** or **DeviceN** color spaces. They are not involved in the rendering of device or CIE-based color spaces, nor are they subject to the conversions described below.)

Note: Some devices provide a native color space that is not one of the three named above but consists of a different combination of colorants. In that case, conversion from the standard device color spaces to the device's native color space is performed by device-dependent means.

Knowing the native color space and other output capabilities of the device, the viewer application can automatically convert the color values specified in a document to those appropriate for the device's native color space. For example, if a document specifies colors in the **DeviceRGB** color space but the device supports grayscale (such as a monochrome display) or *CMYK* (such as a color printer), the viewer application performs the necessary conversions. If the document specifies colors directly in the device's native color space, no conversions are necessary.

The algorithms used to convert among device color spaces are very simple. As perceived by a human viewer, the conversions produce only crude approximations of the original colors. More sophisticated control over color conversion can be achieved by means of CIE-based color specification and rendering. Additionally, device color spaces can be remapped into CIE-based color spaces (see "Default Color Spaces" on page 177).

6.2.1 Conversion between DeviceRGB and DeviceGray

Black, white, and intermediate shades of gray can be considered special cases of *RGB* color. A grayscale value is described by a single number: 0.0 corresponds to black, 1.0 to white, and intermediate values to different gray levels.

A gray level is equivalent to an *RGB* value with all three components the same. In other words, the *RGB* color value equivalent to a specific gray value is simply

$$
\begin{aligned}
red &= gray \\
green &= gray \\
blue &= gray
\end{aligned}
$$

The gray value for a given *RGB* value is computed according to the NTSC video standard, which determines how a color television signal is rendered on a black-and-white television set:

$$gray \;=\; 0.3 \times red + 0.59 \times green + 0.11 \times blue$$

6.2.2 Conversion between DeviceCMYK and DeviceGray

Nominally, a gray level is the complement of the black component of *CMYK*. Therefore, the *CMYK* color value equivalent to a specific gray level is simply

$$
\begin{aligned}
cyan &= 0.0 \\
magenta &= 0.0 \\
yellow &= 0.0 \\
black &= 1.0 - gray
\end{aligned}
$$

To obtain the equivalent gray level for a given *CMYK* value, the contributions of all components must be taken into account:

$$gray \;=\; 1.0 - \min(1.0,\, 0.3 \times cyan + 0.59 \times magenta + 0.11 \times yellow + black)$$

The interactions between the black component and the other three are elaborated below.

6.2.3 Conversion from DeviceRGB to DeviceCMYK

Conversion of a color value from *RGB* to *CMYK* is a two-step process. The first step is to convert the red-green-blue value to equivalent cyan, magenta, and yellow components. The second step is to generate a black component and alter the other components to produce a better approximation of the original color.

The subtractive color primaries cyan, magenta, and yellow are the complements of the additive primaries red, green, and blue. For example, a cyan ink subtracts the red component of white light. In theory, the conversion is very simple:

$$
\begin{aligned}
cyan &= 1.0 - red \\
magenta &= 1.0 - green \\
yellow &= 1.0 - blue
\end{aligned}
$$

For example, a color that is 0.2 red, 0.7 green, and 0.4 blue can also be expressed as $1.0 - 0.2 = 0.8$ cyan, $1.0 - 0.7 = 0.3$ magenta, and $1.0 - 0.4 = 0.6$ yellow.

Logically, only cyan, magenta, and yellow are needed to generate a printing color. An equal level of cyan, magenta, and yellow should create the equivalent level of black. In practice, however, colored printing inks do not mix perfectly; such combinations often form dark brown shades instead of true black. To obtain a truer color rendition on a printer, it is often desirable to substitute true black ink for the mixed-black portion of a color. Most color printers support a black component (the *K* component of *CMYK*). Computing the quantity of this component requires some additional steps:

1. *Black generation* calculates the amount of black to be used when trying to reproduce a particular color.

2. *Undercolor removal* reduces the amounts of the cyan, magenta, and yellow components to compensate for the amount of black that was added by black generation.

The complete conversion from *RGB* to *CMYK* is as follows, where $BG(k)$ and $UCR(k)$ are invocations of the black-generation and undercolor-removal functions, respectively:

$$
\begin{aligned}
c &= 1.0 - red \\
m &= 1.0 - green \\
y &= 1.0 - blue \\
k &= \min(c, m, y)
\end{aligned}
$$

$$
\begin{aligned}
cyan &= \min(1.0, \max(0.0, c - UCR(k))) \\
magenta &= \min(1.0, \max(0.0, m - UCR(k))) \\
yellow &= \min(1.0, \max(0.0, y - UCR(k))) \\
black &= \min(1.0, \max(0.0, BG(k)))
\end{aligned}
$$

In PDF 1.2, the black-generation and undercolor-removal functions are defined as PDF function dictionaries (see Section 3.9, "Functions") that are parameters in the graphics state. They are specified as the values of the **BG** and **UCR** (or **BG2** and **UCR2**) entries in a graphics state parameter dictionary (see Table 4.8 on page 144). Each function is called with a single numeric operand and is expected to return a single numeric result.

The input of both functions is k, the minimum of the intermediate c, m, and y values that have been computed by subtracting the original *red*, *green*, and *blue* components from 1.0. Nominally, k is the amount of black that can be removed from the cyan, magenta, and yellow components and substituted as a separate black component.

The black-generation function computes the black component as a function of the nominal k value. It can simply return its k operand unchanged or it can return a larger value for extra black, a smaller value for less black, or 0.0 for no black at all.

The undercolor-removal function computes the amount to subtract from each of the intermediate c, m, and y values to produce the final cyan, magenta, and yellow components. It can simply return its k operand unchanged or it can return 0.0 (so no color is removed), some fraction of the black amount, or even a negative amount, thereby adding to the total amount of colorant.

The final component values that result after applying black generation and undercolor removal are expected to be in the range 0.0 to 1.0. If a value falls outside this range, the nearest valid value is substituted automatically, without error indication. This is indicated explicitly by invocations of *min* and *max* operations in the formulas above.

The correct choice of black-generation and undercolor-removal functions depends on the characteristics of the output device—for example, how inks mix. Each device is configured with default values that are appropriate for that device.

6.2.4 Conversion from DeviceCMYK to DeviceRGB

Conversion of a color value from *CMYK* to *RGB* is a simple operation that does not involve black generation or undercolor removal:

$$
\begin{aligned}
red &= 1.0 - \min{(1.0, cyan + black)} \\
green &= 1.0 - \min{(1.0, magenta + black)} \\
blue &= 1.0 - \min{(1.0, yellow + black)}
\end{aligned}
$$

In other words, the black component is simply added to each of the other components, which are then converted to their complementary colors by subtracting them each from 1.0.

6.3 Transfer Functions

In PDF 1.2, a *transfer function* adjusts the values of color components to compensate for nonlinear response in an output device and in the human eye. Each component of a device color space—for example, the red component of the **DeviceRGB** space—is intended to represent the perceived lightness or intensity of that color component in proportion to the component's numeric value. Many devices do not actually behave this way, however; the purpose of a transfer function is to compensate for the device's actual behavior. This operation is sometimes called *gamma correction* (not to be confused with the *CIE-based gamut mapping function* performed as part of CIE-based color rendering).

In the sequence of steps for processing colors, the viewer application applies the transfer function *after* performing any needed conversions between color spaces, but *before* applying a halftone function, if necessary. Each color component has its own separate transfer function; there is no interaction between components.

Transfer functions always operate in the native color space of the output device, regardless of the color space in which colors were originally specified. For example, for a *CMYK* device, the transfer functions apply to the device's cyan, magenta, yellow, and black color components, even if the colors were originally specified in, say, the **DeviceRGB** or **CalRGB** color space.

In PDF 1.2, transfer functions are defined as PDF function dictionaries (see Section 3.9, "Functions"). There are two ways to specify transfer functions:

- The *current transfer function* parameter in the graphics state consists of either a single transfer function or an array of four separate transfer functions, one each for red, green, blue, and gray or their complements cyan, magenta, yellow, and black. (If only a single function is specified, it applies to all components.) An *RGB* device uses the first three; a monochrome device uses the gray transfer function only; and a *CMYK* device uses all four. The current transfer function can be specified as the value of the **TR** or **TR2** entry in a graphics state parameter dictionary; see Table 4.8 on page 144.

• The *current halftone* parameter in the graphics state can specify transfer functions as optional entries in *halftone dictionaries* (see Section 6.4.4, "Halftone Dictionaries"). This is the only way to set transfer functions for nonprimary color components, or for any component in devices whose native color space uses components other than the ones listed above. A transfer function specified in a halftone dictionary overrides the corresponding one specified by the current transfer function parameter in the graphics state.

A transfer function is called with a numeric operand in the range 0.0 to 1.0 and must return a number in the same range. The input is the value of a color component in the device's native color space, either specified directly or produced by conversion from some other color space. The output is the transformed component value to be transmitted to the device (after halftoning, if necessary). Both the input and the output are always interpreted as if the color component were additive (red, green, blue, or gray): the greater the numeric value, the lighter the color. If the component is subtractive (cyan, magenta, yellow, black, or a spot color), it is converted to additive form by subtracting it from 1.0 before it is passed to the transfer function. The output of the transfer function is always in additive form, and is passed on to the halftone function in that form.

In addition to their intended use for gamma correction, transfer functions can be used to produce a variety of special, device-dependent effects. For example, on a monochrome device, the PostScript calculator function

    {1 exch sub}

inverts the output colors, producing a negative rendition of the page. In general, this method does not work for color devices; inversion can be more complicated than merely inverting each of the components. Because transfer functions produce device-dependent effects, a page description that is intended to be device-independent should not alter them.

Note: *When the current color space is* **DeviceGray** *and the output device's native color space is* **DeviceCMYK**, *the interpreter uses only the gray transfer function. The* *normal conversion from **DeviceGray** to **DeviceCMYK** produces 0.0 for the cyan, magenta, and yellow components. These components are not passed through their respective transfer functions but are rendered directly, producing output containing no colored inks. This special case exists for compatibility with existing applications that use a transfer function to obtain special effects on monochrome devices, and applies only to colors specified in the **DeviceGray** color space.*

6.4 Halftones

Halftoning is a process by which continuous-tone colors are approximated on an output device that can achieve only a limited number of discrete colors. Colors that the device cannot produce directly are simulated by using patterns of pixels in the colors available. Perhaps the most familiar example is the rendering of gray tones with black and white pixels, as in a newspaper photograph.

Some output devices can reproduce continuous-tone colors directly. Halftoning is not required for such devices; after gamma correction by the transfer functions, the color components are transmitted directly to the device. On devices that do require halftoning, it occurs after all color components have been transformed by the applicable transfer functions. The input to the halftone function consists of continuous-tone, gamma-corrected color components in the device's native color space. Its output consists of pixels in colors the device can reproduce.

PDF provides a high degree of control over details of the halftoning process. For example, in color printing, independent halftone screens can be specified for each of several colorants. When rendering on low-resolution displays, fine control over halftone patterns is needed to achieve the best approximations of gray levels or colors and to minimize visual artifacts.

Note: *Remember that everything pertaining to halftones is, by definition, device-dependent. In general, when a PDF document provides its own halftone specifications, it sacrifices portability. Associated with every output device is a default halftone definition that is appropriate for most purposes. Only relatively sophisticated documents need to define their own halftones to achieve special effects.*

All halftones are defined in device space, unaffected by the current transformation matrix. For correct results, a PDF document that defines a new halftone must make assumptions about the resolution and orientation of device space. The best choice of halftone parameters often depends on specific physical properties of the output device, such as pixel shape, overlap between pixels, and the effects of electronic or mechanical noise.

6.4.1 Halftone Screens

In general, halftoning methods are based on the notion of a *halftone screen*, which divides the array of device pixels into *cells* that can be modified to produce the desired halftone effects. A screen is defined by conceptually laying a uniform rectangular grid over the device pixel array. Each pixel belongs to one cell of the grid; a single cell typically contains many pixels. The screen grid is defined entirely in device space, and is unaffected by modifications to the current transformation matrix. This property is essential to ensure that adjacent areas colored by halftones are properly stitched together without visible "seams."

On a bilevel (black-and-white) device, each cell of a screen can be made to approximate a shade of gray by painting some of the cell's pixels black and some white. Numerically, the gray level produced within a cell is the ratio of white pixels to the total number of pixels in the cell. A cell containing n pixels can render $n + 1$ different gray levels, ranging from all pixels black to all pixels white. A desired gray value g in the range 0.0 to 1.0 is produced by making i pixels white, where $i = \text{floor}(g \times n)$.

The foregoing description also applies to color output devices whose pixels consist of primary colors that are either completely on or completely off. Most color printers, but not color displays, work this way. Halftoning is applied to each color component independently, producing shades of that color.

Color components are presented to the halftoning machinery in additive form, regardless of whether they were originally specified additively (*RGB* or gray) or subtractively (*CMYK* or tint). Larger values of a color component represent lighter colors—greater intensity in an additive device such as a display, or less ink in a subtractive device such as a printer. Transfer functions produce color values in additive form; see Section 6.3, "Transfer Functions."

6.4.2 Spot Functions

A common way of defining a halftone screen is by specifying a *frequency, angle,* and *spot function*. The frequency is the number of halftone cells per inch; the angle indicates the orientation of the grid lines relative to the device coordinate system. As a cell's desired gray level varies from black to white, individual pixels within the cell change from black to white in a well-defined sequence: if a particular gray level includes certain white pixels, lighter grays will include the same white pixels and some additional ones as well. The order in which pixels change from black to white for increasing gray levels is determined by a *spot function*, which specifies that order in an indirect way that minimizes interactions with the screen frequency and angle.

Consider a halftone cell to have its own coordinate system: the center of the cell is the origin and the corners are at coordinates ±1.0 horizontally and vertically. Each pixel in the cell is centered at horizontal and vertical coordinates that both lie in the range −1.0 to +1.0. For each pixel, the spot function is invoked with the pixel's coordinates as input and must return a single number in the range −1.0 to +1.0, defining the pixel's position in the whitening order.

The specific values the spot function returns are not significant; all that matters are the *relative* values returned for different pixels. As a cell's gray level varies from black to white, the first pixel whitened is the one for which the spot function returns the lowest value, the next pixel is the one with the next higher spot function value, and so on. If two pixels have the same spot function value, their relative order is chosen arbitrarily.

PDF provides built-in definitions for many of the most commonly used spot functions. A halftone can simply specify any of these predefined spot functions by name instead of giving an explicit function definition. For example, the name **SimpleDot** designates a spot function whose value is inversely related to a pixel's distance from the center of the halftone cell. This produces a "dot screen" in which the black pixels are clustered within a circle whose area is inversely proportional to the gray level. The predefined function **Line** is a spot function whose value is the distance from a given pixel to a line through the center of the cell, producing a "line screen" in which the white pixels grow away from that line.

Table 6.1 shows the predefined spot functions. The table gives the mathematical definition of each function along with the corresponding PostScript language code as it would be defined in a PostScript calculator function (see Section 3.9.4, "Type 4 (PostScript Calculator) Functions"). The image accompanying each function shows how the relative values of the function are distributed over the halftone cell, indicating the approximate order in which pixels are whitened; pixels corresponding to darker points in the image are whitened later than those corresponding to lighter points. (See implementation note 47 in Appendix H.)

TABLE 6.1 Predefined spot functions

NAME	APPEARANCE	DEFINITION
SimpleDot		$1 - (x^2 + y^2)$ { dup mul exch dup mul add 1 exch sub }
InvertedSimpleDot		$x^2 + y^2 - 1$ { dup mul exch dup mul add 1 sub }
DoubleDot		$\dfrac{\sin(360 \times x)}{2} + \dfrac{\sin(360 \times y)}{2}$ { 360 mul sin 2 div exch 360 mul sin 2 div add }
InvertedDoubleDot		$-\left(\dfrac{\sin(360 \times x)}{2} + \dfrac{\sin(360 \times y)}{2}\right)$ { 360 mul sin 2 div exch 360 mul sin 2 div add neg }
CosineDot		$\dfrac{\cos(180 \times x)}{2} + \dfrac{\cos(180 \times y)}{2}$ { 180 mul cos exch 180 mul cos add 2 div }

Double

$$\frac{\sin\left(360 \times \frac{x}{2}\right)}{2} + \frac{\sin(360 \times y)}{2}$$

{ 360 mul sin 2 div exch 2 div 360 mul sin 2 div add }

InvertedDouble

$$-\left(\frac{\sin\left(360 \times \frac{x}{2}\right)}{2} + \frac{\sin(360 \times y)}{2}\right)$$

{ 360 mul sin 2 div exch 2 div 360 mul sin 2 div add neg }

Line

$$-|y|$$

{ exch pop abs neg }

LineX

$$x$$

{ pop }

LineY

$$y$$

{ exch pop }

Round

$$if\ |x| + |y| \le 1\ then\ 1 - (x^2 + y^2)$$
$$else\ (|x| - 1)^2 + (|y| - 1)^2 - 1$$

```
{ abs  exch abs
  2 copy add  1 le
                { dup mul  exch dup mul  add  1 exch sub }
                { 1 sub dup mul  exch 1 sub dup mul  add  1 sub }
                ifelse }
```

Ellipse

$$let\ w = (4 \times |x|) + (3 \times |y|) - 3$$

$$if\ w < 0\ then\quad 1 - \frac{x^2 + \left(\dfrac{|y|}{0.75}\right)^2}{4}$$

$$else\ if\ w > 1\ then\quad \frac{(1 - |x|)^2 + \left(\dfrac{1 - |y|}{0.75}\right)^2}{4} - 1$$

$$else\ 0.5 - w$$

```
{ abs  exch abs  2 copy 3 mul  exch 4 mul  add  3 sub  dup 0 lt
            { pop  dup mul  exch .75 div  dup mul  add
              4 div  1 exch sub }
            { dup 1 gt
                        { pop  1 exch sub  dup mul
                          exch 1 exch sub  .75 div  dup mul  add
                          4 div  1 sub }
                        { .5 exch sub  exch pop  exch pop }
                        ifelse }
            ifelse }
  ifelse }
```

EllipseA

$$1 - (x^2 + 0.9 \times y^2)$$

```
{ dup mul  .9 mul  exch dup mul  add  1 exch sub }
```

InvertedEllipseA

$$x^2 + 0.9 \times y^2 - 1$$

```
{ dup mul  .9 mul  exch dup mul  add  1 sub }
```

EllipseB

$$1 - \sqrt{x^2 + \frac{5}{8} \times y^2}$$

{ dup 5 mul 8 div mul exch dup mul exch add sqrt
1 exch sub }

EllipseC

$$1 - (0.9 \times x^2 + y^2)$$

{ dup mul exch dup mul .9 mul add 1 exch sub }

InvertedEllipseC

$$0.9 \times x^2 + y^2 - 1$$

{ dup mul exch dup mul .9 mul add 1 sub }

Square

$$-\max(|x|, |y|)$$

{ abs exch abs 2 copy lt
{ exch }
if
pop neg }

Cross

$$-\min(|x|, |y|)$$

{ abs exch abs 2 copy gt
{ exch }
if
pop neg }

Rhomboid

$$\frac{0.9 \times |x| + |y|}{2}$$

{ abs exch abs 0.9 mul add 2 div }

Diamond

$$if\,|x|+|y| \leq 0.75\ then\ 1-(x^2+y^2)$$
$$else\ if\,|x|+|y| \leq 1.23\ then\ 1-(0.85 \times |x|+|y|)$$
$$else\,(|x|-1)^2+(|y|-1)^2-1$$

```
{ abs  exch abs  2 copy add  .75 le
        { dup mul  exch dup mul  add  1 exch sub }
        { 2 copy add  1.23 le
            { .85 mul  add  1 exch sub }
            { 1 sub dup mul  exch 1 sub dup mul  add  1 sub }
          ifelse }
      ifelse }
```

Figure 6.1 illustrates the effects of some of the predefined spot functions.

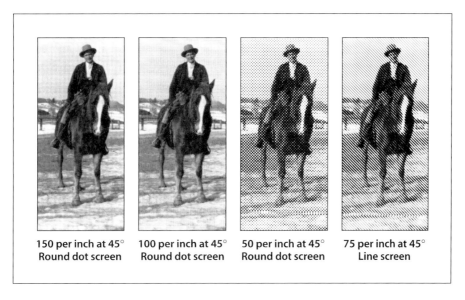

| 150 per inch at 45° | 100 per inch at 45° | 50 per inch at 45° | 75 per inch at 45° |
| Round dot screen | Round dot screen | Round dot screen | Line screen |

FIGURE 6.1 *Various halftoning effects*

6.4.3 Threshold Arrays

Another way to define a halftone screen is with a *threshold array* that directly controls individual device pixels in a halftone cell. This technique provides a high degree of control over halftone rendering. It also permits halftone cells to be arbitrary rectangles, whereas those controlled by a spot function are always square.

A threshold array is much like a sampled image—a rectangular array of pixel values—but is defined entirely in device space. Depending on the halftone type, the threshold values occupy 8 or 16 bits each. Threshold values nominally represent gray levels in the usual way, from 0 for black up to the maximum (255 or 65,535) for white. The threshold array is replicated to tile the entire device space: each pixel in device space is mapped to a particular sample in the threshold array. On a bilevel device, where each pixel is either black or white, halftoning with a threshold array proceeds as follows:

1. For each device pixel that is to be painted with some gray level, consult the corresponding threshold value from the threshold array.

2. If the requested gray level is less than the threshold value, paint the device pixel black; otherwise, paint it white. Gray levels in the range 0.0 to 1.0 correspond to threshold values from 0 to the maximum available (255 or 65,535).

Note: A threshold value of 0 is treated as if it were 1; therefore, a gray level of 0.0 paints all pixels black, regardless of the values in the threshold array.

This scheme easily generalizes to monochrome devices with multiple bits per pixel. For example, if there are 2 bits per pixel, each pixel can directly represent one of four different gray levels: black, dark gray, light gray, or white, encoded as 0, 1, 2, and 3, respectively. For any device pixel that is specified with some in-between gray level, the halftoning algorithm consults the corresponding value in the threshold array to determine whether to use the next lower or next higher representable gray level. In this situation, the threshold values do not represent absolute gray levels, but rather gradations between any two adjacent representable gray levels.

A halftone defined in this way can also be used with color displays that have a limited number of values for each color component. The red, green, and blue components are simply treated independently as gray levels, applying the appropriate threshold array to each. (This technique also works for a screen defined as a spot function, since the spot function is used to compute a threshold array internally.)

6.4.4 Halftone Dictionaries

In PDF 1.2, the graphics state includes a *current halftone* parameter, which determines the halftoning process to be used by the painting operators. The current halftone can be specified as the value of the **HT** entry in a graphics state parameter dictionary; see Table 4.8 on page 144. It may be defined by either a dictionary or a stream, depending on the type of halftone; the term *halftone dictionary* will be used generically in this section to refer to either a dictionary object or the dictionary portion of a stream object.

Every halftone dictionary must have a **HalftoneType** entry whose value is an integer specifying the overall type of halftone definition. The remaining entries in the dictionary are interpreted according to this type. PDF supports the halftone types listed in Table 6.2.

TABLE 6.2   PDF halftone types

TYPE	MEANING
1	Defines a single halftone screen by a *frequency, angle,* and *spot function.*
5	Defines an arbitrary number of halftone screens, one for each colorant or color component (including both primary and spot colorants). The keys in this dictionary are names of colorants; the values are halftone dictionaries of other types, each defining the halftone screen for a single colorant.
6	Defines a single halftone screen by a threshold array containing 8-bit sample values.
10	Defines a single halftone screen by a threshold array containing 8-bit sample values, representing a halftone cell that may have a nonzero screen angle.
16	*(PDF 1.3)* Defines a single halftone screen by a threshold array containing 16-bit sample values, representing a halftone cell that may have a nonzero screen angle.

The dictionaries representing these halftone types contain the same entries as the corresponding PostScript language halftone dictionaries (as described in Section 7.4 of the *PostScript Language Reference*, Third Edition), with the following exceptions:

• The PDF dictionaries may contain a **Type** entry with the value **Halftone**, identifying the type of PDF object that the dictionary describes.

• Spot functions and transfer functions are represented by function objects instead of PostScript procedures.

• Threshold arrays are specified as streams instead of files.

- In type 5 halftone dictionaries, the keys for colorants must be name objects; they may not be strings as they may in PostScript.

Halftone dictionaries have an optional entry, **HalftoneName**, that identifies the desired halftone by name. In PDF 1.3, if this entry is present, all other entries, including **HalftoneType**, are optional. At rendering time, if the output device has a halftone with the specified name, that halftone will be used, overriding any other halftone parameters specified in the dictionary. This provides a way for PDF documents to select the proprietary halftones supplied by some device manufacturers, which would not otherwise be accessible because they are not explicitly defined in PDF. If there is no **HalftoneName** entry, or if the requested halftone name does not exist on the device, the halftone's parameters are defined by the other entries in the dictionary, if any. If no other entries are present, the default halftone is used.

Type 1 Halftones

Table 6.3 describes the contents of a halftone dictionary of type 1, which defines a halftone screen in terms of its frequency, angle, and spot function.

TABLE 6.3	Entries in a type 1 halftone dictionary	
KEY	**TYPE**	**VALUE**
Type	name	*(Optional)* The type of PDF object that this dictionary describes; if present, must be **Halftone** for a halftone dictionary.
HalftoneType	integer	*(Required)* A code identifying the halftone type that this dictionary describes; must be 1 for this type of halftone.
HalftoneName	string	*(Optional)* The name of the halftone dictionary.
Frequency	number	*(Required)* The screen frequency, measured in halftone cells per inch in device space.
Angle	number	*(Required)* The screen angle, in degrees of rotation counterclockwise with respect to the device coordinate system. (Note that most output devices have left-handed device spaces; on such devices, a counterclockwise angle in device space will correspond to a clockwise angle in default user space and on the physical medium.)
SpotFunction	function or name	*(Required)* A function object defining the order in which device pixels within a screen cell are adjusted for different gray levels, or the name of one of the predefined spot functions (see Table 6.1 on page 359).

| AccurateScreens | boolean | *(Optional)* A flag specifying whether to invoke a special halftone algorithm that is extremely precise, but computationally expensive; see below for further discussion. Default value: *false*. |
| TransferFunction | function or name | *(Optional)* A transfer function, which overrides the corresponding transfer function in the graphics state for the same component. This entry is required if the dictionary is an element in a type 5 halftone dictionary (see "Type 5 Halftones" on page 373) and represents either a nonprimary or nonstandard primary color component (see Section 6.3, "Transfer Functions"). The name Identity may be used to specify the identity function. |

If the optional entry **AccurateScreens** is present with a boolean value of *true*, a highly precise halftoning algorithm is substituted in place of the standard one; if the **AccurateScreens** entry is *false* or is not present, ordinary halftoning is used. Accurate halftoning achieves the requested screen frequency and angle with very high accuracy, whereas ordinary halftoning adjusts them so that a single screen cell is quantized to device pixels. High accuracy is important mainly for making color separations on high-resolution devices. However, it may be computationally expensive and so is ordinarily disabled.

In principle, PDF permits the use of halftone screens with arbitrarily large cells—in other words, arbitrarily low frequencies. However, cells that are very large relative to the device resolution or that are oriented at unfavorable angles may exceed the capacity of available memory. If this happens, an error will occur. The **AccurateScreens** feature often requires very large amounts of memory to achieve the highest accuracy.

Example 6.1 shows a halftone dictionary for a type 1 halftone.

Example 6.1

```
28 0 obj
   << /Type /Halftone
      /HalftoneType 1
      /Frequency 120
      /Angle 30
      /SpotFunction /CosineDot
      /TransferFunction /Identity
   >>
endobj
```

Type 6 Halftones

A type 6 halftone defines a halftone screen with a threshold array. The halftone is represented as a stream containing the threshold values; the parameters defining the halftone are specified by entries in the stream dictionary (see Table 6.4). The **Width** and **Height** entries specify the dimensions of the threshold array in device pixels; the stream must contain **Width** × **Height** bytes, each representing a single threshold value. Threshold values are defined in device space in the same order as image samples in image space (see Figure 4.30 on page 247), with the first value at device coordinates $(0, 0)$ and horizontal coordinates changing faster than vertical.

TABLE 6.4   Entries in a stream dictionary for a type 6 halftone

KEY	TYPE	VALUE
Type	name	*(Optional)* The type of PDF object that this dictionary describes; if present, must be **Halftone** for a stream dictionary representing a halftone.
HalftoneType	integer	*(Required)* A code identifying the halftone type that this dictionary describes; must be 6 for this type of halftone.
HalftoneName	string	*(Optional)* The name of the halftone dictionary.
Width	integer	*(Required)* The width of the threshold array, in device pixels.
Height	integer	*(Required)* The height of the threshold array, in device pixels.
TransferFunction	function or name	*(Optional)* A transfer function, which overrides the corresponding transfer function in the graphics state for the same component. This entry is required if the dictionary is an element in a type 5 halftone dictionary (see "Type 5 Halftones" on page 373) and represents either a nonprimary or nonstandard primary color component (see Section 6.3, "Transfer Functions"). The name Identity may be used to specify the identity function.

Type 10 Halftones

Although type 6 halftones can be used to specify a threshold array with a zero screen angle, they make no provision for other angles. The type 10 halftone removes this restriction and allows the use of threshold arrays for halftones with nonzero screen angles as well.

Halftone cells at nonzero angles can be difficult to specify, because they may not line up well with scan lines and because it may be difficult to determine where a given sampled point goes. The type 10 halftone addresses these difficulties by dividing the halftone cell into a pair of squares that line up at zero angles with the output device's pixel grid. The squares contain the same information as the original cell, but are much easier to store and manipulate. In addition, they can be mapped easily into the internal representation used for all rendering.

Figure 6.2 shows a halftone cell with a frequency of 38.4 cells per inch and an angle of 50.2 degrees, represented graphically in device space at a resolution of 300 dots per inch. Each asterisk in the figure represents a location in device space that is mapped to a specific location in the threshold array.

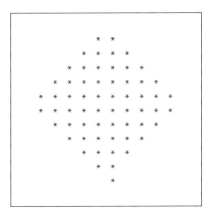

FIGURE 6.2 *Halftone cell with a nonzero angle*

Figure 6.3 shows how the halftone cell can be divided into two squares. If the squares and the original cell are tiled across device space, the area to the right of the upper square maps exactly into the empty area of the lower square, and vice versa (see Figure 6.4). The last row in the first square is immediately adjacent to the first row in the second and starts in the same column.

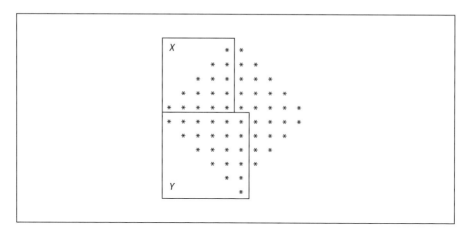

FIGURE 6.3 *Angled halftone cell divided into two squares*

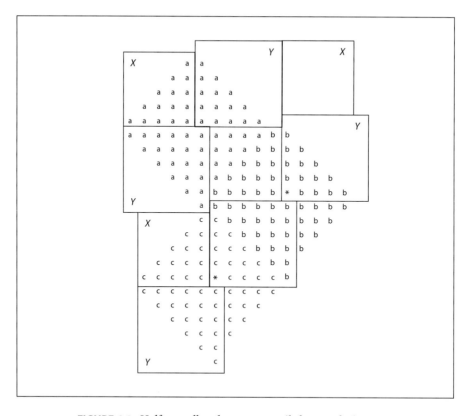

FIGURE 6.4 *Halftone cell and two squares tiled across device space*

Any halftone cell can be divided in this way. The side of the upper square (X) is equal to the horizontal displacement from a point in one halftone cell to the corresponding point in the adjacent cell, such as those marked by asterisks in Figure 6.4. The side of the lower square (Y) is the vertical displacement between the same two points. The frequency of a halftone screen constructed from squares with sides X and Y is thus given by

$$frequency = \frac{resolution}{\sqrt{X^2 + Y^2}}$$

and the angle by

$$angle = atan\left(\frac{Y}{X}\right)$$

Like a type 6 halftone, a type 10 halftone is represented as a stream containing the threshold values, with the parameters defining the halftone specified by entries in the stream dictionary (see Table 6.5); the **Xsquare** and **Ysquare** entries replace the type 6 halftone's **Width** and **Height** entries.

TABLE 6.5 Entries in a stream dictionary for a type 10 halftone

KEY	TYPE	VALUE
Type	name	*(Optional)* The type of PDF object that this dictionary describes; if present, must be **Halftone** for a stream dictionary representing a halftone.
HalftoneType	integer	*(Required)* A code identifying the halftone type that this dictionary describes; must be 10 for this type of halftone.
HalftoneName	string	*(Optional)* The name of the halftone dictionary.
Xsquare	integer	*(Required)* The side of square X, in device pixels; see below.
Ysquare	integer	*(Required)* The side of square Y, in device pixels; see below.
TransferFunction	function or name	*(Optional)* A transfer function, which overrides the corresponding transfer function in the graphics state for the same component. This entry is required if the dictionary is an element in a type 5 halftone dictionary (see "Type 5 Halftones" on page 373) and represents either a nonprimary or nonstandard primary color component (see Section 6.3, "Transfer Functions"). The name Identity may be used to specify the identity function.

The **Xsquare** and **Ysquare** entries specify the dimensions of the two squares in device pixels; the stream must contain $\mathbf{Xsquare}^2 + \mathbf{Ysquare}^2$ bytes, each representing a single threshold value. The contents of square X are specified first, followed by those of square Y. Threshold values within each square are defined in device space in the same order as image samples in image space (see Figure 4.30 on page 247), with the first value at device coordinates $(0, 0)$ and horizontal coordinates changing faster than vertical.

Type 16 Halftones

Like type 10, a type 16 halftone *(PDF 1.3)* defines a halftone screen with a threshold array and allows nonzero screen angles. In type 16, however, each element of the threshold array is 16 bits wide instead of 8. This allows the threshold array to distinguish 65,536 levels of color rather than only 256 levels. The threshold array can consist of either one or two rectangles. If two rectangles are specified, they will tile the device space as shown in Figure 6.5. The last row in the first rectangle is immediately adjacent to the first row in the second and starts in the same column.

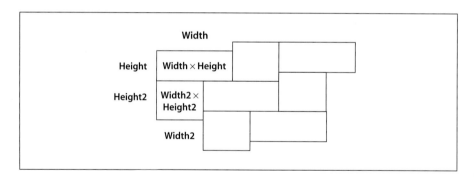

FIGURE 6.5 *Tiling of device space in a type 16 halftone*

A type 16 halftone, like type 6 and type 10, is represented as a stream containing the threshold values, with the parameters defining the halftone specified by entries in the stream dictionary (see Table 6.6). The dimensions of the first (or only) rectangle are defined by the dictionary's **Width** and **Height** entries; those of the second, optional rectangle are defined by the optional entries **Width2** and **Height2**. Each threshold value is represented as 2 bytes, with the high-order byte first. The stream must thus contain $2 \times \mathbf{Width} \times \mathbf{Height}$ bytes if there is only one rectangle, or $2 \times (\mathbf{Width} \times \mathbf{Height} + \mathbf{Width2} \times \mathbf{Height2})$ bytes if there are two. The contents of the first rectangle are specified first, followed by those of the second rectangle. Threshold values within each rectangle are defined in device space in the same order as image samples in image space (see Figure 4.30 on page 247), with the first value at device coordinates (0, 0) and horizontal coordinates changing faster than vertical.

TABLE 6.6   Entries in a stream dictionary for a type 16 halftone

KEY	TYPE	VALUE
Type	name	*(Optional)* The type of PDF object that this dictionary describes; if present, must be **Halftone** for a stream dictionary representing a halftone.
HalftoneType	integer	*(Required)* A code identifying the halftone type that this dictionary describes; must be 16 for this type of halftone.
HalftoneName	string	*(Optional)* The name of the halftone dictionary.
Width	integer	*(Required)* The width of the first (or only) rectangle in the threshold array, in device pixels.
Height	integer	*(Required)* The height of the first (or only) rectangle in the threshold array, in device pixels.
Width2	integer	*(Optional)* The width of the optional second rectangle in the threshold array, in device pixels. If this entry is present, the **Height2** entry must be present as well; if this entry is absent, the **Height2** entry must also be absent and the threshold array has only one rectangle.
Height2	integer	*(Optional)* The height of the optional second rectangle in the threshold array, in device pixels.
TransferFunction	function or name	*(Optional)* A transfer function, which overrides the corresponding transfer function in the graphics state for the same component. This entry is required if the dictionary is an element in a type 5 halftone dictionary (see "Type 5 Halftones," below) and represents either a nonprimary or nonstandard primary color component (see Section 6.3, "Transfer Functions"). The name Identity may be used to specify the identity function.

Type 5 Halftones

Some devices, particularly color printers, require separate halftones for each individual colorant. Also, devices that can produce named separations may require individual halftones for each separation. Halftone dictionaries of type 5 allow individual halftones to be specified for an arbitrary number of colorants or color components.

A type 5 halftone dictionary (Table 6.7) is a composite dictionary containing independent halftone definitions for multiple colorants. Its keys are name objects representing the names of individual colorants or color components. The values associated with these keys are other halftone dictionaries, each defining the halftone screen and transfer function for a single colorant or color component. The component halftone dictionaries may be of any supported type except 5.

TABLE 6.7   Entries in a type 5 halftone dictionary

KEY	TYPE	VALUE
Type	name	(*Optional*) The type of PDF object that this dictionary describes; if present, must be **Halftone** for a halftone dictionary.
HalftoneType	number	(*Required*) A code identifying the halftone type that this dictionary describes; must be 5 for this type of halftone.
HalftoneName	string	(*Optional*) The name of the halftone dictionary.
any colorant name	dictionary or stream	(*Required, one per colorant*) The halftone corresponding to the colorant or color component named by the key. The halftone may be of any type other than 5. Note that the key must be a name object; strings are not permitted, as they are in type 5 PostScript halftone dictionaries.
Default	dictionary or stream	(*Required*) A halftone to be used for any colorant or color component that does not have an entry of its own. The value may not be a type 5 halftone. If there are any nonprimary colorants, the default halftone must have a transfer function.

The colorants or color components represented in a type 5 halftone dictionary fall into two categories:

- Primary color components for the standard native device color spaces (**Red**, **Green**, and **Blue** for **DeviceRGB**; **Cyan**, **Magenta**, **Yellow**, and **Black** for **DeviceCMYK**; **Gray** for **DeviceGray**).

- Nonstandard color components for use as spot colorants in **Separation** and **DeviceN** color spaces. Some of these may also be used as process colorants if the native color space is nonstandard.

The dictionary must also contain an entry whose key is **Default**; the value of this entry is a halftone dictionary to be used for any color component that does not have an entry of its own.

When a halftone dictionary of some other type appears as the value of an entry in a type 5 halftone dictionary, it applies only to the single colorant or color component named by that entry's key. This is in contrast to such a dictionary's being used as the current halftone parameter in the graphics state, which applies to all color components. If nonprimary colorants are requested when the current halftone is defined by any means other than a type 5 halftone dictionary, the gray halftone screen and transfer function are used for all such colorants.

Example 6.2 shows a type 5 halftone dictionary with the primary color components for a *CMYK* device. In this example, the halftone dictionaries for the color components and for the default all use the same spot function.

Example 6.2

```
27  0  obj
    <<  /Type  /Halftone
        /HalftoneType  5
        /Cyan  31 0 R
        /Magenta  32 0 R
        /Yellow  33 0 R
        /Black  34 0 R
        /Default  35 0 R
    >>
endobj

31  0  obj
    <<  /Type  /Halftone
        /HalftoneType  1
        /Frequency  89.827
        /Angle  15
        /SpotFunction  /Round
        /AccurateScreens  true
    >>
endobj
```

```
32 0 obj
    << /Type /Halftone
       /HalftoneType 1
       /Frequency 89.827
       /Angle 75
       /SpotFunction /Round
       /AccurateScreens true
    >>
endobj

33 0 obj
    << /Type /Halftone
       /HalftoneType 1
       /Frequency 90.714
       /Angle 0
       /SpotFunction /Round
       /AccurateScreens true
    >>
endobj

34 0 obj
    << /Type /Halftone
       /HalftoneType 1
       /Frequency 89.803
       /Angle 45
       /SpotFunction /Round
       /AccurateScreens true
    >>
endobj

35 0 obj
    << /Type /Halftone
       /HalftoneType 1
       /Frequency 90.000
       /Angle 45
       /SpotFunction /Round
       /AccurateScreens true
    >>
endobj
```

6.5 Scan Conversion Details

The final step of rendering is *scan conversion.* As discussed in Section 2.1.4, "Scan Conversion," the viewer application executes a scan conversion algorithm to paint graphics, text, and images in the raster memory of the output device.

The specifics of the scan conversion algorithm are not defined as part of PDF. Different implementations can perform scan conversion in different ways; techniques that are appropriate for one device may be inappropriate for another. Still, it is useful to have a general understanding of how scan conversion works, particularly when creating PDF documents intended for viewing on a display. At the low resolutions typical of displays, variations of even one pixel's width can have a noticeable effect on the appearance of painted shapes.

The following sections describe the scan conversion algorithms that are typical of Adobe Acrobat products. (These details also apply to Adobe PostScript products, yielding consistent results when a viewer application prints a document on a PostScript printer.) Most scan conversion details are not under program control, but a few are; the parameters for controlling them are described here.

6.5.1 Flatness Tolerance

The *flatness tolerance* controls the maximum permitted distance in device pixels between the mathematically correct path and an approximation constructed from straight line segments, as shown in Figure 6.6. Flatness can be specified as the operand of the **i** operator (see Table 4.7 on page 142) or as the value of the **FL** entry in a graphics state parameter dictionary (see Table 4.8 on page 144). It must be a positive number; smaller values yield greater precision at the cost of more computation.

Note: Although the figure exaggerates the difference between the curved and flattened paths for the sake of clarity, the purpose of the flatness tolerance is to control the precision of curve rendering, not to draw inscribed polygons. If the parameter's value is large enough to cause visible straight line segments to appear, the result is unpredictable.

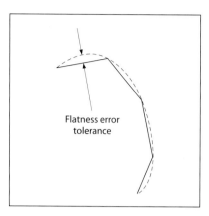

Flatness error
tolerance

FIGURE 6.6 *Flatness tolerance*

6.5.2 Smoothness Tolerance

The *smoothness tolerance (PDF 1.3)* controls the quality of smooth shading (type 2 patterns and the **sh** operator), and thus indirectly controls the rendering performance. Smoothness is the allowable color error between a shading approximated by piecewise linear interpolation and the true value of a (possibly nonlinear) shading function. The error is measured for each color component, and the maximum error is used. The allowable error (or tolerance) is expressed as a fraction of the range of the color component, from 0.0 to 1.0. Thus, a smoothness tolerance of 0.1 represents a tolerance of 10 percent in each color component. Smoothness can be specified as the value of the **SM** entry in a graphics state parameter dictionary (see Table 4.8 on page 144).

Each output device may have internal limits on the maximum and minimum tolerances attainable. For example, setting smoothness to 1.0 may result in an internal smoothness of 0.5 on a high-quality color device, while setting it to 0.0 on the same device may result in an internal smoothness of 0.01 if an error of that magnitude is imperceptible on the device.

The smoothness tolerance may also interact with the accuracy of color conversion. In the case of a color conversion defined by a sampled function, the conversion function is unknown. Thus, the error may be sampled at too low a frequency, in which case the accuracy defined by the smoothness tolerance cannot be guaranteed. In most cases, however, where the conversion function is smooth and continuous, the accuracy should be within the specified tolerance.

The effect of the smoothness tolerance is similar to that of the flatness tolerance. Note, however, that flatness is measured in device-dependent units of pixel width, whereas smoothness is measured as a fraction of color component range.

6.5.3 Scan Conversion Rules

The following rules determine which device pixels a painting operation will affect. All references to coordinates and pixels are in device space. A *shape* is a path to be painted with the current color or with an image. Its coordinates are mapped into device space, but not rounded to device pixel boundaries. At this level, curves have been flattened to sequences of straight lines, and all "insideness" computations have been performed.

Pixel boundaries always fall on integer coordinates in device space. A pixel is a square region identified by the location of its corner with minimum horizontal and vertical coordinates. The region is *half-open*, meaning that it includes its lower but not its upper boundaries. More precisely, for any point whose real-number coordinates are (x, y), let $i = \text{floor}(x)$ and $j = \text{floor}(y)$. The pixel that contains this point is the one identified as (i, j). The region belonging to that pixel is defined to be the set of points (x', y') such that $i \leq x' < i + 1$ and $j \leq y' < j + 1$. Like pixels, shapes to be painted by filling and stroking operations are also treated as half-open regions that include the boundaries along their "floor" sides, but not along their "ceiling" sides.

A shape is scan-converted by painting any pixel whose square region intersects the shape, no matter how small the intersection is. This ensures that no shape ever disappears as a result of unfavorable placement relative to the device pixel grid, as might happen with other possible scan conversion rules. The area covered by painted pixels is always at least as large as the area of the original shape. This rule applies both to fill operations and to strokes with nonzero width. Zero-width strokes are done in a device-dependent manner that may include fewer pixels than the rule implies.

Note: *Normally, the intersection of two regions is defined as the intersection of their interiors. However, for purposes of scan conversion, a filling region is considered to intersect every pixel through which its boundary passes, even if the interior of the filling region is empty. Thus, for example, a zero-width or zero-height rectangle will paint a line 1 pixel wide.*

The region of device space to be painted by a sampled image is determined similarly to that of a filled shape, though not identically. The viewer application transforms the image's source rectangle into device space and defines a half-open region, just as for fill operations. However, only those pixels whose *centers* lie within the region are painted. The position of the center of such a pixel—in other words, the point whose coordinate values have fractional parts of one-half—is mapped back into source space to determine how to color the pixel. There is no averaging over the pixel area; if the resolution of the source image is higher than that of device space, some source samples will not be used.

For clipping, the clipping region consists of the set of pixels that would be included by a fill operation. Subsequent painting operations affect a region that is the intersection of the set of pixels defined by the clipping region with the set of pixels for the region to be painted.

Scan conversion of character glyphs is performed by a different algorithm from the one above. That font rendering algorithm uses hints in the glyph descriptions and techniques that are specialized to glyph rasterization.

6.5.4 Automatic Stroke Adjustment

When a stroke is drawn along a path, the scan conversion algorithm may produce lines of nonuniform thickness because of rasterization effects. In general, the line width and the coordinates of the endpoints, transformed into device space, are arbitrary real numbers not quantized to device pixels. A line of a given width can intersect with different numbers of device pixels, depending on where it is positioned. Figure 6.7 illustrates this effect.

For best results, it is important to compensate for the rasterization effects to produce strokes of uniform thickness. This is especially important in low-resolution display applications. To meet this need, PDF 1.2 provides an optional *stroke adjustment* feature. When stroke adjustment is enabled, the line width and the coordinates of a stroke are automatically adjusted as necessary to produce lines of uniform thickness. The thickness is as near as possible to the requested line width—no more than half a pixel different.

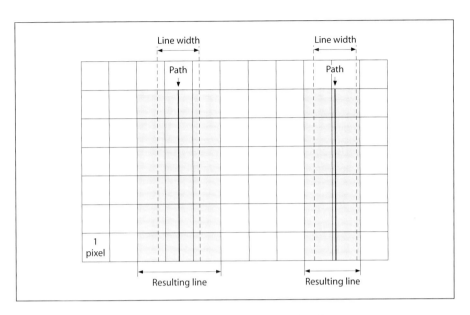

FIGURE 6.7 *Rasterization without stroke adjustment*

Note: If stroke adjustment is enabled and the requested line width, transformed into device space, is less than half a pixel, the stroke is rendered as a single-pixel line. This is the thinnest line that can be rendered at device resolution. It is equivalent to the effect produced by setting the line width to 0 (see Section 6.5.3, "Scan Conversion Rules").

Because automatic stroke adjustment can have a substantial effect on the appearance of lines, a PDF document must be able to control whether the adjustment is to be performed. This can be specified as the value of the **SA** entry in a graphics state parameter dictionary (see Table 4.8 on page 144).

CHAPTER 7

Interactive Features

THIS CHAPTER DESCRIBES those features of PDF that allow a user to interact with a document on the screen, using the mouse and keyboard. These include:

- *Preference settings* to control the way the document is presented on the screen

- *Navigation* facilities for moving through the document in a variety of ways

- *Annotations* for adding text notes, sounds, movies, and other ancillary information to the document

- *Actions* that can be triggered by specified events

- Interactive *forms* for gathering information from the user

7.1 Viewer Preferences

The **ViewerPreferences** entry in a document's catalog (see Section 3.6.1, "Document Catalog") designates a *viewer preferences dictionary (PDF 1.2)* controlling the way the document is to be presented on the screen. If no such dictionary is specified, viewer applications should behave in accordance with their own current user preference settings. Table 7.1 shows the contents of the viewer preferences dictionary. (See implementation note 48 in Appendix H.)

TABLE 7.1 Entries in a viewer preferences dictionary

KEY	TYPE	VALUE
HideToolbar	boolean	*(Optional)* A flag specifying whether to hide the viewer application's tool bars when the document is active. Default value: *false*.
HideMenubar	boolean	*(Optional)* A flag specifying whether to hide the viewer application's menu bar when the document is active. Default value: *false*.

HideWindowUI	boolean	(*Optional*) A flag specifying whether to hide user interface elements in the document's window (such as scroll bars and navigation controls), leaving only the document's contents displayed. Default value: *false.*
FitWindow	boolean	(*Optional*) A flag specifying whether to resize the document's window to fit the size of the first displayed page. Default value: *false.*
CenterWindow	boolean	(*Optional*) A flag specifying whether to position the document's window in the center of the screen. Default value: *false.*
NonFullScreenPageMode	name	(*Optional*) The document's *page mode*, specifying how to display the document on exiting full-screen mode:

		UseNone	Neither document outline nor thumbnail images visible
		UseOutlines	Document outline visible
		UseThumbs	Thumbnail images visible

This entry is meaningful only if the value of the **PageMode** entry in the catalog dictionary (see Section 3.6.1, "Document Catalog") is FullScreen; it is ignored otherwise. Default value: UseNone.

| Direction | name | (*Optional; PDF 1.3*) The predominant reading order for text: |

| | | L2R | Left to right |
| | | R2L | Right to left (including vertical writing systems such as Chinese, Japanese, and Korean) |

This entry has no direct effect on the document's contents or page numbering, but can be used to determine the relative positioning of pages when displayed side by side or printed *n*-up. Default value: L2R.

7.2 Document-Level Navigation

The features described in this section allow a PDF viewer application to present the user with an interactive, global overview of a document in either of two forms:

- As a hierarchical *outline* showing the document's internal structure

- As a collection of *thumbnail images* representing the pages of the document in miniature form

Each item in the outline or each thumbnail image can then be associated with a corresponding *destination* in the document, allowing the user to jump directly to that destination by clicking with the mouse.

7.2.1 Destinations

A *destination* defines a particular view of a document, consisting of the following:

- The page of the document to be displayed

- The location of the display window on that page

- The magnification (zoom) factor to use when displaying the page

Destinations may be associated with outline items (see Section 7.2.2, "Document Outline"), annotations ("Link Annotations" on page 410), or actions ("Go-To Actions" on page 425 and "Remote Go-To Actions" on page 426). In each case, the destination specifies the view of the document to be presented when the outline item or annotation is opened or the action is performed. In addition, the optional **OpenAction** entry in a document's catalog (Section 3.6.1, "Document Catalog") may specify a destination to be displayed when the document is opened. A destination may be specified either explicitly, by an array of parameters defining its properties, or indirectly by name.

Explicit Destinations

Table 7.2 shows the allowed syntactic forms for specifying a destination explicitly in a PDF file. In each case, *page* is an indirect reference to a page object. All coordinate values (*left*, *right*, *top*, and *bottom*) are expressed in the default user space coordinate system. The page's *bounding box* is the smallest rectangle enclosing all of its contents. (If any side of the bounding box lies outside the page's crop box, the corresponding side of the crop box is used instead; see Section 8.6.1, "Page Boundaries," for further discussion of the crop box.)

Note: No page object can be specified for a destination associated with a remote go-to action (see "Remote Go-To Actions" on page 426), because the destination page is in a different PDF document. In this case, the **page** *parameter specifies a page number within the remote document instead of a page object in the current document.*

TABLE 7.2   Destination syntax

SYNTAX	MEANING
[*page* /XYZ *left top zoom*]	Display the page designated by *page*, with the coordinates (*left*, *top*) positioned at the top-left corner of the window and the contents of the page magnified by the factor *zoom*. A null value for any of the parameters *left*, *top*, or *zoom* specifies that the current value of that parameter is to be retained unchanged. A *zoom* value of 0 has the same meaning as a null value.
[*page* /Fit]	Display the page designated by *page*, with its contents magnified just enough to fit the entire page within the window both horizontally and vertically. If the required horizontal and vertical magnification factors are different, use the smaller of the two, centering the page within the window in the other dimension.
[*page* /FitH *top*]	Display the page designated by *page*, with the vertical coordinate *top* positioned at the top edge of the window and the contents of the page magnified just enough to fit the entire width of the page within the window.
[*page* /FitV *left*]	Display the page designated by *page*, with the horizontal coordinate *left* positioned at the left edge of the window and the contents of the page magnified just enough to fit the entire height of the page within the window.
[*page* /FitR *left bottom right top*]	Display the page designated by *page*, with its contents magnified just enough to fit the rectangle specified by the coordinates *left*, *bottom*, *right*, and *top* entirely within the window both horizontally and vertically. If the required horizontal and vertical magnification factors are different, use the smaller of the two, centering the rectangle within the window in the other dimension.
[*page* /FitB]	*(PDF 1.1)* Display the page designated by *page*, with its contents magnified just enough to fit its bounding box entirely within the window both horizontally and vertically. If the required horizontal and vertical magnification factors are different, use the smaller of the two, centering the bounding box within the window in the other dimension.
[*page* /FitBH *top*]	*(PDF 1.1)* Display the page designated by *page*, with the vertical coordinate *top* positioned at the top edge of the window and the contents of the page magnified just enough to fit the entire width of its bounding box within the window.
[*page* /FitBV *left*]	*(PDF 1.1)* Display the page designated by *page*, with the horizontal coordinate *left* positioned at the left edge of the window and the contents of the page magnified just enough to fit the entire height of its bounding box within the window.

Named Destinations

Instead of being defined directly, using the explicit syntax shown in Table 7.2, a destination may be referred to indirectly, using a name object *(PDF 1.1)* or a string *(PDF 1.2)*. This capability is especially useful when the destination is located in another PDF document. For example, a link to the beginning of Chapter 6 in another document might refer to the destination by a name such as Chap6.begin instead of giving an explicit page number in the other document. This would allow the location of the chapter opening to change within the other document without invalidating the link. If an annotation or outline item that refers to a named destination has an associated action, such as a remote go-to action (see "Remote Go-To Actions" on page 426) or a thread action ("Thread Actions" on page 428), the destination is in the file specified by the action's **F** entry, if any; if there is no **F** entry, the destination is in the current file.

In PDF 1.1, the correspondence between name objects and destinations is defined by the **Dests** entry in the document catalog (see Section 3.6.1, "Document Catalog"). The value of this entry is a dictionary in which each key is a destination name and the corresponding value is either an array defining the destination, using the syntax shown in Table 7.2, or a dictionary with a **D** entry whose value is such an array. (The latter form allows additional attributes to be associated with the destination.)

In PDF 1.2, the correspondence between strings and destinations is defined by the **Dests** entry in the document's name dictionary (see Section 3.6.3, "Name Dictionary"). The value of this entry is a name tree (Section 3.8.4, "Name Trees") mapping strings to destinations. (The keys in the name tree may be treated as text strings for display purposes.)

Note: *The use of strings as destination names is a PDF 1.2 feature. If compatibility with earlier versions of PDF is required, only name objects may be used to refer to named destinations. Where such compatibility is not a consideration, however, applications that generate large numbers of named destinations should use the string form of representation instead, since there are essentially no implementation limits.*

7.2.2 Document Outline

A PDF document may optionally display a *document outline* on the screen, allowing the user to navigate interactively from one part of the document to another. The outline consists of a tree-structured hierarchy of *outline items* (sometimes called *bookmarks*), which serve as a "visual table of contents" to display the document's structure to the user. The user can interactively open and close individual items by clicking them with the mouse. When an item is open, its immediate children in the hierarchy become visible on the screen; each child may in turn be open or closed, selectively revealing or hiding further parts of the hierarchy. When an item is closed, all of its descendants in the hierarchy are hidden. Clicking the text of any visible item with the mouse *activates* the item, causing the viewer application to jump to a destination or trigger an action associated with the item.

The root of a document's outline hierarchy is an *outline dictionary* specified by the **Outlines** entry in the document catalog (see Section 3.6.1, "Document Catalog"). Table 7.3 shows the contents of this dictionary. Each individual outline item within the hierarchy is defined by an *outline item dictionary* (Table 7.4). The items at each level of the hierarchy form a linked list, chained together through their **Prev** and **Next** entries and accessed through the **First** and **Last** entries in the parent item (or in the outline dictionary in the case of top-level items). When displayed on the screen, the items at a given level appear in the order in which they occur in the linked list.

Note: *In PDF 1.2, an additional entry in the outline item dictionary, named **AA** (additional actions), was defined but was never implemented. In PDF 1.3, the **AA** entry is obsolete for outline items and should be ignored.*

		TABLE 7.3 Entries in an outline dictionary
KEY	**TYPE**	**VALUE**
Type	name	*(Optional)* The type of PDF object that this dictionary describes; if present, must be **Outlines** for an outline dictionary.
First	dictionary	*(Required; must be an indirect reference)* An outline item dictionary representing the first top-level item in the outline.
Last	dictionary	*(Required; must be an indirect reference)* An outline item dictionary representing the last top-level item in the outline.
Count	integer	*(Required if the document has any open outline entries)* The total number of open items at all levels of the outline. This entry should be omitted if there are no open outline items.

TABLE 7.4   Entries in an outline item dictionary

KEY	TYPE	VALUE
Title	text string	*(Required)* The text to be displayed on the screen for this item.
Parent	dictionary	*(Required; must be an indirect reference)* The parent of this item in the outline hierarchy. The parent of a top-level item is the outline dictionary itself.
Prev	dictionary	*(Required for all but the first item at each level; must be an indirect reference)* The previous item at this outline level.
Next	dictionary	*(Required for all but the last item at each level; must be an indirect reference)* The next item at this outline level.
First	dictionary	*(Required if the item has any descendants; must be an indirect reference)* The first of this item's immediate children in the outline hierarchy.
Last	dictionary	*(Required if the item has any descendants; must be an indirect reference)* The last of this item's immediate children in the outline hierarchy.
Count	integer	*(Required if the item has any descendants)* If the item is open, the total number of its open descendants at all lower levels of the outline hierarchy. If the item is closed, a negative integer whose absolute value specifies how many descendants would appear if the item were reopened.
Dest	name, string, or array	*(Optional; not permitted if an **A** entry is present)* The destination to be displayed when this item is activated (see Section 7.2.1, "Destinations"; see also implementation note 49 in Appendix H).
A	dictionary	*(Optional; PDF 1.1; not permitted if a **Dest** entry is present)* The action to be performed when this item is activated (see Section 7.5, "Actions").
SE	dictionary	*(Optional; PDF 1.3; must be an indirect reference)* The structure element to which the item refers (see "Structure Hierarchy" on page 486).

Note: The ability to associate an outline item with a structural element (such as the beginning of a chapter) is a PDF 1.3 feature. For backward compatibility with earlier PDF versions, such an item should also specify a destination corresponding to an area of a page where the contents of the designated structural element are displayed.

Example 7.1 shows a typical outline dictionary and outline item dictionary. See Appendix G for an example of a complete outline hierarchy.

Example 7.1

```
21  0  obj
    <<  /Count  6
        /First  22 0 R
        /Last  29 0 R
    >>
endobj

22  0  obj
    <<  /Title  (Chapter 1)
        /Parent  21 0 R
        /Next  26 0 R
        /First  23 0 R
        /Last  25 0 R
        /Count  3
        /Dest  [3 0 R  /XYZ  0 792 0]
    >>
endobj
```

7.2.3 Thumbnail Images

A PDF document may define *thumbnail images* representing the contents of its pages in miniature form. A viewer application can then display these images on th : screen, allowing the user to navigate to a page by clicking its thumbnail image with the mouse.

Note: Thumbnail images are not required, and may be included for some pages and not for others.

The thumbnail image for a page is an image XObject specified by the **Thumb** entry in the page object (see "Page Objects" on page 77). It has the usual structure for an image dictionary (Section 4.8.4, "Image Dictionaries"), but only the required entries **Width**, **Height**, **ColorSpace**, and **BitsPerComponent** are significant; all other entries, including **Subtype**, are ignored if present. (If **Subtype** is specified, its value must be **Image**.) The image's color space must be either **DeviceGray** or **DeviceRGB**, or an **Indexed** space based on one of these. Example 7.2 shows a typical thumbnail image definition.

Example 7.2

```
12 0 obj
   << /Width  76
        /Height  99
        /ColorSpace  /DeviceRGB
        /BitsPerComponent  8
        /Length  13 0 R
        /Filter  [/ASCII85Decode  /DCTDecode]
   >>
stream
s4IA>!"M;*Ddm8XA,IT0!!3,S!/(=R!<E3%!<N<(!WrK*!WrN,
… Omitted data …
endstream
endobj

13  0 obj                                % Length of stream
   …
endobj
```

7.3 Page-Level Navigation

This section describes PDF facilities that allow the user to navigate from page to page within a document. These include:

- *Page labels* for numbering or otherwise identifying individual pages

- *Article threads* that chain together sequences of content items within the document that are logically connected but not physically sequential

- *Presentations* that display the document in the form of a "slide show," advancing from one page to the next either automatically or under user control

For another important form of page-level navigation, see "Link Annotations" on page 410.

7.3.1 Page Labels

Each page in a PDF document is identified by an integer *page index* that expresses the page's relative position within the document. In addition, a document may optionally define *page labels (PDF 1.3)* to identify each page visually on the screen or in print. Page labels and page indices need not coincide: the indices are fixed, running consecutively through the document starting from 0 for the first page, but the labels can be specified in any way that is appropriate for the particular document. For example, if the document begins with 12 pages of front matter numbered in roman numerals and the remainder of the document is numbered in arabic, then the first page would have a page index of 0 and a page label of i, the twelfth page would have index 11 and label xii, and the thirteenth page would have index 12 and label 1.

For purposes of page labeling, a document can be divided into *labeling ranges,* each of which is a contiguous set of pages using the same numbering system. Pages within a range are numbered sequentially in ascending order. A page's label consists of a numeric portion based on its position within its labeling range, optionally preceded by a *label prefix* denoting the range itself. For example, the pages in an appendix might be labeled with decimal numeric portions prefixed with the string A–; the resulting page labels would be A–1, A–2, and so on.

A document's labeling ranges are defined by the **PageLabels** entry in the document catalog (see Section 3.6.1, "Document Catalog"). The value of this entry is a number tree (Section 3.8.5, "Number Trees"), each of whose keys is the page index of the first page in a labeling range; the corresponding value is a *page label dictionary* defining the labeling characteristics for the pages in that range. The tree must include a value for page index 0. Table 7.5 shows the contents of a page label dictionary. (See implementation note 50 in Appendix H.) Example 7.3 shows a document with pages labeled

   i, ii, iii, iv, 1, 2, 3, A–8, A–9, …

Example 7.3

```
1 0 obj
  << /Type /Catalog
     /PageLabels << /Nums [ 0 << /S /r >>      % A number tree containing
                            4 << /S /D >>      %   three page label dictionaries
                            7 << /S /D
                                 /P (A–)
                                 /St 8
                               >>
                          ]
                 >>
     ...
  >>
endobj
```

TABLE 7.5 **Entries in a page label dictionary**

KEY	TYPE	VALUE
Type	name	*(Optional)* The type of PDF object that this dictionary describes; if present, must be **PageLabel** for a page label dictionary.
S	name	*(Optional)* The numbering style to be used for the numeric portion of each page label:

D	Decimal arabic numerals
R	Uppercase roman numerals
r	Lowercase roman numerals
A	Uppercase letters (A to Z for the first 26 pages, AA to ZZ for the next 26, and so on)
a	Lowercase letters (a to z for the first 26 pages, aa to zz for the next 26, and so on)

There is no default numbering style; if no **S** entry is present, page labels will consist solely of a label prefix with no numeric portion. For example, if the **P** entry (below) specifies the label prefix Contents, each page will simply be labeled Contents with no page number. (If the **P** entry is also missing or empty, the page label will be an empty string.)

KEY	TYPE	VALUE
P	text string	*(Optional)* The label prefix for page labels in this range.
St	integer	*(Optional)* The value of the numeric portion for the first page label in the range. Subsequent pages will be numbered sequentially from this value, which must be greater than or equal to 1. Default value: 1.

7.3.2 Articles

Some types of document may contain sequences of content items that are logically connected but not physically sequential. For example, a news story may begin on the first page of a newsletter and run over onto one or more nonconsecutive interior pages. To represent such sequences of physically discontiguous but logically related items, a PDF document may define one or more *articles (PDF 1.1)*. The sequential flow of an article is defined by an *article thread*; the individual content items that make up the article are called *beads* on the thread. PDF viewer applications can provide navigation facilities to allow the user to follow a thread from one bead to the next.

The optional **Threads** entry in the document catalog (see Section 3.6.1, "Document Catalog") holds an array of *thread dictionaries* (Table 7.6) defining the document's articles. Each individual bead within a thread is represented by a *bead dictionary* (Table 7.7). The thread dictionary's **F** entry points to the first bead in the thread; the beads are then chained together sequentially in a doubly linked list through their **N** (next) and **V** (previous) entries. In addition, for each page on which article beads appear, the page object (see "Page Objects" on page 77) should contain a **B** entry whose value is an array of indirect references to the beads on the page, in drawing order.

TABLE 7.6 Entries in a thread dictionary

KEY	TYPE	VALUE
Type	name	*(Optional)* The type of PDF object that this dictionary describes; if present, must be **Thread** for a thread dictionary.
F	dictionary	*(Required; must be an indirect reference)* The first bead in the thread.
I	dictionary	*(Optional)* A thread information dictionary containing information about the thread, such as its title, author, and creation date. The contents of this dictionary are similar to those of the document information dictionary (see Section 8.2, "Document Information Dictionary").

TABLE 7.7 Entries in a bead dictionary

KEY	TYPE	VALUE
Type	name	*(Optional)* The type of PDF object that this dictionary describes; if present, must be **Bead** for a bead dictionary.
T	dictionary	*(Required for the first bead of a thread; optional for all others; must be an indirect reference)* The thread to which this bead belongs.
		Note: *In PDF 1.1, this entry is permitted only for the first bead of a thread. In PDF 1.2 and higher, it is permitted for any bead but required only for the first.*
N	dictionary	*(Required; must be an indirect reference)* The next bead in the thread. In the last bead, this entry points to the first.
V	dictionary	*(Required; must be an indirect reference)* The previous bead in the thread. In the first bead, this entry points to the last.
P	dictionary	*(Required; must be an indirect reference)* The page object representing the page on which this bead appears.
R	rectangle	*(Required)* A rectangle specifying the location of this bead on the page.

Example 7.4 shows a thread with three beads.

Example 7.4

```
22 0 obj
    << /F 23 0 R
       /I  << /Title (Man Bites Dog) >>
    >>
endobj

23 0 obj
    << /T 22 0 R
       /N 24 0 R
       /V 25 0 R
       /P 8 0 R
       /R [158 247 318 905]
    >>
endobj

24 0 obj
    << /T 22 0 R
       /N 25 0 R
       /V 23 0 R
       /P 8 0 R
       /R [322 246 486 904]
    >>
endobj

25 0 obj
    << /T 22 0 R
       /N 23 0 R
       /V 24 0 R
       /P 10 0 R
       /R [157 254 319 903]
    >>
endobj
```

7.3.3 Presentations

Some PDF viewer applications may allow a document to be displayed in the form of a *presentation* or "slide show," advancing from one page to the next either automatically or under user control. A page object (see "Page Objects" on page 77) may contain two optional entries, **Dur** and **Trans** *(PDF 1.1)*, to specify how to display that page in presentation mode.

The **Dur** entry in the page object specifies the page's *display duration* (also called its *advance timing*): the maximum length of time, in seconds, that the page will be displayed before the presentation automatically advances to the next page. (The user can advance the page manually before the specified time has expired.) If no **Dur** key is specified in the page object, the page does not advance automatically.

The **Trans** entry in the page object contains a *transition dictionary* describing the style and duration of the visual transition to use when moving from another page to the given page during a presentation. Table 7.8 shows the contents of the transition dictionary. (Some of the entries shown are needed only for certain transition styles, as indicated in the table.)

TABLE 7.8 Entries in a transition dictionary

KEY	TYPE	VALUE
Type	name	*(Optional)* The type of PDF object that this dictionary describes; if present, must be **Trans** for a transition dictionary.
D	number	*(Optional)* The duration of the transition effect, in seconds. Default value: 1.
S	name	*(Optional)* The *transition style* to use when moving to this page from another during a presentation:

	Split	Two lines sweep across the screen, revealing the new page. The lines may be either horizontal or vertical and may move inward from the edges of the page or outward from the center, as specified by the **Dm** and **M** entries, respectively.
	Blinds	Multiple lines, evenly spaced across the screen, synchronously sweep in the same direction to reveal the new page. The lines may be either horizontal or vertical, as specified by the **Dm** entry. Horizontal lines move downward, vertical lines to the right.
	Box	A rectangular box sweeps inward from the edges of the page or outward from the center, as specified by the **M** entry, revealing the new page.
	Wipe	A single line sweeps across the screen from one edge to the other in the direction specified by the **Di** entry, revealing the new page.
	Dissolve	The old page "dissolves" gradually to reveal the new one.
	Glitter	Similar to Dissolve, except that the effect sweeps across the page in a wide band moving from one side of the screen to the other in the direction specified by the **Di** entry.
	R	The new page simply replaces the old one with no special transition effect; the **D** entry is ignored.

Default value: R.

| **Dm** | name | *(Optional; Split and Blinds transition styles only)* The dimension in which the specified transition effect occurs: |

| | | H | Horizontal |
| | | V | Vertical |

Default value: H.

| **M** | name | *(Optional; Split and Box transition styles only)* The direction of motion for the specified transition effect: |

| | | I | Inward from the edges of the page |
| | | O | Outward from the center of the page |

Default value: I.

| **Di** | number | *(Optional; Wipe and Glitter transition styles only)* The direction in which the specified transition effect moves, expressed in degrees counterclockwise starting from a left-to-right direction. (Note that this differs from the page object's **Rotate** entry, which is measured clockwise from the top.) Only the following values are valid: |

		0	Left to right
		90	Bottom to top (Wipe only)
		180	Right to left (Wipe only)
		270	Top to bottom
		315	Top-left to bottom-right (Glitter only)

Default value: 0.

Figure 7.1 illustrates the relationship between transition duration (**D** in the transition dictionary) and display duration (**Dur** in the page object). Note that the transition duration specified for a page (page 2 in the figure) governs the transition *to* that page from another page; the transition *from* the page is governed by the next page's transition duration.

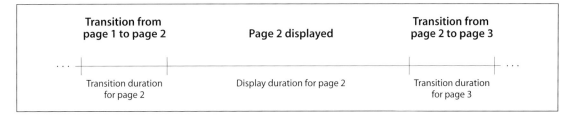

FIGURE 7.1 *Presentation timing*

Example 7.5 shows the presentation parameters for a page to be displayed for 5 seconds. Before the page is displayed, there is a 3.5-second transition in which two vertical lines sweep outward from the center to the edges of the page.

Example 7.5

```
10  0  obj
    <<  /Type  /Page
        /Parent  4 0 R
        /Contents  16 0 R
        /Dur  5
        /Trans  <<  /Type  /Trans
                    /D  3.5
                    /S  /Split
                    /Dm  /V
                    /M  /O
                >>
    >>
endobj
```

7.4 Annotations

An *annotation* associates an object such as a note, sound, or movie with a location on a page of a PDF document, or provides a means of interacting with the user via the mouse and keyboard. PDF includes a wide variety of standard annotation types, described in detail in Section 7.4.5, "Annotation Types." Many of them may be displayed in either the *open* or the *closed* state. When closed, they appear on the page in some distinctive form depending on the specific annotation type, such as an icon, a box, or a rubber stamp. When the user *activates* the annotation by clicking it with the mouse, it exhibits its associated object, such as by opening a pop-up window displaying a text note (Figure 7.2) or by playing a sound or a movie.

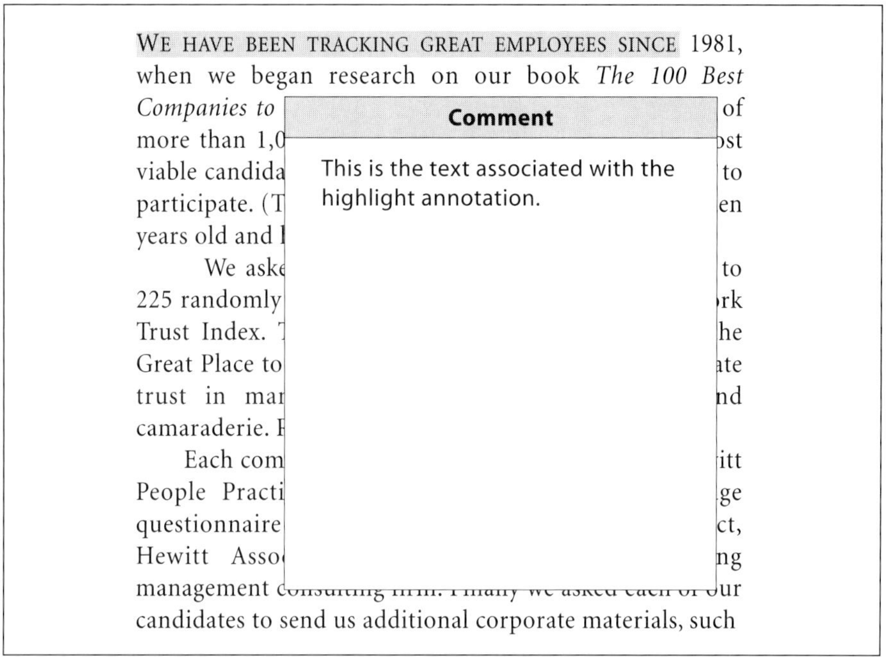

WE HAVE BEEN TRACKING GREAT EMPLOYEES SINCE 1981,
when we began research on our book *The 100 Best
Companies to* [**Comment**   ] of
more than 1,0   ost
viable candida   This is the text associated with the   to
participate. (T   highlight annotation.   en
years old and l

   We aske   to
225 randomly   rk
Trust Index. T   he
Great Place to   ate
trust in mar   nd
camaraderie. F

   Each com   itt
People Practi   ge
questionnaire   ct,
Hewitt Asso   ng
management consulting firm. Finally we asked each of our
candidates to send us additional corporate materials, such

FIGURE 7.2 *Open annotation*

The behavior of each annotation type is implemented by a software module
called an *annotation handler*. Handlers for the standard annotation types are built
directly into the PDF viewer application; handlers for additional types can be
supplied as plug-in extensions.

7.4.1 Annotation Dictionaries

The optional **Annots** entry in a page object (see "Page Objects" on page 77) holds
an array of *annotation dictionaries*, each representing an annotation associated
with the given page. Table 7.9 shows the required and optional entries that are
common to all annotation dictionaries. The dictionary may contain additional
entries specific to a particular annotation type; see the descriptions of individual
annotation types in Section 7.4.5, "Annotation Types," for details.

TABLE 7.9 Entries common to all annotation dictionaries

KEY	TYPE	VALUE
Type	name	*(Optional)* The type of PDF object that this dictionary describes; if present, must be **Annot** for an annotation dictionary.
Subtype	name	*(Required)* The type of annotation that this dictionary describes; see Table 7.13 on page 408 for specific values.
P	dictionary	*(Optional; PDF 1.3; not used in FDF files)* An indirect reference to the page object with which this annotation is associated.
Rect	rectangle	*(Required)* The *annotation rectangle*, defining the location of the annotation on the page in default user space units.
M	date or string	*(Optional; PDF 1.1)* The date and time when the annotation was last modified. The preferred format is a date string as described in Section 3.8.2, "Dates," but viewer applications should be prepared to accept and display a string in any format. (See implementation note 51 in Appendix H.)
F	integer	*(Optional; PDF 1.1)* A set of flags specifying various characteristics of the annotation (see Section 7.4.2, "Annotation Flags"). Default value: 0.
Border	array	*(Optional)* An array specifying the characteristics of the annotation's border. The border is specified as a "rounded rectangle."
		In PDF 1.0, the array consists of three numbers defining the horizontal corner radius, vertical corner radius, and border width, all in default user space units. If the corner radii are 0, the border has square (not rounded) corners; if the border width is 0, no border is drawn. (See implementation note 52 in Appendix H.)
		In PDF 1.1, the array may have a fourth element, an optional *dash array* defining a pattern of dashes and gaps to be used in drawing the border. The dash array is specified in the same format as in the dash pattern parameter of the graphics state (see "Line Dash Pattern" on page 141). For example, a **Border** value of [0 0 1 [3 2]] specifies a border 1 unit wide, with square corners, drawn with 3-unit dashes alternating with 2-unit gaps. Note that no dash phase is specified; the phase is assumed to be 0. (See implementation note 53 in Appendix H.)
		In PDF 1.2 or later, some types of annotation may ignore this entry and use the **BS** entry instead. At the time of publication, all annotation types except widget annotations use the **Border** entry.
		Default value: [0 0 1].

BS	dictionary	*(Optional; PDF 1.2)* A border style dictionary specifying the characteristics of the annotation's border (see Section 7.4.3, "Border Styles"; see also implementation note 54 in Appendix H).
		Note: *At the time of publication, only widget annotations use this entry to specify their border styles; all other annotation types use* **Border** *instead. This entry is used, however, to specify the width and dash pattern for the lines drawn by line, square, circle, and ink annotations.*
AP	dictionary	*(Optional; PDF 1.2)* An *appearance dictionary* specifying how the annotation is presented visually on the page (see Section 7.4.4, "Appearance Streams"; see also implementation note 54 in Appendix H).
AS	name	*(Required if the appearance dictionary* **AP** *contains one or more subdictionaries; PDF 1.2)* The annotation's *appearance state*, which selects the applicable appearance stream from an appearance subdictionary (see Section 7.4.4, "Appearance Streams"; see also implementation note 54 in Appendix H).
C	array	*(Optional; PDF 1.1)* An array of three numbers in the range 0.0 to 1.0, representing the components of a color in the **DeviceRGB** color space. This color will be used for the following purposes:
		• The background of the annotation's icon when closed
		• The title bar of the annotation's pop-up window
		• The border of a link annotation
T	text string	*(Optional; PDF 1.1)* The text label to be displayed in the title bar of the annotation's pop-up window when open and active.
Popup	dictionary	*(Optional; PDF 1.3)* An indirect reference to a pop-up annotation for entering or editing the text associated with this annotation.
A	dictionary	*(Optional; PDF 1.1)* An action to be performed when the annotation is activated (see Section 7.5, "Actions").
		Note: *This entry is not permitted in link annotations if a* **Dest** *entry is present (see "Link Annotations" on page 410). Also note that the* **A** *entry in movie annotations has a different meaning (see "Movie Annotations" on page 418).*
AA	dictionary	*(Optional; PDF 1.2)* An additional-actions dictionary defining the annotation's behavior in response to various trigger events (see Section 7.5.2, "Trigger Events"). At the time of publication, this entry is used only by widget annotations.
StructParents	integer	*(Required if the annotation is a structural content item; PDF 1.3)* The integer key of the annotation's entry in the structural parent tree (see "Finding Structure Elements from Content Items" on page 496).

7.4.2 Annotation Flags

The value of the annotation dictionary's **F** entry is an unsigned 32-bit integer containing flags specifying various characteristics of the annotation. Bit positions within the flag word are numbered from 1 (low-order) to 32 (high-order). Table 7.10 shows the meanings of the flags; all undefined flag bits are reserved and must be set to 0.

TABLE 7.10 Annotation flags

BIT POSITION	NAME	MEANING
1	Invisible	If set, do not display the annotation if it does not belong to one of the standard annotation types and no annotation handler is available. If clear, display such an unknown annotation using an appearance stream specified by its appearance dictionary, if any (see Section 7.4.4, "Appearance Streams").
2	Hidden	*(PDF 1.2)* If set, do not display or print the annotation or allow it to interact with the user, regardless of its annotation type or whether an annotation handler is available. In cases where screen space is limited, the ability to hide and show annotations selectively can be used in combination with appearance streams (see Section 7.4.4, "Appearance Streams") to display auxiliary pop-up information similar in function to online help systems. (See implementation note 55 in Appendix H.)
3	Print	*(PDF 1.2)* If set, print the annotation when the page is printed. If clear, never print the annotation, regardless of whether it is displayed on the screen. This can be useful, for example, for annotations representing interactive pushbuttons, which would serve no meaningful purpose on the printed page. (See implementation note 55 in Appendix H.)
4	NoZoom	*(PDF 1.3)* If set, do not scale the annotation's appearance to match the magnification of the page. The location of the annotation on the page (defined by the upper-left corner of its bounding box) remains fixed, regardless of the page magnification. See below for further discussion.

| 5 | NoRotate | *(PDF 1.3)* If set, do not rotate the annotation's appearance to match the rotation of the page. The upper-left corner of the annotation's bounding box remains in a fixed location on the page, regardless of the page rotation. See below for further discussion. |
| 6 | NoView | *(PDF 1.3)* If set, do not display the annotation on the screen or allow it to interact with the user. The annotation may be printed (depending on the setting of the Print flag), but should be considered hidden for purposes of on-screen display and user interaction. |
| 7 | ReadOnly | *(PDF 1.3)* If set, do not allow the annotation to interact with the user. The annotation may be displayed or printed (depending on the settings of the NoView and Print flags), but should not respond to mouse clicks or change its appearance in response to mouse motions.

Note: *This flag is ignored for widget annotations; its function is subsumed by the ReadOnly flag of the associated form field (see Table 7.45 on page 438).* |

If the NoZoom flag is set, the annotation always maintains the same fixed size on the screen and is unaffected by the magnification level at which the page itself is displayed. Similarly, if the NoRotate flag is set, the annotation retains its original orientation on the screen when the page is rotated (by changing the **Rotate** entry in the page dictionary; see "Page Objects" on page 77).

In either case, the annotation's position is determined by the coordinates of the upper-left corner of its bounding box, as determined from the **Rect** entry in the annotation dictionary and interpreted in the default user space of the page. When the default user space is scaled or rotated, the positions of the other three corners of the annotation's bounding box will be different in the altered user space than they were in the original user space. The viewer application performs this alteration automatically; however, it does not actually change the annotation's **Rect** entry, which continues to describe the annotation's relationship with the unscaled, unrotated user space.

For example, Figure 7.3 shows how an annotation whose NoRotate flag is set remains upright when the page it is on is rotated 90 degrees clockwise. The upper-left corner of the annotation remains at the same point in default user space; the annotation pivots around that point.

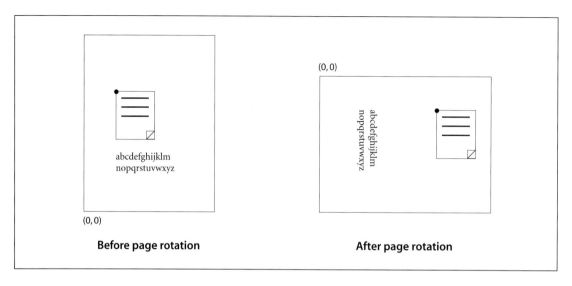

Before page rotation   **After page rotation**

FIGURE 7.3 *Coordinate adjustment with the NoRotate flag*

7.4.3 Border Styles

An annotation may optionally be surrounded by a border when displayed or printed. If present, the border is drawn completely inside the annotation's bounding box. In PDF 1.1, the characteristics of the border are specified by the **Border** entry in the annotation dictionary (see Table 7.9 on page 400). Beginning in PDF 1.2, some types of annotation may instead specify their border characteristics in a *border style dictionary* designated by the annotation's **BS** entry. Table 7.11 summarizes the contents of this dictionary. If neither the **Border** nor the **BS** entry is present, the border is drawn as a solid line with a width of 1 point.

*Note: At the time of publication, only widget annotations use border style dictionaries to specify their border styles; all other annotation types use the **Border** entry instead. Border style dictionaries are used, however, to specify the width and dash pattern for the lines drawn by line, square, circle, and ink annotations.*

TABLE 7.11 Entries in a border style dictionary

KEY	TYPE	VALUE
Type	name	*(Optional)* The type of PDF object that this dictionary describes; if present, must be **Border** for a border style dictionary.
W	number	*(Optional)* The border width in points. If this value is 0, no border is drawn. Default value: 1.
S	name	*(Optional)* The border style:

		S	(Solid) A solid rectangle surrounding the annotation.
		D	(Dashed) A dashed rectangle surrounding the annotation. The dash pattern is specified by the **D** entry (see below).
		B	(Beveled) A simulated embossed rectangle that appears to be raised above the surface of the page.
		I	(Inset) A simulated engraved rectangle that appears to be recessed below the surface of the page.
		U	(Underline) A single line along the bottom of the annotation's bounding box.

Other border styles may be defined in the future. (See implementation note 56 in Appendix H.) Default value: S.

| **D** | array | *(Optional)* A *dash array* defining a pattern of dashes and gaps to be used in drawing a dashed border (border style D above). The dash array is specified in the same format as in the line dash pattern parameter of the graphics state (see "Line Dash Pattern" on page 141). The dash phase is not specified and is assumed to be 0. For example, a **D** entry of [3 2] specifies a border drawn with 3-point dashes alternating with 2-point gaps. Default value: [3]. |

7.4.4 Appearance Streams

Beginning in PDF 1.2, an annotation can specify one or more *appearance streams* as an alternative to the simple border and color characteristics available in earlier versions. This allows the annotation to be presented visually on the page in different ways to reflect its interactions with the user. Each appearance stream is a form XObject (see Section 4.9, "Form XObjects"): a self-contained content stream to be rendered inside the annotation's bounding box.

Before rendering an appearance stream, the viewer application establishes a coordinate system whose origin is at the lower-left corner of the annotation rectangle. Nominally, the coordinates in this space are in default user space units; however, the space may be scaled or rotated with respect to the actual page coordinate system, depending on the values of the annotation's NoZoom and NoRotate flags (see Section 7.4.2, "Annotation Flags"). The form XObject's **Matrix** entry should transform the form coordinate system into that of the annotation. The results are clipped to the annotation's bounding box. All other elements of the graphics state are set to their default values.

An annotation can define as many as three separate appearances:

- The *normal appearance* is used when the annotation is not interacting with the user. This is also the appearance that is used for printing the annotation.

- The *rollover appearance* is used when the user moves the cursor into the annotation's active area without pressing the mouse button.

- The *down appearance* is used when the mouse button is pressed or held down within the annotation's active area.

Note: *As used here, the term* mouse *denotes a generic pointing device that controls the location of a cursor on the screen and has at least one button that can be pressed, held down, and released. See Section 7.5.2, "Trigger Events," for further discussion.*

The normal, rollover, and down appearances are defined in an *appearance dictionary*, which in turn is the value of the **AP** entry in the annotation dictionary (see Table 7.9 on page 400). Table 7.12 shows the contents of the appearance dictionary.

TABLE 7.12 Entries in an appearance dictionary

KEY	TYPE	VALUE
N	stream or dictionary	*(Required)* The annotation's normal appearance.
R	stream or dictionary	*(Optional)* The annotation's rollover appearance. Default value: the value of the **N** entry.
D	stream or dictionary	*(Optional)* The annotation's down appearance. Default value: the value of the **N** entry.

Each entry in the appearance dictionary may contain either a single appearance stream or an *appearance subdictionary*. In the latter case, the subdictionary defines multiple appearance streams corresponding to different *appearance states* of the annotation. For example, an annotation representing an interactive checkbox might have two appearance states named On and Off. Its appearance dictionary might be defined as follows:

```
/AP <<  /N <<  /On formXObject₁
                /Off formXObject₂
          >>
        /D <<  /On formXObject₃
                /Off formXObject₄
          >>
      >>
```

where *formXObject₁* and *formXObject₂* define the checkbox's normal appearance in its checked and unchecked states, while *formXObject₃* and *formXObject₄* provide visual feedback, such as emboldening its outline, when the user clicks it with the mouse. (No **R** entry is defined because no special appearance is needed when the user moves the cursor over the checkbox without pressing the mouse button.) The choice between the checked and unchecked appearance states is determined by the **AS** entry in the annotation dictionary (see Table 7.9 on page 400).

*Note: Some of the standard PDF annotation types, such as movie annotations—as well as all custom annotation types defined by third parties—are implemented through plug-in extensions. If the plug-in for a particular annotation type is not available, PDF viewer applications should display the annotation with its normal (**N**) appearance. Viewer applications should also attempt to provide reasonable behavior (such as displaying nothing at all) if an annotation's **AS** entry designates an appearance state for which no appearance is defined in the appearance dictionary.*

For convenience in managing appearance streams that are used repeatedly, the **AP** entry in a PDF document's name dictionary (see Section 3.6.3, "Name Dictionary") can contain a name tree that maps names to appearance streams. The names have no standard meanings; no PDF objects refer to appearance streams by name.

7.4.5 Annotation Types

PDF supports the standard annotation types listed in Table 7.13. The following sections describe each of these types in detail. Plug-in extensions may add new annotation types, and further standard types may be added in the future. (See implementation note 57 in Appendix H.)

TABLE 7.13 Annotation types	
ANNOTATION TYPE	**DESCRIPTION**
Text	Text annotation
Link	Link annotation
FreeText	*(PDF 1.3)* Free text annotation
Line	*(PDF 1.3)* Line annotation
Square	*(PDF 1.3)* Square annotation
Circle	*(PDF 1.3)* Circle annotation
Highlight	*(PDF 1.3)* Highlight annotation
Underline	*(PDF 1.3)* Underline annotation
StrikeOut	*(PDF 1.3)* Strikeout annotation
Stamp	*(PDF 1.3)* Rubber stamp annotation
Ink	*(PDF 1.3)* Ink annotation
Popup	*(PDF 1.3)* Pop-up annotation
FileAttachment	*(PDF 1.3)* File attachment annotation
Sound	*(PDF 1.2)* Sound annotation
Movie	*(PDF 1.2)* Movie annotation
Widget	*(PDF 1.2)* Widget annotation
TrapNet	*(PDF 1.3)* Trap network annotation

Text Annotations

A *text annotation* represents a "sticky note" attached to a point in the PDF document. When closed, the annotation appears as an icon; when open, it displays a pop-up window containing the text of the note, in a font and size chosen by the viewer application. Table 7.14 shows the annotation dictionary entries specific to this type of annotation.

TABLE 7.14 Additional entries specific to a text annotation

KEY	TYPE	VALUE
Subtype	name	*(Required)* The type of annotation that this dictionary describes; must be **Text** for a text annotation.
Contents	text string	*(Required)* The text to be displayed in the pop-up window when the annotation is opened. Carriage returns may be used to separate the text into paragraphs.
Open	boolean	*(Optional)* A flag specifying whether the annotation should initially be displayed open. Default value: *false* (closed).
Name	name	*(Optional)* The name of an icon to be used in displaying the annotation. Viewer applications should provide predefined icon appearances for at least the following standard names:

Comment	Key	Note
Help	NewParagraph	Paragraph
Insert		

Additional names may be supported as well. Default value: **Note**.

*Note: The annotation dictionary's **AP** entry, if present, takes precedence over the **Name** entry; see Table 7.9 on page 400 and Section 7.4.4, "Appearance Streams."*

Example 7.6 shows the definition of a text annotation.

Example 7.6

```
22 0 obj
    << /Type /Annot
       /Subtype /Text
       /Rect [266 116 430 204]
       /Contents (The quick brown fox ate the lazy mouse.)
    >>
endobj
```

Link Annotations

A *link annotation* represents either a hypertext link to a destination elsewhere in the document (see Section 7.2.1, "Destinations") or an action to be performed (Section 7.5, "Actions"). Table 7.15 shows the annotation dictionary entries specific to this type of annotation.

TABLE 7.15 Additional entries specific to a link annotation

KEY	TYPE	VALUE
Subtype	name	*(Required)* The type of annotation that this dictionary describes; must be **Link** for a link annotation.
Dest	array, name, or string	*(Optional; not permitted if an **A** entry is present)* A destination to be displayed when the annotation is activated (see Section 7.2.1, "Destinations"; see also implementation note 58 in Appendix H).
H	name	*(Optional; PDF 1.2)* The annotation's *highlighting mode,* the visual effect to be used when the mouse button is pressed or held down inside its active area:

N   (None) No highlighting.

I   (Invert) Invert the contents of the annotation's bounding box.

O   (Outline) Invert the annotation's border.

P   (Push) Display the annotation's down appearance, if any (see Section 7.4.4, "Appearance Streams"). If no down appearance is defined, offset the contents of the annotation's bounding box to appear as if it were being "pushed" below the surface of the page.

A highlighting mode other than P overrides any down appearance defined for the annotation. Default value: I.

Note: *In PDF 1.1, highlighting is always done by inverting colors inside the annotation's bounding box.*

| PA | dictionary | *(Optional; PDF 1.3)* A URI action (see "URI Actions" on page 428) formerly associated with this annotation. When Web Capture (Section 8.5, "Web Capture") changes an annotation from a URI to a go-to action ("Go-To Actions" on page 425), it uses this entry to save the data from the original URI action so that it can be changed back in case the target page for the **GoTo** action is subsequently deleted. |

Example 7.7 shows a link annotation that jumps to a destination elsewhere in the document.

Example 7.7

```
93 0 obj
    << /Type /Annot
        /Subtype /Link
        /Rect [71 717 190 734]
        /Border [16 16 1]
        /Dest [3 0 R /FitR –4 399 199 533]
    >>
endobj
```

Free Text Annotations

A *free text annotation (PDF 1.3)* displays text directly on the page. Unlike an ordinary text annotation (see "Text Annotations" on page 409), a free text annotation has no open or closed state; instead of being displayed in a pop-up window, the text is always visible. Table 7.16 shows the annotation dictionary entries specific to this type of annotation.

TABLE 7.16 Additional entries specific to a free text annotation

KEY	TYPE	VALUE
Subtype	name	*(Required)* The type of annotation that this dictionary describes; must be **FreeText** for a free text annotation.
Contents	text string	*(Required)* The text to be displayed.
DA	string	*(Required)* The default appearance string to be used in formatting the text (see "Variable Text" on page 439).
		Note: *The annotation dictionary's* **AP** *entry, if present, takes precedence over the* **DA** *entry; see Table 7.9 on page 400 and Section 7.4.4, "Appearance Streams."*

Line Annotations

A *line annotation (PDF 1.3)* displays a single straight line on the page. When opened, it displays a pop-up window containing the text of the associated note. Table 7.17 shows the annotation dictionary entries specific to this type of annotation.

TABLE 7.17   Additional entries specific to a line annotation

KEY	TYPE	VALUE
Subtype	name	*(Required)* The type of annotation that this dictionary describes; must be **Line** for a line annotation.
Contents	text string	*(Required)* The text to be displayed in the pop-up window when the annotation is opened. Carriage returns may be used to separate the text into paragraphs.
L	array	*(Required)* An array of four numbers, $[x_1\ y_1\ x_2\ y_2]$, specifying the starting and ending coordinates of the line in default user space.
BS	dictionary	*(Optional)* A border style (see Table 7.11 on page 405) specifying the width and dash pattern of the line to be drawn.
		*Note: The annotation dictionary's **AP** entry, if present, takes precedence over the **L** and **BS** entries; see Table 7.9 on page 400 and Section 7.4.4, "Appearance Streams."*

Square and Circle Annotations

Square and *circle annotations (PDF 1.3)* display, respectively, a rectangle or an ellipse on the page. When opened, they display a pop-up window containing the text of the associated note. The rectangle or ellipse is inscribed within the bounding box defined by the annotation dictionary's **Rect** entry (see Table 7.9 on page 400); Figure 7.4 shows an example, using a border width of 18 points. Despite the names *square* and *circle*, the width and height of the bounding box need not be equal. Table 7.18 shows the annotation dictionary entries specific to these types of annotation.

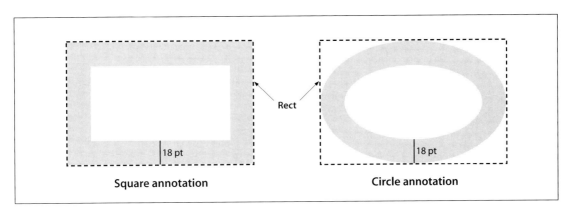

FIGURE 7.4 *Square and circle annotations*

TABLE 7.18 **Additional entries specific to a square or circle annotation**

KEY	TYPE	VALUE
Subtype	name	*(Required)* The type of annotation that this dictionary describes; must be **Square** or **Circle** for a square or circle annotation, respectively.
Contents	text string	*(Required)* The text to be displayed in the pop-up window when the annotation is opened. Carriage returns may be used to separate the text into paragraphs.
BS	dictionary	*(Optional)* A border style (see Table 7.11 on page 405) specifying the line width and dash pattern for drawing the rectangle or ellipse.
		Note: *The annotation dictionary's* **AP** *entry, if present, takes precedence over the* **Rect** *and* **BS** *entries; see Table 7.9 on page 400 and Section 7.4.4, "Appearance Streams."*

Markup Annotations

Markup annotations (PDF 1.3) appear as highlights, underlines, and strikeouts in the text of a document. When opened, they display a pop-up window containing the text of the associated note. Table 7.19 shows the annotation dictionary entries specific to these types of annotation.

TABLE 7.19 Additional entries specific to markup annotations

KEY	TYPE	VALUE
Subtype	name	*(Required)* The type of annotation that this dictionary describes; must be **Highlight**, **Underline**, or **StrikeOut** for a highlight, underline, or strikeout annotation, respectively.
Contents	text string	*(Required)* The text to be displayed in the pop-up window when the annotation is opened. Carriage returns may be used to separate the text into paragraphs.
QuadPoints	array	*(Required)* An array of $8 \times n$ numbers specifying the coordinates of n quadrilaterals in default user space. Each quadrilateral encompasses a word or group of contiguous words in the text underlying the annotation. The coordinates for each quadrilateral are given in the order

$$x_1 \ y_1 \ x_2 \ y_2 \ x_3 \ y_3 \ x_4 \ y_4$$

specifying the quadrilateral's four vertices in counterclockwise order (see Figure 7.5). The text is oriented with respect to the edge connecting points (x_1, y_1) and (x_2, y_2). (See implementation note 59 in Appendix H.)

Note: The annotation dictionary's **AP** *entry, if present, takes precedence over the* **QuadPoints** *entry; see Table 7.9 on page 400 and Section 7.4.4, "Appearance Streams."*

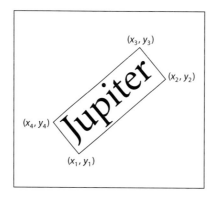

FIGURE 7.5 *QuadPoints specification*

Rubber Stamp Annotations

A *rubber stamp annotation (PDF 1.3)* displays text or graphics intended to look as if they were stamped on the page with a rubber stamp. When opened, it displays a pop-up window containing the text of the associated note. Table 7.20 shows the annotation dictionary entries specific to this type of annotation.

TABLE 7.20   Additional entries specific to a rubber stamp annotation

KEY	TYPE	VALUE
Subtype	name	*(Required)* The type of annotation that this dictionary describes; must be **Stamp** for a rubber stamp annotation.
Contents	text string	*(Required)* The text to be displayed in the pop-up window when the annotation is opened. Carriage returns may be used to separate the text into paragraphs.
Name	name	*(Optional)* The name of an icon to be used in displaying the annotation. Viewer applications should provide predefined icon appearances for at least the following standard names: Approved Experimental NotApproved AsIs Expired NotForPublicRelease Confidential Final Sold Departmental ForComment TopSecret Draft ForPublicRelease Additional names may be supported as well. Default value: **Draft**. *Note: The annotation dictionary's **AP** entry, if present, takes precedence over the **Name** entry; see Table 7.9 on page 400 and Section 7.4.4, "Appearance Streams."*

Ink Annotations

An *ink annotation (PDF 1.3)* represents a freehand "scribble" composed of one or more disjoint paths. When opened, it displays a pop-up window containing the text of the associated note. Table 7.21 shows the annotation dictionary entries specific to this type of annotation.

TABLE 7.21 Additional entries specific to an ink annotation

KEY	TYPE	VALUE
Subtype	name	*(Required)* The type of annotation that this dictionary describes; must be **Ink** for an ink annotation.
Contents	text string	*(Required)* The text to be displayed in the pop-up window when the annotation is opened. Carriage returns may be used to separate the text into paragraphs.
InkList	array	*(Required)* An array of *n* arrays, each representing a stroked path. Each array is a series of alternating *x* and *y* coordinates in default user space, specifying points along the path. When drawn, the points are connected by straight lines or curves in an implementation-dependent way. (See implementation note 60 in Appendix H.)
BS	dictionary	*(Optional)* A border style (see Table 7.11 on page 405) specifying the line width and dash pattern for drawing the paths.
		Note: *The annotation dictionary's **AP** entry, if present, takes precedence over the **InkList** and **BS** entries; see Table 7.9 on page 400 and Section 7.4.4, "Appearance Streams."*

Pop-up Annotations

A *pop-up annotation (PDF 1.3)* displays text in a pop-up window for entry and editing. It typically does not appear alone, but is associated with another annotation, its *parent annotation*, and is used for editing the parent's text. It has no appearance stream or associated actions of its own, and is identified by the **Popup** entry in the parent's annotation dictionary (see Table 7.9 on page 400). Table 7.22 shows the annotation dictionary entries specific to this type of annotation.

TABLE 7.22 Additional entries specific to a pop-up annotation

KEY	TYPE	VALUE
Subtype	name	*(Required)* The type of annotation that this dictionary describes; must be **Popup** for a pop-up annotation.
Parent	dictionary	*(Optional; must be an indirect reference)* The parent annotation with which this pop-up annotation is associated.
		Note: *If this entry is present, the parent annotation's **Contents**, **T**, **C**, and **M** entries (see Table 7.9 on page 400) override those of the pop-up annotation itself.*
Open	boolean	*(Optional)* A flag specifying whether the pop-up annotation should initially be displayed open. Default value: *false* (closed).

File Attachment Annotations

A *file attachment annotation (PDF 1.3)* contains a reference to a file, which typically will be embedded in the PDF file (see Section 3.10.3, "Embedded File
Streams"). For example, a table of data might use a file attachment annotation to
link to a spreadsheet file based on that data; activating the annotation will extract
the embedded file and give the user an opportunity to view it or store it in the file
system. Table 7.23 shows the annotation dictionary entries specific to this type of
annotation.

TABLE 7.23 Additional entries specific to a file attachment annotation

KEY	TYPE	VALUE
Subtype	name	*(Required)* The type of annotation that this dictionary describes; must be **FileAttachment** for a file attachment annotation.
FS	file specification	*(Required)* The file associated with this annotation.
Contents	text string	*(Required)* The text to be displayed in the pop-up window when the annotation is opened. Carriage returns may be used to separate the text into paragraphs.
Name	name	*(Optional)* The name of an icon to be used in displaying the annotation. Viewer applications should provide predefined icon appearances for at least the following standard names:

        Graph   **PushPin**
        Paperclip   **Tag**

    Additional names may be supported as well. Default value: **PushPin**.

    Note: *The annotation dictionary's* **AP** *entry, if present, takes precedence over the* **Name** *entry; see Table 7.9 on page 400 and Section 7.4.4, "Appearance Streams."*

Sound Annotations

A *sound annotation (PDF 1.2)* is analogous to a text annotation, except that instead of a text note, it contains sound recorded from the computer's microphone
or imported from a file. When the annotation is activated, the sound is played.
The annotation behaves like a text annotation in most ways, with a different icon
(by default, a speaker) to indicate that it represents a sound. Table 7.24 shows the
annotation dictionary entries specific to this type of annotation; sounds themselves are discussed in Section 7.7, "Sounds."

TABLE 7.24 Additional entries specific to a sound annotation

KEY	TYPE	VALUE
Subtype	name	*(Required)* The type of annotation that this dictionary describes; must be **Sound** for a sound annotation.
Sound	stream	*(Required)* A sound object defining the sound to be played when the annotation is activated (see Section 7.7, "Sounds").
Contents	text string	*(Optional)* The text to be displayed in the annotation's pop-up window as a description of the sound.
Name	name	*(Optional)* The name of an icon to be used in displaying the annotation. Viewer applications should provide predefined icon appearances for at least the standard names **Speaker** and **Microphone**; additional names may be supported as well. Default value: **Speaker**.
		*Note: The annotation dictionary's **AP** entry, if present, takes precedence over the **Name** entry; see Table 7.9 on page 400 and Section 7.4.4, "Appearance Streams."*

Movie Annotations

A *movie annotation (PDF 1.2)* contains animated graphics and sound to be presented on the computer screen and through the speakers. When the annotation is activated, the movie is played. Table 7.25 shows the annotation dictionary entries specific to this type of annotation; movies themselves are discussed in Section 7.8, "Movies." (See also implementation note 61 in Appendix H.)

TABLE 7.25 Additional entries specific to a movie annotation

KEY	TYPE	VALUE
Subtype	name	*(Required)* The type of annotation that this dictionary describes; must be **Movie** for a movie annotation.
Movie	dictionary	*(Required)* A movie dictionary describing the movie's static characteristics (see Section 7.8, "Movies").
A	boolean or dictionary	*(Optional)* A flag or dictionary specifying whether and how to play the movie when the annotation is activated. If this value is a dictionary, it is a movie activation dictionary (see Section 7.8, "Movies") specifying how to play the movie; if it is the boolean value *true*, the movie should be played using default activation parameters; if it is *false*, the movie should not be played at all. Default value: *true*.

Widget Annotations

Interactive forms (see Section 7.6, "Interactive Forms") use *widget annotations* to represent the appearance of fields and to manage user interactions. As a convenience, when a field has only a single associated widget annotation, the contents of the field dictionary (Section 7.6.2, "Field Dictionaries") and the annotation dictionary may be merged into a single dictionary containing entries that pertain to both a field and an annotation. (This presents no ambiguity, since the contents of the two kinds of dictionary do not conflict.) Table 7.26 shows the annotation dictionary entries specific to this type of annotation; interactive forms and fields are discussed at length in Section 7.6.

TABLE 7.26 Additional entries specific to a widget annotation

KEY	TYPE	VALUE
Subtype	name	*(Required)* The type of annotation that this dictionary describes; must be **Widget** for a widget annotation.
H	name	*(Optional; PDF 1.2)* The annotation's *highlighting mode*, the visual effect to be used when the mouse button is pressed or held down inside its active area:

> N (None) No highlighting.
>
> I (Invert) Invert the contents of the annotation's bounding box.
>
> O (Outline) Invert the annotation's border.
>
> P (Push) Display the annotation's down appearance, if any (see Section 7.4.4, "Appearance Streams"). If no down appearance is defined, offset the contents of the annotation's bounding box to appear as if it were being "pushed" below the surface of the page.
>
> T (Toggle) Same as P (which is preferred).

A highlighting mode other than P overrides any down appearance defined for the annotation. Default value: I.

MK	dictionary	*(Optional; PDF 1.2)* An appearance characteristics dictionary to be used in constructing a dynamic appearance stream specifying the annotation's visual presentation on the page; see "Variable Text" on page 439 for further discussion.

Note: *The name* **MK** *for this entry is of historical significance only and has no direct meaning.*

Trap Network Annotations

A *trap network annotation* defines the trapping characteristics for a page of a PDF document. (*Trapping* is the process of adding marks to a page along color boundaries to avoid unwanted visual artifacts resulting from misregistration of colorants when the page is printed.) A page may have at most one trap network annotation, whose **Subtype** entry has the value **TrapNet** and which is always the last element in the page object's **Annots** array (see "Page Objects" on page 77). See Section 8.6.3, "Trapping Support," for further discussion.

7.5 Actions

Instead of simply jumping to a destination in the document, an annotation or outline item can specify an *action (PDF 1.1)* for the viewer application to perform, such as launching an application, playing a sound, or changing an annotation's appearance state. The optional **A** entry in the annotation or outline item dictionary (see Tables 7.9 on page 400 and 7.4 on page 389) specifies an action to be performed when the annotation or outline item is activated; in PDF 1.2, a variety of other circumstances may trigger an action as well (see Section 7.5.2, "Trigger Events"). In addition, the optional **OpenAction** entry in a document's catalog (Section 3.6.1, "Document Catalog") may specify an action to be performed when the document is opened. PDF includes a wide variety of standard action types, described in detail in Section 7.5.3, "Action Types."

7.5.1 Action Dictionaries

An *action dictionary* defines the characteristics and behavior of an action. Table 7.27 shows the required and optional entries that are common to all action dictionaries. The dictionary may contain additional entries specific to a particular action type; see the descriptions of individual action types in Section 7.5.3, "Action Types," for details.

TABLE 7.27 **Entries common to all action dictionaries**

KEY	TYPE	VALUE
Type	name	*(Optional)* The type of PDF object that this dictionary describes; if present, must be **Action** for an action dictionary.
S	name	*(Required)* The type of action that this dictionary describes; see Table 7.29 on page 424 for specific values.
Next	dictionary or array	*(Optional; PDF 1.2)* The next action, or sequence of actions, to be performed after this one. The value is either a single action dictionary or an array of action dictionaries to be performed in order; see below for further discussion.

The action dictionary's **Next** entry *(PDF 1.2)* allows sequences of actions to be chained together. For example, the effect of clicking a link annotation with the mouse might be to play a sound, jump to a new page, and start up a movie. Note that the **Next** entry is not restricted to a single action, but may contain an array of actions, each of which in turn may have a **Next** entry of its own. The actions may thus form a tree instead of a simple linked list. Actions within each **Next** array are executed in order, each followed in turn by any actions specified in *its* **Next** entry, and so on recursively. Viewer applications should attempt to provide reasonable behavior in anomalous situations; for example, self-referential actions should not be executed more than once, and actions that close the document or otherwise render the next action impossible should terminate the execution sequence. Applications should also provide some mechanism for the user to interrupt and manually terminate a sequence of actions.

Note: *No action should modify its own action dictionary or any other in the action tree in which it resides. The effect of such modification on subsequent execution of actions in the tree is undefined.*

7.5.2 Trigger Events

An annotation, page object, or interactive form field may include an entry named **AA** that specifies an *additional-actions dictionary (PDF 1.2)*, extending the set of events that can trigger the execution of an action. Table 7.28 shows the contents of such a dictionary. (See implementation notes 62 and 63 in Appendix H.)

TABLE 7.28   Entries in an additional-actions dictionary

KEY	TYPE	VALUE
E	dictionary	(*Optional; annotations only*) An action to be performed when the cursor enters the annotation's active area.
X	dictionary	(*Optional; annotations only*) An action to be performed when the cursor exits the annotation's active area.
D	dictionary	(*Optional; annotations only*) An action to be performed when the mouse button is pressed inside the annotation's active area.
U	dictionary	(*Optional; annotations only*) An action to be performed when the mouse button is released inside the annotation's active area. **Note:** *For backward compatibility, the* **A** *entry in an annotation dictionary, if present, takes precedence over this entry (see Table 7.15 on page 410).*
O	dictionary	(*Optional; pages only*) An action to be performed when the page is opened (for example, when the user navigates to it from the next or previous page or via a link annotation or outline entry). This action is independent of any that may be defined by the **OpenAction** entry in the document catalog (see Section 3.6.1, "Document Catalog"), and is executed after such an action. (See implementation note 64 in Appendix H.)
C	dictionary	(*Optional; pages only*) An action to be performed when the page is closed (for example, when the user navigates to the next or previous page or follows a link annotation or an outline entry). This action applies to the page being closed, and is executed before any other page is opened. (See implementation note 64 in Appendix H.)
Fo	dictionary	(*Optional; widget annotations only*) An action to be performed when the annotation receives the input focus.
Bl	dictionary	(*Optional; widget annotations only*) An action to be performed when the annotation is "blurred" (loses the input focus).
K	dictionary	(*Optional; PDF 1.3; form fields only*) A JavaScript action to be performed when the user types a keystroke into a text or combo box or modifies the selection in a scrollable list. This allows the keystroke to be checked for validity and rejected or modified.
F	dictionary	(*Optional; PDF 1.3; form fields only*) A JavaScript action to be performed before the field is formatted to display its current value. This allows the field's value to be modified before formatting.
V	dictionary	(*Optional; PDF 1.3; form fields only*) A JavaScript action to be performed when the field's value is changed. This allows the new value to be checked for validity.
C	dictionary	(*Optional; PDF 1.3; form fields only*) A JavaScript action to be performed when the value of another field changes, in order to recalculate the value of this field. The order in which the document's fields are recalculated is defined by the **CO** entry in the interactive form dictionary (see Section 7.6.1, "Interactive Form Dictionary").

*Note: Although the table lists two different entries with the same name (**C**), the two do not conflict, because they apply to different types of object. The **C** entry stands for "close" for a page object and "calculate" for an interactive form field.*

For purposes of the trigger events **E** (enter), **X** (exit), **D** (down), and **U** (up), the term *mouse* denotes a generic pointing device with the following characteristics:

- A selection button that can be *pressed*, *held down*, and *released*. If there is more than one mouse button, this is typically the left button.

- A notion of *location*—that is, an indication of where on the screen the device is pointing. This is typically denoted by a screen cursor.

- A notion of *focus*—that is, which element in the document is currently interacting with the user. In many systems, this is denoted by a blinking caret, a focus rectangle, or a color change.

PDF viewer applications must ensure the presence of such a device in order for the corresponding actions to be executed correctly. Mouse-related trigger events are subject to the following constraints:

- An **E** (enter) event can occur only when the mouse button is up.

- An **X** (exit) event cannot occur without a preceding **E** event.

- A **U** (up) event cannot occur without a preceding **E** and **D** event.

- In the case of overlapping or nested annotations, entering a second annotation's active area causes an **X** event to occur for the first annotation.

*Note: The field-related trigger events **K** (keystroke), **F** (format), **V** (validate), and **C** (calculate) are not defined for button fields (see "Button Fields" on page 444). Note that the effects of an action triggered by one of these events are limited only by the action itself and can occur outside the described scope of the event. For example, even though the **F** event is used to trigger actions that format field values prior to display, it is possible for an action triggered by this event to perform a calculation or make any other modification to the document.*

*Note also that these field-related trigger events can occur either through user interaction or programmatically, such as in response to the **NeedAppearances** entry in the interactive form dictionary (see Section 7.6.1, "Interactive Form Dictionary"), importation of FDF data (Section 7.6.6, "Forms Data Format"), or JavaScript actions ("JavaScript Actions" on page 458). For example, the user's modifying a field value can trigger a cascade of calculations and further formatting and validation for other fields in the document.*

7.5.3 Action Types

PDF supports the standard action types listed in Table 7.29. The following sections describe each of these types in detail. Plug-in extensions may add new action types.

TABLE 7.29 Action types

ACTION TYPE	DESCRIPTION
GoTo	Go to a destination in the current document.
GoToR	("Go-to remote") Go to a destination in another document.
Launch	Launch an application, usually to open a file.
Thread	Begin reading an article thread.
URI	Resolve a uniform resource identifier.
Sound	*(PDF 1.2)* Play a sound.
Movie	*(PDF 1.2)* Play a movie.
Hide	*(PDF 1.2)* Set an annotation's Hidden flag.
Named	*(PDF 1.2)* Execute an action predefined by the viewer application.
SubmitForm	*(PDF 1.2)* Send data to a uniform resource locator.
ResetForm	*(PDF 1.2)* Set fields to their default values.
ImportData	*(PDF 1.2)* Import field values from a file.
JavaScript	*(PDF 1.3)* Execute a JavaScript script.

Note: *Previous versions of the PDF specification described an action type known as the* set-state action; *this type of action is now considered obsolete and its use is no longer recommended. An additional action type, the* no-op action, *was defined in PDF 1.2 but never implemented; it is no longer defined and should be ignored.*

Go-To Actions

A *go-to action* changes the view to a specified destination (page, location, and magnification factor). Table 7.30 shows the action dictionary entries specific to this type of action.

TABLE 7.30 Additional entries specific to a go-to action		
KEY	**TYPE**	**VALUE**
S	name	*(Required)* The type of action that this dictionary describes; must be **GoTo** for a go-to action.
D	name, string, or array	*(Required)* The destination to jump to (see Section 7.2.1, "Destinations").

Specifying a go-to action in the **A** entry of a link annotation or outline entry (see Tables 7.15 on page 410 and 7.4 on page 389) has the same effect as specifying the destination directly via the **Dest** entry. For example, the link annotation shown in Example 7.8, which uses a go-to action, has the same effect as the one in Example 7.7 on page 411, which specifies the destination directly. However, the go-to action is less compact and is not compatible with PDF 1.0, so using a direct destination is preferable.

Example 7.8

```
93  0  obj
    <<  /Type  /Annot
        /Subtype  /Link
        /Rect  [71  717  190  734]
        /Border  [16  16  1]
        /A  <<  /Type  /Action
                /S  /GoTo
                /D  [3 0 R  /FitR  -4 399 199 533]
            >>
    >>
endobj
```

Remote Go-To Actions

A *remote go-to action* is similar to an ordinary go-to action, but jumps to a destination in another PDF file instead of the current file. Table 7.31 shows the action dictionary entries specific to this type of action.

TABLE 7.31 Additional entries specific to a remote go-to action

KEY	TYPE	VALUE
S	name	*(Required)* The type of action that this dictionary describes; must be **GoToR** for a remote go-to action.
F	file specification	*(Required)* The file in which the destination is located.
D	name, string, or array	*(Required)* The destination to jump to (see Section 7.2.1, "Destinations"). If the value is an array defining an explicit destination (as described under "Explicit Destinations" on page 385), its first element must be a page number within the remote document instead of an indirect reference to a page object in the current document. The first page is numbered 0.
NewWindow	boolean	*(Optional; PDF 1.2)* A flag specifying whether to open the destination document in a new window. If this flag is *false*, the destination document will replace the current document in the same window. If this entry is absent, the viewer application should behave in accordance with the current user preference.

Launch Actions

A *launch action* launches an application or opens or prints a document. Table 7.32 shows the action dictionary entries specific to this type of action.

TABLE 7.32 Additional entries specific to a launch action

KEY	TYPE	VALUE
S	name	*(Required)* The type of action that this dictionary describes; must be **Launch** for a launch action.
F	file specification	*(Required if none of the entries **Win**, **Mac**, or **Unix** is present)* The application to be launched or the document to be opened or printed. If this entry is absent and the viewer application does not understand any of the alternative entries, it should do nothing.

Win	dictionary	*(Optional)* A dictionary containing Windows-specific launch parameters (see Table 7.33; see also implementation note 65 in Appendix H).
Mac	(undefined)	*(Optional)* Macintosh-specific launch parameters; not yet defined.
Unix	(undefined)	*(Optional)* UNIX-specific launch parameters; not yet defined.
NewWindow	boolean	*(Optional; PDF 1.2)* A flag specifying whether to open the destination document in a new window. If this flag is *false*, the destination document will replace the current document in the same window. If this entry is absent, the viewer application should behave in accordance with the current user preference. This entry is ignored if the file designated by the **F** entry is not a PDF document.

The optional **Win**, **Mac**, and **Unix** entries allow the action dictionary to include platform-specific parameters for launching the designated application. If no such entry is present for the given platform, the **F** entry is used instead. Table 7.33 shows the platform-specific launch parameters for the Windows platform; those for the Macintosh and UNIX platforms are not yet defined at the time of publication.

TABLE 7.33 Windows-specific launch parameters

KEY	TYPE	VALUE
F	string	*(Required)* The file name of the application to be launched or the document to be opened or printed, in standard Windows pathname format. If the name string includes a backslash character (\), the backslash must itself be preceded by a backslash.
		Note: *This value must be a simple string; it is not a file specification.*
D	string	*(Optional)* A string specifying the default directory in standard DOS syntax.
O	string	*(Optional)* A string specifying the operation to perform:
		open Open a document. print Print a document.
		If the **F** entry designates an application instead of a document, this entry is ignored and the application is launched. Default value: open.
P	string	*(Optional)* A parameter string to be passed to the application designated by the **F** entry. This entry should be omitted if **F** designates a document.

Thread Actions

A *thread action* jumps to a specified bead on an article thread (see Section 7.3.2, "Articles"), in either the current document or a different one. Table 7.34 shows the action dictionary entries specific to this type of action.

TABLE 7.34 Additional entries specific to a thread action

KEY	TYPE	VALUE
S	name	(Required) The type of action that this dictionary describes; must be **Thread** for a thread action.
F	file specification	(Optional) The file containing the desired thread. If this entry is absent, the thread is in the current file.
D	dictionary, integer, or text string	(Required) The desired destination thread, specified in one of the following forms: • An indirect reference to a thread dictionary (see Section 7.3.2, "Articles"). In this case, the thread must be in the current file. • The index of the thread within the **Threads** array of its document's catalog (see Section 3.6.1, "Document Catalog"). The first thread in the array has index 0. • The title of the thread, as specified in its thread information dictionary (see Table 7.6 on page 394). If two or more threads have the same title, the one appearing first in the document catalog's **Threads** array will be used.
B	dictionary or integer	(Optional) The desired bead in the destination thread, specified in one of the following forms: • An indirect reference to a bead dictionary (see Section 7.3.2, "Articles"). In this case, the thread must be in the current file. • The index of the bead within its thread. The first bead in a thread has index 0.

URI Actions

A *uniform resource identifier* (URI) is a string that identifies (*resolves* to) a resource on the Internet—typically a file that is the destination of a hypertext link, although it can also resolve to a query or other entity. A *URI action* causes a URI to be resolved. Table 7.35 shows the action dictionary entries specific to this type of action. (See implementation notes 66 and 67 in Appendix H.)

TABLE 7.35   Additional entries specific to a URI action

KEY	TYPE	VALUE
S	name	*(Required)* The type of action that this dictionary describes; must be **URI** for a URI action.
URI	string	*(Required)* The uniform resource identifier to resolve, encoded in 7-bit ASCII.
IsMap	boolean	*(Optional)* A flag specifying whether to track the mouse position when the URI is resolved (see below). Default value: *false*.
		This entry applies only to actions triggered by the user's clicking an annotation; it is ignored for actions associated with outline items or with a document's **OpenAction** entry.

If the **IsMap** flag is *true* and the user has triggered the URI action by clicking an annotation with the mouse, the coordinates of the mouse position at the time the action is performed should be transformed from device space to user space and then offset relative to the upper-left corner of the annotation rectangle (that is, the value of the **Rect** entry in the annotation with which the URI action is associated). For example, if the mouse coordinates in user space are (x_m, y_m) and the annotation rectangle is extends from (ll_x, ll_y) at the lower-left to (ur_x, ur_y) at the upper-right, the final coordinates (x_f, y_f) are as follows:

$$x_f = x_m \quad ll_x$$
$$y_f = ur_y - y_m$$

If the resulting coordinates (x_f, y_f) are fractional, they should be rounded to the nearest integer values. They are then appended to the URI to be resolved, separated by commas and preceded by a question mark. For example:

http://www.adobe.com/intro?100,200

To support URI actions, a PDF document's catalog (see Section 3.6.1, "Document Catalog") may include a *URI dictionary*. At the time of publication, only one entry is defined for such a dictionary (see Table 7.36).

TABLE 7.36 Entry in a URI dictionary

KEY	TYPE	VALUE
Base	string	*(Optional)* The *base URI* to be used in resolving relative URI references. URI actions within the document may specify URIs in partial form, to be interpreted relative to this base address. If no base URI is specified, such partial URIs will be interpreted relative to the location of the document itself. The use of this entry is parallel to that of the body element <BASE>, as described in section 2.7.2 of Internet RFC 1866, *Hypertext Markup Language 2.0 Proposed Standard* (see the Bibliography).

The **Base** entry allows the URI of the document itself to be recorded in situations in which the document may be accessed out of context. For example, if a document has been moved to a new location but contains relative links to other documents that have not, the **Base** entry could be used to refer such links to the true location of the other documents, rather than that of the moved document.

Sound Actions

A *sound action (PDF 1.2)* plays a sound through the computer's speakers. Table 7.37 shows the action dictionary entries specific to this type of action; sounds themselves are discussed in Section 7.7, "Sounds."

TABLE 7.37 Additional entries specific to a sound action

KEY	TYPE	VALUE
S	name	*(Required)* The type of action that this dictionary describes; must be **Sound** for a sound action.
Sound	stream	*(Required)* A sound object defining the sound to be played (see Section 7.7, "Sounds"; see also implementation note 68 in Appendix H).
Volume	number	*(Optional)* The volume at which to play the sound, in the range −1.0 to 1.0. Higher values denote greater volume; negative values mute the sound. Default value: 1.0.
Synchronous	boolean	*(Optional)* A flag specifying whether to play the sound synchronously or asynchronously. If this flag is *true*, the viewer application will retain control, allowing no further user interaction other than canceling the sound, until the sound has been completely played. Default value: *false*.

| Repeat | boolean | *(Optional)* A flag specifying whether to repeat the sound indefinitely. If this entry is present, the **Synchronous** entry is ignored. Default value: *false*. |
| Mix | boolean | *(Optional)* A flag specifying whether to mix this sound with any other sound already playing. If this flag is *false*, any previously playing sound will be stopped before starting this sound; this can be used to stop a repeating sound (see **Repeat**, above). Default value: *false*. |

Movie Actions

A *movie action (PDF 1.2)* can be used to play a movie in a floating window or within the rectangle of a movie annotation (see "Movie Annotations" on page 418 and Section 7.8, "Movies"). The movie annotation must be associated with the page that is the destination of the link annotation or outline item containing the movie action, or with the page object with which the action is associated. (See implementation note 69 in Appendix H.)

The contents of a movie action dictionary are identical to those of a movie activation dictionary (see Table 7.71 on page 471), with the additional entries shown in Table 7.38. The contents of the activation dictionary associated with the movie annotation are ignored; the information specified in the movie action dictionary is used instead.

TABLE 7.38 Additional entries specific to a movie action

KEY	TYPE	VALUE
S	name	*(Required)* The type of action that this dictionary describes; must be **Movie** for a movie action.
Annot	dictionary	*(Optional)* An indirect reference to a movie annotation identifying the movie to be played.
T	text string	*(Optional)* The title of a movie annotation identifying the movie to be played.
		Note: *The dictionary must include either an **Annot** or a **T** entry, but not both.*
Operation	name	*(Optional)* The operation to be performed on the movie:
		Play — Start playing the movie, using the play mode specified by the dictionary's **Mode** entry (see Table 7.70 on page 471). If the movie is currently paused, it is repositioned to the beginning before playing (or to the starting point specified by the dictionary's **Start** entry, if present).

Stop   Stop playing the movie.

Pause   Pause a playing movie.

Resume   Resume a paused movie.

Default value: Play.

Hide Actions

A *hide action (PDF 1.2)* hides or shows one or more annotations on the screen by setting or clearing their Hidden flags (see Section 7.4.2, "Annotation Flags"). This type of action can be used in combination with appearance streams and trigger events (Sections 7.4.4, "Appearance Streams," and 7.5.2, "Trigger Events") to display pop-up help information on the screen. For example, the **E** (enter) and **X** (exit) trigger events in an annotation's additional-actions dictionary can be used to show and hide the annotation when the user rolls the cursor in and out of its active area on the page; this can be used to pop up a help label describing the effect of clicking the mouse at that location on the page. Table 7.39 shows the action dictionary entries specific to this type of action. (See implementation notes 70 and 71 in Appendix H.)

KEY	TYPE	VALUE
	TABLE 7.39 Additional entries specific to a hide action	
S	name	*(Required)* The type of action that this dictionary describes; must be **Hide** for a hide action.
T	dictionary, string, or array	*(Required)* The annotation or annotations to be hidden or shown, specified in any of the following forms: • An indirect reference to an annotation dictionary • A string giving the fully qualified field name of an interactive form field whose associated widget annotation or annotations are to be affected (see "Field Names" on page 438) • An array of such dictionaries or strings
H	boolean	*(Optional)* A flag indicating whether to hide (*true*) or show (*false*) the annotation. Default value: *true*.

Named Actions

Table 7.40 lists several *named actions (PDF 1.2)* that PDF viewer applications are expected to support; further names may be added in the future. (See implementation notes 72 and 73 in Appendix H.)

TABLE 7.40 Named actions

NAME	ACTION
NextPage	Go to the next page of the document.
PrevPage	Go to the previous page of the document.
FirstPage	Go to the first page of the document.
LastPage	Go to the last page of the document.

Note: Viewer applications may support additional, nonstandard named actions, but any document using them will not be portable. If the viewer encounters a named action that is inappropriate for a viewing platform, or if the viewer does not recognize the name, it should take no action.

Table 7.41 shows the action dictionary entries specific to named actions.

TABLE 7.41 Additional entries specific to named actions

KEY	TYPE	VALUE
S	name	*(Required)* The type of action that this dictionary describes; must be **Named** for a named action.
N	name	*(Required)* The name of the action to be performed (see Table 7.40).

Form Actions

Four additional action types (submit-form, reset-form, import-data, and JavaScript) are defined for use with interactive forms. See Section 7.6.4, "Form Actions," for details.

7.6 Interactive Forms

An *interactive form (PDF 1.2)*—sometimes referred to as an *AcroForm*—is a collection of *fields* for gathering information interactively from the user. A PDF document may contain any number of fields appearing on any combination of pages, all of which make up a single, global interactive form spanning the entire document. Arbitrary subsets of these fields can be imported or exported from the document; see Section 7.6.4, "Form Actions."

Note: *Interactive forms should not be confused with form XObjects (see Section 4.9, "Form XObjects"). Despite the similarity of names, the two are different, unrelated types of object.*

Each field in a document's interactive form is defined by a *field dictionary* (see Section 7.6.2, "Field Dictionaries"). For purposes of definition and naming, the fields can be organized hierarchically and can inherit attributes from their ancestors in the field hierarchy. A field's children in the hierarchy may also include widget annotations (see "Widget Annotations" on page 419) that define its appearance on the page; such a field is called a *terminal field.*

As a convenience, when a field has only a single associated widget annotation, the contents of the field dictionary and the annotation dictionary (Section 7.4.1, "Annotation Dictionaries") may be merged into a single dictionary containing entries that pertain to both a field and an annotation. (This presents no ambiguity, since the contents of the two kinds of dictionary do not conflict.) If such an object defines an appearance stream, the appearance must be consistent with the object's current value as a field.

Note: *Fields containing text whose contents are not known in advance may need to construct their appearance streams dynamically instead of defining them statically in an appearance dictionary; see "Variable Text" on page 439.*

7.6.1 Interactive Form Dictionary

The contents and properties of a document's interactive form are defined by an *interactive form dictionary* that is referenced from the **AcroForm** entry in the document catalog (see Section 3.6.1, "Document Catalog"). Table 7.42 shows the contents of this dictionary.

		TABLE 7.42 **Entries in the interactive form dictionary**
KEY	**TYPE**	**VALUE**
Fields	array	*(Required)* An array of references to each of the document's *root fields* (those with no ancestors in the field hierarchy).
NeedAppearances	boolean	*(Optional)* A flag specifying whether to construct appearance streams and appearance dictionaries for all widget annotations in the document (see "Variable Text" on page 439). Default value: *false*.
SigFlags	integer	*(Optional; PDF 1.3)* A set of flags specifying various document-level characteristics related to signature fields (see Table 7.43, below, and "Signature Fields" on page 451). Default value: 0.
CO	array	*(Required if any fields in the document have additional-actions dictionaries containing a **C** entry; PDF 1.3)* An array of indirect references to field dictionaries with calculation actions, defining the *calculation order* in which their values will be recalculated when the value of any field changes (see Section 7.5.2, "Trigger Events").
DR	dictionary	*(Optional)* A document-wide default value for the **DR** attribute of variable text fields (see "Variable Text" on page 439).
DA	string	*(Optional)* A document-wide default value for the **DA** attribute of variable text fields (see "Variable Text" on page 439).
Q	integer	*(Optional)* A document-wide default value for the **Q** attribute of variable text fields (see "Variable Text" on page 439).

The value of the interactive form dictionary's **SigFlags** entry is an unsigned 32-bit integer containing flags specifying various document-level characteristics related to signature fields (see "Signature Fields" on page 451). Bit positions within the flag word are numbered from 1 (low-order) to 32 (high-order). Table 7.43 shows the meanings of the flags; all undefined flag bits are reserved and must be set to 0.

TABLE 7.43 Signature flags

BIT POSITION	NAME	MEANING
1	SignaturesExist	If set, the document contains at least one signature field. This flag allows a viewer application to enable user interface items (such as menu items or push-buttons) related to signature processing without having to scan the entire document for the presence of signature fields.
2	AppendOnly	If set, the document contains signatures that may be invalidated if the file is saved (written) in a way that alters its previous contents, such as with the "optimize" option. Merely updating the file by appending new information to the end of the previous version is safe (see Section G.6, "Updating Example"). Viewer applications can use this flag to present a user requesting an optimized save with an additional alert box warning that signatures will be invalidated and requiring explicit confirmation before continuing with the operation.

7.6.2 Field Dictionaries

Each field in a document's interactive form is defined by a *field dictionary*, which must be an indirect object. The field dictionaries may be organized hierarchically into one or more tree structures. Many field attributes are *inheritable*, meaning that if they are not explicitly specified for a given field, their values are taken from those of its parent in the field hierarchy. Such inheritable attributes are designated as such in the tables below; the designation *(Required; inheritable)* means that an attribute must be defined for every field, whether explicitly in its own field dictionary or by inheritance from an ancestor in the hierarchy. Table 7.44 shows those entries that are common to all field dictionaries, regardless of type; those that pertain only to a particular type of field are described in the relevant sections below.

TABLE 7.44 Entries common to all field dictionaries

KEY	TYPE	VALUE
FT	name	*(Required for terminal fields; inheritable)* The type of field that this dictionary describes:
		Btn Button (see "Button Fields" on page 444) **Tx** Text (see "Text Fields" on page 448) **Ch** Choice (see "Choice Fields" on page 449) **Sig** *(PDF 1.3)* Signature (see "Signature Fields" on page 451)
		Note: *This entry may be present in a nonterminal field (one whose descendants are themselves fields) in order to provide an inheritable* **FT** *value. However, a nonterminal field does not logically have a type of its own; it is merely a container for inheritable attributes that are intended for descendant terminal fields of any type.*
Parent	dictionary	*(Required if this field is the child of another in the field hierarchy; absent otherwise)* The field that is the immediate parent of this one (the field, if any, whose **Kids** array includes this field). A field can have at most one parent; that is, it can be included in the **Kids** array of at most one other field.
Kids	array	*(Optional)* An array of indirect references to the immediate children of this field.
T	text string	*(Optional)* The partial field name (see "Field Names," below; see also implementation notes 74 and 75 in Appendix H).
TU	text string	*(Optional; PDF 1.3)* The *user name* to be used when generating error or status messages for the field.
TM	text string	*(Optional; PDF 1.3)* The *mapping name* to be used when exporting interactive form field data from the document.
Ff	integer	*(Optional; inheritable)* A set of flags specifying various characteristics of the field (see Table 7.45). Default value: 0.
V	(various)	*(Optional; inheritable)* The field's value, whose format varies depending on the field type; see the descriptions of individual field types for further information.
DV	(various)	*(Optional; inheritable)* The default value to which the field reverts when a reset-form action is executed (see "Reset-Form Actions" on page 457). The format of this value is the same as that of **V**.
AA	dictionary	*(Optional; PDF 1.2)* An additional-actions dictionary defining the field's behavior in response to various trigger events (see Section 7.5.2, "Trigger Events"). This entry has exactly the same meaning as the **AA** entry in an annotation dictionary (see Section 7.4.1, "Annotation Dictionaries").

The value of the field dictionary's **Ff** entry is an unsigned 32-bit integer containing flags specifying various characteristics of the field. Bit positions within the flag word are numbered from 1 (low-order) to 32 (high-order). The flags shown in Table 7.45 are common to all types of field; flags that apply only to specific field types are discussed in the sections describing those types. All undefined flag bits are reserved and must be set to 0.

TABLE 7.45   Field flags common to all field types

BIT POSITION	NAME	MEANING
1	ReadOnly	If set, the user may not change the value of the field. Any associated widget annotations will not interact with the user; that is, they will not respond to mouse clicks or change their appearance in response to mouse motions. This flag is useful for fields whose values are computed or imported from a database.
2	Required	If set, the field must have a value at the time it is exported by a submit-form action (see "Submit-Form Actions" on page 454).
3	NoExport	If set, the field must not be exported by a submit-form action (see "Submit-Form Actions" on page 454).

Field Names

The **T** entry in the field dictionary (see Table 7.44 on page 437) holds a text string defining the field's *partial field name*. The *fully qualified field name* is not explicitly defined, but is constructed from the partial field names of the field and all of its ancestors. For a field with no parent, the partial and fully qualified names are the same; for a field that is the child of another field, the fully qualified name is formed by appending the child field's partial name to the parent's fully qualified name, separated by a period (.):

    parent's_full_name.child's_partial_name

For example, if a field with the partial field name PersonalData has a child whose partial name is Address, which in turn has a child with the partial name ZipCode, then the fully qualified name of this last field would be

    PersonalData.Address.ZipCode

Thus all fields descended from a common ancestor will share the ancestor's fully qualified field name as a common prefix in their own fully qualified names.

It is possible for different field dictionaries to have the same fully qualified field name if they are descendants of a common ancestor with that name and have no partial field names (**T** entries) of their own. Such field dictionaries are different representations of the same underlying field; they should differ only in properties that specify their visual appearance. In particular, field dictionaries with the same fully qualified field name must have the same field type (**FT**), value (**V**), and default value (**DV**).

Variable Text

When the contents and properties of a field are known in advance, its visual appearance can be specified by an appearance stream defined in the PDF file itself (see Section 7.4.4, "Appearance Streams," and "Widget Annotations" on page 419). In some cases, however, the field may contain text whose value is not known until viewing time. Examples include text boxes to be filled in with text typed by the user from the keyboard and scrollable list boxes whose contents are determined interactively at the time the document is displayed.

In such cases, the PDF document cannot provide a statically defined appearance stream for displaying the field; rather, the viewer application must construct an appearance stream dynamically at viewing time. The dictionary entries shown in Table 7.46 provide general information about the field's appearance that can be combined with the specific text it contains to construct an appearance stream.

TABLE 7.46   **Additional entries common to all fields containing variable text**

KEY	TYPE	VALUE
DR	dictionary	*(Required; inheritable)* A resource dictionary (see Section 3.7.2, "Resource Dictionaries") containing default resources (such as fonts, patterns, or color spaces) to be used by the appearance stream. At a minimum, this dictionary must contain a **Font** entry specifying the resource name and font dictionary of the default font for displaying the field's text. (See implementation note 76 in Appendix H.)
DA	string	*(Required; inheritable)* The *default appearance string,* containing a sequence of valid page-content graphics or text-state operators defining such properties as the field's text size and color.

Q   integer   *(Optional; inheritable)* A code specifying the field's *quadding* (text justification) attribute:

    0   Left-justified
    1   Centered
    2   Right-justified

Default value: 0.

The new appearance stream becomes the normal appearance (**N**) in the appearance dictionary associated with the field's widget annotation (see Table 7.12 on page 406). (If the widget annotation has no appearance dictionary, the viewer application must create one and store it in the annotation dictionary's **AP** entry.) The appearance stream—which, like all appearance streams, is a form XObject—has the contents of its form dictionary initialized as follows:

- The resource dictionary (**Resources**) is set to the value of the field dictionary's **DR** entry.

- The lower-left corner of the bounding box (**BBox**) is set to coordinates (0, 0) in the form coordinate system. The box's top and right coordinates are taken from the dimensions of the annotation rectangle (the **Rect** entry in the widget annotation dictionary).

- All other entries in the appearance stream's form dictionary are set to their default values (see Section 4.9, "Form XObjects").

The contents of the appearance stream are as follows:

```
/Tx  BMC                                    % Begin marked content with tag Tx
    q                                       % Save graphics state
        … Any required graphics state changes, such as clipping …
        BT                                  % Begin text object
            … Default appearance string (DA) …
            … Text-positioning and text-showing operators to show the variable text …
        ET                                  % End text object
    Q                                       % Restore graphics state
EMC                                         % End marked content
```

The **BMC** (begin marked content) and **EMC** (end marked content) operators are discussed in Section 8.4.2, "Marked Content"; **q** (save graphics state) and **Q** (restore graphics state) in Section 4.3.3, "Graphics State Operators"; and **BT** (begin text object) and **ET** (end text object) in Section 5.3, "Text Objects."

The default appearance string (**DA**) contains any graphics state or text state operators needed to establish the graphics state parameters, such as text size and color, for displaying the field's variable text. Only operators that are allowed within text objects may occur in this string (see Figure 4.1 on page 122). At a minimum, the string must include a **Tf** (text font) operator along with its two operands, *font* and *size*. The specified *font* value must match a resource name in the **Font** entry of the default resource dictionary (**DR**). A zero value for *size* means that the font is to be *auto-sized*: its size is computed as a function of the height of the annotation rectangle.

The default appearance string should contain at most one **Tm** (text matrix) operator. If this operator is present, the viewer application should replace the *x* and *y* translation components with positioning information it determines to be appropriate, based on the field value, the quadding (**Q**) attribute, and any layout rules it employs. If the default appearance string contains no **Tm** operator, the viewer should insert one in the appearance stream, with appropriate *x* and *y* translation components, after the default appearance string and before the text-positioning and text-showing operators for the variable text.

To update an existing appearance stream to reflect a new field value, the viewer application should first copy any needed resources from the field's **DR** dictionary into the stream's **Resources** dictionary. (If the **DR** and **Resources** dictionaries contain resources with the same name, the one already in the **Resources** dictionary should be left intact, *not* replaced with the corresponding value from the **DR** dictionary.) The viewer application should then replace the existing contents of the appearance stream from

    /Tx BMC

to the matching

    EMC

with the corresponding new contents as shown above. (If the existing appearance stream contains no marked content with tag Tx, the new contents should be appended to the end of the original stream.)

The optional **MK** entry in the field's widget annotation dictionary (see Table 7.26 on page 419) can be used to provide an *appearance characteristics dictionary (PDF 1.2)* containing additional information for constructing the annotation's appearance stream. Table 7.47 shows the contents of this dictionary.

TABLE 7.47 **Entries in an appearance characteristics dictionary**

KEY	TYPE	VALUE
R	integer	*(Optional)* The number of degrees by which the widget annotation is rotated counterclockwise relative to the page. The value must be a multiple of 90. Default value: 0.
BC	array	*(Optional)* An array of numbers in the range 0.0 to 1.0 specifying the color of the widget annotation's border. The number of array elements determines the color space in which the color is defined: 0 No color; transparent 1 **DeviceGray** 3 **DeviceRGB** 4 **DeviceCMYK**
BG	array	*(Optional)* An array of numbers in the range 0.0 to 1.0 specifying the color of the widget annotation's background. The number of array elements determines the color space, as described above for **BC**.
CA	text string	*(Optional; button fields only)* The widget annotation's *normal caption*, displayed when it is not interacting with the user. **Note:** *Unlike the remaining entries listed below, which apply only to widget annotations associated with pushbutton fields (see "Pushbuttons" on page 444), the* **CA** *entry can be used with any type of button field, including checkboxes ("Checkboxes" on page 445) and radio buttons ("Radio Buttons" on page 446).*
RC	text string	*(Optional; pushbutton fields only)* The widget annotation's *rollover caption*, displayed when the user rolls the cursor into its active area without pressing the mouse button.
AC	text string	*(Optional; pushbutton fields only)* The widget annotation's *alternate (down) caption*, displayed when the mouse button is pressed within its active area.
I	stream	*(Optional; pushbutton fields only; must be an indirect reference)* A form XObject defining the widget annotation's *normal icon*, displayed when it is not interacting with the user.
RI	stream	*(Optional; pushbutton fields only; must be an indirect reference)* A form XObject defining the widget annotation's *rollover icon*, displayed when the user rolls the cursor into its active area without pressing the mouse button.

IX	stream	*(Optional; pushbutton fields only; must be an indirect reference)* A form XObject defining the widget annotation's *alternate (down) icon*, displayed when the mouse button is pressed within its active area.
IF	dictionary	*(Optional; pushbutton fields only)* An icon fit dictionary (see Table 7.64 on page 466) specifying how to display the widget annotation's icon within its annotation rectangle. If present, the icon fit dictionary applies to all of the annotation's icons (normal, rollover, and alternate).
TP	integer	*(Optional; pushbutton fields only)* A code indicating where to position the text of the widget annotation's caption relative to its icon:

0	No icon; caption only
1	No caption; icon only
2	Caption below the icon
3	Caption above the icon
4	Caption to the right of the icon
5	Caption to the left of the icon
6	Caption overlaid directly on the icon

Default value: 0.

7.6.3 Field Types

Interactive forms support the following field types:

- *Button fields* represent interactive controls on the screen that the user can manipulate with the mouse. They include *pushbuttons*, *checkboxes*, and *radio buttons*.

- *Text fields* are boxes or spaces in which the user can enter text from the keyboard.

- *Choice fields* contain several text items, at most one of which may be selected as the field value. They include scrollable *list boxes* and *combo boxes*.

- *Signature fields* represent electronic "signatures" for authenticating the identity of a user. They can include purely mathematical authentication methods such as public/private-key encrypted document digests, or biometric forms of identification such as handwritten signatures, fingerprints, or retinal scans.

The following sections describe each of these field types in detail. Further types may be added in the future.

Button Fields

A *button field* (field type **Btn**) represents an interactive control on the screen that the user can manipulate with the mouse. It may be any of the following:

- A *pushbutton* is a purely interactive control that responds immediately to user input without retaining a permanent value.

- A *checkbox* toggles between two states, on and off.

- *Radio buttons* are a set of related toggles, at most one of which may be on at any given time; selecting any one of the buttons automatically deselects all the others.

The various types of button field are distinguished by flags in the **Ff** entry, as shown in Table 7.48.

TABLE 7.48 Field flags specific to button fields		
BIT POSITION	**NAME**	**MEANING**
17	Pushbutton	If set, the field is a pushbutton that does not retain a permanent value.
16	Radio	If set, the field is a set of radio buttons; if clear, the field is a checkbox. This flag is meaningful only if the Pushbutton flag is clear.
15	NoToggleToOff	*(Radio buttons only)* If set, exactly one radio button must be selected at all times; clicking the currently selected button has no effect. If clear, clicking the selected button deselects it, leaving no button selected.

Pushbuttons

The simplest type of field is a *pushbutton field*, which has a field type of **Btn** and the Pushbutton flag (see Table 7.48) set. Because this type of button retains no permanent value, it does not use the **V** and **DV** entries in the field dictionary (see Table 7.44 on page 437).

Checkboxes

A *checkbox field* toggles between two states, on and off, when manipulated by the user with the mouse or keyboard. Its field type is **Btn** and its Pushbutton and Radio flags (see Table 7.48) are both clear. Each state can have a separate appearance, defined by an appearance stream in the appearance dictionary of the field's widget annotation (see Section 7.4.4, "Appearance Streams"). The **V** entry in the field dictionary (see Table 7.44 on page 437) holds a name object representing the checkbox's appearance state, which is used to select the appropriate appearance from the appearance dictionary. The appearance for the off state is optional, but if present must be stored in the appearance dictionary under the name Off. The recommended name for the on state is Yes, but this is not required. Example 7.9 shows a typical checkbox definition.

Example 7.9

```
1 0 obj
    << /FT /Btn
        /T (Urgent)
        /V /Yes
        /AS /Yes
        /AP << /N << /Yes 2 0 R >>
            >>
    >>
endobj

2 0 obj
    << /Resources 20 0 R
        /Length 104
    >>
stream
    q
        0  0  1  rg
        BT
            /ZaDb  12  Tf
            0  0  Td
            (8)  Tj
        ET
    Q
endstream
endobj
```

Radio Buttons

A *radio button field* is a set of related toggle controls, at most one of which may be on at any given time; selecting any one of the buttons automatically deselects all the others. The field type is **Btn**, the Pushbutton flag (see Table 7.48 on page 444) is clear, and the Radio flag is set. This type of button field has an additional flag, NoToggleToOff, which specifies, if set, that exactly one of the radio buttons must be selected at all times. In this case, clicking the currently selected button has no effect; if the NoToggleToOff flag is clear, clicking the selected button deselects it, leaving no button selected.

The **Kids** entry in the radio button field's field dictionary (see Table 7.44 on page 437) holds an array of widget annotations representing the individual buttons in the set, each of which is a separate checkbox field in its own right. The parent field's **V** entry holds a name object corresponding to the appearance state of whichever child field is currently in the on state; the default value for this entry is Off. Example 7.10 shows the object definitions for a set of radio buttons.

Example 7.10

```
10  0  obj                          % Radio button field
    << /FT /Btn
       /Ff ...                      % ... Radio flag = 1, Pushbutton = 0 ...
       /T (Credit card)
       /V /MasterCard
       /Kids [ 11 0 R
               12 0 R
             ]
    >>
endobj

11  0  obj                          % First checkbox
    << /Parent 10 0 R
       /AS /MasterCard
       /AP << /N << /MasterCard  8 0 R
                    /Off  9 0 R
                 >>
              >>
    >>
endobj
```

```
12 0 obj                                    % Second checkbox
   << /Parent  10 0 R
      /AS  /Off
      /AP  << /N  << /Visa  8 0 R
                    /Off  9 0 R
                 >>
            >>
   >>
endobj

8 0 obj                                     % Appearance stream for "on" state
   << /Resources  20 0 R
      /Length  104
   >>
stream
   q
      0 0 1 rg
      BT
         /ZaDb  12  Tf
         0  0  Td
         (8)  Tj
      ET
   Q
endstream
endobj

9 0 obj                                     % Appearance stream for "off" state
   << /Resources  20 0 R
      /Length  104
   >>
stream
   q
      0  0  1 rg
      BT
         /ZaDb  12  Tf
         0  0  Td
         (4)  Tj
      ET
   Q
endstream
endobj
```

Text Fields

A *text field* (field type **Tx**) is a box or space in which the user can enter text from the keyboard. The text may be restricted to a single line or may be allowed to span multiple lines, depending on the setting of the Multiline flag in the field dictionary's **Ff** entry (see Tables 7.44 on page 437 and 7.49, below).

	TABLE 7.49	**Field flags specific to text fields**
BIT POSITION	**NAME**	**MEANING**
13	Multiline	If set, the field may contain multiple lines of text; if clear, the field's text is restricted to a single line.
14	Password	If set, the field is intended for entering a secure password that should not be echoed visibly to the screen. Characters typed from the keyboard should instead be echoed in some unreadable form, such as asterisks or bullet characters.
		To protect password confidentiality, viewer applications should never store the value of the text field in the PDF file if this flag is set.

The field's text is held in a text string in the **V** (value) entry of the field dictionary. The contents of this text string are used to construct an appearance stream for displaying the field, as described under "Variable Text" on page 439; the text is presented in a single style (font, size, color, and so forth), as specified by the **DA** (default appearance) string. Besides the usual entries common to all types of field (see Table 7.44 on page 437), the field dictionary for a text field can contain the additional entry shown in Table 7.50.

	TABLE 7.50	**Additional entry specific to a text field**
KEY	**TYPE**	**VALUE**
MaxLen	integer	*(Optional, inheritable)* The maximum length of the field's text, in characters.

Example 7.11 shows the object definitions for a typical text field.

Example 7.11

```
6 0 obj
    << /FT /Tx
        /Ff ...                                    % Set Multiline flag
        /T (Silly prose)
        /DR 21 0 R
        /DA (0 0 1 rg /Ti 12 Tf)
        /V (The quick brown fox ate the lazy mouse)
        /AP << /N 5 0 R >>
    >>
endobj

5 0 obj
    << /Resources 21 0 R
        /Length 172
    >>
stream
    /Tx BMC
        BT
            0 0 1 rg
            /Ti 12 Tf
            1 0 0 1 100 100 Tm
            0 0 Td
            (The quick brown fox ) Tj
            0 −13 Td
            (ate the lazy mouse.) Tj
        ET
    EMC
endstream
endobj
```

Choice Fields

A *choice field* (field type **Ch**) contains several text items, at most one of which may be selected as the field value. The items may be presented to the user in either of two forms:

• A scrollable *list box*

• A *combo box* consisting of a drop list optionally accompanied by an editable text box in which the user can type a value other than the predefined choices

The various types of choice field are distinguished by flags in the **Ff** entry, as shown in Table 7.51. Table 7.52 shows the field dictionary entries specific to choice fields.

TABLE 7.51 Field flags specific to choice fields

BIT POSITION	NAME	MEANING
18	Combo	If set, the field is a combo box; if clear, the field is a list box.
19	Edit	If set, the combo box includes an editable text box as well as a drop list; if clear, it includes only a drop list. This flag is meaningful only if the Combo flag is set.
20	Sort	If set, the field's option items should be sorted alphabetically. This flag is intended for use by form authoring tools, not by PDF viewer applications; viewers should simply display the options in the order in which they occur in the **Opt** array (see Table 7.52, below).

TABLE 7.52 Additional entries specific to a choice field

KEY	TYPE	VALUE
Opt	array	*(Required; inheritable)* An array of options to be presented to the user. Each element of the array is either a text string representing one of the available options or a two-element array consisting of a text string together with a default appearance string for constructing the item's appearance dynamically at viewing time (see "Variable Text" on page 439; see also implementation note 77 in Appendix H).
TI	integer	*(Optional, inheritable)* For scrollable list boxes, the *top index* (the index in the **Opt** array of the first option visible in the list).

The **Opt** array specifies the list of options to be presented to the user. Each option is represented by a text string to be displayed on the screen as the name of the option. The corresponding element of the **Opt** array may contain either this text string by itself or a two-element array with the text string as its first element. In the latter case, the second element of the array is a default appearance string to be used in constructing a dynamic appearance stream, as described under "Variable

Text" on page 439. The field dictionary's **V** (value) entry (see Table 7.44 on page 437) contains a text string identifying which of the available options is currently selected.

Example 7.12 shows a typical choice field definition.

Example 7.12

```
<< /FT /Ch
   /Ff ...
   /T (Body Color)
   /V (Blue)
   /Opt [ (Red)
          (My favorite color)
          (Blue)
        ]
>>
```

Signature Fields

A *signature field (PDF 1.3)* represents an electronic "signature" for authenticating the identity of a user. The signature may be purely mathematical, such as a public/private-key encrypted document digest, or it may be a biometric form of identification such as a handwritten signature, fingerprint, or retinal scan. The specific form of authentication used is implemented by a plug-in *signature handler.* Third-party handler writers are encouraged to register their handler names with Adobe; see Appendix E.

Note: The specification for public-key digital signature authentication is available in the Adobe document PDF Public-Key Digital Signature and Encryption Specification *(see the Bibliography).*

The field dictionary representing a signature field contains the standard entries described in Table 7.44 on page 437. The field type (**FT**) is **Sig**, the field value (**V**) is a *signature dictionary* specifying various attributes of the signature field, and the default value (**DV**) is a signature dictionary containing default values for reinitializing the contents of the **V** dictionary in response to a reset-form action (see "Reset-Form Actions" on page 457). Filling in ("signing") the signature field entails updating at least the **V** entry, and usually also the **AP** entry of the associated widget annotation. Exporting a signature field typically exports the **T, V,** and **AP** entries.

Table 7.53 shows the contents of the signature dictionary. Signature handlers are free to use or omit those entries that are marked optional in the table, but are encouraged to use them in a standard way if they are used at all. In addition, specific signature handlers may add private entries of their own. To avoid name duplication, it is suggested that the keys for all such private entries be prefixed with the registered handler name followed by a period.

TABLE 7.53 **Entries in a signature dictionary**

KEY	TYPE	VALUE
Type	name	*(Optional)* The type of PDF object that this dictionary describes; if present, must be **Sig** for a signature dictionary.
Filter	name	*(Required; inheritable)* The name of the signature handler to be used for authenticating the field's contents, such as **Adobe.PPKLite**, **Entrust.PPKEF**, **CICI.SignIt**, or **VeriSign.PPKVS**.
SubFilter	name	*(Optional)* The name of a specific submethod of the specified handler.
ByteRange	array	*(Required)* An array of pairs of integers (starting byte offset, length in bytes) describing the exact byte range for the digest calculation. Multiple discontiguous byte ranges may be used to describe a digest that does not include the signature token itself.
Contents	string	*(Required)* The encrypted signature token.
Name	text string	*(Optional)* The name of the person or authority signing the document.
M	date	*(Optional)* The time of signing. Depending on the signature handler, this may be a normal unverified computer time or a time generated in a verifiable way from a secure time server.
Location	text string	*(Optional)* The CPU host name or physical location of the signing.
Reason	text string	*(Optional)* The reason for the signing, such as (I agree…).

The **DV** (default value) entry in the field dictionary may specify a signature dictionary for an unsigned field that is preloaded with default values for some entries. Signature handlers are free to use or ignore these values in initializing the **V** dictionary for a signed field. The default dictionary may include default values for private entries belonging to multiple handlers; a given handler should use only those entries that are pertinent to itself and strip out the others.

Like any other field, a signature field may actually be described by a widget annotation dictionary containing entries pertaining to an annotation as well as a field (see "Widget Annotations" on page 419). The annotation rectangle (**Rect**) in such a dictionary gives the position of the field on its page. For signature fields (such as PPK signatures) that are not intended to be visible, the annotation rectangle may have zero height and width.

The appearance dictionary (**AP**) of a signature field's widget annotation defines the field's visual appearance on the page (see Section 7.4.4, "Appearance Streams"). For a signature field that has not been filled in, the normal appearance is usually blank. If no plug-in signature handler is available for a given signing method, the normal appearance for a signature that has been filled in should simply show an appropriate representation of the signature: text, ink strokes representing a handwritten signature, a bitmap of a fingerprint, or any other representation appropriate for the particular signing method. If an appropriate signature handler is available, three appearances are possible:

- The *unvalidated* appearance represents a signature that has not yet been validated by the signature handler.

- The *valid* appearance represents a signature that has been validated and accepted by the signature handler.

- The *invalid* appearance represents a signature that has been validated and rejected by the signature handler.

When the signature handler is invoked to validate the signature, it should alter the signature's appearance from unvalidated to either valid or invalid. It is suggested that the unvalidated appearance contain an overprinted yellow question mark, the invalid appearance an overprinted red X, and the valid appearance the logo of the signature handler underprinted as a watermark.

7.6.4 Form Actions

Interactive forms support four special types of action in addition to those described in Section 7.5.3, "Action Types":

- *Submit-form actions* transmit the names and values of selected interactive form fields to a specified uniform resource locator (URL), presumably the address of a World Wide Web server that will process them and send back a response.

- *Reset-form actions* reset selected interactive form fields to their default values.

- *Import-data actions* import Forms Data Format (FDF) data into the document's interactive form from a specified file.

- *JavaScript actions (PDF 1.3)* cause a script to be compiled and executed by the JavaScript interpreter.

Submit-Form Actions

A *submit-form action* transmits the names and values of selected interactive form fields to a specified uniform resource locator (URL), presumably the address of a World Wide Web server that will process them and send back a response. Table 7.54 shows the action dictionary entries specific to this type of action.

TABLE 7.54 Additional entries specific to a submit-form action

KEY	TYPE	VALUE
S	name	*(Required)* The type of action that this dictionary describes; must be **SubmitForm** for a submit-form action.
F	file specification	*(Required)* A URL file specification (see Section 3.10.4, "URL Specifications") giving the uniform resource locator (URL) of the script at the Web server that will process the submission.
Fields	array	*(Optional)* An array identifying which fields to include in the submission or which to exclude, depending on the setting of the Include/Exclude flag in the **Flags** entry (see Table 7.55). Each element of the array is either an indirect reference to a field dictionary or *(PDF 1.3)* a string representing the fully qualified name of a field. Elements of both kinds may be mixed in the same array.
		If this entry is omitted, the Include/Exclude flag is ignored; all fields in the document's interactive form are submitted except those whose NoExport flag (see Table 7.45 on page 438) is set. (Fields with no values may also be excluded, depending on the setting of the IncludeNoValueFields flag; see Table 7.55.) See the text following Table 7.55 for further discussion.
Flags	integer	*(Optional; inheritable)* A set of flags specifying various characteristics of the action (see Table 7.55). Default value: 0.

The value of the action dictionary's **Flags** entry is an unsigned 32-bit integer containing flags specifying various characteristics of the action. Bit positions within the flag word are numbered from 1 (low-order) to 32 (high-order). Table 7.55 shows the meanings of the flags; all undefined flag bits are reserved and must be set to 0.

TABLE 7.55 Flags for submit-form actions

BIT POSITION	NAME	MEANING
1	Include/Exclude	If clear, the **Fields** array (see Table 7.54) specifies which fields to include in the submission. (All descendants of the specified fields in the field hierarchy are submitted as well.) If set, the **Fields** array tells which fields to exclude; all fields in the document's interactive form are submitted *except* those listed in the **Fields** array and those whose NoExport flag (see Table 7.45 on page 438) is set.
2	IncludeNoValueFields	If set, all fields designated by the **Fields** array and the Include/Exclude flag are submitted, regardless of whether they have a value (**V** entry in the field dictionary); for fields without a value, only the field name is transmitted. If clear, fields without a value are not submitted.
3	ExportFormat	If set, field names and values are submitted in HTML Form format. If clear, they are submitted in Forms Data Format (FDF); see Section 7.6.6, "Forms Data Format."
4	GetMethod	If set, field names and values are submitted using an HTTP GET request; if clear, they are submitted using a POST request. This flag is meaningful only when the ExportFormat flag is set; if ExportFormat is clear, this flag must also be clear.

5	SubmitCoordinates	If set, the coordinates of the mouse click that caused the submit-form action are transmitted as part of the form data. The coordinate values are relative to the upper-left corner of the field's widget annotation. They are represented in the data in the format

$$name.x=xval\&name.y=yval$$

where *name* is the field's mapping name (**TM** in the field dictionary) if present, otherwise the field name. If the value of the **TM** entry is a single space character, both the name and the dot following it are suppressed, resulting in the format

$$x=xval\&y=yval$$

This flag is meaningful only when the ExportFormat flag is set; if ExportFormat is clear, this flag must also be clear.

The set of fields whose names and values are to be submitted is defined by the **Fields** array in the action dictionary (Table 7.54) together with the Include/Exclude and IncludeNoValueFields flags in the **Flags** entry (Table 7.55). Each element of the **Fields** array identifies an interactive form field, either by an indirect reference to its field dictionary or *(PDF 1.3)* by its fully qualified field name (see "Field Names" on page 438). If the Include/Exclude flag is clear, the submission consists of all fields listed in the **Fields** array, along with any descendants of these fields in the field hierarchy. If the Include/Exclude flag is set, the submission consists of all fields in the document's interactive form *except* those listed in the **Fields** array.

Note: *The NoExport flag in the field dictionary's* **Ff** *entry (see Tables 7.44 on page 437 and 7.45 on page 438) takes precedence over the action's* **Fields** *array and Include/Exclude flag. Fields whose NoExport flag is set are* never *included in a submit-form action.*

Field names and values may be submitted either in HTML Form format or in Forms Data Format (FDF), depending on the setting of the action's Export-Format flag. (HTML Form format is described in Internet RFC 1866, *Hypertext Markup Language 2.0 Proposed Standard*; see the Bibliography. FDF is described in Section 7.6.6, "Forms Data Format"; see also implementation note 78 in Appendix H.) The name submitted for each field is its fully qualified name (see "Field Names" on page 438), and the value is that specified by the **V** entry in its field dictionary.

*Note: For pushbutton fields submitted in FDF, the value submitted is that of the **AP** entry in the field's widget annotation dictionary. If the submit-form action dictionary contains no **Fields** entry, such pushbutton fields are not submitted at all.*

Fields with no value (that is, whose field dictionary does not contain a **V** entry) are ordinarily not included in the submission. The submit-form action's Include-NoValueFields flag overrides this behavior; if this flag is set, such valueless fields are included in the submission by name only, with no associated value.

Reset-Form Actions

A *reset-form action* resets selected interactive form fields to their default values; that is, it sets the value of the **V** entry in the field dictionary to that of the **DV** key (see Table 7.44 on page 437). If no default value is defined for a field, its **V** entry is removed. For fields that can have no value (such as pushbuttons), the action has no effect. Table 7.56 shows the action dictionary entries specific to this type of action.

TABLE 7.56   Additional entries specific to a reset-form action

KEY	TYPE	VALUE
S	name	(*Required*) The type of action that this dictionary describes; must be **ResetForm** for a reset-form action.
Fields	array	(*Optional*) An array identifying which fields to reset or which to exclude from resetting, depending on the setting of the Include/Exclude flag in the **Flags** entry (see Table 7.57). Each element of the array is either an indirect reference to a field dictionary or (*PDF 1.3*) a string representing the fully qualified name of a field. Elements of both kinds may be mixed in the same array.
		If this entry is omitted, the Include/Exclude flag is ignored; all fields in the document's interactive form are reset.
Flags	integer	(*Optional; inheritable*) A set of flags specifying various characteristics of the action (see Table 7.57). Default value: 0.

The value of the action dictionary's **Flags** entry is an unsigned 32-bit integer containing flags specifying various characteristics of the action. Bit positions within the flag word are numbered from 1 (low-order) to 32 (high-order). At the time of publication, only one flag is defined for this type of action; Table 7.57 shows its meaning. All undefined flag bits are reserved and must be set to 0.

TABLE 7.57 Flag for reset-form actions

BIT POSITION	NAME	MEANING
1	Include/Exclude	If clear, the **Fields** array (see Table 7.54) specifies which fields to reset. (All descendants of the specified fields in the field hierarchy are reset as well.) If set, the **Fields** array tells which fields to exclude from resetting; all fields in the document's interactive form are reset *except* those listed in the **Fields** array.

Import-Data Actions

An *import-data action* imports Forms Data Format (FDF) data into the document's interactive form from a specified file (see Section 7.6.6, "Forms Data Format"). Table 7.58 shows the action dictionary entries specific to this type of action.

TABLE 7.58 Additional entries specific to an import-data action

KEY	TYPE	VALUE
S	name	*(Required)* The type of action that this dictionary describes; must be **ImportData** for an import-data action.
F	file specification	*(Required)* The FDF file from which to import the data. (See implementation notes 79 and 80 in Appendix H.)

JavaScript Actions

A *JavaScript action (PDF 1.3)* causes a script to be compiled and executed by the JavaScript interpreter. Depending on the nature of the script, this can cause various interactive form fields in the document to update their values or change their visual appearances. Netscape's *Client-Side JavaScript Reference* and Adobe Technical Note #5186, *Acrobat Forms JavaScript Object Specification* (see the Bibliography) give details on the contents and effects of JavaScript scripts.

TABLE 7.59 Additional entries specific to a JavaScript action

KEY	TYPE	VALUE
S	name	*(Required)* The type of action that this dictionary describes; must be **JavaScript** for a JavaScript action.
JS	string or stream	*(Required)* A string or stream containing the JavaScript script to be executed.
		*Note: **PDFDocEncoding** or Unicode encoding (the latter identified by the Unicode prefix U+FEFF) are used to encode the contents of the string or stream. (See implementation note 81 in Appendix H.)*

To support the use of parameterized function calls in JavaScript scripts, the **JavaScript** entry in a PDF document's name dictionary (see Section 3.6.3, "Name Dictionary") can contain a name tree mapping names to document-level JavaScript actions. When the document is opened, all of the actions in this name tree are executed, defining JavaScript functions for use by other scripts in the document.

Note: The names associated with individual JavaScript actions in the name dictionary serve merely as a convenient means for organizing and packaging scripts. The names are arbitrary and need not bear any relation to the JavaScript name space itself.

7.6.5 Named Pages

The optional **Pages** entry *(PDF 1.3)* in a document's name dictionary (see Section 3.6.3, "Name Dictionary") contains a name tree that maps names to individual pages within the document. Naming a page allows it to be referenced in two different ways:

- An import-data action can add the named page to the document into which FDF is being imported, either as a page or as a button appearance.

- A script executed by a JavaScript action can add the named page to the current document as a regular page.

A named page that is to be visible to the user should be left in the page tree (see *Section 3.6.2, "Page Tree"*), with a reference to it in the appropriate leaf node of the name dictionary's **Pages** tree. If the page is not to be displayed by the viewer application, it should be referenced from the name dictionary's **Templates** tree instead. Such invisible pages should have an object type of **Template** rather than **Page**, and should have no **Parent** or **B** entry (see Table 3.17 on page 77). Regardless of whether the page is named in the **Pages** or **Templates** tree or whether it is added to a document by an import-data or JavaScript action, the new copy is not itself named.

7.6.6 Forms Data Format

This section describes Forms Data Format (FDF), the file format used for interactive form data *(PDF 1.2)*. FDF is used when submitting form data to a server, receiving the response, and incorporating it into the interactive form. It can also be used to export form data to stand-alone files that can be stored, transmitted electronically, and imported back into the corresponding PDF interactive form. In addition, beginning in PDF 1.3, it can be used to define a container for annotations that are separate from the PDF document to which they apply.

FDF is based on PDF; it uses the same syntax (see Section 3.1, "Lexical Conventions") and basic object types (Section 3.2, "Objects"), and has essentially the same file structure (Section 3.4, "File Structure"). However, it differs from PDF in the following ways:

- The cross-reference table (Section 3.4.3, "Cross-Reference Table") is optional.

- FDF files cannot be updated (see Section 3.4.5, "Incremental Updates"); objects can only be of generation 0, and no two objects can have the same object number.

- The document structure is much simpler than PDF, since the body of an FDF document consists of only one required object.

- The length of a stream may not be specified by an indirect object.

FDF uses the MIME type application/vnd.fdf. On the Windows and UNIX platforms, FDF files have the extension .fdf; on the Macintosh, they have file type 'FDF '.

FDF File Structure

An FDF file is structured in essentially the same way as a PDF file, but need contain only those elements required for the export and import of interactive form and annotation data. It consists of three required and one optional element (see Figure 7.6):

- A one-line *header* identifying the version number of the FDF specification to which the file conforms

- A *body* containing the objects that make up the content of the file

- An optional *cross-reference table* containing information about the objects in the file

- A *trailer* giving the location of various objects within the body of the file

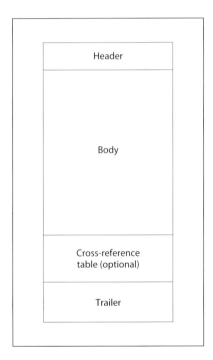

FIGURE 7.6 *FDF file structure*

FDF Header

The first line of an FDF file is a *header* identifying the version number of the FDF specification to which the file conforms. For a file conforming to FDF version 1.2 (the latest version at the time of publication), the header should be

    %FDF–1.2

FDF Body

The *body* of an FDF file consists of a sequence of indirect objects representing the file's catalog (see "FDF Catalog" on page 463), together with any additional objects that the catalog may reference. The objects are of the same basic types described in Section 3.2, "Objects." Just as in PDF, objects in FDF can be direct or indirect.

FDF Trailer

The *trailer* of an FDF file enables an application reading the file to find significant objects quickly within the body of the file. The last line of the file contains only the end-of-file marker, %%EOF. This is preceded by the *trailer dictionary*, consisting of the keyword **trailer** followed by a series of one or more key-value pairs enclosed in double angle brackets. The only required key is **Root**, whose value is an indirect reference to the file's catalog dictionary (see Table 7.60). The trailer may optionally contain additional entries for objects that are referenced from within the catalog.

Thus the trailer has the following overall structure:

    trailer
        << Root c 0 R
            key₂ value₂
            ...
            keyₙ valueₙ
        >>
    %%EOF

where c is the object number of the file's catalog dictionary.

TABLE 7.60   Entry in an FDF trailer dictionary

KEY	TYPE	VALUE
Root	dictionary	*(Required; must be an indirect reference)* The catalog object for this FDF file (see "FDF Catalog," below).

FDF Catalog

The root node of an FDF file's object hierarchy is the *catalog* dictionary, located via the **Root** entry in the file's trailer (see "FDF Trailer," above). The only required entry in the catalog is **FDF** (see Table 7.61). Its value is an *FDF dictionary* (Table 7.62), which in turn contains references to other objects describing the file's contents.

TABLE 7.61   Entry in an FDF catalog dictionary

KEY	TYPE	VALUE
FDF	dictionary	*(Required)* The FDF dictionary for this file (see Table 7.62).

TABLE 7.62   Entries in an FDF dictionary

KEY	TYPE	VALUE
F	file specification	*(Optional)* The *source file* or *target file*: the PDF document file that this FDF file was exported from or is intended to be imported into.
ID	array	*(Optional)* An array of two strings taken from the **ID** entry in the trailer dictionary (see Section 3.4.4, "File Trailer") of the source or target file designated by **F**. Each string is a file identifier (see Section 8.3, "File Identifiers"). The first identifier is established permanently when the source or target file is created; the second is changed each time the file is updated.
Fields	array	*(Optional)* An array of FDF field dictionaries (see "FDF Fields," below) describing the root fields (those with no ancestors in the field hierarchy) to be exported or imported. This entry and the **Pages** entry may not both be present.
Status	string	*(Optional)* A status string to be displayed indicating the result of an action, typically a submit-form action (see "Submit-Form Actions" on page 454). The string is encoded with **PDFDocEncoding**. (See implementation note 82 in Appendix H.) This entry and the **Pages** entry may not both be present.

Pages	array	*(Optional; PDF 1.3)* An array of FDF page dictionaries (see "FDF Pages" on page 467) describing new pages to be added to a PDF target document. The **Fields** and **Status** entries may not be present together with this entry.
Encoding	name	*(Optional; PDF 1.3)* The encoding to be used for any FDF field value or option (**V** or **Opt** in the field dictionary; see Table 7.63) that is a string and does not begin with the Unicode prefix U+FEFF. The default is **PDFDocEncoding**. (See implementation note 83 in Appendix H.)
Annots	array	*(Optional; PDF 1.3)* An array of FDF annotation dictionaries (see "FDF Annotation Dictionaries" on page 468).

FDF Fields

Each field in an FDF file is described by an *FDF field dictionary*. Table 7.63 shows the contents of this type of dictionary. Most of the entries have the same form and meaning as the corresponding entries in a field dictionary (Tables 7.44 on page 437, 7.46 on page 439, 7.50 on page 448, and 7.52 on page 450) or a widget annotation dictionary (Tables 7.9 on page 400 and 7.26 on page 419). Unless otherwise indicated in the table, importing a field causes the values of the entries in the FDF field dictionary to replace those of the corresponding entries in the field with the same fully qualified name in the target document. (See implementation notes 84–89 in Appendix H.)

TABLE 7.63 Entries in an FDF field dictionary

KEY	TYPE	VALUE
Kids	array	*(Optional)* An array of indirect references to the immediate children of this field.
T	text string	*(Required)* The partial field name (see "Field Names" on page 438).
V	(various)	*(Optional)* The field's value, whose format varies depending on the field type; see the descriptions of individual field types in Section 7.6.3 for further information.
Ff	integer	*(Optional)* A set of flags specifying various characteristics of the field (see Tables 7.45 on page 438, 7.48 on page 444, 7.49 on page 448, and 7.51 on page 450). When imported into an interactive form, the value of this entry replaces that of the **Ff** entry in the form's corresponding field dictionary. If this field is present, the **SetFf** and **ClrFf** entries, if any, are ignored.
SetFf	integer	*(Optional)* A set of flags to be set (turned on) in the **Ff** entry of the form's corresponding field dictionary. Bits equal to 1 in **SetFf** cause the corresponding bits in **Ff** to be set to 1. This entry is ignored if an **Ff** entry is present in the FDF field dictionary.

ClrFf	integer	*(Optional)* A set of flags to be cleared (turned off) in the **Ff** entry of the form's corresponding field dictionary. Bits equal to 1 in **ClrFf** cause the corresponding bits in **Ff** to be set to 0. If a **SetFf** entry is also present in the FDF field dictionary, it is applied before this entry. This entry is ignored if an **Ff** entry is present in the FDF field dictionary.
F	integer	*(Optional)* A set of flags specifying various characteristics of the field's widget annotation (see Section 7.4.2, "Annotation Flags"). When imported into an interactive form, the value of this entry replaces that of the **F** entry in the form's corresponding annotation dictionary. If this field is present, the **SetF** and **ClrF** entries, if any, are ignored.
SetF	integer	*(Optional)* A set of flags to be set (turned on) in the **F** entry of the form's corresponding widget annotation dictionary. Bits equal to 1 in **SetF** cause the corresponding bits in **F** to be set to 1. This entry is ignored if an **F** entry is present in the FDF field dictionary.
ClrF	integer	*(Optional)* A set of flags to be cleared (turned off) in the **F** entry of the form's corresponding widget annotation dictionary. Bits equal to 1 in **ClrF** cause the corresponding bits in **F** to be set to 0. If a **SetF** entry is also present in the FDF field dictionary, it is applied before this entry. This entry is ignored if an **F** entry is present in the FDF field dictionary.
AP	dictionary	*(Optional)* An appearance dictionary specifying the appearance of a pushbutton field (see "Pushbuttons" on page 444). The appearance dictionary's contents are as shown in Table 7.12 on page 406, except that the values of the **N**, **R**, and **D** entries must all be streams.
APRef	dictionary	*(Optional; PDF 1.3)* A dictionary holding references to external PDF files containing the pages to use for the appearances of a pushbutton field. This dictionary is similar to an appearance dictionary (see Table 7.12 on page 406), except that the values of the **N**, **R**, and **D** entries must all be named page reference dictionaries (Table 7.67 on page 468). This entry is ignored if an **AP** entry is present.
IF	dictionary	*(Optional; PDF 1.3; button fields only)* An icon fit dictionary (see Table 7.64) specifying how to display a button field's icon within the annotation rectangle of its widget annotation.
Opt	array	*(Required; choice fields only)* An array of options to be presented to the user. Each element of the array can take either of two forms: • A text string representing one of the available options • A two-element array consisting of a text string representing one of the available options and a default appearance string for constructing the item's appearance dynamically at viewing time (see "Variable Text" on page 439)

A	dictionary	*(Optional)* An action to be performed when this annotation is activated (see Section 7.5, "Actions").
AA	dictionary	*(Optional)* An additional-actions dictionary defining the field's behavior in response to various trigger events (see Section 7.5.2, "Trigger Events").

In an FDF field dictionary representing a button field, the optional **IF** entry holds an *icon fit dictionary (PDF 1.3)* specifying how to display the button's icon within the annotation rectangle of its widget annotation. Table 7.64 shows the contents of this type of dictionary.

TABLE 7.64   Entries in an icon fit dictionary

KEY	TYPE	VALUE
SW	name	*(Required)* The circumstances under which the icon should be scaled inside the annotation rectangle:

    A   Always scale.
    B   Scale only when the icon is bigger than the annotation rectangle.
    S   Scale only when the icon is smaller than the annotation rectangle.
    N   Never scale.

Default value: A.

S	name	*(Required)* The type of scaling to use:

    A   *Anamorphic scaling*: scale the icon to fill the annotation rectangle exactly, without regard to its original aspect ratio (ratio of width to height).

    P   *Proportional scaling*: scale the icon to fit the width or height of the annotation rectangle while maintaining the icon's original aspect ratio. If the required horizontal and vertical scaling factors arc diffcrcnt, usc thc smaller of the two, centering the icon within the annotation rectangle in the other dimension.

Default value: P.

A	array	*(Required)* An array of two numbers between 0.0 and 1.0 indicating the fraction of leftover space to allocate at the left and bottom of the icon. A value of [0.0 0.0] positions the icon at the bottom-left corner of the annotation rectangle; a value of [0.5 0.5] centers it within the rectangle. This entry is used only if the icon is scaled proportionally. Default value: [0.5 0.5].

FDF Pages

The optional **Pages** field in an FDF dictionary (see Table 7.62 on page 463) contains an array of *FDF page dictionaries (PDF 1.3)* describing new pages to be added to the target document. Table 7.65 shows the contents of this type of dictionary.

TABLE 7.65   Entries in an FDF page dictionary

KEY	TYPE	VALUE
Templates	array	*(Required)* An array of *FDF template dictionaries* (see Table 7.66) describing the named pages that serve as templates on the page.
Info	dictionary	*(Optional)* An *FDF page information dictionary* containing additional information about the page. At the time of publication, no entries have been defined for this dictionary.

An *FDF template dictionary* contains information describing a named page that serves as a template. Table 7.66 shows the contents of this type of dictionary.

TABLE 7.66   Entries in an FDF template dictionary

KEY	TYPE	VALUE
TRef	dictionary	*(Required)* A named page reference dictionary (see Table 7.67) specifying the location of the template.
Fields	array	*(Optional)* An array of references to FDF field dictionaries (see Table 7.63) describing the root fields to be imported (those with no ancestors in the field hierarchy).
Rename	boolean	*(Optional)* A flag specifying whether fields imported from the template may be renamed in the event of name conflicts with existing fields; see below for further discussion. Default value: *true*.

The names of fields imported from a template may sometimes conflict with those of existing fields in the target document. This can occur, for example, if the same template page is imported more than once or if two different templates have fields with the same names. If the **Rename** flag in the FDF template dictionary is *true*, fields with such conflicting names are renamed to guarantee their uniqueness. If **Rename** is *false*, the fields are not renamed; this results in multiple fields with the same name in the target document. Each time the FDF file provides attributes for a given field name, all fields with that name will be updated. (See implementation notes 90 and 91 in Appendix H.)

The **TRef** entry in an FDF template dictionary holds a *named page reference dictionary* describing the location of external templates or page elements. Table 7.67 shows the contents of this type of dictionary.

TABLE 7.67   Entries in an FDF named page reference dictionary

KEY	TYPE	VALUE
Name	string	*(Required)* The name of the referenced page.
F	file specification	*(Optional)* The file containing the named page. If this key is absent, it is assumed that the page resides in the associated PDF file.

FDF Annotation Dictionaries

Each annotation dictionary in an FDF file must have a **Page** entry (see Table 7.68) indicating the page of the source document to which the annotation is attached.

TABLE 7.68   Additional entry for annotation dictionaries in an FDF file

KEY	TYPE	VALUE
Page	integer	*(Required for annotations in FDF files)* The ordinal page number on which this annotation should appear, where page 0 is the first page.

7.7 Sounds

A *sound object (PDF 1.2)* is a stream containing sample values that define a sound to be played through the computer's speakers. The **Sound** entry in a sound annotation or sound action dictionary (see Tables 7.24 on page 418 and 7.37 on page 430) identifies a sound object representing the sound to be played when the annotation is activated.

Since a sound object is a stream, it can contain any of the standard entries common to all streams, as described in Table 3.4 on page 35. In particular, if it contains an **F** (file specification) entry, then the sound is defined in an external file. This must be a self-describing sound file, containing all information needed to render the sound; no additional information need be present in the PDF file.

Note: *The AIFF, AIFF-C (Macintosh), RIFF (.wav), and snd (.au) file formats are all self-describing.*

If no **F** entry is present, the sound object itself contains the sample data and all other information needed to define the sound. Table 7.69 shows the additional dictionary entries specific to a sound object.

KEY	TYPE	VALUE
		TABLE 7.69 Additional entries specific to a sound object
Type	name	*(Optional)* The type of PDF object that this dictionary describes; if present, must be **Sound** for a sound object.
R	number	*(Required)* The sampling rate, in samples per second.
C	integer	*(Optional)* The number of sound channels. Default value: 1. (See implementation note 92 in Appendix H.)
B	integer	*(Optional)* The number of bits per sample value per channel. Default value: 8.
E	name	*(Optional)* The format of the sample data:
		Raw Unspecified or unsigned values in the range 0 to $2^B - 1$
		Signed Twos-complement values
		muLaw µ-law encoded samples
		ALaw A-law encoded samples
		Default value: Raw.
CO	name	*(Optional)* The sound compression format used on the sample data. (Note that this is separate from any stream compression specified by the sound object's **Filter** entry; see Table 3.4 on page 35 and "Filters" on page 36.) If this entry is absent, then no sound compression has been used; the data contains sampled waveforms to be played at **R** samples per second per channel.
CP	(various)	*(Optional)* Optional parameters specific to the sound compression format used.
		Note: *At the time of publication, no standard values have been defined for the **CO** and **CP** entries.*

Sample values are stored in the stream with the most significant bits first ("big-endian" order for samples larger than 8 bits). Samples that are not a multiple of 8 bits are packed into consecutive bytes, starting at the most significant end. If a sample extends across a byte boundary, the most significant bits are placed in the first byte, followed by less significant bits in subsequent bytes. For dual-channel stereophonic sounds, the samples are stored in an interleaved format, with each sample value for the left channel (channel 1) preceding the corresponding sample for the right (channel 2).

To maximize the portability of PDF documents containing embedded sounds, Adobe recommends that PDF viewer applications and plug-in extensions support at least the following formats (assuming the platform has sufficient hardware and OS support to play sounds at all):

R	8000, 11,025, or 22,050 samples per second
C	1 or 2 channels
B	8 or 16 bits per channel
E	Raw, Signed, or muLaw encoding

If the encoding (**E**) is Raw or Signed, then **R** must be 11,025 or 22,050 samples per channel. If the encoding is muLaw, then **R** must be 8000 samples per channel, **C** must be 1 channel, and **B** must be 8 bits per channel. Sound players should be prepared to convert between formats, downsample rates, and combine channels as necessary to render sound on the target platform.

7.8 Movies

PDF includes the ability to embed *movies* within a document by means of movie annotations (see "Movie Annotations" on page 418). Despite the name, a movie may consist entirely of sound with no visible images to be displayed on the screen. The **Movie** and **A** (activation) entries in the movie annotation dictionary refer, respectively, to a *movie dictionary* (Table 7.70) describing the static characteristics of the movie and a *movie activation dictionary* (Table 7.71) specifying how it should be presented.

TABLE 7.70 Entries in a movie dictionary

KEY	TYPE	VALUE
F	file specification	*(Required)* A file specification identifying a self-describing movie file. **Note:** *The format of a "self-describing movie file" is left unspecified, and there is no guarantee of portability.*
Aspect	array	*(Optional)* The width and height of the movie's bounding box, in pixels, specified as [*width height*]. This entry should be omitted for a movie consisting entirely of sound with no visible images.
Rotate	integer	*(Optional)* The number of degrees by which the movie is rotated clockwise relative to the page. The value must be a multiple of 90. Default value: 0.
Poster	boolean or stream	*(Optional)* A flag or stream specifying whether and how to display a *poster image* representing the movie. If this value is a stream, it contains an image XObject (see Section 4.8, "Images") to be displayed as the poster; if it is the boolean value *true*, the poster image should be retrieved from the movie file itself; if it is *false*, no poster should be displayed. Default value: *false*.

TABLE 7.71 Entries in a movie activation dictionary

KEY	TYPE	VALUE
Start	(various)	*(Optional)* The starting time of the movie segment to be played. Movie time values are expressed in units of time based on a *time scale*, which defines the number of units per second; the default time scale is defined in the movie data itself. The starting time is nominally a 64-bit integer, specified as follows: • If it is representable as an integer (subject to the implementation limit for integers, as described in Appendix C), it should be specified as such. • If it is not representable as an integer, it should be specified as an 8-byte string representing a 64-bit twos-complement integer, most significant byte first. • If it is expressed in a time scale different from that of the movie itself, it is represented as an array of two values: an integer or string denoting the starting time, as above, followed by an integer specifying the time scale in units per second. If this entry is omitted, the movie is played from the beginning.
Duration	(various)	*(Optional)* The duration of the movie segment to be played, specified in the same form as **Start**. Negative values specify that the movie is to be played backward. If this entry is omitted, the movie is played to the end.

Rate	number	*(Optional)* The initial speed at which to play the movie. If the value of this entry is negative, the movie is played backward with respect to **Start** and **Duration**. Default value: 1.0.
Volume	number	*(Optional)* The initial sound volume at which to play the movie, in the range −1.0 to 1.0. Higher values denote greater volume; negative values mute the sound. Default value: 1.0.
ShowControls	boolean	*(Optional)* A flag specifying whether to display a movie controller bar while playing the movie. Default value: *false*.
Mode	name	*(Optional)* The *play mode* for playing the movie:

Once	Play once and stop.
Open	Play and leave the movie controller bar open.
Repeat	Play repeatedly from beginning to end until stopped.
Palindrome	Play continuously forward and backward until stopped.

Default value: Once.

Synchronous	boolean	*(Optional)* A flag specifying whether to play the movie synchronously or asynchronously. If this value is *true*, the movie player will retain control until the movie is completed or dismissed by the user; if *false*, it will return control to the viewer application immediately after starting the movie. Default value: *false*.
FWScale	array	*(Optional)* The magnification factor at which to play the movie. The presence of this entry implies that the movie is to be played in a floating window; if the entry is absent, it will be played in the annotation rectangle.

The value of the entry is an array of two integers, [*numerator denominator*], denoting a rational magnification factor for the movie. The final window size, in pixels, is

$$(numerator \div denominator) \times \textbf{Aspect}$$

where the value of **Aspect** is taken from the movie dictionary (see Table 7.70).

FWPosition	array	*(Optional)* For floating play windows, the relative position of the window on the screen. The value is an array of two numbers

[*horiz vert*]

each in the range 0.0 to 1.0, denoting the relative horizontal and vertical position of the movie window with respect to the screen. For example, the value [0.5 0.5] centers the window on the screen. Default value: [0.5 0.5].

CHAPTER 8

Document Interchange

THE FEATURES DESCRIBED in this chapter do not affect the final appearance of a document. Rather, they allow it to include higher-level information that is useful for the interchange of documents among applications. They include:

- *Procedure sets* that define the implementation of PDF operators

- A *document information dictionary* containing general information such as the document's title, author, and creation and modification dates

- *File identifiers* for reliable reference from one PDF file to another

- *Page-piece dictionaries*, *marked-content operators*, and *logical structure* facilities, all of which allow applications that process PDF documents to embed private data in a document for their own use

- The *Web Capture* plug-in extension, which creates PDF files from Internet-based or locally resident HTML, PDF, GIF, JPEG, and ASCII text files

- Facilities supporting prepress production workflows, such as the generation of *color separations*, *traps*, and low-resolution *proxies* for high-resolution images

8.1 Procedure Sets

The PDF operators used in content streams are grouped into categories of related operators called *procedure sets* (see Table 8.1). Each procedure set corresponds to a named resource containing the implementations of the operators in that procedure set. The **ProcSet** entry in a content stream's resource dictionary (see Section 3.7.2, "Resource Dictionaries") holds an array consisting of the names of the procedure sets used in that content stream. These procedure sets are used only when the content stream is printed to a PostScript output device; the names identify PostScript procedure sets that must be sent to the device to interpret the

PDF operators in the content stream. Each element of this array must be one of the predefined names shown in Table 8.1. (See implementation note 93 in Appendix H.)

	TABLE 8.1 Predefined procedure sets
NAME	**CATEGORY OF OPERATORS**
PDF	Painting and graphics state
Text	Text
ImageB	Grayscale images or image masks
ImageC	Color images
ImageI	Indexed (color-table) images

Note: This feature is considered obsolescent. Applications that generate PDF should continue to specify procedure sets for compatibility with existing viewer applications; however, viewers should not depend on the correctness of this information.

8.2 Document Information Dictionary

A PDF document may include a *document information dictionary* containing general information such as the document's title, author, and creation and modification dates. Such global information about the document itself (as opposed to its content or structure) is called *metadata*, and is intended to assist in cataloguing and searching for documents in external databases.

The document information dictionary is the value of the optional **Info** entry in the trailer of the PDF file (see Section 3.4.4, "File Trailer"); Table 8.2 shows its contents. Any entry whose value is not known should be omitted from the dictionary, rather than included with an empty string as its value. (See implementation note 94 in Appendix H.)

TABLE 8.2 **Entries in a document information dictionary**

KEY	TYPE	VALUE
Title	text string	*(Optional; PDF 1.1)* The document's title.
Author	text string	*(Optional)* The name of the person who created the document.
Subject	text string	*(Optional; PDF 1.1)* The subject of the document.
Keywords	text string	*(Optional; PDF 1.1)* Keywords associated with the document.
Creator	text string	*(Optional)* If the document was converted to PDF from another format, the name of the application (for example, Adobe FrameMaker®) that created the original document from which it was converted.
Producer	text string	*(Optional)* If the document was converted to PDF from another format, the name of the application (for example, Acrobat Distiller) that converted it to PDF.
CreationDate	date	*(Optional)* The date the document was created, in human-readable form (see Section 3.8.2, "Dates").
ModDate	date	*(Optional; PDF 1.1)* The date the document was last modified, in human-readable form (see Section 3.8.2, "Dates").
Trapped	name	*(Optional; PDF 1.3)* A name object indicating whether the document has been modified to include trapping information (see Section 8.6.3, "Trapping Support"):

	True	The document has been fully trapped; no further trapping is needed. (Note that this is the name True, not the boolean value *true*.)
	False	The document has not yet been trapped; any desired trapping must still be done. (Note that this is the name False, not the boolean value *false*.)
	Unknown	Either it is unknown whether the document has been trapped, or it has been partly but not yet fully trapped; some additional trapping may still be needed.

Default value: Unknown.

The value of this entry may be set automatically by the software creating the document's trapping information or may only be known to a human operator and entered manually.

Entries in the document information dictionary may be added or changed by users or extensions (see implementation note 95 in Appendix H). Some extensions may also choose to permit searches on the contents of the dictionary. To facilitate browsing and editing, all keys in the dictionary are fully spelled out, not abbreviated. New keys should be chosen with care so that they make sense to users.

Note: *Although viewer applications can store custom metadata in the document information dictionary, it is inappropriate to store private content or structural information there; such information should be stored in the document catalog instead (see Section 3.6.1, "Document Catalog").*

Example 8.1 shows a typical document information dictionary.

Example 8.1

```
1  0  obj
    << /Title  (PostScript Language Reference, Third Edition)
       /Author  (Adobe Systems Incorporated)
       /Creator  (Adobe® FrameMaker® 5.5.3 for Power Macintosh)
       /Producer  (Acrobat® Distiller™ 3.01 for Power Macintosh)
       /CreationDate  (D:19970915110347-08'00')
       /ModDate  (D:19990209153925-08'00')
    >>
endobj
```

8.3 File Identifiers

PDF files may contain references to other PDF files (see Section 3.10, "File Specifications"). Simply storing a file name, however, even in a platform-independent format, does not guarantee that the file can be found. Even if the file still exists and its name has not been changed, different server software applications may identify it in different ways. For example, servers running on DOS platforms must convert all file names to 8 characters and a 3-character extension; different servers may use different strategies for converting longer file names to this format.

External file references can be made more reliable by including a *file identifier (PDF 1.1)* in the file itself and using it in addition to the normal platform-based file designation. Matching the identifier in the file reference with the one in the file itself confirms whether the desired file was found.

File identifiers are defined by the optional **ID** entry in a PDF file's trailer dictionary (see Section 3.4.4, "File Trailer"; see also implementation note 96 in Appendix H). The value of this entry is an array of two strings. The first string is a permanent identifier based on the contents of the file at the time it was originally created, and does not change when the file is incrementally updated. The second string is a changing identifier based on the file's contents at the time it was last updated. When a file is first written, both identifiers are set to the same value. If both identifiers match when a file reference is resolved, it is very likely that the correct file has been found; if only the first identifier matches, then a different version of the correct file has been found.

To help ensure the uniqueness of file identifiers, it is recommend that they be computed using a message digest algorithm such as MD5 (described in Internet RFC 1321, *The MD5 Message-Digest Algorithm*; see the Bibliography), using the following information (see implementation note 97 in Appendix H):

- The current time

- A string representation of the file's location, usually a pathname

- The size of the file in bytes

- The values of all entries in the file's document information dictionary (see Section 8.2, "Document Information Dictionary")

8.4 Application Data

The PDF features described in this section allow applications that generate or process PDF files to embed private data within a document for their own use. Examples include information on object grouping for a graphics editor or the layer information used by Adobe Photoshop®. Such private data can convey information meaningful to the application that produces it, but is typically ignored by general-purpose PDF viewer applications. It can be stored in a PDF document in any of three ways:

- In a *page-piece dictionary* (Section 8.4.1) associated with an individual page or a form XObject

- Embedded in a content stream by means of *marked-content operators* (Section 8.4.2)

- In a *structure hierarchy* global to the entire document (Section 8.4.3)

8.4.1 Page-Piece Dictionaries

The optional **PieceInfo** entry in a page object or a form dictionary (see Tables 3.17 on page 77 and 4.41 on page 264) can hold a *page-piece dictionary (PDF 1.3)* containing private application data associated with a PDF page or a form XObject. Applications can use this dictionary as a place to store any private data they wish in connection with that page or form.

As Table 8.3 shows, a page-piece dictionary may contain any number of entries, each keyed by the name of a distinct application or of a "well-known" data type recognized by a family of applications. The value associated with each key is an *application data dictionary* containing the private data to be used by the application. The **Private** entry may have a value of any data type, but typically it will be a dictionary containing all of the private data needed by the application other than the actual content of the page or form.

TABLE 8.3 Entries in a page-piece dictionary

KEY	TYPE	VALUE
any application name or well-known data type	dictionary	An application data dictionary (see Table 8.4).

TABLE 8.4 Entries in an application data dictionary

KEY	TYPE	VALUE
LastModified	date	*(Required)* The date and time when the contents of the page or form were most recently modified by this application.
Private	(any)	*(Optional)* Any private data appropriate to the application, typically in the form of a dictionary.

The **LastModified** entry indicates when this application last altered the content of the page or form. If the page-piece dictionary contains several application data dictionaries, their modification dates can be compared with those in the corresponding entry of the page object or form dictionary (see Tables 3.17 on page 77 and 4.41 on page 264) to ascertain which application data dictionary corresponds to the current content of the page or form. Because some platforms may use only an approximate value for the date and time or may not deal correctly with differing time zones, modification dates are compared only for equality and not for sequential ordering.

Note: *It is possible for two or more application data dictionaries to have the same modification date. Applications can use this capability to define multiple or extended versions of the same data format. For example, suppose that earlier versions of an application use an application data dictionary named* **PictureEdit**, *while later versions of the same application extend the data to include additional items not previously used. The original data could continue to be kept in the* **PictureEdit** *dictionary, with the additional items placed in a new dictionary named* **PictureEditExtended**. *This allows the earlier versions of the application to continue to work as before, while later versions are able to locate and use the extended data items.*

8.4.2 Marked Content

Marked-content operators (PDF 1.2) identify a portion of a PDF content stream as a *marked-content element* of interest to a particular application or PDF plug-in extension. Marked-content elements and the operators that mark them fall into two categories:

- The **MP** and **DP** operators designate a single *marked-content point* in the content stream.

- The **BMC**, **BDC**, and **EMC** operators bracket a *marked-content sequence* of objects within the content stream. Note that this is not simply a sequence of bytes in the content stream, but of complete graphics objects. Each object is fully qualified by the parameters of the graphics state in which it is rendered.

A graphics application, for example, might use marked content to identify a set of related objects as a "group" to be processed as a single unit. A text-processing application might use it to maintain a connection between a footnote marker in the body of a document and the corresponding footnote text at the bottom of the page. Table 8.5 summarizes the marked-content operators.

TABLE 8.5 Marked-content operators

OPERANDS	OPERATOR	DESCRIPTION
tag	**MP**	Designate a marked-content point. *tag* is a name object indicating the role or significance of the point.
tag properties	**DP**	Designate a marked-content point with an associated property list. *tag* is a name object indicating the role or significance of the point; *properties* is either an in-line dictionary containing the property list or a name object associated with it in the **Properties** subdictionary of the current resource dictionary (see "Property Lists" on page 481).
tag	**BMC**	Begin a marked-content sequence terminated by a balancing **EMC** operator. *tag* is a name object indicating the role or significance of the sequence.
tag properties	**BDC**	Begin a marked-content sequence with an associated property list, terminated by a balancing **EMC** operator. *tag* is a name object indicating the role or significance of the sequence; *properties* is either an in-line dictionary containing the property list or a name object associated with it in the **Properties** subdictionary of the current resource dictionary (see "Property Lists" on page 481).
—	**EMC**	End a marked-content sequence begun by a **BMC** or **BDC** operator.

All marked-content operators except **EMC** take a *tag* operand indicating the role or significance of the marked-content element to the processing application. All such tags must be registered with Adobe Systems (see Appendix E) to avoid conflicts between different applications marking the same content stream. In addition to the tag operand, the **DP** and **BDC** operators specify a *property list* containing further information associated with the marked content. Property lists are discussed further under "Property Lists," below.

Marked-content operators may appear only *between* graphics objects in the content stream; they may not occur within a graphics object or between a graphics state operator and its operands. Marked-content sequences may be nested one within another, but each sequence must be entirely contained within a single content stream; it may not cross page boundaries, for example.

Note: The **Contents** *entry of a page object (see "Page Objects" on page 77), which may be either a single stream or an array of streams, is considered a single stream with respect to marked-content sequences.*

When the marked-content operators **BMC**, **BDC**, and **EMC** are combined with the text object operators **BT** and **ET** (see Section 5.3, "Text Objects"), each pair of matching operators (**BMC**...**EMC**, **BDC**...**EMC**, or **BT**...**ET**) must be properly (separately) nested. That is, the sequences

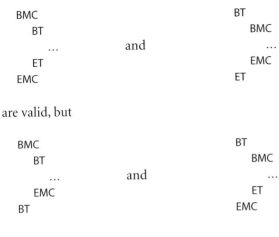

BMC
  BT
    ...   and
  ET
EMC

BT
  BMC
    ...
  EMC
ET

are valid, but

BMC
  BT
    ...   and
  EMC
BT

BT
  BMC
    ...
  ET
EMC

are not.

Property Lists

The marked-content operators **DP** and **BDC** associate a *property list* with a marked-content element within a content stream. This is a dictionary containing private information meaningful to the program (application or plug-in extension) creating the marked content. Although the dictionary may contain any entries the program wishes to place there, it is suggested that any particular program use the entries in a consistent way; for example, the values associated with a given key should always be of the same type (or small set of types).

If all of the values in a property list dictionary are direct objects, the dictionary may be written in-line in the content stream as a direct object. If any of the values are indirect references to objects outside the content stream, the property list dictionary must instead be defined as a named resource in the **Properties** subdictionary of the current resource dictionary (see Section 3.7.2, "Resource Dictionaries") and then referenced by name as the *properties* operand of the **DP** or **BDC** operator.

Marked Content and Clipping

Some PDF path and text objects are defined purely for their effect on the current clipping path, without themselves actually being painted on the page. This occurs when a path object is defined using the operator sequence **W n** or **W* n** (see Section 4.4.3, "Clipping Path Operators") or when a text object is painted in text rendering mode 7 (see Section 5.2.5, "Text Rendering Mode"). Such clipped, unpainted path or text objects are called *clipping objects*. When a clipping object falls within a marked-content sequence, it is not considered part of the sequence unless the entire sequence consists only of clipping objects. In Example 8.2, for instance, the marked-content sequence tagged Clip includes the text string (Clip me), but not the rectangular path that defines the clipping boundary.

Example 8.2

```
/Clip  BMC
    100  100  10  10  re  W  n          % Clipping path
    (Clip me)  Tj                       % Object to be clipped
EMC
```

Only when a marked-content sequence consists entirely of clipping objects are the clipping objects considered part of the sequence. In this case, the sequence is known as a *marked clipping sequence*. Such sequences may be nested. In Example 8.3, for instance, multiple lines of text are used to clip a subsequent graphics object (in this case, a filled path). Each line of text is bracketed within a separate marked clipping sequence, tagged Pgf; the entire series is bracketed in turn by an outer marked clipping sequence, tagged Clip. Note, however, that the marked-content sequence tagged ClippedText is *not* a marked clipping sequence, since it contains a filled rectangular path that is not a clipping object. The clipping objects belonging to the Clip and Pgf sequences are therefore not considered part of the ClippedText sequence.

Example 8.3

```
/ClippedText  BMC
    /Clip  <<...>>
        BDC
            BT
                7  Tr                        % Begin text clip mode
                /Pgf  BMC
                    (Line 1)  Tj
                EMC
                /Pgf  BMC
                    (Line)  '
                    ( 2)  Tj
                EMC
            ET                               % Set current text clip
        EMC
        100  100  10  10  re  f              % Filled path
    EMC
```

The precise rules governing marked clipping sequences are as follows:

- A *clipping object* is a path object ended by the operator sequence **W n** or **W* n** or a text object painted in text rendering mode 7.

- An *invisible graphics object* is a path object ended by the operator **n** only (with no preceding **W** or **W***) or a text object painted in text rendering mode 3.

- A *visible graphics object* is a path object ended by any operator other than **n**, a text object painted in any text rendering mode other than 3 or 7, or any XObject invoked by the **Do** operator.

- An *empty marked-content element* is a marked-content point or a marked-content sequence that encloses no graphics objects.

- A *marked clipping sequence* is a marked-content sequence that contains at least one clipping object and no visible graphics objects.

- Clipping objects and marked clipping sequences are considered part of an enclosing marked-content sequence only if it is a marked clipping sequence.

- Invisible graphics objects and empty marked-content elements are always considered part of an enclosing marked-content sequence, regardless of whether it is a marked clipping sequence.

- The **q** (save) and **Q** (restore) operators may not occur within a marked clipping sequence.

Example 8.4 illustrates the application of these rules. Marked-content sequence S4 is a marked clipping sequence, because it contains a clipping object (clipping path 2) and no visible graphics objects. Clipping path 2 is therefore considered part of sequence S4. Marked-content sequences S1, S2, and S3 are *not* marked clipping sequences, since they each include at least one visible graphics object. Thus clipping paths 1 and 2 are not part of any of these three sequences.

Example 8.4

```
/S1  BMC
   /S2  BMC
      /S3  BMC
         0  0  m
         100  100  l
         0  100  l  W  n              % Clipping path 1

         0  0  m
         200  200  l
         0  100  l  f                 % Filled path
      EMC

      /S4  BMC
         0  0  m
         300  300  l
         0  100  l  W  n              % Clipping path 2
      EMC
   EMC
   100  100  10  10  re  f            % Filled path
EMC
```

In Example 8.5, marked-content sequence S1 is a marked clipping sequence, because the only graphics object it contains is a clipping path. Thus the empty marked-content sequence S3 and the marked-content point P1 are both part of sequence S2, and S2, S3, and P1 are all part of sequence S1.

Example 8.5

```
/S1  BMC
   … Clipping path …
   /S2  BMC
      /S3  BMC
      EMC
      /P1  DP
   EMC
EMC
```

In Example 8.6, marked-content sequences S1 and S4 are marked clipping sequences, because the only object they contain is a clipping path. Hence the clipping path is part of sequences S1 and S4; S3 is part of S2; and S2, S3, and S4 are all part of S1.

Example 8.6

```
/S1  BMC
    /S2  BMC
        /S3  BMC
        EMC
    EMC

    /S4  BMC
        … Clipping path …
    EMC
EMC
```

8.4.3 Logical Structure

PDF's *logical structure* facilities *(PDF 1.3)* provide a mechanism for incorporating structural information about a document's content into a PDF file. Such information might include, for example, the organization of the document into chapters and sections or the identification of special elements such as figures, tables, and footnotes. The logical structure facilities are extensible, allowing applications that produce PDF files to choose what structural information to include and how to represent it, while enabling PDF consumers to navigate a file without knowing the producer's structural conventions.

PDF logical structure shares basic features with standard document markup languages such as HTML, SGML, and XML. A document's logical structure is expressed as a hierarchy of *structure elements*, each represented by a dictionary object. Like their counterparts in other markup languages, PDF structure elements can have content and attributes. Their content can consist of references to document content, references to other structure elements, or both. In PDF, however, rendered document content takes over the role occupied by text in HTML, SGML, and XML.

A PDF document's logical structure is stored separately from its visible content, with pointers from each to the other. This separation allows the ordering and nesting of logical elements to be entirely independent of the order and location of graphics objects on the document's pages.

Structure Hierarchy

The logical structure of a document is described by a hierarchy of objects called the *structure hierarchy* or *structure tree*. At the root of the hierarchy is a dictionary object called the *structure tree root*, located via the **StructTreeRoot** entry in the document catalog (see Section 3.6.1, "Document Catalog"). The remainder of the hierarchy is formed of intermediate nodes called *structure elements*. At the leaves of the tree are individual *content items* associated with structure elements; these may be marked-content elements, complete PDF objects, or other structure elements. Tables 8.6 and 8.7 show the contents of the structure tree root and a structure element, respectively.

TABLE 8.6 Entries in the structure tree root

KEY	TYPE	VALUE
Type	name	*(Required)* The type of PDF object that this dictionary describes; must be **StructTreeRoot** for a structure tree root.
K	dictionary or array	*(Optional)* The immediate child or children of the structure tree root in the structure hierarchy. The value may be either a dictionary representing a single structure element or an array of such dictionaries.
IDTree	name tree	*(Required if any structure elements have element identifiers)* A name tree that maps element identifiers (see Table 8.7) to the structure elements they denote.
ParentTree	number tree	*(Required if any structure element contains PDF objects or marked-content sequences as content items)* A number tree (see Section 3.8.5, "Number Trees") used in finding the structure elements to which content items belong. Each integer key in the number tree corresponds to a single page of the document or to an individual object (such as an annotation or an XObject) that is a content item in its own right. The integer key is given as the value of the **StructParents** entry in that object (see "Finding Structure Elements from Content Items" on page 496). For an object that is a content item, the associated value is an indirect reference to the object's parent element (the structure element that contains it as a content item). For a page object or content stream containing marked-content

sequences that are content items, the value is an array of references to the parent elements of those marked-content sequences. See "Finding Structure Elements from Content Items" on page 496 for further discussion.

ParentTreeNextKey	integer	*(Optional)* An integer greater than any key in the parent tree, to be used as a key for the next entry added to the tree.
RoleMap	dictionary	*(Optional)* A dictionary mapping the names of structure types used in the document to their approximate equivalents in the proposed set of standard structure types (see "Structure Types" on page 489).
ClassMap	dictionary	*(Optional)* A dictionary mapping name objects designating attribute classes to the corresponding attribute objects or arrays of attribute objects (see "Attribute Classes" on page 500).

TABLE 8.7 Entries in a structure element dictionary

KEY	TYPE	VALUE
Type	name	*(Optional)* The type of PDF object that this dictionary describes; if present, must be **StructElem** for a structure element.
S	name	*(Required)* The *structure type*, a name object identifying the nature of the structure element and its role within the document, such as a chapter, paragraph, or footnote (see "Structure Types," below). Names of structure types must conform to the guidelines described in Appendix E.
P	dictionary	*(Required; must be an indirect reference)* The structure element that is the immediate parent of this one in the structure hierarchy.
ID	string	*(Optional)* The *element identifier,* a string designating this structure element. The string must be unique among all elements in the document's structure hierarchy. The **IDTree** entry in the structure tree root (see Table 8.6, above) defines the correspondence between element identifiers and the structure elements they denote.
Pg	dictionary	*(Optional; must be an indirect reference)* A page object representing a page on which some or all of the content items designated by the **K** entry are rendered.

K	(various)	*(Optional)* The contents of this structure element, which may consist of one or more marked-content sequences, PDF objects, and other structure elements. The value of this entry may be any of the following:

- An integer marked-content identifier denoting a marked-content sequence

- A marked-content reference dictionary denoting a marked-content sequence

- An object reference dictionary denoting a PDF object

- A structure element dictionary denoting another structure element

- An array, each of whose elements is one of the objects listed above

See "Structure Content" on page 489 for further discussion of each of these forms of representation.

A	(various)	*(Optional)* The attribute object or objects, if any, associated with this structure element. Each attribute object is either a dictionary or a stream; the value of this entry may be either a single attribute object or an array of such objects together with their revision numbers (see "Structure Attributes" on page 500 and "Attribute Revision Numbers" on page 501).
C	name or array	*(Optional)* The attribute class or classes, if any, to which this structure element belongs. The value of this entry may be either a single class name or an array of class names together with their revision numbers (see "Attribute Classes" on page 500 and "Attribute Revision Numbers" on page 501).
R	integer	*(Optional)* The current revision number of this structure element (see "Attribute Revision Numbers" on page 501). The value must be a non-negative integer. Default value: 0.
T	text string	*(Optional)* The title of the structure element, a text string representing it in human-readable form. The title should characterize the specific structure element, such as Chapter 1, rather than merely a generic element type, such as Chapter.
Alt	text string	*(Optional)* An alternate representation of the structure element's contents in human-readable form, for use by viewer applications that cannot process the contents.

Structure Types

Every structure element has a *structure type*, a name object that identifies the nature of the structure element and its role within the document (such as a chapter, paragraph, or footnote). To facilitate data interchange among PDF applications, Adobe has proposed a set of standard structure types, defined in Adobe Technical Note #5401, *Standard Element Types for Logical Structure in PDF*. Applications are not required to adopt them, however, but may use any names they wish for their structure types.

Where names other than the standard ones are used, a *role map* may be provided in the structure tree root, mapping the structure types used in the document to their nearest equivalents in the standard set. For example, a structure type named Chap used in the document might be mapped to the standard type Chapter. The equivalence need not be exact; the role map merely indicates an approximate analogy between types, allowing applications other than the one creating a document to handle its nonstandard structure elements in a reasonable way.

Note: *The same structure type may occur as both a key and a value in the role map, and circular chains of association are explicitly permitted. A single role map can thus define a bidirectional mapping. An application using the role map should follow the chain of associations until it either finds a structure type it recognizes or returns to one it has already encountered.*

Structure Content

The content of a structure element may consist of one or more *content items* of any of the following kinds:

- Marked-content sequences embedded within content streams

- Complete PDF objects such as annotations and XObjects

- Other structure elements

The **K** entry in a structure element dictionary can have as its value either a single object denoting one of these items or an array of such objects. Items of any or all three kinds may be mixed in the same content array. The following sections describe how each kind of content item is denoted in a structure element's **K** entry.

Marked-Content Sequences as Content Items

For a sequence of graphics operators in a content stream to be included in the content of a structure element, they must be bracketed as a marked-content sequence between **BDC** and **EMC** operators (see Section 8.4.2, "Marked Content"). Furthermore, the marked-content sequence must have a property list (see "Property Lists" on page 481) containing an **MCID** entry. This entry defines an integer *marked-content identifier* that uniquely identifies the marked-content sequence within its content stream. The structure element can then refer to the sequence by specifying its content stream and its marked-content identifier within the stream.

Note: *Although the tag associated with a marked-content sequence is not directly related to the document's logical structure, it should be the same as the structure type of the associated structure element.*

In the general case, a structure element refers to a marked-content sequence by means of a dictionary object called a *marked-content reference*. Table 8.8 shows the contents of this type of dictionary.

TABLE 8.8   Entries in a marked-content reference dictionary

KEY	TYPE	VALUE
Type	name	*(Required)* The type of PDF object that this dictionary describes; must be **MCR** for a marked-content reference.
Pg	dictionary	*(Optional; must be an indirect reference)* The page object representing the page on which the graphics objects in the marked-content sequence are rendered. This entry overrides any **Pg** entry in the structure element containing the marked-content reference; it is required if the structure element has no such entry.
Stm	stream	*(Optional; must be an indirect reference)* The content stream containing the marked-content sequence. This entry is needed only if the marked-content sequence resides in some other content stream associated with the page—for example, in a form XObject (see Section 4.9, "Form XObjects") or an annotation's appearance stream (Section 7.4.4, "Appearance Streams"). Default value: the content stream of the page identified by **Pg**.
StmOwn	(any)	*(Optional; must be an indirect reference)* The PDF object owning the stream identified by **Stm**—for example, the annotation to which an appearance stream belongs.
MCID	integer	*(Required)* The marked-content identifier of the marked-content sequence within its content stream.

Example 8.7 illustrates the use of a marked-content reference to refer to a marked-content sequence within the content stream of a page; Example 8.8 shows its use with a marked-content sequence in a different type of content stream (in this case, a form XObject).

*Note: These examples omit required **StructParents** entries in the objects used as content items (see "Finding Structure Elements from Content Items" on page 496).*

Example 8.7

```
1 0 obj                                % Structure element
   << /Type  /StructElem
       /S  /P                          % Structure type
       /P  ...                         % Parent in structure hierarchy
       /K << /Type  /MCR
             /Pg  2 0 R                % Page containing the marked-content sequence
             /MCID  0                  % Marked-content identifier
         >>
   >>
endobj

2 0 obj                                % Page object
   << /Type  /Page
       /Contents  3 0 R                % Content stream
       ...
   >>
endobj

3 0 obj                                % Page's content stream
   << /Length  ...  >>
stream
   ...
   /P << /MCID  0 >>                    % Start of marked-content sequence
      BDC
         (Here is some text)  TJ
         ...
      EMC                              % End of marked-content sequence
   ...
endstream
endobj
```

Example 8.8

```
1 0 obj                             % Structure element
    << /Type /StructElem
        /S /P                       % Structure type
        /P ...                      % Parent in structure hierarchy
        /K << /Type /MCR
            /Pg 2 0 R               % Page containing the marked-content sequence
            /Stm 4 0 R              % Stream containing the marked-content sequence
            /MCID 0                 % Marked-content identifier
        >>
    >>
endobj

2 0 obj                                     % Page object
    << /Type /Page
        /Resources << /XObject << /Fm4 4 0 R >>     % Resource dictionary
                    >>                              %   containing form XObject
        /Contents 3 0 R                             % Content stream
        ...
    >>
endobj

3 0 obj                         % Page's content stream
    << /Length ... >>
stream
    ...
    /Fm4 Do                     % Paint form XObject
    ...
endstream
endobj

4 0 obj                         % Form XObject
    << /Type /XObject
        /Subtype /Form
        /Length ...
    >>
stream
    ...
    /P << /MCID 0 >>            % Start of marked-content sequence
        BDC
            (Here is some text) TJ
            ...
        EMC                     % End of marked-content sequence
    ...
endstream
endobj
```

In the common case where all or most of the marked-content sequences in a structure element's content are on the same page, the **Pg** entry identifying the page can be supplied in the structure element dictionary itself (Table 8.7 on page 487), rather than in a separate marked-content reference for each sequence. Often, this allows the marked-content reference to be dispensed with entirely and the sequence identified in the structure element's **K** entry by simply giving its integer marked-content identifier directly. Example 8.9 shows an illustration.

Example 8.9

```
1 0 obj                              % Structure element
   << /Type  /StructElem
      /S  /P                         % Structure type
      /P  …                          % Parent in structure hierarchy
      /Pg  2 0 R                     % Page containing the marked-content sequence
      /K  0                          % Marked-content identifier
   >>
endobj

2 0 obj                              % Page object
   << /Type  /Page
      /Contents  3 0 R               % Content stream
      …
   >>
endobj

3 0 obj                              % Page's content stream
   << /Length  … >>
stream
   …
   /P  << /MCID  0 >>                % Start of marked-content sequence
      BDC
         (Here is some text)  TJ
         …
      EMC                            % End of marked-content sequence
   …
endstream
endobj
```

PDF Objects as Content Items

When a structure element's content includes an entire PDF object, such as an XObject or an annotation, that is associated with a page but not directly included in the page's content stream, the object is identified in the structure element's **K** entry by an *object reference dictionary* (see Table 8.9). Note that this form of reference is used only for entire objects; if the referenced content forms only part of the object's content stream, it is instead handled as a marked-content sequence, as described in the preceding section.

TABLE 8.9 Entries in an object reference dictionary

KEY	TYPE	VALUE
Type	name	*(Required)* The type of PDF object that this dictionary describes; must be **OBJR** for an object reference.
Pg	dictionary	*(Optional; must be an indirect reference)* The page object representing the page on which the object is rendered. This entry overrides any **Pg** entry in the structure element containing the object reference; it is required if the structure element has no such entry.
Obj	(any)	*(Required; must be an indirect reference)* The referenced object.

*Note: If the referenced object is rendered on multiple pages, each rendering requires a separate object reference; but if it is rendered multiple times on the same page, just a single object reference suffices to identify all of them. (If it is important to distinguish between multiple renditions of the same XObject on the same page, they should be accessed via marked-content sequences enclosing particular invocations of the **Do** operator, rather than via object references.)*

Structure Elements as Content Items

One structure element can contain another as a content item simply by referring to the other structure element in its **K** entry. Example 8.10 shows a structure element containing other structure elements as content items, along with a marked-content sequence from a page's content stream.

Example 8.10

```
1 0  obj                           % Containing structure element
   << /Type  /StructElem
       /S  /MixedContainer          % Structure type
       /P  …                        % Parent in structure hierarchy
       /Pg  2 0 R                   % Page containing the marked-content sequence
       /K  [ 4 0 R                  % Three content items: a structure element
          0                         %    a marked-content sequence
            5 0 R                   %    another structure element
         ]
   >>
endobj

2 0  obj                           % Page object
   << /Type  /Page
       /Contents  3 0 R            % Content stream
       …
   >>
endobj

3 0  obj                           % Page's content stream
   << /Length  … >>
stream
   …
   /P  << /MCID  0 >>              % Start of marked-content sequence
      BDC
         (Here is some text)  TJ
         …
      EMC                          % End of marked-content sequence
   …
endstream
endobj

4 0  obj                           % First contained structure element
   << /Type  /StructElem
       …
   >>
endobj

5 0  obj                           % Second contained structure element
   << /Type  /StructElem
       …
   >>
endobj
```

Finding Structure Elements from Content Items

Because a stream cannot contain object references, there is no way for content items that are marked-content sequences to refer directly back to their parent structure elements (the ones to which they belong as content items). Instead, a different mechanism, the *structural parent tree*, is provided for this purpose. For consistency, content items that are entire PDF objects, such as XObjects, also use the parent tree to refer to their parent structure elements.

The parent tree is a number tree (see Section 3.8.5, "Number Trees"), accessed via the **ParentTree** entry in a document's structure tree root (Table 8.6 on page 486). The tree contains an entry for each object that is a content item of at least one structure element and for each content stream containing at least one marked-content sequence that is a content item. The key for each entry is an integer given as the value of the **StructParents** entry in the object (see below). The values of these entries are as follows:

- For an object identified as a content item by means of an object reference (see "PDF Objects as Content Items" on page 494), the value is an indirect reference to the parent structure element.

- For a content stream containing marked-content sequences that are content items, the value is an array of indirect references to the sequences' parent structure elements. The array element corresponding to each sequence is found by using the sequence's marked-content identifier as a zero-based index into the array.

Note: Because marked-content identifiers serve as indices into an array in the structural parent tree, their assigned values should be as small as possible to conserve space in the array.

The **ParentTreeNextKey** entry in the structure tree root holds an integer value greater than any that is currently in use as a key in the structural parent tree. Whenever a new entry is added to the parent tree, it uses the current value of **ParentTreeNextKey** as its key; the value is then incremented to prepare for the next new entry to be added.

To locate the relevant parent tree entry, each object or content stream that is represented in the tree must contain a special dictionary entry, **StructParents** (see Table 8.10). Depending on the type of content item, this entry may appear in the page object of a page containing marked-content sequences, in the stream dictionary of a form or image XObject, in an annotation dictionary, or in any other type of object dictionary that is included as a content item in a structure element. Its value is the integer key under which the entry corresponding to the object is to be found in the structural parent tree.

TABLE 8.10 **Additional dictionary entry for structure element access**

KEY	TYPE	VALUE
StructParents	integer	*(Required for all objects that are structural content items or contain such items; PDF 1.3)* The integer key of this object's entry in the structural parent tree.

For a content item identified by an object reference, the parent structure element can thus be found by using the value of the **StructParents** entry in the item's object dictionary as a retrieval key in the structural parent tree (found in the **ParentTree** entry of the structure tree root). The corresponding value retrieved from the parent tree is a reference to the parent structure element (see Example 8.11).

Example 8.11

```
1 0 obj                       % Parent structure element
   << /Type /StructElem
      …
      /K << /Type /OBJR       % Object reference
            /Pg  2 0 R        % Page containing the form XObject
            /Obj  4 0 R       % Reference to form XObject
         >>
   >>
endobj

2 0 obj                       % Page object
   << /Type /Page
      /Resources  << /XObject << /Fm4  4 0 R >>    % Resource dictionary
                  >>                               %    containing form XObject
      /Contents  3 0 R        % Content stream
      …
   >>
endobj
```

```
3 0 obj                        % Page's content stream
   << /Length ... >>
stream
   …
   /Fm4  Do                    % Paint form XObject
   …
endstream
endobj
4  0 obj                       % Form XObject
   << /Type  /XObject
      /Subtype  /Form
      /Length  …
      /StructParents  6        % Parent tree key
   >>
stream
   …
endstream
endobj
100  0 obj                     % Parent tree (accessed from structure tree root)
   << /Nums [ 0  101 0 R
             1  102 0 R
             …
             6  1 0 R          % Entry for page object 2; points back
             …                 %    to parent structure element
           ]
   >>
endobj
```

For a content item that is a marked-content sequence, the retrieval method is similar but slightly more complicated. Because a marked-content sequence is not an object in its own right, its parent tree key is found in the **StructParents** entry of the page object or other content stream in which the sequence resides. The value retrieved from the parent tree is not a reference to the parent structure element itself, but rather an array of such references—one for each marked-content sequence contained within that content stream. The parent structure element for the given sequence is found by using the sequence's marked-content identifier as an index in this array (see Example 8.12).

Example 8.12

```
1  0  obj                          % Parent structure element
    << /Type  /StructElem
        …
        /Pg  20R                   % Page containing the marked-content sequence
        /K  0                      % Marked-content identifier
    >>
endobj

2  0  obj                          % Page object
    << /Type  /Page
        /Contents  30R             % Content stream
        /StructParents  6          % Parent tree key
        …
    >>
endobj

3  0  obj                          % Page's content stream
    << /Length  …  >>
stream
    …
    /P  <</MCID  0>>               % Start of marked-content sequence
        BDC
            (Here is some text)  TJ
        …
        EMC                        % End of marked-content sequence
    …
endstream
endobj

100  0  obj                        % Parent tree (accessed from structure tree root)
    << /Nums  [  0  1010R
                 1  1020R
                 …
                 6  [10R]          % Entry for page object 2; array element at index 0
                 …                 %    points back to parent structure element
             ]
    >>
endobj
```

Structure Attributes

An application or plug-in extension that processes logical structure can attach additional information, called *attributes*, to any structure element. The attribute information is held in an *attribute object* associated with the structure element. Any dictionary or stream can serve as an attribute object by including an **O** entry (see Table 8.11) identifying the application or plug-in that owns the attribute information; the owner can then add any additional entries it wishes to the object to hold the attributes.

TABLE 8.11 Entry common to all attribute objects

KEY	TYPE	VALUE
O	name	*(Required)* The name of the application or plug-in extension owning the attribute data. The name must conform to the guidelines described in Appendix E.

Any application can attach attributes to any structure element, even one created by another application. Multiple applications can attach attributes to the same structure element; the **A** entry in the structure element dictionary (see Table 8.7 on page 487) can hold either a single attribute object or an array of such objects, together with *revision numbers* for coordinating attributes created by different owners (see "Attribute Revision Numbers" on page 501). An application creating or destroying the second attribute object for a structure element is responsible for converting the value of the **A** entry from a single object to an array or vice versa, as well as for maintaining the integrity of the revision numbers. No inherent order is defined for the attribute objects in an **A** array, but it is considered good form to add new objects at the end of the array so that the first array element is the one belonging to the application that originally created the structure element.

Attribute Classes

If many structure elements share the same set of attribute values, they can be defined as an *attribute class* sharing the identical attribute object. Structure elements refer to the class by name; the association between class names and attribute objects is defined by a dictionary called the *class map*, kept in the **Class-Map** entry of the structure tree root (see Table 8.6 on page 486). Each key in the class map is a name object denoting the name of a class; the corresponding value is an attribute object or an array of such objects. Class names must conform to the guidelines described in Appendix E.

Note: Despite the name, PDF attribute classes are unrelated to the concept of a class in object-oriented programming languages such as Java and C++. Attribute classes are strictly a mechanism for storing attribute information in a more compact form; they have no inheritance properties like those of true object-oriented classes.

The **C** entry in a structure element dictionary (see Table 8.7 on page 487) contains a class name or an array of class names (typically accompanied by revision numbers as well; see "Attribute Revision Numbers," below). For each class named in the **C** entry, the corresponding attribute object or objects are considered to be attached to the given structure element along with those identified in the element's **A** entry.

Attribute Revision Numbers

When an application modifies a structure element or its contents, the change may affect the validity of attribute information attached to that structure element by other applications. A system of *revision numbers* allows applications to detect such changes made by other applications and update their own attribute information accordingly.

A structure element's revision number is kept in the **R** entry in the structure element dictionary (see Table 8.7 on page 487). Initially, the revision number is 0 (the default value if no **R** entry is present); each time an application modifies the structure element or any of its content items, it must signal the change by incrementing the revision number. Note that the revision number is not the same thing as the generation number associated with an indirect object (see Section 3.2.9, "Indirect Objects"); the two are completely separate concepts.

As described below, each attribute object attached to a structure element carries an associated revision number. Each time an attribute object is created or modified, its revision number is set equal to the current value of the structure element's **R** entry. By comparing the attribute object's revision number with that of the structure element, an application can tell whether the contents of the attribute object are still current or whether they have been outdated by more recent changes in the underlying structure element.

Because a single attribute object may be associated with more than one structure element (whose revision numbers may differ), the revision number is not stored directly in the attribute object itself, but rather in the array that associates the attribute object with the structure element. This allows the same attribute object to carry different revision numbers with respect to different structure elements. In the general case, each attribute object in a structure element's **A** array is represented by a pair of array elements, the first containing the attribute object itself and the second the integer revision number associated with it in this structure element. Similarly, the structure element's **C** array contains a pair of elements for each attribute class, the first containing the class name and the second the associated revision number. (Revision numbers equal to 0 can be omitted from both the **A** and **C** arrays; an attribute object or class name that is not followed by an integer array element is understood to have a revision number of 0.)

Note: A structure element's revision number changes only when the structure element itself or any of its content items is modified. Changes in an attached attribute object do not *change the structure element's revision number (though they may cause the attribute object's revision number to be updated to match it).*

Occasionally, an application may make such extensive changes to a structure element that they are likely to invalidate all previous attribute information associated with it. In this case, instead of incrementing the structure element's revision number, the application may choose to delete all unknown attribute objects from its **A** and **C** arrays. These two actions are mutually exclusive: the application should *either* increment the structure element's revision number *or* remove its attribute objects, but not both. Note that any application creating attribute objects must be prepared for the possibility that they may be deleted at any time by another application.

Example of Logical Structure

Example 8.13 shows portions of a PDF file with a simple document structure. The structure tree root (object 300) contains elements with structure types **Chap** (object 301) and **Para** (object 304). The **Chap** element, titled Chapter 1, contains elements with types **Head1** (object 302) and **Para** (object 303). The example also illustrates the structure of a parent tree (object 400) mapping content items back to their parent structure elements, and an ID tree (object 403) mapping element identifiers to the structure elements they denote.

Example 8.13

```
 1  0  obj                                  % Document catalog
    << /Type  /Catalog
        /Pages  100 0 R                      % Page tree
        /StructTreeRoot  300 0 R             % Structure tree root
    >>
 endobj

100  0  obj                                 % Page tree
    << /Type  /Pages
        /Kids [  101 1 R                     % First page object
               102 0 R                       % Second page object
            ]
        /Count  2                            % Page count
    >>
 endobj

101  1  obj                                 % First page object
    << /Type  /Page
        /Parent  100 0 R                     % Parent is the page tree
        /Resources  << /Font  << /F1  6 0 R  % Font resources
                                 /F12  7 0 R
                     >>
                 /ProcSet [/PDF /Text]       % Procedure sets
            >>
        /MediaBox [0  0  612  792]           % Media box
        /Contents  201 0 R                   % Content stream
        /StructParents  0                    % Parent tree key
    >>
 endobj

201  0  obj                                 % Content stream for first page
    << /Length  … >>
 stream
    1  1  1  rg
    0  0  612  792  re  f
    BT                                       % Start of text object

        /Head1  << /MCID  0 >>               % Start of marked-content sequence 0
            BDC
                0  0  0  rg
                /F1  1  Tf
                30  0  0  30  18  732  Tm
                (This is a first level heading. Hello world:)  Tj
                1.1333  TL
                T*
                (goodbye universe.)  Tj
            EMC                              % End of marked-content sequence 0
```

```
        /Para << /MCID 1 >>                    % Start of marked-content sequence 1
            BDC
                /F12 1 Tf
                14 0 0 14 18 660.8 Tm
                (This is the first paragraph, which spans pages. It has four fairly short and \
concise sentences. This is the next to last ) Tj
            EMC                                % End of marked-content sequence 1

        ET                                     % End of text object
    endstream
    endobj

    102 0 obj                                  % Second page object
        << /Type /Page
            /Parent 100 0 R                    % Parent is the page tree
            /Resources << /Font << /F1 6 0 R   % Font resources
                                   /F12 7 0 R
                                >>
                          /ProcSet [/PDF /Text] % Procedure sets
                       >>
            /MediaBox [0 0 612 792]            % Media box
            /Contents 202 0 R                  % Content stream
            /StructParents 1                   % Parent tree key
        >>
    endobj

    202 0 obj                                  % Content stream for second page
        << /Length ... >>
    stream
        1 1 1 rg
        0 0 612 792 re f
        BT                                     % Start of text object

        /Para << /MCID 0 >>                    % Start of marked-content sequence 0
            BDC
                0 0 0 rg
                /F12 1 Tf
                14 0 0 14 18 732 Tm
                (sentence. This is the very last sentence of the first paragraph.) Tj
            EMC                                % End of marked-content sequence 0

        /Para << /MCID 1 >>                    % Start of marked-content sequence 1
            BDC
                /F12 1 Tf
                14 0 0 14 18 570.8 Tm
                (This is the second paragraph. It has four fairly short and concise sentences. \
This is the next to last ) Tj
            EMC                                % End of marked-content sequence 1
```

```
            /Para  << /MCID  2 >>                    % Start of marked-content sequence 2
               BDC
                   1.1429  TL
                   T*
               (sentence.This is the very last sentence of the second paragraph.)  Tj
               EMC                                    % End of marked-content sequence 2

        ET                                           % End of text object
    endstream
    endobj

    300  0  obj                                      % Structure tree root
       << /Type /StructTreeRoot
          /K [  301 0 R                              % Two children: a chapter
                304 0 R                               %    and a paragraph
             ]
          /RoleMap  << /Chap  /Chapter               % Mapping to standard structure types
                       /Head1  /H
                       /Para  /P
                    >>
          /ParentTree  400 0 R                       % Number tree for parent elements
          /ParentTreeNextKey  2                      % Next key to use in parent tree
          /IDTree  403 0 R                           % Name tree for element identifiers
       >>
    endobj

    301  0  obj                                      % Structure element for a chapter
       << /Type  /StructElem
          /S  /Chap
          /ID  (Chap1)                               % Element identifier
          /T  (Chapter 1)                            % Human-readable title
          /P  300 0 R                                % Parent is the structure tree root
          /K [  302 0 R                              % Two children: a section head
                303 0 R                               %    and a paragraph
             ]
       >>
    endobj

    302  0  obj                                      % Structure element for a section head
       << /Type  /StructElem
          /S  /Head1
          /ID  (Sec1.1)                              % Element identifier
          /T  (Section 1.1)                          % Human-readable title
          /P  301 0 R                                % Parent is the chapter
          /Pg  101 1 R                               % Page containing content items
          /K  0                                      % Marked-content sequence 0
       >>
    endobj
```

```
303  0  obj                                    % Structure element for a paragraph
   << /Type /StructElem
      /S /Para
      /ID (Para1)                              % Element identifier
      /P  301 0 R                              % Parent is the chapter
      /Pg  101 1 R                             % Page containing first content item
      /K [ 1                                   % Marked-content sequence 1
            << /Type /MCR                      % Marked-content reference to second item
               /Pg  102 0 R                    % Page containing second item
               /MCID  0                        % Marked-content sequence 0
            >>
         ]
   >>
endobj

304  0  obj                                    % Structure element for another paragraph
   << /Type /StructElem
      /S /Para
      /ID (Para2)                              % Element identifier
      /P  300 0 R                              % Parent is the structure tree root
      /Pg  102 0 R                             % Page containing content items
      /K [1  2]                                % Marked-content sequences 1 and 2
   >>
endobj

400  0  obj                                    % Parent tree
   << /Nums [ 0  401 0 R                       % Parent elements for first page
              1  402 0 R                       % Parent elements for second page
            ]
   >>
endobj

401  0  obj                                    % Array of parent elements for first page
   [ 302 0 R                                   % Parent of marked-content sequence 0
     303 0 R                                   % Parent of marked-content sequence 1
   ]
endobj

402  0  obj                                    % Array of parent elements for second page
   [ 303 0 R                                   % Parent of marked-content sequence 0
     304 0 R                                   % Parent of marked-content sequence 1
     304 0 R                                   % Parent of marked-content sequence 2
   ]
endobj
```

```
403  0  obj                              % ID tree root node
   << /Kids  [404 0 R]  >>               % Reference to leaf node
endobj

404  0  obj                              % ID tree leaf node
   << /Limits   [ (Chap1) (Sec1.3) ]     % Least and greatest keys in tree
      /Names   [ (Chap1)  301 0 R        % Mapping from element identifiers
                 (Sec1.1)  302 0 R       %    to structure elements
                 (Sec1.2)  303 0 R
                 (Sec1.3)  304 0 R
               ]
   >>
endobj
```

8.5 Web Capture

Web Capture is a PDF 1.3 feature that allows information from Internet-based or locally resident HTML, PDF, GIF, JPEG, and ASCII text files to be imported into a PDF file. This feature is implemented in the Adobe Acrobat 4.0 viewer by a Web Capture plug-in extension (sometimes called AcroSpider). The information in the Web Capture data structures enables viewer applications to perform the following operations:

• Save locally and preserve the visual appearance of material from the World Wide Web

• Retrieve additional material from the Web and add it to an existing PDF file

• Update or modify existing material previously captured from the Web

• Find source information for material captured from the Web, such as the URL (if any) from which it was captured

• Find all material in a PDF file that was generated from a given URL

• Find all material in a PDF file that matches a given digital identifier (MD5 hash)

The information needed to perform these operations is recorded in two data structures in the PDF file:

- The *Web Capture information dictionary* holds document-level information related to Web Capture.

- The Web Capture *content database* keeps track of the material retrieved by Web Capture and where it came from, enabling Web Capture to avoid needlessly downloading material that is already present in the file.

The following sections provide a detailed overview of these structures. See Appendix C for information about implementation limits in Web Capture.

Note: The following discussion centers on HTML and GIF files, although Web Capture handles other file types as well.

8.5.1 Web Capture Information Dictionary

The optional **SpiderInfo** entry in the document catalog (see Section 3.6.1, "Document Catalog") holds an optional *Web Capture information dictionary* containing document-level information related to Web Capture. Table 8.12 shows the contents of this dictionary.

TABLE 8.12 Entries in a Web Capture information dictionary

KEY	TYPE	VALUE
V	number	*(Required)* The Web Capture version number. For PDF 1.3, the version number is 1.0.
		Note: This value is a single real number, not a major and minor version number. Thus, for example, a version number of 1.2 would be considered greater than 1.15.
C	array	*(Optional)* An array of indirect references to Web Capture command dictionaries (see "Command Dictionaries" on page 520) describing commands that were used in building the PDF file. The commands appear in the array in the order in which they were executed in building the file.

8.5.2 Content Database

Web Capture retrieves HTML files from URLs and converts them into PDF. The resulting PDF file may contain the contents of multiple HTML pages. Conversely, since HTML pages do not have a fixed size, a single HTML page may give rise to multiple PDF pages. To keep track of the correspondences, Web Capture maintains a *content database* mapping URLs and digital identifiers to PDF objects such as pages and XObjects. By looking up digital identifiers in the database, Web Capture can determine whether newly downloaded content is identical to content already retrieved from a different URL. This allows it to perform optimizations such as storing only one copy of an image that is referenced by multiple HTML pages.

Web Capture's content database is organized into *content sets*. Each content set is a dictionary holding information about a group of related PDF objects generated from the same source data. Content sets are of two subtypes: *page sets* and *image sets*. When Web Capture converts an HTML file into PDF pages, for example, it creates a page set to hold information about the pages. Similarly, when it converts a GIF image into one or more image XObjects, it creates an image set describing those XObjects.

The content set corresponding to a given data source can be accessed in either of two ways:

- By the URL from which it was retrieved

- By a digital identifier generated from the source data itself (see "Digital Identifiers" on page 512)

The **URLS** and **IDS** entries in a PDF document's name dictionary (see Section 3.6.3, "Name Dictionary") contain name trees mapping URLs and digital identifiers, respectively, to Web Capture content sets. Figure 8.1 shows a simple example. An HTML file retrieved from the URL <http://www.adobe.com/> has been converted into three pages in the PDF file. The entry for that URL in the **URLS** name tree points to a page set containing the three pages. Similarly, the **IDS** name tree contains an entry pointing to the same page set, associated with the digital identifier calculated from the HTML source (the string shown in the figure as 904B…1EA2).

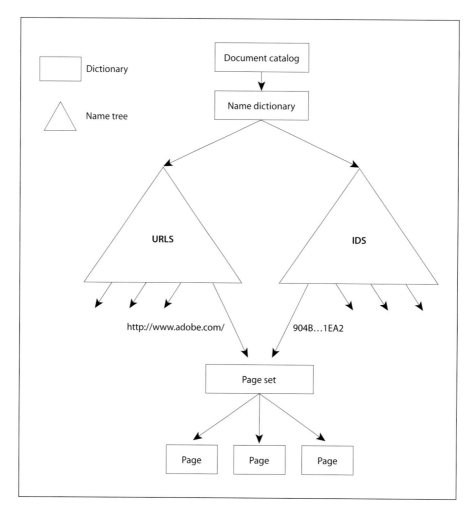

FIGURE 8.1 *Simple Web Capture file structure*

Entries in the **URLS** and **IDS** name trees may refer to an array of content sets instead of just a single content set. The content sets need not have the same subtype, but may include both page sets and image sets. In Figure 8.2, for example, a GIF file has been retrieved from a URL (<http://www.adobe.com/getacro.gif>) and converted into a single PDF page. As in Figure 8.1, a page set has been created to hold information about the new page. However, since the retrieval also resulted in a new image XObject, an image set has also been created. Instead of pointing directly to a single content set, the **URLS** and **IDS** entries point to an array containing both the page set and the image set.

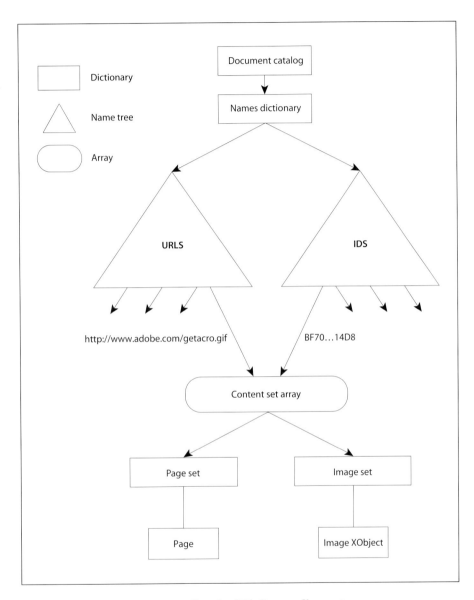

FIGURE 8.2 *Complex Web Capture file structure*

URL Strings

URLs associated with Web Capture content sets must be reduced to a predictable, canonical form before being used as keys in the **URLS** name tree. The following steps describe how to perform this reduction, using terminology from Internet RFCs 1738, *Uniform Resource Locators*, and 1808, *Relative Uniform Resource Locators* (see the Bibliography). This algorithm is relevant for HTTP, FTP, and file URLs:

1. If the URL is relative, make it absolute.

2. If the URL contains one or more number sign characters (#), strip the leftmost number sign and any characters after it.

3. Convert the scheme section to lowercase ASCII.

4. If there is a host section, convert it to lowercase ASCII.

5. If the scheme is file and the host is localhost, strip the host section.

6. If there is a port section and the port is the default port for the given protocol (80 for HTTP or 21 for FTP), strip the port section.

7. If the path section contains dot (.) or double-dot (..) subsequences, transform the path as described in section 4 of RFC 1808.

Note: Because the percent character (%) is "unsafe" according to RFC 1738 and is also the escape character for encoded characters, it is not possible in general to distinguish a URL with unencoded characters from one with encoded characters. For example, it is impossible to decide whether the sequence %00 represents a single encoded null character or a sequence of three unencoded characters. Hence no number of encoding or decoding passes on a URL will ever cause it to reach a stable state. Empirically, URLs embedded in HTML files have unsafe characters encoded with one encoding pass, and Web servers perform one decoding pass on received paths (though CGI scripts are free to make their own decisions). Canonical URLs are thus assumed to have undergone one and only one encoding pass. A URL whose initial encoding state is known can be safely transformed into a URL that has undergone only one encoding pass.

Digital Identifiers

Digital identifiers associated with Web Capture content sets by the **IDS** name tree are generated using the MD5 message-digest algorithm (described in Internet

RFC 1321, *The MD5 Message-Digest Algorithm*; see the Bibliography). The exact data passed to the algorithm depends on the type of content set and the nature of the identifier being calculated.

For a page set, the source data itself is passed to the MD5 algorithm first, followed by strings representing the digital identifiers of any auxiliary data files (such as images) referenced in the source data, in the order in which they are first referenced. (If an auxiliary file is referenced more than once, its identifier is passed only the first time.) This produces a composite identifier representing the visual appearance of the pages in the page set. Two HTML source files that are identical, but for which the referenced images contain different data—for example, if they have been generated by a script or are pointed to by relative URLs—will not produce the same identifier.

Note: *When the source data is taken from a PDF file, the identifier will be generated solely from the contents of that file; there is no auxiliary data. (See also implementation note 98 in Appendix H.)*

A page set can also have a *text identifier*, calculated by applying the MD5 algorithm to just the rendered text present in the source data. For an HTML file, for example, the text identifier is based solely on the text between markup tags; no images are used in the calculation.

For an image set, the digital identifier is calculated by passing the source data for the original image to the MD5 algorithm. For example, the identifier for an image set created from a GIF image is calculated from the contents of the GIF itself.

Unique Name Generation

In generating PDF pages from a data source, Web Capture converts items such as hypertext links and HTML form fields into corresponding named destinations and interactive form fields. These items must have names that do not conflict with those of existing items in the file. Also, when updating the file, Web Capture may need to locate all destinations and fields constructed for a given page set. Accordingly, each destination or field is given a unique name, derived from its original name but constructed so as to avoid conflicts with similarly named items in other page sets.

Note: *As used here, the term* name *refers to a string, not a name object.*

The unique name is formed by appending an encoded form of the page set's digital identifier string to the original name of the destination or field. The identifier string must be encoded to remove characters that have special meaning in destinations and fields. For example, since the period character (.) is used as the field separator in interactive form field names, it must not appear in the identifier portion of the unique name; it is therefore encoded internally as two bytes, 92 and 112, corresponding to the ASCII characters \p. Note that since the backslash character (\) has special meaning for the syntax of string objects, it must be preceded by another backslash when written in the PDF file. For example, if the original digital identifier string were

    alpha.beta

this would be encoded internally as

    alpha\pbeta

and written in the PDF file as

    alpha\\pbeta

Similarly, the null character (character code 0) is encoded internally as the two bytes 92 and 48, corresponding to the ASCII characters \0. If the original digital identifier string were

    alphaØbeta

(where Ø denotes the null character), it would be encoded internally as

    alpha\0beta

and written in the PDF file as

    alpha\\0beta

Finally, the backslash character itself is encoded internally as the two bytes 92 and 92, corresponding to the characters \\. In written form, each of these in turn requires a preceding backslash. Thus the digital identifier string

    alpha\beta

would be encoded internally as

alpha\\beta

and written in the PDF file as

alpha\\\\beta

If the name is used for an interactive form field, there is an additional encoding to ensure uniqueness and compatibility with interactive forms. Each byte in the source string, encoded as described above, is replaced by two bytes in the destination string. The first byte in each pair is 65 (corresponding to the ASCII character A) plus the high-order 4 bits of the source byte; the second byte is 65 plus the low-order 4 bits of the source byte.

8.5.3 Content Sets

A Web Capture *content set* is a dictionary describing a set of PDF objects generated from the same source data. It may include information common to all the objects in the set as well as about the set itself. Table 8.13 shows the contents of this type of dictionary.

TABLE 8.13 Entries common to all content sets

KEY	TYPE	VALUE
Type	name	*(Optional)* The type of PDF object that this dictionary describes; if present, must be **SpiderContentSet** for a Web Capture content set.
S	name	*(Required)* The subtype of content set that this dictionary describes: **SPS** ("Spider page set") A page set **SIS** ("Spider image set") An image set
ID	string	*(Required)* The digital identifier of the content set (see "Digital Identifiers" on page 512). If the content set has been located via the **URLS** name tree, this allows its related entry in the **IDS** name tree to be found.
O	array	*(Required)* An array of indirect references to the objects belonging to the content set. The order of objects in the array is undefined in general, but may be restricted by specific content set subtypes.

SI	dictionary or array	*(Required)* A source information dictionary (see Section 8.5.4, "Source Information"), or an array of such dictionaries, describing the sources from which the objects belonging to the content set were created.
CT	string	*(Optional)* The *content type*, a string characterizing the source from which the objects belonging to the content set were created. The string should conform to the content type specification described in Internet RFC 2045, *Multipurpose Internet Mail Extensions (MIME) Part One: Format of Internet Message Bodies* (see the Bibliography). For example, for a page set consisting of a group of PDF pages created from an HTML file, the content type would be text/html.
TS	date	*(Optional)* A time stamp giving the date and time at which the content set was created.

Page Sets

A *page set* is a content set containing a group of PDF page objects generated from a common source, such as an HTML file. The pages are listed in the **O** array (see Table 8.13) in the same order in which they were initially added to the file. A single page object may not belong to more than one page set. Table 8.14 shows the content set dictionary entries specific to this type of content set.

TABLE 8.14 Additional entries specific to a page set

KEY	TYPE	VALUE
S	name	*(Required)* The subtype of content set that this dictionary describes; must be **SPS** ("Spider page set") for a page set.
T	text string	*(Optional)* The title of the page set, a text string representing it in human-readable form.
TID	string	*(Optional)* A text identifier generated from the text of the page set, as described in "Digital Identifiers" on page 512.

The optional **TID** (text identifier) entry may be used to store an identifier generated from the text of the pages belonging to the page set (see "Digital Identifiers" on page 512). This identifier may be used, for example, to determine whether the text of a document has changed. A text identifier may not be appropriate for some page sets (such as those with no text), and should be omitted in these cases.

Image Sets

An *image set* is a content set containing a group of image XObjects generated from a common source, such as multiple frames of an animated GIF. (Web Capture 4.0 will always generate a single image XObject for a given image.) A single XObject may not belong to more than one image set. Table 8.15 shows the content set dictionary entries specific to this type of content set.

TABLE 8.15   Additional entries specific to an image set

KEY	TYPE	VALUE
S	name	*(Required)* The subtype of content set that this dictionary describes; must be **SIS** ("Spider image set") for an image set.
R	integer or array	*(Required)* The reference counts (see below) for the image XObjects belonging to the image set. For an image set containing a single XObject, the value is simply the integer reference count for that XObject. If the image set contains multiple XObjects, the value is an array of reference counts parallel to the **O** array (see Table 8.13 on page 515); that is, each element in the **R** array holds the reference count for the image XObject at the corresponding position in the **O** array.

Each image XObject in an image set has a reference count indicating the number of PDF pages referring to that XObject. The reference count is incremented whenever Web Capture creates a new page referring to the XObject (including copies of already existing pages) and decremented whenever such a page is destroyed. (The reference count is incremented or decremented only once per page, regardless of the number of times the XObject may be referenced by that same page.) When the reference count reaches 0, it is assumed that there are no remaining pages referring to the XObject, and that it can be removed from the image set's **O** array. (See implementation note 99 in Appendix H.)

8.5.4   Source Information

The **SI** entry in a content set dictionary (see Table 8.13 on page 515) identifies one or more *source information dictionaries* containing information about the locations from which the source data for the content set was retrieved. Table 8.16 shows the contents of this type of dictionary.

TABLE 8.16 **Entries in a source information dictionary**

KEY	TYPE	VALUE
AU	string or dictionary	*(Required)* A string or URL alias dictionary (see "URL Alias Dictionaries," below) identifying the URLs from which the source data was retrieved.
TS	date	*(Optional)* A time stamp giving the most recent date and time at which the content set's contents were known to be up to date with the source data.
E	date	*(Optional)* An expiration stamp giving the date and time at which the content set's contents should be considered out of date with the source data.
S	integer	*(Optional)* A code indicating the type of form submission, if any, by which the source data was accessed (see "Submit-Form Actions" on page 454):
		0 Not accessed via a form submission
		1 Accessed via an HTTP GET form submission
		2 Accessed via an HTTP POST form submission
		Should be present only in source information dictionaries associated with page sets. Default value: 0.
C	dictionary	*(Optional; must be an indirect reference)* A command dictionary (see "Command Dictionaries" on page 520) describing the command that caused the source data to be retrieved. Should be present only in source information dictionaries associated with page sets.

In the simplest case, the content set's **SI** entry just contains a single source information dictionary. However, it is not uncommon for the same source data to be accessible via two or more unrelated URLs. When Web Capture detects such a condition (by comparing digital identifiers), it generates a single content set from the source data, containing just one copy of the relevant PDF pages or image XObjects, but creates multiple source information dictionaries describing the separate ways in which the original source data can be accessed. It then stores an array containing these multiple source information dictionaries as the value of the **SI** entry in the content set dictionary.

A source information dictionary's **AU** (aliased URLs) entry identifies the URLs from which the source data was retrieved. If there is only one such URL, a simple string suffices as the value of this entry. If multiple URLs map to the same location through redirection, the **AU** value is a URL alias dictionary representing them (see "URL Alias Dictionaries," below).

Note: *For file size efficiency, it is recommended that the entire URL alias dictionary (excluding the URL strings) be represented as a direct object, as its internal structure should never be shared or externally referenced.*

The **TS** (time stamp) entry allows each source location associated with a content set to have its own time stamp. This is necessary because the time stamp in the content set dictionary itself (see Table 8.13 on page 515) merely refers to the creation date of the content set. A hypothetical "Update Content Set" command might reset the time stamp in the source information dictionary to the current time if it found the that the source data had not changed since the time stamp was last set.

The **E** (expiration) entry specifies an expiration date for each source location associated with a content set. If the current date and time are later than those specified, the contents of the content set should be considered out of date with the original source.

URL Alias Dictionaries

When a URL is accessed via HTTP, a response header may be returned indicating that the requested data is to be found at a different URL. This *redirection* process may be repeated in turn at the new URL, and can potentially continue indefinitely. It is not uncommon to find multiple URLs that all lead eventually to the same destination through one or more redirections. A *URL alias dictionary* represents such a set of URL chains leading to a common destination. Table 8.17 shows the contents of this type of dictionary.

TABLE 8.17 Entries in a URL alias dictionary

KEY	TYPE	VALUE
U	string	*(Required)* The destination URL to which all of the chains specified by the **C** entry lead.
C	array	*(Optional)* An array of one or more arrays of strings, each representing a chain of URLs leading to the common destination specified by **URL**.

The **C** (chains) entry should be omitted if the URL alias dictionary contains only one URL. If **C** is present, its value is an array of arrays, each representing a chain of URLs leading to the common destination. Within each chain, the URLs are stored as strings in the order in which they occur in the redirection sequence. The common destination (the last URL in a chain) may be omitted, since it is already identified by the **URL** entry. (See implementation note 100 in Appendix H.)

Command Dictionaries

A Web Capture *command dictionary* represents a command executed by Web Capture to retrieve one or more pieces of source data that were used to create new pages or modify existing pages. The entries in this dictionary represent parameters that were originally specified interactively by the user who requested that the Web content be captured. This information is recorded so that the command can subsequently be repeated to update the captured content. Table 8.18 shows the contents of this type of dictionary.

		TABLE 8.18 Entries in a command dictionary
KEY	**TYPE**	**VALUE**
URL	string	*(Required)* The initial URL from which source data was requested.
L	integer	*(Optional)* The number of levels of pages retrieved from the initial URL. Default value: 1.
F	integer	*(Optional)* A set of flags specifying various characteristics of the command (see Table 8.19). Default value: 0.
P	string or stream	*(Optional)* Data that was posted to the URL.
CT	string	*(Optional)* A content type describing the data posted to the URL. Default value: application/x–www–form–urlencoded.
H	string	*(Optional)* Additional HTTP request headers sent to the URL.
S	dictionary	*(Optional)* A command settings dictionary containing settings used in the conversion process (see "Command Settings" on page 522).

The **URL** entry specifies the initial URL for the retrieval command. The **L** (levels) entry specifies the number of levels of pages requested to be retrieved from this URL. If the **L** entry is omitted, its value is assumed to be 1, denoting retrieval of the initial URL only.

The value of the command dictionary's **F** entry is an unsigned 32-bit integer containing flags specifying various characteristics of the command. Bit positions within the flag word are numbered from 1 (low-order) to 32 (high-order). Table 8.19 shows the meanings of the flags; all undefined flag bits are reserved and must be set to 0.

TABLE 8.19   Web Capture command flags

BIT POSITION	NAME	MEANING
1	SameSite	If set, pages were retrieved only from the host specified in the initial URL.
2	SamePath	If set, pages were retrieved only from the path specified in the initial URL (see below).
3	Submit	If set, the command represents a form submission (see below).

The SamePath flag, if set, indicates that pages were retrieved only if they were in the same path specified in the initial URL. A page is considered to be in the same path if its scheme and network location components (as defined in Internet RFC 1808, *Relative Uniform Resource Locators*) match those of the initial URL and its path component matches up to and including the last forward slash (/) character in the initial URL. For example, the URL

    http://www.adobe.com/fiddle/faddle/foo.html

is considered to be in the same path as the initial URL

    http://www.adobe.com/fiddle/initial.html

The comparison is case-insensitive for the scheme and network location components and case-sensitive for the path component.

If the Submit flag is set, the command represents a form submission. If no **P** (posted data) entry is present, the submitted data is encoded in the URL (an HTTP GET form submission). If **P** is present, the command represents an HTTP POST form submission. In this case, the value of the Submit flag is ignored. If the posted data is small enough, it may be represented by a string; for large amounts of data, a stream is recommended, as it can offer compression.

The **CT** (content type) entry is relevant only for POST requests. It describes the content type of the posted data, as described in Internet RFC 2045, *Multipurpose Internet Mail Extensions (MIME), Part One: Format of Internet Message Bodies* (see the Bibliography).

The **H** (headers) entry specifies additional HTTP request headers that were sent in the request for the URL. Each header line in the string is terminated with a carriage return and a line feed. For example:

(Referer: http://frumble.com\015\012From: veeble@frotz.com\015\012)

The HTTP request header format is specified in Internet RFC 2068, *Hypertext Transfer Protocol—HTTP/1.1* (see the Bibliography).

The **S** (settings) entry specifies a command settings dictionary (see the next section). holding settings specific to the conversion engines. If this entry is omitted, default values are assumed. It is recommended that command settings dictionaries be shared by any command dictionaries that use the same settings.

Command Settings

The **S** (settings) entry in a command dictionary contains a *command settings dictionary,* which holds settings for conversion engines used in converting the results of the command to PDF. Table 8.20 shows the contents of this type of dictionary.

KEY	TYPE	VALUE
	TABLE 8.20 Entries in a command settings dictionary	
G	dictionary	*(Optional)* A dictionary containing global conversion engine settings relevant to all conversion engines. If this key is absent, default settings will be used.
C	dictionary	*(Optional)* Settings for specific conversion engines. Each key in this dictionary is the internal name of a conversion engine (see below). The associated value is a dictionary containing the settings associated with that conversion engine. If the settings for a particular conversion engine are not found in the dictionary, default settings will be used.

Each key in the **C** dictionary is the internal name of a conversion engine, which should be a name object of the following form:

/ *company*:*product*:*version*:*contentType*

where

company is the name (or abbreviation) of the company that created the conversion engine.

product is the name of the conversion engine. This field may be left blank, but the trailing colon character is still required.

version is the version of the conversion engine.

contentType is an identifier for the content type that the settings are associated with. This is required because some converters may handle multiple content-types.

For example:

```
/ADBE:H2PDF:1.0:HTML
```

Note that all fields in the internal name are case-sensitive. The *company* field must conform to the naming guidelines described in Appendix E; the values of the other fields are unrestricted, except that they must not contain a colon (:).

Note: *It must be possible to make a deep copy of a command settings dictionary without explicit knowledge of the settings it may contain. To facilitate this operation, the directed graph of PDF objects rooted by the command settings dictionary must be entirely self-contained; that is, it must not contain any object referred to from elsewhere in the PDF file.*

8.5.5 Object Attributes Related to Web Capture

A given page object or image XObject can belong to at most one Web Capture content set, called its *parent content set*. However, the object has no direct pointer to its parent content set; such a pointer might present problems for an application that traces all pointers from an object to determine, for example, what resources the object depends on. Instead, the object's **ID** entry (see Tables 3.17 on page 77 and 4.35 on page 249) contains the digital identifier of the parent content set, which can be used to locate the parent content set via the **IDS** name tree in the document's name dictionary. (If the **IDS** entry for the identifier contains an array of content sets, the parent can be found by searching the array for the content set whose **O** entry includes the child object.)

In the course of creating PDF pages from HTML files, Web Capture frequently scales the contents down to fit on fixed-sized pages. The **PZ** (preferred zoom) entry in a page object (see "Page Objects" on page 77) specifies a magnification factor by which the page can be scaled to undo the downscaling and view the page at its original size. That is, when the page is viewed at the preferred magnification factor, one unit in default user space will correspond to one original source pixel.

8.6 Prepress Support

This section describes features of PDF that support prepress production workflows:

- The specification of page boundaries governing various aspects of the prepress process, such as cropping, bleed, and trimming (Section 8.6.1, "Page Boundaries")

- Information for generating color separations for pages in a document (Section 8.6.2, "Separation Dictionaries")

- Support for the generation of traps to minimize the visual effects of misregistration between multiple colorants (Section 8.6.3, "Trapping Support")

- The Open Prepress Interface (OPI) for creating low-resolution proxies for high-resolution images (Section 8.6.4, "Open Prepress Interface (OPI)")

8.6.1 Page Boundaries

A PDF page may be prepared either for a finished medium, such as a sheet of paper, or as part of a prepress process in which the content of the page is placed on an intermediate medium, such as film or an imposed reproduction plate. In the latter case, it is important to distinguish between the intermediate page and the finished page. The intermediate page may often include additional production-related content, such as bleeds or printer marks, that falls outside the boundaries of the finished page. To handle such cases, a PDF page can define as many as five separate boundaries to control various aspects of the imaging process:

- The *media box* defines the maximum imageable area of the physical medium on which the page is to be printed (equivalent to the PostScript page device parameter **PageSize**). It may include any extended area surrounding the finished page for bleed, printing marks, or other such purposes. Content falling outside this boundary can safely be discarded without affecting the meaning of the PDF file.

• The *crop box* defines the region to which the contents of the page are to be clipped (cropped) when displayed or printed. Unlike the other boxes, the crop box has no defined meaning in terms of physical page geometry or intended use; it merely imposes clipping on the page contents. The default value is the page's media box.

• The *bleed box (PDF 1.3)* defines the region to which the contents of the page should be clipped when output in a production environment. This may include any extra "bleed area" needed to accommodate the physical limitations of cutting, folding, and trimming equipment. The actual printed page may include printing marks that fall outside the bleed box. The default value is the page's crop box.

• The *trim box (PDF 1.3)* defines the intended dimensions of the finished page after trimming. It may be smaller than the media box, to allow for production-related content such as printing instructions, cut marks, or color bars. The default value is the page's crop box.

• The *art box (PDF 1.3)* defines the extent of the page's meaningful content (including potential white space) as intended by the page's creator. The default value is the page's crop box.

These boundaries are specified by the **MediaBox**, **CropBox**, **BleedBox**, **TrimBox**, and **ArtBox** entries, respectively, in the page object dictionary (see Table 3.17 on page 77). All of them are rectangles expressed in default user space units. The crop, bleed, trim, and art boxes should not ordinarily extend beyond the boundaries of the media box; if they do, they will be effectively reduced to their intersection with the media box. Figure 8.3 illustrates the relationships among these boundaries. (The crop box is not shown in the figure because it has no defined relationship with any of the other boundaries.)

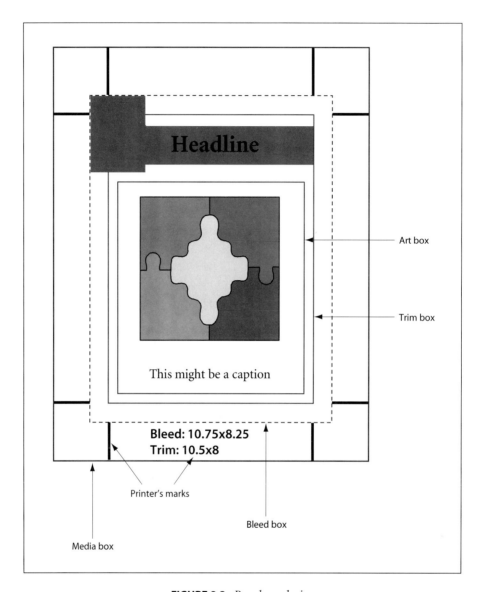

FIGURE 8.3 *Page boundaries*

How the various boundaries are used depends on the purpose to which the page is being put. Typical purposes might include the following:

• *Placing the content of a page in another application.* The art box determines the boundary of the content that is to be placed in the application. Depending on the applicable usage conventions, the placed content may be clipped to either the art box or the bleed box. (For example, a quarter-page advertisement to be placed on a magazine page might be clipped to the art box on the two sides of the ad that face into the middle of the page and to the bleed box on the two sides that bleed over the edge of the page.) The media box and trim box are ignored.

- *Printing a finished page.* This case is typical of desktop or shared page printers, in which the page content is positioned directly on the final output medium. The art box and bleed box are ignored. The trim box, if present, should be the same as the media box.

- *Printing an intermediate page for use in a prepress process.* The art box is ignored. The bleed box defines the boundary of the content to be imaged. The trim box specifies the positioning of the content on the medium; it may also be used to generate cut or fold marks outside the bleed box. Content falling within the media box but outside the bleed box may or may not be imaged, depending on the specific production process being used.

- *Building an imposition of multiple pages on a press sheet.* The art box is ignored. The bleed box defines the clipping boundary of the content to be imaged; content outside the bleed box will be ignored. The trim box specifies the positioning of the page's content within the imposition. Cut and fold marks are typically generated for the imposition as a whole.

In the scenarios above, an application that interprets the bleed, trim, and art boxes for some purpose will typically alter the crop box so as to impose the clipping that those boxes prescribe.

8.6.2 Separation Dictionaries

In high-end printing workflows, pages are ultimately produced as sets of *separations*, one per colorant (see "Separation Color Spaces" on page 183). Ordinarily, each page in a PDF file is treated as a composite page that paints graphics objects using all the process colorants and perhaps some spot colorants as well. In other words, all separations for a page are generated from a single PDF description of that page.

However, in some workflows, pages are pre-separated prior to the generation of the PDF file. In a pre-separated PDF file, the separations for a page are described as separate page objects, each painting only a single colorant (usually specified as

DeviceGray). When this is done, additional information is needed to identify the actual colorant associated with each separation and to group together the page objects representing all the separations for a given page. This information is contained in a *separation dictionary (PDF 1.3)* in the **SeparationInfo** entry of each page object (see "Page Objects" on page 77). Table 8.21 shows the contents of this type of dictionary.

TABLE 8.21 Entries in a separation dictionary

KEY	TYPE	VALUE
Pages	array	(Required) An array of indirect references to page objects representing separations of the same document page. One of the page objects in the array must be the one with which this separation dictionary is associated, and all of them must have separation dictionaries (**SeparationInfo** entries) containing **Pages** arrays identical to this one.
DeviceColorant	name or string	(Required) The name of the device colorant to be used in rendering this separation, such as Cyan or PANTONE 35 CV.
ColorSpace	array	(Optional) An array defining a color space of type **Separation** or **DeviceN** (see "Separation Color Spaces" on page 183 and "DeviceN Color Spaces" on page 186). This provides additional information about the color specified by **DeviceColorant**—in particular, the alternate color space and tint transform function that would be used to represent the colorant as a process color. This information enables a viewer application to preview the separation in a color that approximates the device colorant.

The value of **DeviceColorant** must match the space's colorant name (if it is a **Separation** space) or be one of the space's colorant names (if it is a **DeviceN** space). |

8.6.3 Trapping Support

On devices such as offset printing presses, which mark multiple colorants on a single sheet of physical medium, mechanical limitations of the device can cause imprecise alignment, or *misregistration*, between colorants. This can produce unwanted visual artifacts such as brightly colored gaps or bands around the edges of printed objects. In high-quality reproduction of color documents, such artifacts are commonly avoided by creating an overlap, called a *trap*, between areas of adjacent color.

Figure 8.4 shows an example of trapping. The light and medium grays represent two different colorants, which are used to paint the background and the glyph denoting the letter A. The first figure shows the intended result, with the two colorants properly registered. The second figure shows what happens when the colorants are misregistered. In the third figure, traps have been overprinted along the boundaries, obscuring the artifacts caused by the misregistration. (For emphasis, the traps are shown here in dark gray; in actual practice, their color would be similar to one of the adjoining colors.)

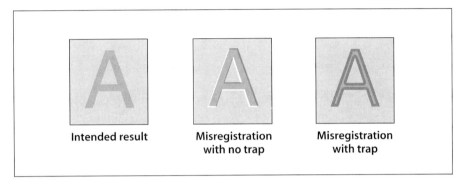

FIGURE 8.4 *Trapping example*

Trapping can be implemented by the application generating a PDF file, by some intermediate application that adds traps to a PDF document, or by the raster image processor (RIP) that produces final output. In the last two cases, the trapping process is controlled by a set of *trapping instructions*, which define two kinds of information:

- *Trapping zones* within which traps should be created

- *Trapping parameters* specifying the nature of the traps within each zone

Trapping zones and trapping parameters are discussed fully in sections 6.3.2 and 6.3.3, respectively, of the *PostScript Language Reference*, Third Edition. Trapping instructions are not directly specified in a PDF file (as they are in a PostScript file); instead, they are specified in a *job ticket* that accompanies the PDF file or can be embedded within it. Job tickets are described in Adobe Technical Note #5620, *Portable Job Ticket Format*.

When trapping is performed prior to the production of final output, the resulting traps are placed in the PDF file for subsequent use. The traps themselves are described as a content stream in a trap network annotation (see below). The stream dictionary can include additional entries describing the method that was used to produce the traps and other information about their appearance.

Trap Network Annotations

A complete set of traps generated for a given page under a specified set of trapping instructions is called a *trap network (PDF 1.3)*. It is a form XObject containing graphics objects for painting the required traps on the page. A page may have more than one trap network based on different trapping instructions, presumably intended for different output devices. All of the trap networks for a given page are contained in a single *trap network annotation* (see Section 7.4, "Annotations"). There can be at most one trap network annotation per page, which must be the last element in the page's **Annots** array (see "Page Objects" on page 77). This ensures that the trap network is printed after all of the page's other contents. (See implementation note 101 in Appendix H.)

Individual trap networks associated with the page are defined as appearance streams in the **N** (normal) subdictionary of the trap network annotation's appearance dictionary (see Section 7.4.4, "Appearance Streams"). The keys used to identify trap networks within the **N** subdictionary are arbitrary. The trap network annotation's **AS** (appearance state) entry designates one of them as the *current trap network*, the one that the annotation is currently displaying or printing.

*Note: The trap network annotation's appearance dictionary may include **R** (rollover) or **D** (down) subdictionaries, but appearances defined in either of these subdictionaries will never be printed.*

Like all annotations, a trap network annotation is defined by an annotation dictionary (see Section 7.4.1, "Annotation Dictionaries"); its annotation type is **TrapNet**. The **AP** (appearances), **AS** (appearance state), and **F** (flags) entries (which ordinarily are optional) must be present, with the Print and ReadOnly flags set and all others clear (see Section 7.4.2, "Annotation Flags"). Table 8.22 shows the additional annotation dictionary entries specific to this type of annotation.

TABLE 8.22 **Additional entries specific to a trap network annotation**

KEY	TYPE	VALUE
Subtype	name	*(Required)* The type of annotation that this dictionary describes; must be **TrapNet** for a trap network annotation.
Version	array	*(Required)* An unordered array of all objects present in the page description at the time the trap networks were generated and that, if changed, could affect the appearance of the page. The array must include the following objects:
		• All content streams identified in the page object's **Contents** entry (see "Page Objects" on page 77)
		• All resource objects (other than procedure sets) in the page's resource dictionary (see Section 3.7.2, "Resource Dictionaries")
		• All resource objects (other than procedure sets) in the resource dictionaries of any form XObjects on the page (see Section 4.9, "Form XObjects")
		• All OPI dictionaries associated with XObjects on the page (see Section 8.6.4, "Open Prepress Interface (OPI)")
AnnotStates	array	*(Required)* An array of name objects representing the appearance states (value of the **AS** entry) for annotations associated with the page. The appearance states must be listed in the same order as the annotations in the page's **Annots** array (see "Page Objects" on page 77). For an annotation with no **AS** entry, the corresponding array element should be null. No appearance state should be included for the trap network annotation itself.
FontFauxing	array	*(Optional)* An array of font dictionaries representing fonts that were "fauxed" (replaced by substitute fonts) during the generation of trap networks for the page.

The **Version** array identifies elements of the page's content that might be changed by an editing application and thus invalidate its trap networks. Because there is only one **Version** array per trap network annotation (and thus per page), any application generating a new trap network must also verify the validity of existing trap networks by enumerating the objects identified in the array and verifying that the results exactly match the array's current contents. Any trap networks found to be invalid must be regenerated. (See implementation note 102 in Appendix H.)

Trap Network Appearances

Each entry in the **N** (normal) subdictionary of a trap network annotation's appearance dictionary holds an appearance stream defining a trap network associated with the given page. Like all appearances, a trap network is a stream object defining a form XObject (see Section 4.9, "Form XObjects"). The body of the stream contains the graphics objects needed to paint the traps making up the trap network. Its dictionary entries include, besides the standard entries for a form dictionary, the additional entries shown in Table 8.23.

TABLE 8.23 Additional entries specific to a trap network appearance stream

KEY	TYPE	VALUE
PCM	name	*(Required)* The name of the process color model that was assumed when this trap network was created; equivalent to the PostScript page device parameter **ProcessColorModel** (see Section 6.2.5 of the *PostScript Language Reference*, Third Edition). Valid values are **DeviceGray**, **DeviceRGB**, **DeviceCMYK**, **DeviceCMY**, **DeviceRGBK**, and **DeviceN**.
SeparationColorNames	array	*(Optional)* An array of names identifying the colorants that were assumed when this network was created; equivalent to the PostScript page device parameter of the same name (see Section 6.2.5 of the *PostScript Language Reference*, Third Edition). Colorants implied by the process color model **PCM** are available automatically and need not be explicitly declared. If this entry is absent, the colorants implied by **PCM** are assumed.
TrapRegions	array	*(Optional)* An array of indirect references to **TrapRegion** objects defining the page's trapping zones and the associated trapping parameters, as described in Adobe Technical Note #5620, *Portable Job Ticket Format*. These references are to objects comprising portions of a job ticket that is embedded in the PDF file. When the trapping zones and parameters are defined by an external job ticket (or by some other means), this entry is absent.
TrapStyles	text string	*(Optional)* A human-readable text string that applications can use to describe this trap network to the user (for example, to allow switching between trap networks).

*Note: Separated PDF files (see Section 8.7.1, "Separation Information") cannot be trapped, because traps are defined along the borders between different colors and a separated file uses only one color. Separation must therefore occur after trapping, not before. An application separating a trapped PDF file is responsible for calculating new **Version** arrays for the separated trap networks.*

8.6.4   Open Prepress Interface (OPI)

The workflow in a prepress environment often involves multiple applications in areas such as graphic design, page layout, word processing, photo manipulation, and document construction. As pieces of the final document are moved from one application to another, it is useful to separate the data of high-resolution images, which can be quite large—in some cases, many times the size of the rest of the document combined—from that of the document itself. The *Open Prepress Interface (OPI)* is a mechanism, originally developed by Aldus® Corporation, for creating low-resolution placeholders, or *proxies*, for such high-resolution images. The proxy typically consists of a downsampled version of the full-resolution image, to be used for screen display and proofing. Before the document is printed, it passes through a filter known as an *OPI server*, which replaces the proxies with the original full-resolution images.

In PostScript programs, OPI proxies are defined by PostScript code surrounded by special *OPI comments*, which specify such information as the placement and cropping of the image and adjustments to its size, rotation, color, and other attributes. In PDF, proxies are embedded in a document as image or form XObjects with an associated *OPI dictionary (PDF 1.2)* containing the same information conveyed in PostScript by the OPI comments. Two versions of OPI are supported, versions 1.3 and 2.0. In OPI 1.3, a proxy consisting of a single image, with no changes in the graphics state, may be represented as an image XObject; otherwise it must be a form XObject. In OPI 2.0, the proxy always entails changes in the graphics state and hence must be represented as a form XObject. (See implementation notes 103 and 104 in Appendix H.)

An XObject representing an OPI proxy must contain an **OPI** entry in its image or form dictionary (see Tables 4.35 on page 249 and 4.41 on page 264). The value of this entry is an *OPI version dictionary* (Table 8.24) identifying the version of OPI to which the proxy corresponds. This dictionary consists of a single entry, whose key is the name **1.3** or **2.0** and whose value is the OPI dictionary defining the proxy's OPI attributes.

TABLE 8.24 Entry in an OPI version dictionary

KEY	TYPE	VALUE
version number	dictionary	*(Required; PDF 1.2)* An OPI dictionary specifying the attributes of this proxy (see Tables 8.25 and 8.26). The key for this entry must be the name **1.3** or **2.0**, identifying the version of OPI to which the proxy corresponds.

Note: *As in any other PDF dictionary, the key in an OPI version dictionary must be a name object. The OPI version dictionary would thus be written in the PDF file in either the form*

        `<< /1.3 d 0 R >>`   % OPI 1.3 dictionary

or

        `<< /2.0 d 0 R >>`   % OPI 2.0 dictionary

where d is the object number of the corresponding OPI dictionary.

Tables 8.25 and 8.26 describe the contents of the OPI dictionaries for OPI 1.3 and OPI 2.0, respectively, along with the corresponding PostScript OPI comments. The dictionary entries are listed in the order in which the corresponding OPI comments should appear in a PostScript program. Complete details on the meanings of these entries and their effects on OPI servers can be found in *OPI: Open Prepress Interface Specification 1.3* (available from Adobe) and Adobe Technical Note #5660, *Open Prepress Interface (OPI) Specification, Version 2.0*.

TABLE 8.25 Entries in a version 1.3 OPI dictionary

KEY	TYPE	OPI COMMENT	VALUE
Type	name		*(Optional)* The type of PDF object that this dictionary describes; if present, must be **OPI** for an OPI dictionary.
Version	number		*(Required)* The version of OPI to which this dictionary refers; must be the number 1.3 (not the name 1.3, as in an OPI version dictionary).
F	file specification	%ALDImageFilename	*(Required)* The external file containing the image corresponding to this proxy. (See implementation note 105 in Appendix H.)

ID	string	%ALDImageID	*(Optional)* An identifying string denoting the image.
Comments	text string	%ALDObjectComments	*(Optional)* A human-readable comment, typically containing instructions or suggestions to the operator of the OPI server on how to handle the image.
Size	array	%ALDImageDimensions	*(Required)* An array of two integers of the form [*pixelsWide pixelsHigh*] specifying the dimensions of the image in pixels.
CropRect	rectangle	%ALDImageCropRect	*(Required)* An array of four integers of the form [*left top right bottom*] specifying the portion of the image to be used.
CropFixed	array	%ALDImageCropFixed	*(Optional)* An array with the same form and meaning as **CropRect**, but expressed in real numbers instead of integers. Default value: **CropRect**.

Position	array	%ALDImagePosition	*(Required)* An array of eight numbers of the form
			
			    $[ll_x\ \ ll_y\ \ ul_x\ \ ul_y\ \ ur_x\ \ ur_y\ \ lr_x\ \ lr_y]$
			
			specifying the location on the page of the cropped image, where (ll_x, ll_y) are the user space coordinates of the lower-left corner, (ul_x, ul_y) those of the upper-left corner, (ur_x, ur_y) those of the upper-right corner, and (lr_x, lr_y) those of the lower-right corner. The specified coordinates must define a parallelogram; that is, they must satisfy the conditions
			
			    $ul_x - ll_x = ur_x - lr_x$
			
			and
			
			    $ul_y - ll_y = ur_y - lr_y$
			
			The combination of **Position** and **CropRect** determines the image's scaling, rotation, reflection, and skew.

Resolution	array	%ALDImageResolution	*(Optional)* An array of two numbers of the form

[*horizRes vertRes*]

specifying the resolution of the image in samples per inch.

ColorType	name	%ALDImageColorType	*(Optional)* The type of color specified by the **Color** entry. Valid values are Process, Spot, and Separation. Default value: Spot.

Color	array	%ALDImageColor	*(Optional)* An array of four numbers and a string of the form

[*C M Y K colorName*]

specifying the value and name of the color in which the image is to be rendered. The values of *C*, *M*, *Y*, and *K* must all be in the range 0.0 to 1.0. Default value: [0.0 0.0 0.0 1.0 (Black)].

Tint	number	%ALDImageTint	*(Optional)* A number in the range 0.0 to 1.0 specifying the concentration of the color specified by **Color** in which the image is to be rendered. Default value: 1.0.
Overprint	boolean	%ALDImageOverprint	*(Optional)* A flag specifying whether the image is to overprint (*true*) or knock out (*false*) underlying marks on other separations. Default value: *false.*
ImageType	array	%ALDImageType	*(Optional)* An array of two integers of the form

[*samples bits*]

specifying the number of samples per pixel and bits per sample in the image.

GrayMap	array	%ALDImageGrayMap	*(Optional)* An array of 2^n integers in the range 0 to 65,535 (where *n* is the number of bits per sample) recording changes made to the brightness or contrast of the image.
Transparency	boolean	%ALDImageTransparency	*(Optional)* A flag specifying whether white pixels in the image are to be treated as transparent. Default value: *true.*

Tags	array	%ALDImageAsciiTag<*NNN*>	*(Optional)* An array of pairs of the form

$$[tagNum_1\ tagText_1\ ...\ tagNum_n\ tagText_n]$$

where each *tagNum* is an integer representing a TIFF tag number and each *tagText* is a string representing the corresponding ASCII tag value.

TABLE 8.26 Entries in a version 2.0 OPI dictionary

KEY	TYPE	OPI COMMENT	VALUE
Type	name		*(Optional)* The type of PDF object that this dictionary describes; if present, must be **OPI** for an OPI dictionary.
Version	number		*(Required)* The version of OPI to which this dictionary refers; must be the number 2 or 2.0 (not the name 2.0, as in an OPI version dictionary).
F	file specification	%%ImageFilename	*(Required)* The external file containing the low-resolution proxy image. (See implementation note 105 in Appendix H.)
MainImage	string	%%MainImage	*(Optional)* The pathname of the file containing the full-resolution image corresponding to this proxy, or any other identifying string that uniquely identifies the full-resolution image.
Tags	array	%%TIFFASCIITag	*(Optional)* An array of pairs of the form $$[tagNum_1\ tagText_1\ ...\ tagNum_n\ tagText_n]$$ where each *tagNum* is an integer representing a TIFF tag number and each *tagText* is a string or an array of strings representing the corresponding ASCII tag value.
Size	array	%%ImageDimensions	*(Optional; see note below)* An array of two numbers of the form [*width height*] specifying the dimensions of the image in pixels.
CropRect	rectangle	%%ImageCropRect	*(Optional; see note below)* An array of four numbers of the form [*left top right bottom*] specifying the portion of the image to be used.

| | | | Note: The **Size** and **CropRect** entries should either both be present or both absent. If present, they must satisfy the conditions |

$$0 \leq \textit{left} < \textit{right} \leq \textit{width}$$

and

$$0 \leq \textit{top} < \textit{bottom} \leq \textit{height}$$

(Note that in this coordinate space, the positive y axis extends vertically downward; hence the requirement that top < bottom.)

| **Overprint** | boolean | %%ImageOverprint | *(Optional)* A flag specifying whether the image is to overprint (*true*) or knock out (*false*) underlying marks on other separations. Default value: *false*. |

| **Inks** | name or array | %%ImageInks | *(Optional)* A name object or array specifying the colorants to be applied to the image. The value may be the name full_color or registration or an array of the form |

$$[\text{/monochrome } \textit{name}_1 \textit{ tint}_1 \text{ ... } \textit{name}_n \textit{ tint}_n]$$

where each *name* is a string representing the name of a colorant and each *tint* is a real number in the range 0.0 to 1.0 specifying the concentration of that colorant to be applied.

| **IncludedImageDimensions** | | | |
| | array | %%IncludedImageDimensions | *(Optional)* An array of two integers of the form |

$$[\textit{pixelsWide } \textit{pixelsHigh}]$$

specifying the dimensions of the included image in pixels.

| **IncludedImageQuality** | | | |
| | number | %%IncludedImageQuality | *(Optional)* A number indicating the quality of the included image. Valid values are 1, 2, and 3. |

APPENDIX A

Operator Summary

THIS APPENDIX LISTS all the operators used in PDF content streams, in alphabetical order. Corresponding PostScript language operators are given in Table A.1 only when they are exact or near-exact equivalents of the PDF operators. Table and page references are to the place in the text where each operator is introduced.

TABLE A.1   PDF content stream operators

OPERATOR	POSTSCRIPT EQUIVALENT	DESCRIPTION	TABLE	PAGE
b	closepath, fill, stroke	Close, fill, and stroke path using nonzero winding number rule	4.10	152
B	fill, stroke	Fill and stroke path using nonzero winding number rule	4.10	152
b*	closepath, eofill, stroke	Close, fill, and stroke path using even-odd rule	4.10	152
B*	eofill, stroke	Fill and stroke path using even-odd rule	4.10	152
BDC		*(PDF 1.2)* Begin marked-content sequence with property list	8.5	480
BI		Begin in-line image object	4.38	260
BMC		*(PDF 1.2)* Begin marked-content sequence	8.5	480
BT		Begin text object	5.4	286
BX		*(PDF 1.1)* Begin compatibility section	3.19	84
c	curveto	Append curved segment to path (three control points)	4.9	149
cm	concat	Concatenate matrix to current transformation matrix	4.7	143
cs	setcolorspace	*(PDF 1.1)* Set color space for nonstroking operations	4.21	198
CS	setcolorspace	*(PDF 1.1)* Set color space for stroking operations	4.21	198

d	**setdash**	Set line dash pattern	4.7	143
d0	**setcharwidth**	Set glyph width in Type 3 font	5.10	303
d1	**setcachedevice**	Set glyph width and bounding box in Type 3 font	5.10	303
Do		Invoke named XObject	4.34	243
DP		*(PDF 1.2)* Define marked-content point with property list	8.5	480
EI		End in-line image object	4.38	260
EMC		*(PDF 1.2)* End marked-content sequence	8.5	480
ET		End text object	5.4	286
EX		*(PDF 1.1)* End compatibility section	3.19	84
f	**fill**	Fill path using nonzero winding number rule	4.10	152
F	**fill**	Fill path using nonzero winding number rule (obsolete)	4.10	152
f*	**eofill**	Fill path using even-odd rule	4.10	152
g	**setgray**	Set gray level for nonstroking operations	4.21	199
G	**setgray**	Set gray level for stroking operations	4.21	199
gs		*(PDF 1.2)* Set parameters from graphics state parameter dictionary	4.7	143
h	**closepath**	Close subpath	4.9	149
i	**setflat**	Set flatness tolerance	4.7	143
ID		Begin in-line image data	4.38	260
j	**setlinejoin**	Set line join style	4.7	143
J	**setlinecap**	Set line cap style	4.7	143
k	**setcmykcolor**	Set *CMYK* color for nonstroking operations	4.21	199
K	**setcmykcolor**	Set *CMYK* color for stroking operations	4.21	199
l	**lineto**	Append straight line segment to path	4.9	149
m	**moveto**	Begin new subpath	4.9	149
M	**setmiterlimit**	Set miter limit	4.7	143
MP		*(PDF 1.2)* Define marked-content point	8.5	480
n		End path without filling or stroking	4.10	152
q	**gsave**	Save graphics state	4.7	142

Q	grestore	Restore graphics state	4.7	142
re		Append rectangle to path	4.9	149
rg	setrgbcolor	Set *RGB* color for nonstroking operations	4.21	199
RG	setrgbcolor	Set *RGB* color for stroking operations	4.21	199
ri		Set color rendering intent	4.7	143
s	closepath, stroke	Close and stroke path	4.10	152
S	stroke	Stroke path	4.10	152
sc	setcolor	*(PDF 1.1)* Set color for nonstroking operations	4.21	198
SC	setcolor	*(PDF 1.1)* Set color for stroking operations	4.21	199
scn	setcolor	*(PDF 1.2)* Set color for nonstroking operations (**ICCBased** and special color spaces)	4.21	199
SCN	setcolor	*(PDF 1.2)* Set color for stroking operations (**ICCBased** and special color spaces)	4.21	199
sh	shfill	*(PDF 1.3)* Paint area defined by shading pattern	4.24	214
T*		Move to start of next text line	5.5	288
Tc		Set character spacing	5.2	280
Td		Move text position	5.5	287
TD		Move text position and set leading	5.5	287
Tf	selectfont	Set text font and size	5.2	280
Tj	show	Show text	5.6	289
TJ		Show text, allowing individual glyph positioning	5.6	289
TL		Set text leading	5.2	280
Tm		Set text matrix and text line matrix	5.5	288
Tr		Set text rendering mode	5.2	280
Ts		Set text rise	5.2	280
Tw		Set word spacing	5.2	280
Tz		Set horizontal text scaling	5.2	280
v	curveto	Append curved segment to path (initial point replicated)	4.9	149
w	setlinewidth	Set line width	4.7	143
W	clip	Set clipping path using nonzero winding number rule	4.11	156

W*	eoclip	Set clipping path using even-odd rule	4.11	156
y	curveto	Append curved segment to path (final point replicated)	4.9	149
'		Move to next line and show text	5.6	289
"		Set word and character spacing, move to next line, and show text	5.6	289

APPENDIX B

Operators in Type 4 Functions

THIS APPENDIX SUMMARIZES the PostScript operators that can appear in a type 4 function, as discussed in Section 3.9.4, "Type 4 (PostScript Calculator) Functions." For details on these operators, see the *PostScript Language Reference*, Third Edition.

B.1 Arithmetic Operators

num_1 num_2	**add**	sum	Return num_1 plus num_2
num_1 num_2	**div**	$quotient$	Return num_1 divided by num_2
int_1 int_2	**idiv**	$quotient$	Return int_1 divided by int_2 as an integer
int_1 int_2	**mod**	$remainder$	Return remainder after dividing int_1 by int_2
num_1 num_2	**mul**	$product$	Return num_1 times num_2
num_1 num_2	**sub**	$difference$	Return num_1 minus num_2
num_1	**abs**	num_2	Return absolute value of num_1
num_1	**neg**	num_2	Return negative of num_1
num_1	**ceiling**	num_2	Return ceiling of num_1
num_1	**floor**	num_2	Return floor of num_1
num_1	**round**	num_2	Round num_1 to nearest integer
num_1	**truncate**	num_2	Remove fractional part of num_1
num	**sqrt**	$real$	Return square root of num
num den	**atan**	$angle$	Return arc tangent of num/den in degrees
$angle$	**cos**	$real$	Return cosine of $angle$ degrees
$angle$	**sin**	$real$	Return sine of $angle$ degrees
$base$ $exponent$	**exp**	$real$	Raise $base$ to $exponent$ power
num	**ln**	$real$	Return natural logarithm (base e)
num	**log**	$real$	Return common logarithm (base 10)
num	**cvi**	int	Convert to integer
num	**cvr**	$real$	Convert to real

B.2   Relational, Boolean, and Bitwise Operators

any_1 any_2 **eq** *bool*		Test equal
any_1 any_2 **ne** *bool*		Test not equal
num_1 num_2 **ge** *bool*		Test greater than or equal
num_1 num_2 **gt** *bool*		Test greater than
num_1 num_2 **le** *bool*		Test less than or equal
num_1 num_2 **lt** *bool*		Test less than
$bool_1|int_1$ $bool_2|int_2$ **and** $bool_3|int_3$		Perform logical|bitwise and
$bool_1|int_1$ **not** $bool_2|int_2$		Perform logical|bitwise not
$bool_1|int_1$ $bool_2|int_2$ **or** $bool_3|int_3$		Perform logical|bitwise inclusive or
$bool_1|int_1$ $bool_2|int_2$ **xor** $bool_3|int_3$		Perform logical|bitwise exclusive or
– **true** *true*		Return boolean value *true*
– **false** *false*		Return boolean value *false*
int_1 *shift* **bitshift** int_2		Perform bitwise shift of int_1 (positive is left)

B.3   Conditional Operators

bool {*expr*} **if** –	Execute *expr* if *bool* is *true*
bool {$expr_1$} {$expr_2$} **ifelse** –	Execute $expr_1$ if *bool* is *true*, $expr_2$ if *false*

B.4   Stack Operators

any **pop** –	Discard top element
any_1 any_2 **exch** any_2 any_1	Exchange top two elements
any **dup** *any any*	Duplicate top element
any_1 ... any_n n **copy** any_1 ... any_n any_1 ... any_n	Duplicate top n elements
any_n ... any_0 n **index** any_n ... any_0 any_n	Duplicate arbitrary element
any_{n-1} ... any_0 n j **roll** $any_{(j-1)\bmod n}$ $\cdots$ any_0 any_{n-1} ... $any_{j\bmod n}$	Roll n elements up j times

APPENDIX C

Implementation Limits

IN GENERAL, PDF does not restrict the size or quantity of things described in the file format, such as numbers, arrays, images, and so on. However, a PDF viewer application running on a particular processor and in a particular operating environment does have such limits. If a viewer application attempts to perform an action that exceeds one of the limits, it will display an error.

PostScript interpreters also have implementation limits, listed in Appendix B of the *PostScript Language Reference*, Third Edition. It is possible to construct a PDF file that does not violate viewer application limits but will not print on a PostScript printer. Keep in mind that these limits vary according to the PostScript language level, interpreter version, and the amount of memory available to the interpreter.

This appendix describes typical limits for Acrobat. These limits fall into two main classes:

- *Architectural limits*. The hardware on which a viewer application executes imposes certain constraints. For example, an integer is usually represented in 32 bits, limiting the range of allowed integers. In addition, the design of the software imposes other constraints, such as a limit to the number of elements in an array or string.

- *Memory limits*. The amount of memory available to a viewer application limits the number of memory-consuming objects that can be held simultaneously.

PDF itself has one architectural limit: Because ten digits are allocated to byte offsets, the size of a file is limited to 10^{10} bytes (approximately 10 gigabytes).

C.1 General Implementation Limits

Table C.1 describes the architectural limits for Acrobat viewer applications running on 32-bit machines. Because Acrobat implementations are subject to these limits, applications producing PDF files are strongly advised to remain within them. Note, however, that memory limits will often be exceeded before architectural limits (such as the limit on the number of indirect objects) are reached.

TABLE C.1 Architectural limits

QUANTITY	LIMIT	DESCRIPTION
integer	2,147,483,647	Largest integer value; equal to $2^{31} - 1$.
	−2,147,483,648	Smallest integer value; equal to -2^{31}.
real	±32,767	Largest and smallest real values (approximate).
	±1/ 65,536	Nonzero real values closest to 0 (approximate); equal to $\pm 10^{-38}$. Values closer than these are automatically converted to 0.
	5	Significant number of decimal digits of precision in fractional part (approximate).
array	8191	Maximum length of an array, in elements.
dictionary	4095	Maximum capacity of a dictionary, in entries.
string	65,535	Maximum length of a string, in bytes.
name	127	Maximum length of a name, in bytes.
indirect object	8,388,607	Maximum number of indirect objects in a PDF file.
CID	65,535	Maximum value of a CID (character identifier).
DeviceN components	8	Maximum number of colorants or color components in a **DeviceN** color space.

Acrobat has some additional architectural limits:

• Thumbnail images may be no larger than 106 by 106 samples, and should be created at one-eighth scale for 8.5-by-11-inch and A4-size pages.

• The minimum allowed page size in Acrobat 4.0 is 3 by 3 units in default user space (approximately 0.04 by 0.04 inch); the maximum is 14,400 by 14,400 units (200 by 200 inches). (See implementation note 106 in Appendix H.)

- The magnification factor of a view is constrained to be between approximately 8 percent and 3200 percent. These limits are not fixed; they vary with the size of the page being displayed, as well as with the size of the pages previously viewed within the file.

- When Acrobat reads a PDF file with a damaged or missing cross-reference table, it attempts to rebuild the table by scanning all the objects in the file. However, the generation numbers of deleted entries are lost if the cross-reference table is missing or severely damaged. Reconstruction fails if any object identifiers do not appear at the start of a line or if the **endobj** keyword does not appear at the start of a line. Also, reconstruction fails if a stream contains a line beginning with the word **endstream**, aside from the required **endstream** that delimits the end of the stream.

Memory limits cannot be characterized as precisely as architectural limits can, because the amount of available memory and the ways in which it is allocated vary from one product to another. Memory is automatically reallocated from one use to another when necessary: when more memory is needed for a particular purpose, it can be taken away from memory allocated to another purpose if that memory is currently unused or its use is nonessential (a cache, for example). Also, data is often saved to a temporary file when memory is limited. Because of this behavior, it is not possible to state limits for such items as the number of pages, number of text annotations or hypertext links on a page, number of graphics objects on a page, or number of fonts on a page or in a document.

C.2 Implementation Limits Affecting Web Capture

The data structures constructed by the Web Capture plug-in extension (*PDF 1.3*; see Section 8.5) depend on the maximum length of an array, k, which is 8191 elements in the Acrobat 4 implementation.

- A content set array can associate at most k content sets with a given name.

- A content set can reference at most k objects.

- There can be at most k source information dictionaries associated with a single content set.

- An URL alias dictionary can contain at most k chains, and each chain can contain at most k URLs.

- A maximum of k command dictionaries can be stored in the **C** array of the Web Capture information dictionary.

- There can be at most $k \div 2$ entries in the **C** dictionary of a Web Capture command settings dictionary.

APPENDIX D

Character Sets and Encodings

THIS APPENDIX LISTS the character sets and encodings that are assumed to be predefined in any PDF viewer application. Only simple fonts, encompassing Latin text and some symbols, are described here. See "Predefined CMaps" on page 320 for a list of predefined CMaps for CID-keyed fonts.

Section D.1, "Latin Character Set and Encodings," describes the entire character set for Adobe's standard Latin-text fonts. This is the character set supported by the Times, Helvetica, and Courier font families, which are among the 14 standard predefined fonts (see "The Standard Type 1 Fonts" on page 296). For each named character, an octal character code is given in four different encodings: **StandardEncoding**, **MacRomanEncoding**, **WinAnsiEncoding**, and **PDFDocEncoding** (see Table D.1). Unencoded characters are indicated by a dash (—).

Section D.2, "Expert Set and MacExpertEncoding," describes the so-called "expert" character set, which contains additional characters useful for sophisticated typography, such as small capitals, ligatures, and fractions. For each named character, an octal character code is given in **MacExpertEncoding**. Note that the built-in encoding in an expert font program is usually different from **MacExpertEncoding**.

Sections D.3, "Symbol Set and Encoding," and D.4, "ZapfDingbats Set and Encoding," describe the character sets and built-in encodings for the Symbol and ZapfDingbats font programs, which are among the standard 14 predefined fonts. These fonts have built-in encodings that are unique to each font. (The characters for ZapfDingbats are ordered by code instead of by name, since the names in that font are meaningless.)

TABLE D.1   Latin-text encodings

ENCODING	DESCRIPTION
StandardEncoding	Adobe standard Latin-text encoding. This is the built-in encoding defined in Type 1 Latin-text font programs (but generally not in TrueType font programs). PDF does not have a predefined encoding named **StandardEncoding**. However, it is useful to describe this encoding, since a font's built-in encoding can be used as the base encoding from which differences are specified in an encoding dictionary.
MacRomanEncoding	Mac OS standard encoding for Latin text in western European languages. PDF has a predefined encoding named **MacRomanEncoding** that can be used with both Type 1 and TrueType fonts.
WinAnsiEncoding	Windows code page 1252, often called the "Windows ANSI" encoding. This is the standard Windows encoding for Latin text in western European languages. PDF has a predefined encoding named **WinAnsiEncoding** that can be used with both Type 1 and TrueType fonts.
PDFDocEncoding	Encoding for text strings in a PDF document *outside* the document's content streams. This is one of two encodings (the other being Unicode) that can be used to represent text strings; see Section 3.8.1, "Text Strings." PDF does not have a predefined encoding named **PDFDocEncoding**; it is not customary to use this encoding to show text from fonts.
MacExpertEncoding	An encoding for use with expert fonts—ones containing the expert character set. PDF has a predefined encoding named **MacExpertEncoding**. Despite its name, it is not a platform-specific encoding; however, only certain fonts have the appropriate character set for use with this encoding. No such fonts are among the standard 14 predefined fonts.

D.1 Latin Character Set and Encodings

CHAR	NAME	STD	MAC	WIN	PDF	CHAR	NAME	STD	MAC	WIN	PDF
		CHAR CODE (OCTAL)						CHAR CODE (OCTAL)			
A	A	101	101	101	101	Œ	OE	352	316	214	226
Æ	AE	341	256	306	306	Ó	Oacute	—	356	323	323
Á	Aacute	—	347	301	301	Ô	Ocircumflex	—	357	324	324
Â	Acircumflex	—	345	302	302	Ö	Odieresis	—	205	326	326
Ä	Adieresis	—	200	304	304	Ò	Ograve	—	361	322	322
À	Agrave	—	313	300	300	Ø	Oslash	351	257	330	330
Å	Aring	—	201	305	305	Õ	Otilde	—	315	325	325
Ã	Atilde	—	314	303	303	P	P	120	120	120	120
B	B	102	102	102	102	Q	Q	121	121	121	121
C	C	103	103	103	103	R	R	122	122	122	122
Ç	Ccedilla	—	202	307	307	S	S	123	123	123	123
D	D	104	104	104	104	Š	Scaron	—	—	212	227
E	E	105	105	105	105	T	T	124	124	124	124
É	Eacute	—	203	311	311	Þ	Thorn	—	—	336	336
Ê	Ecircumflex	—	346	312	312	U	U	125	125	125	125
Ë	Edieresis	—	350	313	313	Ú	Uacute	—	362	332	332
È	Egrave	—	351	310	310	Û	Ucircumflex	—	363	333	333
Ð	Eth	—	—	320	320	Ü	Udieresis	—	206	334	334
€	Euro[1]	—	—	200	240	Ù	Ugrave	—	364	331	331
F	F	106	106	106	106	V	V	126	126	126	126
G	G	107	107	107	107	W	W	127	127	127	127
H	H	110	110	110	110	X	X	130	130	130	130
I	I	111	111	111	111	Y	Y	131	131	131	131
Í	Iacute	—	352	315	315	Ý	Yacute	—	—	335	335
Î	Icircumflex	—	353	316	316	Ÿ	Ydieresis	—	331	237	230
Ï	Idieresis	—	354	317	317	Z	Z	132	132	132	132
Ì	Igrave	—	355	314	314	Ž	Zcaron[2]	—	—	216	231
J	J	112	112	112	112	a	a	141	141	141	141
K	K	113	113	113	113	á	aacute	—	207	341	341
L	L	114	114	114	114	â	acircumflex	—	211	342	342
Ł	Lslash	350	—	—	225	´	acute	302	253	264	264
M	M	115	115	115	115	ä	adieresis	—	212	344	344
N	N	116	116	116	116	æ	ae	361	276	346	346
Ñ	Ntilde	—	204	321	321	à	agrave	—	210	340	340
O	O	117	117	117	117	&	ampersand	046	046	046	046

CHAR	NAME	CHAR CODE (OCTAL)				CHAR	NAME	CHAR CODE (OCTAL)			
		STD	MAC	WIN	PDF			STD	MAC	WIN	PDF
å	aring	—	214	345	345	ê	ecircumflex	—	220	352	352
∧	asciicircum	136	136	136	136	ë	edieresis	—	221	353	353
~	asciitilde	176	176	176	176	è	egrave	—	217	350	350
*	asterisk	052	052	052	052	8	eight	070	070	070	070
@	at	100	100	100	100	…	ellipsis	274	311	205	203
ã	atilde	—	213	343	343	—	emdash	320	321	227	204
b	b	142	142	142	142	–	endash	261	320	226	205
\	backslash	134	134	134	134	=	equal	075	075	075	075
|	bar	174	174	174	174	ð	eth	—	—	360	360
{	braceleft	173	173	173	173	!	exclam	041	041	041	041
}	braceright	175	175	175	175	¡	exclamdown	241	301	241	241
[	bracketleft	133	133	133	133	f	f	146	146	146	146
]	bracketright	135	135	135	135	fi	fi	256	336	—	223
˘	breve	306	371	—	030	5	five	065	065	065	065
¦	brokenbar	—	—	246	246	fl	fl	257	337	—	224
•	bullet[3]	267	245	225	200	ƒ	florin	246	304	203	206
c	c	143	143	143	143	4	four	064	064	064	064
ˇ	caron	317	377	—	031	/	fraction	244	332	—	207
ç	ccedilla	—	215	347	347	g	g	147	147	147	147
¸	cedilla	313	374	270	270	ß	germandbls	373	247	337	337
¢	cent	242	242	242	242	`	grave	301	140	140	140
ˆ	circumflex	303	366	210	032	>	greater	076	076	076	076
:	colon	072	072	072	072	«	guillemotleft[4]	253	307	253	253
,	comma	054	054	054	054	»	guillemotright[4]	273	310	273	273
©	copyright	—	251	251	251	‹	guilsinglleft	254	334	213	210
¤	currency[1]	250	333	244	244	›	guilsinglright	255	335	233	211
d	d	144	144	144	144	h	h	150	150	150	150
†	dagger	262	240	206	201	˝	hungarumlaut	315	375	—	034
‡	daggerdbl	263	340	207	202	-	hyphen[5]	055	055	055	055
°	degree	—	241	260	260	i	i	151	151	151	151
¨	dieresis	310	254	250	250	í	iacute	—	222	355	355
÷	divide	—	326	367	367	î	icircumflex	—	224	356	356
$	dollar	044	044	044	044	ï	idieresis	—	225	357	357
˙	dotaccent	307	372	—	033	ì	igrave	—	223	354	354
ı	dotlessi	365	365	—	232	j	j	152	152	152	152
e	e	145	145	145	145	k	k	153	153	153	153
é	eacute	—	216	351	351	l	l	154	154	154	154

CHAR	NAME	STD	MAC	WIN	PDF	CHAR	NAME	STD	MAC	WIN	PDF
<	less	074	074	074	074	q	q	161	161	161	161
¬	logicalnot	—	302	254	254	?	question	077	077	077	077
ł	lslash	370	—	—	233	¿	questiondown	277	300	277	277
m	m	155	155	155	155	"	quotedbl	042	042	042	042
¯	macron	305	370	257	257	„	quotedblbase	271	343	204	214
−	minus	—	—	—	212	"	quotedblleft	252	322	223	215
μ	mu	—	265	265	265	"	quotedblright	272	323	224	216
×	multiply	—	—	327	327	'	quoteleft	140	324	221	217
n	n	156	156	156	156	'	quoteright	047	325	222	220
9	nine	071	071	071	071	‚	quotesinglbase	270	342	202	221
ñ	ntilde	—	226	361	361	'	quotesingle	251	047	047	047
#	numbersign	043	043	043	043	r	r	162	162	162	162
o	o	157	157	157	157	®	registered	—	250	256	256
ó	oacute	—	227	363	363	°	ring	312	373	—	036
ô	ocircumflex	—	231	364	364	s	s	163	163	163	163
ö	odieresis	—	232	366	366	š	scaron	—	—	232	235
œ	oe	372	317	234	234	§	section	247	244	247	247
˛	ogonek	316	376	—	035	;	semicolon	073	073	073	073
ò	ograve	—	230	362	362	7	seven	067	067	067	067
1	one	061	061	061	061	6	six	066	066	066	066
½	onehalf	—	—	275	275	/	slash	057	057	057	057
¼	onequarter	—	—	274	274		space[6]	040	040	040	040
¹	onesuperior	—	—	271	271	£	sterling	243	243	243	243
ª	ordfeminine	343	273	252	252	t	t	164	164	164	164
º	ordmasculine	353	274	272	272	þ	thorn	—	—	376	376
ø	oslash	371	277	370	370	3	three	063	063	063	063
õ	otilde	—	233	365	365	¾	threequarters	—	—	276	276
p	p	160	160	160	160	³	threesuperior	—	—	263	263
¶	paragraph	266	246	266	266	˜	tilde	304	367	230	037
(	parenleft	050	050	050	050	™	trademark	—	252	231	222
)	parenright	051	051	051	051	2	two	062	062	062	062
%	percent	045	045	045	045	²	twosuperior	—	—	262	262
.	period	056	056	056	056	u	u	165	165	165	165
·	periodcentered	264	341	267	267	ú	uacute	—	234	372	372
‰	perthousand	275	344	211	213	û	ucircumflex	—	236	373	373
+	plus	053	053	053	053	ü	udieresis	—	237	374	374
±	plusminus	—	261	261	261	ù	ugrave	—	235	371	371

CHAR	NAME	CHAR CODE (OCTAL)				CHAR	NAME	CHAR CODE (OCTAL)			
		STD	MAC	WIN	PDF			STD	MAC	WIN	PDF
_	underscore	137	137	137	137	ÿ	ydieresis	—	330	377	377
v	v	166	166	166	166	¥	yen	245	264	245	245
w	w	167	167	167	167	z	z	172	172	172	172
x	x	170	170	170	170	ž	zcaron[2]	—	—	236	236
y	y	171	171	171	171	0	zero	060	060	060	060
ý	yacute	—	—	375	375						

1. In PDF 1.3, the Euro character was added to the Adobe standard Latin character set. It is encoded as 200 in **WinAnsiEncoding** and 240 in **PDFDocEncoding**, assigning codes that were previously unused. Apple changed the Mac OS Latin-text encoding for code 333 from the currency character to the Euro character. However, this incompatible change has *not* been reflected in PDF's **MacRomanEncoding**, which continues to map code 333 to currency. If the Euro character is desired, an encoding dictionary can be used to specify this single difference from **MacRomanEncoding**.

2. In PDF 1.3, the existing Zcaron and zcaron characters were added to **WinAnsiEncoding** as the previously unused codes 216 and 236.

3. In **WinAnsiEncoding**, all unused codes greater than 40 map to the bullet character. However, only code 225 is specifically assigned to the bullet character; other codes are subject to future reassignment.

4. The character names guillemotleft and guillemotright are misspelled. The correct spelling for this punctuation character is *guillemet*. However, the misspelled names are the ones actually used in the fonts and encodings containing these characters.

5. The hyphen character is also encoded as 255 in **WinAnsiEncoding**. The meaning of this duplicate code is "soft hyphen," but it is typographically the same as hyphen.

6. The space character is also encoded as 312 in **MacRomanEncoding** and as 240 in **WinAnsiEncoding**. The meaning of this duplicate code is "nonbreaking space," but it is typographically the same as space.

D.2　Expert Set and MacExpertEncoding

CHAR	NAME	CODE	CHAR	NAME	CODE
Æ	AEsmall	276	J	Jsmall	152
Á	Aacutesmall	207	K	Ksmall	153
Â	Acircumflexsmall	211	Ł	Lslashsmall	302
´	Acutesmall	047	L	Lsmall	154
Ä	Adieresissmall	212	¯	Macronsmall	364
À	Agravesmall	210	M	Msmall	155
Å	Aringsmall	214	N	Nsmall	156
A	Asmall	141	Ñ	Ntildesmall	226
Ã	Atildesmall	213	Œ	OEsmall	317
˘	Brevesmall	363	ó	Oacutesmall	227
B	Bsmall	142	ô	Ocircumflexsmall	231
ˇ	Caronsmall	256	ö	Odieresissmall	232
Ç	Ccedillasmall	215	˛	Ogoneksmall	362
¸	Cedillasmall	311	ò	Ogravesmall	230
ˆ	Circumflexsmall	136	ø	Oslashsmall	277
C	Csmall	143	o	Osmall	157
¨	Dieresissmall	254	õ	Otildesmall	233
˙	Dotaccentsmall	372	P	Psmall	160
D	Dsmall	144	Q	Qsmall	161
É	Eacutesmall	216	°	Ringsmall	373
Ê	Ecircumflexsmall	220	R	Rsmall	162
Ë	Edieresissmall	221	š	Scaronsmall	247
È	Egravesmall	217	S	Ssmall	163
E	Esmall	145	Þ	Thornsmall	271
Ð	Ethsmall	104	˜	Tildesmall	176
F	Fsmall	146	T	Tsmall	164
`	Gravesmall	140	Ú	Uacutesmall	234
G	Gsmall	147	Û	Ucircumflexsmall	236
H	Hsmall	150	Ü	Udieresissmall	237
˝	Hungarumlautsmall	042	ù	Ugravesmall	235
í	Iacutesmall	222	U	Usmall	165
î	Icircumflexsmall	224	V	Vsmall	166
ï	Idieresissmall	225	W	Wsmall	167
ì	Igravesmall	223	X	Xsmall	170
I	Ismall	151	ý	Yacutesmall	264

CHAR	NAME	CODE	CHAR	NAME	CODE
Ÿ	Ydieresissmall	330	4	fouroldstyle	064
Y	Ysmall	171	4	foursuperior	335
ž	Zcaronsmall	275	/	fraction	057
z	Zsmall	172	-	hyphen	055
&	ampersandsmall	046	-	hypheninferior	137
a	asuperior	201	-	hyphensuperior	321
b	bsuperior	365	i	isuperior	351
¢	centinferior	251	l	lsuperior	361
¢	centoldstyle	043	m	msuperior	367
¢	centsuperior	202	9	nineinferior	273
:	colon	072	9	nineoldstyle	071
₡	colonmonetary	173	9	ninesuperior	341
,	comma	054	n	nsuperior	366
,	commainferior	262	.	onedotenleader	053
,	commasuperior	370	⅛	oneeighth	112
$	dollarinferior	266	1	onefitted	174
$	dollaroldstyle	044	½	onehalf	110
$	dollarsuperior	045	1	oneinferior	301
d	dsuperior	353	1	oneoldstyle	061
8	eightinferior	245	¼	onequarter	107
8	eightoldstyle	070	1	onesuperior	332
8	eightsuperior	241	⅓	onethird	116
e	esuperior	344	o	osuperior	257
¡	exclamdownsmall	326	(	parenleftinferior	133
!	exclamsmall	041	(	parenleftsuperior	050
ff	ff	126	)	parenrightinferior	135
ffi	ffi	131	)	parenrightsuperior	051
ffl	ffl	132	.	period	056
fi	fi	127	.	periodinferior	263
–	figuredash	320	·	periodsuperior	371
⅝	fiveeighths	114	¿	questiondownsmall	300
5	fiveinferior	260	?	questionsmall	077
5	fiveoldstyle	065	r	rsuperior	345
5	fivesuperior	336	Rp	rupiah	175
fl	fl	130	;	semicolon	073
4	fourinferior	242	⅞	seveneighths	115

CHAR	NAME	CODE	CHAR	NAME	CODE
7	seveninferior	246	—	threequartersemdash	075
7	sevenoldstyle	067	3	threesuperior	334
7	sevensuperior	340	t	tsuperior	346
6	sixinferior	244	..	twodotenleader	052
6	sixoldstyle	066	2	twoinferior	252
6	sixsuperior	337	2	twooldstyle	062
	space	040	2	twosuperior	333
s	ssuperior	352	⅔	twothirds	117
⅜	threeeighths	113	0	zeroinferior	274
3	threeinferior	243	o	zerooldstyle	060
3	threeoldstyle	063	0	zerosuperior	342
¾	threequarters	111			

D.3 Symbol Set and Encoding

CHAR	NAME	CODE	CHAR	NAME	CODE
A	Alpha	101	↔	arrowboth	253
B	Beta	102	⇔	arrowdblboth	333
X	Chi	103	⇓	arrowdbldown	337
Δ	Delta	104	⇐	arrowdblleft	334
E	Epsilon	105	⇒	arrowdblright	336
H	Eta	110	⇑	arrowdblup	335
€	Euro	240	↓	arrowdown	257
Γ	Gamma	107	—	arrowhorizex	276
ℑ	Ifraktur	301	←	arrowleft	254
I	Iota	111	→	arrowright	256
K	Kappa	113	↑	arrowup	255
Λ	Lambda	114		arrowvertex	275
M	Mu	115	*	asteriskmath	052
N	Nu	116		bar	174
Ω	Omega	127	β	beta	142
O	Omicron	117	{	braceleft	173
Φ	Phi	106	}	braceright	175
Π	Pi	120	⎧	bracelefttp	354
Ψ	Psi	131	⎨	braceleftmid	355
ℜ	Rfraktur	302	⎩	braceleftbt	356
P	Rho	122	⎫	bracerighttp	374
Σ	Sigma	123	⎬	bracerightmid	375
T	Tau	124	⎭	bracerightbt	376
Θ	Theta	121	⎪	braceex	357
Υ	Upsilon	125	[	bracketleft	133
ϒ	Upsilon1	241	]	bracketright	135
Ξ	Xi	130	⎡	bracketlefttp	351
Z	Zeta	132	⎢	bracketleftex	352
ℵ	aleph	300	⎣	bracketleftbt	353
α	alpha	141	⎤	bracketrighttp	371
&	ampersand	046	⎥	bracketrightex	372
∠	angle	320	⎦	bracketrightbt	373
⟨	angleleft	341	•	bullet	267
⟩	angleright	361	↵	carriagereturn	277
≈	approxequal	273	χ	chi	143

CHAR	NAME	CODE	CHAR	NAME	CODE
⊗	circlemultiply	304	∫	integralbt	365
⊕	circleplus	305	∩	intersection	307
♣	club	247	ι	iota	151
:	colon	072	κ	kappa	153
,	comma	054	λ	lambda	154
≅	congruent	100	<	less	074
©	copyrightsans	343	≤	lessequal	243
©	copyrightserif	323	∧	logicaland	331
°	degree	260	¬	logicalnot	330
δ	delta	144	∨	logicalor	332
♦	diamond	250	◊	lozenge	340
÷	divide	270	−	minus	055
·	dotmath	327	′	minute	242
8	eight	070	μ	mu	155
∈	element	316	×	multiply	264
…	ellipsis	274	9	nine	071
∅	emptyset	306	∉	notelement	317
ε	epsilon	145	≠	notequal	271
=	equal	075	⊄	notsubset	313
≡	equivalence	272	ν	nu	156
η	eta	150	#	numbersign	043
!	exclam	041	ω	omega	167
∃	existential	044	ϖ	omega1	166
5	five	065	ο	omicron	157
ƒ	florin	246	1	one	061
4	four	064	(	parenleft	050
/	fraction	244	)	parenright	051
γ	gamma	147	⎛	parenlefttp	346
∇	gradient	321	⎜	parenleftex	347
>	greater	076	⎝	parenleftbt	350
≥	greaterequal	263	⎞	parenrighttp	366
♥	heart	251	⎟	parenrightex	367
∞	infinity	245	⎠	parenrightbt	370
∫	integral	362	∂	partialdiff	266
⌠	integraltp	363	%	percent	045
⎮	integralex	364	.	period	056

CHAR	NAME	CODE	CHAR	NAME	CODE
⊥	perpendicular	136	~	similar	176
φ	phi	146	6	six	066
φ	phi1	152	/	slash	057
π	pi	160		space	040
+	plus	053	♠	spade	252
±	plusminus	261	϶	suchthat	047
∏	product	325	Σ	summation	345
⊂	propersubset	314	τ	tau	164
⊃	propersuperset	311	∴	therefore	134
∝	proportional	265	θ	theta	161
ψ	psi	171	ϑ	theta1	112
?	question	077	3	three	063
√	radical	326	™	trademarksans	344
	radicalex	140	™	trademarkserif	324
⊆	reflexsubset	315	2	two	062
⊇	reflexsuperset	312	_	underscore	137
®	registersans	342	∪	union	310
®	registerserif	322	∀	universal	042
ρ	rho	162	υ	upsilon	165
″	second	262	℘	weierstrass	303
;	semicolon	073	ξ	xi	170
7	seven	067	0	zero	060
σ	sigma	163	ζ	zeta	172
ς	sigma1	126			

D.4 ZapfDingbats Set and Encoding

CHAR	NAME	CODE	CHAR	NAME	CODE	CHAR	NAME	CODE	CHAR	NAME	CODE
	space	040		a30	103		a65	146		a109	253
	a1	041		a31	104		a66	147		a120	254
	a2	042		a32	105		a67	150		a121	255
	a202	043		a33	106		a68	151		a122	256
	a3	044		a34	107		a69	152		a123	257
	a4	045		a35	110		a70	153		a124	260
	a5	046		a36	111		a71	154		a125	261
	a119	047		a37	112		a72	155		a126	262
	a118	050		a38	113		a73	156		a127	263
	a117	051		a39	114		a74	157		a128	264
	a11	052		a40	115		a203	160		a129	265
	a12	053		a41	116		a75	161		a130	266
	a13	054		a42	117		a204	162		a131	267
	a14	055		a43	120		a76	163		a132	270
	a15	056		a44	121		a77	164		a133	271
	a16	057		a45	122		a78	165		a134	272
	a105	060		a46	123		a79	166		a135	273
	a17	061		a47	124		a81	167		a136	274
	a18	062		a48	125		a82	170		a137	275
	a19	063		a49	126		a83	171		a138	276
	a20	064		a50	127		a84	172		a139	277
	a21	065		a51	130		a97	173		a140	300
	a22	066		a52	131		a98	174		a141	301
	a23	067		a53	132		a99	175		a142	302
	a24	070		a54	133		a100	176		a143	303
	a25	071		a55	134		a101	241		a144	304
	a26	072		a56	135		a102	242		a145	305
	a27	073		a57	136		a103	243		a146	306
	a28	074		a58	137		a104	244		a147	307
	a6	075		a59	140		a106	245		a148	310
	a7	076		a60	141		a107	246		a149	311
	a8	077		a61	142		a108	247		a150	312
	a9	100		a62	143		a112	250		a151	313
	a10	101		a63	144		a111	251		a152	314
	a29	102		a64	145		a110	252		a153	315

CHAR	NAME	CODE	CHAR	NAME	CODE	CHAR	NAME	CODE	CHAR	NAME	CODE
❺	a154	316	↗	a192	332	➡	a176	346	⧑	a184	363
❻	a155	317	⇀	a166	333	◗	a177	347	↘	a197	364
❼	a156	320	➔	a167	334	➡	a178	350	⇒	a185	365
❽	a157	321	→	a168	335	⇨	a179	351	↗	a194	366
❾	a158	322	→	a169	336	⇨	a193	352	↙	a198	367
❿	a159	323	⇢	a170	337	⇐	a180	353	↠	a186	370
➔	a160	324	⇛	a171	340	⇒	a199	354	↗	a195	371
→	a161	325	➡	a172	341	⇨	a181	355	⇥	a187	372
↔	a163	326	➤	a173	342	⇨	a200	356	↤	a188	373
↕	a164	327	➤	a162	343	⇨	a182	357	⇥	a189	374
↘	a196	330	➤	a174	344	⇨	a201	361	⇥	a190	375
➔	a165	331	➡	a175	345	⊃	a183	362	⇒	a191	376

APPENDIX E

PDF Name Registry

THIS APPENDIX DISCUSSES a registry, maintained for developers by Adobe Systems, that contains private names and formats used by PDF producers or Acrobat plug-in extensions.

Acrobat enables third parties to add private data to PDF documents and to add plug-in extensions that change viewer behavior based on this data. However, Acrobat users have certain expectations when opening a PDF document, no matter what plug-ins are available. PDF enforces certain restrictions on private data in order to meet these expectations.

A PDF producer or Acrobat viewer plug-in extension may define new types of action, destination, annotation, security, and file system handlers. If a user opens a PDF document and the plug-in that implements the new type of object is unavailable, the viewer will behave as described in Appendix H.

A PDF producer or Acrobat plug-in extension may also add keys to any PDF object that is implemented as a dictionary, except the trailer dictionary. In addition, a PDF producer or Acrobat plug-in may create tags that indicate the role of marked-content operators *(PDF 1.2)*, as described in Section 8.4.2, "Marked Content."

To avoid conflicts with third-party names and with future versions of PDF, Adobe maintains a registry for certain private names and formats. Developers must only add private data that conforms to the registry rules. The registry includes three classes:

• *First class*—names and data formats that are of value to a wide range of developers. All names defined in any version of the PDF specification are first-class names. Plug-in extensions that are publicly available should often use first-class names for their private data. First-class names and data formats must be registered with Adobe and will be made available for all developers to use. To submit a private name and format for consideration as first-class, contact Adobe at either of the following addresses:

Adobe Solutions Network
Adobe Systems Incorporated
345 Park Avenue
San Jose, CA 95110-2704

<acrodevsup@adobe.com>

- *Second class*—names that are applicable to a specific developer. (Adobe does not register second-class data formats.) Adobe distributes second-class names by registering developer-specific prefixes, which must be used as the first characters in the names of all private data added by the developer. Adobe will not register the same prefix to two different developers, thereby ensuring that different developers' second-class names will not conflict. Each developer must ensure that it does not itself use the same name in conflicting ways. Contact Adobe (at either of the addresses listed above) to request a prefix for second-class names.

- *Third class*—names that can be used only in files that will never be seen by other third parties, because they may conflict with third-class names defined by others. Third-class names all begin with a specific prefix reserved by Adobe for private plug-in extensions. This prefix, which is XX, must be used as the first characters in the names of all private data added by the developer. It is not necessary to contact Adobe to register third-class names.

Note: *New keys for a document's information dictionary (which the trailer points to) or a thread information dictionary (in the I entry of the thread dictionary) need not be registered.*

APPENDIX F

Linearized PDF

A LINEARIZED PDF FILE is one that has been organized in a special way to enable efficient incremental access in a network environment. The file is valid PDF in all respects, and is compatible with all existing viewers and other PDF applications. Enhanced viewer applications can recognize that a PDF file has been linearized and can take advantage of that organization (as well as added "hint" information) to enhance viewing performance.

The Linearized PDF file organization is an optional feature available beginning in PDF 1.2. Its primary goal is to achieve the following behavior:

- When a document is opened, display the first page as quickly as possible. The first page to be viewed can be an arbitrary page of the document, not necessarily page 0 (though opening at page 0 is most common).

- When the user requests another page of an open document (for example, by going to the next page or by following a link to an arbitrary page), display that page as quickly as possible.

- When data for a page is delivered over a slow channel, display the page incrementally as it arrives. To the extent possible, display the most useful data first.

- Permit user interaction, such as following a link, to be performed even before the entire page has been received and displayed.

This behavior should be achieved for documents of arbitrary size. The total number of pages in the document should have little or no effect on the user-perceived performance of viewing any particular page.

The primary focus of Linearized PDF is optimized viewing of read-only PDF documents. It is intended that the Linearized PDF will be generated once and read many times. Incremental update is still permitted, but the resulting PDF is no longer linearized and subsequently will be treated as ordinary PDF. Linearizing it again may require reprocessing the entire file; see Section F.4.6, "Accessing an Updated File," for details.

Linearized PDF requires two additions to the PDF specification:

* Rules for the ordering of objects in the PDF file

* Additional data structures, called *hint tables*, that enable efficient navigation within the document

Both of these additions are relatively simple to describe; however, using them effectively requires a deeper understanding of their purpose. Consequently, this appendix goes considerably beyond a simple specification of these PDF extensions, to include background, motivation, and strategies.

* Section F.1, "Background and Assumptions," provides background information about the properties of the World Wide Web that are relevant to the design of Linearized PDF.

* Section F.2, "Linearized PDF Document Structure," specifies the file format and object-ordering requirements of Linearized PDF.

* Section F.3, "Hint Tables," specifies the detailed representation of the hint tables.

* Section F.4, "Access Strategies," outlines strategies for accessing Linearized PDF over a network, which in turn determine the optimal way to organize the PDF file itself.

The reader is assumed to be familiar with the basic architecture of the Web, including terms such as URL, HTTP, and MIME.

F.1 Background and Assumptions

The principal problem addressed by the Linearized PDF design is the access of
PDF documents through the World Wide Web. This environment has the following important properties:

- The access protocol (HTTP) is a transaction consisting of a request and a response. The client presents a request in the form of a URL, and the server sends
  a response consisting of one or more MIME-tagged data blocks.

- After a transaction has completed, obtaining more data requires a new request-
  response transaction. The connection between client and server does not ordinarily persist beyond the end of a transaction, although some implementations
  may attempt to cache the open connection in order to expedite subsequent
  transactions with the same server.

- Round-trip delay can be significant. A request-response transaction can take
  up to several seconds, independent of the amount of data requested.

- The data rate may be limited. A typical bottleneck is a slow modem link between the client and the Internet service provider.

These properties are generally shared by other wide-area network architectures
besides the Web. Also, CD-ROMs share some of these properties, since they have
relatively slow seek times and limited data rates compared to magnetic media.
The remainder of this appendix focuses on the Web.

There are some additional properties of the HTTP protocol that are relevant to
the problem of accessing PDF files efficiently. These properties may not all be
shared by other protocols or network environments.

- When a PDF file is initially accessed (such as by following a URL hyperlink
  from some other document), the file type is not known to the client. Therefore,
  the client initiates a transaction to retrieve the entire document and then
  inspects the MIME tag of the response as it arrives. Only at that point is the
  document known to be PDF. Additionally, with a properly configured server
  environment, the length of the document becomes known at that time.

- The client can abort a response while the transaction is still in progress, if it de-
  cides that the remainder of the data is not of immediate interest. In HTTP,
  aborting the transaction requires closing the connection, which will interfere
  with the strategy of caching the open connection between transactions.

- The client can request retrieval of portions of a document by specifying one or more byte ranges (by offset and count) in the HTTP request headers. Each range can be relative to either the beginning or the end of the file. The client can specify as many ranges as it wants in the request, and the response will consist of multiple blocks, each properly tagged.

- The client can initiate multiple concurrent transactions in an attempt to obtain multiple responses in parallel. This is commonly done, for instance, to retrieve in-line images referenced from an HTML document. This strategy is not always reliable and may backfire if the transactions interfere with each other by competing for scarce resources in the server or the communication channel.

  Note: Extensive experimentation has determined that having multiple concurrent transactions does not work very well for PDF in some important environments. Therefore, Linearized PDF is designed to enable good performance to be achieved using only one transaction at a time. In particular, this means that the client must have sufficient information to determine the byte ranges for all the objects required to display a given page of the PDF file, so that it can specify all those byte ranges in a single request.

Finally, the following additional assumptions are made about the PDF viewer application and its local environment:

- The viewer application has plenty of local temporary storage available. It should rarely need to retrieve a given portion of a PDF document more than once from the server.

- The viewer application is able to display PDF data quickly once it has been received. The performance bottleneck is assumed to be in the transport system (throughput or round-trip delay), not in the processing of data after it arrives.

The consequence of these assumptions is that it may be advantageous for the client to do considerable extra work in order to minimize delays due to communications. Such work includes maintaining local caches and reordering actions according to when the needed data becomes available.

F.2 Linearized PDF Document Structure

Except as noted below, all elements of a Linearized PDF file are as specified in Section 3.4, "File Structure," and all indirect objects in the file are numbered sequentially in two groups, based on their order of appearance in the file.

- The first group consists of the document catalog, certain other document-level objects, and all objects belonging to the first page of the document. These are numbered sequentially starting at the first object number after the last number of the second group. (The stream containing the hint tables, called a *hint stream*, may be numbered out of sequence; see Section F.2.5, "Hint Streams (Parts 5 and 10).")

- The second group consists of all remaining objects in the document, including all pages after the first, all shared objects (objects referenced from more than one page, not counting objects referenced from the first page), and so forth. These are numbered sequentially starting at 1.

These groups of objects are indexed by precisely two cross-reference table sections, located as shown in Example F.1. The composition of these groups is discussed in more detail in the sections that follow (ordered by the part number as shown in this example, with one section for parts 5 and 10). All objects have a generation number of 0.

Example F.1

Part 1: Header

```
%PDF–1.1
% … Binary characters …
```

Part 2: Linearization parameters

```
43 0 obj
    << /Linearized  1.0       % Version
       /L  54567              % File length
       /H  [475  598]         % Primary hint stream offset and length (part 5)
       /O  45                 % Object number of first page's page object (part 6)
       /E  5437               % Offset of end of first page
       /N  11                 % Number of pages in document
       /T  52786              % Offset of first entry in main cross-reference table (part 11)
    >>
endobj
```

Part 3: First-page cross-reference table and trailer

```
xref
43  14
0000000052  00000  n
0000000392  00000  n
0000001073  00000  n
```
… *Cross-reference entries for remaining objects in the first page* …
```
0000000475  00000  n
trailer
    << /Size  57              % Total number of cross-reference table entries in document
       /Prev  52776           % Offset of main cross-reference table (part 11)
       /Root  44 0 R          % Indirect reference to catalog (part 4)
       … Any other entries, such as Info and Encrypt …        % (part 9)
    >>
startxref
0                             % Dummy cross-reference table offset
%%EOF
```

Part 4: Document catalog and other required document-level objects

```
44  0  obj
    << /Type  /Catalog
       /Pages  42 0 R
    >>
endobj
```

… *Other objects* …

Part 5: Primary hint stream (may precede or follow part 6)

```
56  0  obj
    << /Length  457
       … Possibly other stream attributes, such as Filter …
       /Prev  52776           % Offset of main cross-reference table (part 11)
       /P  0                  % Position of page offset hint table
       /S  221                % Position of shared objects hint table
       … Possibly entries for other hint tables …
    >>
stream
    … Page offset hint table …
    … Shared objects hint table …
    … Possibly other hint tables …
endstream
endobj
```

Part 6: First page (may precede or follow part 5)

```
45  0  obj
    <<  /Type  /Page
         ...
    >>
endobj
```

... Outline hierarchy (if the PageMode value in the document catalog is UseOutlines) ...

... Objects for first page, including both shared and nonshared objects ...

Part 7: Remaining pages

```
1  0  obj
    <<  /Type  /Page
         ... Other page attributes, such as MediaBox, Parent, and Contents ...
    >>
endobj
```

... Nonshared objects for this page ...

... Each successive page followed by its nonshared objects ...

... Last page followed by its nonshared objects ...

Part 8: Shared objects for all pages except the first

... Shared objects ...

Part 9: Objects not associated with pages, if any

... Other objects ...

Part 10: Overflow hint stream (optional)

... Overflow hint stream ...

Part 11: Main cross-reference table and trailer

```
xref
0  43
0000000000  65535  f
... Cross-reference entries for all except first page's objects ...
trailer
    /O  45                    % Object number of first page's page object (part 6)
    <<  /Size  43 >>          % Trailer need not contain other entries; in particular,
startxref                     %    it should not have a Prev entry
257                           % Offset of first-page cross-reference table (part 3)
%%EOF
```

F.2.1 Header (Part 1)

The Linearized PDF file begins with the standard header line (see Section 3.4.1, "File Header"). Linearization is independent of PDF version number and can be applied to any PDF file of version 1.1 or greater.

The "binary characters" following the percent sign on the second line are characters with codes 128 or greater, as recommended in Section 3.4.1, "File Header."

F.2.2 Linearization Parameters (Part 2)

Following the header, the first object in the body of the file (part 2) must be an indirect dictionary object containing the parameters listed in Table F.1. All values in this dictionary must be direct objects. Note that there are no references to this dictionary anywhere in the document. (However, there is a normal entry for it in the first-page cross-reference table, part 3.)

TABLE F.1 Linearization parameters

PARAMETER	TYPE	VALUE
Linearized	number	*(Required)* A version identification for the linearized format. As usual, a change in the integer part indicates an incompatible change in the linearized format, and a change in the fractional part indicates an upward-compatible change. The current version is 1.0.
L	integer	*(Required)* The length of the entire file in bytes. This must be exactly equal to the actual length of the PDF file. A mismatch indicates that the PDF is not linearized and must be treated as ordinary PDF, ignoring linearization information. (If the mismatch resulted from appending an update, the linearization information may still be correct but requires validation; see Section F.4.6, "Accessing an Updated File," for details.)
H	array	*(Required)* An array of two or four integers, [*offset$_1$ length$_1$*] or [*offset$_1$ length$_1$ offset$_2$ length$_2$*]. *offset$_1$* is the offset of the primary hint stream from the beginning of the file. (This is the beginning of the stream object, not the beginning of the stream data.) *length$_1$* is the length of this stream (including stream object overhead). If there is an overflow hint stream, *offset$_2$* and *length$_2$* specify its offset and length. (See implementation note 107 in Appendix H.)
O	integer	*(Required)* The object number of the first page's page object.

E	integer	*(Required)* The offset of the end of the first page (the end of part 6 in Example F.1), relative to the beginning of the file.
N	integer	*(Required)* The number of pages in the document.
T	integer	*(Required)* The offset of the first entry of the main cross-reference table (the entry for object number 0), relative to the beginning of the file. Note that this differs from the **Prev** entry in the first-page trailer, which gives the location of the **xref** line that precedes the table.
P	integer	*(Optional)* The page number of the first page (see Section F.2.6, "First Page (Part 6)"). Default value: 0.

The linearization parameter dictionary must be entirely contained within the first 1024 bytes of the PDF file. This limits the amount of data a viewer application must read before deciding whether the file is linearized.

F.2.3 First-Page Cross-Reference Table and Trailer (Part 3)

Part 3 contains the cross-reference table for all the first page's objects (discussed in Section F.2.6, "First Page (Part 6)") as well as for the document catalog and document-level objects appearing before the first page (discussed in Section F.2.4, "Document Catalog and Document-Level Objects (Part 4)"). Additionally, it contains entries for the linearization parameter dictionary (at the beginning) and the primary hint stream (at the end). This table is a valid cross-reference table as defined in Section 3.4.3, "Cross-Reference Table," although its position in the file is rather unconventional. It consists of a single cross-reference subsection, with no free entries.

Below the table is the first-page trailer. The **startxref** line at the end of the trailer gives the offset of the first-page cross-reference table. The trailer's **Prev** entry gives the offset of the main cross-reference table near the end of the file. Again, this is valid PDF, although the trailers are linked in an unusual order. A PDF viewer application that is unaware of linearization interprets the first-page cross-reference table as an update to an original document that is indexed by the main cross-reference table.

The first-page trailer must contain valid **Size** and **Root** entries, as well as any other entries needed to display the document. The **Size** value must be the combined number of entries in both the first-page cross-reference table and the main cross-reference table.

The first-page trailer may optionally end with **startxref**, an integer, and %%EOF, just as in an ordinary trailer. This information is ignored.

F.2.4 Document Catalog and Document-Level Objects (Part 4)

Following the first-page cross-reference table and trailer are the catalog dictionary and other objects that are required when the document is opened. These objects (constituting part 4) include the document catalog dictionary and the values of the following entries, if they are present and are indirect objects:

- The **PageMode** entry in the catalog. (Note that if the value of **PageMode** is Use-Outlines, the outline hierarchy is located in part 6; otherwise, the outline hierarchy, if any, is located in part 9. See Section F.2.9, "Other Objects (Part 9)" for details.)

- The **Threads** entry in the catalog, along with all thread dictionaries it refers to. This does not include the threads' information dictionaries or the individual bead dictionaries belonging to the threads.

- The **OpenAction** entry in the catalog.

- The **AcroForm** entry in the catalog. Only the top-level interactive form dictionary is needed, not the objects that it refers to.

- The **Encrypt** entry in the first-page trailer dictionary. All values in the encryption dictionary must be located here also.

Objects that are not ordinarily needed when the document is opened should not be located here but instead should be at the end of the file; see Section F.2.9, "Other Objects (Part 9)." This includes objects of type **Info**, **Pages**, or **Dests**.

Note that the objects located here are indexed by the first-page cross-reference table, even though they are not logically part of the first page.

F.2.5 Hint Streams (Parts 5 and 10)

The core of the linearization information is stored in data structures known as *hint tables*, whose format is described in Section F.3, "Hint Tables." They provide indexing information that enables the client to construct a single request for all the objects that are needed to display any page of the document or to retrieve certain other information efficiently. The hint tables may contain additional information to optimize access by plug-in extensions to application-specific data.

The hint tables are not logically part of the information content of the document; they can be derived from the document. Any action that changes the document—for instance, appending an incremental update—will invalidate the hint tables. The document will remain a valid PDF file but will no longer be linearized; see Section F.4.6, "Accessing an Updated File," for details.

The hint tables are binary data structures that are enclosed in a stream object. Syntactically, this stream is a normal PDF indirect object. However, there are no references to the stream anywhere in the document, so it is not logically part of the document; an operation that regenerates the document may remove the stream.

Usually, all the hint tables are contained in a single stream, known as the *primary hint stream*. Optionally, there may be an additional stream containing more hints, known as the *overflow hint stream*. The contents of the two hint streams are to be concatenated and treated as if they were a single unbroken stream.

The primary hint stream, which is required, is shown as part 5 in Example F.1. The order of this part and the first-page section, shown as part 6, may be reversed; see Section F.4, "Access Strategies," for considerations on the choice of placement. The overflow hint stream, part 10, is optional. (See implementation note 107 in Appendix H.)

The location and length of the primary hint stream, and of the overflow hint stream if present, are given in the linearization parameter dictionary at the beginning of the file.

The hint streams are assigned the last object numbers in the file—that is, after the object number for the last object in the first page. Their cross-reference table entries are at the end of the first-page cross-reference table. This object number assignment is independent of the physical locations of the hint streams in the file. (This convention keeps their object numbers out of the way of the numbering of the linearized objects.)

The values of all entries in the hint streams' dictionaries must be direct objects, and may contain no indirect object references.

In addition to the standard stream attributes, the dictionary of the primary hint stream contains entries giving the position of the beginning of each hint table in the stream. These positions are given in bytes relative to the beginning of the stream data (after decoding filters, if any, are applied) and with the overflow hint stream concatenated if present. The dictionary of the overflow hint stream should not contain these entries. The keys designating the standard hint tables in the primary hint stream's dictionary are listed in Table F.2; Section F.3, "Hint Tables," documents the format of these hint tables.

TABLE F.2   Standard hint tables

KEY	HINT TABLE
P	*(Required)* Page offset hint table
S	*(Required)* Shared objects hint table
T	*(Present only if thumbnail images exist)* Thumbnails hint table
O	*(Present only if a document outline exists)* Outlines hint table
A	*(Present only if article threads exist)* Thread information hint table
E	*(Present only if named destinations exist)* Named destinations hint table
V	*(Present only if an interactive form dictionary exists)* Interactive form hint table
I	*(Present only if a document information dictionary exists)* Information dictionary hint table
C	*(PDF 1.3; present only if a logical structure hierarchy exists)* Logical structure hint table
L	*(PDF 1.3)* Page label hint table

New keys may be registered for additional hint tables required for new PDF features or for application-specific data accessed by plug-in extensions. See Appendix E for further information.

F.2.6   First Page (Part 6)

As mentioned earlier, this section may either precede or follow the primary hint stream. The starting file offset and length of this section may be determined from the hint tables. In addition, the **E** entry in the linearization parameter dictionary specifies the end of the first page (as an offset relative to the beginning of the file), and the **O** entry gives the object number of the first page's page object.

This part of the file contains all the objects needed to display the first page of the document. Ordinarily, the "first page" is page 0—that is, the leftmost leaf page node in the page tree. However, if the document catalog contains an **OpenAction** entry that specifies opening at some page other than page 0, then that page is the "first page" and should be located here. The page number of the first page is given in the **P** entry of the linearization parameter dictionary. (See also implementation note 108 in Appendix H.)

The objects contained here should include the following:

- The page object for the first page. This must be the first object in this part of the file. Its object number is given in the linearization parameter dictionary. This page object must explicitly specify all required attributes, such as **Resources** and **MediaBox**; the attributes cannot be inherited from ancestor page tree nodes (**Pages** objects).

- The entire outline hierarchy, if the value of the **PageMode** entry in the catalog is UseOutlines. (If the **PageMode** entry is omitted or has some other value and the document has an outline hierarchy, the outline hierarchy appears in part 9; see Section F.2.9, "Other Objects (Part 9)" for details.)

- All objects that the page object refers to, to an arbitrary depth. This includes objects referred to by its **Contents**, **Resources**, **Annots**, and **B** entries, but not **Thumb**.

The order of objects referenced from the page object should facilitate early user interaction and incremental display of the page data as it arrives. The following order is recommended:

1. The **Annots** array and all annotation dictionaries, to a depth sufficient to allow those annotations to be activated. Information required to draw the annotation can be deferred until later, since annotations are always drawn on top of (hence after) the contents.

2. The **B** (beads) array and all bead dictionaries, if any, for this page. If any beads exist for this page, the **B** array is required to be present in the page dictionary. Additionally, each bead in the thread (not just the first bead) must contain a **T** entry referring to the associated thread dictionary.

3. The resource dictionary, but not the resource objects contained in the dictionary.

4. Resource objects, other than the types listed below, in the order that they are first referenced (directly or indirectly) from the content stream. If the contents are represented as an array of streams, each resource object should precede the stream in which it is first referenced. Note that **Font**, **FontDescriptor**, and **Encoding** resources should be included here, but not substitutable font files referenced from font descriptors (see the last item below).

5. The page contents (**Contents**). If large, this should be represented as an array of indirect references to content streams, which in turn are interleaved with the resources they require. If small, the entire contents should be a single content stream preceding the resources.

6. Image XObjects, in the order that they are first referenced. Images are assumed to be large and slow to transfer, so the viewer application defers rendering images until all the other contents have been displayed.

7. **FontFile** streams, which contain the actual definitions of embedded fonts. These are assumed to be large and slow to transfer, so the viewer application uses substitute fonts until the real ones have arrived. Only those fonts for which substitution is possible can be deferred in this way. (Currently, this includes any Type 1 or TrueType font that has a font descriptor with **Flags** bit 6 set, indicating the Adobe standard Latin character set).

See Section F.4, "Access Strategies," for additional discussion about object order and incremental drawing strategies.

F.2.7 Remaining Pages (Part 7)

Part 7 of the Linearized PDF file contains the page objects and nonshared objects for all remaining pages of the file, with the objects for each page grouped together. The pages are contiguous and are ordered by page number. If the first page of the file is not page 0, this section starts with page 0 and skips over the first page when its position in the sequence is reached.

For each page, the objects required to display that page are grouped together, except for resources and other objects that are shared with other pages. Shared objects are located in the shared objects section (part 8). The starting file offset and length of any page can be determined from the hint tables.

The recommended order of objects within a page is essentially the same as in the first page. In particular, the page object must be the first object in each section.

In most cases, unlike for the first page, there will be little benefit from interleaving contents with resources. This is because most resources other than images—fonts in particular—are shared among multiple pages and therefore reside in the shared objects section. Image XObjects usually are not shared, but they should appear at the end of the page's section of the file, since rendering of images is deferred.

F.2.8 Shared Objects (Part 8)

Part 8 of the file contains objects, primarily named resources, that are referenced from more than one page but that are not referenced (directly or indirectly) from the first page. The hint tables contain an index of these objects. For more information on named resources, see Section 3.7.2, "Resource Dictionaries."

The order of these objects is essentially arbitrary. However, wherever a resource consists of a multiple-level structure, all components of the structure should be grouped together. If only the top-level object is referenced from outside the group, the entire group can be described by a single entry in the shared objects hint table. This helps to minimize the size of the shared objects hint table and the number of individual references from entries in the page offset hint table. (See also implementation note 109 in Appendix H.)

F.2.9 Other Objects (Part 9)

Following the shared objects are any other objects that are part of the document but are not required for displaying pages. These objects are divided into functional categories. Objects within each of these categories should be grouped together. The relative order of the categories is unimportant.

- The page tree. This can be located here, since the Linearized PDF viewer never needs to consult it. Note that all **Resources** attributes and other inheritable attributes of the page objects must be pushed down and replicated in each of the leaf page objects (but they may contain indirect references to shared objects).

- Thumbnail images. These should simply be ordered by page number. Note that the thumbnail image for page 0 should be first, even if the first page of the document is some page other than 0. Each thumbnail image consists of one or more objects, which may refer to objects in the thumbnail shared objects section (see the next item).

- Thumbnail shared objects. These are objects that are shared among some or all thumbnail objects and are not referenced from any other objects.

- The outline hierarchy, if not located in part 6. The order of objects should be the same as the order in which they are displayed by the viewer application. This is a preorder traversal of the outline tree, skipping over any subtree that is closed (that is, whose parent's **Count** value is negative); following that should be the subtrees that were skipped over, in the order that they would have appeared if they were all open.

- Thread information dictionaries, referenced from the **I** entries of thread dictionaries. Note that the thread dictionaries themselves are located with the document catalog, and the beads with the individual pages.

- Named destinations. These objects include the value of the **Dests** or **Names** entry in the document catalog and all the destination objects that it refers to. See Section F.4.2, "Opening at an Arbitrary Page."

- The document information dictionary and the objects contained within it.

- The interactive form field hierarchy. This does not include the top-level interactive form dictionary, which is located with the document catalog.

- Other entries in the document catalog that are not referenced from any page.

- *(PDF 1.3)* The logical structure hierarchy.

F.2.10 Main Cross-Reference and Trailer (Part 11)

Part 11 is the cross-reference table for all objects in the PDF file except those listed in the first-page cross-reference table (part 3). As indicated earlier, this cross-reference table plays the role of the original cross-reference table for the file (before any updates are appended). It must conform to the following rules:

- It consists of a single cross-reference subsection, beginning at object number 0.

- The first entry (for object number 0) must be a free entry.

- The remaining entries are for in-use objects, which are numbered consecutively starting at 1.

As indicated earlier, the **startxref** line gives the offset of the first-page cross-reference table. The **Prev** entry of the first-page trailer gives the offset of the main cross-reference table. The main trailer has no **Prev** entry, and in fact does not need to contain any entries other than **Size**.

F.3 Hint Tables

The core of the linearization information is stored in two or more hint tables, as indicated by the attributes of the primary hint stream (see Section F.2.5, "Hint Streams (Parts 5 and 10)"). The format of the standard hint tables is described in this section.

There can be additional hint tables for application-specific data that is accessed by plug-in extensions. A generic format for such hint tables is defined; see Section F.3.4, "Generic Hint Tables." Alternatively, the format of a hint table can be private to the application; see Appendix E for further information.

Each hint table consists of a portion of the stream, beginning at the position in the stream indicated by the corresponding stream attribute. (If there is an over-flow hint stream, its contents are to be appended seamlessly to the primary hint stream; hint table positions are relative to the beginning of this combined stream.) In general, this byte stream is treated as a bit stream, high-order bit first, which is then subdivided into fields of arbitrary width without regard to byte boundaries. However, each hint table begins at a byte boundary.

The hint tables are designed to encode the required information as compactly as possible. Interpreting the hint tables requires reading them sequentially; they are not designed for random access. The client is expected to read and decode the tables once and retain the information for as long as the document remains open.

A hint table encodes the positions of various objects in the file. The representation is either explicit (an offset from the beginning of the file) or implicit (accumulated lengths of preceding objects). Regardless of the representation, the resulting positions must be interpreted as if the primary hint stream itself were not present. That is, a position greater than the *hint stream offset* must have the *hint stream length* added to it in order to determine the actual offset relative to the beginning of the file. (The hint stream offset and hint stream length are the values *offset*$_1$ and *length*$_1$ in the **H** array in the linearization parameter dictionary at the beginning of the file.)

The reason for this rule is that the length of the primary hint stream depends on the information contained within the hint tables, and this is not known until after they have been generated. Any information that gets put into the hint tables must not depend on knowing the primary hint stream's length in advance.

Note that this rule applies only to offsets given in the hint tables and not to offsets given in the cross-reference tables or linearization parameter dictionary. Also, the offset and length of the overflow hint stream, if present, need not be taken into account, since this object follows all other objects in the file.

F.3.1 Page Offset Hint Table

The page offset hint table provides information required for locating each page. Additionally, for each page except the first, it also enumerates all shared objects that the page references, directly or indirectly.

This table begins with a header section, described in Table F.3, followed by one or more per-page entries, described in Table F.4. Note that the items making up each per-page entry are not contiguous; they are broken up with items from entries for other pages. The order of items making up the per-page entries is as follows:

1. Item 1 for all pages, in page order starting with the first page

2. Item 2 for all pages, in page order starting with the first page

3. Item 3 for all pages, in page order starting with the first page

4. Item 4 for all shared objects in the second page, followed by item 4 for all shared objects in the third page, and so on

5. Item 5 for all shared objects in the second page, followed by item 5 for all shared objects in the third page, and so on

6. Item 6 for all pages, in page order starting with the first page

7. Item 7 for all pages, in page order starting with the first page

Note: *All the "bits needed" items in Table F.3, such as item 3, may have values in the range 0 through 32. Although that range requires only 6 bits, 16-bit numbers are used.*

TABLE F.3   Page offset hint table, header section

ITEM	SIZE (BITS)	DESCRIPTION
1	32	The least number of objects in a page (including the page object itself).
2	32	The location of the first page's page object.
3	16	The number of bits needed to represent the difference between the greatest and least number of objects in a page.
4	32	The least length of a page in bytes. This is the least length from the beginning of a page object to the last byte of the last object used by that page.
5	16	The number of bits needed to represent the difference between the greatest and least length of a page, in bytes.
6	32	The least offset to the start of the content stream. (See implementation note 110 in Appendix H.)
7	16	The number of bits needed to represent the difference between the greatest and least offset to the start of the content stream. (See implementation note 111 in Appendix H.)
8	32	The least content stream length. (See implementation note 112 in Appendix H.)
9	16	The number of bits needed to represent the difference between the greatest and least content stream length. (See implementation note 112 in Appendix H.)
10	16	The number of bits needed to represent the greatest number of shared object references.
11	16	The number of bits needed to represent the numerically greatest shared object identifier used by the pages (discussed further in Table F.4, item 4).
12	16	The number of bits needed to represent the numerator of the fractional position for each shared object reference. For each shared object referenced from a page, there is an indication of where in the page's content stream the object is first referenced. That position is given as the numerator of a fraction, whose denominator is specified once for the entire document (in the next item in this table). The fraction is explained in more detail in Table F.4, item 5.
13	16	The denominator of the fractional position for each shared object reference.

TABLE F.4 Page offset hint table, per-page entry

ITEM	SIZE (BITS)	DESCRIPTION
1	See Table F.3, item 3.	A number that, when added to the least number of objects in a page (Table F.3, item 1), gives the number of objects in the page. The first object of the first page has an object number that is the value of the **O** entry in the linearization parameter dictionary at the beginning of the file. The first object of the second page has an object number of 1. Objects numbers for subsequent pages can be determined by accumulating the number of objects in all previous pages.
2	See Table F.3, item 5.	A number that, when added to the least page length (Table F.3, item 4), gives the length of the page in bytes. The location of the first object of the first page can be determined from its object number (the **O** entry in the linearization parameter dictionary) and the cross-reference table entry for that object (see Section F.2.3, "First-Page Cross-Reference Table and Trailer (Part 3)"). The locations of subsequent pages can be determined by accumulating the lengths of all previous pages. Note that it is necessary to skip over the primary hint stream, wherever it is located.
3	See Table F.3, item 10.	The number of shared objects referenced from the page. Note that this must be 0 for the first page, and that the next two items start with the second page.
4	See Table F.3, item 11.	*(One item for each shared object referenced from the page)* A *shared object identifier*—that is, an index into the shared objects hint table (described in Section F.3.2, "Shared Objects Hint Table"). Note that a single entry in the shared objects hint table can designate a group of shared objects, only one of which is referenced from outside the group. That is, shared object identifiers are not directly related to object numbers. This identifier combines with the numerators provided in item 5 to form a *shared object reference.*
5	See Table F.3, item 12.	*(One item for each shared object referenced from the page)* The numerator of the fractional position for each shared object reference, in the same order as the preceding item. The fraction indicates where in the page's content stream the shared object is first referenced. This item is interpreted as the numerator of a fraction whose denominator is specified once for the entire document (Table F.3, item 13). If the denominator is d, a numerator ranging from 0 to $d-1$ indicates the corresponding portion of the page's content stream. For example, if the denominator is 4, a numerator of 0, 1, 2, or 3 indicates that the first reference lies in the first, second, third, or fourth quarter of the content stream, respectively.

There are two (or more) other possible values for the numerator, which indicate that the shared object is not referenced from the content stream but is needed by annotations or other objects that are drawn after the contents. The value d indicates that the shared object is needed before image XObjects and other nonshared objects that are at the end of the page. A value of $d + 1$ or greater indicates that the shared object is needed after those objects.

This method of dividing the page into fractions is only approximate. Determining the first reference to a shared object entails inspecting the unencoded content stream. The relationship between positions in the unencoded and encoded streams is not necessarily linear.

| 6 | See Table F.3, item 7. | A number that, when added to the least offset to the start of the content stream (Table F.3, item 6), gives the offset in bytes of the start of the page's content stream, relative to the beginning of the page. This is the offset of the stream object, not the stream data. (See implementation note 111 in Appendix H.) |
| 7 | See Table F.3, item 9. | A number that, when added to the least content stream length (Table F.3, item 8), gives the length of the page's content stream in bytes. This includes object overhead preceding and following the stream data. (See implementation note 112 in Appendix H.) |

F.3.2 Shared Objects Hint Table

The shared objects hint table gives information required to locate shared objects (see Section F.2.8, "Shared Objects (Part 8)"). Shared objects can be physically located in either of two places: objects that are referenced from the first page are located with the first-page objects (part 6); all other shared objects are located in the shared objects section (part 8).

A single entry in the shared objects hint table can actually describe a group of adjacent objects, under the following condition: Only the first object in the group is referenced from outside the group; the remaining objects in the group are referenced only from other objects in the same group.

The page offset hint table, interactive form hint table, and logical structure hint table refer to an entry in the shared objects hint table by a simple index that is its sequence in the table, counting from 0.

The shared objects hint table consists of a header section, described in Table F.5, followed by one or more shared object group entries, described in Table F.6.

There are two sequences of shared object group entries: the ones for objects located in the first page, followed by the ones for objects located in the shared objects section. The entries have the same format in both cases. Note that the items making up each shared object group entry are not contiguous; they are broken up with items from entries for other shared object groups. The order of items in each sequence is as follows:

1. Item 1 for the first group, item 1 for the second group, and so on

2. Item 2 for the first group, item 2 for the second group, and so on

3. Item 3 for the first group, item 3 for the second group, and so on

4. Item 4 for the first group, item 4 for the second group, and so on

For convenience of representation, the first page is treated as if it consisted entirely of shared objects. That is, the first entry refers to the beginning of the first page and has an object count and length that span all the initial nonshared objects. The next entry refers to a group of shared objects. Subsequent entries span additional groups of either shared or nonshared objects consecutively, until all shared objects in the first page have been enumerated. (Obviously, the entries that refer to nonshared objects will never be used.)

Note: *If there are no shared objects, all of the items in the header section should be zero.*

TABLE F.5 Shared objects hint table, header section

ITEM	SIZE (BITS)	DESCRIPTION
1	32	The object number of the first object in the shared objects section (part 8).
2	32	The location of the first object in the shared objects section.
3	32	The number of shared object entries for the first page.
4	32	The number of shared object entries for the shared objects section. This includes the number of shared object entries for the first page.
5	16	The number of bits needed to represent the greatest number of objects in a shared object group. (See also implementation note 113 in Appendix H.)
6	32	The least length of a shared object group in bytes.
7	16	The number of bits needed to represent the difference between the greatest and least length of a shared object group, in bytes.

TABLE F.6 **Shared objects hint table, shared object group entry**

ITEM	SIZE (BITS)	DESCRIPTION
1	See Table F.5, item 7.	A number that, when added to the least shared object group length (Table F.5, item 6), gives the length of the object group in bytes. The location of the first object of the first page is given in the page offset hint table, header section (Table F.3, item 4). The locations of subsequent object groups can be determined by accumulating the lengths of all previous object groups until all shared objects in the first page have been enumerated. Following that, the location of the first object in the shared objects section can be obtained from the header section of the shared objects hint table (Table F.5, item 2).
2	1	A flag indicating whether the MD5 signature (item 3) is present; its value is 1 if the signature is present and 0 if it is absent. (See also implementation note 114 in Appendix H.)
3	128	*(Only if item 2 is 1)* The MD5 signature, a 16-byte MD5 hash that uniquely identifies the resource that the group of objects represents. This is intended to enable the client to substitute a locally cached copy of the resource instead of reading it from the PDF file. Note that this signature is unrelated to signature fields in interactive forms, as defined in the section "Signature Fields" on page 451.
4	See Table F.5, item 5.	The number of objects in the group. The first object of the first page is the one whose object number is given by the **O** entry in the linearization parameter dictionary at the beginning of the file. Object numbers for subsequent entries can be determined by accumulating the number of objects in all previous entries, until all shared objects in the first page have been enumerated. Following that, the first object in the shared objects section has a number that can be obtained from the header section of the shared objects hint table (Table F.5, item 1). (See also implementation note 115 in Appendix H.)

F.3.3 Thumbnails Hint Table

The thumbnails hint table consists of a header section (described in Table F.7), followed by the thumbnails section, which includes one or more per-page entries (Table F.8), each of which describes the thumbnail image for a single page. The entries are in page number order starting with page 0, even if the document catalog contains an **OpenAction** entry that specifies opening at some page other than page 0. Thumbnail images may exist for some pages and not for others.

TABLE F.7 Thumbnails hint table, header section

ITEM	SIZE (BITS)	DESCRIPTION
1	32	The object number of the first thumbnail image (that is, the thumbnail image that is described by the first entry in the thumbnails section).
2	32	The location of the first thumbnail image, specified as an offset from the beginning of the file to that thumbnail image, minus the length of the thumbnails hint table.
3	32	The number of pages that have thumbnail images.
4	16	The number of bits needed to represent the greatest number of consecutive pages that do not have a thumbnail image.
5	32	The least length of a thumbnail image in bytes.
6	16	The number of bits needed to represent the difference between the greatest and least length of a thumbnail image.
7	32	The least number of objects in a thumbnail image.
8	16	The number of bits needed to represent the difference between the greatest and least number of objects in a thumbnail image.
9	32	The object number of the first object in the thumbnail shared objects section (a subsection of part 8). These are objects (color spaces, for example) that are referenced from some or all thumbnail objects and are not referenced from any other objects. The thumbnail shared objects are undifferentiated; there is no indication of which shared objects are referenced from any given page's thumbnail image.
10	32	The location of the first object in the thumbnail shared objects section, specified as the offset from the beginning of the file to that object, minus the length of the thumbnails hint table.
11	32	The number of thumbnail shared objects.
12	32	The length of the thumbnail shared objects section in bytes.

TABLE F.8   Thumbnails hint table, per-page entry

ITEM	SIZE (BITS)	DESCRIPTION
1	See Table F.7, item 4.	(*Optional*) The number of preceding pages lacking a thumbnail image. This indicates how many pages without a thumbnail image lie between the previous entry's page and this one.
2	See Table F.7, item 8.	A number that, when added to the least number of objects in a thumbnail image (Table F.7, item 7), gives the number of objects in this page's thumbnail image.
3	See Table F.7, item 6.	A number that, when added to the least length of a thumbnail image (Table F.7, item 5), gives the length of this page's thumbnail image in bytes.

The order of items in Table F.8 is as follows:

1. Item 1 for all pages, in page order starting with the first page

2. Item 2 for all pages, in page order starting with the first page

3. Item 3 for all pages, in page order starting with the first page

F.3.4   Generic Hint Tables

Certain categories of objects are associated with the document as a whole rather than with individual pages (see Section F.2.9, "Other Objects (Part 9)"), and it is sometimes useful to provide hints for accessing those objects efficiently. For each category of hints, there is a separate entry in the primary hint stream giving the starting position of the table within the stream (see Section F.2.5, "Hint Streams (Parts 5 and 10)").

There is a generic representation for such hints, specified below. This representation is useful for some standard categories of objects, such as outlines, threads, and named destinations. It may also be useful for application-specific objects accessed by plug-in extensions. It is considerably more convenient for a plug-in to use the generic hint representation than to specify custom hints.

A generic hint table describes a single group of objects that are located together in the PDF file. The entries in this table are listed in Table F.9.

ITEM	SIZE (BITS)	DESCRIPTION
TABLE F.9 **Generic hint table**		
1	32	The object number of the first object in the group.
2	32	The location of the first object in the group.
3	32	The number of objects in the group.
4	32	The length of the object group in bytes.

F.3.5 Interactive Form and Structure Hint Tables

If an interactive form or structure tree root dictionary is present, the interactive form and structure hint tables refer to the contents of those dictionaries; see Section F.2.9, "Other Objects (Part 9)." Interactive forms and logical structure hierarchies can refer to objects that are shared with other parts of the document, in which case the hint table lists those shared objects.

An interactive form or structure hint table begins with the same entries as in a generic hint table, followed by three additional entries, as shown in Table F.10.

ITEM	SIZE (BITS)	DESCRIPTION
TABLE F.10 **Interactive form or structure hint table**		
1	32	The object number of the first object in the group.
2	32	The location of the first object in the group.
3	32	The number of objects in the group.
4	32	The length of the object group in bytes.
5	32	The number of shared object references.
6	16	The number of bits needed to represent the numerically greatest shared object identifier used by the interactive form or the logical structure hierarchy.
7 ...	See Table F.3, item 11.	Starting with item 7, each of the remaining items in this table is a shared object identifier—that is, an index into the shared objects hint table (described in Section F.3.2, "Shared Objects Hint Table").

F.3.6 Other Hint Tables

The outline, thread information, named destinations, page label, and information dictionary hint tables use the generic hint table representation; see Section F.3.4, "Generic Hint Tables." The objects that they refer to are grouped together as described in Section F.2.9, "Other Objects (Part 9)."

F.4 Access Strategies

This section outlines how the client can take advantage of the structure of a Linearized PDF file in order to retrieve and display it efficiently. This material is not formally a part of the Linearized PDF specification, but it may help explain the rationale for the organization.

F.4.1 Opening at the First Page

As indicated earlier, when a document is initially accessed, a request is issued to retrieve the entire file, starting at the beginning. Consequently, Linearized PDF is organized so that all the data required to display the first page is at the beginning of the file. This includes all resources that are referenced from the first page, whether or not they are also referenced from other pages.

The first page is usually but not necessarily page 0. If the document catalog contains an **OpenAction** entry that specifies opening at some page other than page 0, that page will be the one physically located at the beginning of the document. Thus, opening a document at the default place (rather than a specific destination) requires simply waiting for the first-page data to arrive; no additional transactions are required.

In an ordinary PDF viewer application, opening a document requires first positioning to the end to obtain the **startxref** line. Since a Linearized PDF file has the first page's cross-reference table at the beginning, reading the **startxref** line is not necessary. All that is required is to verify that the file length given in the linearization parameter dictionary at the beginning of the file matches the actual length of the file, indicating that no updates have been appended to the PDF file.

The primary hint stream is located either before or after the first-page objects. This means that it will also be retrieved as part of the initial sequential read of the file. The client is expected to interpret and retain all the information in the hint tables. They are reasonably compact and are not designed to be obtained from the file in random pieces.

The client must now decide whether to continue reading the remainder of the document sequentially or to abort the initial transaction and access subsequent pages using separate transactions requesting byte ranges. This decision is a function of the size of the file, the data rate of the channel, and the overhead cost of a transaction.

F.4.2 Opening at an Arbitrary Page

The viewer application may be requested to open a PDF file at an arbitrary page. The page can be specified in one of three ways:

- By page number (remote go-to action, integer page specifier)
- By named destination (remote go-to action, name or string page specifier)
- By thread (thread action)

Additionally, an indexed search results in opening a document by page number. Handling this case efficiently is considered especially important.

As indicated above, when the document is initially opened, it is retrieved sequentially starting at the beginning. As soon as the hint tables have been received, the client has sufficient information to request retrieval of any page of the document given its page number. Therefore, it can abort the initial transaction and issue a new transaction for the target page, as described in Section F.4.3, "Going to Another Page of an Open Document."

The position of the primary hint stream (part 5) with respect to the first-page objects (part 6) determines how quickly this can be done. If the primary hint stream precedes the first-page objects, the initial transaction can be aborted very quickly; however, this is at the cost of increased delay when opening the document at the first page. On the other hand, if the primary hint stream follows the first-page objects, displaying the first page is quicker (since the hint tables are not needed for that), but opening at an arbitrary page is delayed by the time required to receive the first page.

At the time a PDF file is linearized, the decision whether to favor opening at the first page or opening at an arbitrary page must be made.

If an overflow hint stream exists, obtaining it requires issuing an additional transaction. For this reason, inclusion of an overflow hint stream in Linearized PDF, although permitted, is not recommended. The feature exists to allow the linearizer to write the PDF file with space reserved for a primary hint stream of an estimated size, and then go back and fill in the hint tables. If the estimate is too small, the linearizer can append an overflow stream containing the remaining hint table data. This enables the PDF file to be written in one pass, which may be an advantage if the performance of writing PDF is considered important.

Opening at a named destination requires the viewer application first to read the entire **Dests** or **Names** dictionary, for which a hint is present. Using this information, it is possible to determine the page containing the specific destination identified by the name.

Opening at a thread requires the viewer application first to read the entire **Threads** array, which is located with the catalog at the beginning of the document. Using this information, it is possible to determine the page containing the first bead of any thread. Opening at other than the first bead of a thread requires chaining through all the beads until the desired one is reached; there are no hints to accelerate this.

F.4.3 Going to Another Page of an Open Document

Given a page number and the information in the hint tables, it is now straightforward for the client to construct a single request to retrieve any arbitrary page of the document. The request should include:

- The objects of the page itself, whose byte range can be determined from the entry in the page offset hint table.

- The portion of the main cross-reference table referring to those objects. This can be computed from main cross-reference table location (the **T** entry in the linearization parameter dictionary) and the cumulative object number in the page offset hint table.

- The shared objects referenced from the page, whose byte ranges can be determined from information in the shared objects hint table.

- The portion or portions of the main cross-reference table referring to those objects, as described above.

The purpose of the fractions in the page offset hint table is to enable the client to schedule retrieval of the page in a way that allows incremental display of the data as it arrives. It accomplishes this by constructing a request that interleaves pieces of the page contents with the shared resources that the contents refer to. This serves much the same purpose as the physical interleaving that is done for the first page.

F.4.4 Drawing a Page Incrementally

The ordering of objects in pages and the organization of the hint tables are intended to allow progressive update of the display and early opportunities for user interaction when the data is arriving slowly. The viewer application must recognize instances in which the targets of indirect object references have not yet arrived and, where possible, rearrange the order in which it acts on the objects in the page.

The following sequence of actions is recommended:

1. Activate the annotations, but do not draw them yet. Also activate the cursor feedback for any article threads in the page.

2. Begin drawing the contents. Whenever there is a reference to an image XObject that has not yet arrived, skip over it. Whenever there is a reference to a font whose definition is an embedded font file that has not yet arrived, draw the text using a substitute font (if that is possible).

3. Draw the annotations.

4. Draw the images as they arrive, together with anything that overlaps them.

5. Once the embedded font definitions have arrived, redraw the text using the correct fonts, together with anything that overlaps the text.

The last two steps should be done using an off-screen buffer if possible, to avoid objectionable flashing during the redraw process.

F.4.5 Following an Article Thread

As indicated earlier, the bead dictionaries for any article thread that visits a given page are located with that page. This enables the bead rectangles to be activated and proper cursor feedback to be shown.

If the user follows a thread, the viewer application can obtain the object number from the **N** or **P** entry of the bead dictionary. This identifies a target bead, which is located with the page to which it belongs. Given this object number, the viewer application can then go to that page, as discussed in Section F.4.3, "Going to Another Page of an Open Document."

F.4.6 Accessing an Updated File

As stated earlier, if a Linearized PDF file subsequently has an incremental update appended to it, the linearization and hints are no longer valid. Actually, this is not necessarily true, but the viewer application must do some additional work to validate them.

When the viewer application sees that the file is longer than the length given in the linearization parameter dictionary, it must issue an additional transaction to read everything that was appended. It must then analyze the objects in that update to see whether any of them modify objects that are in the first page or that are the targets of hints. If so, it must augment its internal data structures as necessary to take the updates into account.

For a PDF file that has received only a small update, this approach may be worthwhile. Accessing the file this way will be quicker than accessing it without hints or retrieving the entire file before displaying any of it.

APPENDIX G

Example PDF Files

THIS APPENDIX PRESENTS several examples showing the structure of actual PDF files:

- A minimal file that can serve as a starting point for creating other PDF files (and that is the basis of later examples)

- A simple example that displays a text string—the classic "Hello World"—and a simple graphics example that draws lines and shapes

- A fragment of a PDF file that illustrates the structure of the page tree for a large document and, similarly, two fragments that illustrate the structure of an outline tree

- Finally, an example showing the structure of a PDF file as it is updated several times, illustrating multiple body sections, cross-reference sections, and trailers

*Note: The **Length** values of stream objects in the examples and the byte addresses in cross-reference tables are not necessarily accurate.*

G.1 Minimal PDF File

Example G.1 is a PDF file that does not draw anything; it is almost the minimum acceptable PDF file. It is not strictly the minimum acceptable because it contains an **Outlines** object (with a zero count, in which case this object would normally be omitted), a **Contents** object, and a resource dictionary containing a **ProcSet** array. These objects were included to make this file useful as a starting point for creating other, more realistic PDF files.

Table G.1 lists the objects present in this example.

TABLE G.1 Objects in minimal example	
OBJECT NUMBER	**OBJECT TYPE**
1	**Catalog**
2	**Outlines** (outline tree root)
3	**Pages** (page tree node)
4	**Page** (page object)
5	Content stream
6	Procedure set array

Note: When using Example G.1 as a starting point for creating other files, remember to update the **ProcSet** array as needed (see Section 8.1, "Procedure Sets"). Also, remember that the cross-reference table entries may need to have a trailing space (see Section 3.4.3, "Cross-Reference Table").

Example G.1

```
%PDF−1.3
1 0 obj
    << /Type /Catalog
        /Outlines 2 0 R
        /Pages  3 0 R
    >>
endobj

2 0 obj
    << /Type  Outlines
        /Count  0
    >>
endobj

3 0 obj
    << /Type /Pages
        /Kids [4 0 R]
        /Count  1
    >>
endobj
```

```
4 0 obj
   << /Type /Page
      /Parent 3 0 R
      /MediaBox [0 0 612 792]
      /Contents 5 0 R
      /Resources << /ProcSet 6 0 R >>
   >>
endobj

5 0 obj
   << /Length 35 >>
stream
… Page-marking operators …
endstream
endobj

6 0 obj
   [/PDF]
endobj

xref
0 7
0000000000 65535 f
0000000009 00000 n
0000000074 00000 n
0000000120 00000 n
0000000179 00000 n
0000000300 00000 n
0000000384 00000 n

trailer
   << /Size 7
      /Root 1 0 R
   >>
startxref
408
%%EOF
```

G.2 Simple Text String Example

Example G.2 is the classic "Hello World" example built from the preceding example. It displays a single line of text consisting of the string Hello World, illustrating the use of fonts and several text-related PDF operators. The string is displayed in 24-point Helvetica; because Helvetica is one of the 14 standard fonts, no font descriptor is needed.

Table G.2 lists the objects present in this example.

OBJECT NUMBER	OBJECT TYPE
	TABLE G.2 Objects in simple text string example
1	**Catalog**
2	**Outlines** (outline tree root)
3	**Pages** (page tree node)
4	**Page** (page object)
5	Content stream
6	Procedure set array
7	**Font** (Type 1 font)

Example G.2

```
%PDF–1.3
1 0 obj
    << /Type /Catalog
       /Outlines 2 0 R
       /Pages 3 0 R
    >>
endobj

2 0 obj
    << /Type /Outlines
       /Count 0
    >>
endobj
```

```
3 0 obj
   << /Type /Pages
       /Kids [4 0 R]
       /Count 1
   >>
endobj

4 0 obj
   << /Type /Page
       /Parent 3 0 R
       /MediaBox [0 0 612 792]
       /Contents 5 0 R
       /Resources << /ProcSet 6 0 R
                     /Font << /F1 7 0 R >>
                  >>
   >>
endobj

5 0 obj
   << /Length 73 >>
stream
   BT
       /F1 24 Tf
       100 100 Td
       (Hello World) Tj
   ET
endstream
endobj

6 0 obj
   [/PDF /Text]
endobj

7 0 obj
   << /Type /Font
       /Subtype /Type1
       /Name /F1
       /BaseFont /Helvetica
       /Encoding /MacRomanEncoding
   >>
endobj
```

```
xref
0 8
0000000000 65535 f
0000000009 00000 n
0000000074 00000 n
0000000120 00000 n
0000000179 00000 n
0000000364 00000 n
0000000466 00000 n
0000000496 00000 n
trailer
    << /Size 8
        /Root 1 0 R
    >>
startxref
625
%%EOF
```

G.3   Simple Graphics Example

Example G.3 draws a thin black line segment, a thick black dashed line segment, a filled and stroked rectangle, and a filled and stroked cubic Bézier curve. Table G.3 lists the objects present in this example, and Figure G.1 shows the resulting output. (Each shape has a red border, and the rectangle is filled with light blue.)

TABLE G.3   Objects in simple graphics example

OBJECT NUMBER	OBJECT TYPE
1	**Catalog**
2	**Outlines** (outline tree root)
3	**Pages** (page tree node)
4	**Page** (page object)
5	Content stream
6	Procedure set array

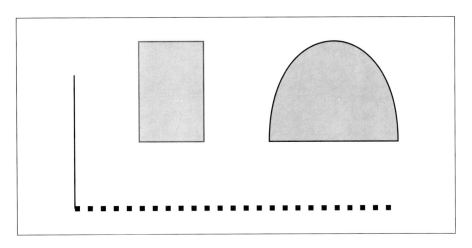

FIGURE G.1   *Visual representation of Example G.3*

Example G.3

```
%PDF–1.3
1  0  obj
    <<  /Type  /Catalog
        /Outlines  2 0 R
        /Pages  3 0 R
    >>
endobj

2  0  obj
    <<  /Type  /Outlines
        /Count  0
    >>
endobj

3  0  obj
    <<  /Type  /Pages
        /Kids  [4 0 R]
        /Count  1
    >>
endobj
```

```
4 0 obj
    << /Type /Page
        /Parent 3 0 R
        /MediaBox [0  0  612  792]
        /Contents  5 0 R
        /Resources << /ProcSet 6 0 R >>
    >>
endobj

5 0 obj
    << /Length 883 >>
stream
    % Draw a black line segment, using the default line width.
    150  250  m
    150  350  l
    S

    % Draw a thicker, dashed line segment.
    4  w                        % Set line width to 4 points
    [4 6] 0 d                   % Set dash pattern to 4 units on, 6 units off
    150  250  m
    400  250  l
    S

    [] 0 d                      % Reset dash pattern to a solid line
    1  w                        % Reset line width to 1 unit

    % Draw a rectangle with a 1–unit red border, filled with light blue.
    1.0  0.0  0.0  RG           % Red for stroke color
    0.5  0.75  1.0  rg          % Light blue for fill color
    200  300  50  75  re
    B

    % Draw a curve filled with gray and with a colored border.
    0.5  0.1  0.2  RG
    0.7  g
    300  300  m
    300  400  400  400  400  300  c
    b
endstream
endobj

6 0 obj
    [/PDF]
endobj
```

```
xref
0 7
0000000000 65535 f
0000000009 00000 n
0000000074 00000 n
0000000120 00000 n
0000000179 00000 n
0000000300 00000 n
0000001532 00000 n

trailer
    << /Size 7
         /Root 1 0 R
    >>
startxref
1556
%%EOF
```

G.4 Page Tree Example

Example G.4 is a fragment of a PDF file illustrating the structure of the page tree for a large document. It contains the page tree nodes for a 62-page document; Figure G.2 shows the structure of this page tree. Numbers in the figure are object numbers corresponding to the objects in the example.

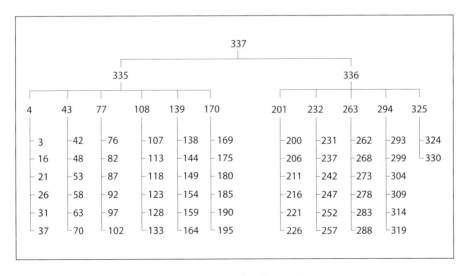

FIGURE G.2 *Page tree for 62-page document*

Example G.4

```
337  0  obj
    <<  /Type  /Pages
        /Kids  [  335 0 R
                  336 0 R
              ]
        /Count  62
    >>
endobj

335  0  obj
    <<  /Type  /Pages
        /Parent  337 0 R
        /Kids  [   4 0 R
                  43 0 R
                  77 0 R
                 108 0 R
                 139 0 R
                 170 0 R
              ]
        /Count  36
    >>
endobj

336  0  obj
    <<  /Type  /Pages
        /Parent  337 0 R
        /Kids  [  201 0 R
                  232 0 R
                  263 0 R
                  294 0 R
                  325 0 R
              ]
        /Count  26
    >>
endobj
```

```
4 0 obj
    << /Type /Pages
        /Parent 335 0 R
        /Kids [ 3 0 R
                16 0 R
                21 0 R
                26 0 R
                31 0 R
                37 0 R
                ]
        /Count 6
    >>
endobj

43 0 obj
    << /Type /Pages
        /Parent 335 0 R
        /Kids [ 42 0 R
                48 0 R
                53 0 R
                58 0 R
                63 0 R
                70 0 R
                ]
        /Count 6
    >>
endobj

77 0 obj
    << /Type /Pages
        /Parent 335 0 R
        /Kids [ 76 0 R
                82 0 R
                87 0 R
                92 0 R
                97 0 R
                102 0 R
                ]
        /Count 6
    >>
endobj
```

```
108  0  obj
    << /Type /Pages
       /Parent 335 0 R
       /Kids [ 107 0 R
               113 0 R
               118 0 R
               123 0 R
               128 0 R
               133 0 R
             ]
       /Count 6
    >>
endobj

139  0  obj
    << /Type /Pages
       /Parent 335 0 R
       /Kids [ 138 0 R
               144 0 R
               149 0 R
               154 0 R
               159 0 R
               164 0 R
             ]
       /Count 6
    >>
endobj

170  0  obj
    << /Type /Pages
       /Parent 335 0 R
       /Kids [ 169 0 R
               175 0 R
               180 0 R
               185 0 R
               190 0 R
               195 0 R
             ]
       /Count 6
    >>
endobj
```

```
201  0  obj
    <<  /Type  /Pages
        /Parent  336 0 R
        /Kids  [  200 0 R
                  206 0 R
                  211 0 R
                  216 0 R
                  221 0 R
                  226 0 R
                ]
        /Count  6
    >>
endobj

232  0  obj
    <<  /Type  /Pages
        /Parent  336 0 R
        /Kids  [  231 0 R
                  237 0 R
                  242 0 R
                  247 0 R
                  252 0 R
                  257 0 R
                ]
        /Count  6
    >>
endobj

263  0  obj
    <<  /Type  /Pages
        /Parent  336 0 R
        /Kids  [  262 0 R
                  268 0 R
                  273 0 R
                  278 0 R
                  283 0 R
                  288 0 R
                ]
        /Count  6
    >>
endobj
```

```
294  0  obj
    << /Type /Pages
        /Parent  336 0 R
        /Kids  [  293 0 R
                  299 0 R
                  304 0 R
                  309 0 R
                  314 0 R
                  319 0 R
               ]
        /Count  6
    >>
endobj

325  0  obj
    << /Type /Pages
        /Parent  336 0 R
        /Kids  [  324 0 R
                  330 0 R
               ]
        /Count  2
    >>
endobj
```

G.5 Outline Tree Example

This section from a PDF file illustrates the structure of an outline tree with six entries. Example G.5 shows the outline with all entries open, as illustrated in Figure G.3.

On-screen appearance	Object number	Count
	21	6
Document	22	4
Section 1	25	0
Section 2	26	1
Subsection 1	27	0
Section 3	28	0
Summary	29	0

FIGURE G.3 *Document outline as displayed in Example G.5*

Example G.5

```
21 0 obj
    << /Type /Outlines
        /First  22 0 R
        /Last  29 0 R
        /Count  6
    >>
endobj

22 0 obj
    << /Title (Document)
        /Parent  21 0 R
        /Next  29 0 R
        /First  25 0 R
        /Last  28 0 R
        /Count  4
        /Dest [3 0 R /XYZ 0 792 0]
    >>
endobj

25 0 obj
    << /Title (Section 1)
        /Parent  22 0 R
        /Next  26 0 R
        /Dest [3 0 R /XYZ null 701 null]
    >>
endobj

26 0 obj
    << /Title (Section 2)
        /Parent  22 0 R
        /Prev  25 0 R
        /Next  28 0 R
        /First  27 0 R
        /Last  27 0 R
        /Count  1
        /Dest [3 0 R /XYZ null 680 null]
    >>
endobj
```

```
27 0 obj
   << /Title (Subsection 1)
      /Parent 26 0 R
      /Dest [3 0 R /XYZ null 670 null]
   >>
endobj

28 0 obj
   << /Title (Section 3)
      /Parent 22 0 R
      /Prev 26 0 R
      /Dest [7 0 R /XYZ null 500 null]
   >>
endobj

29 0 obj
   << /Title (Summary)
      /Parent 21 0 R
      /Prev 22 0 R
      /Dest [8 0 R /XYZ null 199 null]
   >>
endobj
```

Example G.6 is the same as Example G.5, except that one of the outline items has been closed in the display. The outline appears as shown in Figure G.4.

On-screen appearance	Object number	Count
Document	21	5
	22	3
Section 1	25	0
Section 2	26	−1
Section 3	28	0
Summary	29	0

FIGURE G.4 *Document outline as displayed in Example G.6*

Example G.6

```
21 0 obj
    << /Type /Outlines
       /First 22 0 R
       /Last 29 0 R
       /Count 5
    >>
endobj

22 0 obj
    << /Title (Document)
       /Parent 21 0 R
       /Next 29 0 R
       /First 25 0 R
       /Last 28 0 R
       /Count 3
       /Dest [3 0 R /XYZ 0 792 0]
    >>
endobj

25 0 obj
    << /Title (Section 1)
       /Parent 22 0 R
       /Next 26 0 R
       /Dest [3 0 R /XYZ null 701 null]
    >>
endobj

26 0 obj
    << /Title (Section 2)
       /Parent 22 0 R
       /Prev 25 0 R
       /Next 28 0 R
       /First 27 0 R
       /Last 27 0 R
       /Count −1
       /Dest [3 0 R /XYZ null 680 null]
    >>
endobj
```

```
27 0 obj
   << /Title (Subsection 1)
      /Parent 26 0 R
      /Dest [3 0 R /XYZ null 670 null]
   >>
endobj

28 0 obj
   << /Title (Section 3)
      /Parent 22 0 R
      /Prev 26 0 R
      /Dest [7 0 R /XYZ null 500 null]
   >>
endobj

29 0 obj
   << /Title (Summary)
      /Parent 21 0 R
      /Prev 22 0 R
      /Dest [8 0 R /XYZ null 199 null]
   >>
endobj
```

G.6 Updating Example

This example shows the structure of a PDF file as it is updated several times; it illustrates multiple body sections, cross-reference sections, and trailers. In addition, it shows that once an object has been assigned an object identifier, it keeps that identifier until the object is deleted, even if the object is altered. Finally, the example illustrates the reuse of cross-reference entries for objects that have been deleted, along with the incrementing of the generation number after an object has been deleted.

The original file is that shown in Example G.1 on page 598. The updates are divided into four stages, with the file saved after each:

1. Four text annotations are added.

2. The text of one of the annotations is altered.

3. Two of the text annotations are deleted.

4. Three text annotations are added.

The sections following show the segments added to the file at each stage. Throughout this example, objects are referred to by their object identifiers, which are made up of the object number and the generation number, rather than simply by their object numbers as in earlier examples. This is necessary because the example reuses object numbers, so the objects they denote are not unique.

Note: *The tables in these sections show only those objects that are modified during the updating process. Objects from Example G.1 that are not altered during the update are not shown.*

G.6.1 Stage 1: Add Four Text Annotations

Four text annotations are added to the initial file and the file is saved. Table G.4 lists the objects involved in this update.

TABLE G.4 Object use after adding four text annotations	
OBJECT IDENTIFIER	**OBJECT TYPE**
4 0	**Page** (page object)
7 0	Annotation array
8 0	**Annot** (annotation dictionary)
9 0	**Annot** (annotation dictionary)
10 0	**Annot** (annotation dictionary)
11 0	**Annot** (annotation dictionary)

Example G.7 shows the lines added to the file by this update. The page object is updated because an **Annots** entry has been added to it. Note that the file's trailer now contains a **Prev** entry, which points to the original cross-reference section in the file, while the **startxref** value at the end of the trailer points to the cross-reference section added by the update.

Example G.7

```
4 0 obj
    << /Type /Page
       /Parent  3 0 R
       /MediaBox  [0  0  612  792]
       /Contents  5 0 R
       /Resources  << /ProcSet  6 0 R >>
       /Annots  7 0 R
    >>
endobj

7 0 obj
    [ 8 0 R
      9 0 R
      10 0 R
      11 0 R
    ]
endobj

8 0 obj
    << /Type /Annot
       /Subtype /Text
       /Rect  [44  616  162  735]
       /Contents  (Text #1)
       /Open  true
    >>
endobj

9 0 obj
    << /Type /Annot
       /Subtype /Text
       /Rect  [224  668  457  735]
       /Contents  (Text #2)
       /Open  false
    >>
endobj

10 0 obj
    << /Type /Annot
       /Subtype /Text
       /Rect  [239  393  328  622]
       /Contents  (Text #3)
       /Open  true
    >>
endobj
```

```
11  0  obj
    <<  /Type  /Annot
        /Subtype  /Text
        /Rect  [34  398  225  575]
        /Contents  (Text #4)
        /Open  false
    >>
endobj

xref
0  1
0000000000  65535  f
4  1
0000000632  00000  n
7  5
0000000810  00000  n
0000000883  00000  n
0000001024  00000  n
0000001167  00000  n
0000001309  00000  n

trailer
    <<  /Size  12
        /Root  1 0 R
        /Prev  408
    >>
startxref
1452
%%EOF
```

G.6.2   Stage 2: Modify Text of One Annotation

One text annotation is modified and the file is saved. Example G.8 shows the lines added to the file by this update. Note that the file now contains two copies of the object with identifier 10 0 (the text annotation that was modified) and that the added cross-reference section points to the more recent version of the object. This added cross-reference section contains one subsection, containing only an entry for the object that was modified. In addition, the **Prev** entry in the file's trailer has been updated to point to the cross-reference section added in the previous stage, while the **startxref** value at the end of the trailer points to the newly added cross-reference section.

Example G.8

```
10 0 obj
    << /Type /Annot
        /Subtype /Text
        /Rect [239 393 328 622]
        /Contents (Modified Text #3)
        /Open true
    >>
endobj

xref
0 1
0000000000 65535 f
10 1
0000001703 00000 n

trailer
    << /Size 12
        /Root 1 0 R
        /Prev 1452
    >>
startxref
1855
%%EOF
```

G.6.3 Delete Two Annotations

Two text annotations are deleted and the file is saved. Table G.5 lists the objects updated.

TABLE G.5 Object use after deleting two text annotations

OBJECT IDENTIFIER	OBJECT TYPE
7 0	Annotation array
8 0	Free
9 0	Free

The **Annots** array is the only object that is written in this update. It is updated because it now contains two fewer annotations.

Example G.9 shows the lines added when the file was saved. Note that objects with identifiers 8 0 and 9 0 have been deleted, as can be seen from the fact that their entries in the cross-reference section end with the letter **f**.

Example G.9

```
7 0 obj
   [ 10 0 R
     11 0 R
   ]
endobj

xref
0 1
0000000008 65535 f
7 3
0000001978 00000 n
0000000009 00001 f
0000000000 00001 f

trailer
   << /Size 12
        /Root 1 0 R
        /Prev 1855
   >>
startxref
2027
%%EOF
```

The cross-reference section added at this stage contains four entries, representing object number 0, the **Annots** array, and the two deleted text annotations.

• The cross-reference entry for object number 0 is updated because it is the head of the linked list of free objects and must now point to the entry for the newly freed object number 8. The entry for object number 8 points to the entry for object number 9 (the next free entry), while the entry for object number 9 is the last free entry in the cross-reference table, indicated by the fact that it points back to object number 0.

• The entries for the two deleted text annotations are marked as free and as having generation numbers of 1, which will be used for any objects that reuse these cross-reference entries. Keep in mind that, although the two objects have been deleted, they are still present in the file. It is the cross-reference table that records the fact that they have been deleted.

The **Prev** entry in the trailer has again been updated, so that it points to the cross-reference section added in the previous stage, and the **startxref** value points to the newly added cross-reference section.

G.6.4   Stage 4: Add Three Annotations

Finally, three text annotations are added to the file. Table G.6 lists the objects involved in this update.

TABLE G.6 **Object use after adding three text annotations**	
OBJECT IDENTIFIER	**OBJECT TYPE**
7 0	Annotation array
8 1	**Annot** (annotation dictionary)
9 1	**Annot** (annotation dictionary)
12 0	**Annot** (annotation dictionary)

Object numbers 8 and 9, which were used for the two annotations deleted in the previous stage, have been reused; however, the new objects have been given a generation number of 1. In addition, the third text annotation added has been assigned the previously unused object identifier of 12 0.

Example G.10 shows the lines added to the file by this update. The added cross-reference section contains five entries, corresponding to object number 0, the **Annots** array, and the three annotations added. The entry for object number 0 is updated because the previously free entries for object numbers 8 and 9 have been reused. The entry for object number 0 now shows that there are no free entries in the cross-reference table. The **Annots** array is updated to reflect the addition of the three text annotations.

Example G.10

```
7 0 obj
   [ 10 0 R
     11 0 R
     8 1 R
     9 1 R
     12 0 R
   ]
endobj
```

```
8 1 obj
    <<  /Type  /Annot
        /Subtype  /Text
        /Rect  [58  657  172  742]
        /Contents  (New Text #1)
        /Open  true
    >>
endobj

9 1 obj
    <<  /Type  /Annot
        /Subtype  /Text
        /Rect  [389  459  570  537]
        /Contents  (New Text #2)
        /Open  false
    >>
endobj

12 0 obj
    <<  /Type  /Annot
        /Subtype  /Text
        /Rect  [44  253  473  337]
        /Contents  (New Text #3\203a longer text annotation which we will continue \
onto a second line)
        /Open  true
    >>
endobj

xref
0 1
0000000000  65535  f
7 3
0000002216  00000  n
0000002302  00001  n
0000002447  00001  n
12 1
0000002594  00000  n

trailer
    <<  /Size  13
        /Root  1 0 R
        /Prev  2027
    >>
startxref
2814
%%EOF
```

The annotation with object identifier 12 0 illustrates splitting a long text string across multiple lines, as well as the technique for including nonstandard characters in a string. In this case, the character is an ellipsis (…), which is character code 203 (octal) in **PDFDocEncoding**, the encoding used for text annotations.

As in previous updates, the trailer's **Prev** entry and **startxref** value have been updated.

APPENDIX H

Compatibility and Implementation Notes

THE GOAL OF the Adobe Acrobat family of products is to enable people to exchange and view electronic documents easily and reliably. Ideally, this means that any Acrobat viewer application should be able to display the contents of any PDF file, even if the PDF file was created long before or long after the viewer application itself. Of course, new versions of viewer applications are introduced to provide additional capabilities not present before. Furthermore, beginning with Acrobat 2.0, viewer applications may accept plug-in extensions, making some Acrobat 2.0 viewers more capable than others, depending on what extensions are present.

Both the viewer applications and PDF itself have been designed to enable users to view everything in the document that the viewer application understands and to ignore or inform the user about objects not understood. The decision whether to ignore or inform the user is made on a feature-by-feature basis.

The original PDF specification did not define how a viewer application should behave when it reads a file that does not conform to the specification. This appendix provides this information. The PDF version number associated with a file determines how it should be treated when a viewer application encounters a problem.

In addition, this appendix includes notes on the Adobe Acrobat implementation for details that are not strictly defined by the PDF specifications.

H.1 PDF Version Numbers

The header in the first line of a PDF file contains a PDF version number consisting of a major and a minor version. This header takes the form

    %PDF–*M.m*

where *M* is the major and *m* the minor version number.

The major version number is incremented when the PDF specification changes in such a way that existing viewer applications will be unlikely to read a document without serious errors that prevent pages from being viewed. The minor version number reflects changes that do not prevent existing viewer applications from continuing to work, such as the addition of new page description operators.

If PDF changes in a way that existing viewer applications are unlikely to detect, the version number need not change. Such changes might include the addition of private data, such as additional entries in the document catalog, that can be gracefully ignored by applications that do not understand it.

An Acrobat viewer will attempt to read any file with a valid PDF header, even if the version number is more recent than the viewer itself. It will read without errors any file that does not require a plug-in extension, even if the version number is older than the viewer. Some documents may require a plug-in to display an annotation, follow a link, or execute an action. Viewer behavior in this situation is described below in Section H.3, "Implementation Notes." However, a plug-in is never required to display the contents of a page.

When a viewer application opens a document with a major version number newer than it expects, it warns the user that it is unlikely to be able to read the document successfully and that the user will not be able to change or save the document. At the first error related to document processing, the viewer notifies the user that an error has occurred but that no further errors will be reported. (Some errors are always reported, including file I/O errors, extension loading errors, out-of-memory errors, and notifications that a command has failed.) Processing continues if possible. Acrobat does not permit a document with a newer major version number to be inserted into another document.

If a viewer application opens a document with a minor version number newer than it expects, it silently remembers the version number. Only if it encounters an error does it alert the user. At this point it notifies the user that the document is newer than expected, that an error has occurred, and that no further errors will be reported. The document may not be incrementally saved but can be saved to a new file, which will continue to have the new version number. A user may insert a document with a newer minor version into another document. The resulting document can be saved; its version number will be that of the original document or of the document inserted into the original, whichever is greater.

H.2 Dictionary Keys

In general, Acrobat viewers simply ignore dictionary entries that they do not recognize. Adding entries not described in the PDF specification to dictionary objects therefore does not affect the viewers' behavior. See Appendix E for information on how to choose key names that are compatible with future versions of PDF.

If a dictionary object such as an annotation is copied into another document during a page insertion (or in Acrobat 2.0 and 3.0 viewers during a page extraction), all entries are copied. If a value is an indirect reference to another object, that object may be copied as well, depending on the entry.

H.3 Implementation Notes

This section gives details of the implementation of Adobe Acrobat, in the same order in which the corresponding sections appear in the main text.

1.2, "Introduction to PDF 1.3 Features"

1. The native file formats of Adobe Acrobat products are PDF 1.2 for Acrobat 3.0 and PDF 1.3 for Acrobat 4.0.

3.1.2, "Comments"

2. Acrobat viewers do not preserve comments when saving a file.

3.2.4, "Name Objects"

3. In PDF 1.1, the number sign character (#) could be used as part of a name (for example, /A#B), and the specifications did not specifically prohibit embedded spaces (although Adobe generators did not provide a way to write names containing them). In PDF 1.2, the number sign became an escape character, preceding two hexadecimal digits. Thus a 3-character name A-space-B can now be written as /A#20B (since 20 is the hexadecimal code for the space character). This means that the name /A#B is no longer valid, since the number sign is not followed by two hexadecimal digits. A name object with this value must be written as /A#42B, since 42 is the hexadecimal code for the character #.

4. In cases where a PostScript name must be preserved, or where a string is permitted in PostScript but not in PDF, the Acrobat Distiller application uses the # convention as necessary. When an Acrobat viewer generates PostScript, it "inverts" the convention by writing a string, where that is permitted, or a name otherwise. For example, if the string (Adobe Green) were used as a key in a dictionary, the Distiller program would use the name /Adobe#20Green and the viewer would generate (Adobe Green).

3.2.7, "Stream Objects"

5. When a stream specifies an external file, PDF 1.1 parsers ignore the file and always use the bytes between **stream** and **endstream**.

6. Acrobat viewers accept the name **DP** as an abbreviation for the **Decode-Parms** key in any stream dictionary. If both **DP** and **DecodeParms** entries are present, **DecodeParms** takes precedence.

3.2.7, "Stream Objects" (Standard Filters)

7. Acrobat viewers accept the abbreviated filter names shown in Table H.1 in addition to the standard ones. Although the abbreviated names are intended for use only in the context of in-line images (see Section 4.8.6, "In-Line Images"), they are also accepted as filter names in any stream object.

TABLE H.1	Abbreviations for standard filter names
STANDARD FILTER NAME	**ABBREVIATION**
ASCIIHexDecode	AHx
ASCII85Decode	A85
LZWDecode	LZW
FlateDecode	Fl (uppercase F, lowercase L)
RunLengthDecode	RL
CCITTFaxDecode	CCF
DCTDecode	DCT

8. If an unrecognized filter is encountered, Acrobat viewers report the context in which the filter was found. If errors occur while a page is being displayed, only the first error is reported. The subsequent behavior depends on the context, as described in Table H.2. Acrobat operations that process pages, such as the Find command and the Create Thumbnails command, stop as soon as an error occurs.

TABLE H.2	Acrobat behavior with unknown filters
CONTEXT	**BEHAVIOR**
Content stream	Page processing stops.
Indexed color space	The image does not appear, but page processing continues.
Image resource	The image does not appear, but page processing continues.
In-line image	Page processing stops.
Thumbnail image	An error is reported and no more thumbnail images are displayed, but the thumbnails can be deleted and created again.
Form XObject	The form does not appear, but page processing continues.
Type 3 glyph description	The glyph does not appear, but page processing continues. The text position is adjusted based on the glyph width.
Embedded font	The viewer behaves as if the font is not embedded.

9. Versions of the Acrobat viewer prior to 3.0 do not understand the **Flate-Decode** filter. They display an error message indicating that they are unable to process a page.

3.3.6, "DCTDecode Filter"

10. Acrobat 4.0 viewers do not support the combination of the **DCTDecode** filter with any other filter if the encoded data uses the progressive JPEG format. If a version of the Acrobat viewer earlier than 4.0 encounters **DCT-Decode** data encoded in progressive JPEG format, an error occurs that will be handled according to Table H.2.

3.4, "File Structure"

11. The restriction on line length is not enforced by any Acrobat viewer.

12. In PDF 1.3, an exception is made to the restriction on line length in the case of the **Contents** string of a signature dictionary (see "Signature Fields" on page 451).

3.4.1, "File Header"

13. Acrobat viewers require only that the header appear somewhere within the first 1024 bytes of the file.

14. Acrobat viewers will also accept a header of the form

    %!PS–Adobe–*N.n* PDF–*M.m*

3.4.4, "File Trailer"

15. Acrobat viewers require only that the %%EOF marker appear somewhere within the last 1024 bytes of the file.

3.5.2, "Standard Security Handler" (Key Generation Algorithms)

16. In Acrobat 2.0 and 2.1 viewers, the standard security handler uses the empty string if there is no owner password in step 1 of Algorithm 3.3.

3.6.1, "Document Catalog"

17. An additional catalog entry, **AA**, was defined in PDF 1.2, but was never implemented. In PDF 1.3, this entry is obsolete and should be ignored.

18. An earlier version of this specification documented the **PageLayout** entry as being in the viewer preferences dictionary (see Section 7.1, "Viewer Preferences"); it is actually implemented in the document catalog instead.

3.6.2, "Page Tree" (Page Objects)

19. An additional catalog entry, **Hid**, was defined in PDF 1.2, but was never implemented. In PDF 1.3, this entry is obsolete and should be ignored.

20. In a document containing articles, if the first page with an article bead does not have a **B** entry, Acrobat viewers rebuild the **B** array for all pages of the document.

21. In PDF 1.2, additional-actions dictionaries were inheritable; in PDF 1.3, they no longer are.

3.7.1, "Content Streams"

22. Acrobat viewers report an error the first time they find an unknown operator or an operator with too few operands, but continue processing the content stream. No further errors are reported.

3.9.1, "Type 0 (Sampled) Functions"

23. When printing, Acrobat performs only linear interpolation, regardless of the value of the **Order** entry.

3.9.2, "Type 2 (Exponential Interpolation) Functions"

24. Type 2 functions are not defined in PDF 1.2 or earlier versions. Acrobat 3.0 will report an error, "Invalid Function Resource," if it encounters a function of this type.

3.9.3, "Type 3 (Stitching) Functions"

25. Type 3 functions are not defined in PDF 1.2 or earlier versions. Acrobat 3.0 will report an error, "Invalid Function Resource," if it encounters a function of this type.

3.9.4, "Type 4 (PostScript Calculator) Functions"

26. Type 4 functions are not defined in PDF 1.2 or earlier versions. Acrobat 3.0 will report an error, "Invalid Function Resource," if it encounters a function of this type.

27. Acrobat uses single-precision floating-point numbers for all real-number operations in a type 4 function.

4.5.2, "Types of Color Space"

28. If an Acrobat viewer encounters an unknown color space family name, it displays an error specifying the name, but reports no further errors thereafter.

4.5.4, "CIE-Based Color Spaces" (Rendering Intents)

29. Because of the large gamut of most displays, Acrobat viewers ignore the **Intent** entry and always use the **RelativeColorimetric** rendering intent. When printing to a PostScript output device, the Acrobat viewers do not specify a rendering intent unless one was explicitly requested.

4.5.5, "Special Color Spaces" (Multitone Examples)

30. This method of representing multitones is used by Adobe Photoshop® 5.0.2 and subsequent versions when exporting EPS files. Acrobat 4.0 exports Level 3 EPS files using this method, and can also export Level 1 EPS files that use the "Level 1 separation" conventions of Adobe Technical Note #5044, *Color Separation Conventions for PostScript Language Programs*. These conventions are used to emit multitone images as calls to "customcolorimage" with overprinting, which can then be placed in page layout applications such as Adobe PageMaker®, Adobe InDesign™, and QuarkXPress™.

4.6, "Patterns"

31. Acrobat viewers prior to 4.0 do not display patterns on the screen, although they do print them to PostScript output devices.

4.7, "External Objects"

32. If an Acrobat viewer encounters an XObject of an unknown type, it displays an error specifying the type of XObject, but reports no further errors thereafter.

4.8.4, "Image Dictionaries"

33. Image XObjects in PDF 1.2 and earlier versions are all implicitly unmasked images. A PDF consumer that does not recognize the **Mask** entry will treat the image as unmasked without raising an error.

34. All Acrobat viewers ignore the **Name** entry in an image dictionary.

4.8.5, "Masked Images"

35. Explicit masking and color key masking are features of PostScript LanguageLevel 3. Acrobat 4.0 does not attempt to emulate the effect of masked images when printing to LanguageLevel 1 or LanguageLevel 2 output devices; it prints the base image without the mask.

    The Acrobat 4.0 viewer will display masked images, but only when the amount of data in the mask is below a certain limit. Above that, the viewer will display the base image without the mask.

4.9, "Form XObjects"

36. All Acrobat viewers ignore the **Name** entry in a form dictionary.

5.3.2, "Text-Showing Operators"

37. In versions of Acrobat prior to 3.0, the x coordinate of the text position after the **TJ** operator draws a character glyph and moves by any specified offset must not be less than it was before the glyph was drawn.

38. In Acrobat 4.0 and earlier viewers, position adjustments specified by numbers in a **TJ** array are performed incorrectly if the horizontal scaling parameter, T_h, is different from its default value of 100.

5.5.1, "Type 1 Fonts"

39. All Acrobat viewers ignore the **Name** entry in a font dictionary.

5.5.1, "Type 1 Fonts" (The Standard Type 1 Fonts)

40. Acrobat 3.0 and earlier viewers may ignore attempts to override the standard fonts. Also, Acrobat 4.0 and earlier viewers incorrectly allow substitution fonts, such as ArialMT and TimesNewRomanMT, to be specified without **Widths** and **FontDescriptor** entries.

5.5.3, "Font Subsets"

41. For Acrobat 3.0 and earlier viewers, all font subsets whose **BaseFont** names differ only in their tags should have the same font descriptor values and should map character names to glyphs in the same way; otherwise, glyphs may be shown unpredictably. This restriction is eliminated in Acrobat 4.0.

5.5.4, "Type 3 Fonts"

42. In principle, the value of the **Encoding** entry could also be the name of a predefined encoding or an encoding dictionary whose **BaseFont** entry is a predefined encoding. However, Acrobat 4.0 and earlier viewers do not implement this correctly.

43. For compatibility with Acrobat 2.0 and 2.1, the names of resources in a Type 3 font's resource dictionary must match those in the page object's resource dictionary for all pages in which the font is referenced. If backward compatibility is not required, any valid names may be used.

5.6.4, "CMaps"

44. Embedded CMap files, other than **ToUnicode** CMaps, do not work properly in Acrobat 4.0 viewers; this has been corrected in Acrobat 4.05.

5.7, "Font Descriptors"

45. Acrobat viewers prior to version 3.0 ignore the **FontFile3** entry. If a font uses the Adobe standard Latin character set (as defined in Section D.1, "Latin Character Set and Encodings"), Acrobat creates a substitute font. Otherwise, Acrobat displays an error message (once per document) and substitutes any characters in the font with the bullet character.

5.8, "Embedded Font Programs"

46. For simple fonts, font substitution is performed using multiple-master Type 1 fonts. This substitution can be performed only for fonts that use the Adobe standard Latin character set (as defined in Section D.1, "Latin Character Set and Encodings"). In Acrobat 3.0.1 and later, Type 0 fonts that use a CMap whose **CIDSystemInfo** dictionary defines the Adobe-Japan1, Adobe-Korea1, Adobe-GB1, or Adobe-CNS1 character collection can also be substituted. To make a document portable, it is necessary to embed fonts that cannot be substituted. The only exceptions are the Symbol and ITC ZapfDingbats fonts, which are assumed to be present.

6.4.2, "Spot Functions"

47. When the Acrobat Distiller encounters a call to the PostScript **setscreen** or **sethalftone** operator that includes a spot function, it compares the Post-Script code defining the spot function with that of the predefined spot functions shown in Table 6.1. If the code matches one of the predefined functions, Distiller puts the name of that function into the halftone dictionary; Acrobat will then use that function when printing the PDF file to a PostScript output device. If the code does not match any of the predefined spot functions, Distiller samples the specified spot function and generates a function for the halftone dictionary; when printing to a Post-Script device, Acrobat will generate a spot function that interpolates values from that function.

When producing PDF 1.3, Distiller represents the spot function using a Type 4 (PostScript calculator) function whenever possible (see Section 3.9.4, "Type 4 (PostScript Calculator) Functions"). In this case, Acrobat will use this function directly when printing the document.

7.1, "Viewer Preferences"

48. Earlier versions of the PDF specification erroneously described an additional entry, **PageLayout**, as being in the viewer preferences dictionary; it is actually implemented in the document catalog instead (see Section 3.6.1, "Document Catalog").

7.2.2, "Document Outline"

49. Acrobat viewers report an error when a user activates an outline entry whose destination is of an unknown type.

7.3.1, "Page Labels"

50. Acrobat viewers up to version 3.0 ignore the **PageLabels** entry and label pages with decimal numbers starting at 1.

7.4.1, "Annotation Dictionaries"

51. Acrobat viewers update the annotation dictionary's **M** entry only for text annotations.

52. Acrobat viewers ignore the horizontal and vertical corner radii in the annotation dictionary's **Border** entry; the border is always drawn with square corners.

53. Acrobat viewers support a maximum of ten elements in the dash array of the annotation dictionary's **Border** entry.

54. Acrobat 2.0 and 2.1 viewers ignore the annotation dictionary's **BS**, **AP**, and **AS** entries.

7.4.2, "Annotation Flags"

55. Acrobat viewers prior to version 3.0 ignore an annotation's Hidden and Print flags. Annotations that should be hidden are shown; annotations that should be printed are not printed. Acrobat 3.0 ignores the Print flag for text and link annotations.

7.4.3, "Border Styles"

56. If an Acrobat viewer encounters a border style it does not recognize, the border style defaults to S (Solid).

7.4.5, "Annotation Types"

57. Acrobat viewers display annotations whose types they do not recognize in closed form, with an icon containing a question mark. Such an annotation can be selected, moved, or deleted, but if the user attempts to open it, an alert appears giving the annotation type and reporting that a required plug-in is unavailable.

7.4.5, "Annotation Types" (Link Annotations)

58. Acrobat viewers report an error when a user activates a link annotation whose destination is of an unknown type.

7.4.5, "Annotation Types" (Markup Annotations)

59. In Acrobat 4.0, the text is oriented with respect to the vertex with the smallest y value (or the leftmost of those, if there are two such vertices) and the next vertex in a counterclockwise direction, regardless of whether these are the first two points in the **QuadPoints** array.

7.4.5, "Annotation Types" (Ink Annotations)

60. Acrobat viewers always connect the points along each path with straight lines.

7.4.5, "Annotation Types" (Movie Annotations)

61. Acrobat viewers report the following error when they encounter an annotation of type **Movie**: "The Plug-in required by this 'Movie' annotation is unavailable." The annotation is displayed as a gray rectangle with a question mark.

7.5.2, "Trigger Events"

62. In PDF 1.2, the additional-actions dictionary could contain entries named **NP** (next page), **PP** (previous page), **FP** (first page), and **LP** (last page). The actions associated with these entries were never implemented; as of PDF 1.3, these entries are obsolete and should be ignored.

63. In PDF 1.2, additional-actions dictionaries were inheritable; in PDF 1.3, they no longer are.

64. In Acrobat 3.0, the **O** and **C** events in a page object's additional-actions dictionary are ignored if the display is not in a page-oriented mode. In Acrobat 4.0, the actions associated with these events are executed if the viewer is in a page-oriented or single-column mode; they are ignored if it is in a multiple-column mode.

7.5.3, "Action Types" (Launch Actions)

65. The Acrobat viewer for Windows uses the Windows function ShellExecute to launch an application. The **Win** dictionary entries correspond to the parameters of ShellExecute.

7.5.3, "Action Types" (URI Actions)

66. URI actions are resolved by the Acrobat WebLink plug-in extension.

67. If the appropriate plug-in extension (WebLink) is not present, Acrobat viewers report the following error when a link annotation that uses a URI action is activated: "The plug-in required by this URI action is not available."

7.5.3, "Action Types" (Sound Actions)

68. In PDF 1.2, the value of the **Sound** entry was allowed to be a file specification. That is no longer supported, but the same effect can be achieved by using an external stream.

7.5.3, "Action Types" (Movie Actions)

69. Acrobat viewers prior to version 3.0 report an error when they encounter an action of type **Movie**.

7.5.3, "Action Types" (Hide Actions)

70. Acrobat viewers prior to version 3.0 report the following error when encountering an action of type **Hide**: "The plug-in needed for this **Hide** action is not available."

71. In Acrobat viewers, the change in an annotation's Hidden flag as a result of a hide action is temporary, in the sense that the user can subsequently close the document without being prompted to save changes, and the effect of the hide action will be lost. However, if the user does explicitly save the document before closing, such changes *will* be saved and will thus become permanent.

7.5.3, "Action Types" (Named Actions)

72. Acrobat viewers prior to version 3.0 report the following error when encountering an action of type **Named**: "The plug-in needed for this **Named** action is not available."

73. Acrobat viewers extend the list of named actions in Table 7.40 to include most of the menu item names available in the viewer. For further details, see the listing of menu item names in the Acrobat Plug-In Developer's SDK.

7.6.2, "Field Dictionaries"

74. Beginning in Acrobat 3.0, partial field names may not contain a period.

75. Acrobat versions 3.0 and later do not support Unicode encoding of field names.

7.6.2, "Field Dictionaries" (Variable Text)

76. Acrobat viewers may insert additional entries in the **DR** resource dictionary, such as **Encoding**, as a convenience for keeping track of objects being used to construct form fields. Such objects are not actually resources and are not referenced from the appearance stream.

7.6.3, "Field Types" (Choice Fields)

77. In Acrobat 3.0, the **Opt** array must be homogenous: its elements must be either all text strings or all arrays.

7.6.4, "Form Actions" (Submit-Form Actions)

78. In Acrobat viewers, if the response to a submit-form action uses Forms Data Format (FDF), then the URL must end in #FDF so that it will be recognized as such by the Acrobat software and handled properly. Conversely, if the response is in any other format, the URL should not end in #FDF.

7.6.4, "Form Actions" (Import-Data Actions)

79. Acrobat viewers set the **F** entry to a relative file specification locating the FDF file with respect to the current PDF document file. If the designated FDF file is not found when the import-data action is performed, Acrobat tries to locate the file in a few "well-known" locations depending on the host platform. On the Windows platform, for example, it looks in the directory from which Acrobat was loaded, the current directory, the System directory, the Windows directory, and any directories listed in the PATH environment variable; on the Macintosh, it looks in the Preferences folder and the Acrobat folder.

80. When performing an import-data action, Acrobat viewers import the contents of the FDF file into the current document's interactive form, ignoring the **F** and **ID** entries in the FDF file itself.

7.6.4, "Form Actions" (JavaScript Actions)

81. Because JavaScript 1.2 is not Unicode-compatible, **PDFDocEncoding** and the Unicode encoding are translated to a platform-specific encoding prior to interpretation by the JavaScript engine.

7.6.6, "Forms Data Format" (FDF Catalog)

82. The Acrobat implementation of interactive forms displays the value of the **Status** entry, if any, in an alert note when importing an FDF file.

83. The only **Encoding** value supported by Acrobat 4.0 is Shift–JIS. If any other value is specified, the default, **PDFDocEncoding**, will be used.

7.6.6, "Forms Data Format" (FDF Fields)

84. Of all the possible entries shown in Table 7.63 on page 464, Acrobat 3.0 will export only the **V** entry when generating FDF, and Acrobat 4.0 will ex-

port only the **V** and **AP** entries. It will, however, import FDF files containing fields using any of the described entries.

85. If the FDF dictionary in an FDF file received as a result of a submit-form action contains an **F** entry specifying a form other than the one currently being displayed, Acrobat fetches the specified form before importing the FDF file.

86. When exporting a form to an FDF file, Acrobat sets the **F** entry in the FDF dictionary to a relative path from the location of the FDF file to that of the file from which it was exported.

87. If an FDF file being imported contains fields whose fully qualified names are not present in the form, Acrobat will discard those fields. This feature can be useful, for example, if an FDF file containing commonly used fields (such as name and address) is used to populate various types of form, not all of which necessarily include all of the fields available in the FDF file.

88. As shown in Table 7.63 on page 464, the only required entry in the field dictionary is **T**. One possible use for exporting FDF with fields containing **T** entries but no **V** entries is to indicate to a server which fields are desired in the FDF files returned in response. For example, a server accessing a database might use this information to decide whether to transmit all fields in a record or just some selected ones. As noted in note 87 above, the Acrobat implementation of interactive forms will ignore fields in the imported FDF file that do not exist in the form.

89. The Acrobat implementation of forms allows the option of submitting the data in a submit-form action in HTML Form format. This is for the benefit of existing server scripts written to process such forms. Note, however, that any such existing scripts that generate new HTML forms in response will need to be modified to generate FDF instead.

7.6.6, "Forms Data Format" (FDF Pages)

90. Acrobat renames fields by prepending a page number, a template name, and an ordinal number to the field name. The ordinal number corresponds to the order in which the template is applied to a page, with 0 being the first template specified for the page. For example, if the first template used on the fifth page has the name Template and has the **Rename** flag set to *true*, fields defined in that template will be renamed by prepending the character string P5.Template_0. to their field names.

91. Adobe Extreme™ printing systems require that the **Rename** flag be *true*.

7.7, "Sounds"

92. Acrobat supports a maximum of two sound channels.

8.1, "Procedure Sets"

93. Acrobat viewers respond to requests for unknown procedure sets by warning the user that a required procedure set is unavailable and canceling the printing operation.

8.2, "Document Information Dictionary"

94. Acrobat viewers impose a limit of 255 bytes on any string appearing as a value in the document information dictionary.

95. Acrobat viewers display the contents of the document information dictionary in the Document Info dialog box.

8.3, "File Identifiers"

96. Although the **ID** entry is not required, all Adobe applications that produce PDF files include this entry. Acrobat adds this entry when saving a file if it is not already present.

97. Adobe applications pass the suggested information to the MD5 message digest algorithm to calculate file identifiers. Note that the calculation of the file identifier need not be reproducible; all that matters is that the identifier is likely to be unique. For example, two implementations of this algorithm might use different formats for the current time; this will cause them to produce different file identifiers for the same file created at the same time, but does not affect the uniqueness of the identifier.

8.5.2, "Content Database" (Digital Identifiers)

98. The Acrobat Web Capture plug-in treats external streams referenced within a PDF file as auxiliary data. Such streams are not used in generating the digital identifier.

8.5.3, "Content Sets" (Image Sets)

99. In Acrobat 4.0, if the indirect reference to an image XObject is not removed from the **O** array when its reference count reaches 0, the XObject will never be garbage-collected during a save operation. The image set's reference to the XObject may thus be considered a weak one that is relevant only for caching purposes; when the last strong reference goes away, so does the weak one.

8.5.4, "Source Information" (URL Alias Dictionaries)

100. URL alias dictionaries should use an indirect object reference to a shared string for each URL. These strings can then be shared among the chains and with other data structures.

8.6.3, "Trapping Support"

101. Older viewers may fail to maintain the trap network annotation's required position at the end of the **Annots** array.

102. Older viewers may fail to validate trapping networks before printing.

8.6.4, "Open Prepress Interface (OPI)"

103. The Acrobat 3.0 Distiller application converts OPI comments into OPI dictionaries; when the Acrobat 3.0 viewer prints a PDF file to a PostScript file or printer, it converts the OPI dictionary back to OPI comments. However, the OPI information has no effect on the displayed image or form XObject.

104. Acrobat viewer and Distiller applications prior to 4.0 do not support OPI 2.0.

105. In Acrobat 3.0, the value of the **F** entry in an OPI dictionary must be a string.

C.1, "General Implementation Limits"

106. In Acrobat viewers prior to 4.0, the minimum allowed page size is 72 by 72 units in default user space (1 inch by 1 inch); the maximum is 3240 by 3240 units (45 by 45 inches).

F.2.2, "Linearization Parameters (Part 2)"
F.2.5, "Hint Streams (Parts 5 and 10)"

107.   Acrobat does not currently support reading or writing files that have an overflow hint stream.

F.2.6, "First Page (Part 6)"

108.   Acrobat always treats page 0 as the first page for linearization, regardless of the value of **OpenAction**.

F.2.8, "Shared Objects (Part 8)"

109.   Acrobat does not generate shared object groups containing more than one object.

F.3.1, "Page Offset Hint Table"

110.   Acrobat sets item 6 in the header section of the page offset hint table to 0 when writing a linearized file, and assumes it is 0 when reading a linearized file.

111.   In Acrobat, item 7 in the header section of the page offset hint table is unused and always set to 1. In addition, item 6 in each per-page entry is set to 0; thus the byte offset of the start of the content stream is equal to the least offset to the start of the content stream (item 6 in the header section).

112.   Acrobat 4.0 always sets item 8 equal to 0. It also sets item 9 equal to the value of item 5, and sets item 7 of each per-page hint table entry (Table F.4) to be the same as item 2 of the per-page entry. Acrobat ignores all of these entries when reading the file. Item 8 in Table F.3 should be set to the same as item 4 for a valid table.

F.3.2, "Shared Objects Hint Table"

113.   In Acrobat, item 5 in the header section of the shared objects hint table is unused and is always set to 1.

114.   MD5 signatures are not implemented in Acrobat; item 2 in a shared object group entry must be 0.

115.   Acrobat does not support more than one shared object in a group; item 4 in a shared object group entry should always be 1.

Bibliography

THIS BIBLIOGRAPHY PROVIDES details on books and documents, from both Adobe Systems and other sources, that are referred to in this book.

Resources from Adobe Systems Incorporated

All of these resources from Adobe Systems are available on the Adobe Solutions Network (ASN) Developer Program site on the World Wide Web, located at

<http://partners.adobe.com/asn/developer/>

Document version numbers and dates given in this Bibliography are the latest at the time of publication; more recent versions may be found on the Web site.

The ASN can also be contacted as follows:

Adobe Solutions Network
Adobe Systems Incorporated
345 Park Avenue
San Jose, CA 95110-2704

(800) 685-3510 (from North America)
(206) 675-6145 (from other areas)

<acrodevsup@adobe.com>

Adobe Glyph List, Version 1.2. Available through the document *Unicode and Glyph Names* in the Type Technology Forum on the ASN Developer Program Web site.

Adobe Type 1 Font Format, Addison-Wesley, Reading, MA, 1990. Explains the internal organization of a PostScript Type 1 font program. Also see Adobe Technical Note #5015, *Type 1 Font Format Supplement.*

OPI: Open Prepress Interface Specification 1.3. Also see Adobe Technical Note #5660, *Open Prepress Interface (OPI) Specification, Version 2.0.*

PDF Public-Key Digital Signature and Encryption Specification. Available in the Adobe Acrobat Software Development Kit (SDK), on either the ASN Developer Program Web site or the Acrobat SDK CD.

PostScript Language Reference, Third Edition, Addison-Wesley, Reading, MA, 1999.

Technical Notes:

- Technical Note #5001, *PostScript Language Document Structuring Conventions Specification, Version 3.0*

- Technical Note #5004, *Adobe Font Metrics File Format Specification, Version 4.1*

  Adobe font metrics (AFM) files are available through the Type Technology Forum on the ASN Developer Program Web site.

- Technical Note #5014, *Adobe CMap and CID Font Files Specification, Version 1.0*

- Technical Note #5015, *Type 1 Font Format Supplement*

- Technical Note #5044, *Color Separation Conventions for PostScript Language Programs*

- Technical Note #5088, *Font Naming Issues*

- Technical Note #5092, *CID-Keyed Font Technology Overview*

- Technical Note #5116, *Supporting the DCT Filters in PostScript Level 2*

- Technical Note #5176, *The Compact Font Format Specification*

- Technical Note #5177, *The Type 2 Charstring Format*

- Technical Note #5186, *Acrobat Forms JavaScript Object Specification, Version 4.05*

- Technical Note #5401, *Standard Element Types for Logical Structure in PDF*

- Technical Note #5620, *Portable Job Ticket Format, Version 1.1*

- Technical Note #5660, *Open Prepress Interface (OPI) Specification, Version 2.0*

Other Resources

Aho, A. V., Hopcroft, J. E., and Ullman, J. D., *Data Structures and Algorithms*, Addison-Wesley, Reading, MA, 1983. Includes a discussion of balanced trees.

Apple Computer, Inc., *TrueType Reference Manual*. Available on the Web at <http://fonts.apple.com/TTRefMan/index.html>.

Arvo, J. (ed.), *Graphics Gems II*, Academic Press, 1994. The section "Geometrically Continuous Cubic Bézier Curves" by Hans-Peter Seidel describes the mathematics used to smoothly join two cubic Bézier curves.

Fairchild, M. D., *Color Appearance Models*, Addison-Wesley, Reading, MA, 1997. Covers color vision, basic colorimetry, color appearance models, cross-media color reproduction, and the current CIE standards activities. Updates, software, and color appearance data are available at <http://www.cis.rit.edu/people/faculty/fairchild/CAM.html>.

Foley, J. D. et al., *Computer Graphics: Principles and Practice*, Addison-Wesley, Reading, MA, 1996. (First edition was Foley, J. D. and van Dam, A., *Fundamentals of Interactive Computer Graphics*, Addison-Wesley, Reading, MA, 1982.) Covers many graphics-related topics, including a thorough treatment of the mathematics of Bézier cubics and Gouraud shadings.

Glassner, A. S. (ed.), *Graphics Gems*, Academic Press, 1993. The section "An Algorithm for Automatically Fitting Digitized Curves" by Philip J. Schneider describes an algorithm for determining the set of Bézier curves approximating an arbitrary set of user-provided points. Appendix 2 contains an implementation of the algorithm, written in the C programming language. Other sections relevant to the mathematics of Bézier curves include "Solving the Nearest-Point-On-Curve Problem" and "A Bézier Curve-Based Root-Finder," both by Philip J. Schneider, and "Some Properties of Bézier Curves" by Ronald Goldman. The source code appearing in the appendix is available via anonymous FTP, as described in the preface to *Graphics Gems III* (edited by D. Kirk; see its entry below).

Hewlett-Packard Corporation, *PANOSE Classification Metrics Guide*. Available at <http://www.fonts.com/hp/panose/>.

Hunt, R. W. G., *The Reproduction of Colour*, 5th ed., Fisher Books, England, 1996. A comprehensive general reference on color reproduction; includes an introduction to the CIE system.

International Color Consortium, *ICC Profile Format Specification*. Available with related documents at <http://www.color.org>.

International Electrotechnical Commission (IEC), IEC/3WD 61966-2.1, *Colour Measurement and Management in Multimedia Systems and Equipment, Part 2.1: Default RGB Colour Space—sRGB.* Available at <http://www.srgb.com/sRGBstandard.pdf>.

International Organization for Standardization (ISO). The following standards are available through <http://www.iso.ch>:

- ISO 639, *Codes for the Representation of Names of Languages*

- ISO 3166, *Codes for the Representation of Names of Countries and Their Subdivisions*

- ISO/IEC 8824-1, *Abstract Syntax Notation One (ASN.1): Specification of Basic Notation*

- ISO/IEC 10918-1, *Digital Compression and Coding of Continuous-Tone Still Images* (informally known as the JPEG standard, for the Joint Photographic Experts Group, the organization that developed the standard)

International Telecommunication Union (ITU), Recommendations T.4 and T.6. These standards for Group 3 and Group 4 facsimile encoding (which replace those formerly provided in the CCITT *Blue Book*, Volume VII.3) can be ordered from ITU at <http://www.itu.int>.

Internet Engineering Task Force (IETF) Requests for Comments (RFCs). The following RFCs are available through <http://www.rfc-editor.org>:

- RFC 1321, *The MD5 Message-Digest Algorithm*

- RFC 1738, *Uniform Resource Locators*

- RFC 1808, *Relative Uniform Resource Locators*

- RFC 1866, *Hypertext Markup Language 2.0 Proposed Standard*

- RFC 1950, *ZLIB Compressed Data Format Specification, Version 3.3*

- RFC 1951, *DEFLATE Compressed Data Format Specification, Version 1.3*

- RFC 2045, *Multipurpose Internet Mail Extensions (MIME) Part One: Format of Internet Message Bodies*

- RFC 2046, *Multipurpose Internet Mail Extensions (MIME) Part Two: Media Types*

- RFC 2068, *Hypertext Transfer Protocol—HTTP/1.1*

- RFC 2083, *PNG (Portable Network Graphics) Specification, Version 1.0*

Kirk, D. (ed.), *Graphics Gems III*, Academic Press, 1994. The section "Interpolation Using Bézier Curves" by Gershon Elber contains an algorithm for calculating a Bézier curve that passes through a user-specified set of points. The algorithm uses not only cubic Bézier curves, which are supported in PDF, but also higher-order Bézier curves. The appendix contains an implementation of the algorithm, written in the C programming language. The source code appearing in the appendix is available via anonymous FTP, as described in the book's preface.

Lunde, K., *CJKV Information Processing*, O'Reilly & Associates, Sebastopol, CA, 1999. The CMap programs that define all of the predefined CMaps are available at <ftp://ftp.oreilly.com/pub/examples/nutshell/cjkv/adobe/>.

Microsoft Corporation, *TrueType 1.0 Font Files Technical Specification*. Available at <http://www.microsoft.com/typography/tt/tt.htm>.

Netscape Communications Corporation, *Client-Side JavaScript Reference*. Available through Netscape's developer site at <http://developer.netscape.com>.

Pennebaker, W. B. and Mitchell, J. L., *JPEG: Still Image Data Compression Standard*, Van Nostrand Reinhold, New York, 1992.

Unicode Consortium, *The Unicode Standard, Version 2.0*, Addison-Wesley, Reading, MA, 1996. The latest information is available at <http://www.unicode.org>.

Index

B

B entry
 in page object 78
 in sound object 469, 470
 in thread action dictionary 428
B path-painting operator 152, 539
b path-painting operator 152, 539
B* path-painting operator 152, 539
b* path-painting operator 152, 539
B5pc–H CJK CMap name 320
B5pc–V CJK CMap name 320
Background entry in shading dictionary 216
backslash, in literal strings 28, 29, 108, 514
balanced tree 75
Base entry in URI dictionary 430
base image 255
base parameter for **Indexed** color space 181
BaseEncoding entry in encoding dictionary 307
BaseFont entry
 in CIDFont dictionary 315
 in Type 0 font dictionary 327
 in Type 1 font dictionary 294
BBox entry
 in shading dictionary 216
 in type 1 form dictionary 264
 in type 1 pattern dictionary 204, 205
BC entry in appearance characteristics dictionary 442
BDC marked-content operator 479, 480, 481, 539
bead dictionaries 393–394
beginbfchar CMap construction operator 326, 328
beginbfrange CMap construction operator 326, 328
begincidchar CMap construction operator 326, 328
begincidrange CMap construction operator 326, 328
begincmap CMap construction operator 325
begincodespacerange CMap construction operator 325, 328
beginnotdefchar CMap construction operator 326, 329
beginnotdefrange CMap construction operator 326, 329
bevel join, illustrated 140
Bézier curves 150–151, 232
 construction of, 149
BG entry
 in appearance characteristics dictionary 442
 in graphics state parameter dictionary 145
BG2 entry in graphics state parameter dictionary 145
BI in-line image operator 259, 260, 539
bilevel output devices 10

bitshift operator in type 4 functions 105, 544
BitsPerComponent entry
 in filter parameter dictionary for **LZWDecode** and **FlateDecode** 47
 in image dictionary 250
 in in-line image object 261
 in thumbnail image dictionary 390
 in type 4 shading dictionary 226, 229
 in type 5 shading dictionary 231
 in type 6 shading dictionary 235
BitsPerCoordinate entry
 in type 4 shading dictionary 226, 229
 in type 5 shading dictionary 231
 in type 6 shading dictionary 235
BitsPerFlag entry
 in type 4 shading dictionary 226, 229
 in type 6 shading dictionary 235
BitsPerSample entry in type 0 function dictionary 98, 100
bitwise operators in type 4 functions 105
 summary of 544
BI entry in additional-actions dictionary 422
black generation 352, 353
 graphics state parameter 136
BlackIs1 entry in **CCITTFaxDecode** filter parameter dictionary 52
BlackPoint entry
 in **CalGray** color space dictionary 168
 in **CalRGB** color space dictionary 169, 170
 in **Lab** color space dictionary 172
bleed box 525
BleedBox entry in page object 78, 525
blend circles 222
Blinds transition style 396
BMC marked-content operator 479, 480, 481, 539
body
 of FDF file 461, 462
 of PDF file 55, 57
bookmarks 388
boolean data type 87
boolean objects 26
boolean operators in type 4 functions 105
 summary of 544
Border entry in annotation dictionary 400, 404
 implementation notes about 634
border style dictionary 404
border styles 404
 implementation notes about 635
Bounds entry in type 3 function dictionary 103
Box transition style 396
BPC entry in in-line image object 261

Colophon

THIS BOOK WAS PRODUCED using Adobe® FrameMaker®, Adobe Illustrator®, Adobe Photoshop®, Adobe Acrobat® Distiller®, and other application software packages that support the PostScript® page description language and Type 1 fonts. The type used is from the Adobe Minion® and Myriad® families. Heads are set in Myriad MM 565 Semibold, 600 Normal, and the body text is set in 10.5-on-13-point Minion.

Authors—Jim Meehan, Ed Taft, Steve Chernicoff, Caroline Rose

Key Contributors—Nabeel Al-Shamma, Steven Kelley Amerige, Tim Bienz, Richard Cohn, Matt Foley, Ron Gentile, Jim King, Bennett Leeds, Carl Orthlieb, Roberto Perelman, Paul Rovner, Ed Rowe, Craig Rublee, Mike Schuster, John Warnock, Bob Wulff, Steve Zilles

Reviewers—L. Peter Deutsch, Mark Donohoe, Martin Fox, David Gelphman, Brian Havlin, John Nash, Terry O'Donnell, Jim Pravetz, Dick Sites, Lydia Stang, and numerous others at Adobe Systems and elsewhere

Editing and Book Production—Steve Chernicoff, Caroline Rose

Index—Michael Loo

Illustrations—Carl Yoshihara, Wendy Bell, Dayna Porterfield, Lisa Ferdinandsen, Carol Keller, Kim Arney

Book Design—Sharon Anderson

Publication Management—Robert Morrish, Susan Walton